Production - Hiroko Mizuno
         Tomoe Tsutsumi

Originally published in Japanese as *Futatsu no Supika 8, 9*
by MEDIA FACTORY, Inc., Tokyo 2005
Futatsu no Supika first serialized in Gekkan Comic Flapper,
MEDIA FACTORY, Inc., 2001-2009

This is a work of fiction.

ISBN: 978-1-935654-13-1

Manufactured in Canada

First Edition

Vertical, Inc.
451 Park Avenue South, 7th Floor
New York, NY 10016
www.vertical-inc.com

Notes on the Translation

P. 54

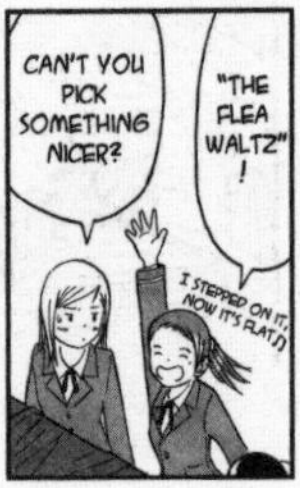
"THE FLEA WALTZ"!
CAN'T YOU PICK SOMETHING NICER?
I STEPPED ON IT, NOW IT'S FLAT!

"The Flea Waltz," which requires frequent striking of the sharp (i.e. black) keys, is popular worldwide as a piano practice piece. Its name, however, varies from language to language. The Japanese one translates as "I Stepped on a Cat" and has lyrics to go with it as Kei demonstrates.

P. 257

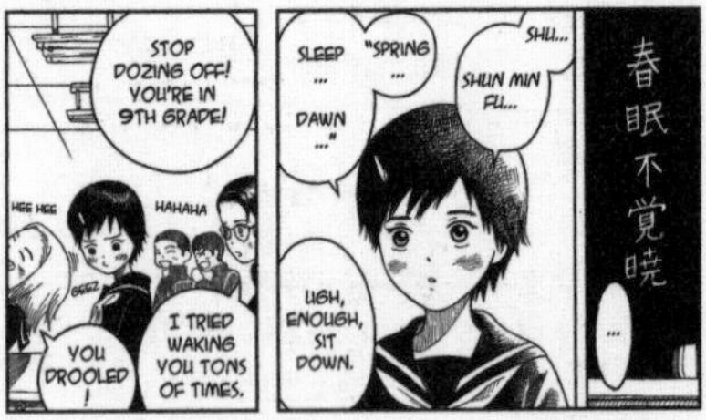
春眠不覚暁
...
SHU...
SHUN MIN FU...
"SPRING ...
SLEEP ... DAWN ..."
UGH, ENOUGH, SIT DOWN.
STOP DOZING OFF! YOU'RE IN 9TH GRADE!
HAHAHA
HEE HEE
GEEZ
I TRIED WAKING YOU TONS OF TIMES.
YOU DROOLED!

Japanese students are taught to read classic Chinese poetry. Similarities between the two languages don't extend far beyond the shared characters so the lessons can be challenging. The first line of "Spring Dawn," by eighth-century Chinese poet Meng Haoran, reads: "In spring I sleep past dawn." Note that Japanese primary and secondary education follows a 6-3-3 scheme so that ninth grade is the last year of middle school. (At Tokyo Space School, there exists a thirteenth grade for the most qualified students as became clear in this volume.) The academic year begins and ends in spring in Japan, and graduation ceremonies are often associated with cherry blossoms as in this story.

P. 282

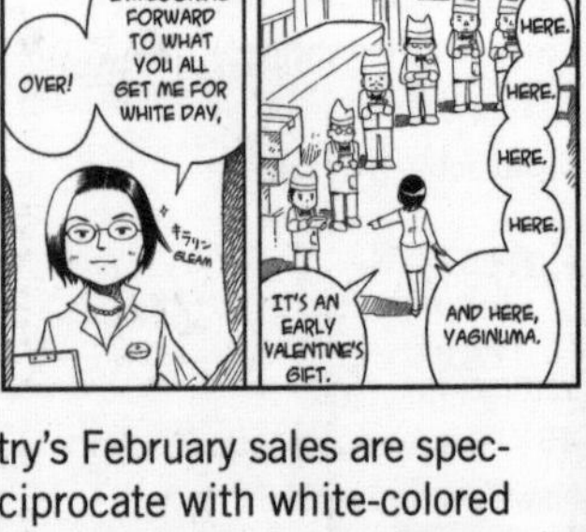
HERE.
HERE.
HERE.
HERE.
AND HERE, YAGINUMA.
IT'S AN EARLY VALENTINE'S GIFT.
I'M LOOKING FORWARD TO WHAT YOU ALL GET ME FOR WHITE DAY,
OVER!
キラリン GLEAM

St. Valentine's Day is significant in Japan but with a local twist, thanks to the confectionery industry's role in promoting the foreign concept: women (but not men) give *chocolate* to their romantic interests on February 14. Lonely-hearts with neither partners nor fans also receive them, however, from women friends and coworkers in a face-saving gesture. The industry's February sales are spectacular as a result. Recipients are supposed to reciprocate with white-colored sweets on March 14, "White Day," according to the perspicacious marketers.

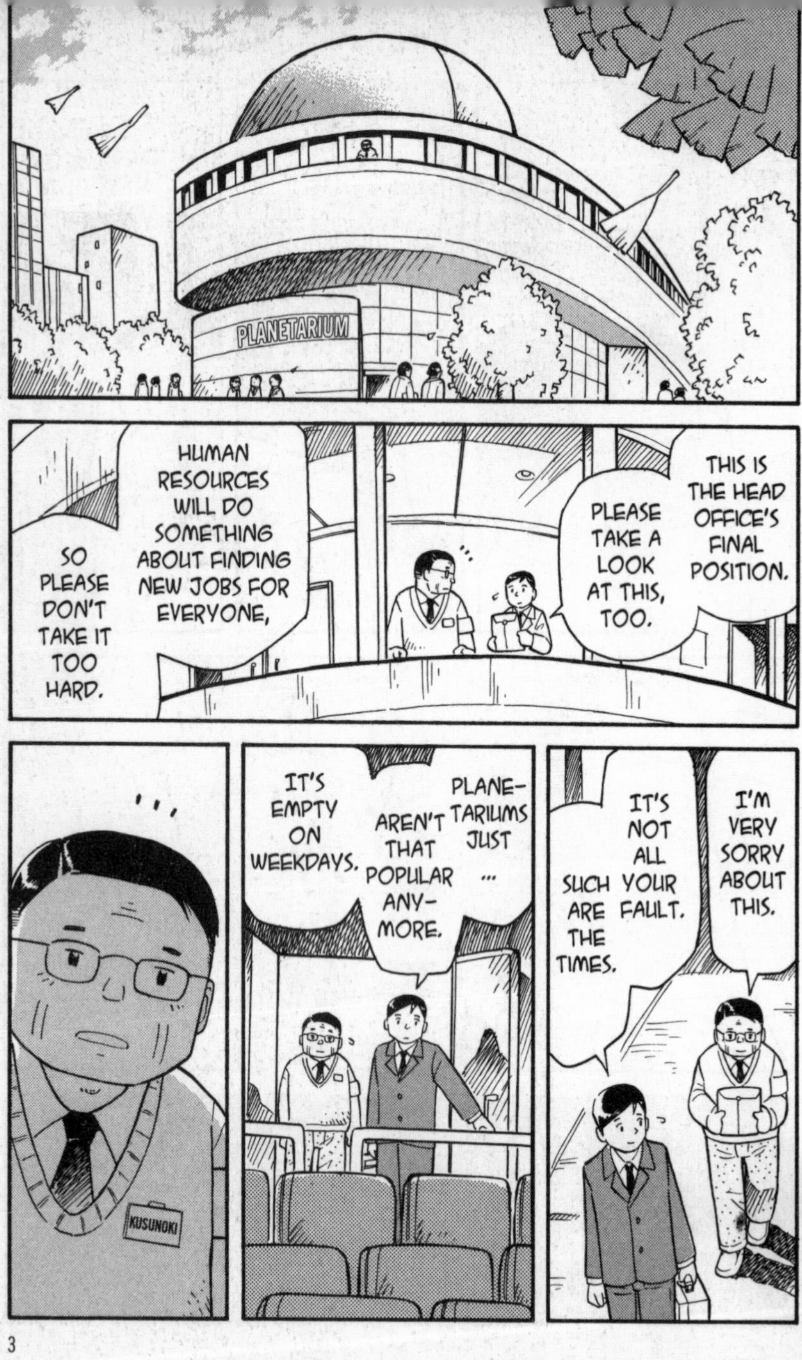
PLANETARIUM
THIS IS THE HEAD OFFICE'S FINAL POSITION.
PLEASE TAKE A LOOK AT THIS, TOO.
HUMAN RESOURCES WILL DO SOMETHING ABOUT FINDING NEW JOBS FOR EVERYONE,
SO PLEASE DON'T TAKE IT TOO HARD.
I'M VERY SORRY ABOUT THIS.
IT'S NOT ALL YOUR FAULT.
SUCH ARE THE TIMES.
PLANETARIUMS JUST ...
AREN'T THAT POPULAR ANYMORE.
IT'S EMPTY ON WEEKDAYS.
...
KUSUNOKI

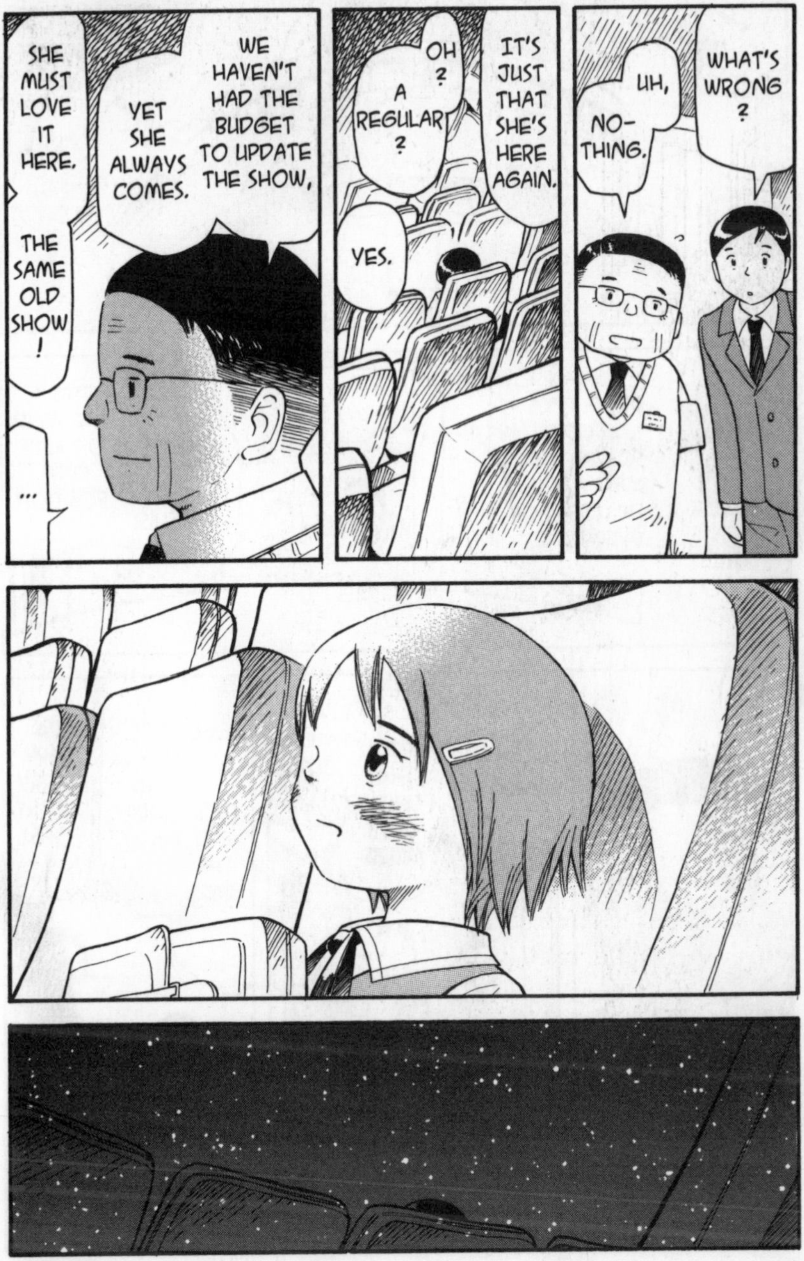
WHAT'S WRONG?
UH, NOTHING.
IT'S JUST THAT SHE'S HERE AGAIN.
OH? A REGULAR?
YES.
WE HAVEN'T HAD THE BUDGET TO UPDATE THE SHOW,
YET SHE ALWAYS COMES.
SHE MUST LOVE IT HERE.
THE SAME OLD SHOW!
...

MISSION:39

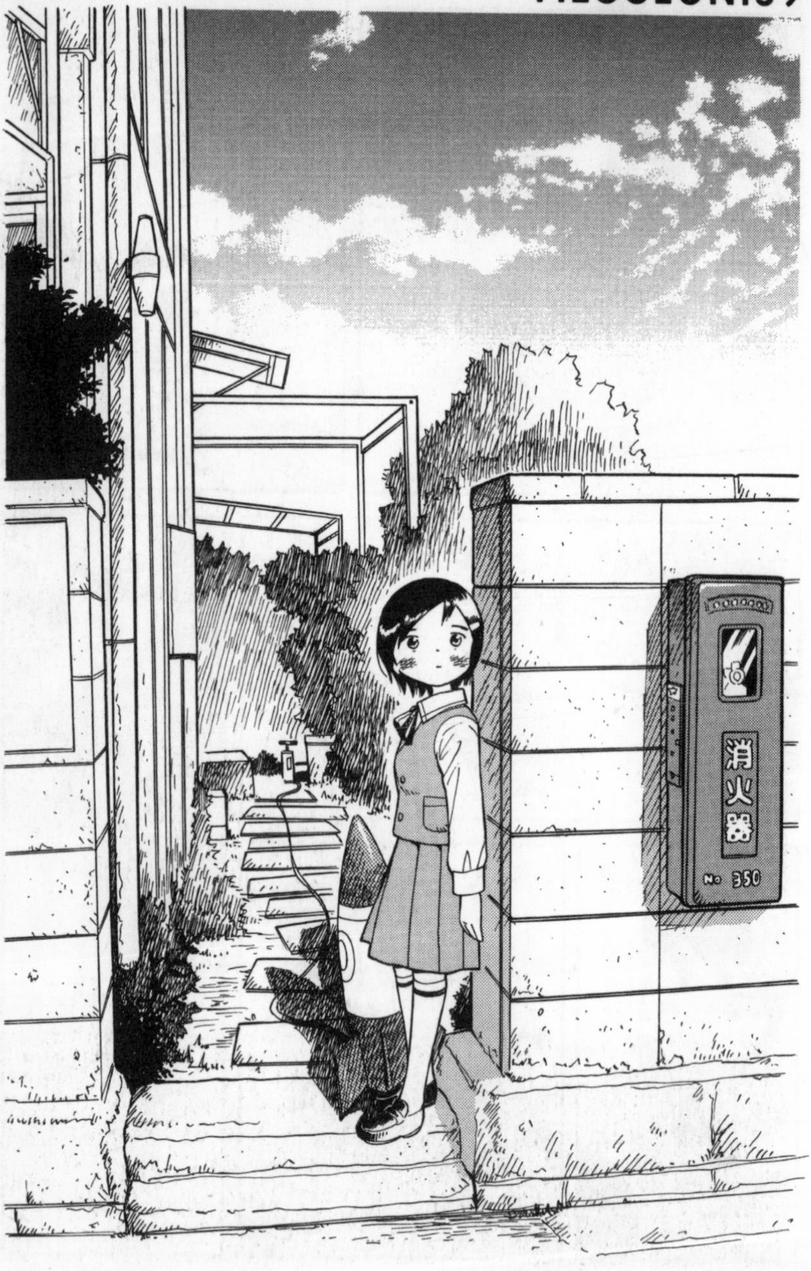
消火器
No 350

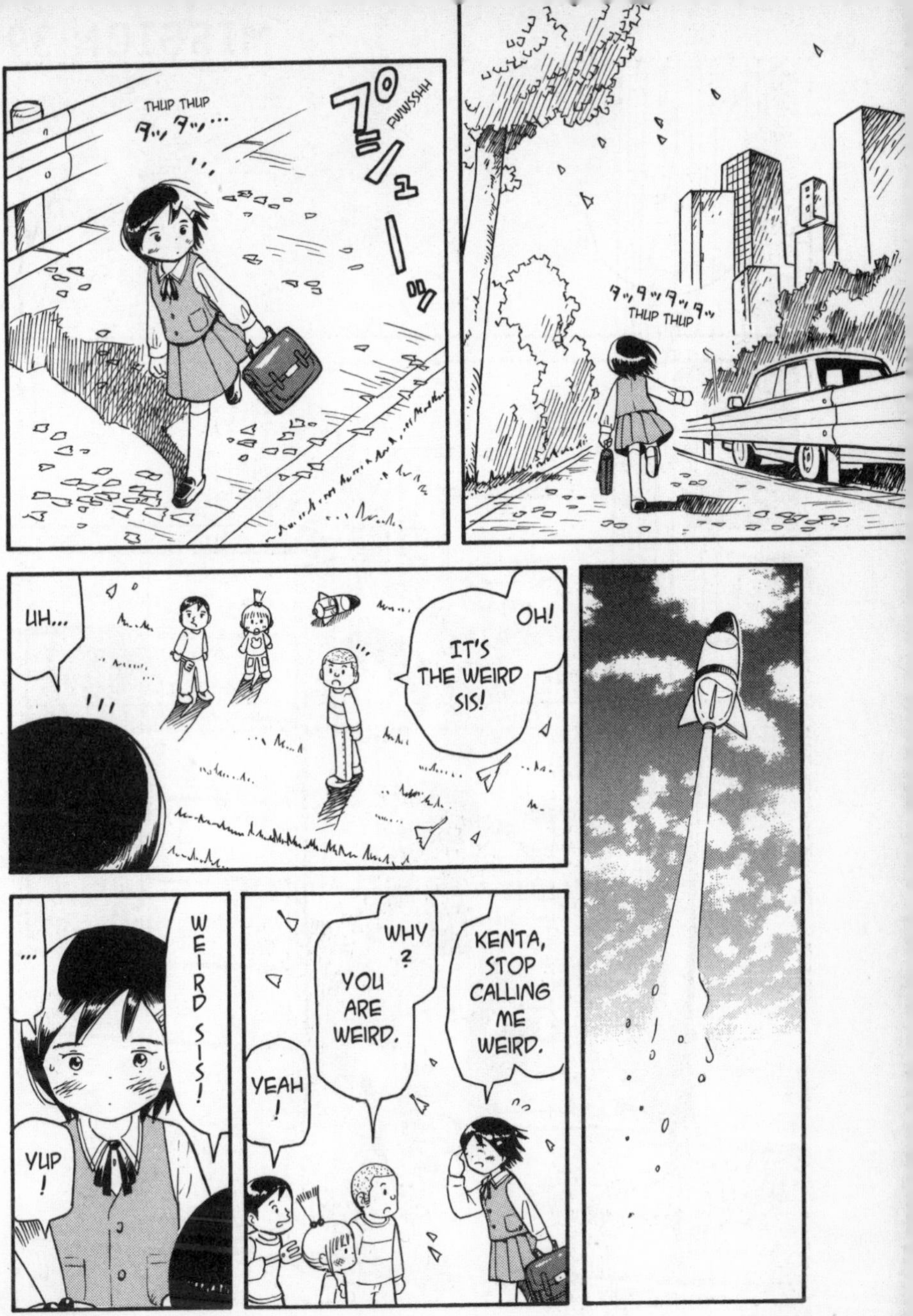
タッタッタッタッ
THUP THUP
THUP THUP
タッタッ…
プシューッ
PWUSSHH
OH!
IT'S THE WEIRD SIS!
UH...
KENTA, STOP CALLING ME WEIRD.
WHY?
YOU ARE WEIRD.
YEAH!
WEIRD SIS!
...
YUP!

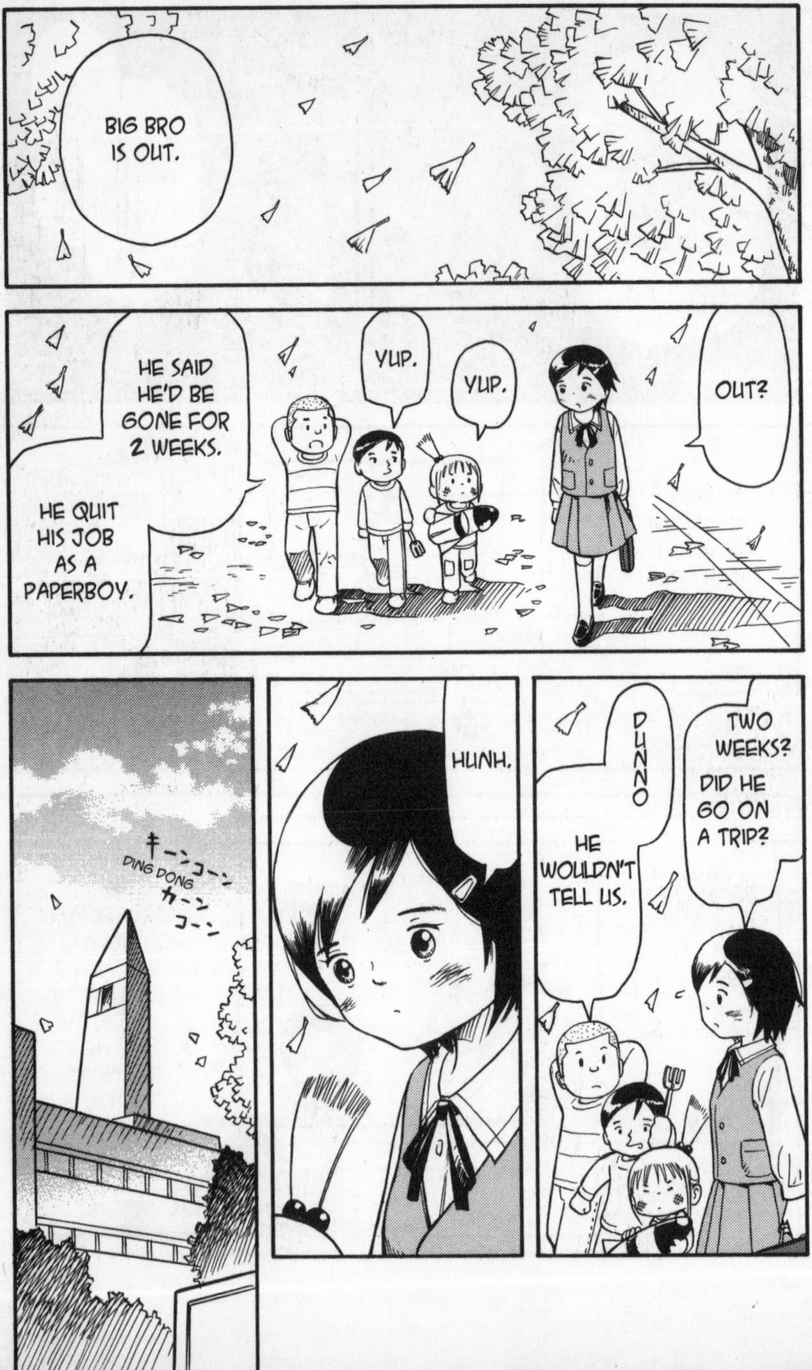
BIG BRO IS OUT.
OUT?
YUP.
YUP.
HE SAID HE'D BE GONE FOR 2 WEEKS.
HE QUIT HIS JOB AS A PAPERBOY.
TWO WEEKS? DID HE GO ON A TRIP?
DUNNO
HE WOULDN'T TELL US.
HUNH.
キーンコーン
DING DONG
カーンコーン

A SUPER-NOVA, OR STELLAR EXPLOSION
IS A PHENOMENON THAT OCCURS AT THE END OF A SUN'S LIFE.
SINCE THE SUPERNOVAS ARE AS BRIGHT AS AN ENTIRE GALAXY,
NEARBY EXPLOSIONS ARE VISIBLE WITH THE NAKED EYE.
IN EARLIER TIMES, BEFORE TELESCOPES AND OBSERVATIONAL EQUIPMENT, SCIENTISTS MISTOOK THE EXPLOSIONS FOR THE BIRTH OF A STAR, HENCE THE NAME "NOVA."
BUT WE NOW KNOW THAT THE EXPLOSIONS ARE IN FACT MADE BY DYING STARS.

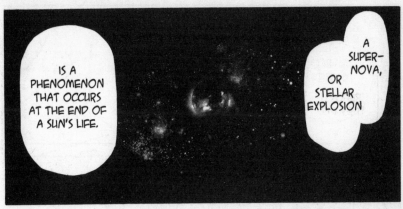

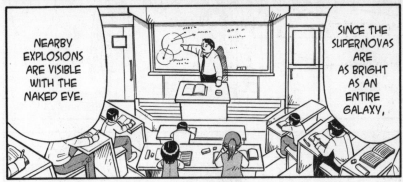

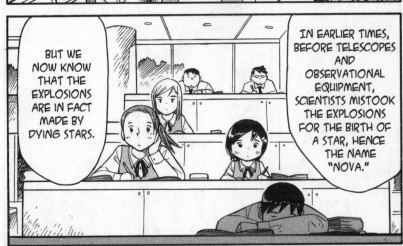

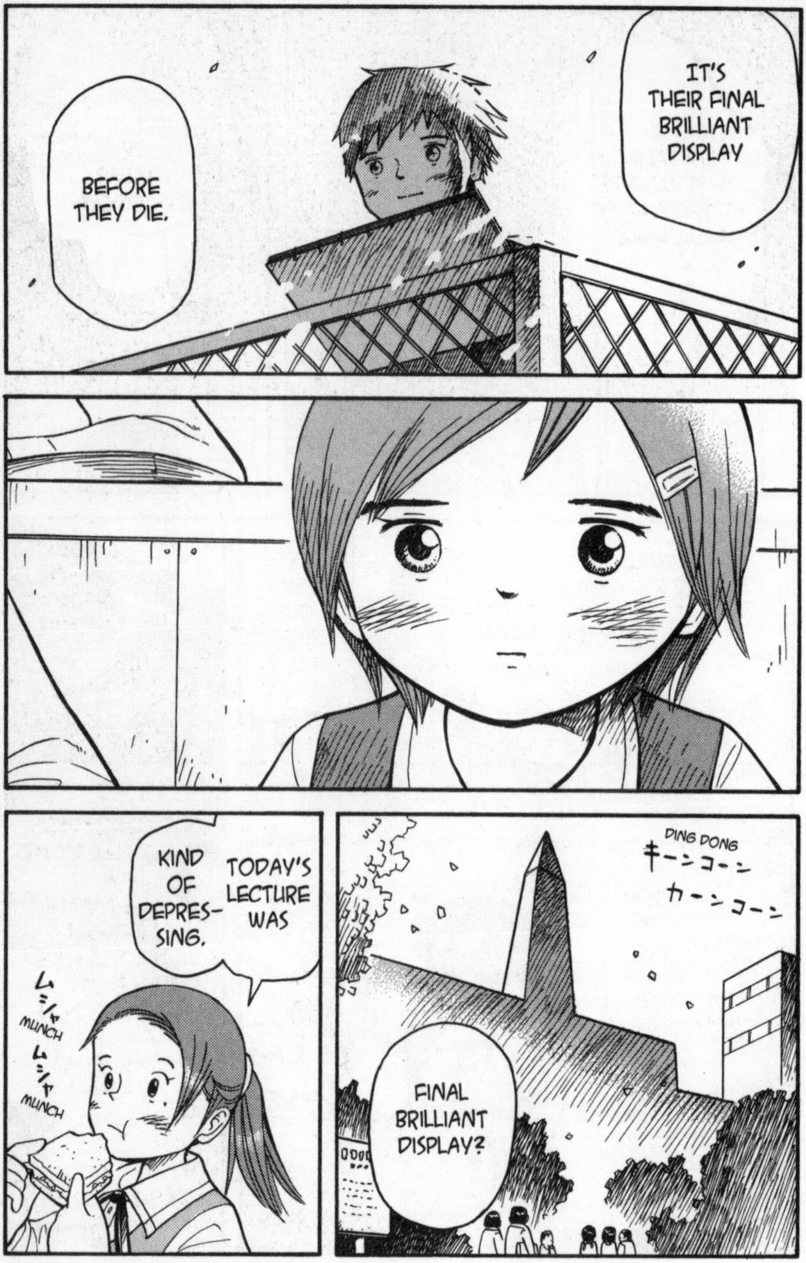
IT'S THEIR FINAL BRILLIANT DISPLAY
BEFORE THEY DIE.
DING DONG
キーンコーン
カーンコーン
FINAL BRILLIANT DISPLAY?
TODAY'S LECTURE WAS
KIND OF DEPRES-SING.
ムシャ
MUNCH
ムシャ
MUNCH

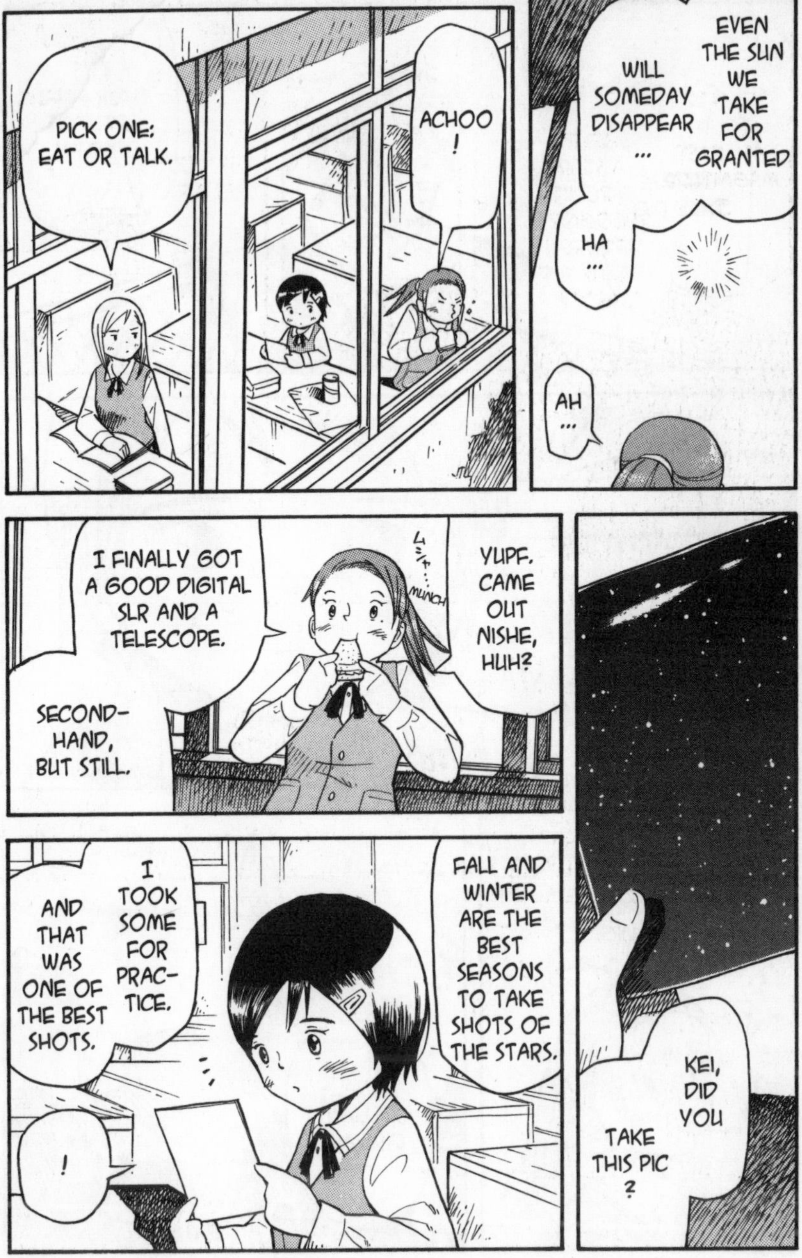
EVEN THE SUN WE TAKE FOR GRANTED
WILL SOMEDAY DISAPPEAR ...
HA ...
AH ...
ACHOO !
PICK ONE: EAT OR TALK.
KEI, DID YOU
TAKE THIS PIC ?
YUPF. CAME OUT NISHE, HUH?
ムシャ… MUNCH
I FINALLY GOT A GOOD DIGITAL SLR AND A TELESCOPE.
SECOND-HAND, BUT STILL.
FALL AND WINTER ARE THE BEST SEASONS TO TAKE SHOTS OF THE STARS.
I TOOK SOME FOR PRAC-TICE.
AND THAT WAS ONE OF THE BEST SHOTS.
!

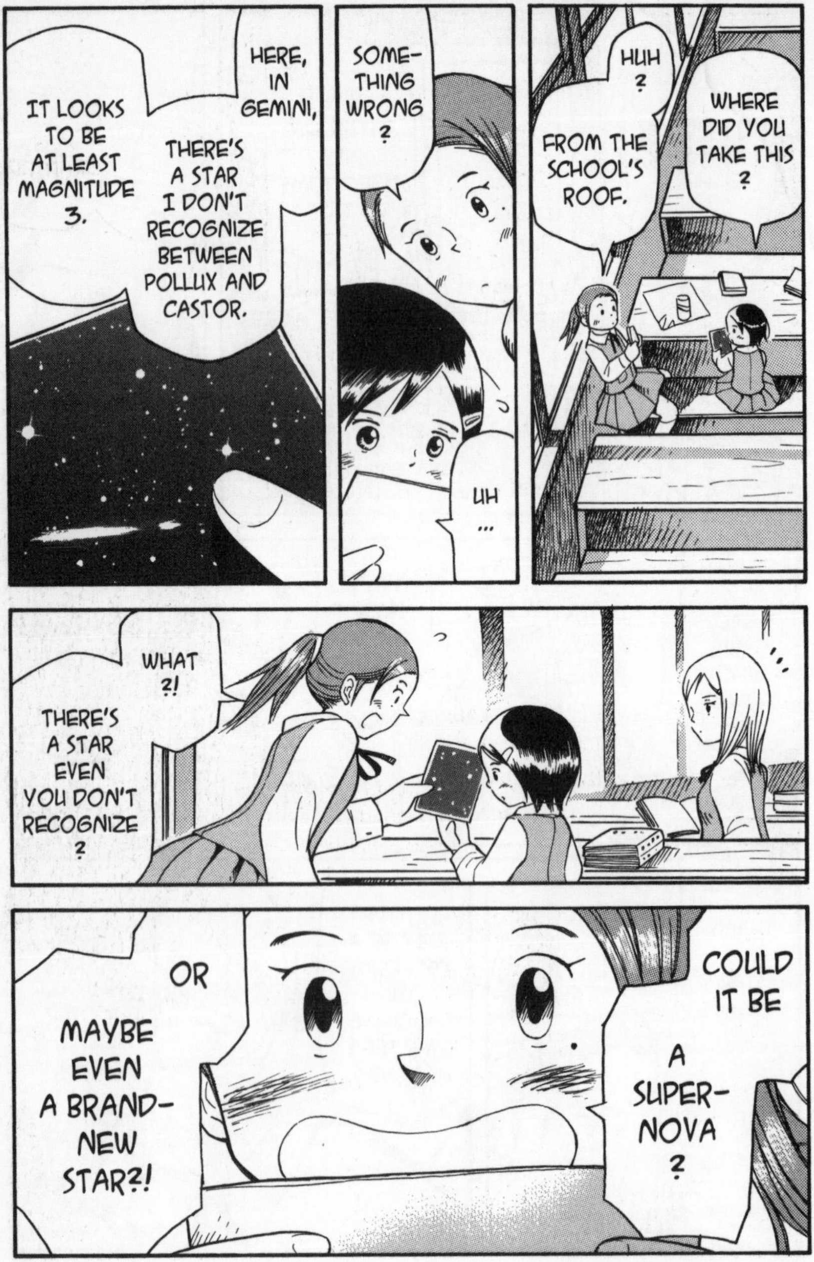
WHERE DID YOU TAKE THIS?
HUH?
FROM THE SCHOOL'S ROOF.
SOME-THING WRONG?
UH...
HERE, IN GEMINI,
THERE'S A STAR I DON'T RECOGNIZE BETWEEN POLLUX AND CASTOR.
IT LOOKS TO BE AT LEAST MAGNITUDE 3.
WHAT?!
THERE'S A STAR EVEN YOU DON'T RECOGNIZE?
COULD IT BE
A SUPER-NOVA?
OR
MAYBE EVEN A BRAND-NEW STAR?!

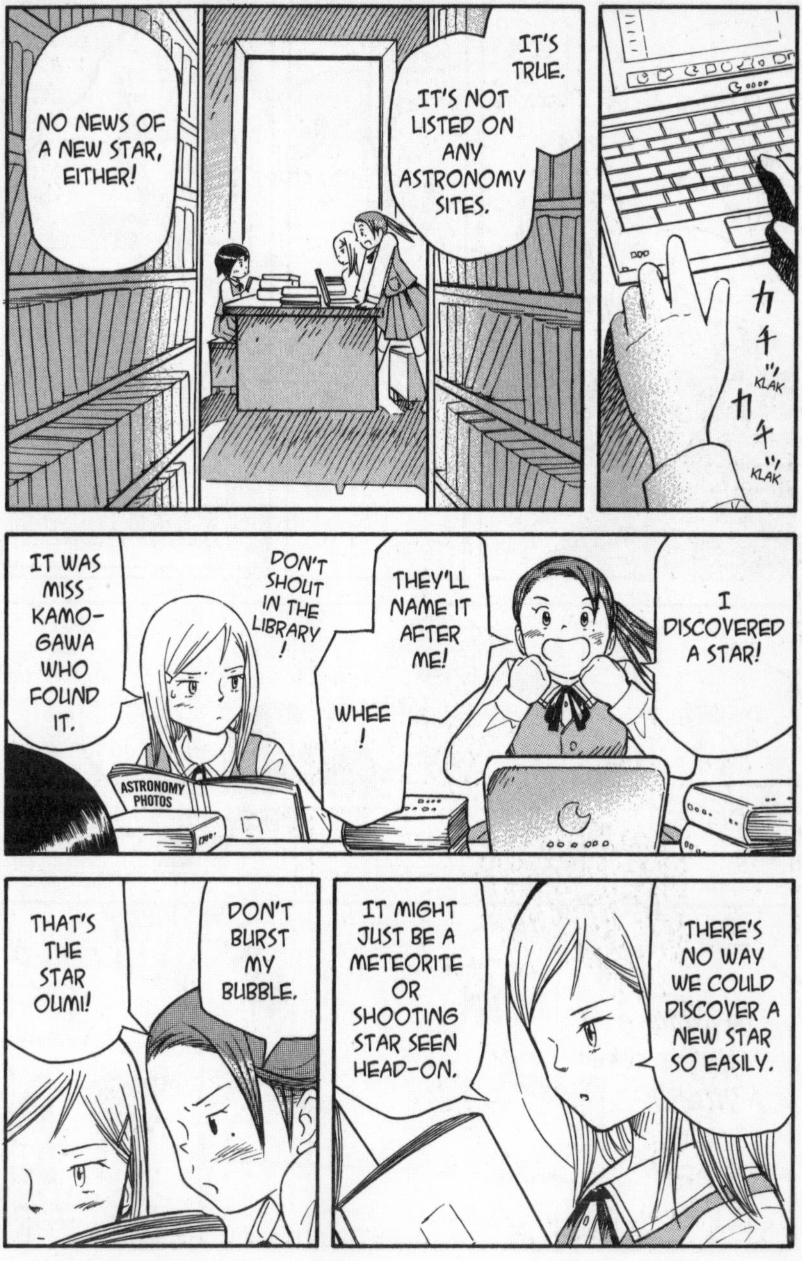
カチッ
KLAK
カチッ
KLAK
IT'S TRUE.
IT'S NOT LISTED ON ANY ASTRONOMY SITES.
NO NEWS OF A NEW STAR, EITHER!
I DISCOVERED A STAR!
THEY'LL NAME IT AFTER ME!
WHEE!
DON'T SHOUT IN THE LIBRARY!
IT WAS MISS KAMOGAWA WHO FOUND IT.
ASTRONOMY PHOTOS
THERE'S NO WAY WE COULD DISCOVER A NEW STAR SO EASILY.
IT MIGHT JUST BE A METEORITE OR SHOOTING STAR SEEN HEAD-ON.
DON'T BURST MY BUBBLE.
THAT'S THE STAR OUMI!

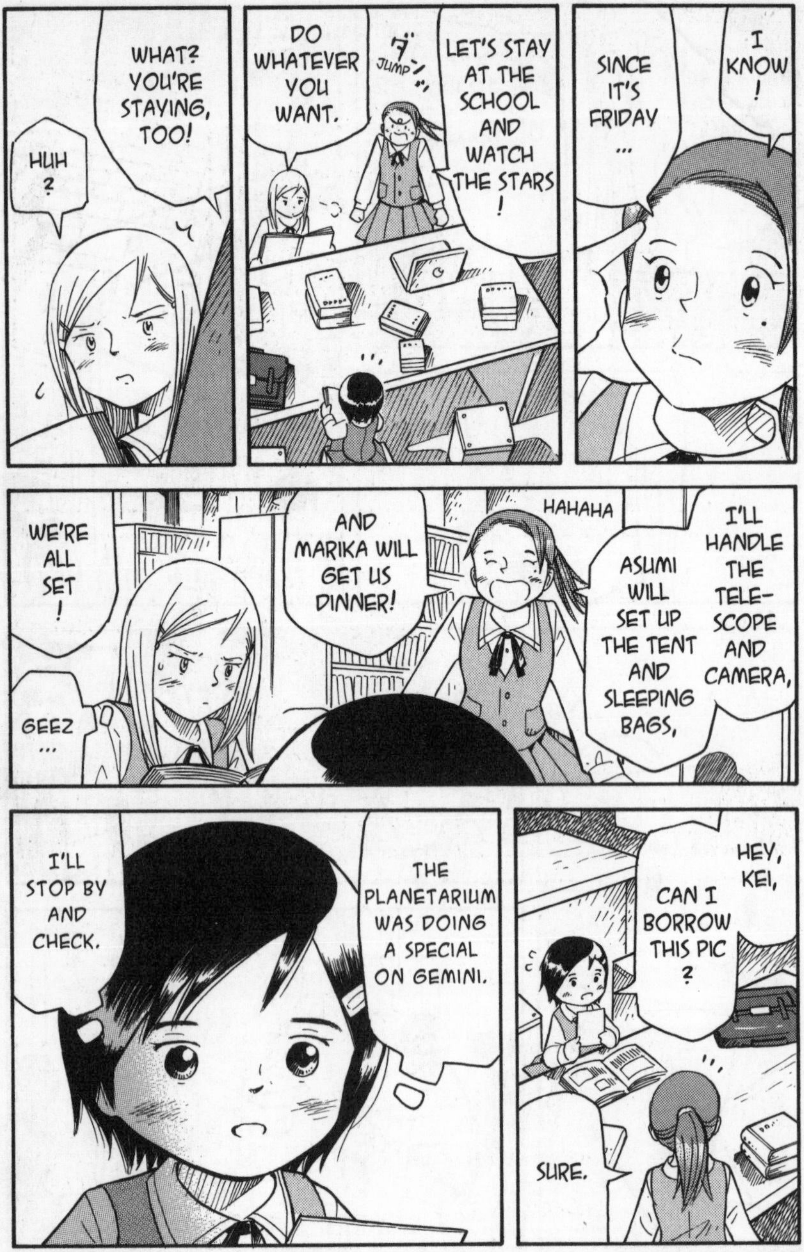
I KNOW!
SINCE IT'S FRIDAY ...
LET'S STAY AT THE SCHOOL AND WATCH THE STARS!
ヴン JUMP
DO WHATEVER YOU WANT.
WHAT? YOU'RE STAYING, TOO!
HUH?
I'LL HANDLE THE TELE-SCOPE AND CAMERA,
ASUMI WILL SET UP THE TENT AND SLEEPING BAGS,
HAHAHA
AND MARIKA WILL GET US DINNER!
WE'RE ALL SET!
GEEZ ...
HEY, KEI,
CAN I BORROW THIS PIC?
SURE.
THE PLANETARIUM WAS DOING A SPECIAL ON GEMINI.
I'LL STOP BY AND CHECK.

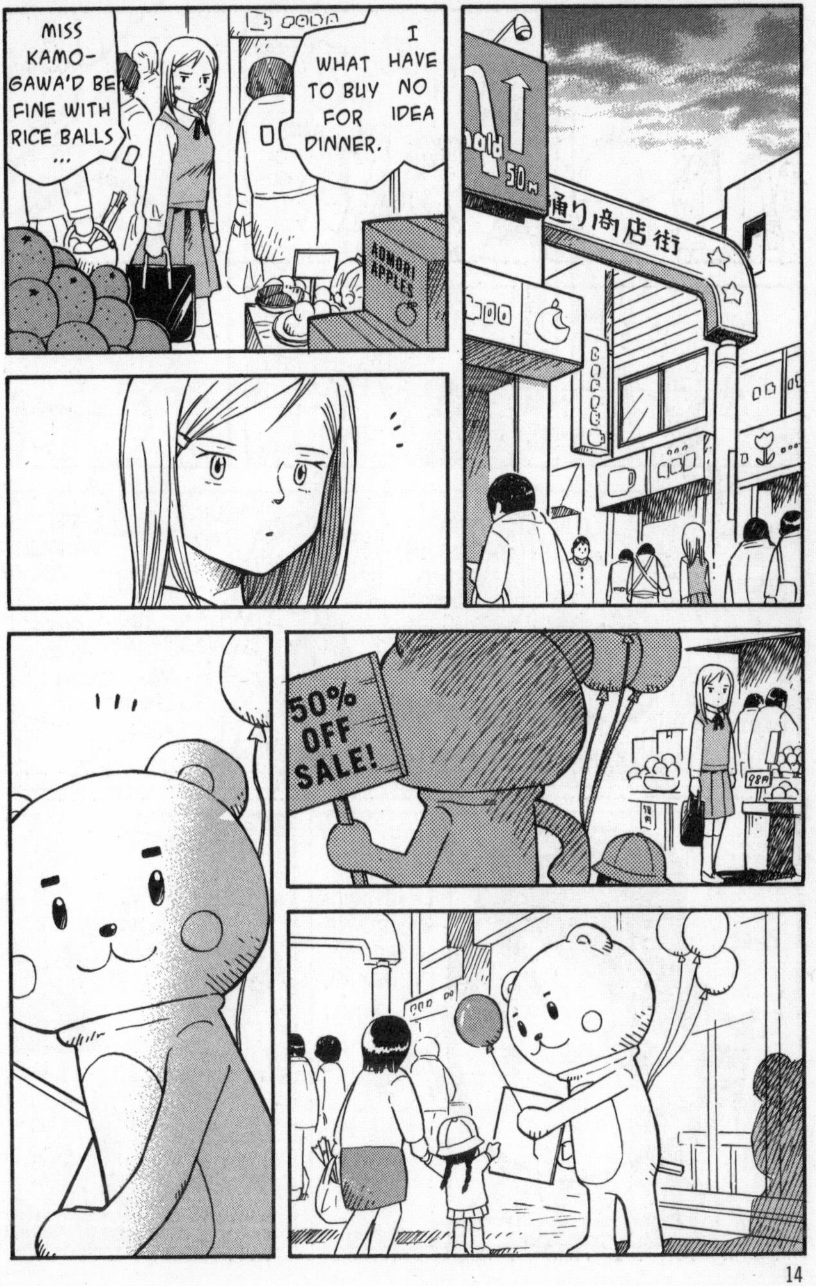
通り商店街
50m
I HAVE NO IDEA WHAT TO BUY FOR DINNER.
MISS KAMO-GAWA'D BE FINE WITH RICE BALLS ...
AOMORI APPLES
50% OFF SALE!

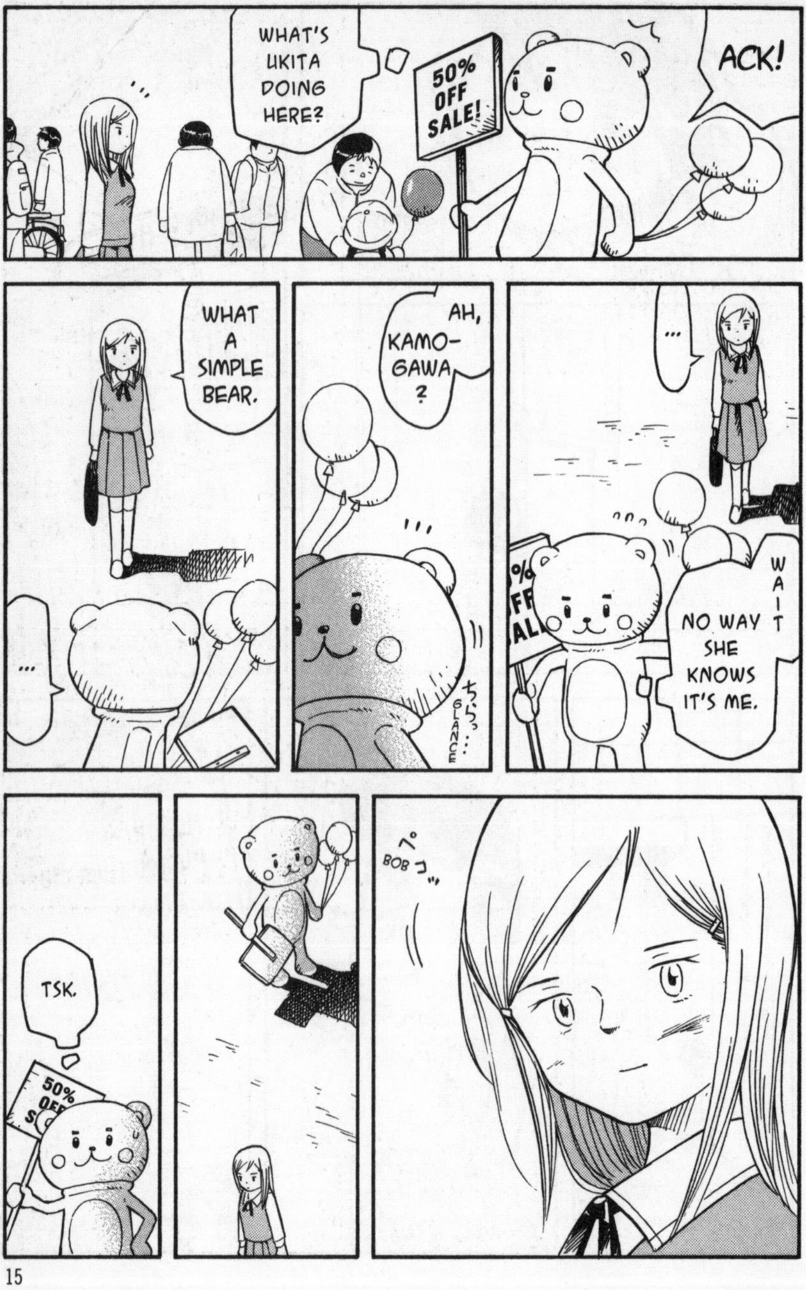
ACK!
WHAT'S UKITA DOING HERE?
...
WAIT
NO WAY SHE KNOWS IT'S ME.
AH, KAMOGAWA?
GLANCE
WHAT A SIMPLE BEAR.
...
BOB
TSK.

THUP...
タッ…

PLANETARIUM

THUP THUP
タッタッ タッタッ

！

ガガ…
SLIDE

HUH
?

CLOSED
?

Notice:
Planetarium closed

As of today,
November 29th,
this planetarium is
shutting down.
Thank you for
your years of support.

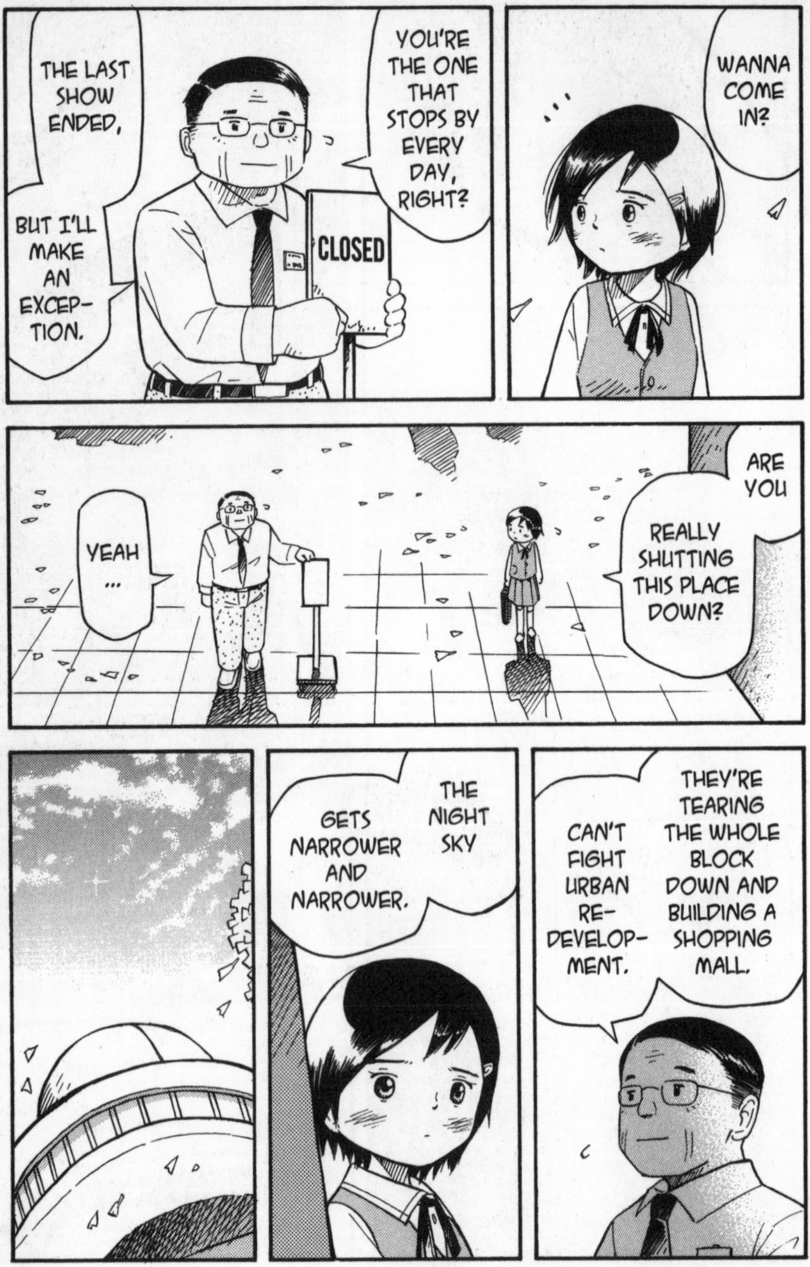
WANNA COME IN?
...
YOU'RE THE ONE THAT STOPS BY EVERY DAY, RIGHT?
CLOSED
THE LAST SHOW ENDED,
BUT I'LL MAKE AN EXCEPTION.
ARE YOU REALLY SHUTTING THIS PLACE DOWN?
YEAH ...
THEY'RE TEARING THE WHOLE BLOCK DOWN AND BUILDING A SHOPPING MALL.
CAN'T FIGHT URBAN RE-DEVELOPMENT.
THE NIGHT SKY GETS NARROWER AND NARROWER.

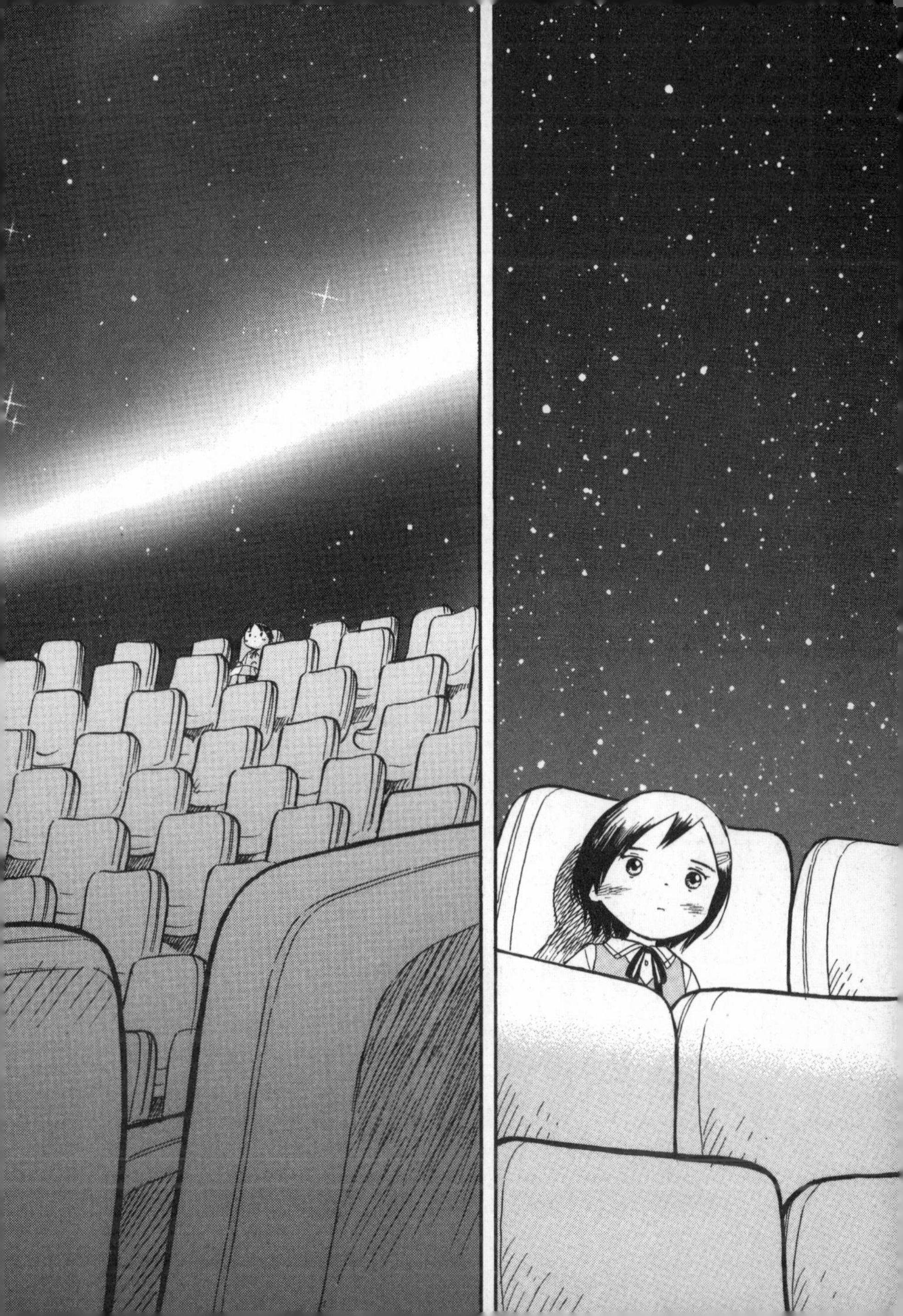

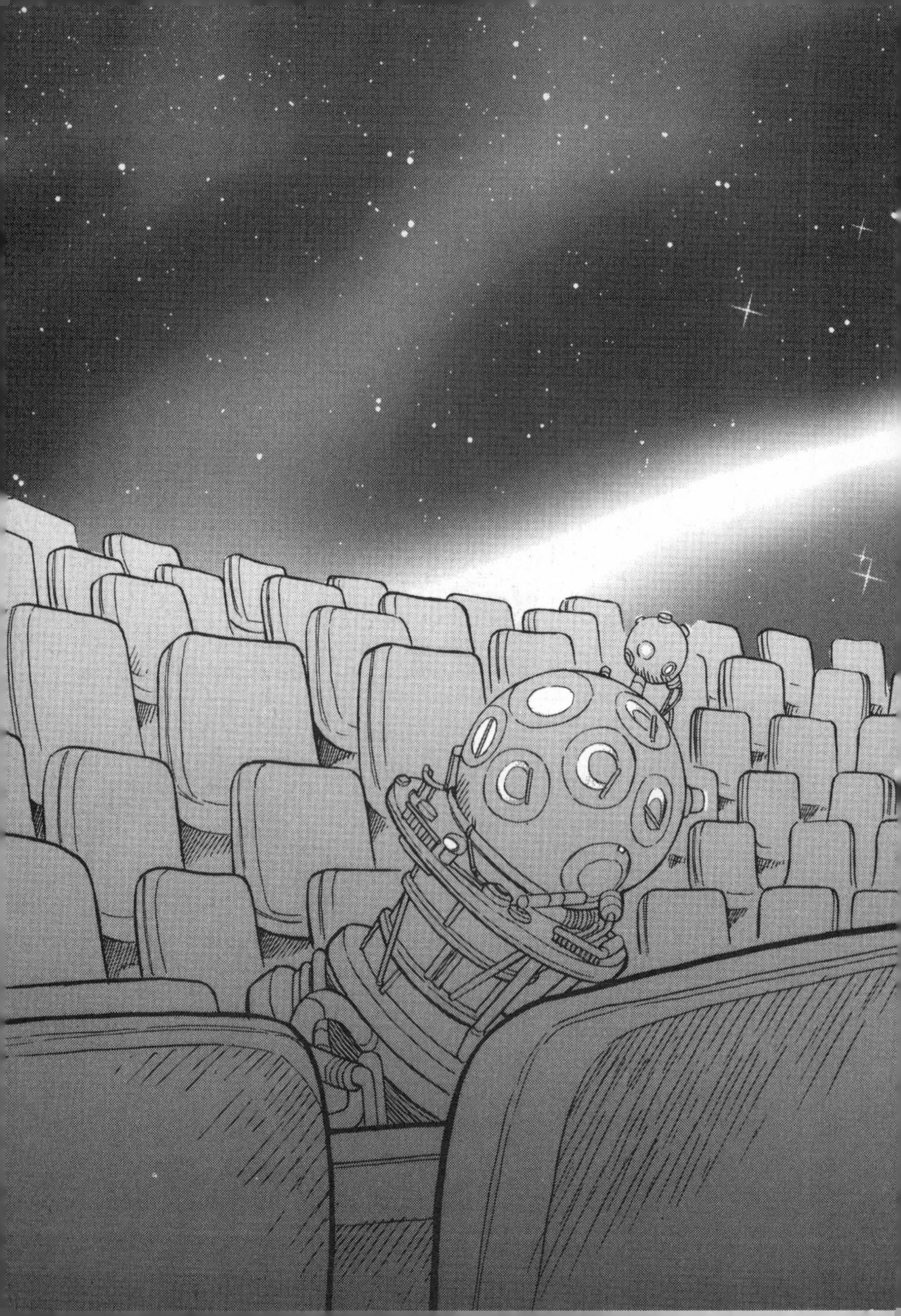

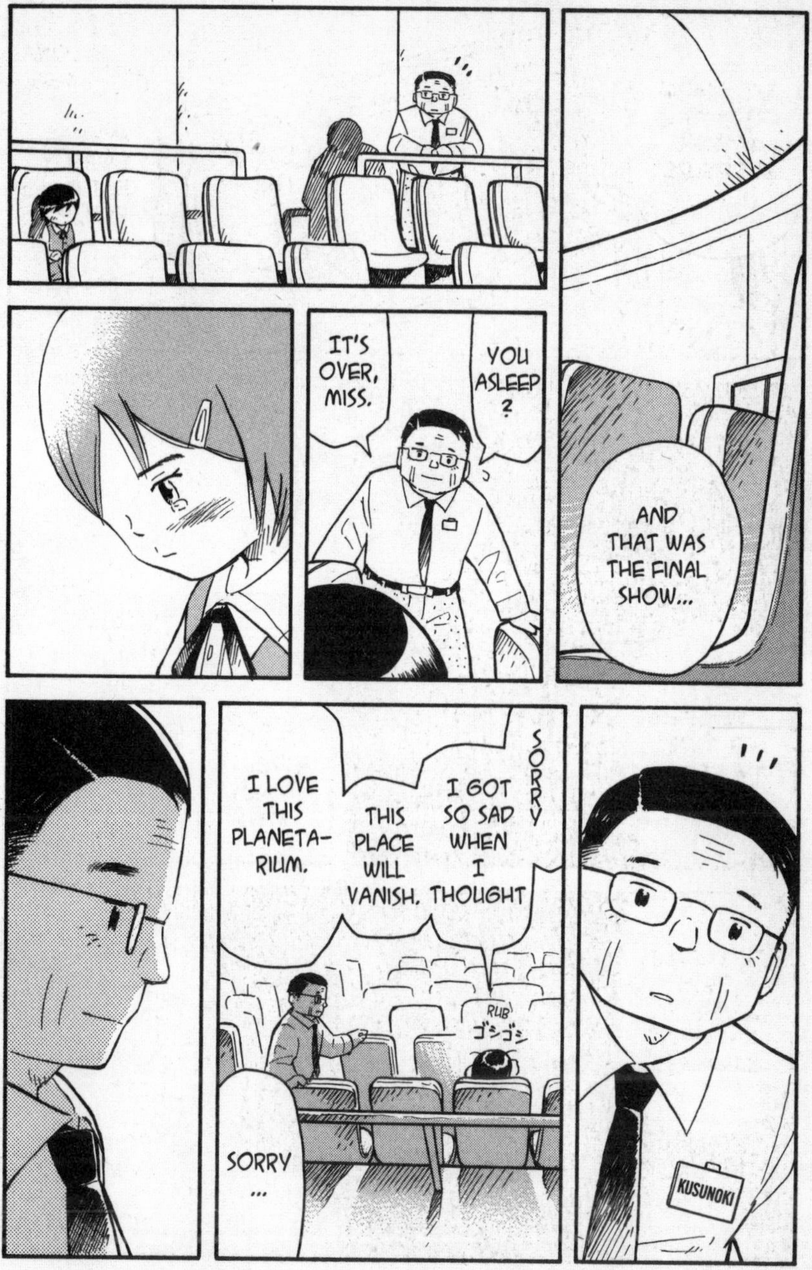
AND THAT WAS THE FINAL SHOW...
YOU ASLEEP?
IT'S OVER, MISS.
KUSUNOKI
SORRY
I GOT SO SAD WHEN I THOUGHT THIS PLACE WILL VANISH.
I LOVE THIS PLANETARIUM.
RUB
ゴシゴシ
SORRY...

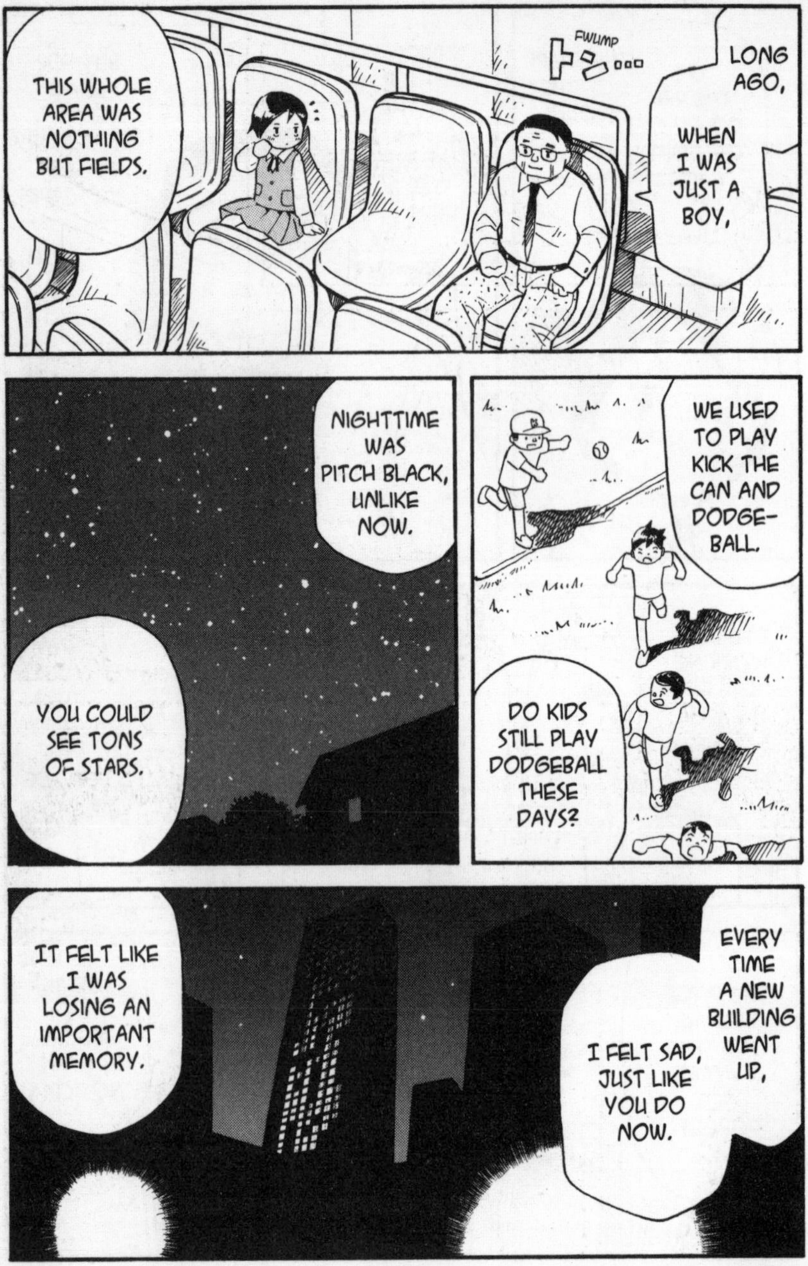
FWUMP
LONG AGO,
WHEN I WAS JUST A BOY,
THIS WHOLE AREA WAS NOTHING BUT FIELDS.
WE USED TO PLAY KICK THE CAN AND DODGE-BALL.
DO KIDS STILL PLAY DODGEBALL THESE DAYS?
NIGHTTIME WAS PITCH BLACK, UNLIKE NOW.
YOU COULD SEE TONS OF STARS.
EVERY TIME A NEW BUILDING WENT UP,
I FELT SAD, JUST LIKE YOU DO NOW.
IT FELT LIKE I WAS LOSING AN IMPORTANT MEMORY.

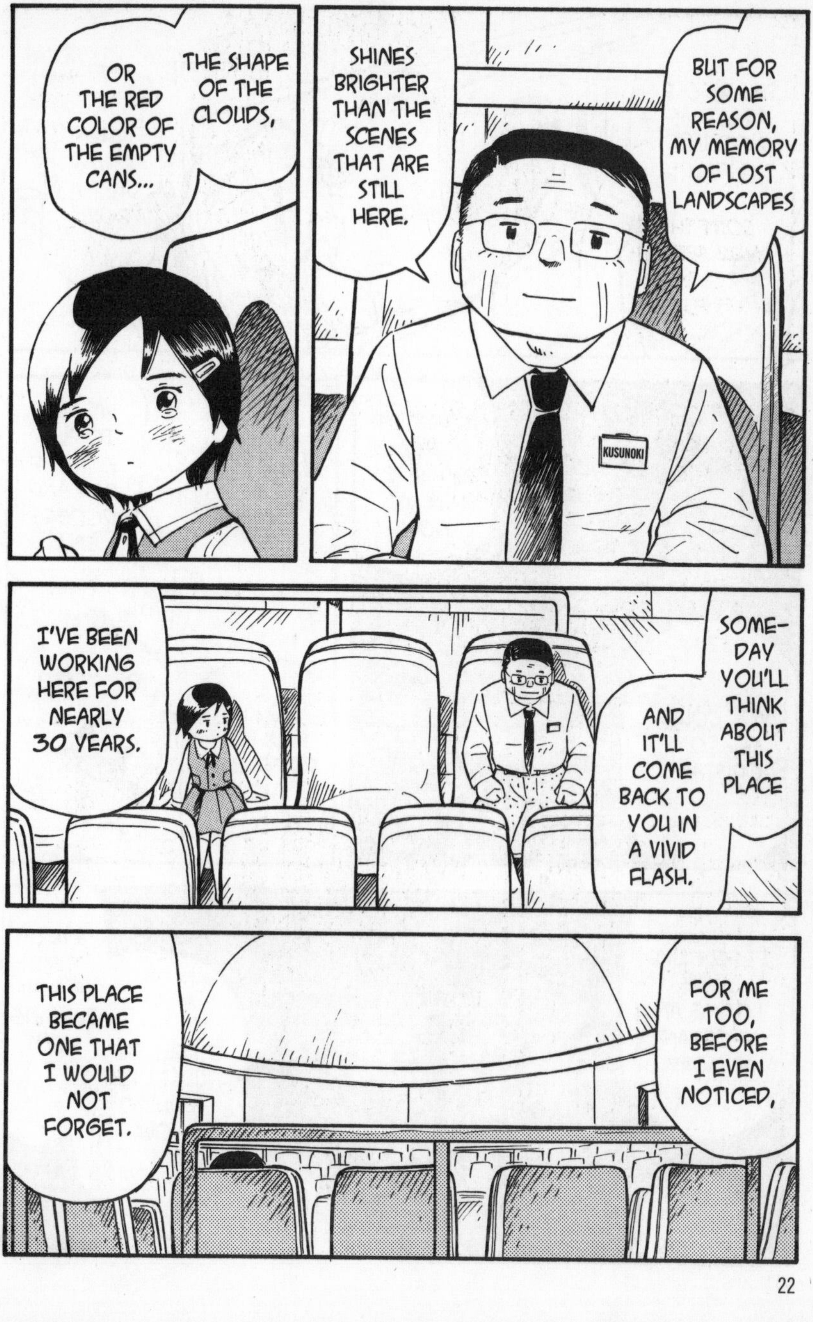
BUT FOR SOME REASON, MY MEMORY OF LOST LANDSCAPES
SHINES BRIGHTER THAN THE SCENES THAT ARE STILL HERE.
KUSUNOKI
THE SHAPE OF THE CLOUDS,
OR THE RED COLOR OF THE EMPTY CANS...
SOME-DAY YOU'LL THINK ABOUT THIS PLACE
AND IT'LL COME BACK TO YOU IN A VIVID FLASH.
I'VE BEEN WORKING HERE FOR NEARLY 30 YEARS.
FOR ME TOO, BEFORE I EVEN NOTICED,
THIS PLACE BECAME ONE THAT I WOULD NOT FORGET.

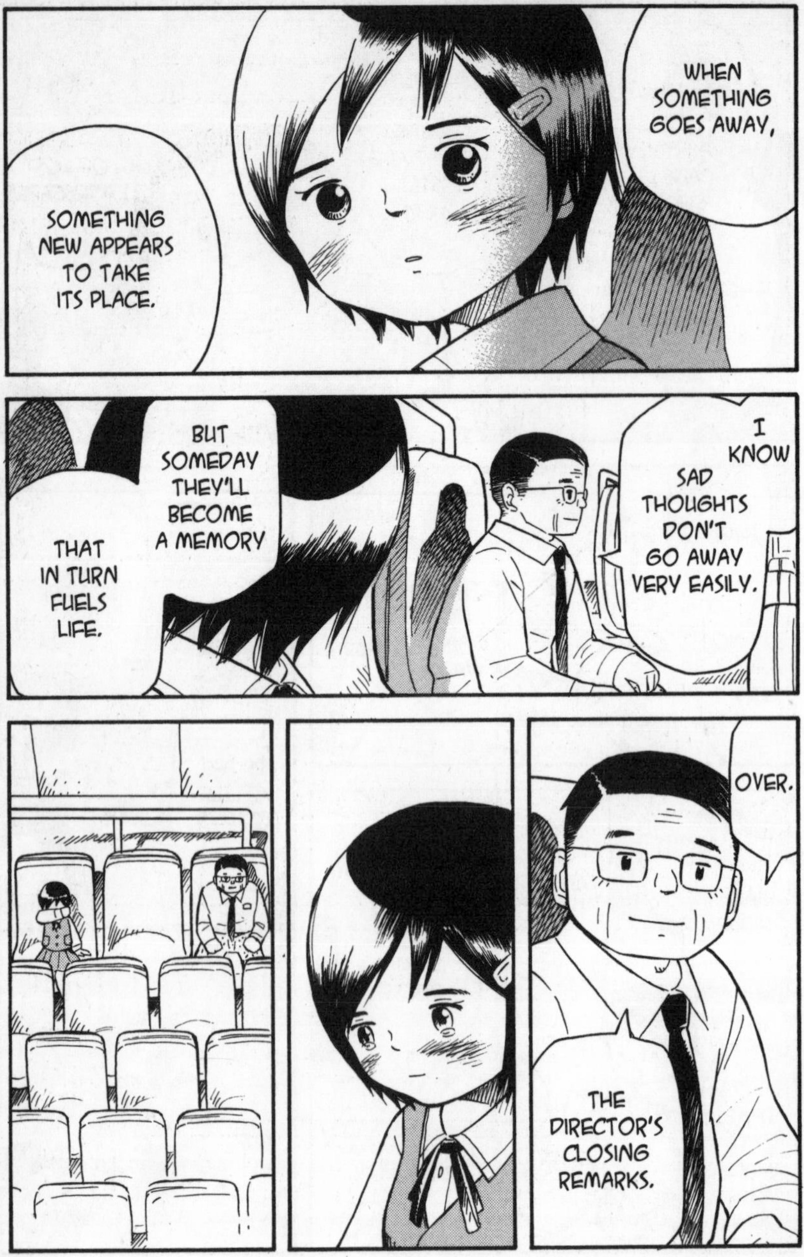
WHEN SOMETHING GOES AWAY,
SOMETHING NEW APPEARS TO TAKE ITS PLACE.
I KNOW
SAD THOUGHTS DON'T GO AWAY VERY EASILY.
BUT SOMEDAY THEY'LL BECOME A MEMORY
THAT IN TURN FUELS LIFE.
OVER.
THE DIRECTOR'S CLOSING REMARKS.

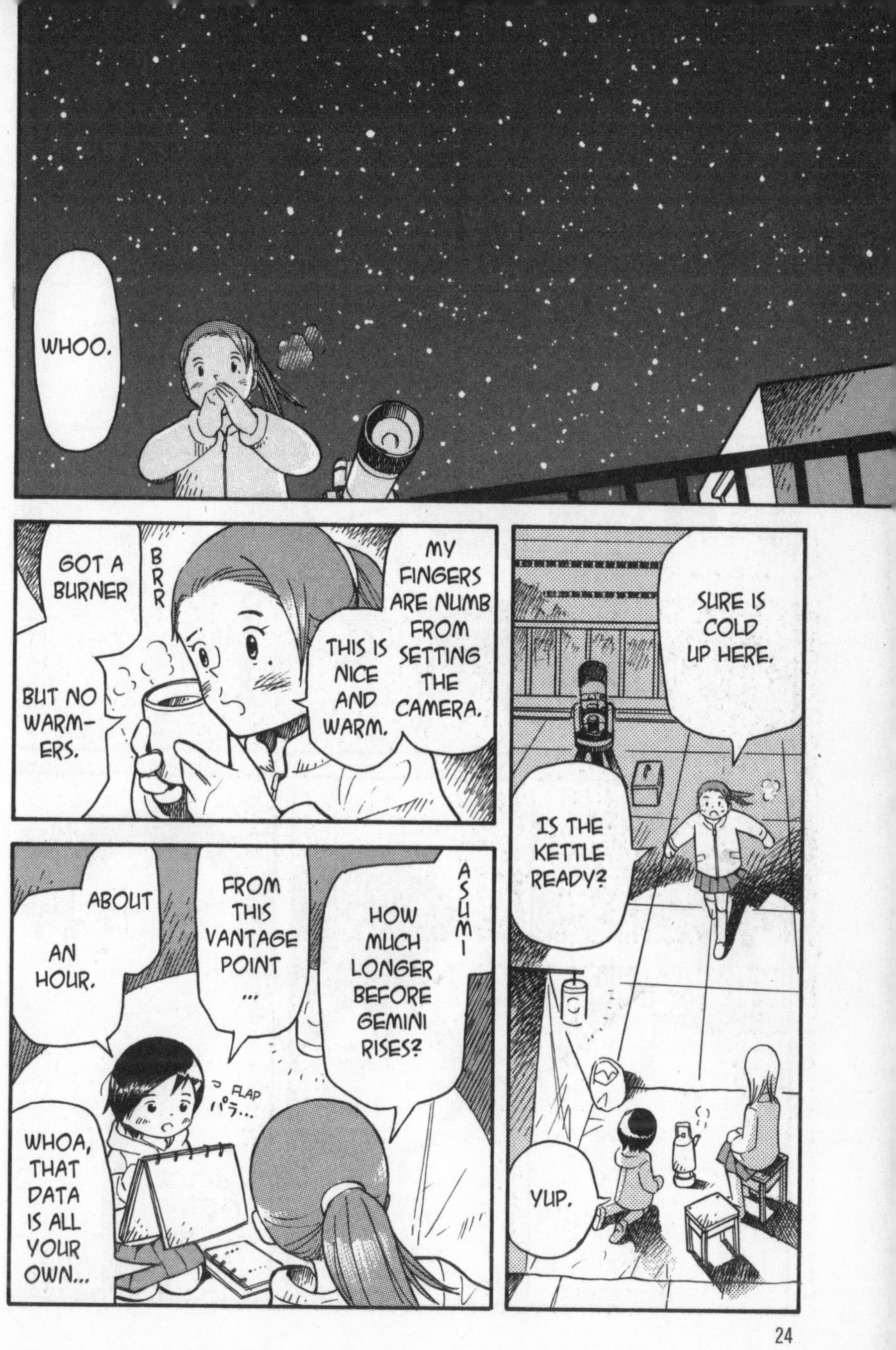
WHOO.
SURE IS COLD UP HERE.
IS THE KETTLE READY?
YUP.
MY FINGERS ARE NUMB FROM SETTING THE CAMERA.
THIS IS NICE AND WARM.
BRR
GOT A BURNER
BUT NO WARMERS.
ASUMI
HOW MUCH LONGER BEFORE GEMINI RISES?
FROM THIS VANTAGE POINT ...
ABOUT
AN HOUR.
FLAP パラ...
WHOA, THAT DATA IS ALL YOUR OWN...

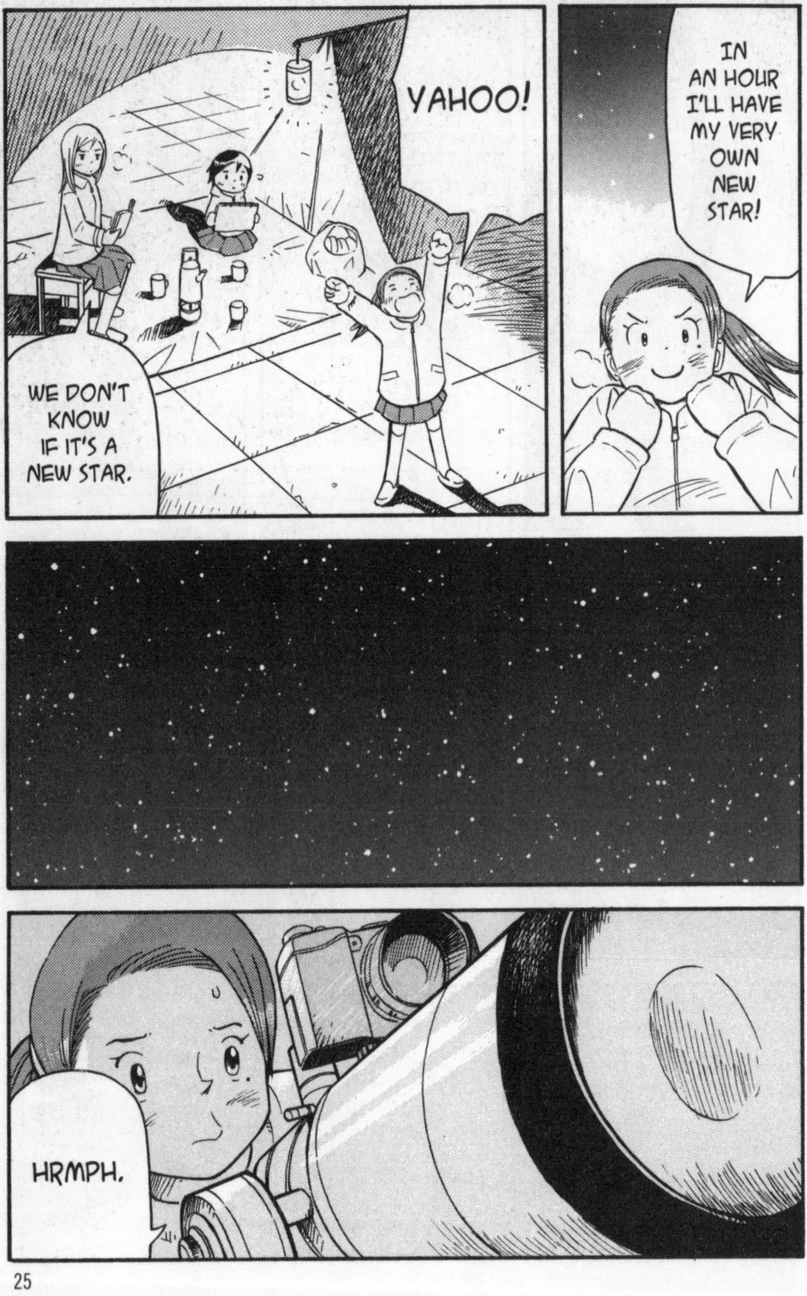
IN AN HOUR I'LL HAVE MY VERY OWN NEW STAR!
YAHOO!
WE DON'T KNOW IF IT'S A NEW STAR.
HRMPH.

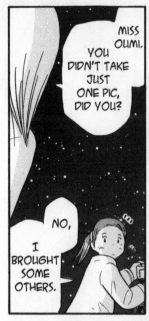

I CAN'T FIND IT.
MAYBE IT WASN'T A STAR BUT A SUPER-NOVA.
THOSE FADE IN AS LITTLE AS TWO MONTHS.
NO WAY ...
MISS OUMI. YOU DIDN'T TAKE JUST ONE PIC, DID YOU?
NO, I BROUGHT SOME OTHERS.
THESE ARE ALL.
IT WAS AROUND GEMINI IN THE OTHER SHOT.
IF THAT'S NOT A NEW STAR, WHAT IS IT?

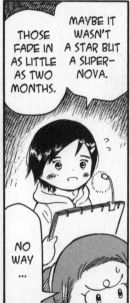

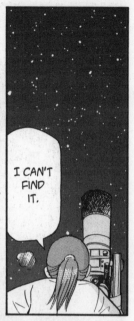

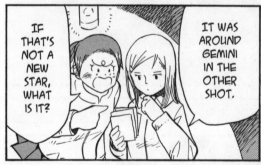

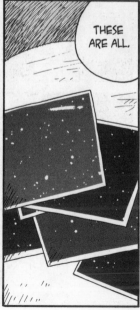

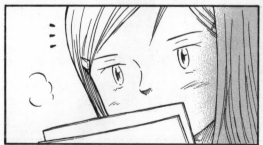

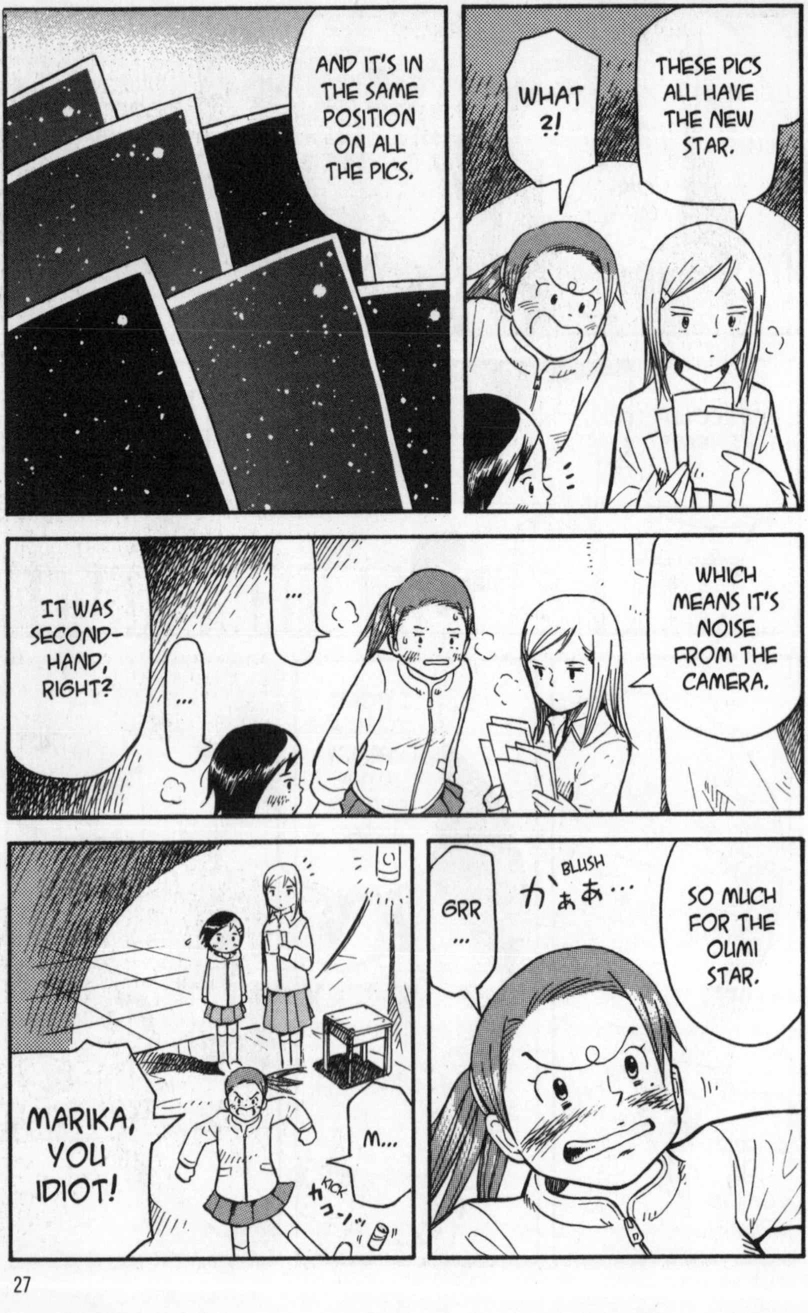
THESE PICS ALL HAVE THE NEW STAR.
WHAT?!
AND IT'S IN THE SAME POSITION ON ALL THE PICS.
WHICH MEANS IT'S NOISE FROM THE CAMERA.
...
...
IT WAS SECOND-HAND, RIGHT?
SO MUCH FOR THE OUMI STAR.
BLUSH
かぁあ…
GRR ...
M...
MARIKA, YOU IDIOT!
KICK
カコーンッ

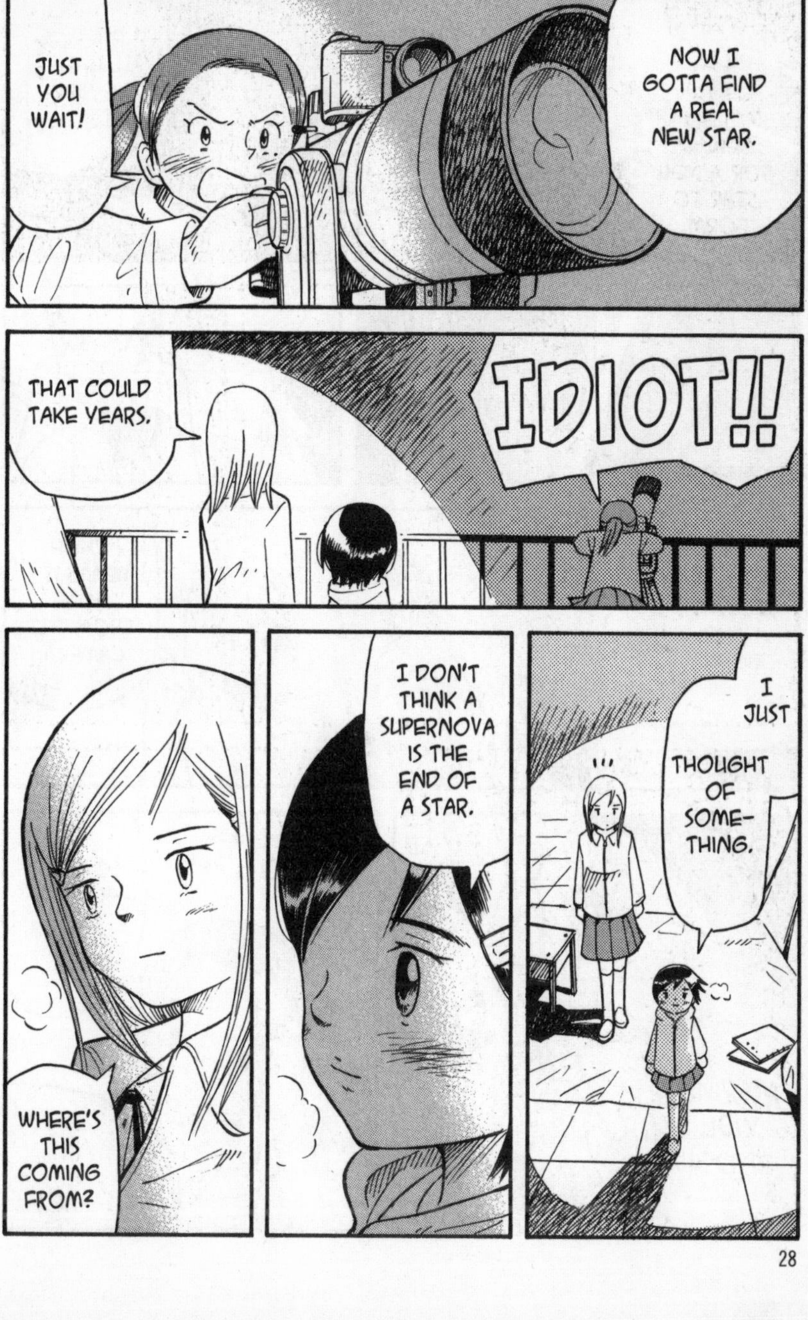
NOW I GOTTA FIND A REAL NEW STAR.
JUST YOU WAIT!
IDIOT!!
THAT COULD TAKE YEARS.
I JUST THOUGHT OF SOME-THING.
I DON'T THINK A SUPERNOVA IS THE END OF A STAR.
WHERE'S THIS COMING FROM?

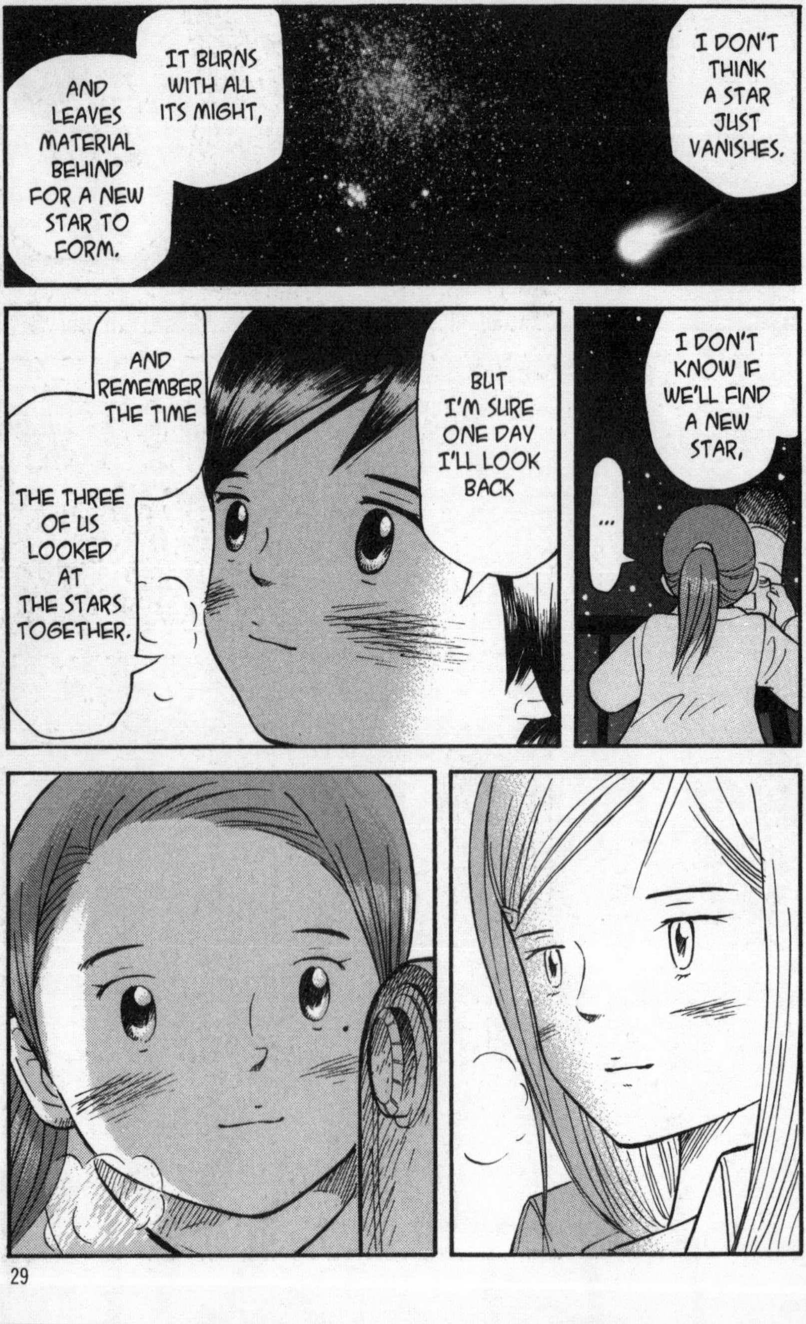
I DON'T THINK A STAR JUST VANISHES.
IT BURNS WITH ALL ITS MIGHT,
AND LEAVES MATERIAL BEHIND FOR A NEW STAR TO FORM.
I DON'T KNOW IF WE'LL FIND A NEW STAR,
...
BUT I'M SURE ONE DAY I'LL LOOK BACK
AND REMEMBER THE TIME
THE THREE OF US LOOKED AT THE STARS TOGETHER.

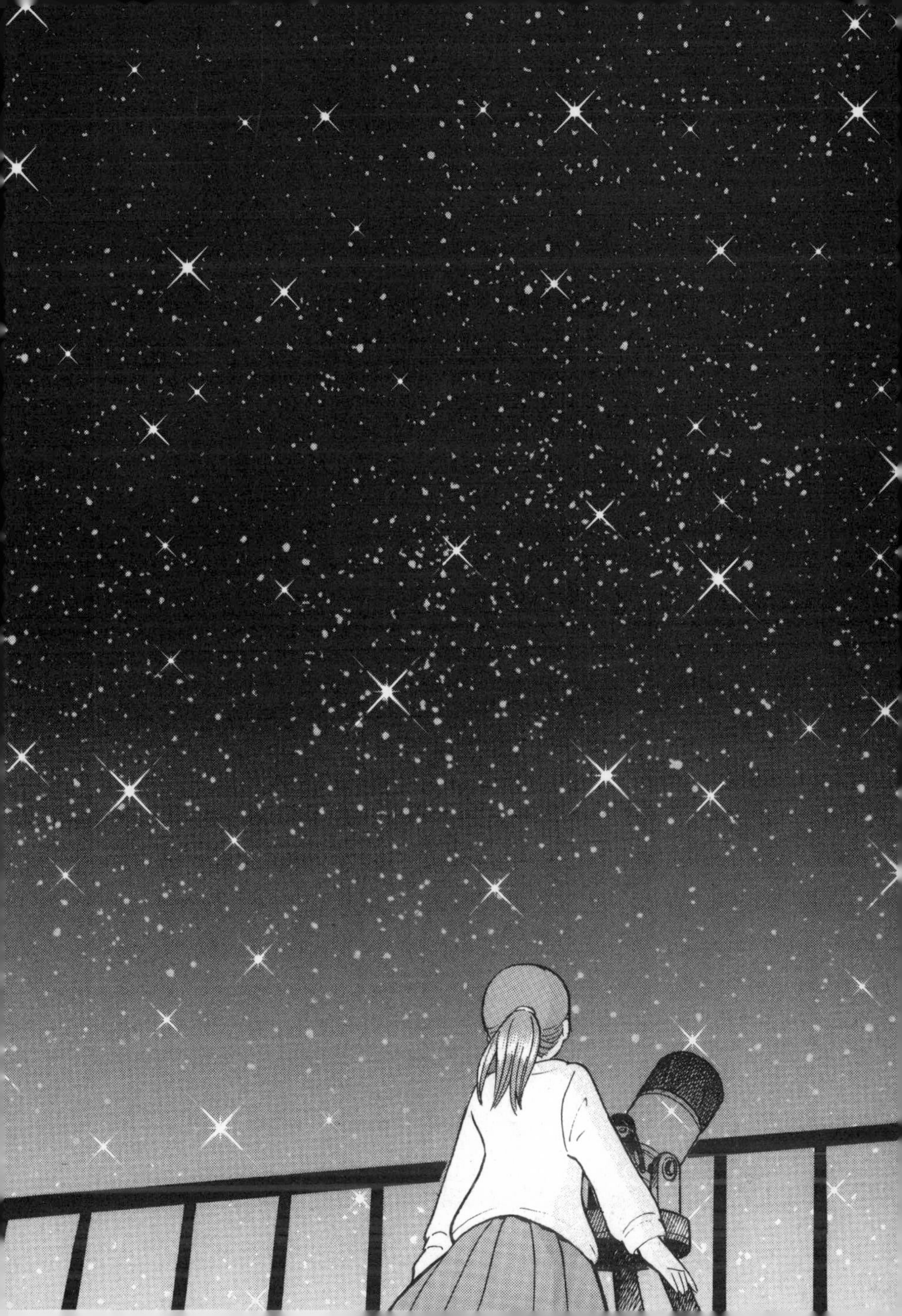

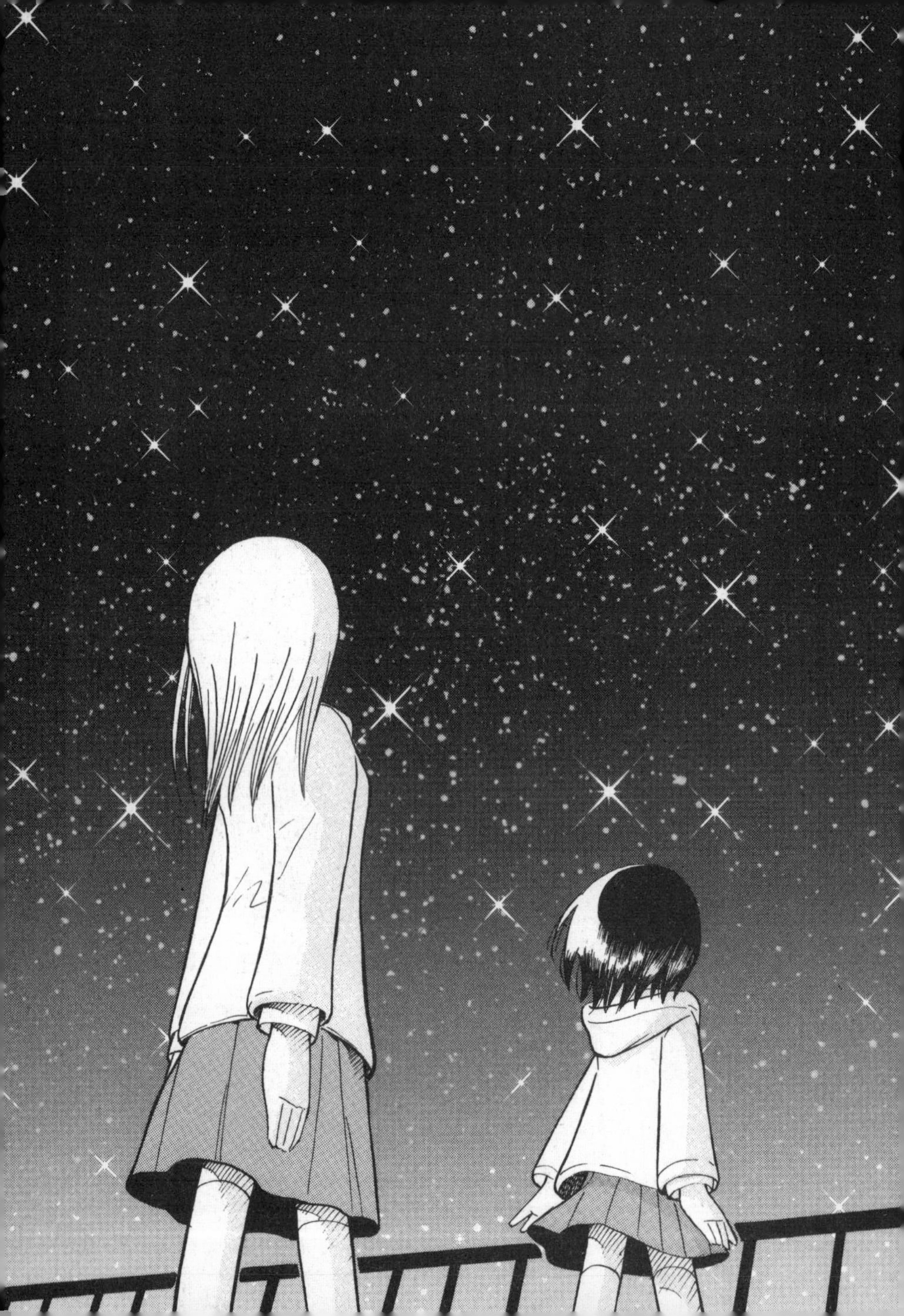

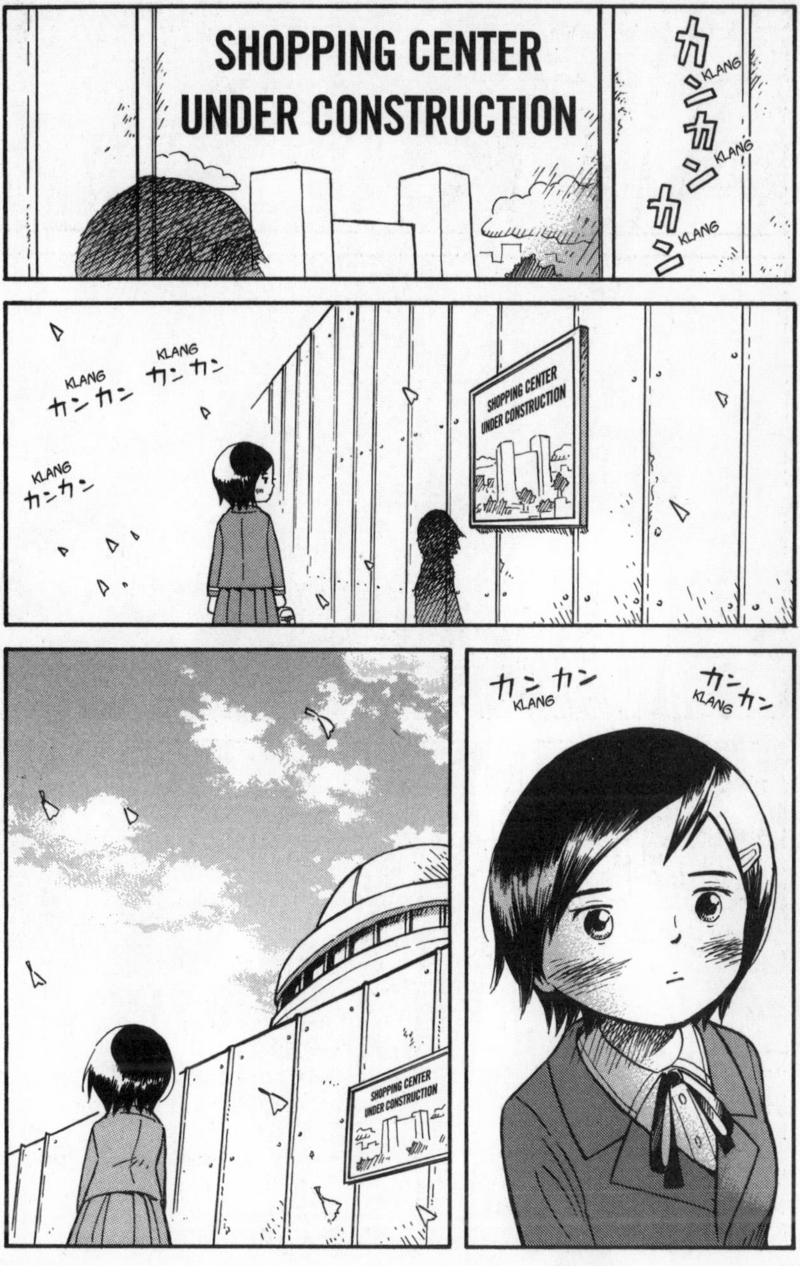
SHOPPING CENTER
UNDER CONSTRUCTION
カン KLANG
カン KLANG
カン KLANG
KLANG カンカン
KLANG カンカン
SHOPPING CENTER
UNDER CONSTRUCTION
KLANG カンカン
カンカン KLANG
カンカン KLANG
SHOPPING CENTER
UNDER CONSTRUCTION

Shu Suzuki

KLATCH

Suzuki
Shu Su
Shu
☆☆☆☆
Shu Suzuki
☆☆☆☆☆☆☆

FLUTTER

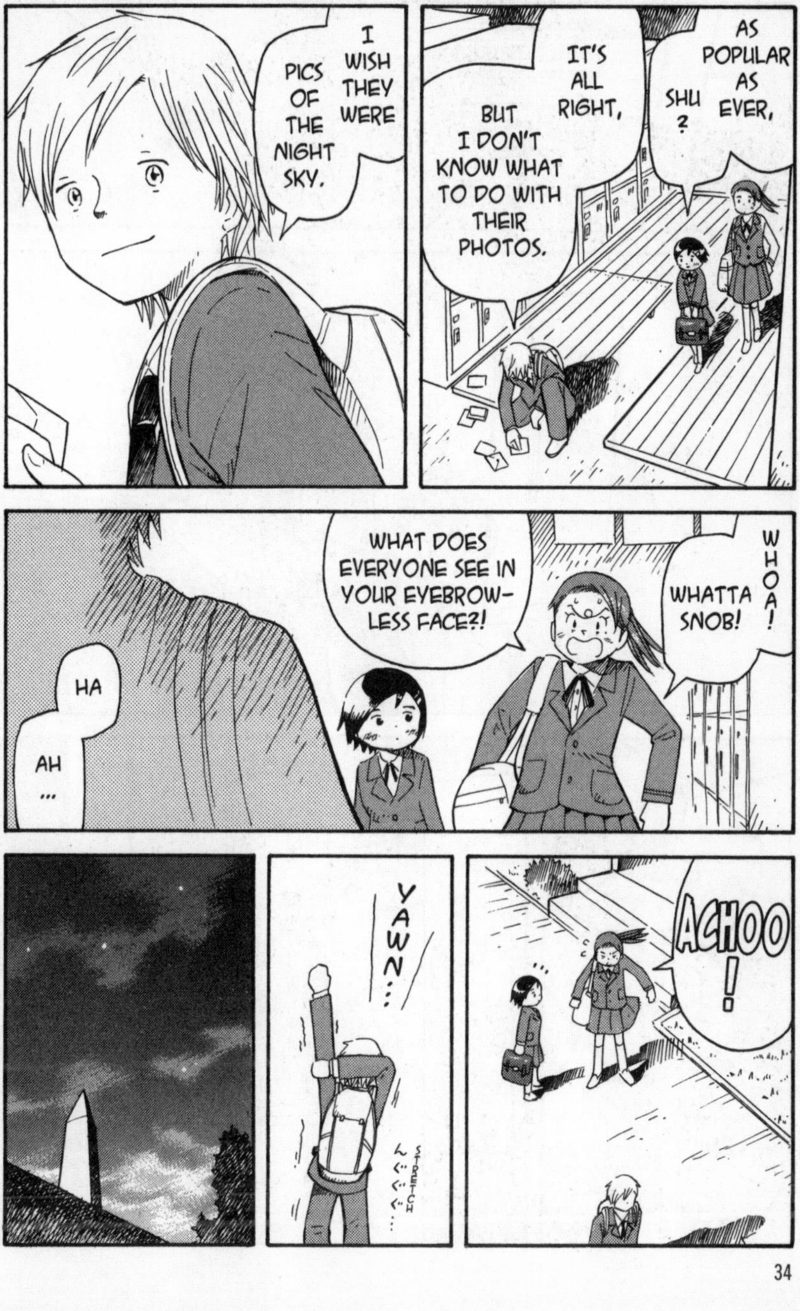
AS POPULAR AS EVER, SHU?
IT'S ALL RIGHT, BUT I DON'T KNOW WHAT TO DO WITH THEIR PHOTOS.
I WISH THEY WERE PICS OF THE NIGHT SKY.
WHOA!
WHATTA SNOB!
WHAT DOES EVERYONE SEE IN YOUR EYEBROW-LESS FACE?!
HA AH...
ACHOO!
YAWN...
STRETCH

MISSION:40

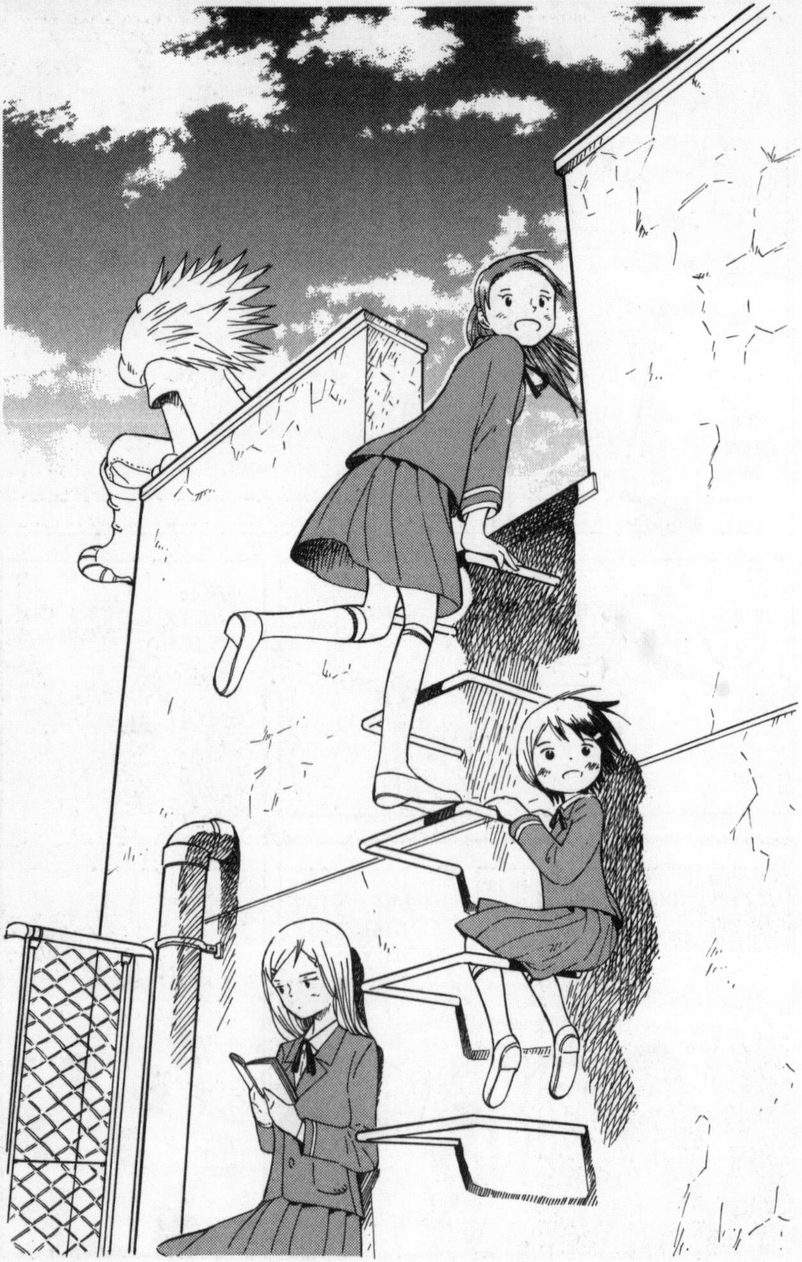

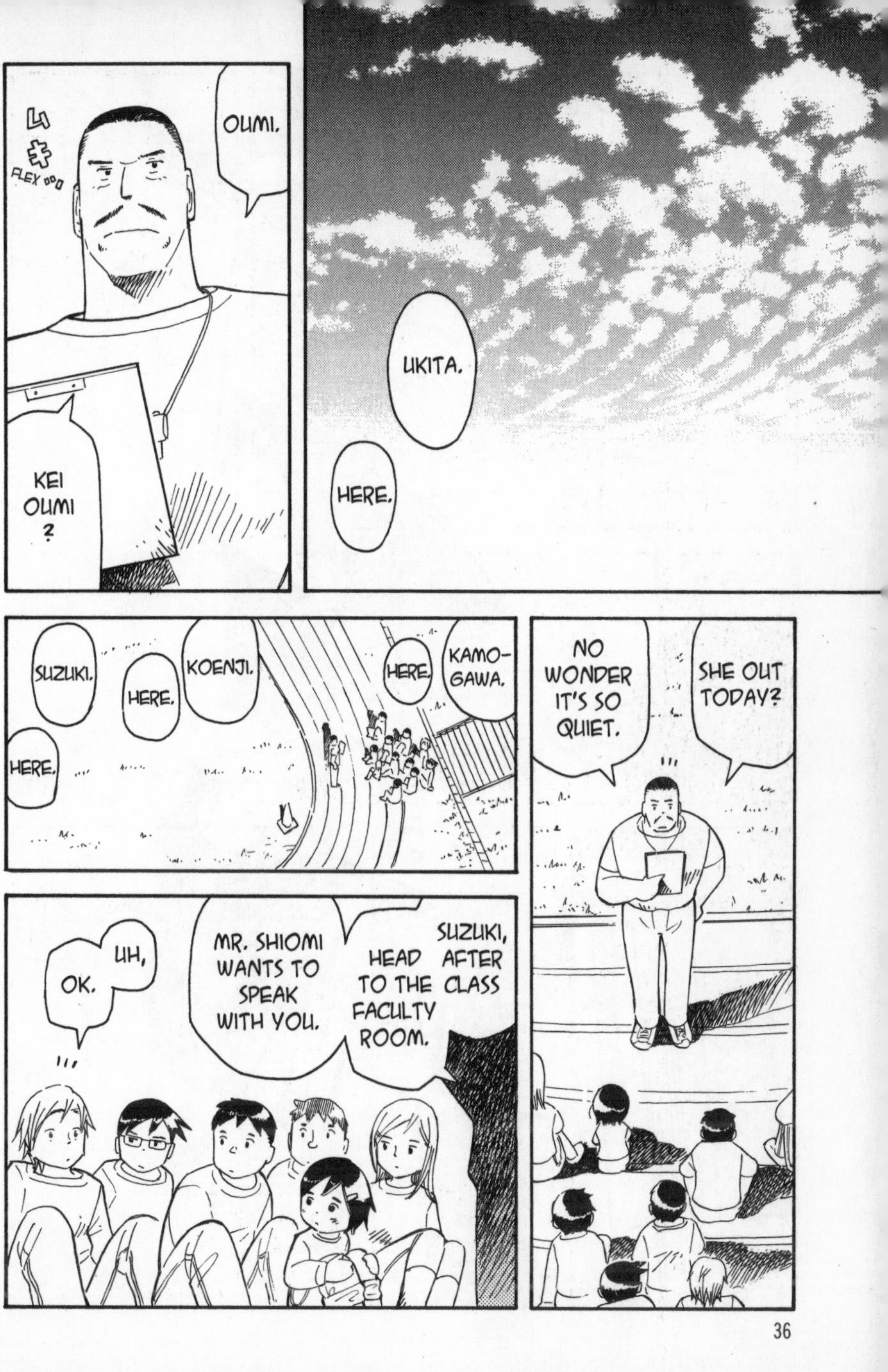
UKITA.
HERE.
OUMI.
FLEX
KEI OUMI?
SHE OUT TODAY?
NO WONDER IT'S SO QUIET.
KAMOGAWA.
HERE.
KOENJI.
HERE.
SUZUKI.
HERE.
SUZUKI, AFTER CLASS HEAD TO THE FACULTY ROOM.
MR. SHIOMI WANTS TO SPEAK WITH YOU.
UH, OK.

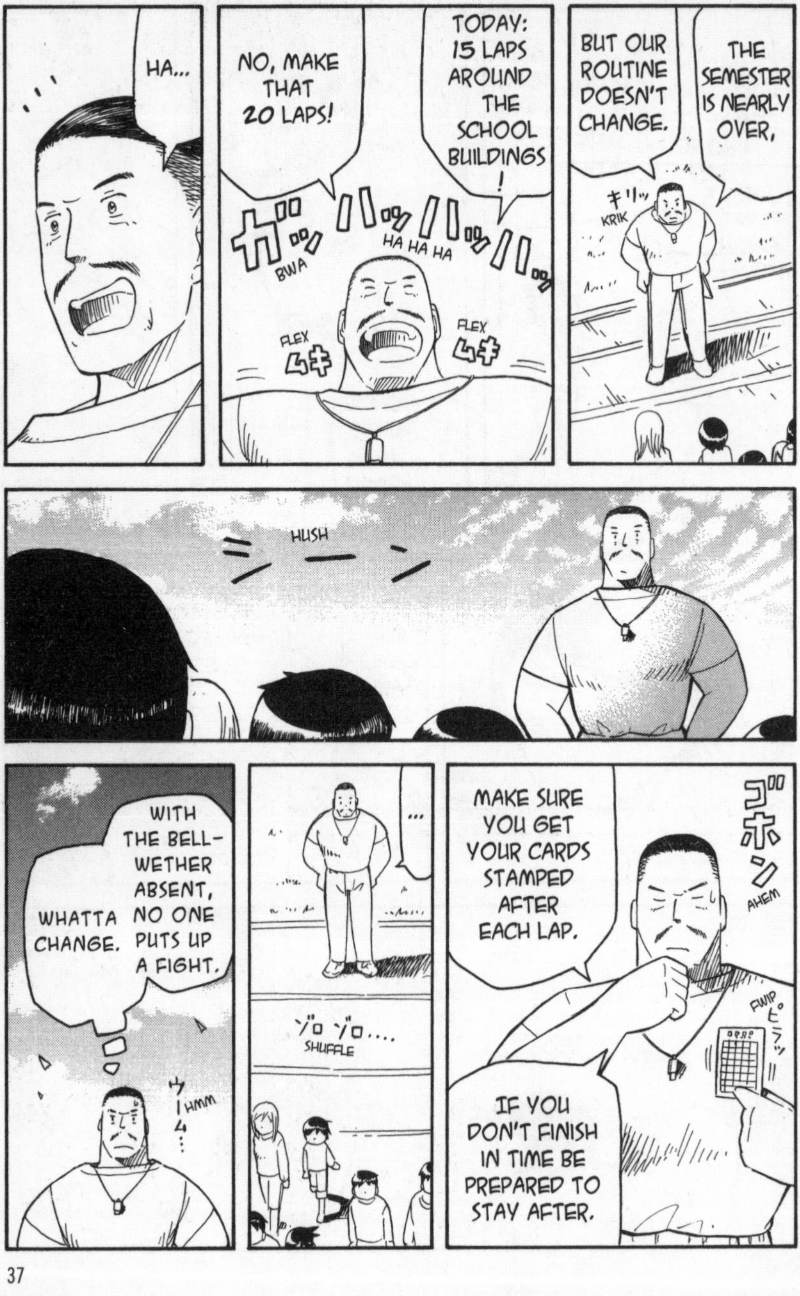
THE SEMESTER IS NEARLY OVER,
BUT OUR ROUTINE DOESN'T CHANGE.
キリッ
KRIK
TODAY: 15 LAPS AROUND THE SCHOOL BUILDINGS!
NO, MAKE THAT 20 LAPS!
ガッハッハッハッハッ
BWA HA HA HA
ムキ
FLEX
ムキ
FLEX
HA...
HUSH
MAKE SURE YOU GET YOUR CARDS STAMPED AFTER EACH LAP.
ゴホン
AHEM
IF YOU DON'T FINISH IN TIME BE PREPARED TO STAY AFTER.
ピラッ
FWIP
...
ゾロゾロ....
SHUFFLE
WITH THE BELL-WETHER ABSENT, NO ONE PUTS UP A FIGHT.
WHATTA CHANGE.
ウーム...
HMM

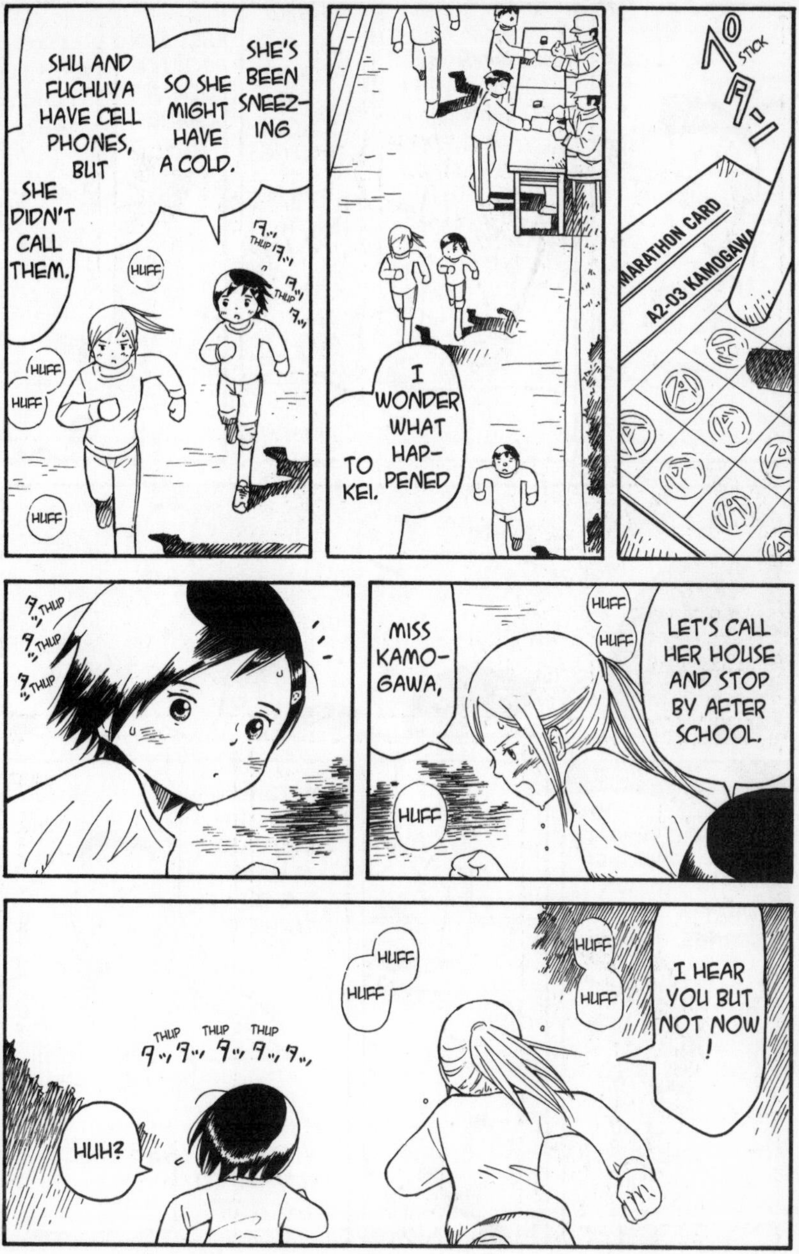
STICK
MARATHON CARD
A2-03 KAMOGAWA
I WONDER WHAT HAP-PENED
TO KEI.
SHE'S BEEN SNEEZ-ING
SO SHE MIGHT HAVE A COLD.
SHU AND FUCHUYA HAVE CELL PHONES, BUT
SHE DIDN'T CALL THEM.
THUP THUP THUP
HUFF
HUFF
HUFF
HUFF
HUFF
HUFF
LET'S CALL HER HOUSE AND STOP BY AFTER SCHOOL.
MISS KAMO-GAWA,
HUFF
THUP THUP THUP
HUFF
HUFF
I HEAR YOU BUT NOT NOW!
HUFF
HUFF
THUP THUP THUP
HUH?

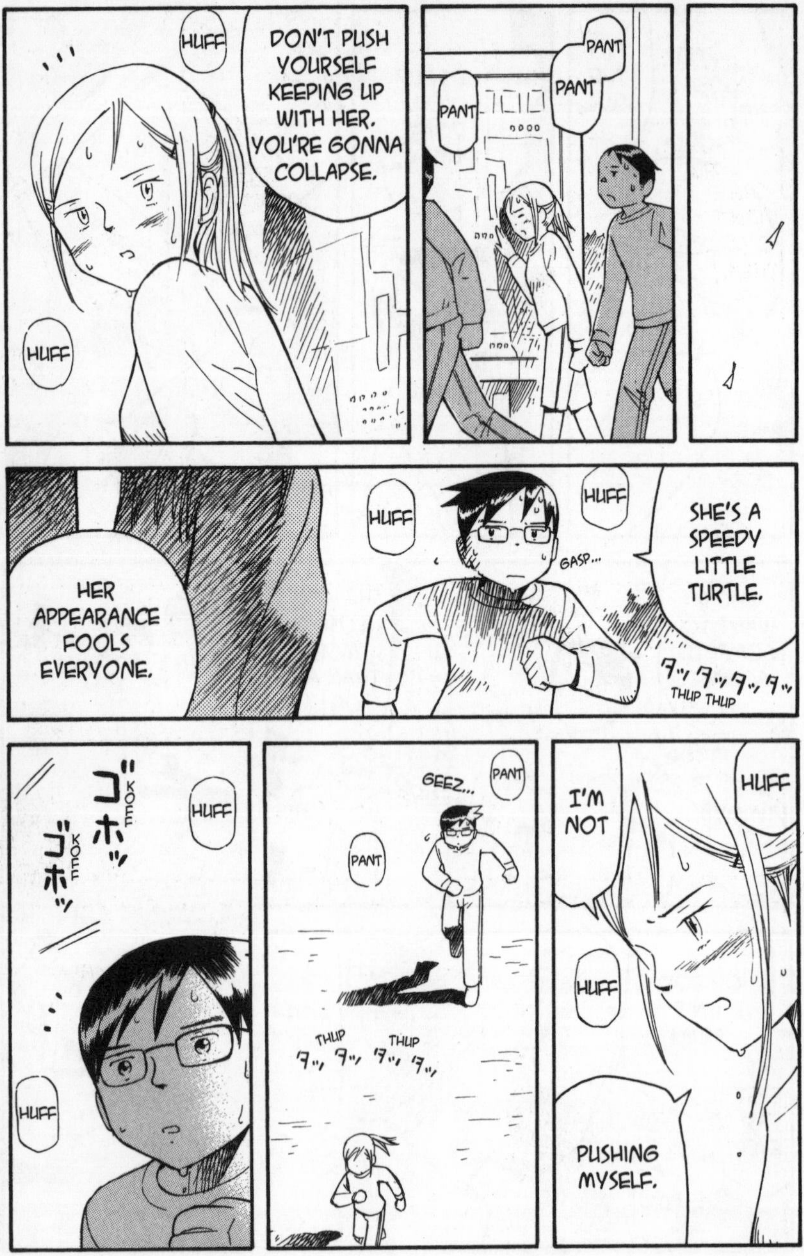
PANT
PANT
PANT
HUFF
DON'T PUSH YOURSELF KEEPING UP WITH HER. YOU'RE GONNA COLLAPSE.
HUFF
SHE'S A SPEEDY LITTLE TURTLE.
HUFF
HUFF
GASP...
タッタッタッタッ
THUP THUP
HER APPEARANCE FOOLS EVERYONE.
HUFF
I'M NOT
HUFF
PUSHING MYSELF.
PANT
GEEZ...
PANT
THUP
THUP
タッ タッ タッ タッ
ゴホッ
KOFF
ゴホッ
KOFF
HUFF
HUFF

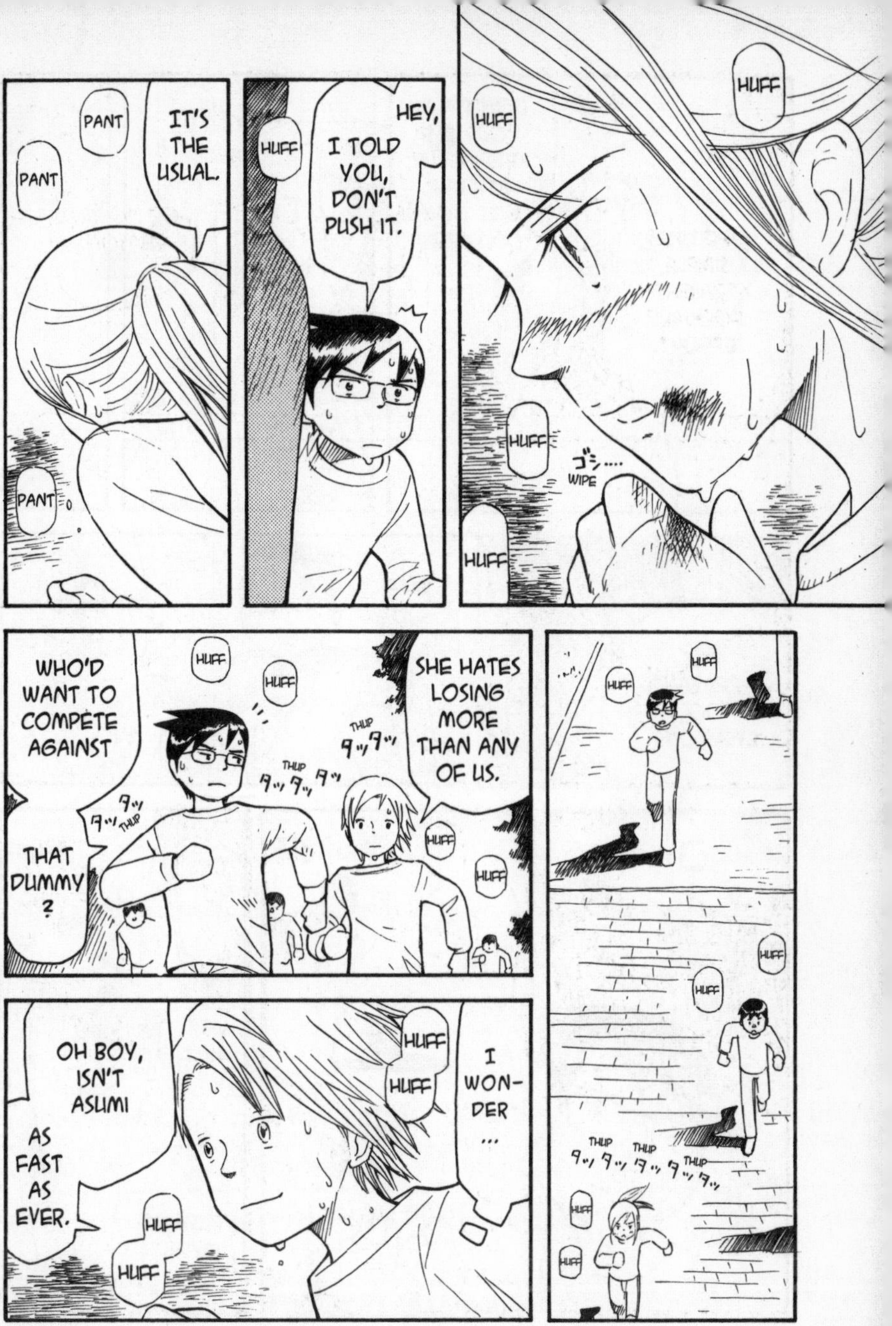
HUFF
HUFF
HUFF
ゴシ….
WIPE
HUFF
HEY, I TOLD YOU, DON'T PUSH IT.
HUFF
IT'S THE USUAL.
PANT
PANT
PANT
HUFF
HUFF
HUFF
HUFF
THUP
タッ タッ タッ タッ タッ
HUFF
HUFF
SHE HATES LOSING MORE THAN ANY OF US.
HUFF
HUFF
THUP
タッタッ
THUP
タッ タッ タッ
タッ タッ
THUP
WHO'D WANT TO COMPETE AGAINST THAT DUMMY?
HUFF
HUFF
I WON-DER ...
HUFF
HUFF
OH BOY, ISN'T ASUMI AS FAST AS EVER.
HUFF
HUFF

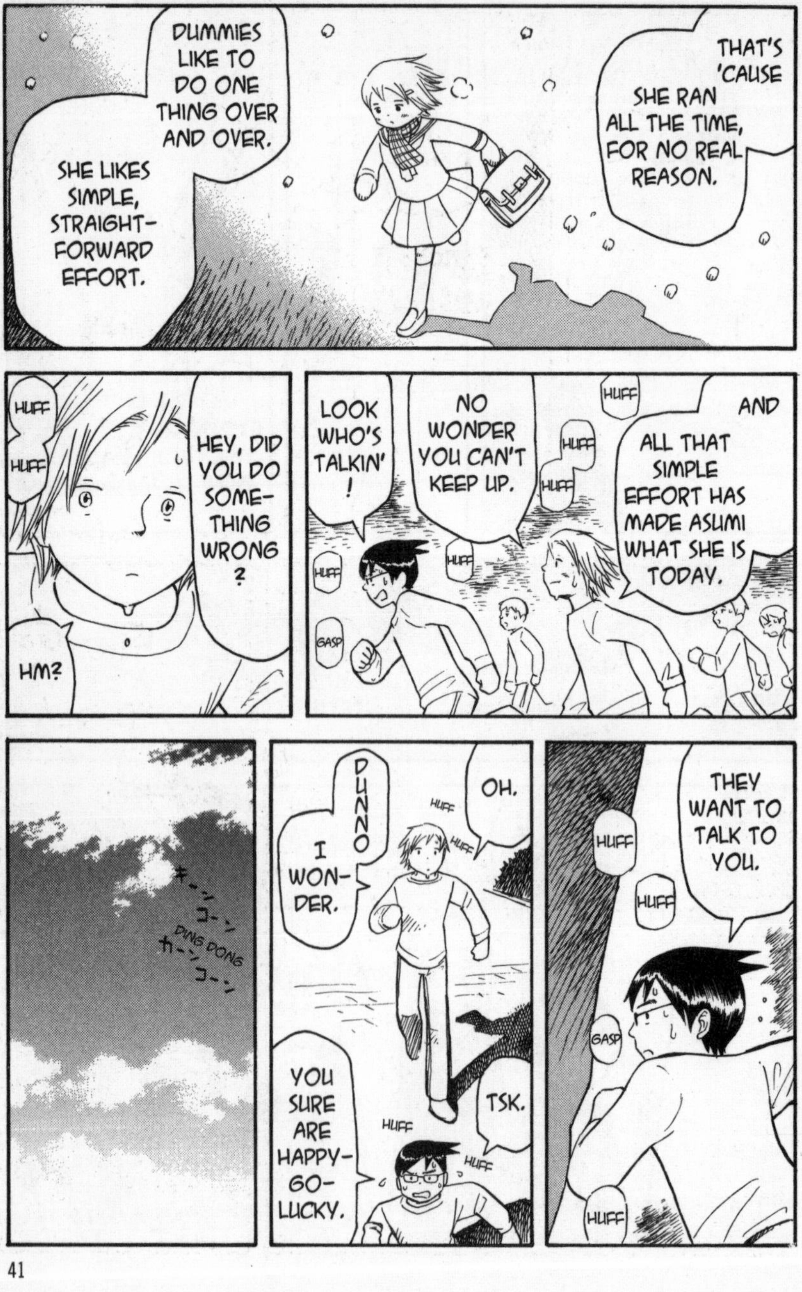
THAT'S 'CAUSE SHE RAN ALL THE TIME, FOR NO REAL REASON.
DUMMIES LIKE TO DO ONE THING OVER AND OVER.
SHE LIKES SIMPLE, STRAIGHT-FORWARD EFFORT.
HUFF
AND ALL THAT SIMPLE EFFORT HAS MADE ASUMI WHAT SHE IS TODAY.
HUFF
HUFF
NO WONDER YOU CAN'T KEEP UP.
HUFF
LOOK WHO'S TALKIN'!
HUFF
GASP
HEY, DID YOU DO SOME-THING WRONG?
HUFF
HUFF
HM?
THEY WANT TO TALK TO YOU.
HUFF
HUFF
GASP
HUFF
OH.
HUFF
HUFF
DUNNO
I WON-DER.
TSK.
HUFF
HUFF
YOU SURE ARE HAPPY-GO-LUCKY.
キーン
コーン
DING DONG
カーン
コーン

ガラ
SLIDE
ガラ...
EXCUSE ME NOW.
...
WHEW...
星通り商店街

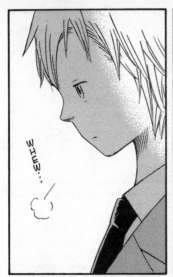

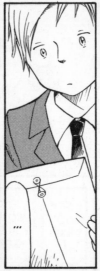

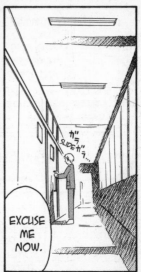

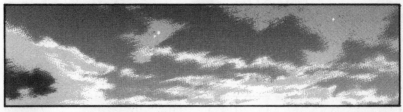

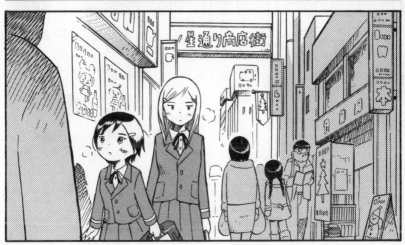

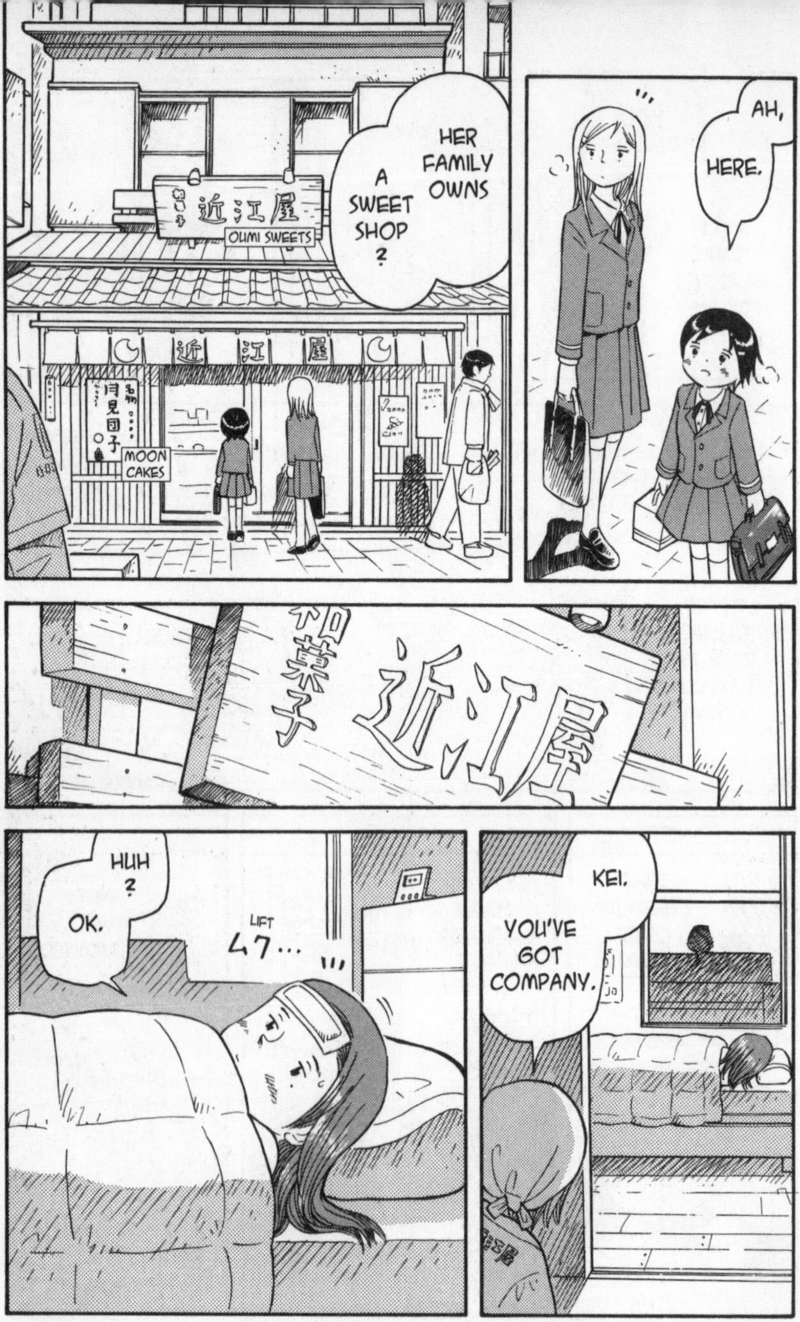
AH, HERE.
HER FAMILY OWNS A SWEET SHOP?
近江屋
OUMI SWEETS
近江屋
名物 月見団子
MOON CAKES
近江屋
KEI. YOU'VE GOT COMPANY.
HUH? OK.
LIFT
ムク...

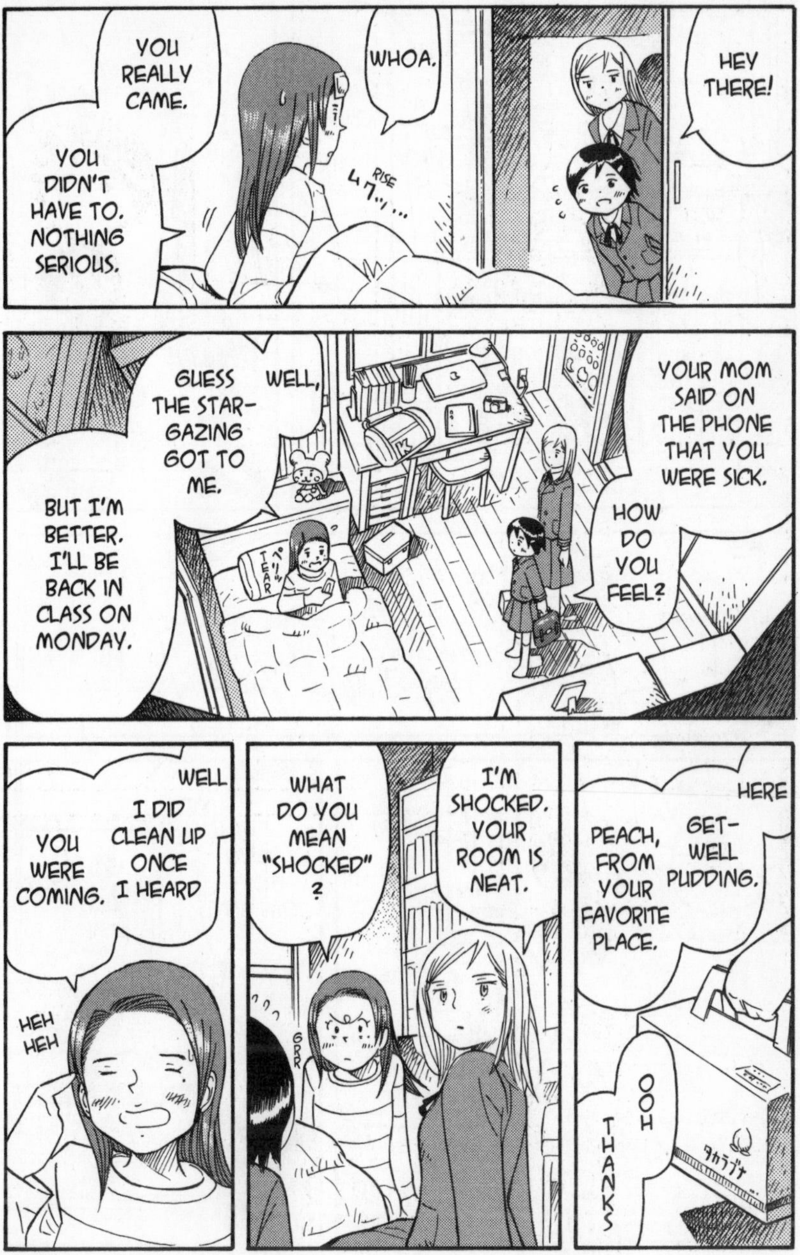
HEY THERE!
WHOA.
RISE
YOU REALLY CAME.
YOU DIDN'T HAVE TO. NOTHING SERIOUS.
YOUR MOM SAID ON THE PHONE THAT YOU WERE SICK.
HOW DO YOU FEEL?
TEAR
WELL, GUESS THE STAR-GAZING GOT TO ME.
BUT I'M BETTER. I'LL BE BACK IN CLASS ON MONDAY.
HERE
GET-WELL PUDDING.
PEACH, FROM YOUR FAVORITE PLACE.
OOH
THANKS
I'M SHOCKED. YOUR ROOM IS NEAT.
WHAT DO YOU MEAN "SHOCKED"?
GRR
WELL
I DID CLEAN UP ONCE I HEARD
YOU WERE COMING.
HEH HEH

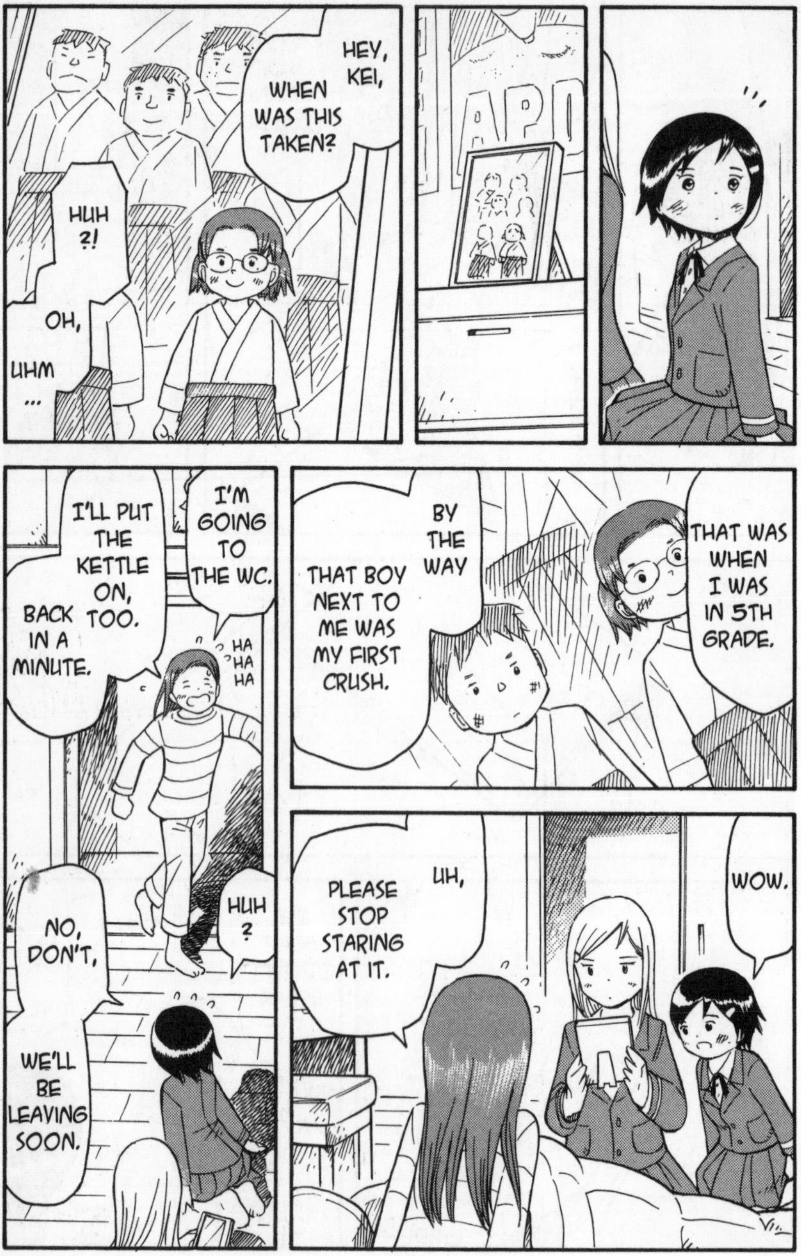
HEY, KEI,
WHEN WAS THIS TAKEN?
HUH ?!
OH,
UHM ...
THAT WAS WHEN I WAS IN 5TH GRADE.
BY THE WAY
THAT BOY NEXT TO ME WAS MY FIRST CRUSH.
WOW.
UH,
PLEASE STOP STARING AT IT.
I'M GOING TO THE WC.
I'LL PUT THE KETTLE ON, TOO.
BACK IN A MINUTE.
HA HA HA
HUH ?
NO, DON'T,
WE'LL BE LEAVING SOON.

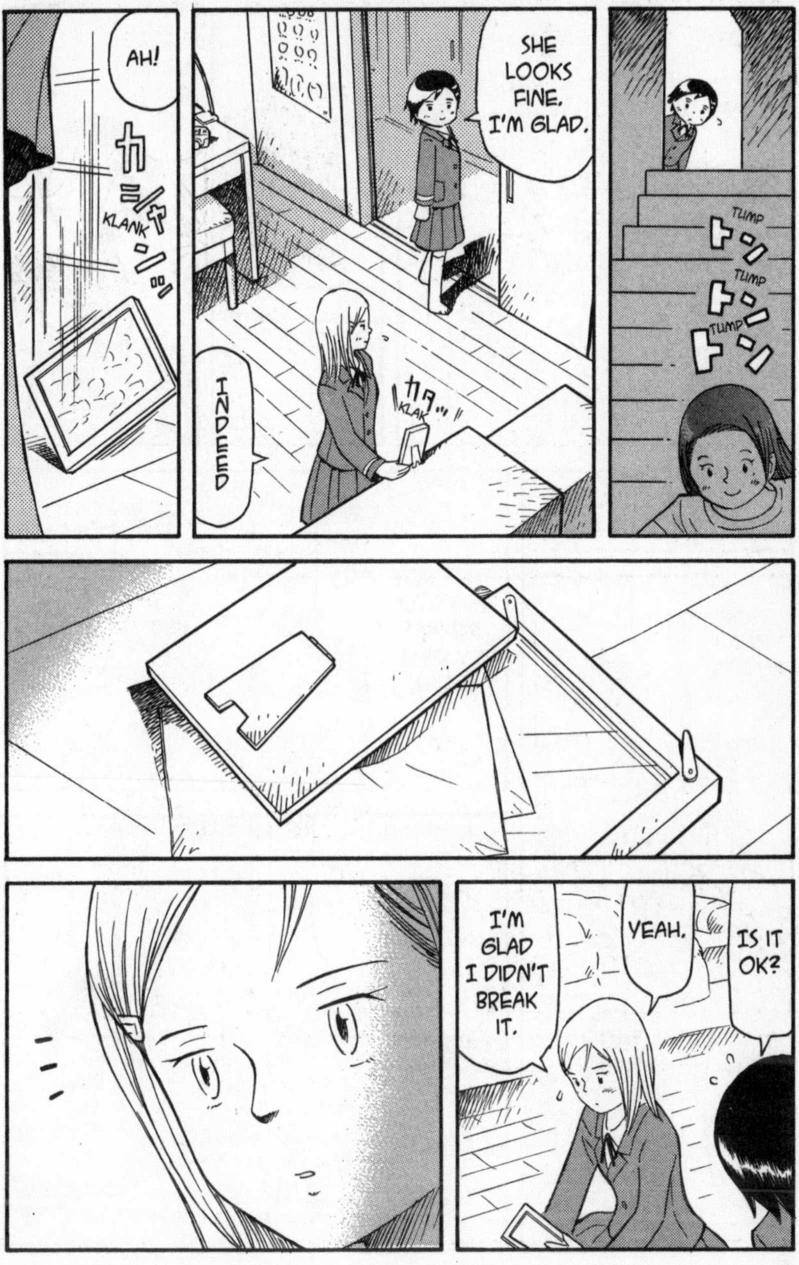
トン TUMP
トン TUMP
トン TUMP
SHE LOOKS FINE. I'M GLAD.
INDEED
カタッ KLAK
AH!
KLANK
IS IT OK?
YEAH.
I'M GLAD I DIDN'T BREAK IT.

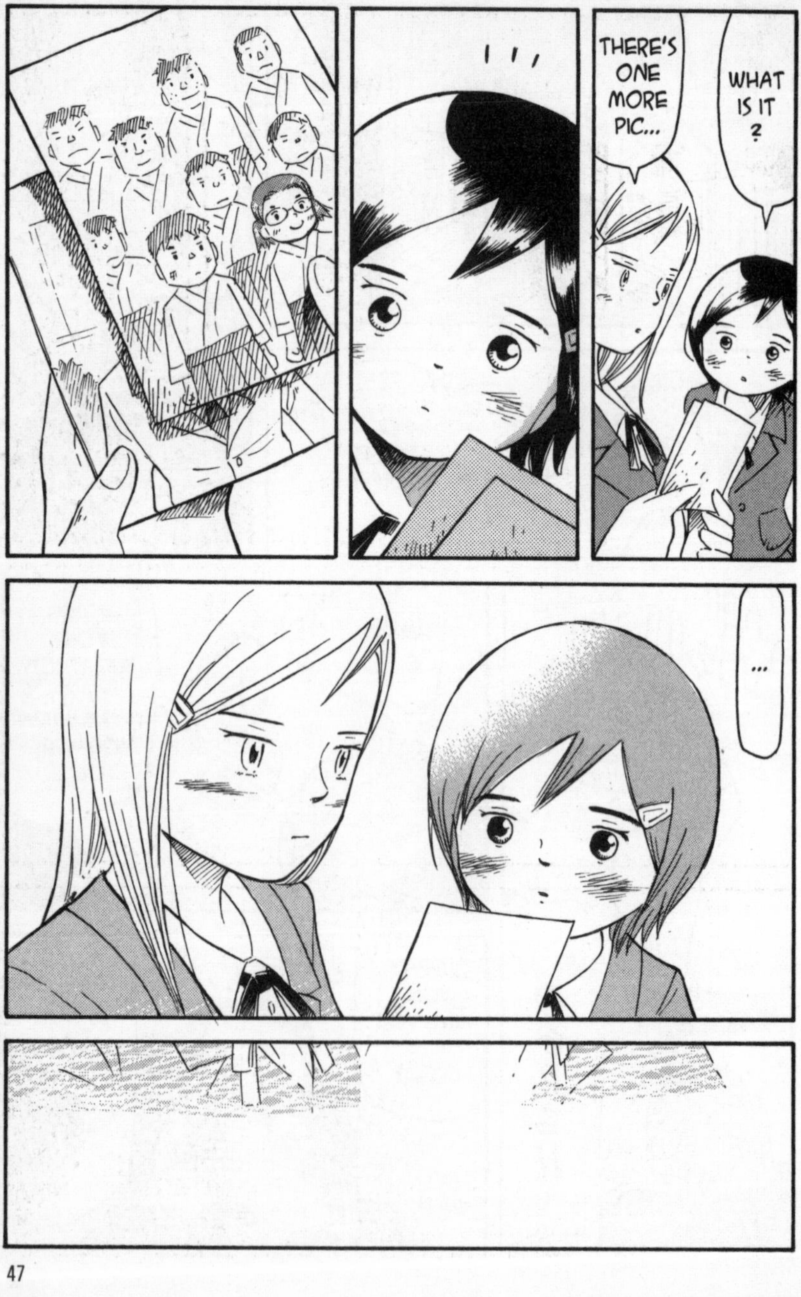
WHAT IS IT ?
THERE'S ONE MORE PIC...
...

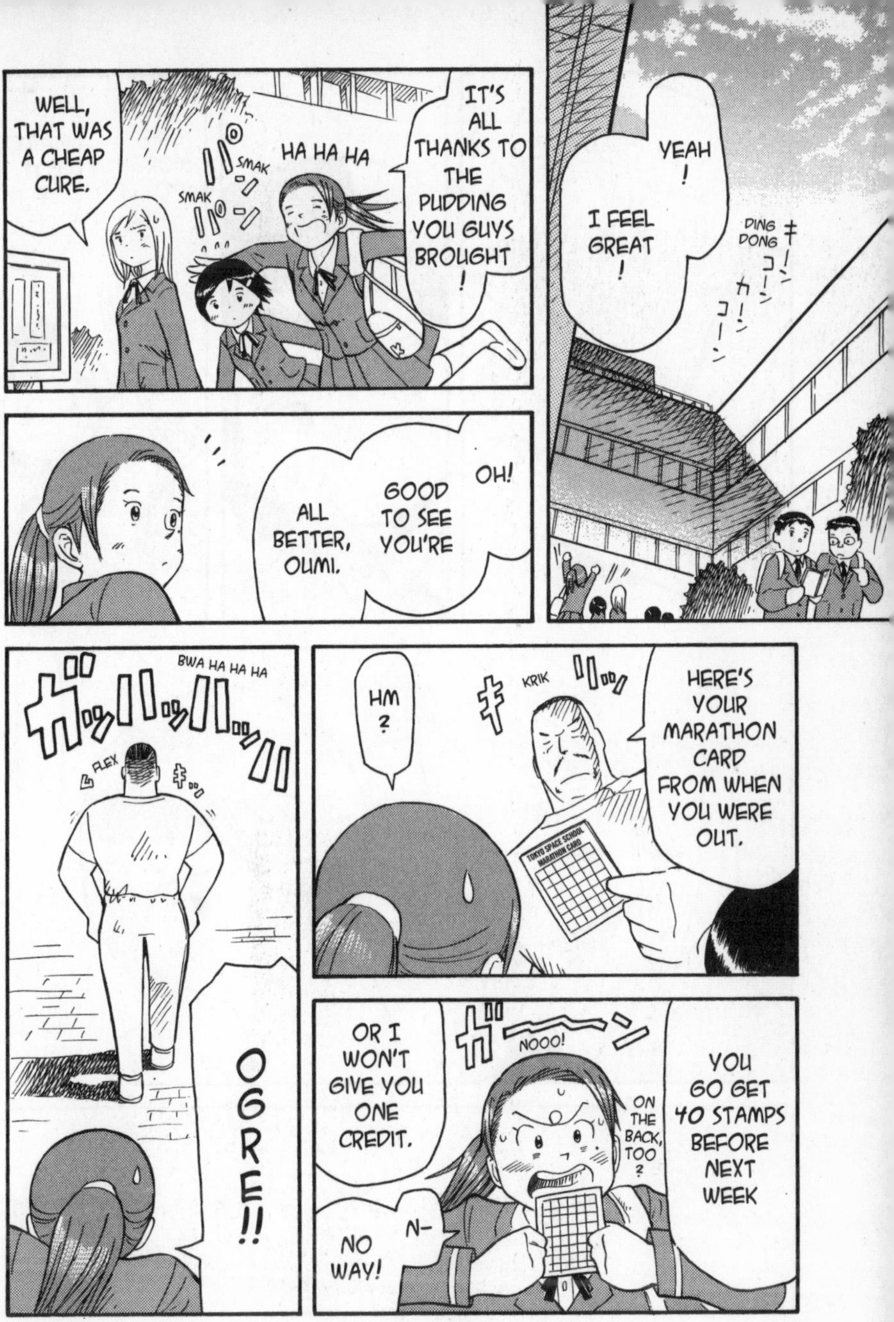
YEAH!
I FEEL GREAT!
DING DONG
IT'S ALL THANKS TO THE PUDDING YOU GUYS BROUGHT!
HA HA HA
SMAK
SMAK
WELL, THAT WAS A CHEAP CURE.
OH!
GOOD TO SEE YOU'RE
ALL BETTER, OUMI.
HERE'S YOUR MARATHON CARD FROM WHEN YOU WERE OUT.
KRIK
HM?
TOKYO SPACE SCHOOL MARATHON CARD
YOU GO GET 40 STAMPS BEFORE NEXT WEEK
OR I WON'T GIVE YOU ONE CREDIT.
NOOO!
ON THE BACK, TOO?
N-
NO WAY!
BWA HA HA HA
FLEX
OGRE!!

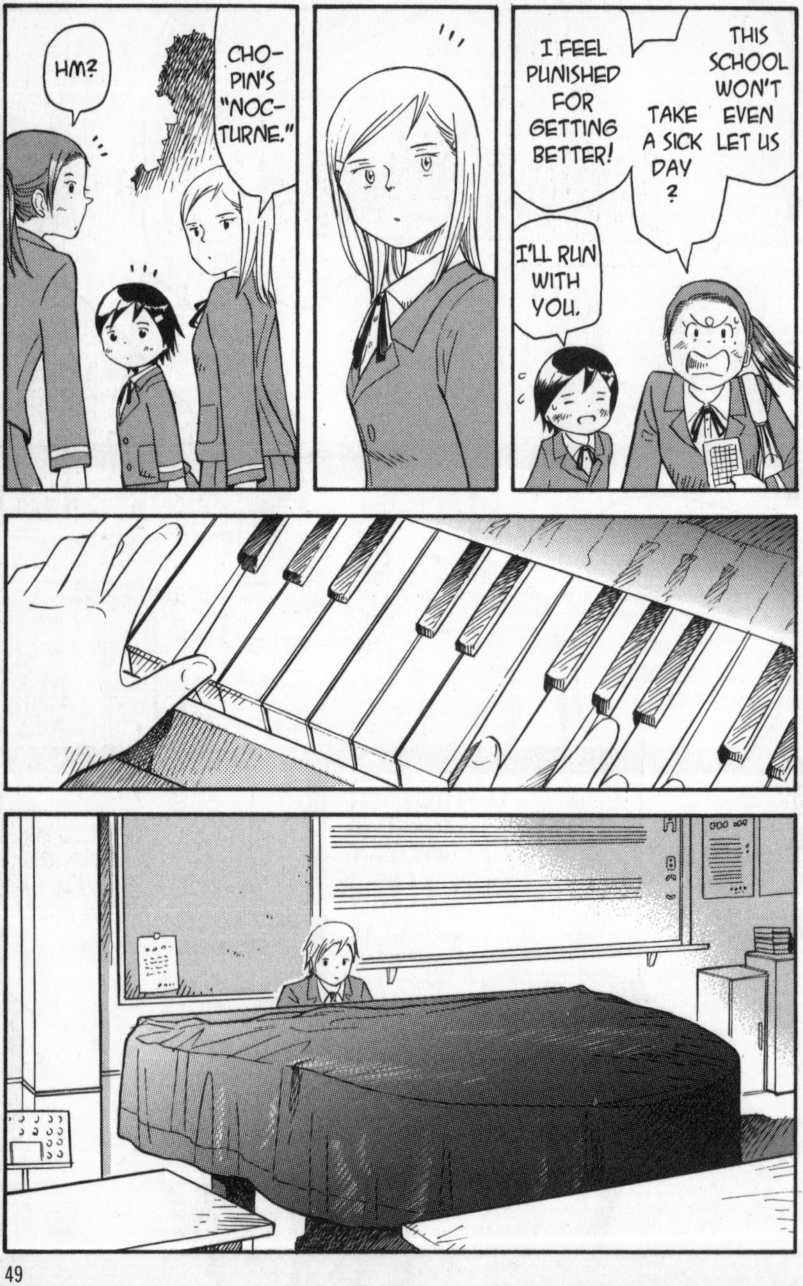
THIS SCHOOL WON'T EVEN LET US TAKE A SICK DAY?
I FEEL PUNISHED FOR GETTING BETTER!
I'LL RUN WITH YOU.
CHO-PIN'S "NOC-TURNE."
HM?

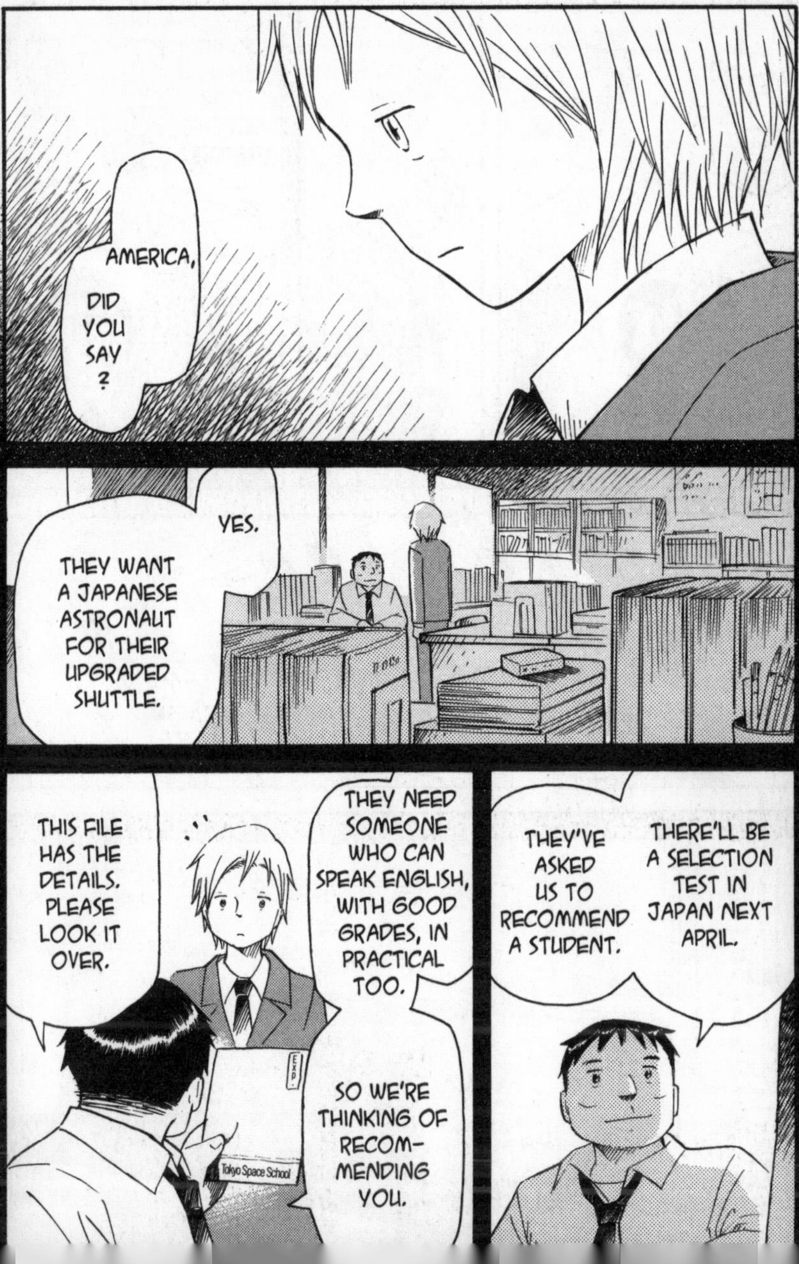
AMERICA, DID YOU SAY?
YES.
THEY WANT A JAPANESE ASTRONAUT FOR THEIR UPGRADED SHUTTLE.
THEY'VE ASKED US TO RECOMMEND A STUDENT.
THERE'LL BE A SELECTION TEST IN JAPAN NEXT APRIL.
THEY NEED SOMEONE WHO CAN SPEAK ENGLISH, WITH GOOD GRADES, IN PRACTICAL TOO.
SO WE'RE THINKING OF RECOM-MENDING YOU.
THIS FILE HAS THE DETAILS. PLEASE LOOK IT OVER.
Tokyo Space School

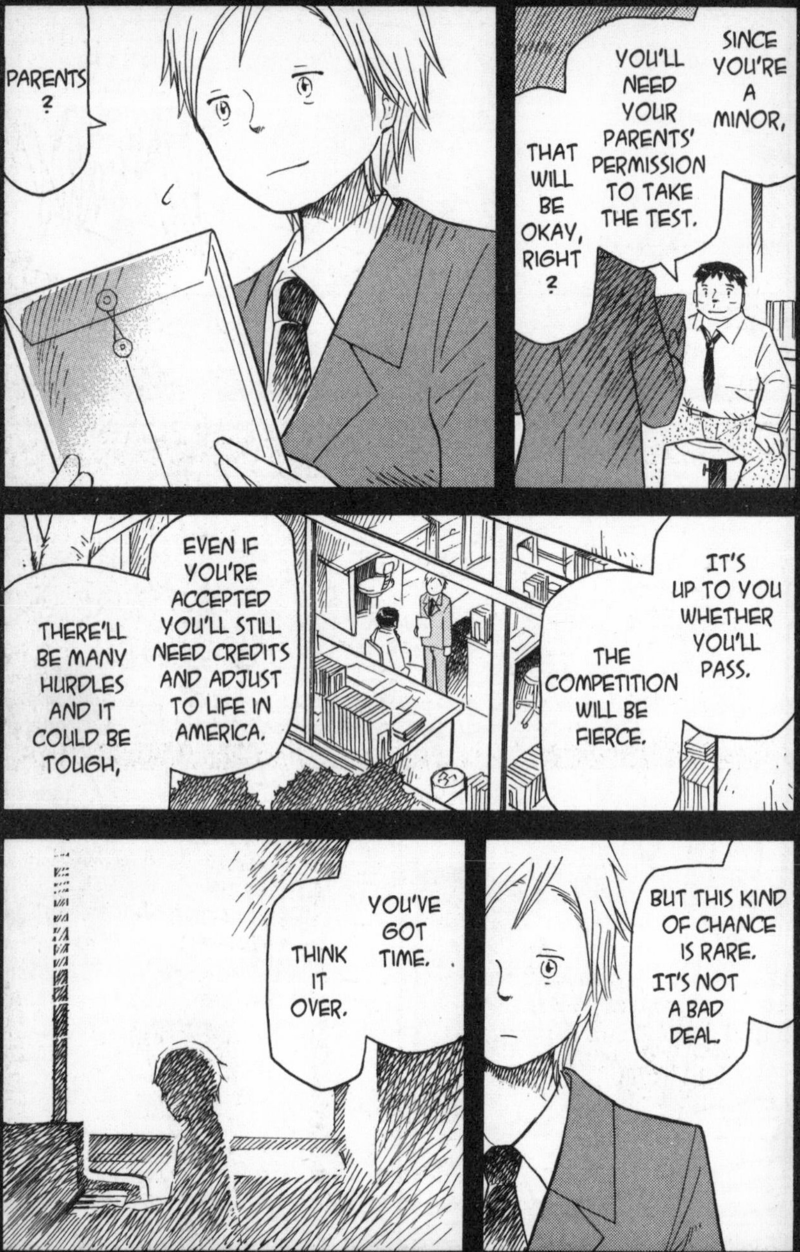
SINCE YOU'RE A MINOR,
YOU'LL NEED YOUR PARENTS' PERMISSION TO TAKE THE TEST.
THAT WILL BE OKAY, RIGHT?
PARENTS?
IT'S UP TO YOU WHETHER YOU'LL PASS.
THE COMPETITION WILL BE FIERCE.
EVEN IF YOU'RE ACCEPTED YOU'LL STILL NEED CREDITS AND ADJUST TO LIFE IN AMERICA.
THERE'LL BE MANY HURDLES AND IT COULD BE TOUGH,
BUT THIS KIND OF CHANCE IS RARE.
IT'S NOT A BAD DEAL.
YOU'VE GOT TIME.
THINK IT OVER.

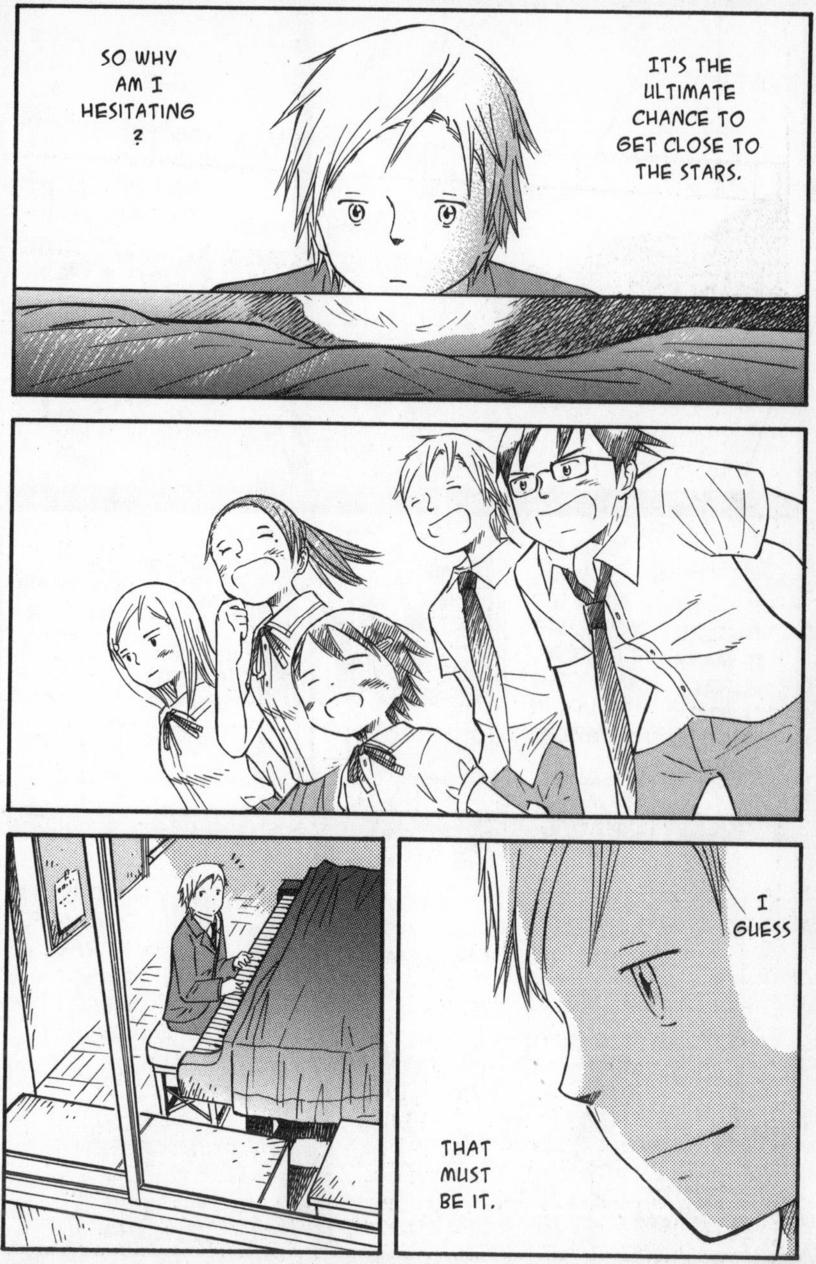
IT'S THE ULTIMATE CHANCE TO GET CLOSE TO THE STARS.
SO WHY AM I HESITATING ?
I GUESS
THAT MUST BE IT.

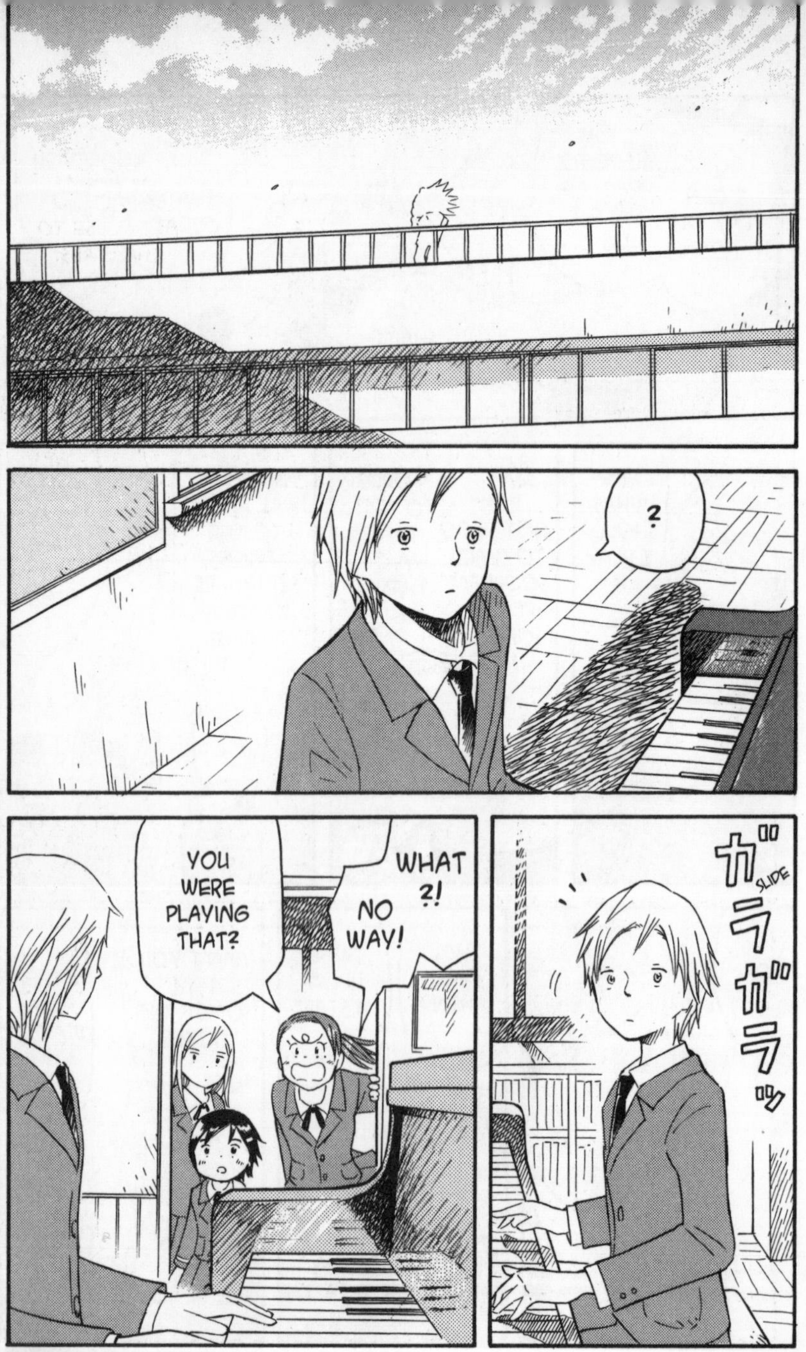
?
ガラガラッ
SLIDE
WHAT?!
NO WAY!
YOU WERE PLAYING THAT?

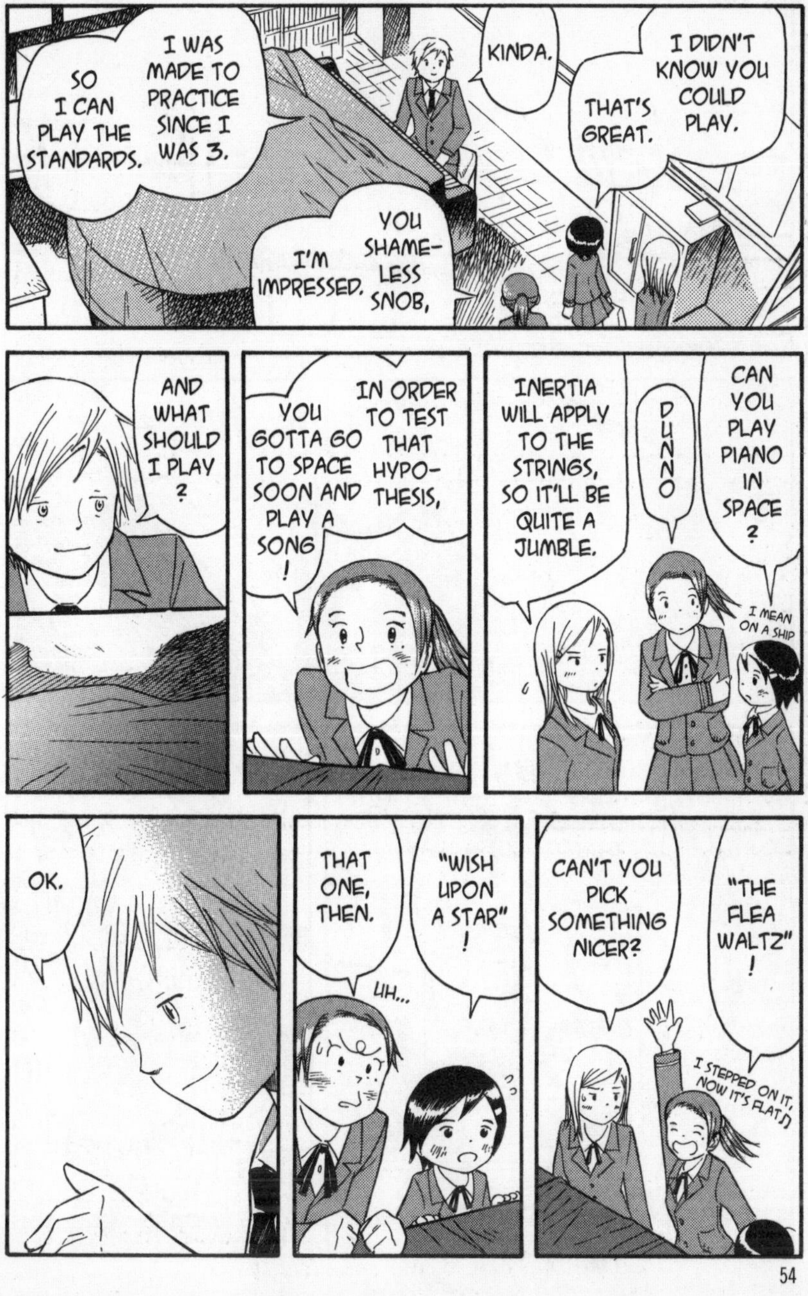
I DIDN'T KNOW YOU COULD PLAY. THAT'S GREAT.
KINDA.
I WAS MADE TO PRACTICE SINCE I WAS 3. SO I CAN PLAY THE STANDARDS.
YOU SHAMELESS SNOB, I'M IMPRESSED.
CAN YOU PLAY PIANO IN SPACE?
I MEAN ON A SHIP
DUNNO
INERTIA WILL APPLY TO THE STRINGS, SO IT'LL BE QUITE A JUMBLE.
IN ORDER TO TEST THAT HYPOTHESIS, YOU GOTTA GO TO SPACE SOON AND PLAY A SONG!
AND WHAT SHOULD I PLAY?
"THE FLEA WALTZ"!
CAN'T YOU PICK SOMETHING NICER?
I STEPPED ON IT, NOW IT'S FLAT♫
"WISH UPON A STAR"!
THAT ONE, THEN.
UH...
OK.

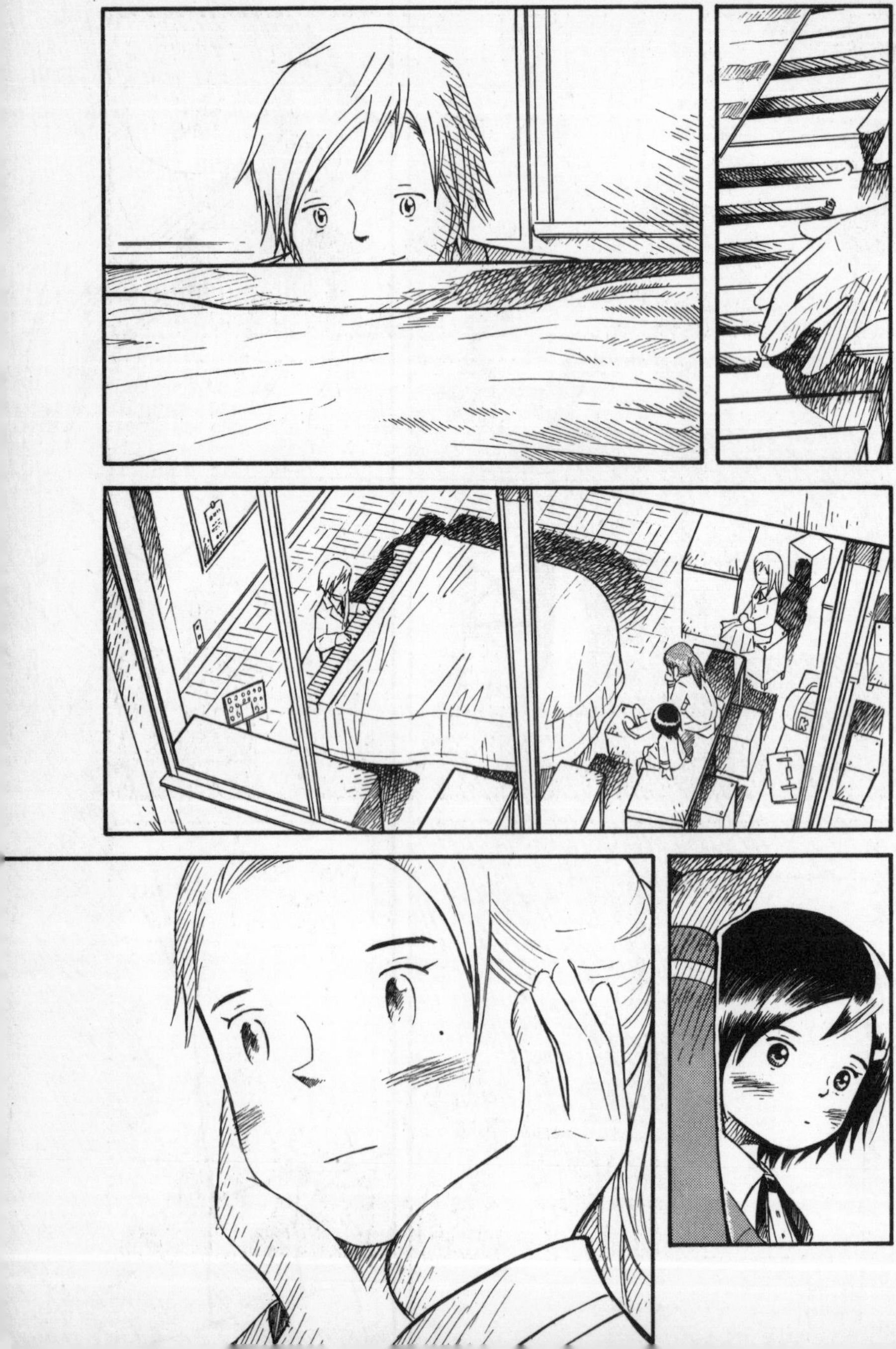

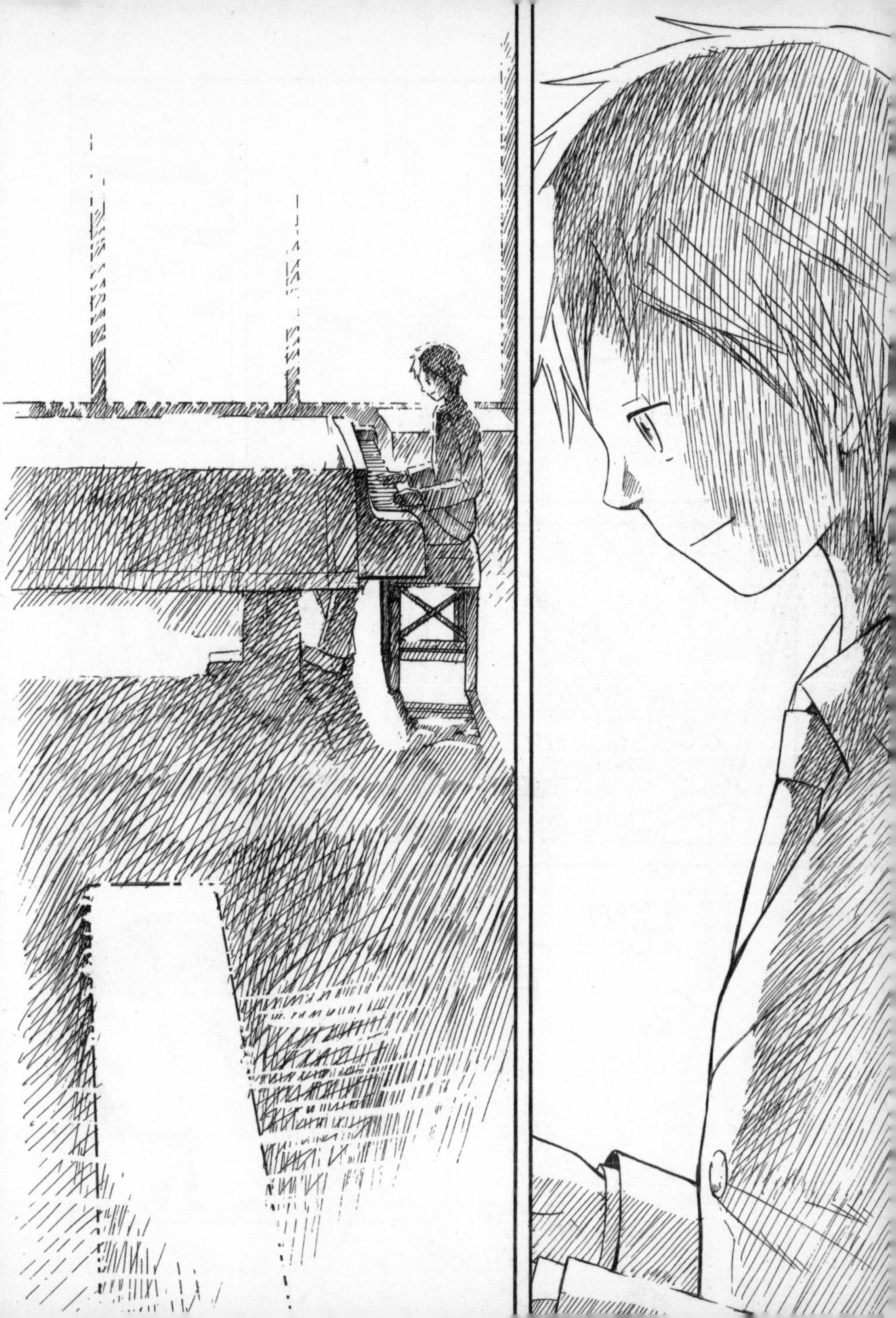

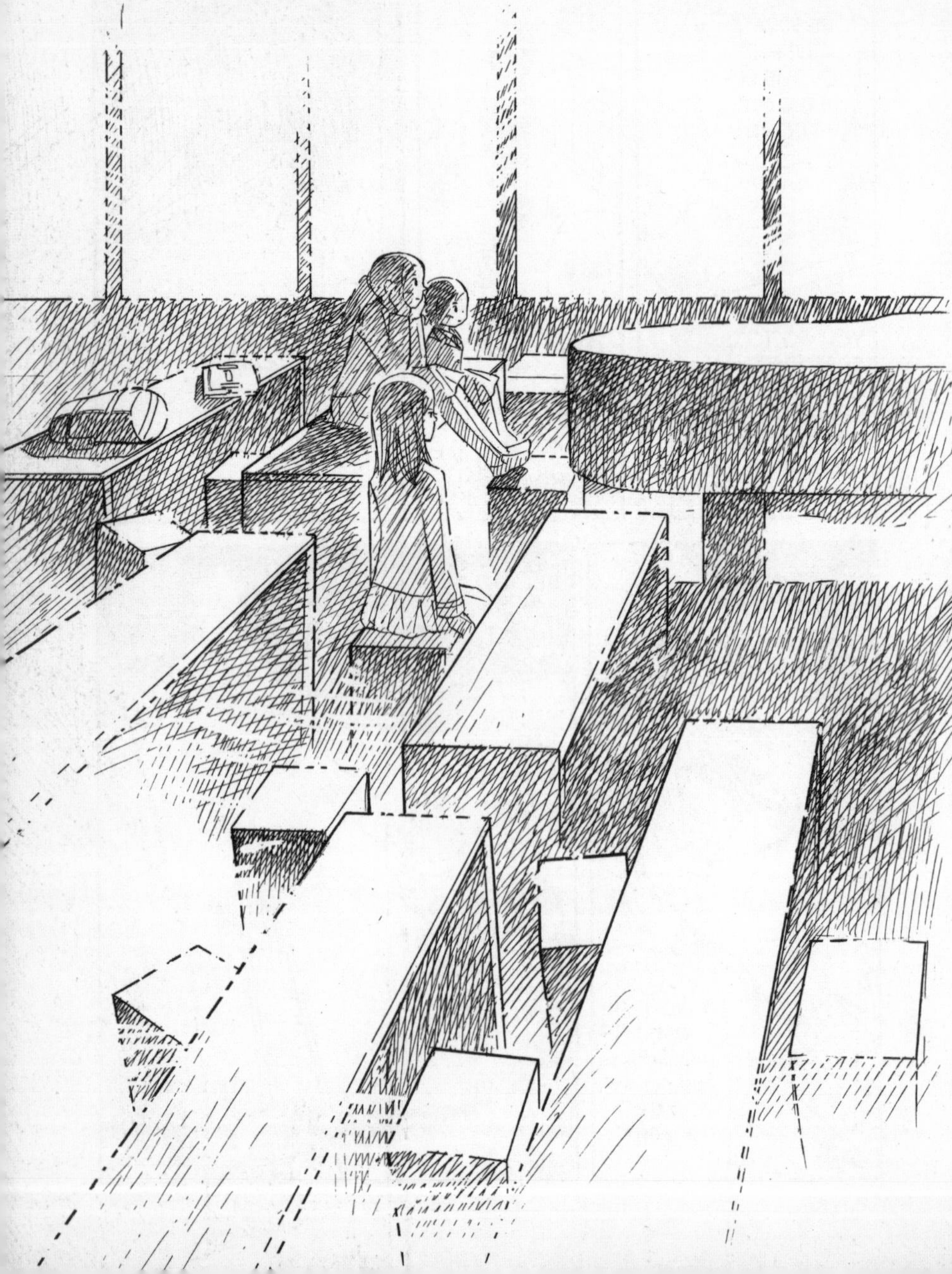

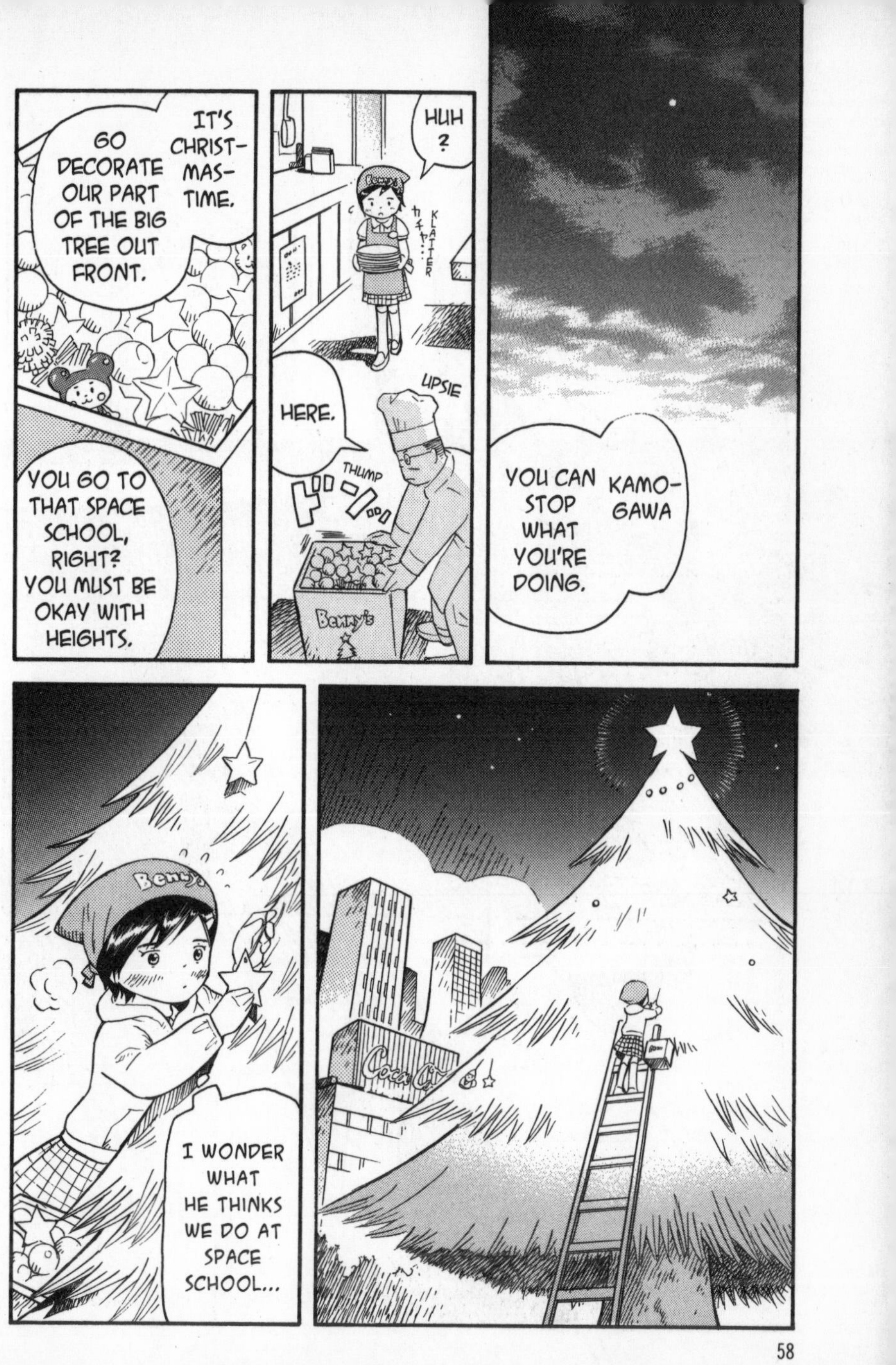
KAMOGAWA
YOU CAN STOP WHAT YOU'RE DOING.
HUH?
KLATTER
UPSIE
HERE.
THUMP
IT'S CHRISTMASTIME.
GO DECORATE OUR PART OF THE BIG TREE OUT FRONT.
YOU GO TO THAT SPACE SCHOOL, RIGHT? YOU MUST BE OKAY WITH HEIGHTS.
Benny's
Coca Cola
I WONDER WHAT HE THINKS WE DO AT SPACE SCHOOL...

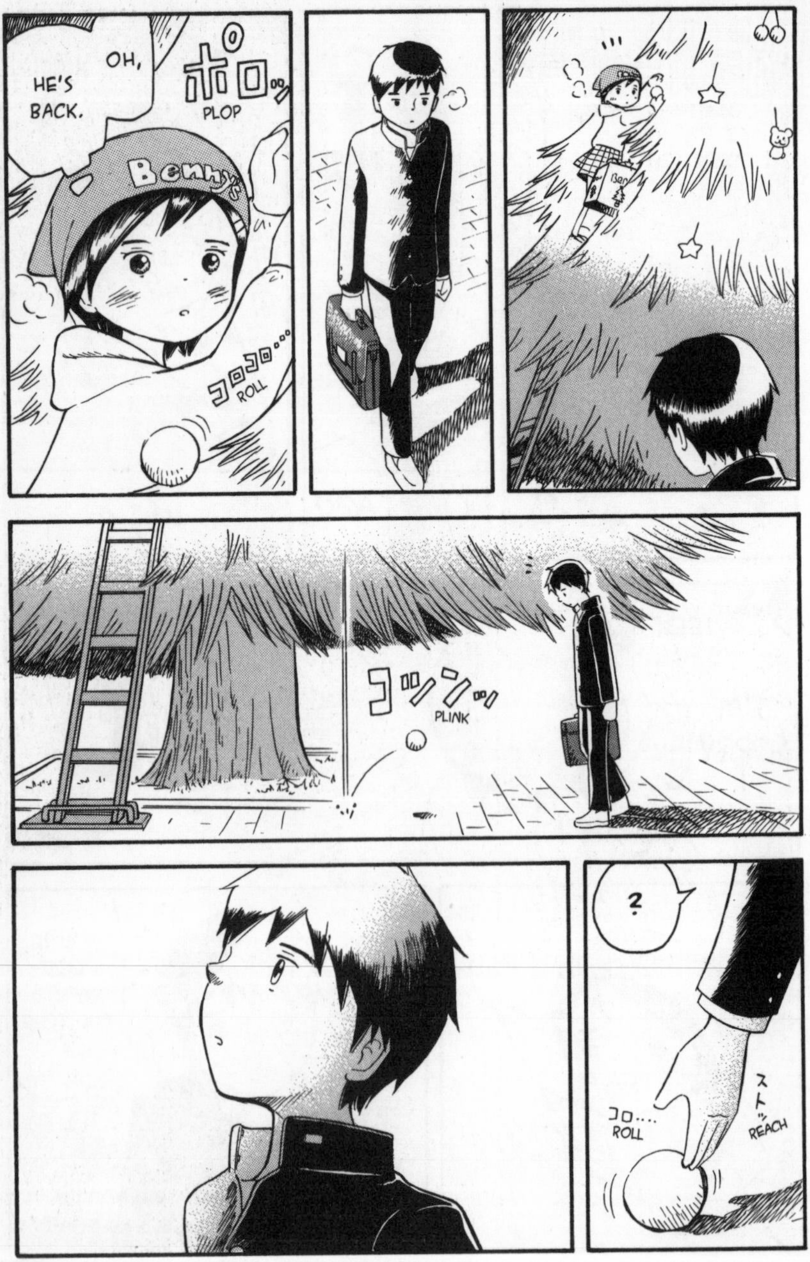
ポロッ
PLOP
OH, HE'S BACK.
Benny's
コロコロ
ROLL
コンッ
PLINK
?
ストッ
REACH
コロ....
ROLL

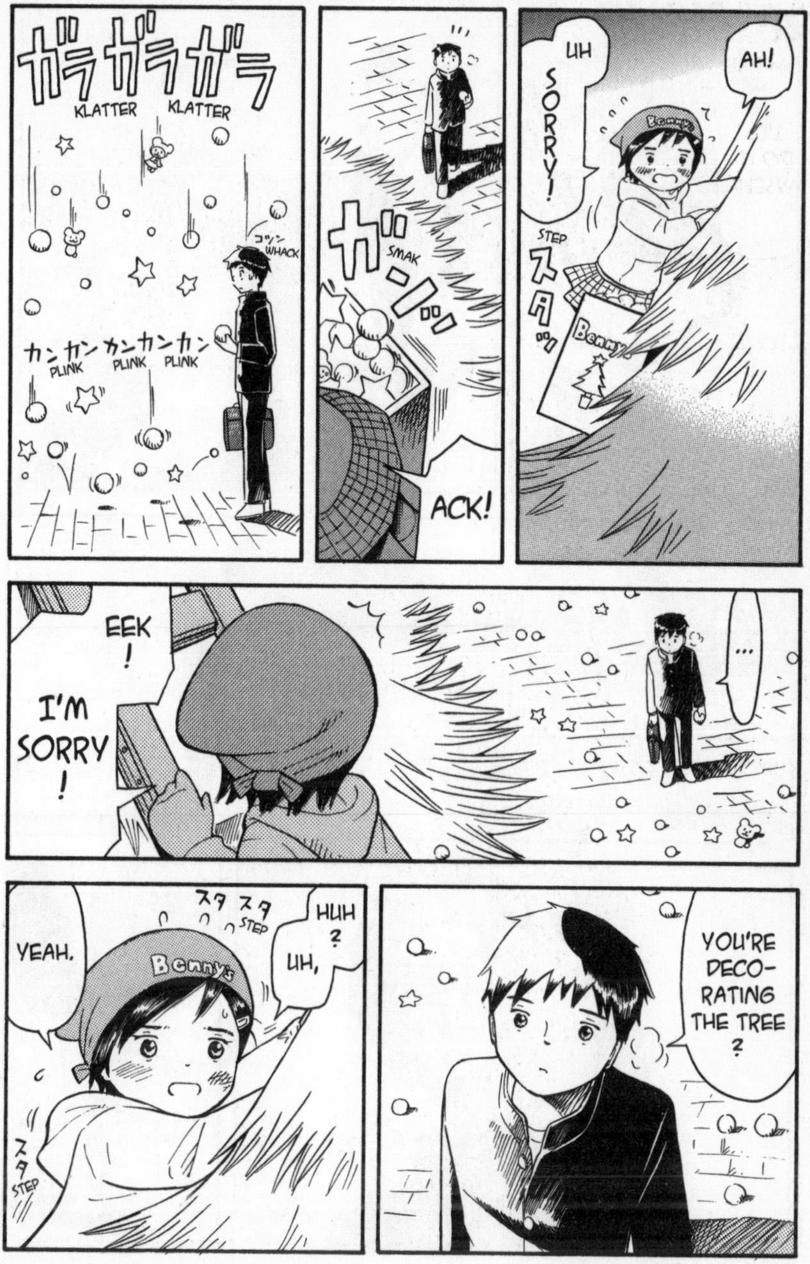
AH!
UH SORRY!
スタッ
STEP
ガン
SMAK
ACK!
ガラガラガラ
KLATTER KLATTER
コツン
WHACK
カンカンカンカンカン
PLINK PLINK PLINK
...
EEK!
I'M SORRY!
YOU'RE DECO-RATING THE TREE?
HUH? UH,
スタ スタ
STEP
YEAH.
スタ
STEP

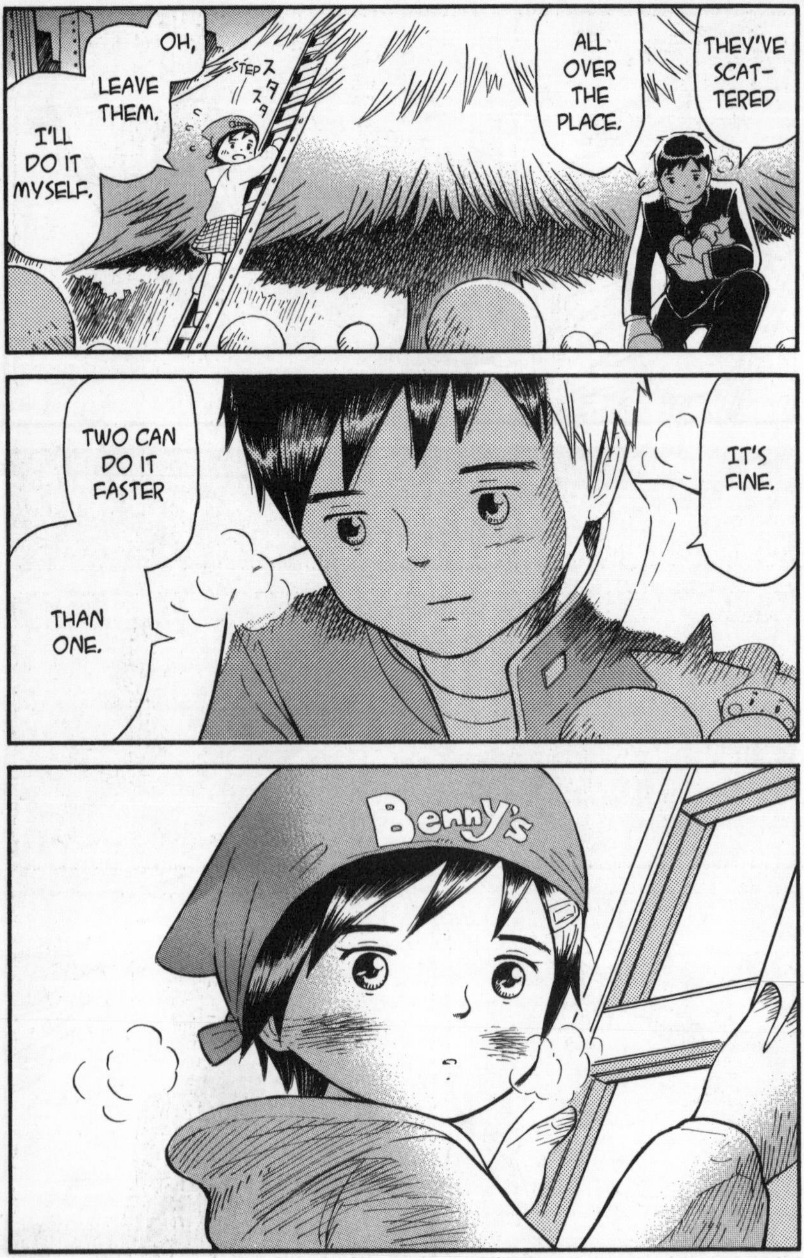
THEY'VE SCAT-TERED
ALL OVER THE PLACE.
OH,
LEAVE THEM.
STEP スタスタ
I'LL DO IT MYSELF.
IT'S FINE.
TWO CAN DO IT FASTER
THAN ONE.

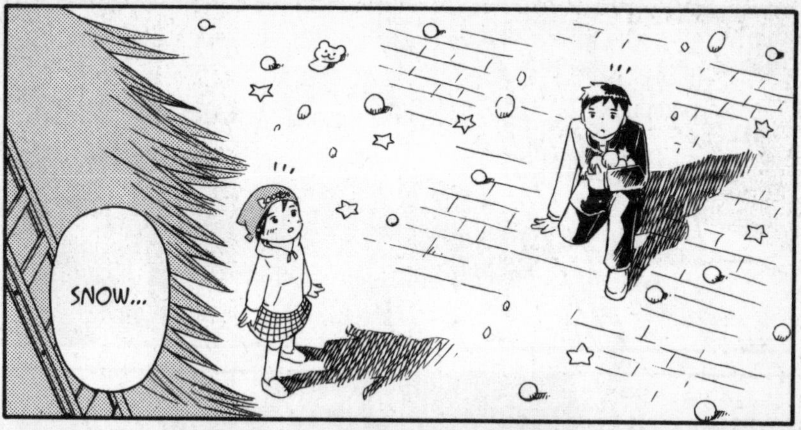
SNOW...

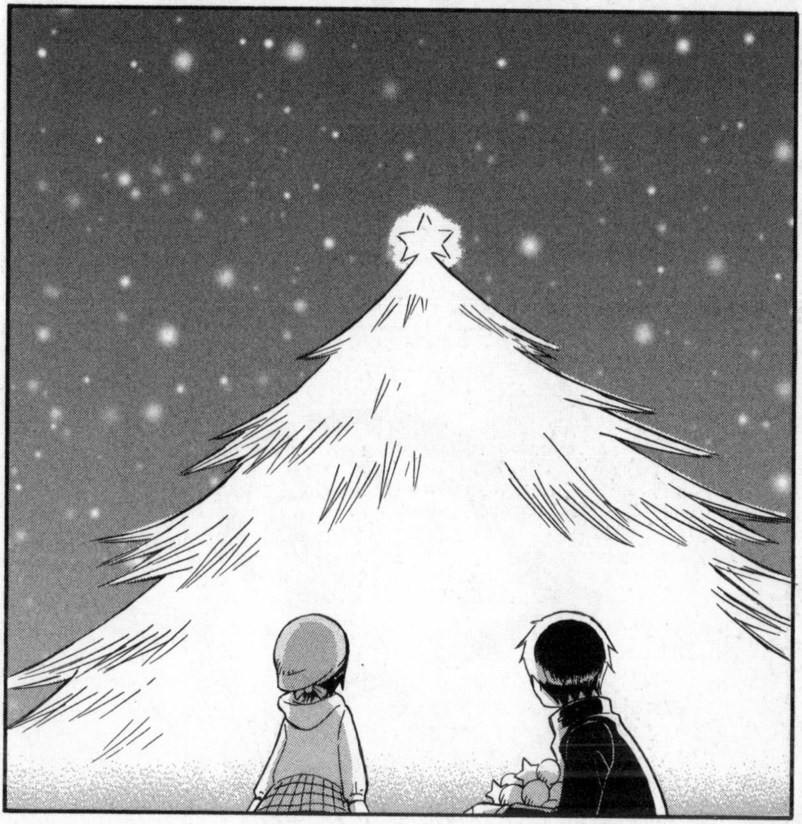

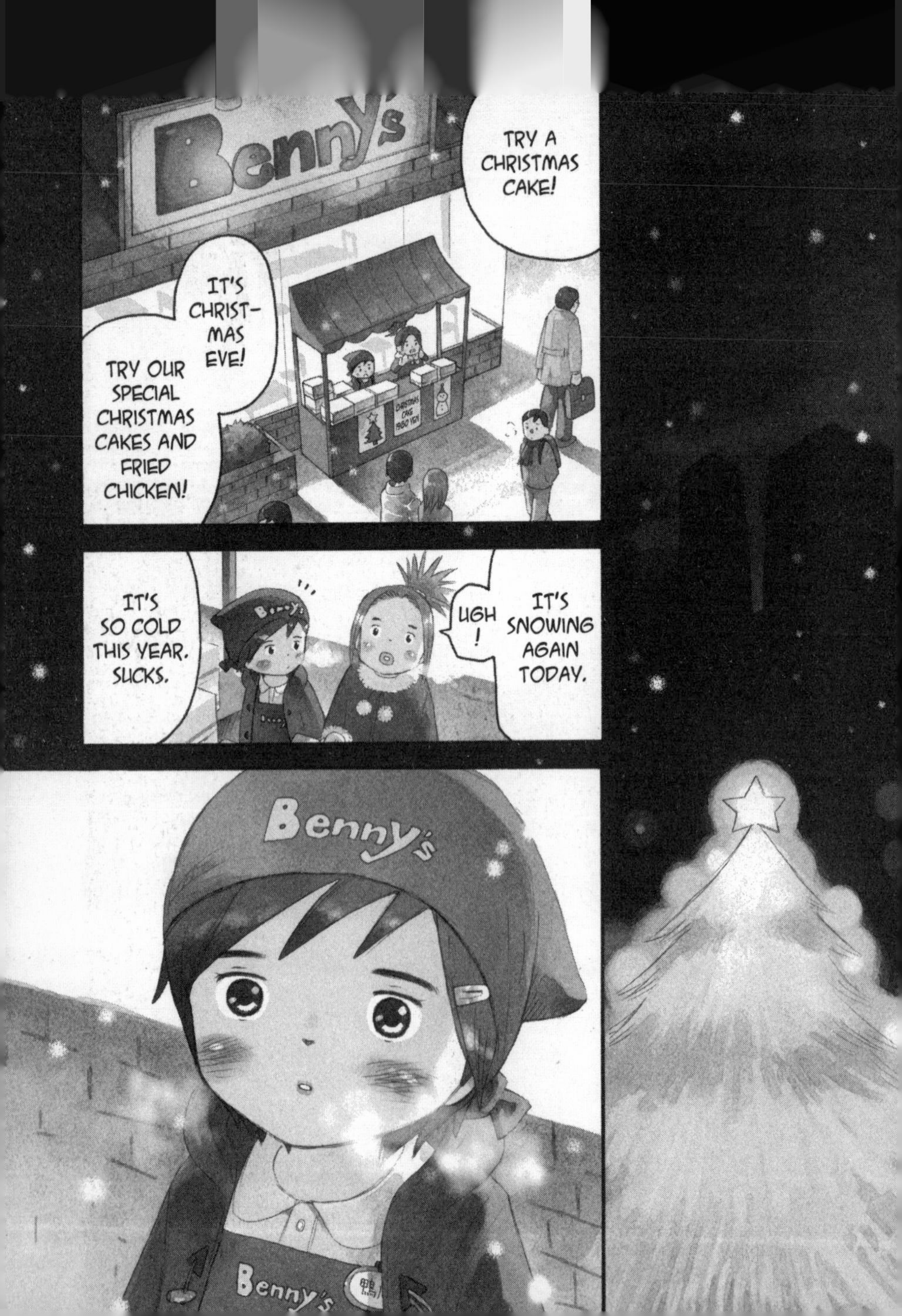
Benny's
TRY A CHRISTMAS CAKE!
IT'S CHRIST-MAS EVE!
TRY OUR SPECIAL CHRISTMAS CAKES AND FRIED CHICKEN!
IT'S SNOWING AGAIN TODAY.
UGH!
IT'S SO COLD THIS YEAR. SUCKS.
Benny's
Benny's

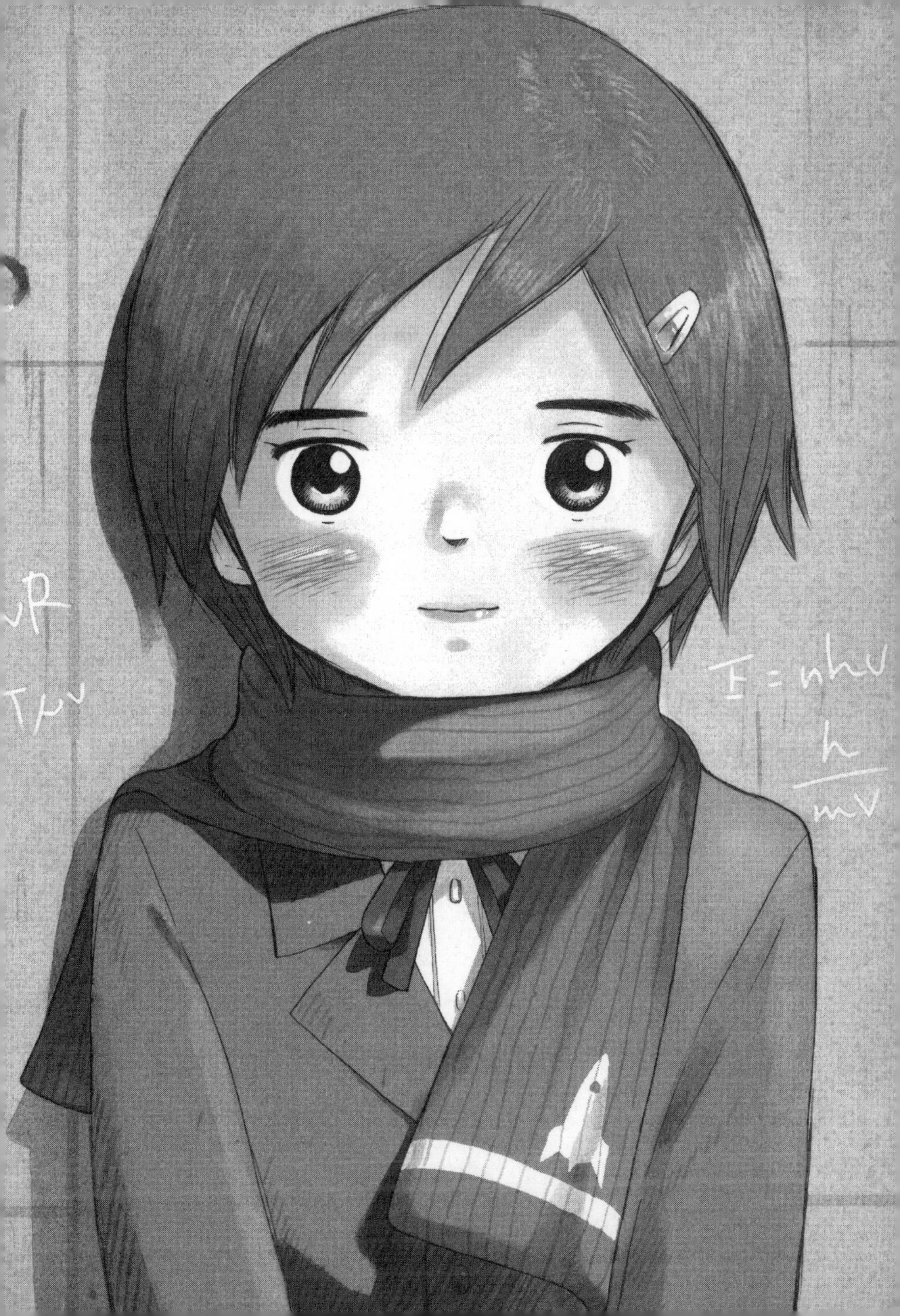
E = nhν
h/mv

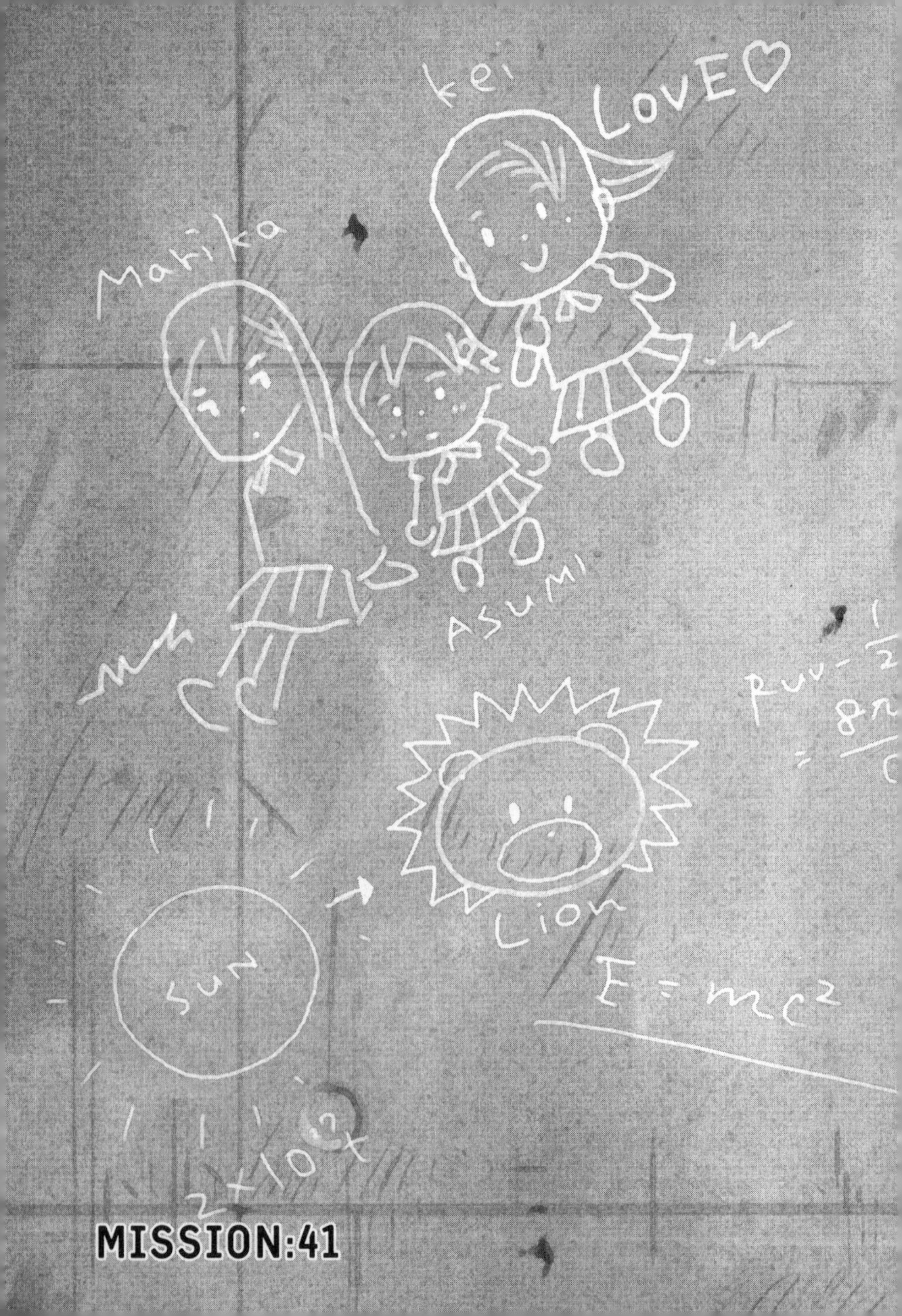
kei
LOVE
Marika
ASUMI
Lion
SUN
E = mc²

MISSION:41

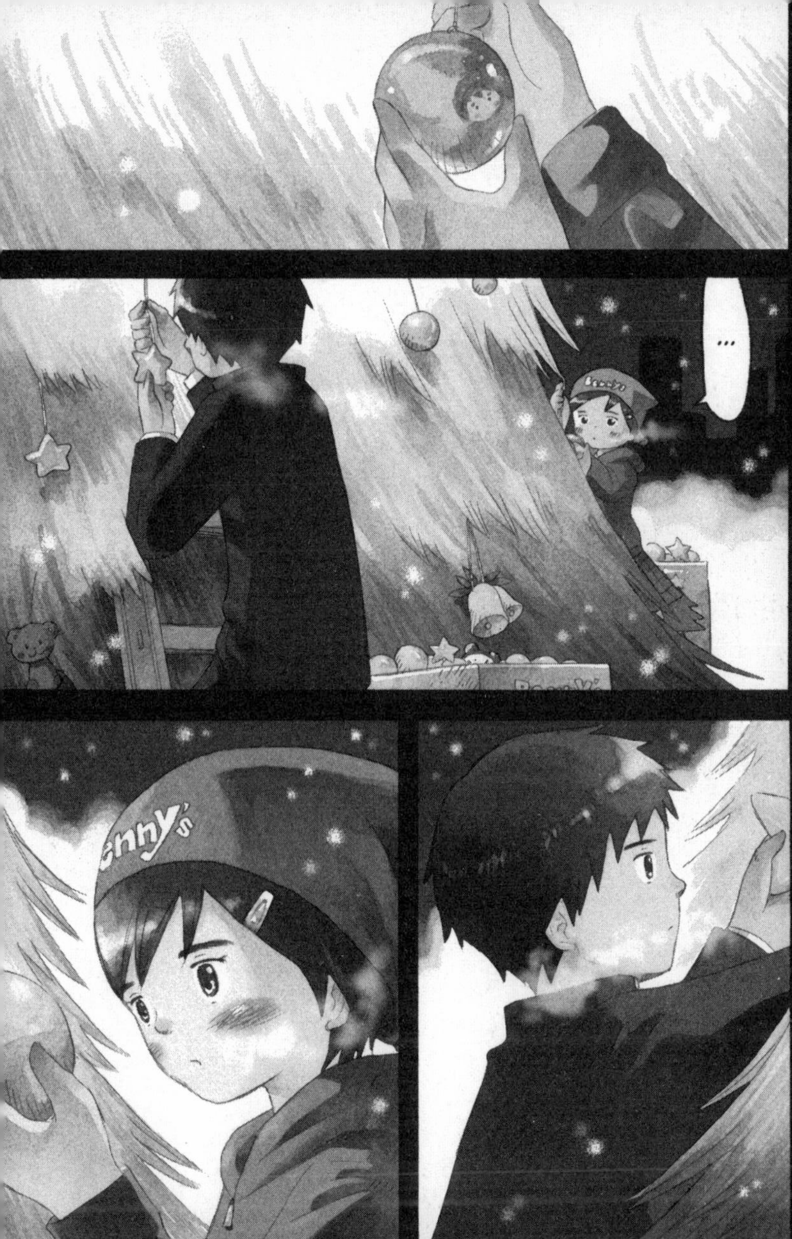
...

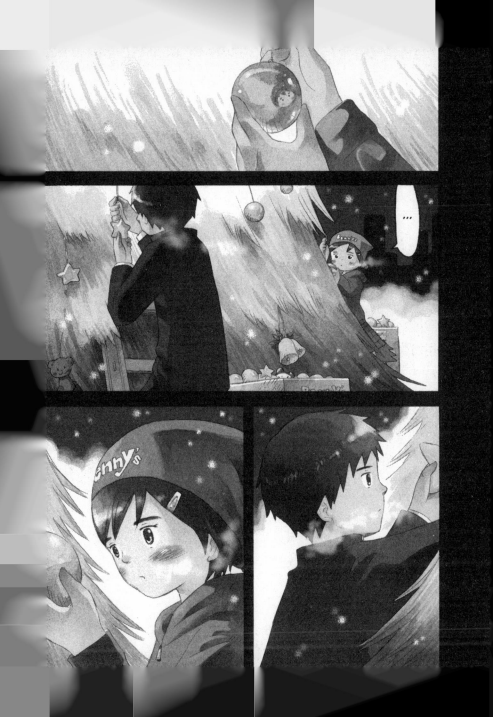

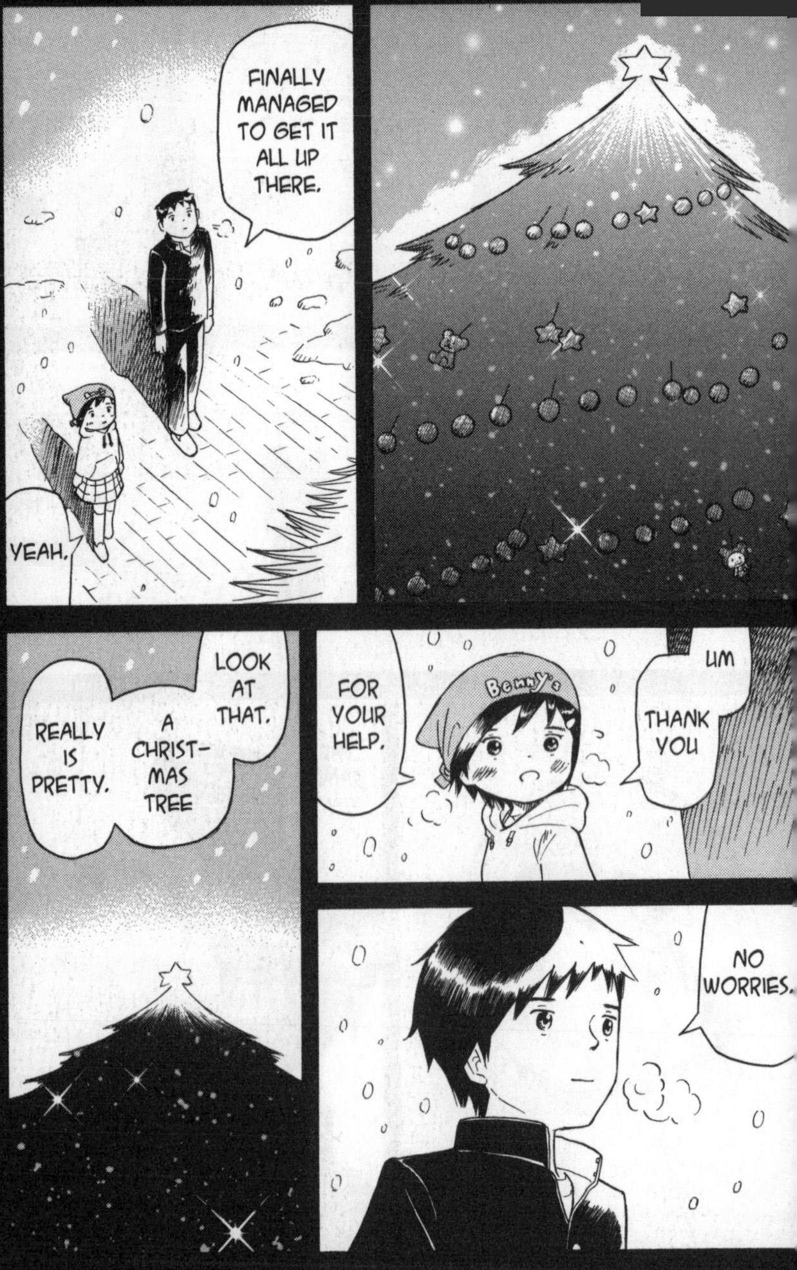
FINALLY MANAGED TO GET IT ALL UP THERE.
YEAH.
UM
THANK YOU
FOR YOUR HELP.
Benny's
NO WORRIES.
LOOK AT THAT.
A CHRIST-MAS TREE
REALLY IS PRETTY.

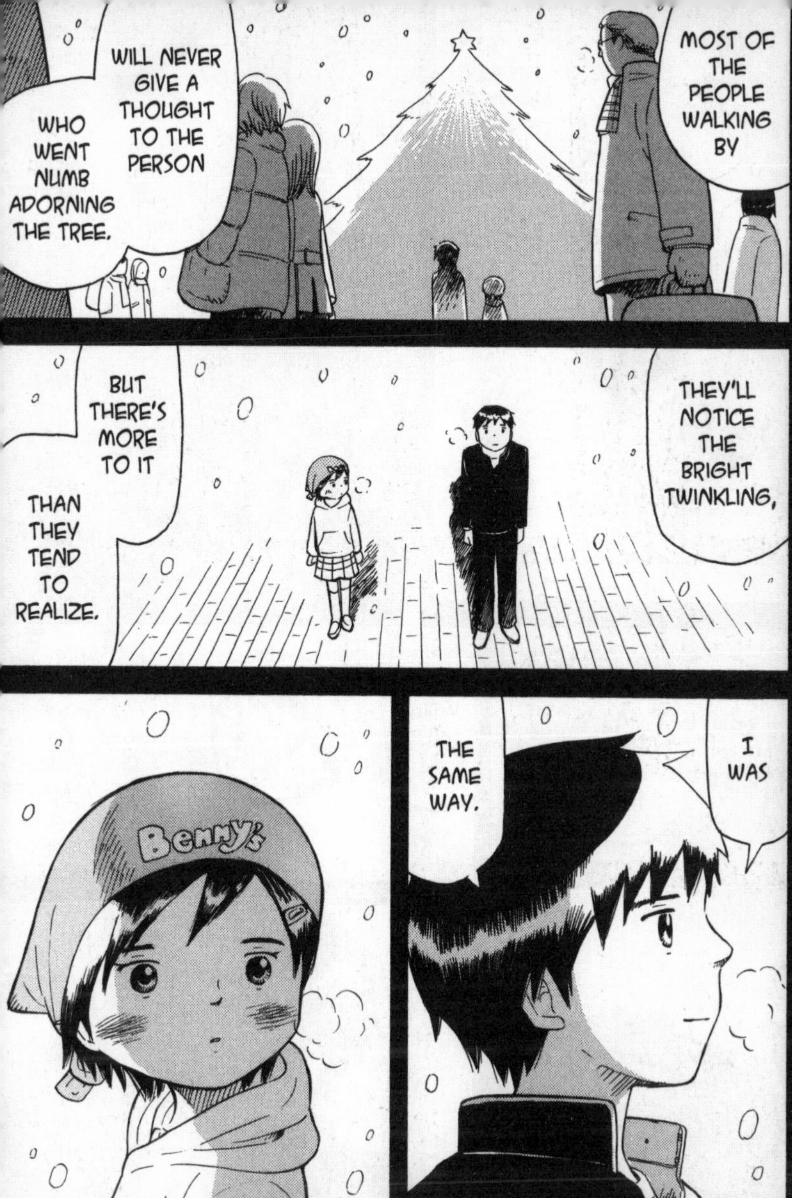
MOST OF THE PEOPLE WALKING BY
WILL NEVER GIVE A THOUGHT TO THE PERSON
WHO WENT NUMB ADORNING THE TREE.
THEY'LL NOTICE THE BRIGHT TWINKLING,
BUT THERE'S MORE TO IT
THAN THEY TEND TO REALIZE.
I WAS
THE SAME WAY.
Benny's

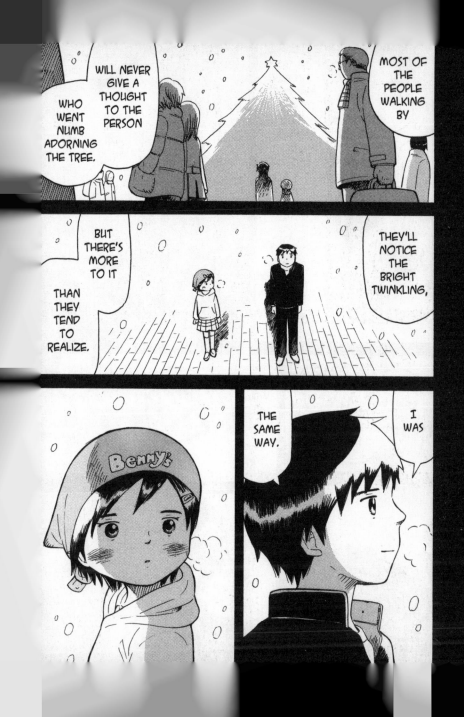

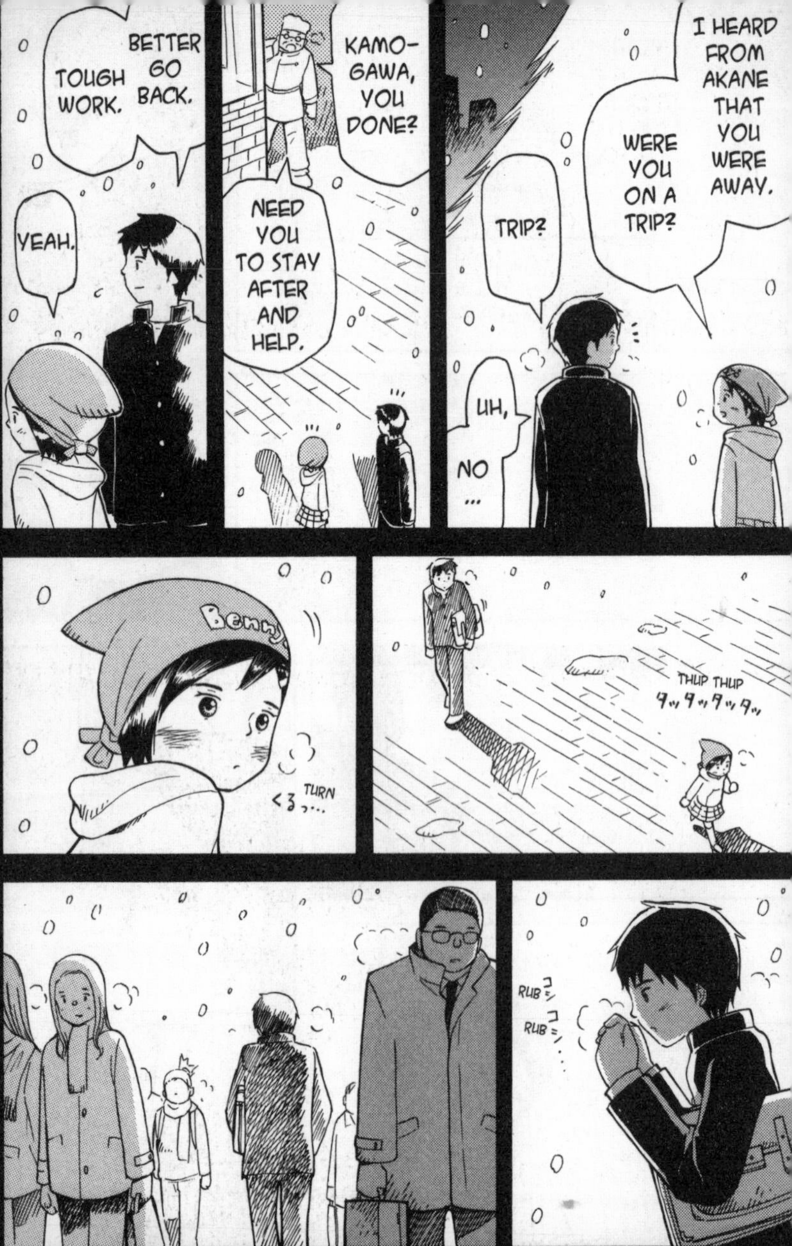
I HEARD FROM AKANE THAT YOU WERE AWAY.
WERE YOU ON A TRIP?
TRIP?
UH,
NO ...
KAMO-GAWA, YOU DONE?
NEED YOU TO STAY AFTER AND HELP.
BETTER GO BACK.
TOUGH WORK.
YEAH.
THUP THUP
タッタッタッタッ
Benny
TURN
くるっ…
RUB
RUB

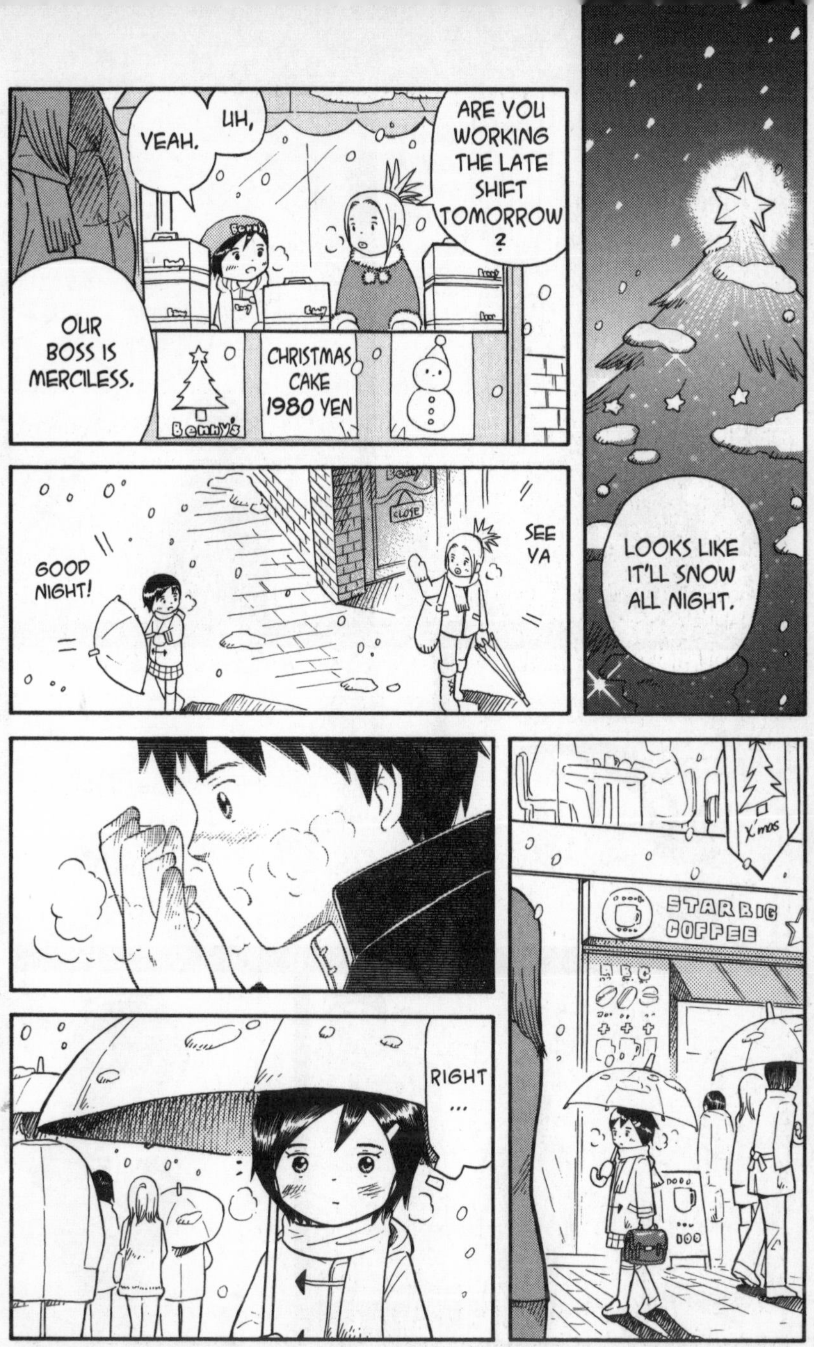
LOOKS LIKE IT'LL SNOW ALL NIGHT.
ARE YOU WORKING THE LATE SHIFT TOMORROW?
UH,
YEAH.
OUR BOSS IS MERCILESS.
CHRISTMAS CAKE 1980 YEN
Benny's
SEE YA
GOOD NIGHT!
X'mas
STARBIG COFFEE
RIGHT ...

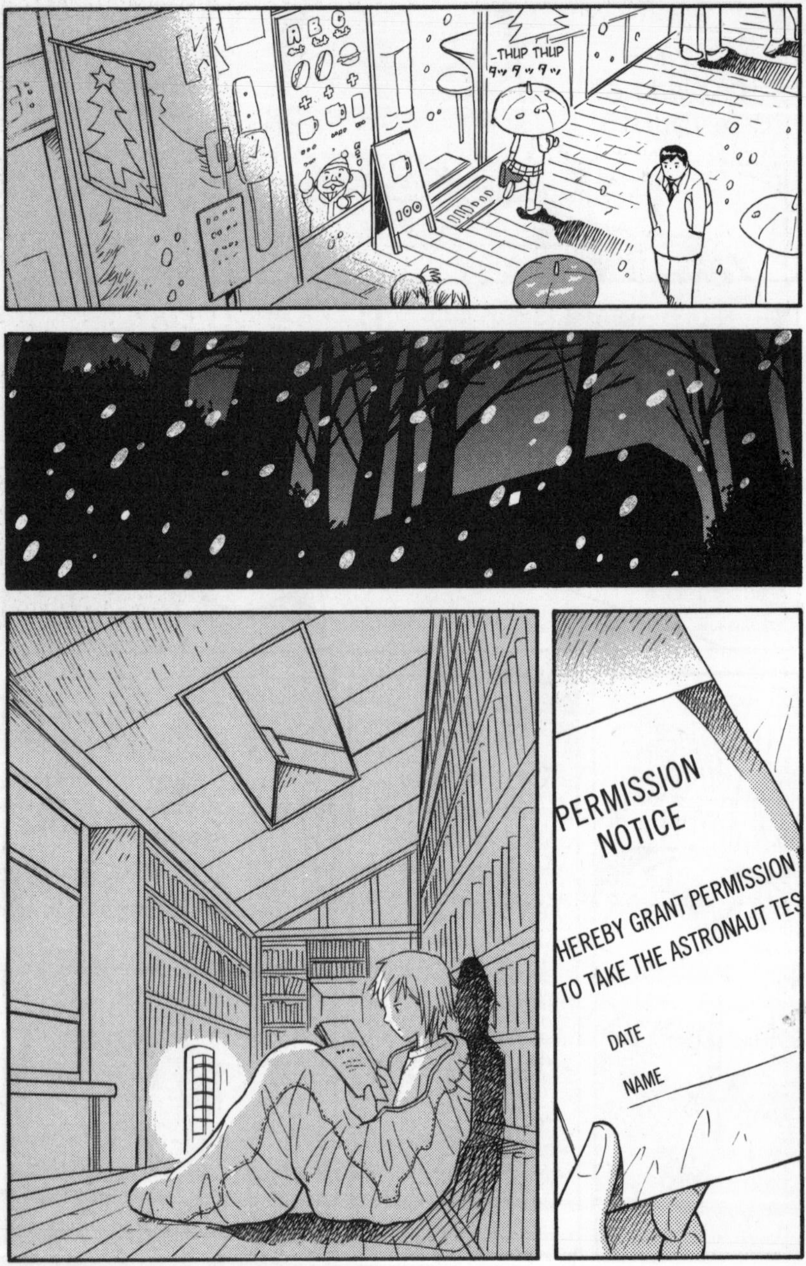
THUP THUP
タッタッタッ
PERMISSION
NOTICE
HEREBY GRANT PERMISSION
TO TAKE THE ASTRONAUT TES
DATE
NAME

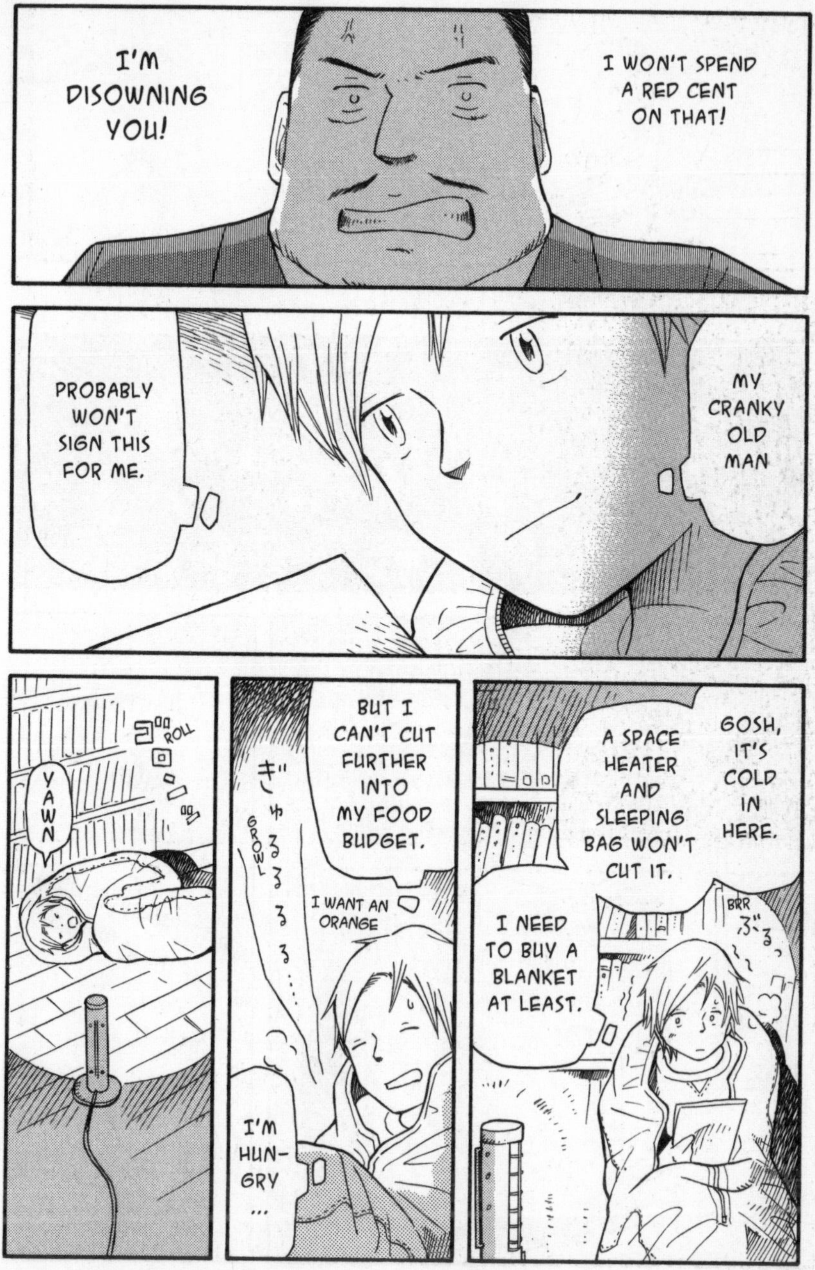
I WON'T SPEND A RED CENT ON THAT!
I'M DISOWNING YOU!
MY CRANKY OLD MAN
PROBABLY WON'T SIGN THIS FOR ME.
GOSH, IT'S COLD IN HERE.
A SPACE HEATER AND SLEEPING BAG WON'T CUT IT.
BRR ぶる
I NEED TO BUY A BLANKET AT LEAST.
BUT I CAN'T CUT FURTHER INTO MY FOOD BUDGET.
ぎゅるるるる……
GROWL
I WANT AN ORANGE
I'M HUN-GRY …
ROLL
YAWN

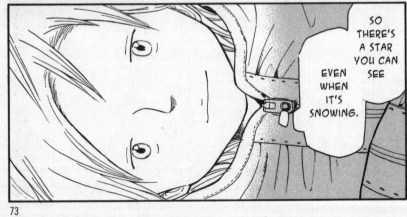

SO THERE'S A STAR YOU CAN SEE EVEN WHEN IT'S SNOWING.

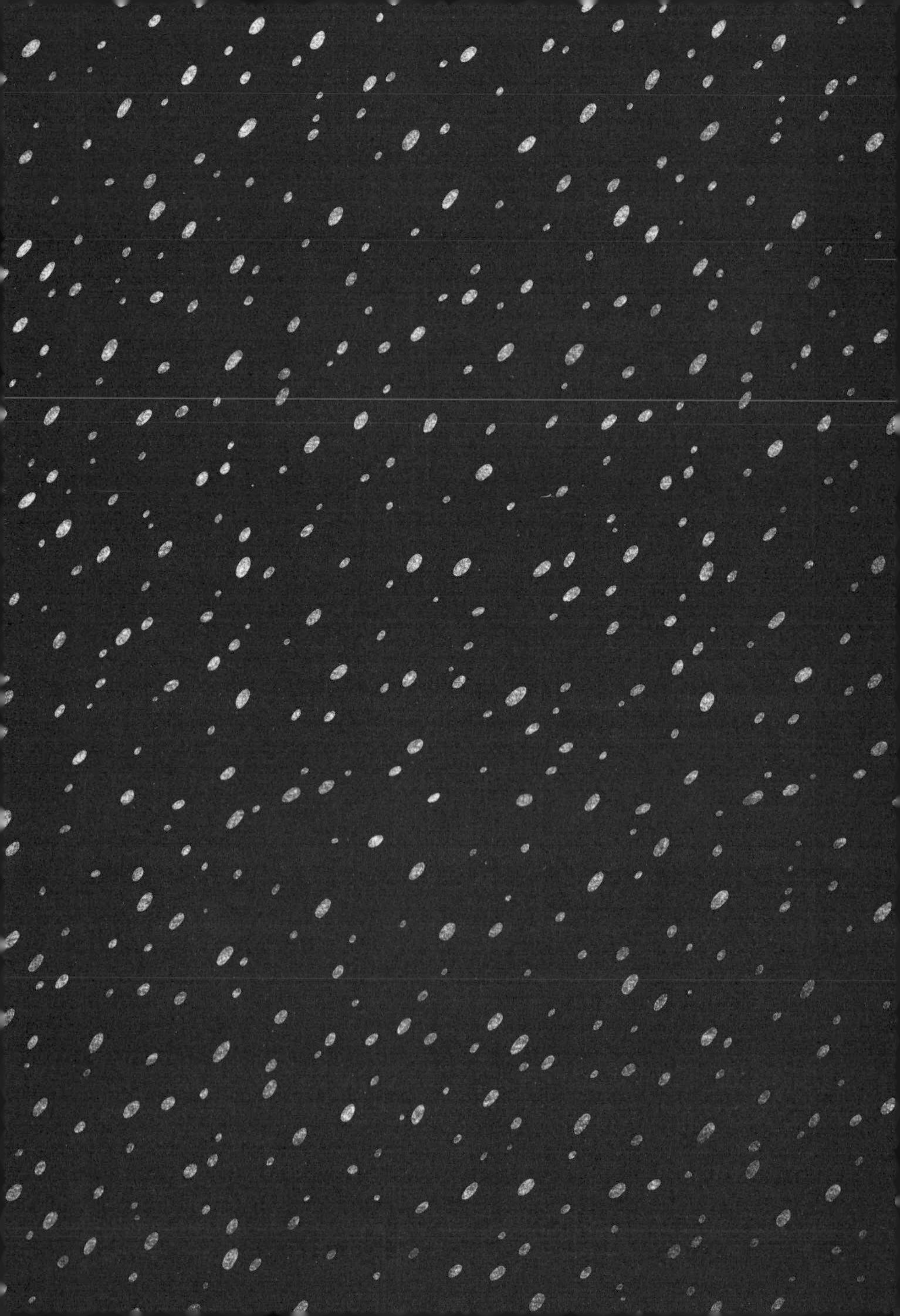

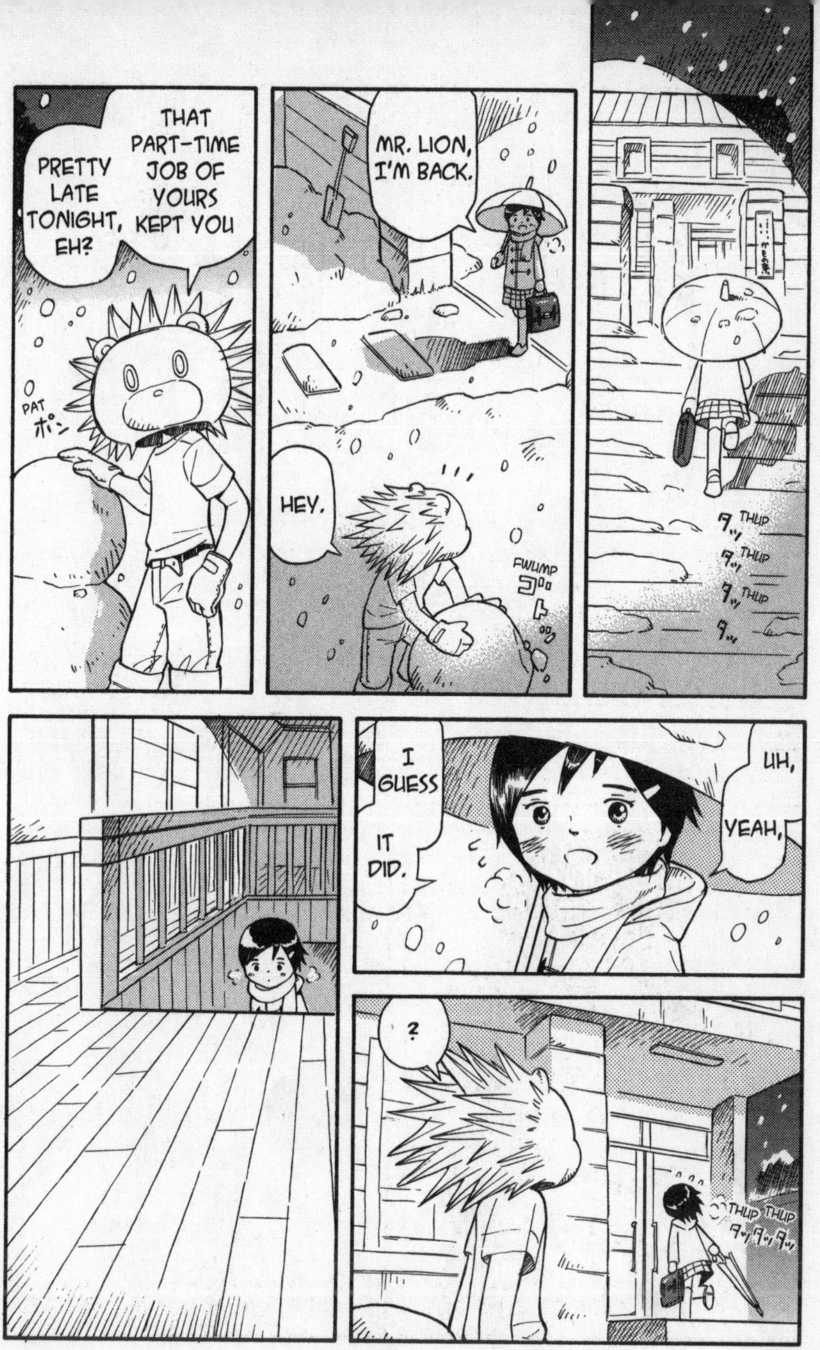
THUP
THUP
THUP
MR. LION, I'M BACK.
HEY.
FWUMP
THAT PART-TIME JOB OF YOURS KEPT YOU
PRETTY LATE TONIGHT, EH?
PAT
UH, YEAH,
I GUESS IT DID.
?
THUP THUP

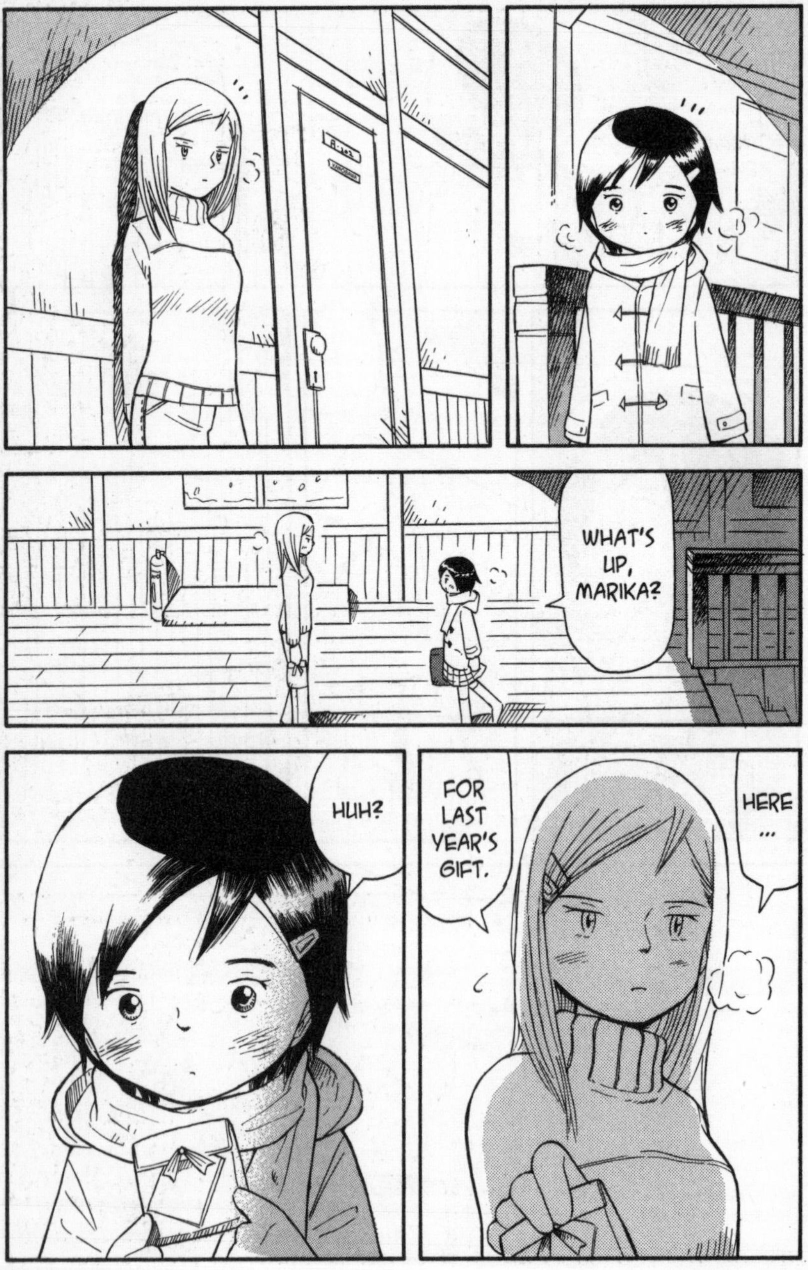
WHAT'S UP, MARIKA?
HERE ...
FOR LAST YEAR'S GIFT.
HUH?

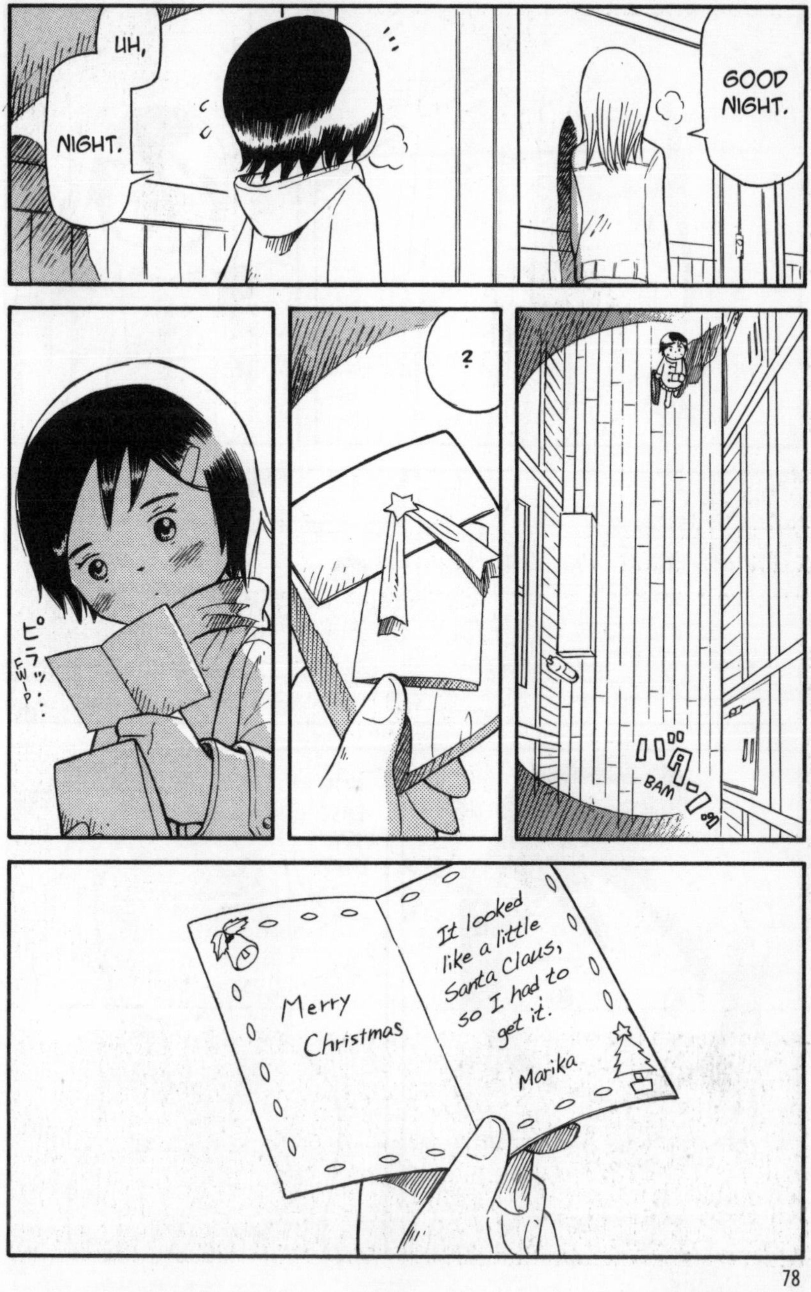
GOOD NIGHT.
UH,
NIGHT.
BAM
?
ピラッ…
FWIP
It looked like a little Santa Claus, so I had to get it.
Merry Christmas
Marika

KEY
RING
?

ガサ
RUSTLE

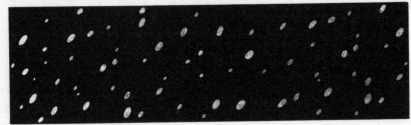

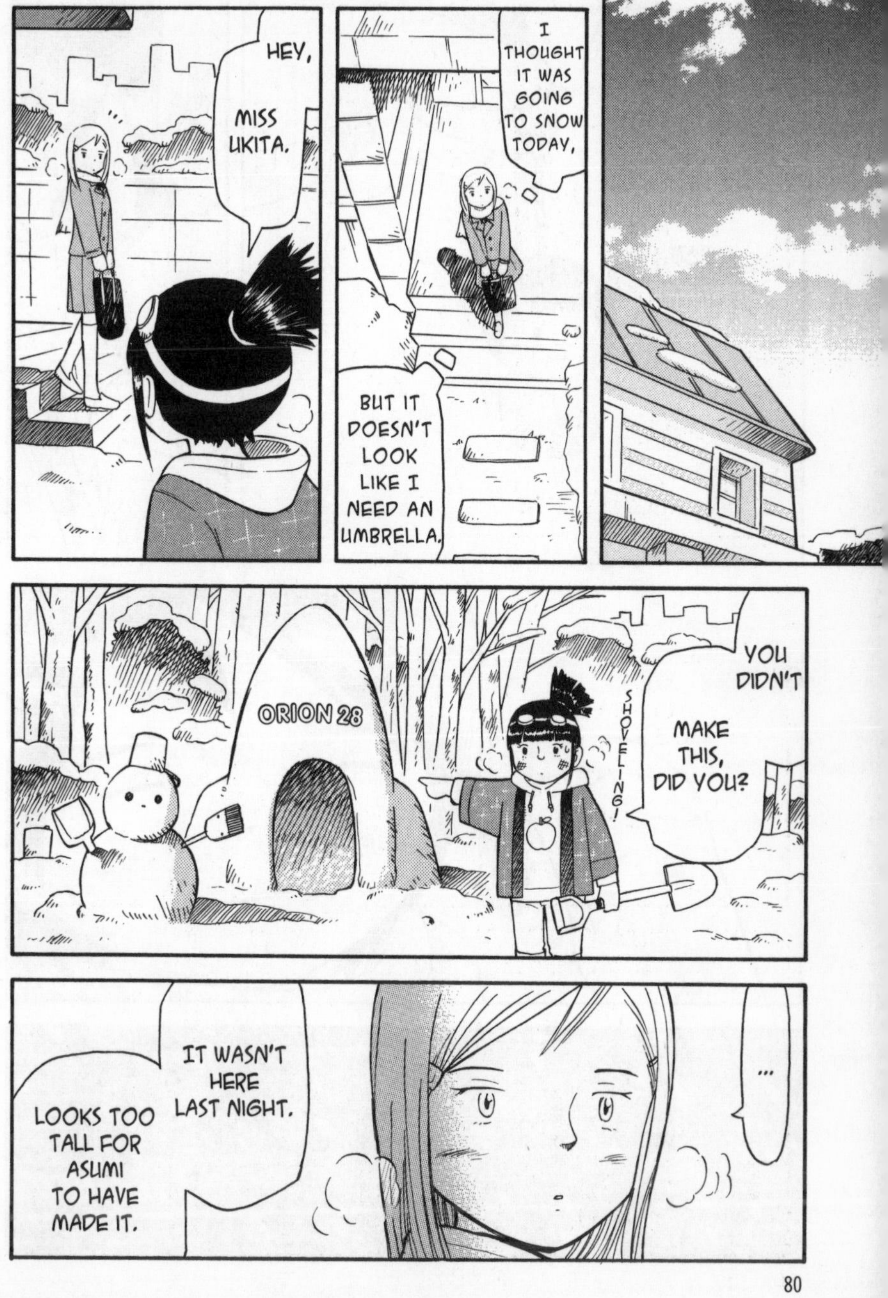
I THOUGHT IT WAS GOING TO SNOW TODAY,
BUT IT DOESN'T LOOK LIKE I NEED AN UMBRELLA.
HEY,
MISS UKITA.
YOU DIDN'T
MAKE THIS, DID YOU?
SHOVELING!
ORION 28
...
IT WASN'T HERE LAST NIGHT.
LOOKS TOO TALL FOR ASUMI TO HAVE MADE IT.

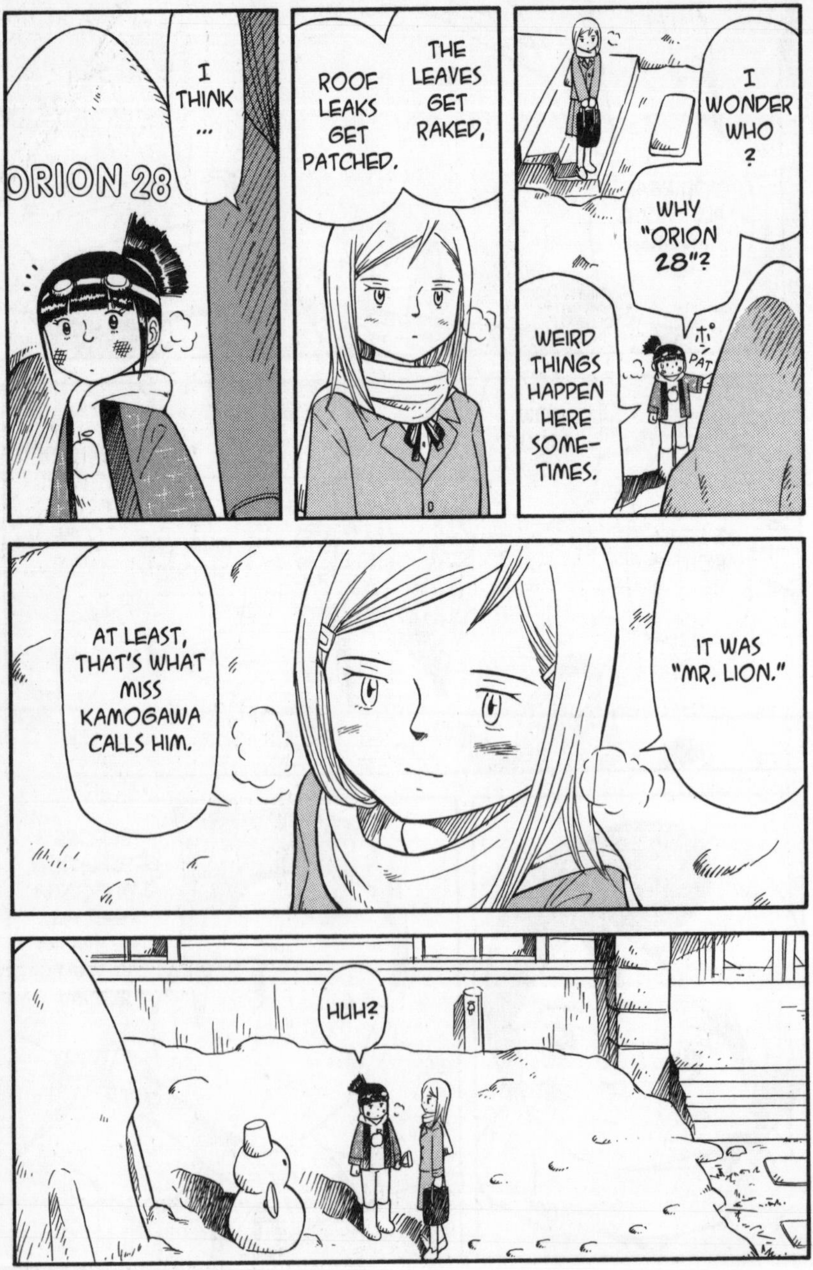
I WONDER WHO?
WHY "ORION 28"?
ポ
PAT
WEIRD THINGS HAPPEN HERE SOME-TIMES.
THE LEAVES GET RAKED,
ROOF LEAKS GET PATCHED.
I THINK ...
ORION 28
IT WAS "MR. LION."
AT LEAST, THAT'S WHAT MISS KAMOGAWA CALLS HIM.
HUH?

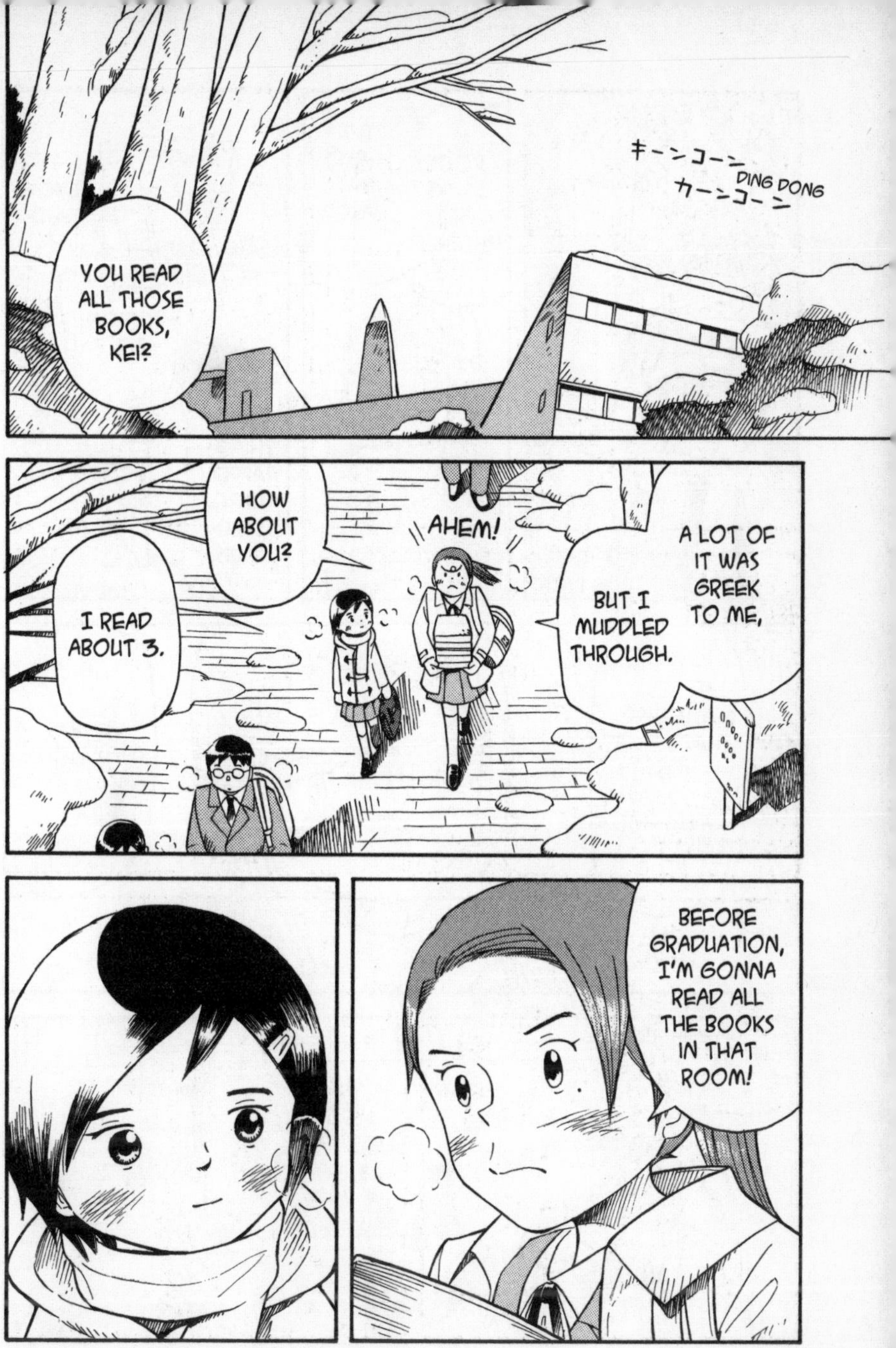
キーンコーン
DING DONG
カーンコーン
YOU READ ALL THOSE BOOKS, KEI?
A LOT OF IT WAS GREEK TO ME,
BUT I MUDDLED THROUGH.
AHEM!
HOW ABOUT YOU?
I READ ABOUT 3.
BEFORE GRADUATION, I'M GONNA READ ALL THE BOOKS IN THAT ROOM!

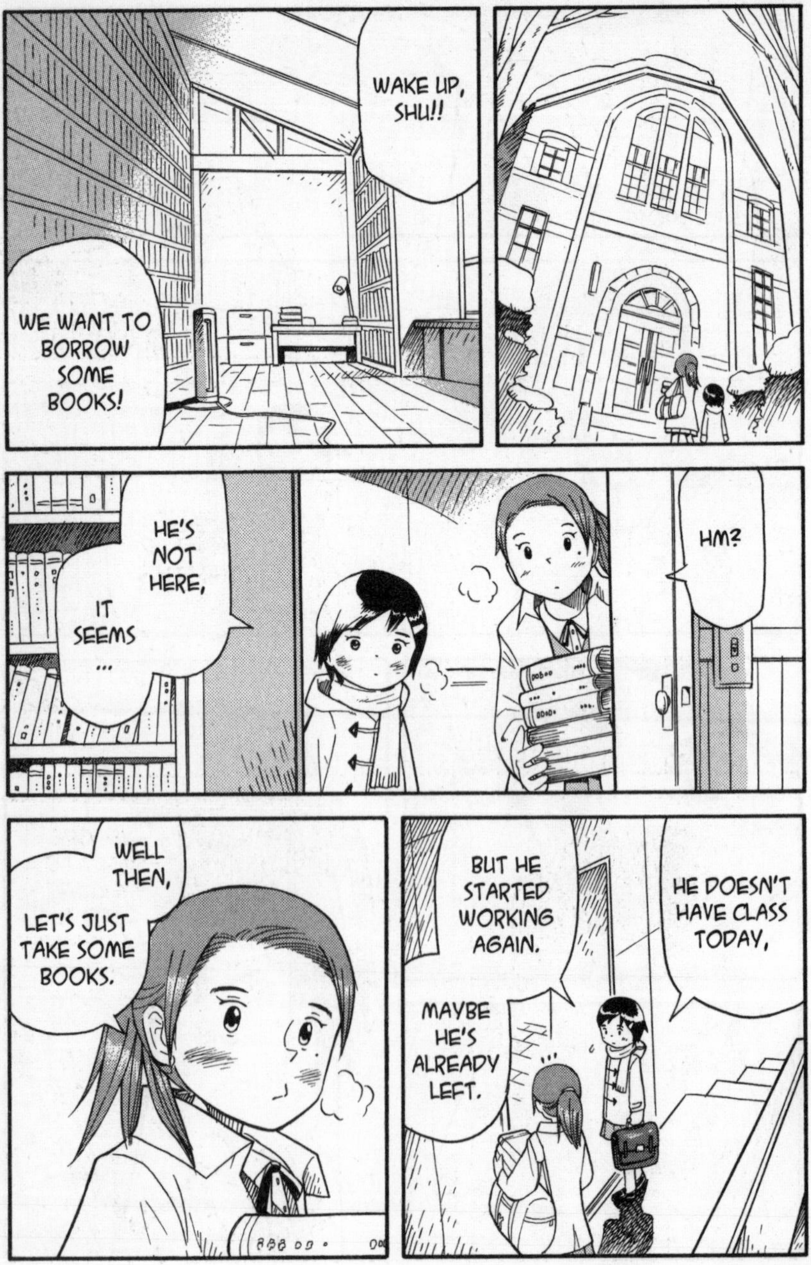
WAKE UP, SHU!!
WE WANT TO BORROW SOME BOOKS!
HM?
HE'S NOT HERE,
IT SEEMS ...
HE DOESN'T HAVE CLASS TODAY,
BUT HE STARTED WORKING AGAIN.
MAYBE HE'S ALREADY LEFT.
WELL THEN,
LET'S JUST TAKE SOME BOOKS.

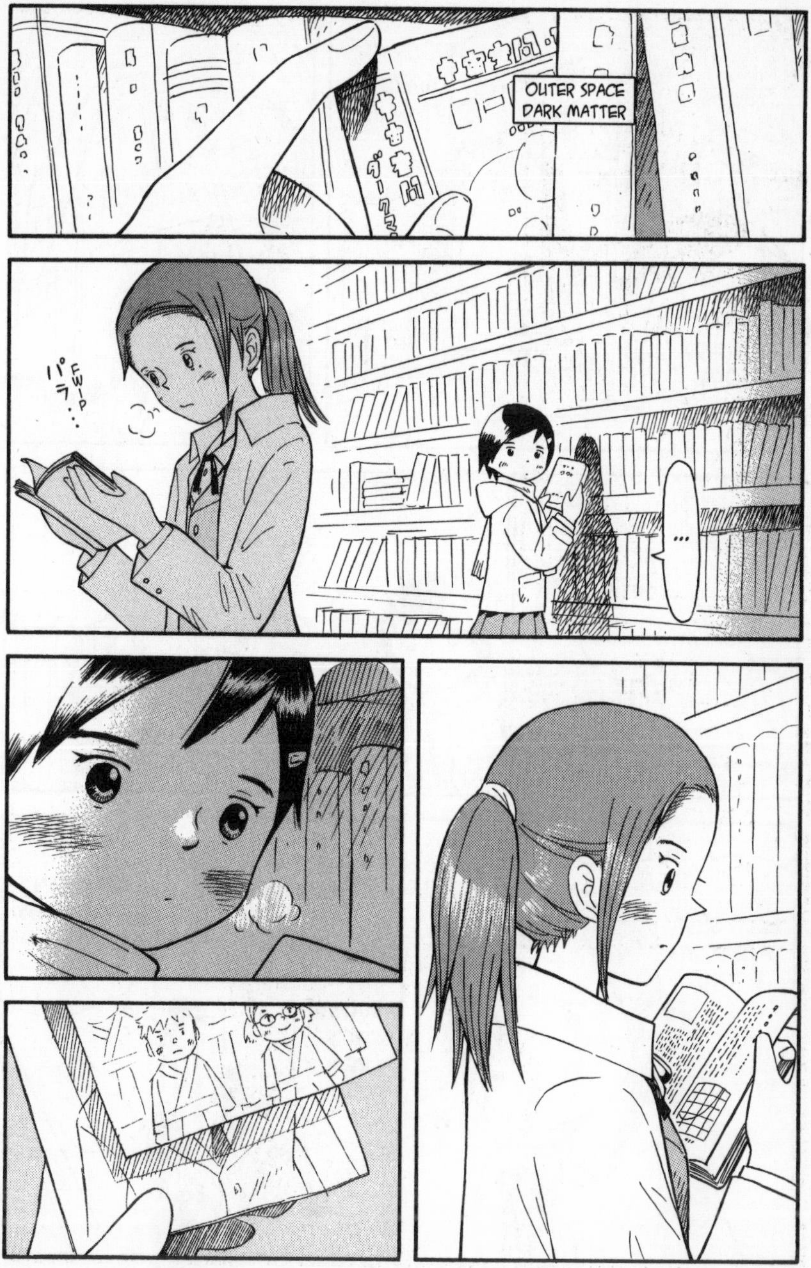
OUTER SPACE
DARK MATTER
...
パラ FWIP...

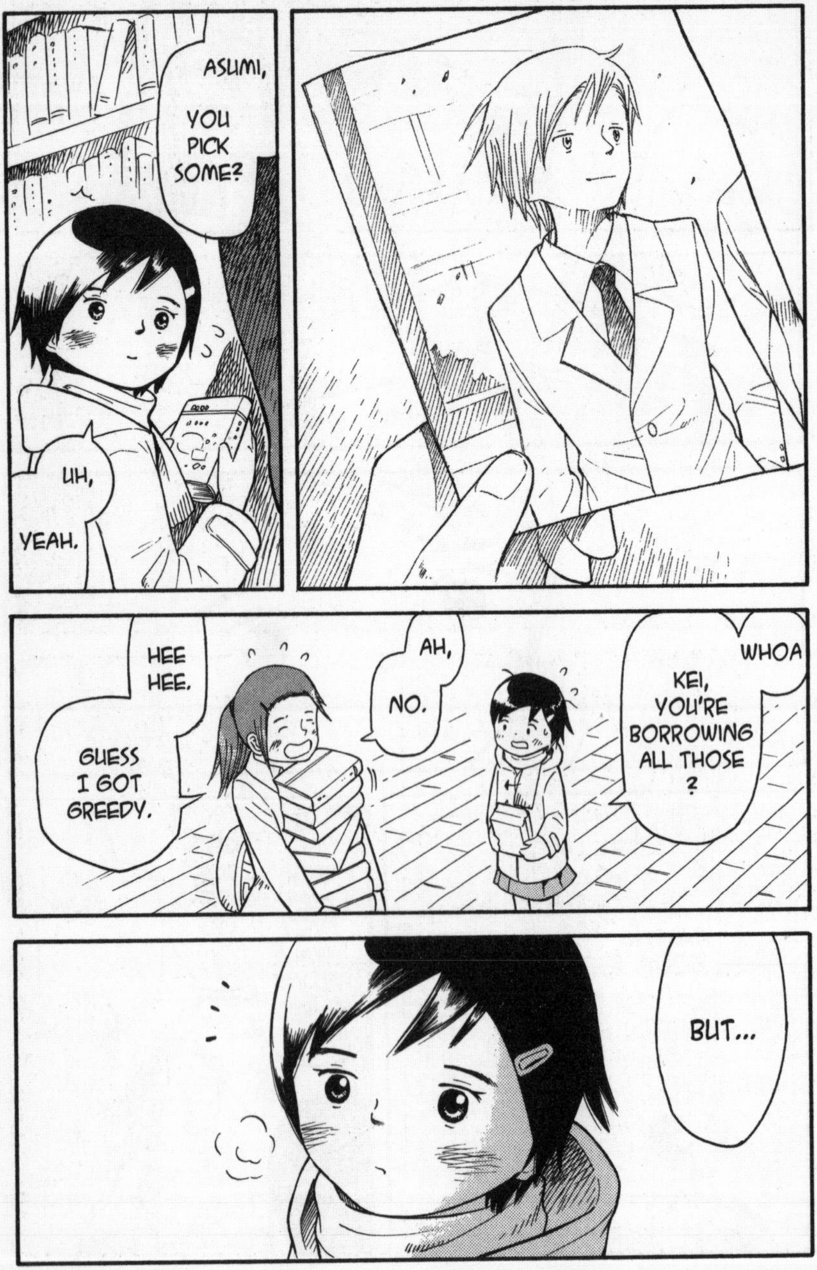
ASUMI, YOU PICK SOME?
UH, YEAH.
WHOA
KEI, YOU'RE BORROWING ALL THOSE ?
AH, NO.
HEE HEE. GUESS I GOT GREEDY.
BUT...

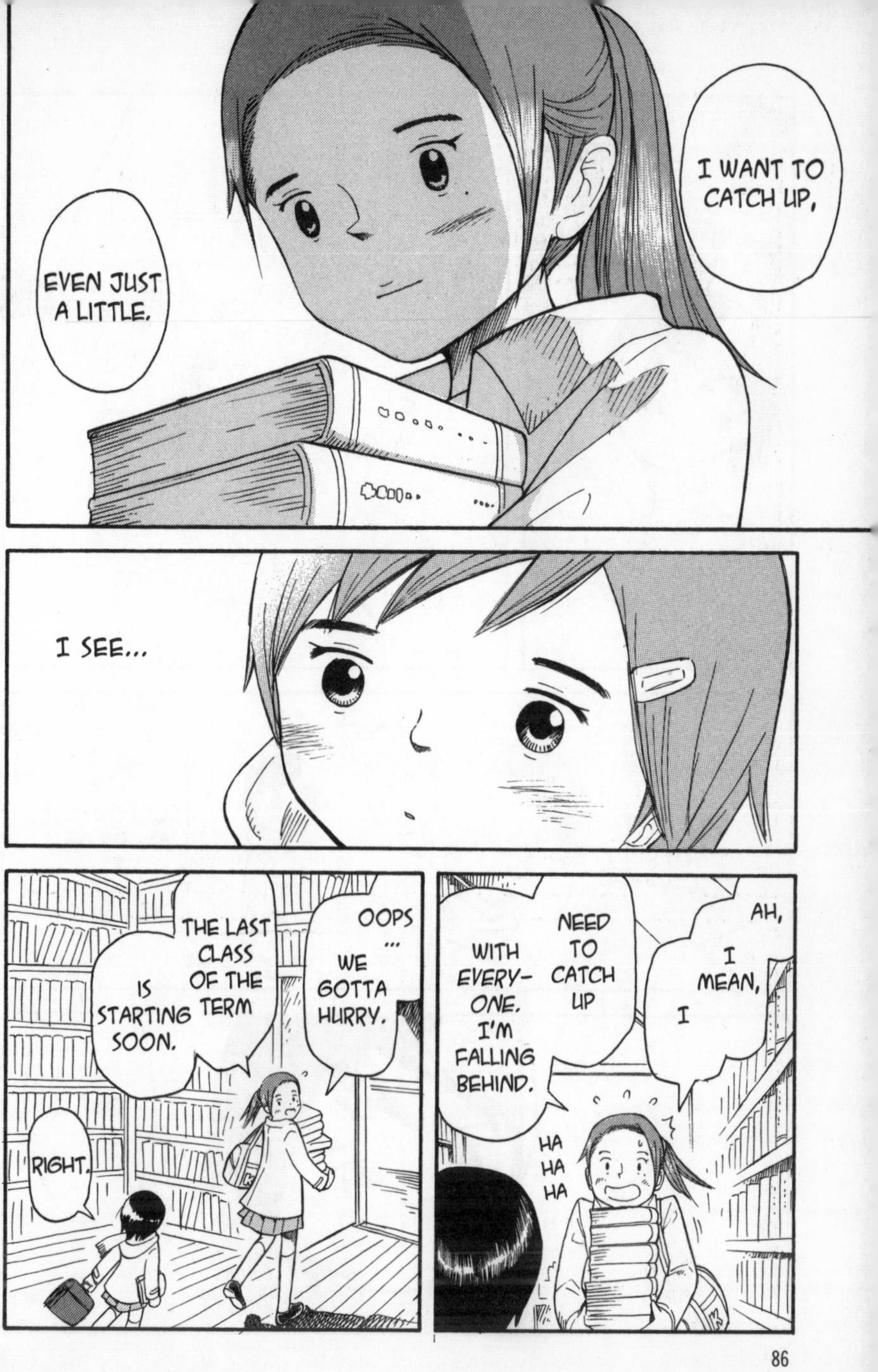
I WANT TO CATCH UP,
EVEN JUST A LITTLE.
I SEE...
AH, I MEAN, I
NEED TO CATCH UP WITH EVERY-ONE. I'M FALLING BEHIND.
HA HA HA
OOPS ... WE GOTTA HURRY.
THE LAST CLASS OF THE TERM IS STARTING SOON.
RIGHT.

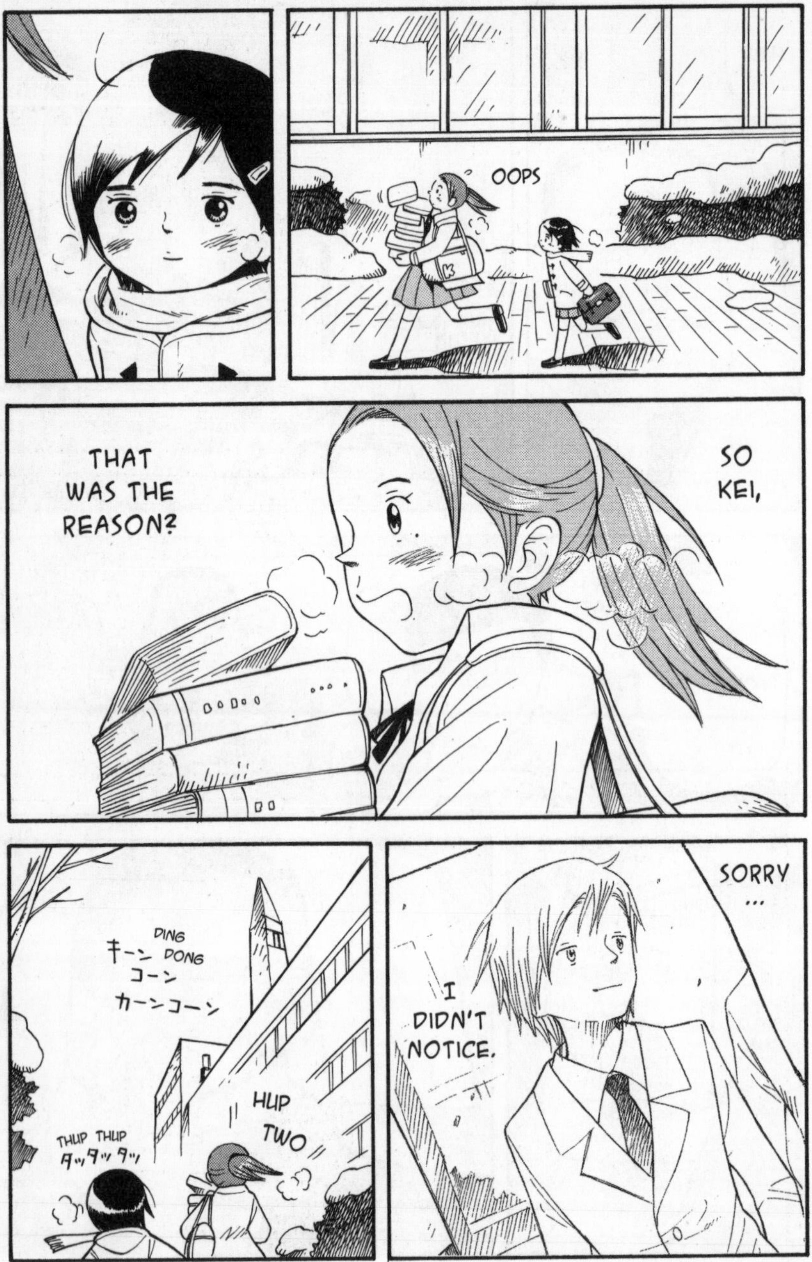
OOPS
SO KEI,
THAT WAS THE REASON?
SORRY ...
I DIDN'T NOTICE.
DING DONG
キーン
コーン
カーンコーン
HUP TWO
THUP THUP
タッタッタッ

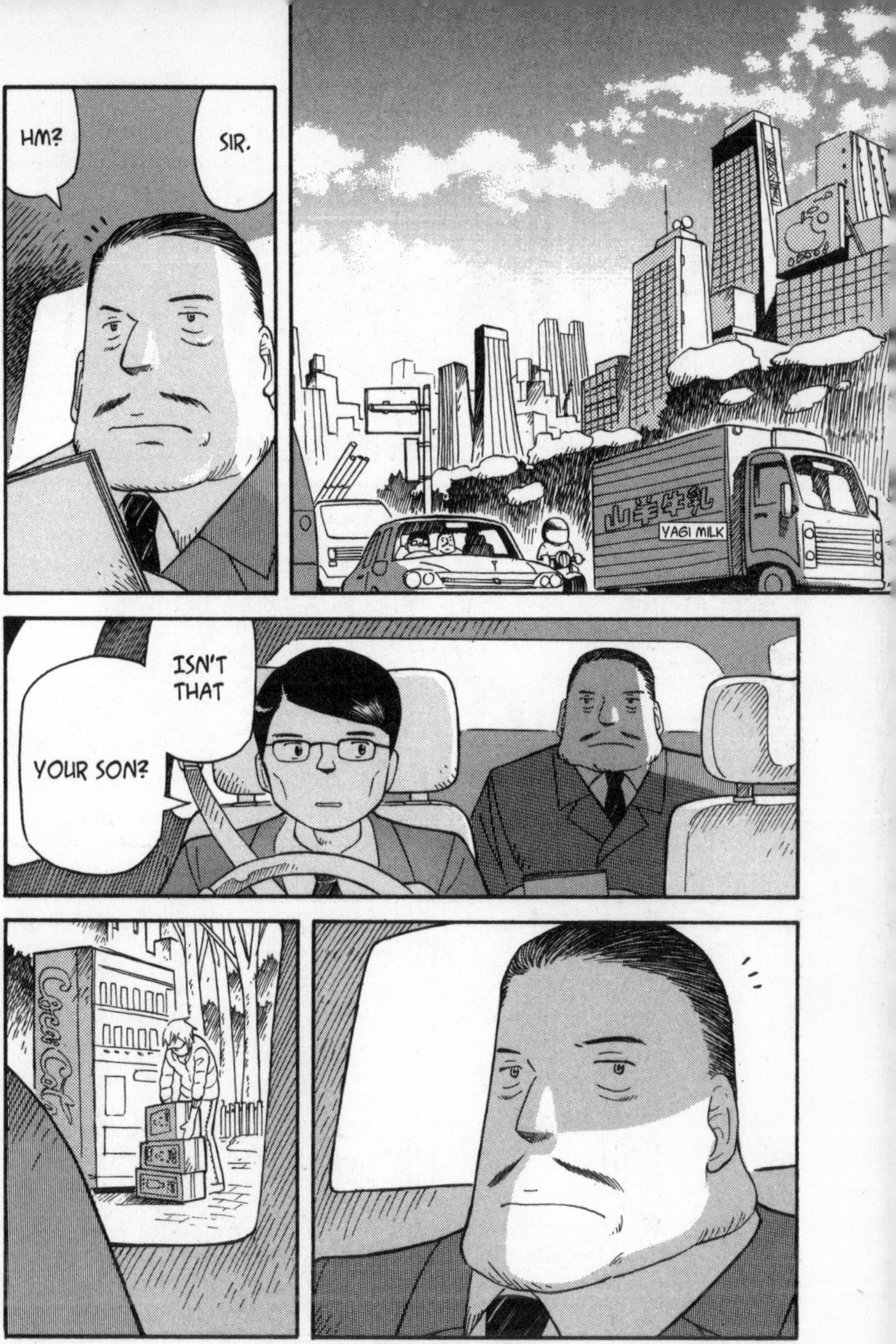
YAGI MILK
SIR.
HM?
ISN'T THAT
YOUR SON?

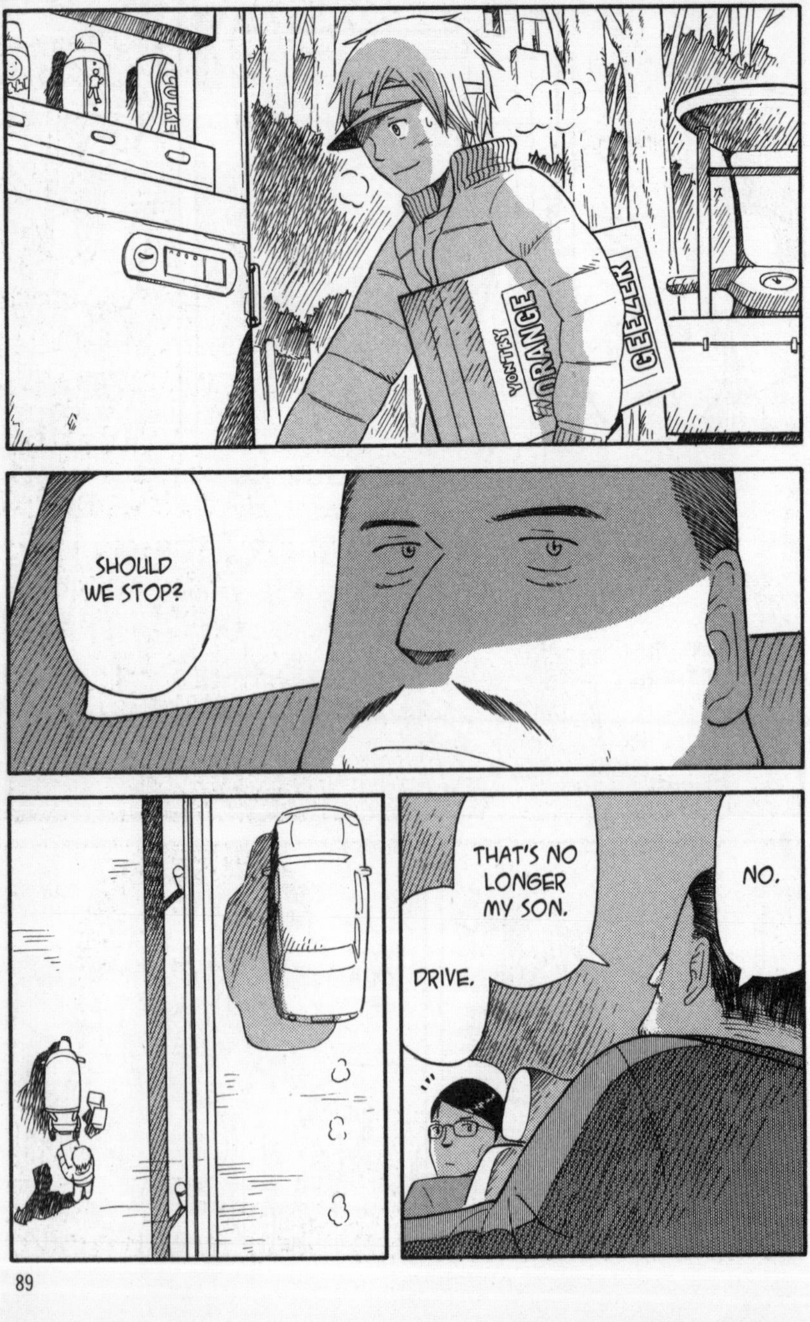
ORANGE
GEEZER
SHOULD WE STOP?
NO.
THAT'S NO LONGER MY SON.
DRIVE.

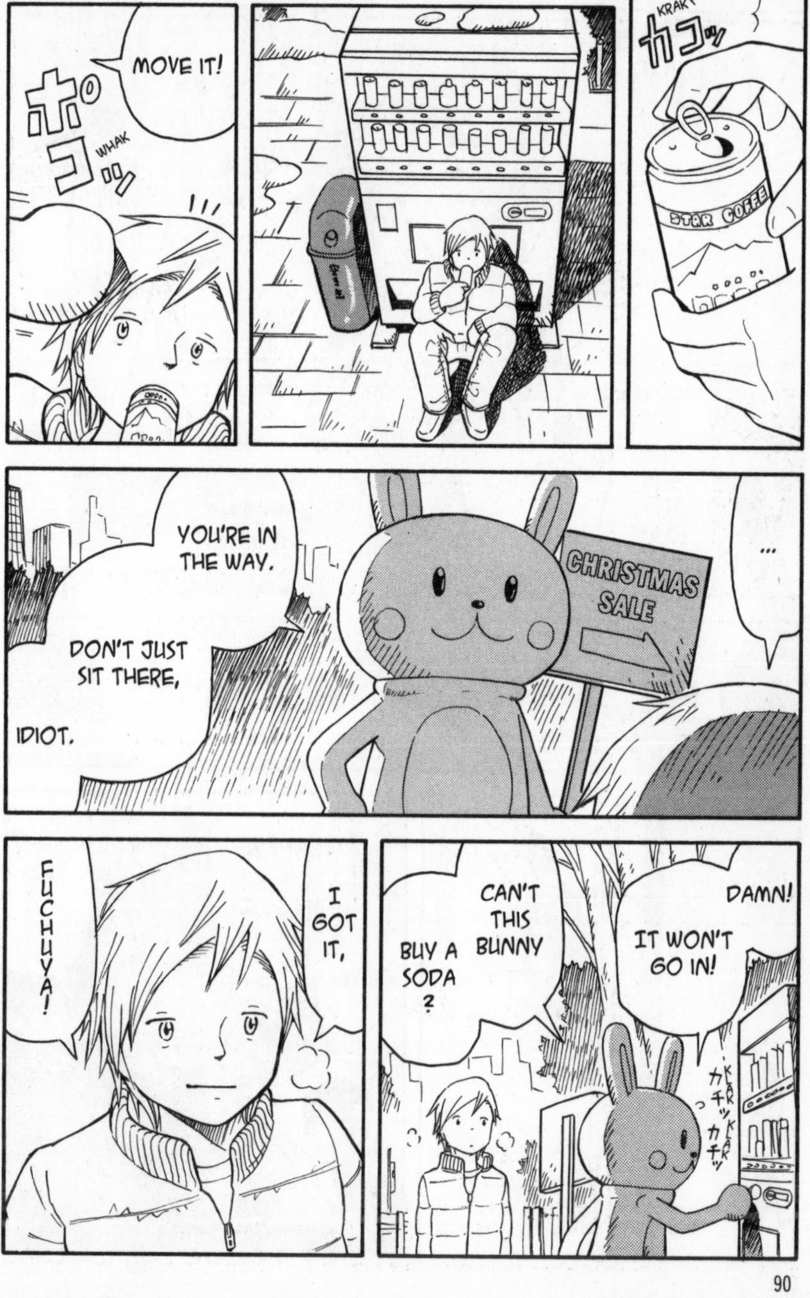
KRAK
カコッ
STAR COFFE
MOVE IT!
ポコッ
WHAK
...
CHRISTMAS SALE
YOU'RE IN THE WAY.
DON'T JUST SIT THERE,
IDIOT.
DAMN!
IT WON'T GO IN!
CAN'T THIS BUNNY
BUY A SODA?
KAK カチッ
KAK カチッ
I GOT IT,
FUCHUYA!

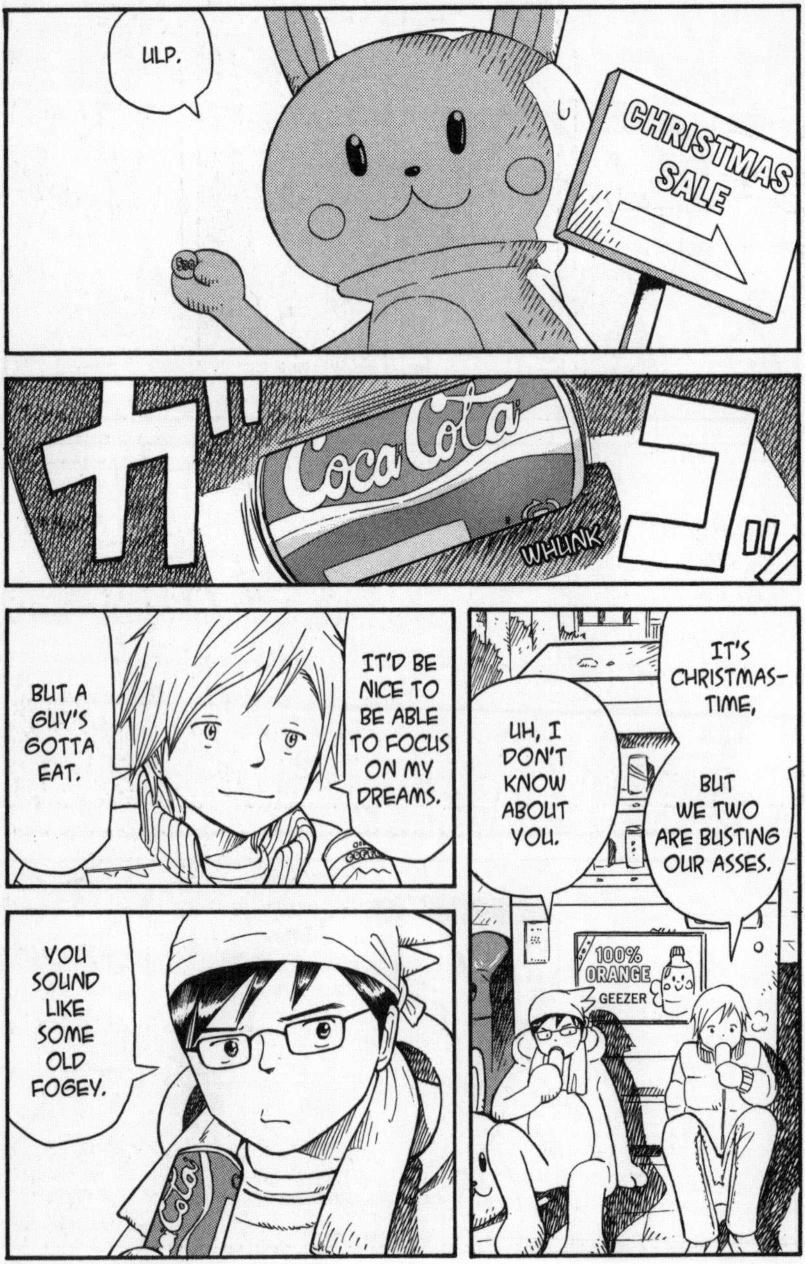
ULP.
CHRISTMAS SALE
WHUNK
IT'S CHRISTMAS-TIME,
BUT WE TWO ARE BUSTING OUR ASSES.
UH, I DON'T KNOW ABOUT YOU.
100% ORANGE
GEEZER
IT'D BE NICE TO BE ABLE TO FOCUS ON MY DREAMS.
BUT A GUY'S GOTTA EAT.
YOU SOUND LIKE SOME OLD FOGEY.

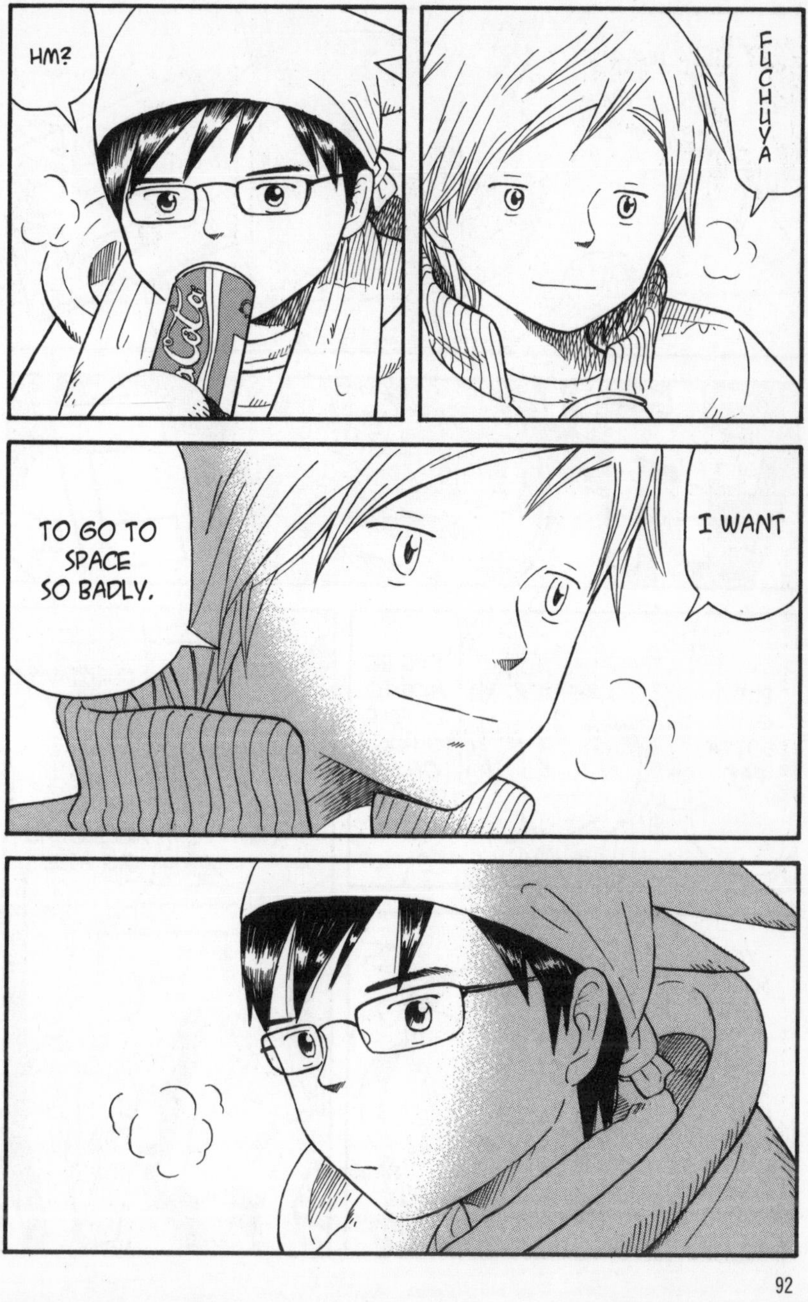
FUCHUYA
HM?
I WANT
TO GO TO SPACE SO BADLY.

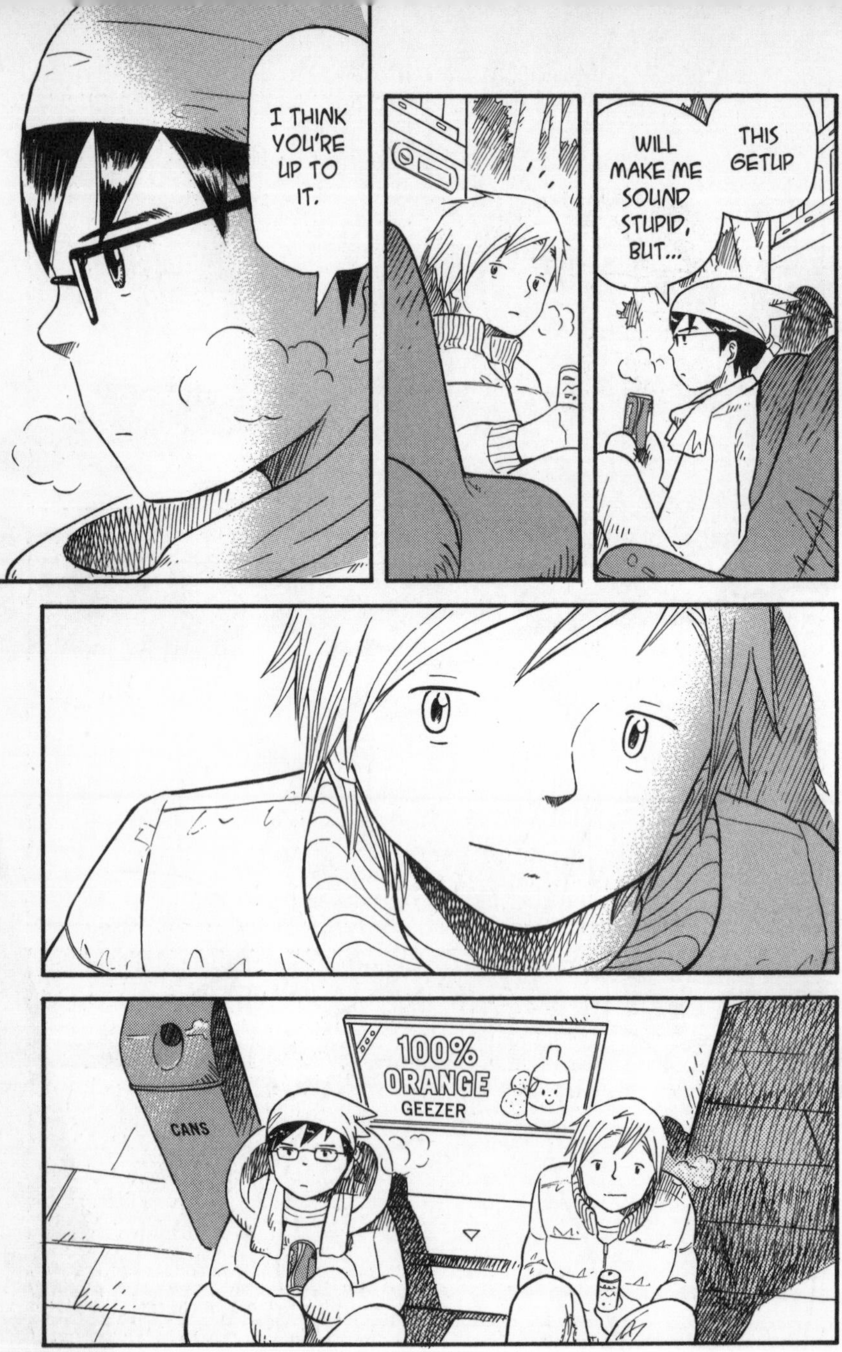
THIS GETUP
WILL MAKE ME SOUND STUPID, BUT...
I THINK YOU'RE UP TO IT.
100% ORANGE
GEEZER
CANS

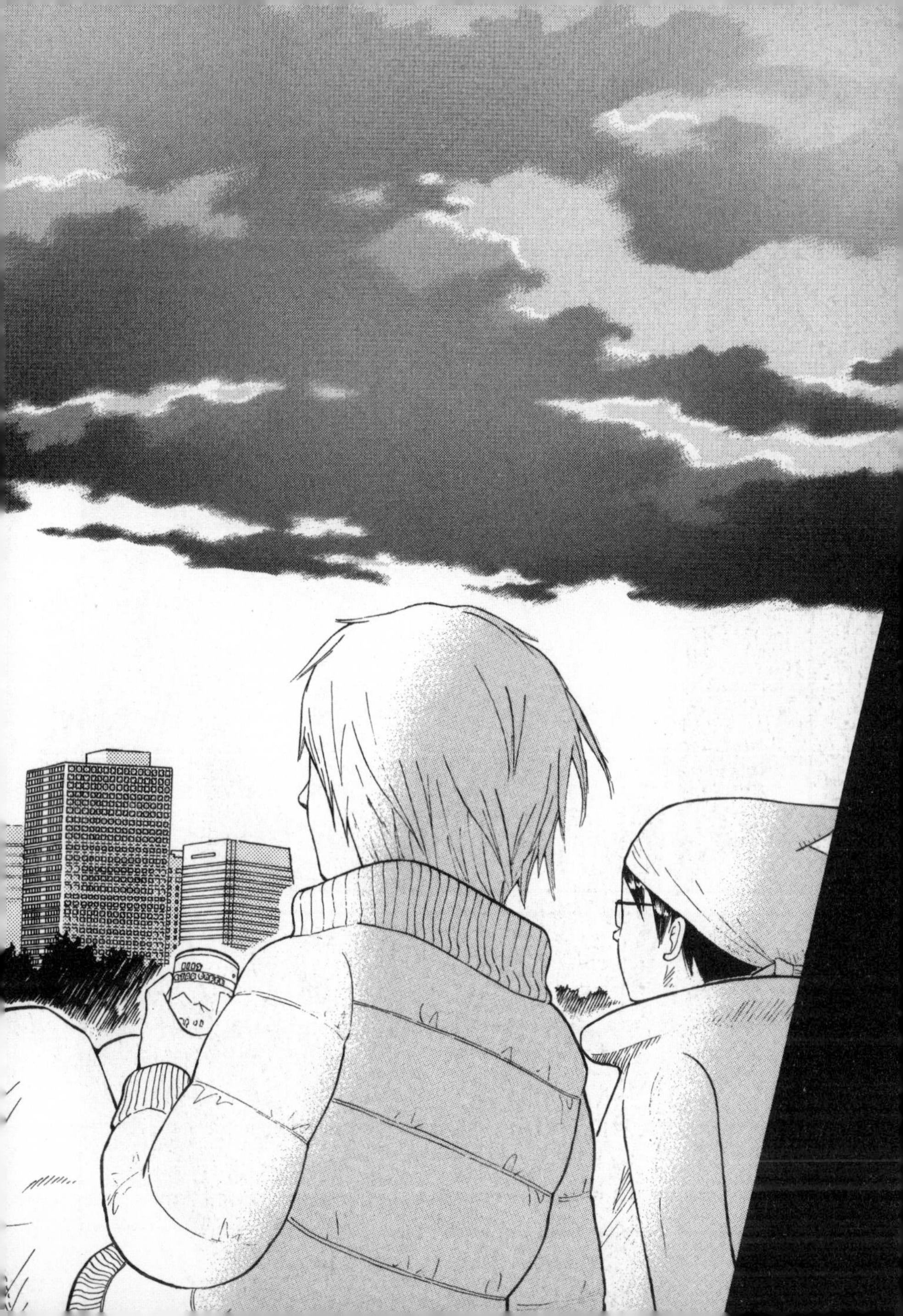

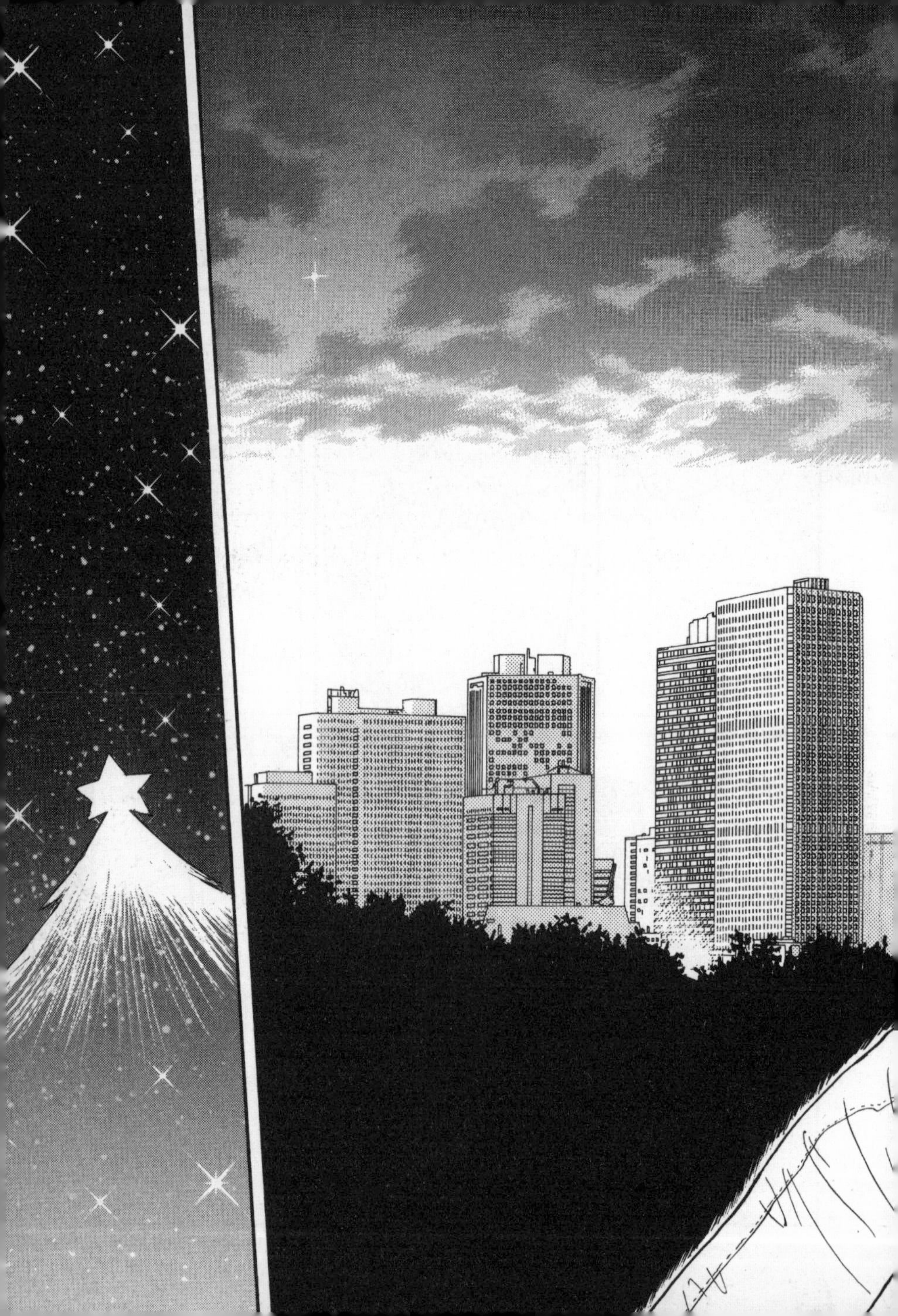

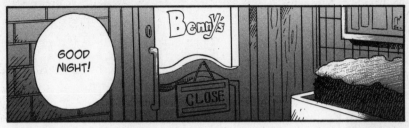

Benny's
CLOSE
GOOD NIGHT!
AH, KAMO-GAWA.
WAVE
YES?
HERE'S A LEFTOVER CAKE.
A CHRISTMAS GIFT FROM THE MANAGER FOR ALL YOUR WORK.
Benny's
THERE'S ONLY ONE, SO KEEP IT A SECRET
FROM NATSU-ME.
I HEARD THAT.
WHOA!
YOU'RE STILL HERE?
PERFECT.

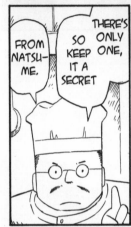

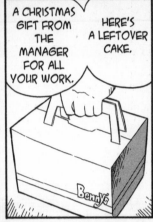

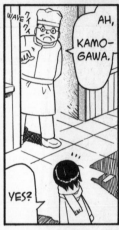

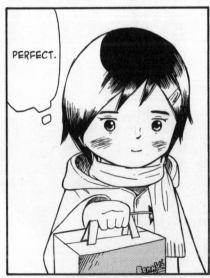

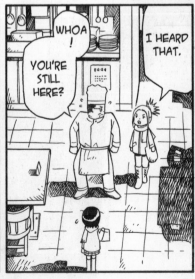

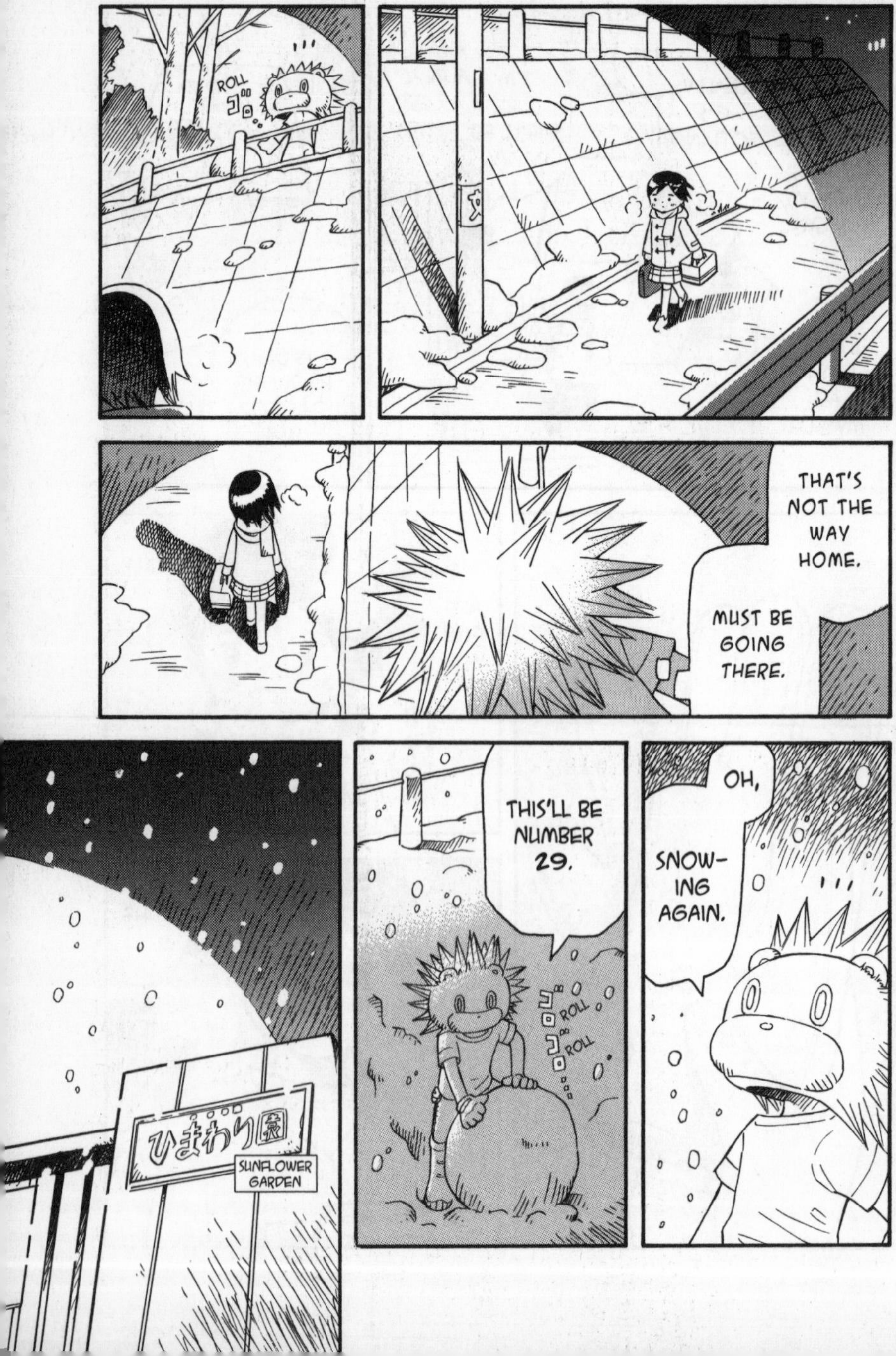
ROLL
ゴロ
THAT'S NOT THE WAY HOME.
MUST BE GOING THERE.
OH,
SNOWING AGAIN.
THIS'LL BE NUMBER 29.
ゴロ ROLL
ゴロ ROLL
ひまわり園
SUNFLOWER GARDEN

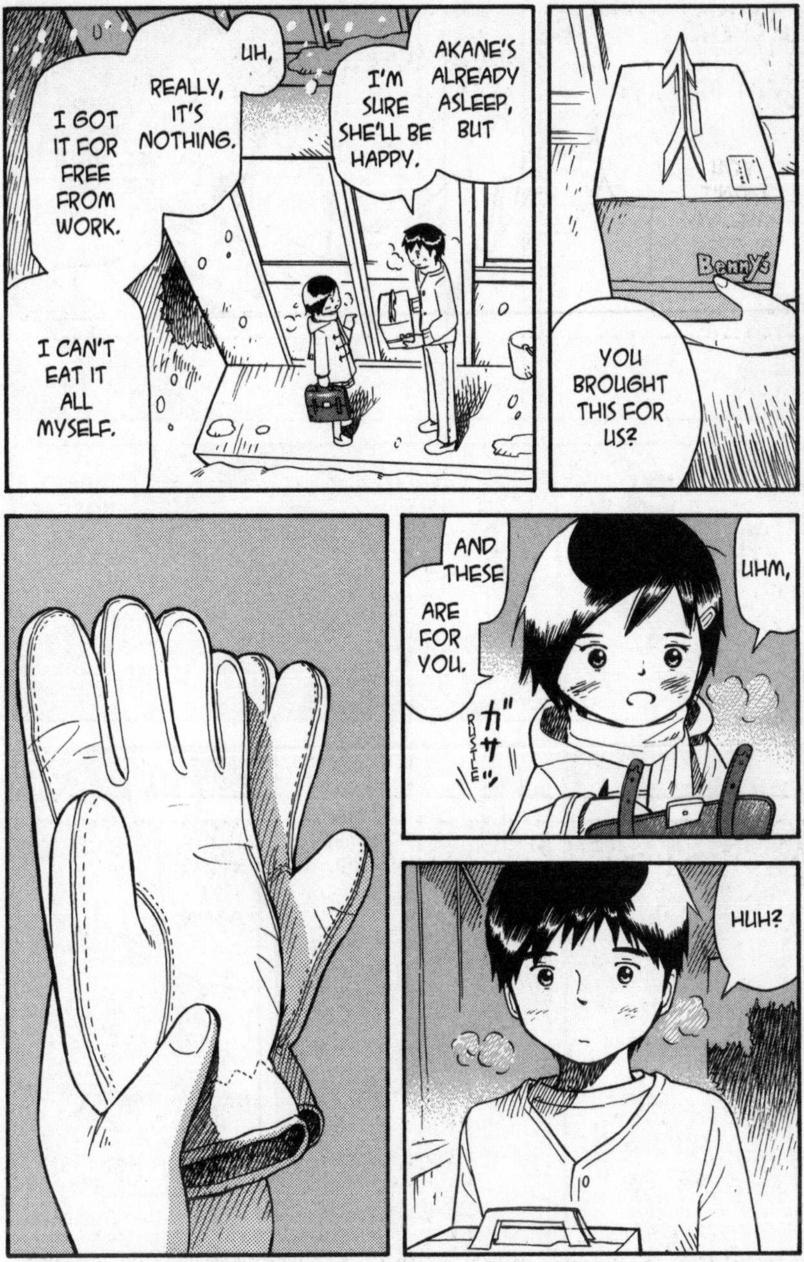
YOU BROUGHT THIS FOR US?
AKANE'S ALREADY ASLEEP, BUT
I'M SURE SHE'LL BE HAPPY.
UH,
REALLY, IT'S NOTHING.
I GOT IT FOR FREE FROM WORK.
I CAN'T EAT IT ALL MYSELF.
Benny's
UHM,
AND THESE
ARE FOR YOU.
ガサッ
RUSTLE
HUH?

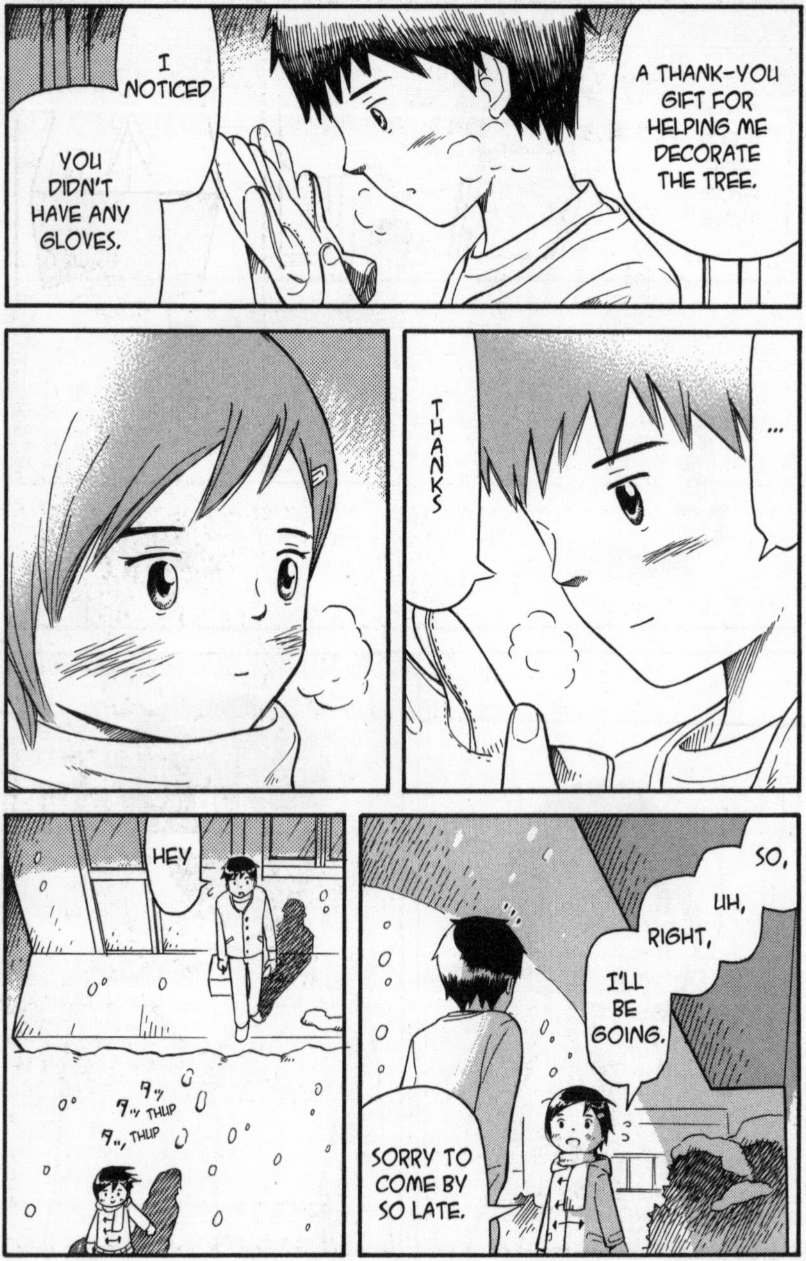
A THANK-YOU GIFT FOR HELPING ME DECORATE THE TREE.
I NOTICED
YOU DIDN'T HAVE ANY GLOVES.
...
THANKS
SO,
UH,
RIGHT,
I'LL BE GOING.
SORRY TO COME BY SO LATE.
HEY
タッ
タッ THUP
タッ THUP

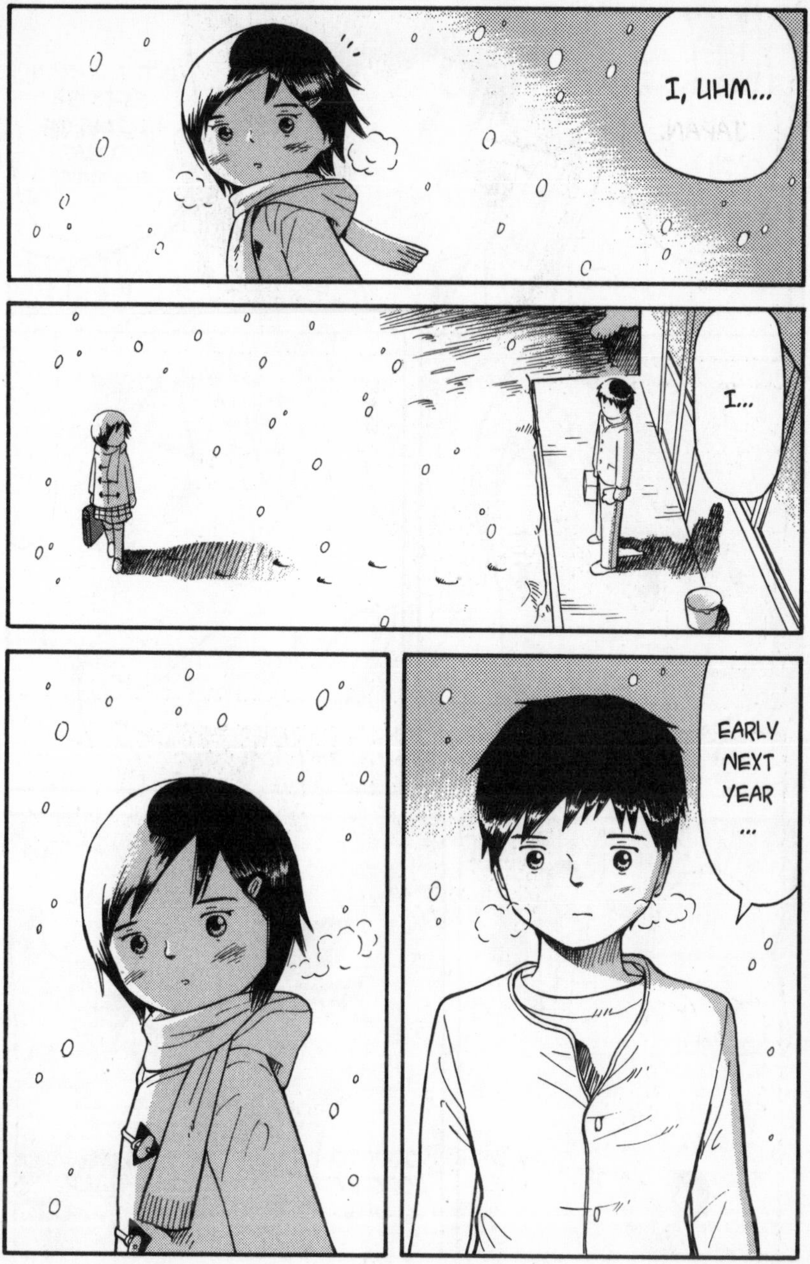
I, UHM...
I...
EARLY NEXT YEAR ...

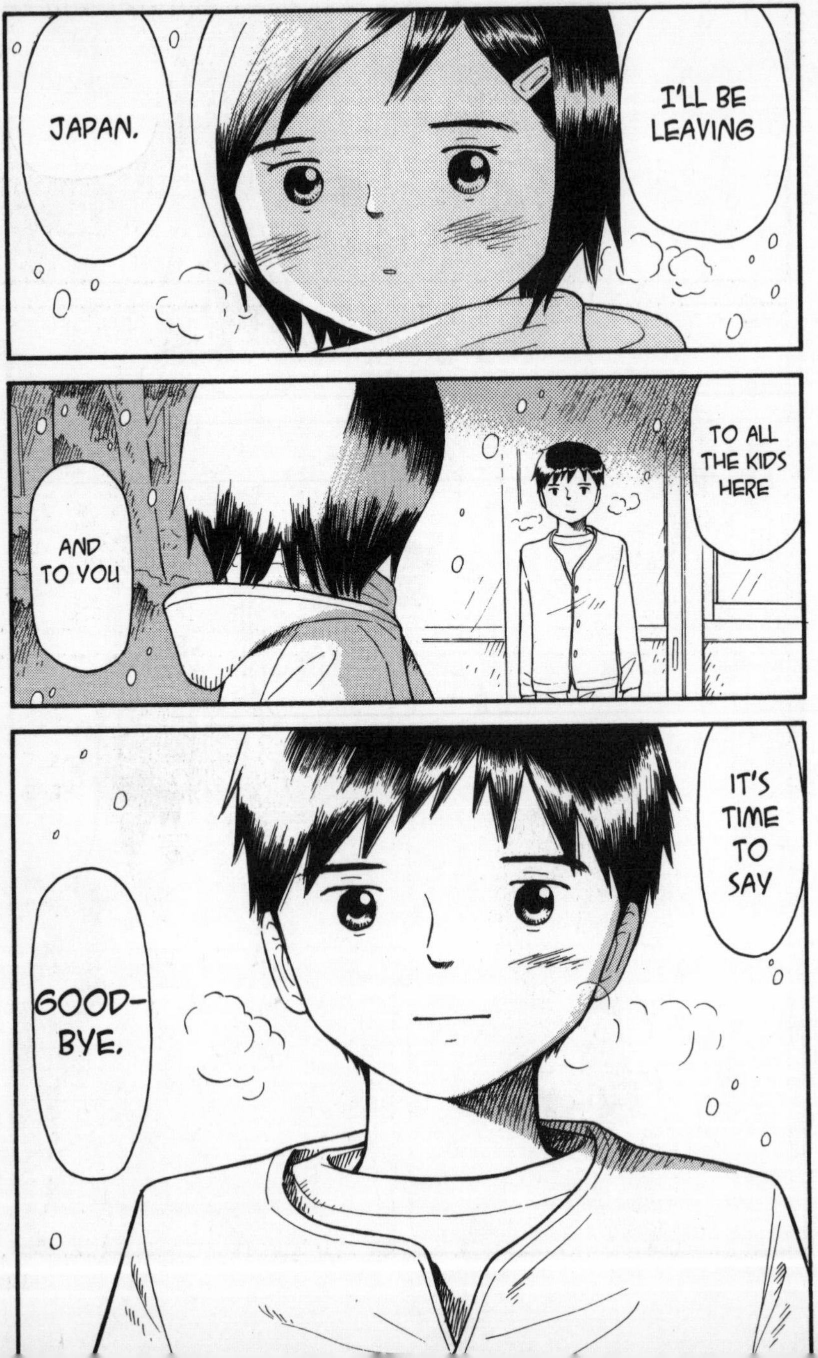
I'LL BE LEAVING
JAPAN.
TO ALL THE KIDS HERE
AND TO YOU
IT'S TIME TO SAY
GOOD-BYE.

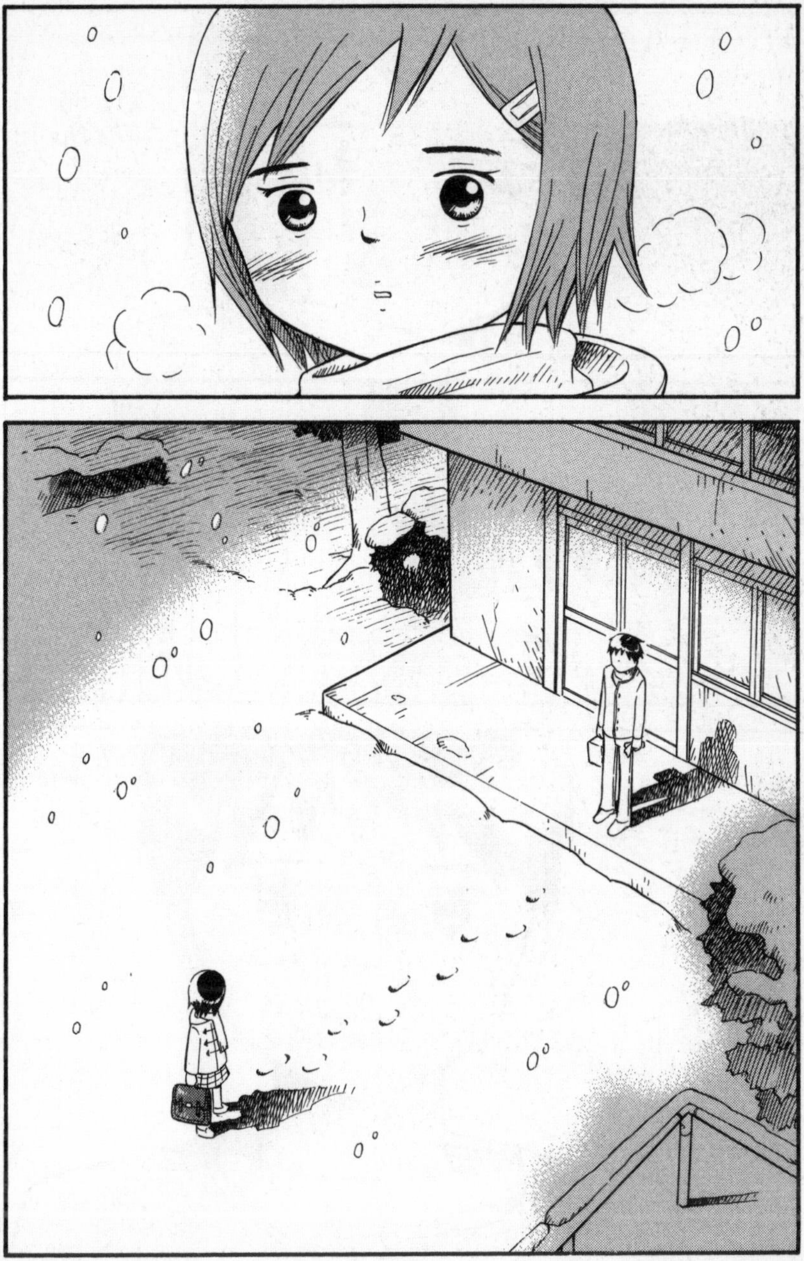

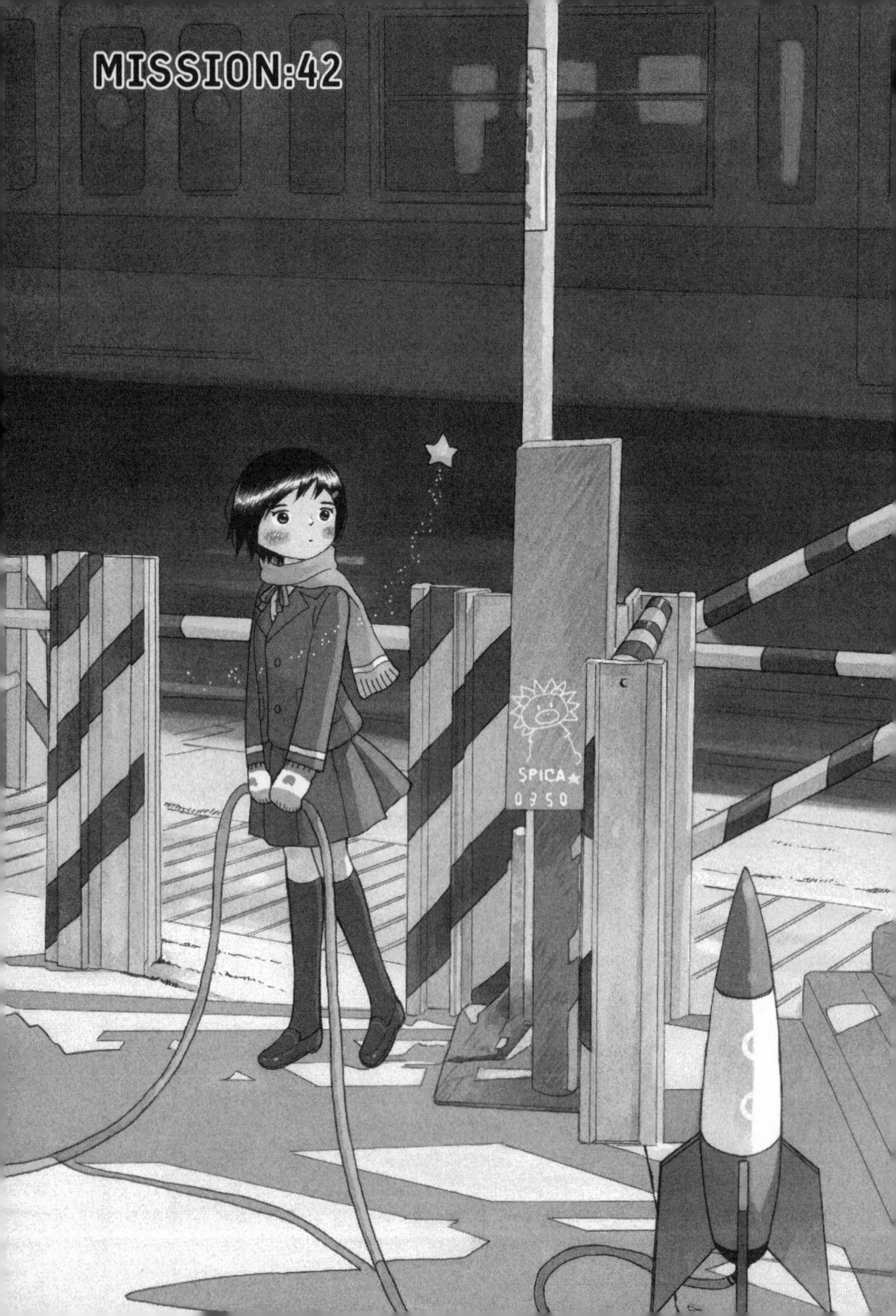
MISSION:42
SPICA★
0350

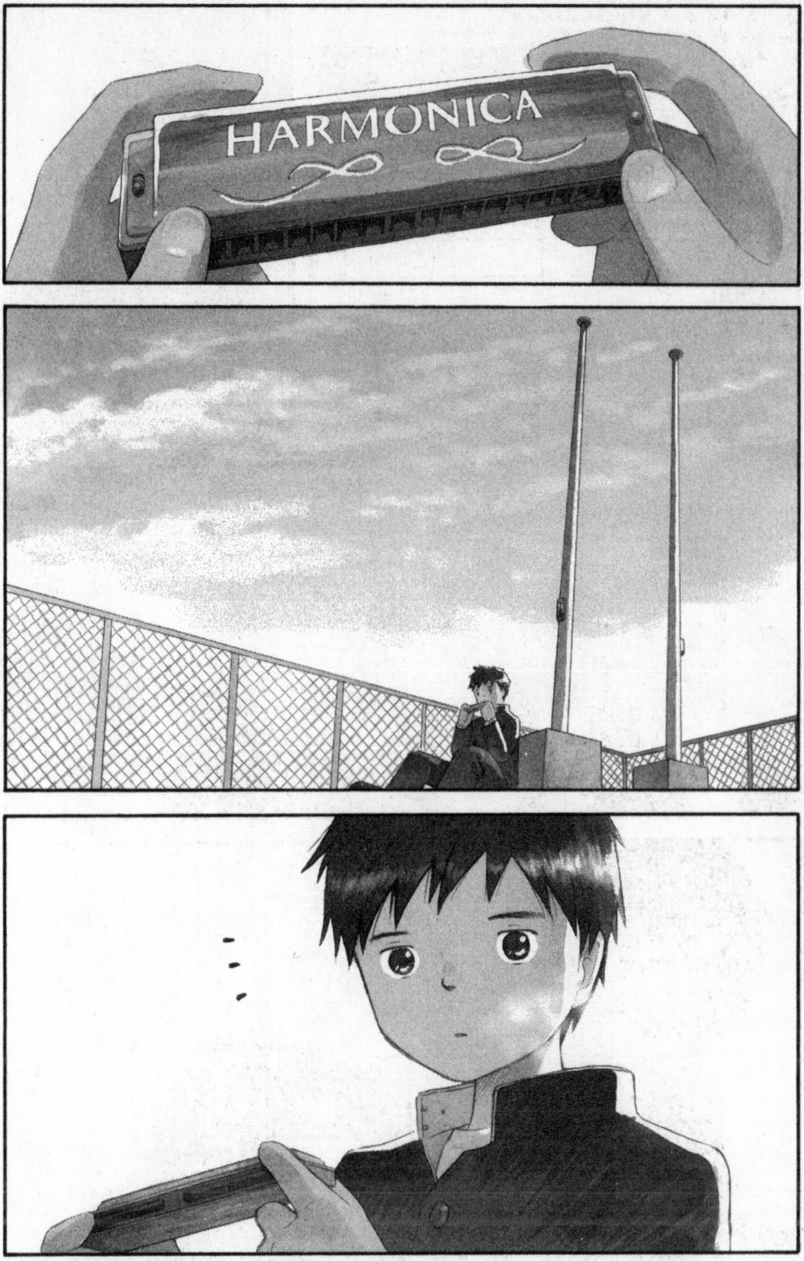
HARMONICA

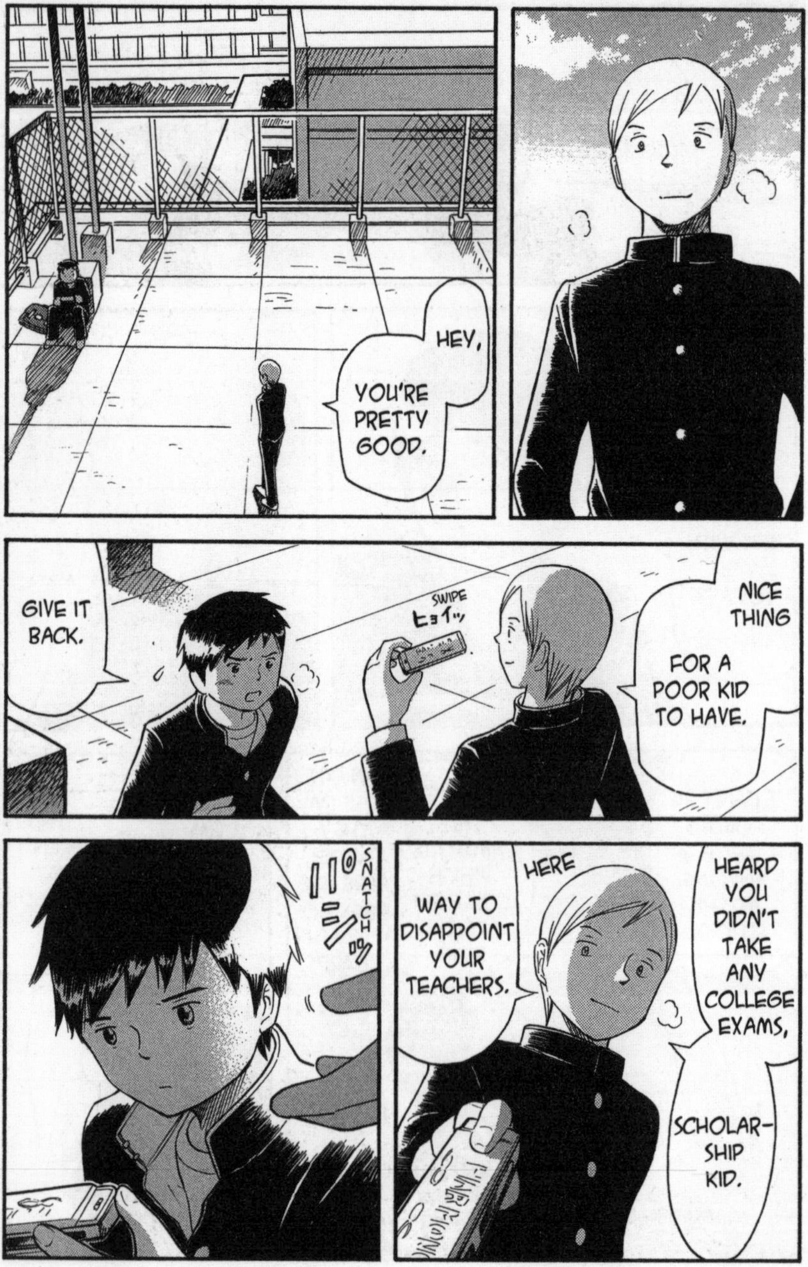
HEY, YOU'RE PRETTY GOOD.
NICE THING FOR A POOR KID TO HAVE.
SWIPE
ヒョイッ
GIVE IT BACK.
HEARD YOU DIDN'T TAKE ANY COLLEGE EXAMS,
HERE
WAY TO DISAPPOINT YOUR TEACHERS.
SCHOLAR-SHIP KID.
SNATCH

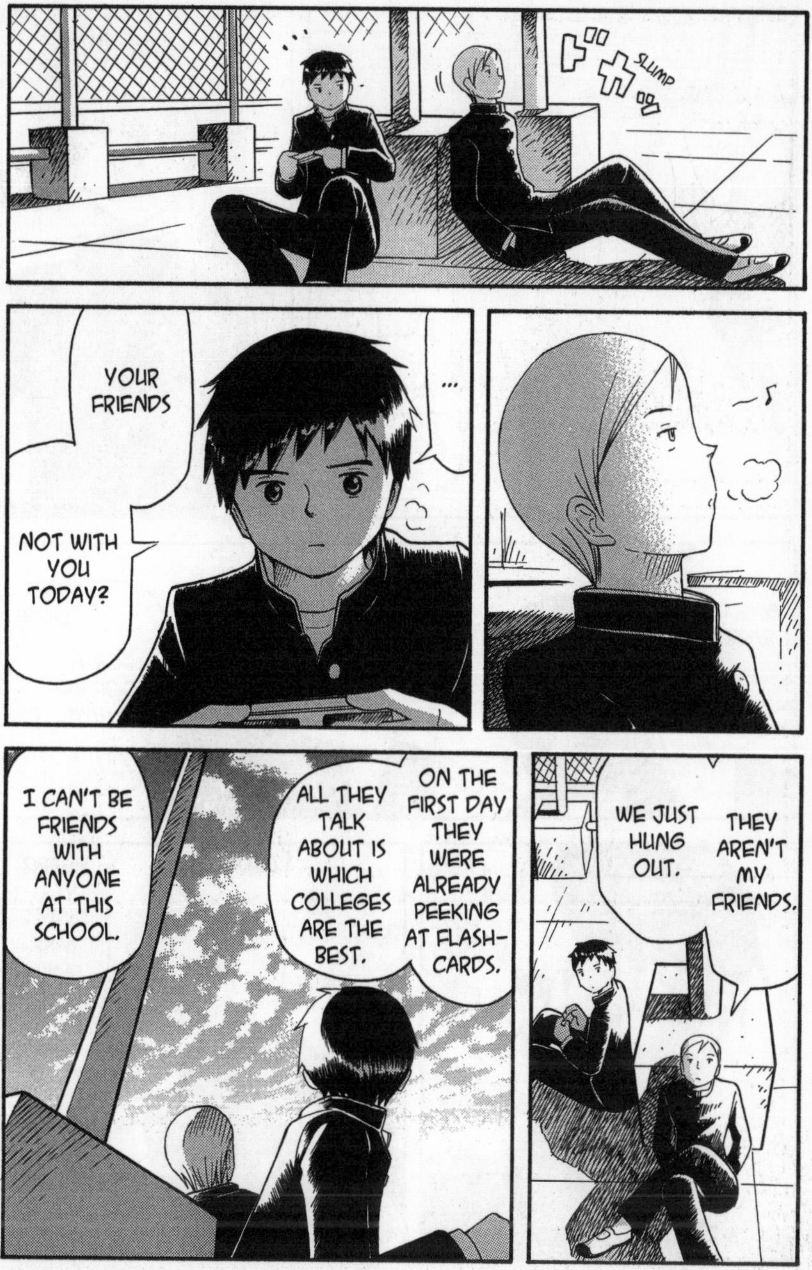
SLUMP
...
YOUR FRIENDS
NOT WITH YOU TODAY?
THEY AREN'T MY FRIENDS.
WE JUST HUNG OUT.
ON THE FIRST DAY THEY WERE ALREADY PEEKING AT FLASH-CARDS.
ALL THEY TALK ABOUT IS WHICH COLLEGES ARE THE BEST.
I CAN'T BE FRIENDS WITH ANYONE AT THIS SCHOOL.

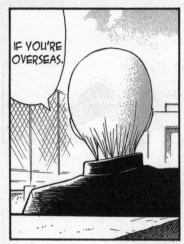

...
I CAN'T PICK ON YOU
IF YOU'RE OVERSEAS.
I'M HERE TO SAY GOODBYE.

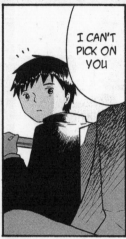

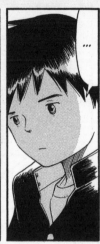

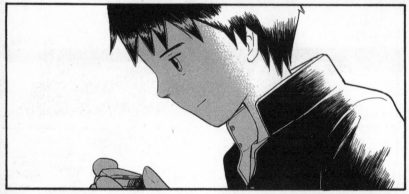

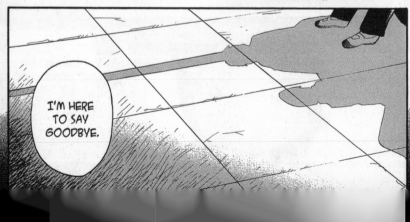

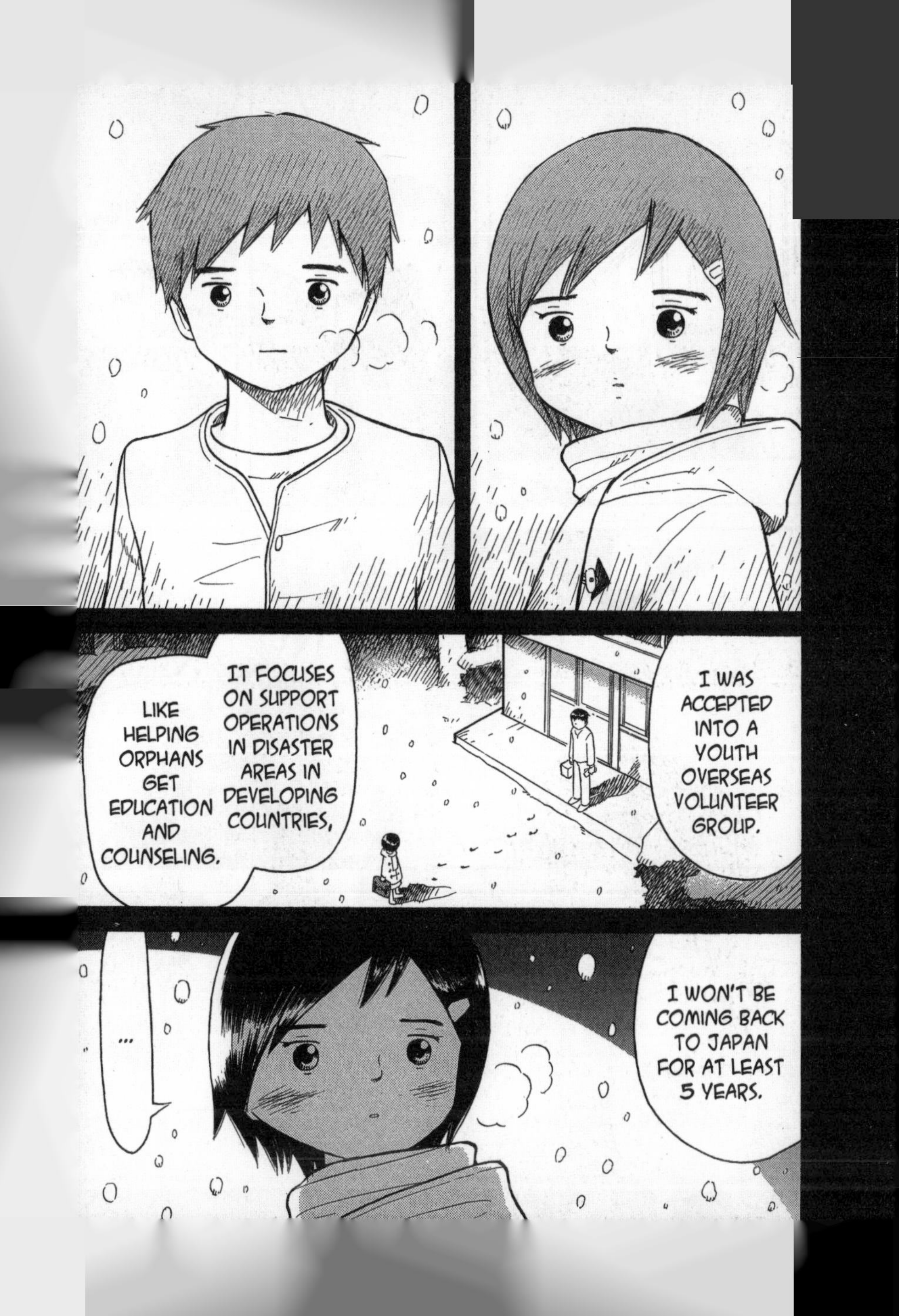
I WAS ACCEPTED INTO A YOUTH OVERSEAS VOLUNTEER GROUP.
IT FOCUSES ON SUPPORT OPERATIONS IN DISASTER AREAS IN DEVELOPING COUNTRIES,
LIKE HELPING ORPHANS GET EDUCATION AND COUNSELING.
I WON'T BE COMING BACK TO JAPAN FOR AT LEAST 5 YEARS.
...

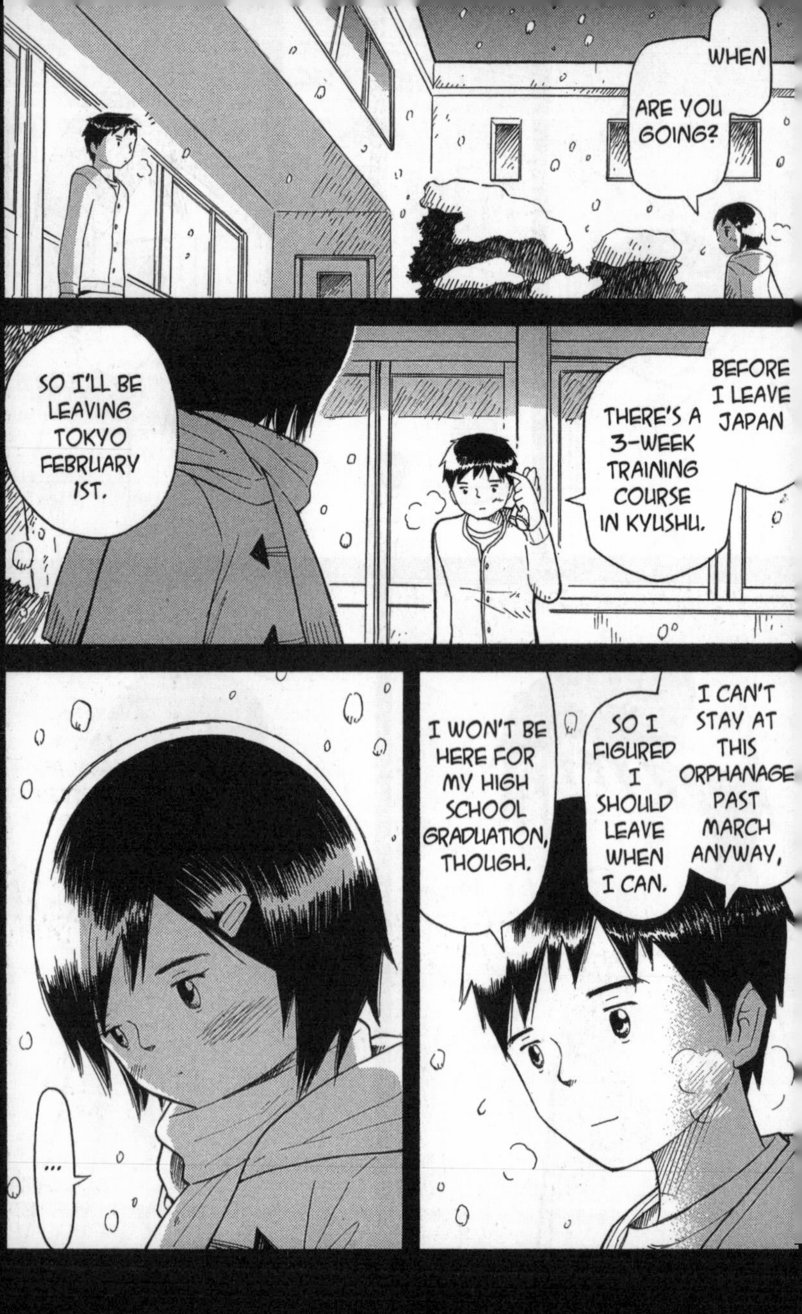
WHEN ARE YOU GOING?
BEFORE I LEAVE JAPAN
THERE'S A 3-WEEK TRAINING COURSE IN KYUSHU.
SO I'LL BE LEAVING TOKYO FEBRUARY 1ST.
I CAN'T STAY AT THIS ORPHANAGE PAST MARCH ANYWAY,
SO I FIGURED I SHOULD LEAVE WHEN I CAN.
I WON'T BE HERE FOR MY HIGH SCHOOL GRADUATION, THOUGH.
...

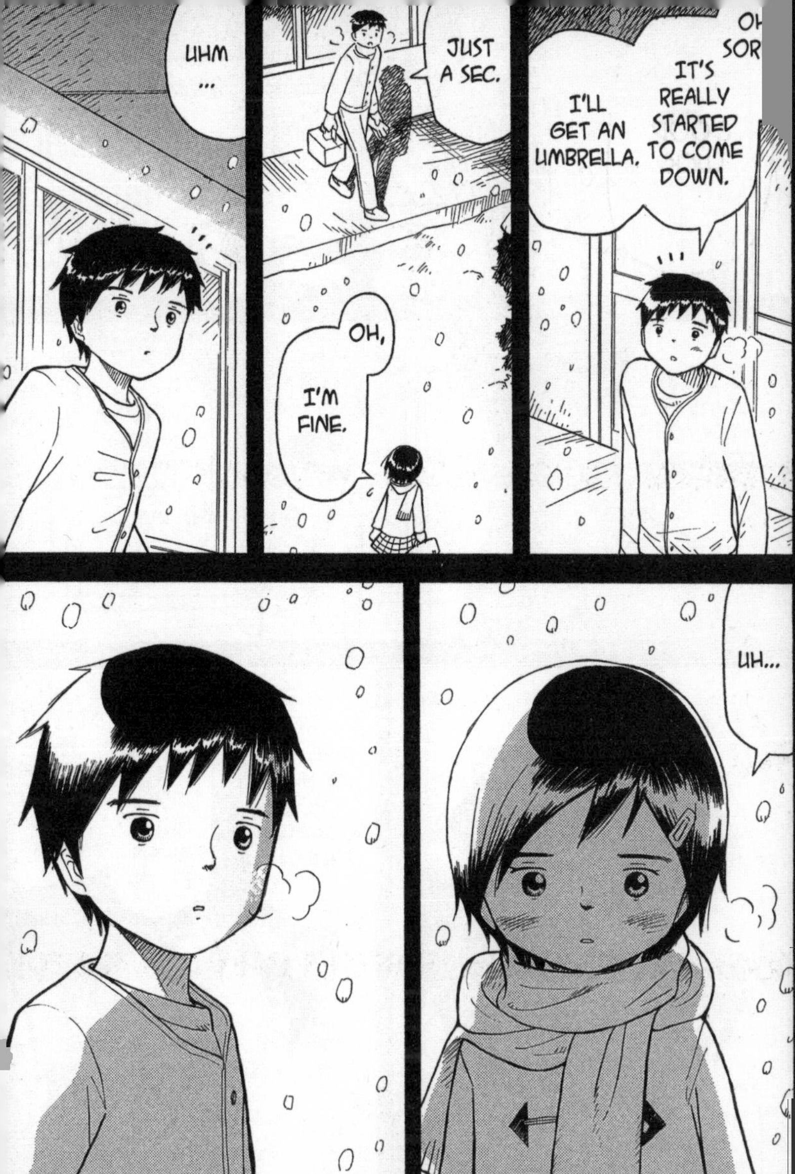
OH SOR
IT'S REALLY STARTED TO COME DOWN.
I'LL GET AN UMBRELLA.
JUST A SEC.
OH,
I'M FINE.
UHM ...
UH...

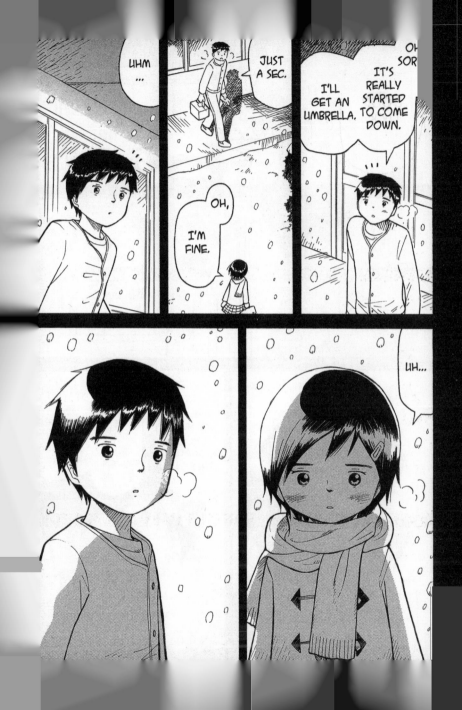

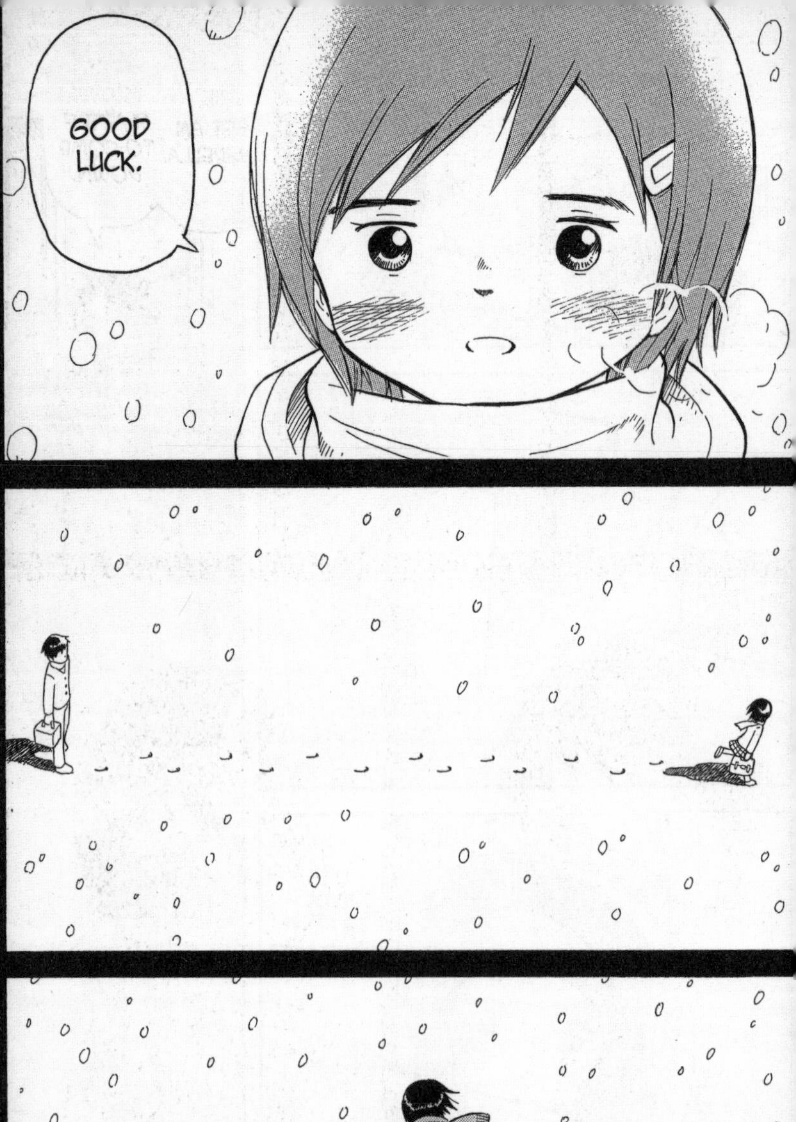
GOOD LUCK.

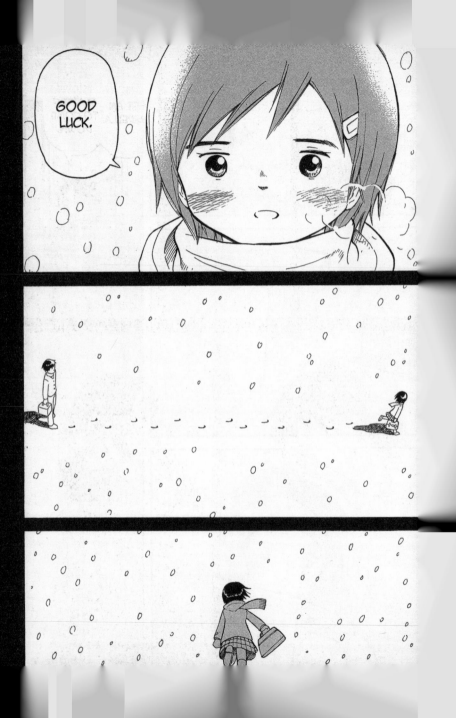

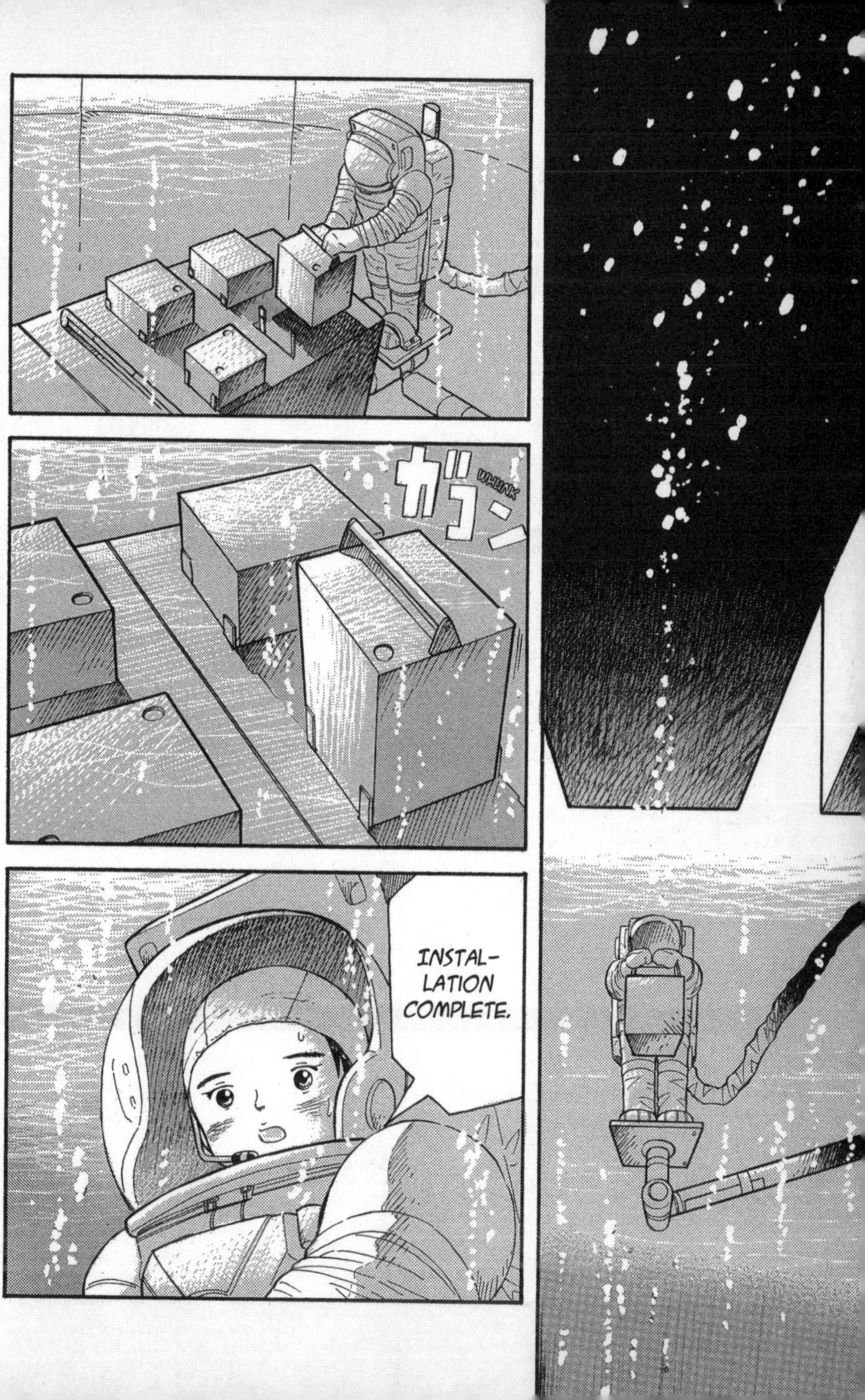
ガゴン
WHLINK
INSTAL-
LATION
COMPLETE.

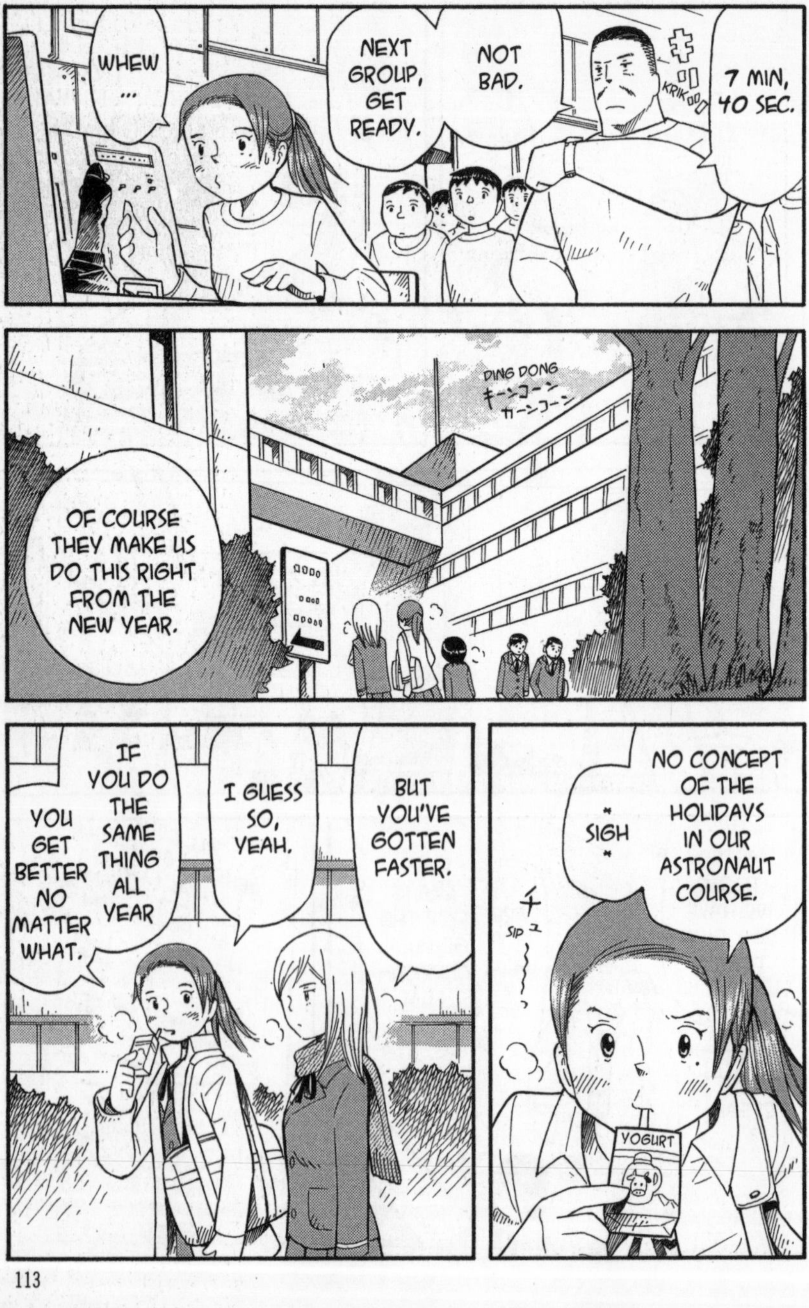
7 MIN, 40 SEC.
KRIK
NOT BAD.
NEXT GROUP, GET READY.
WHEW ...
DING DONG
キーンコーン
カーンコーン
OF COURSE THEY MAKE US DO THIS RIGHT FROM THE NEW YEAR.
NO CONCEPT OF THE HOLIDAYS IN OUR ASTRONAUT COURSE.
SIGH
SIP
YOGURT
BUT YOU'VE GOTTEN FASTER.
I GUESS SO, YEAH.
IF YOU DO THE SAME THING ALL YEAR
YOU GET BETTER NO MATTER WHAT.

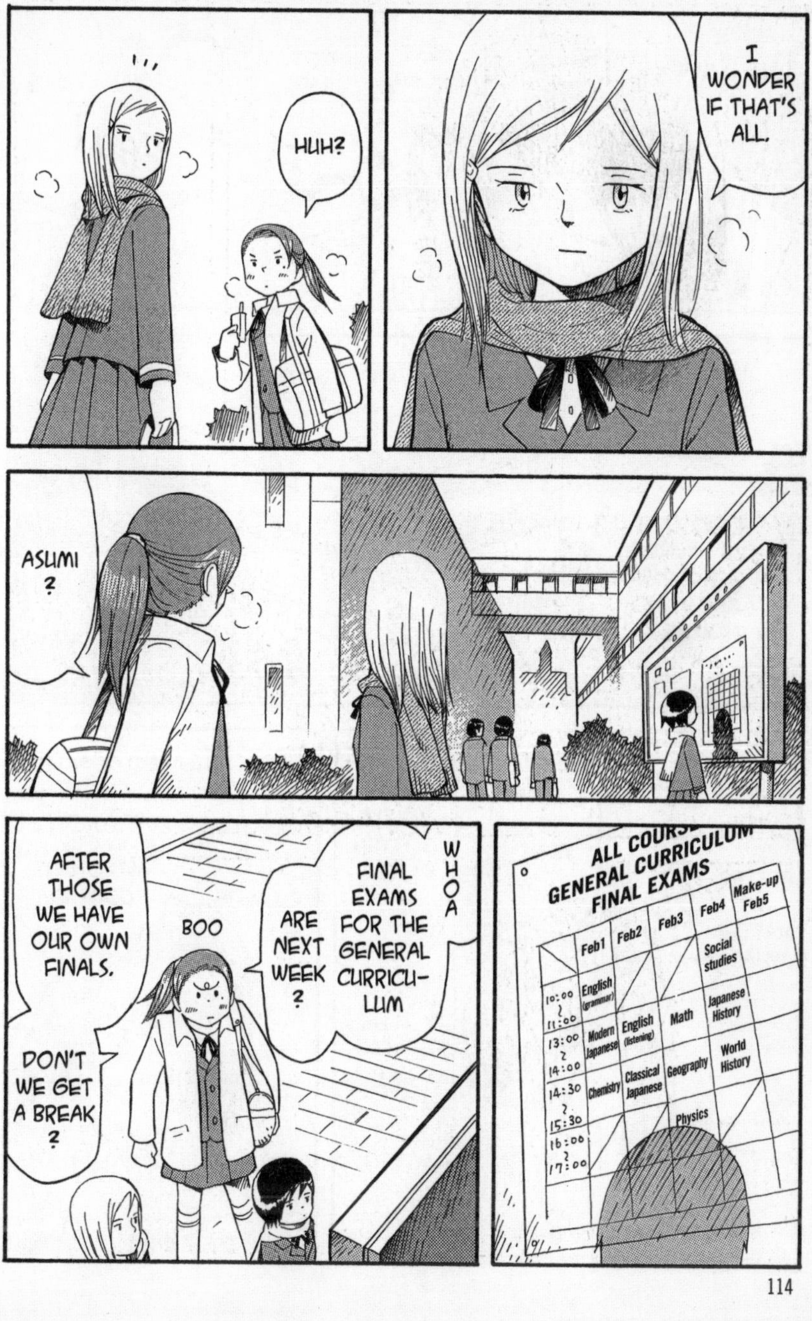
I WONDER IF THAT'S ALL.
HUH?
ASUMI?
ALL COURS
GENERAL CURRICULUM
FINAL EXAMS
Feb1 Feb2 Feb3 Feb4 Make-up Feb5
10:00 ~ 11:00 English (grammar) Social studies
13:00 ~ 14:00 Modern Japanese English (listening) Math Japanese History
14:30 ~ 15:30 Chemistry Classical Japanese Geography World History
16:00 ~ 17:00 Physics
WHOA
FINAL EXAMS FOR THE GENERAL CURRICULUM ARE NEXT WEEK?
BOO
AFTER THOSE WE HAVE OUR OWN FINALS.
DON'T WE GET A BREAK?

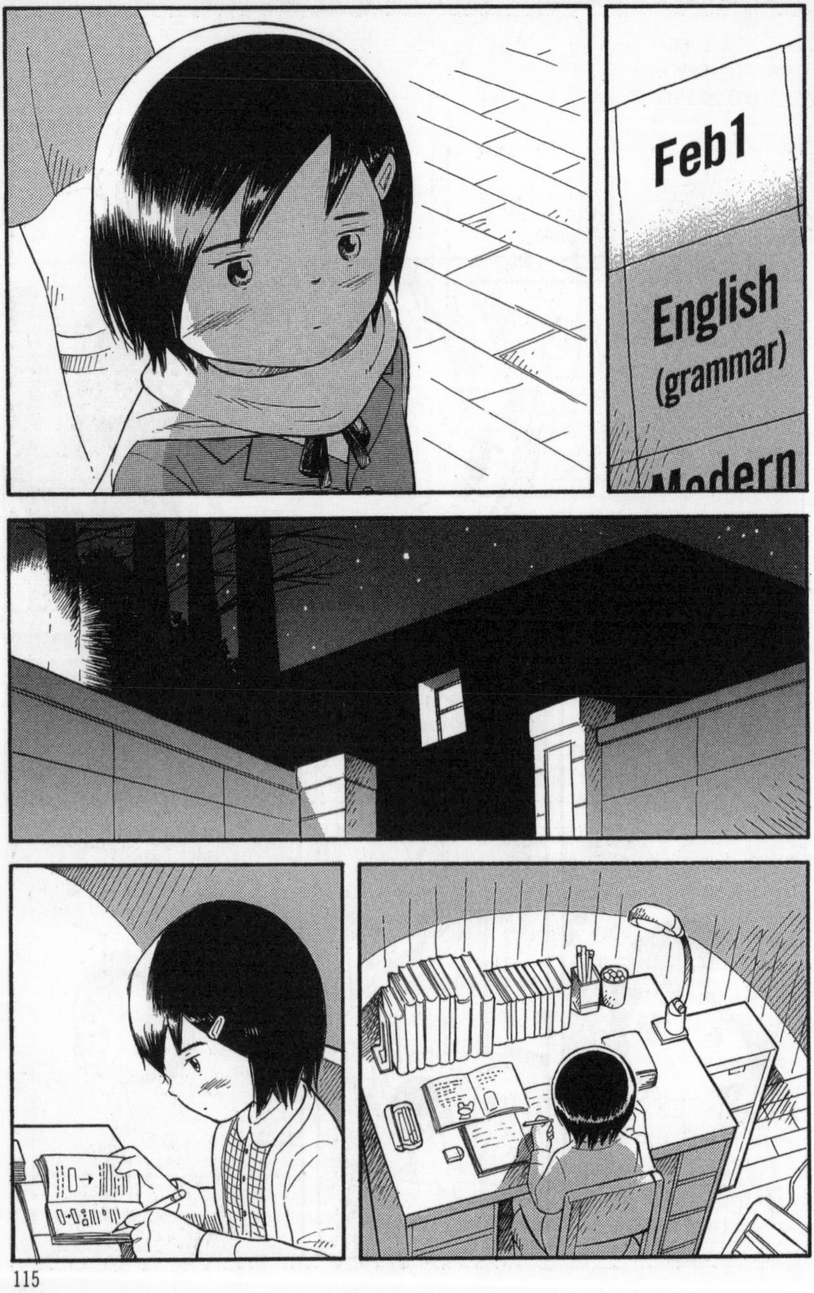
Feb1
English
(grammar)
Modern

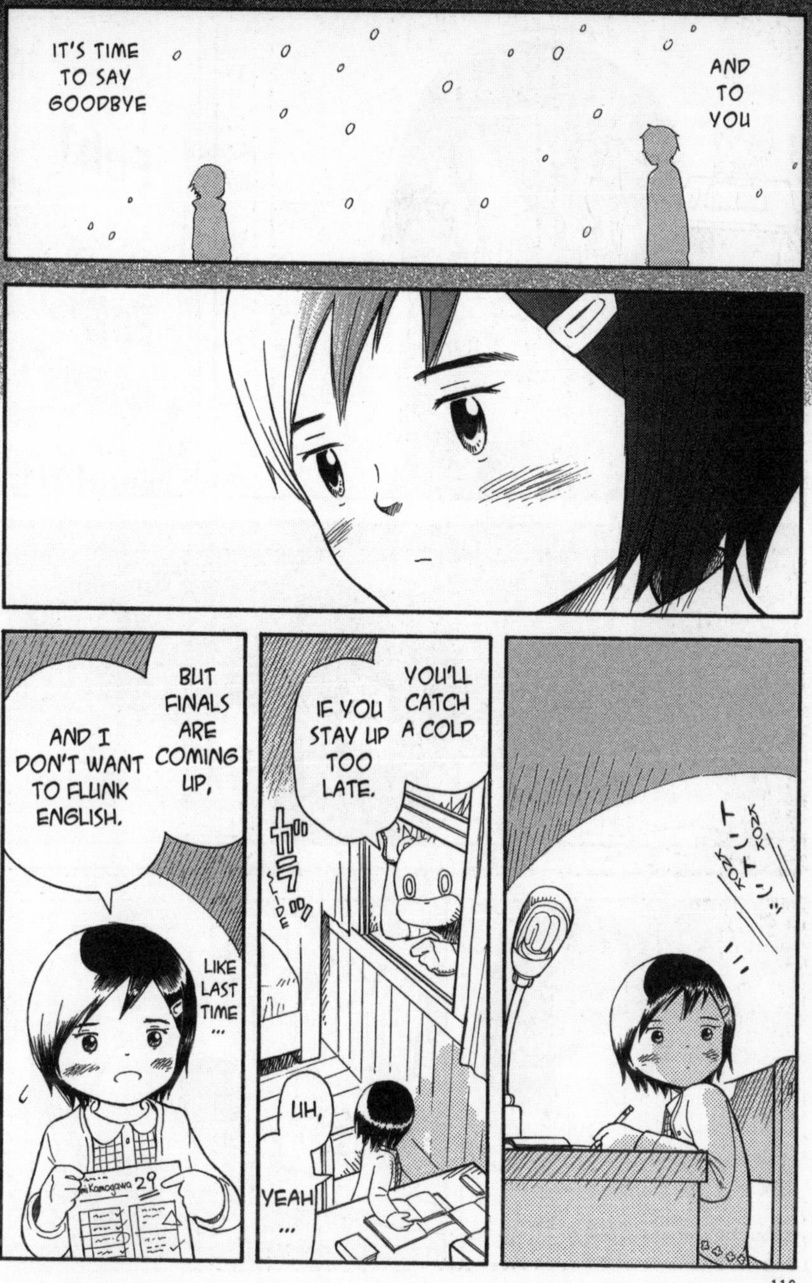
IT'S TIME TO SAY GOODBYE
AND TO YOU
KNOK KNOK
トン トン
!!!
カラ
SLIDE
YOU'LL CATCH A COLD
IF YOU STAY UP TOO LATE.
UH,
YEAH ...
BUT FINALS ARE COMING UP,
AND I DON'T WANT TO FLUNK ENGLISH.
LIKE LAST TIME ...
Kamogawa 29

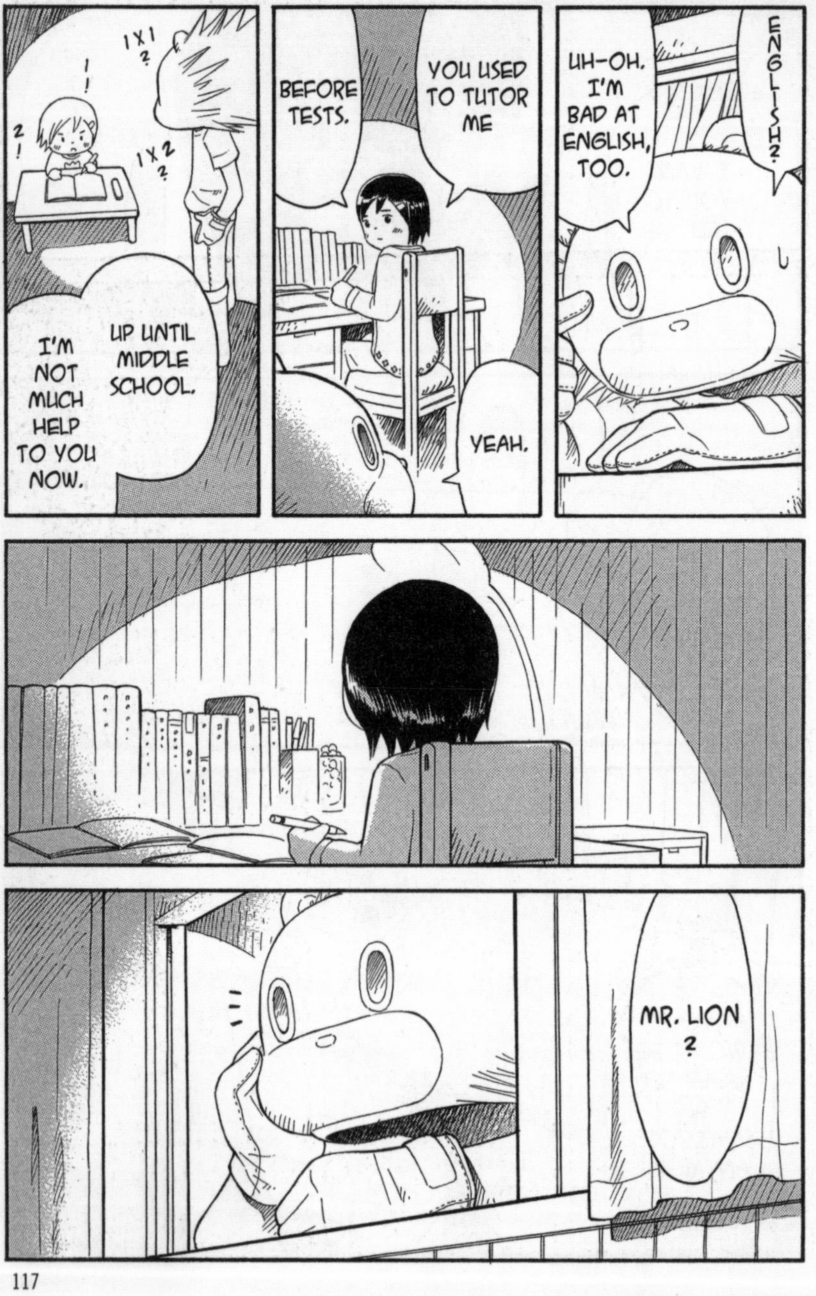
ENGLISH?
UH-OH. I'M BAD AT ENGLISH, TOO.
YOU USED TO TUTOR ME
BEFORE TESTS.
YEAH.
1X1?
!!
1X2?
2!
UP UNTIL MIDDLE SCHOOL.
I'M NOT MUCH HELP TO YOU NOW.
MR. LION?

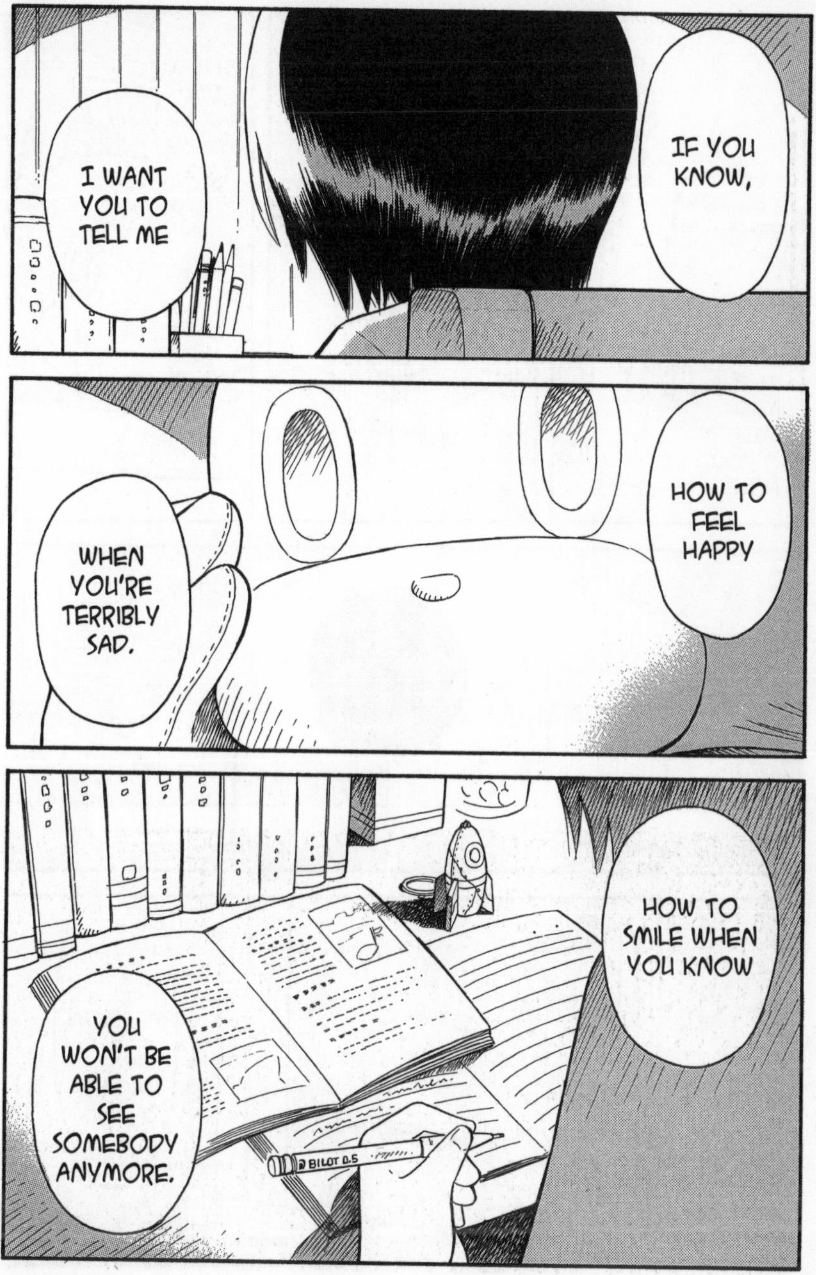
IF YOU KNOW,
I WANT YOU TO TELL ME
HOW TO FEEL HAPPY
WHEN YOU'RE TERRIBLY SAD.
HOW TO SMILE WHEN YOU KNOW
YOU WON'T BE ABLE TO SEE SOMEBODY ANYMORE.
BILOT 0.5

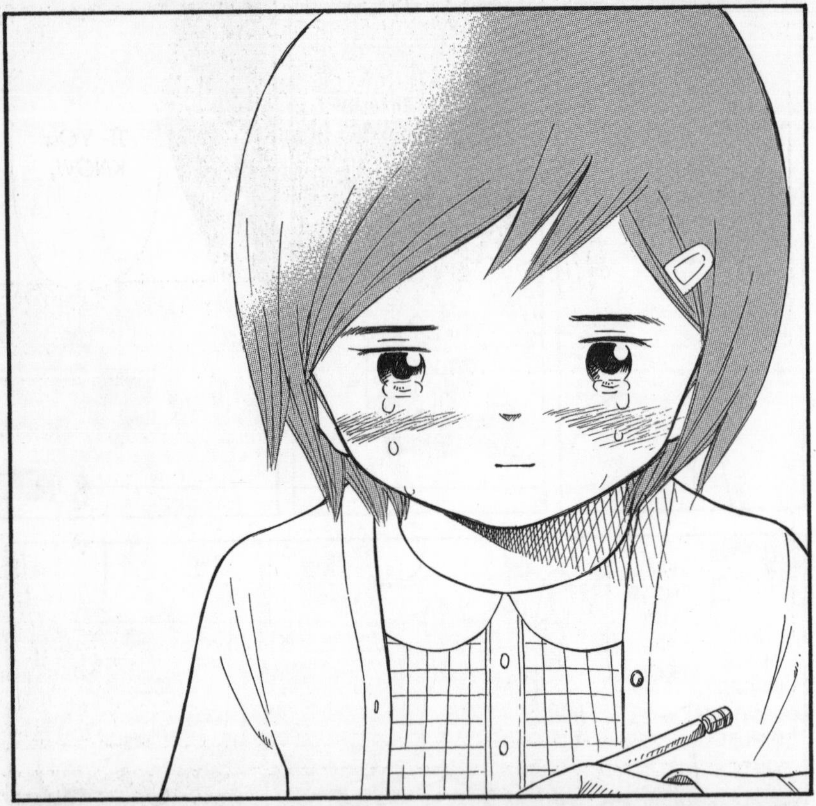

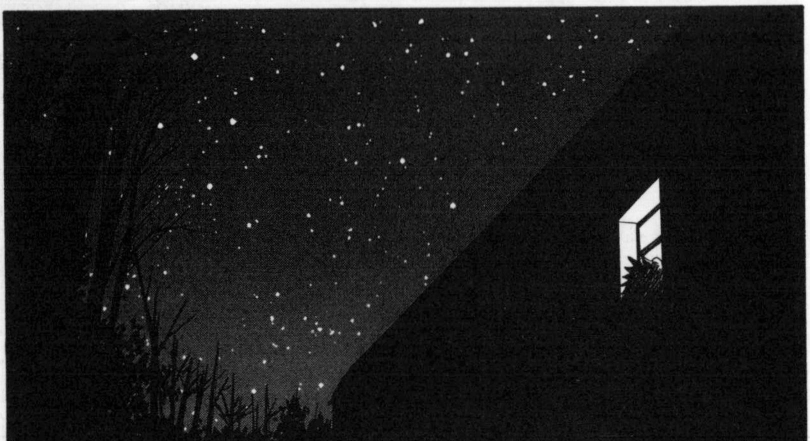

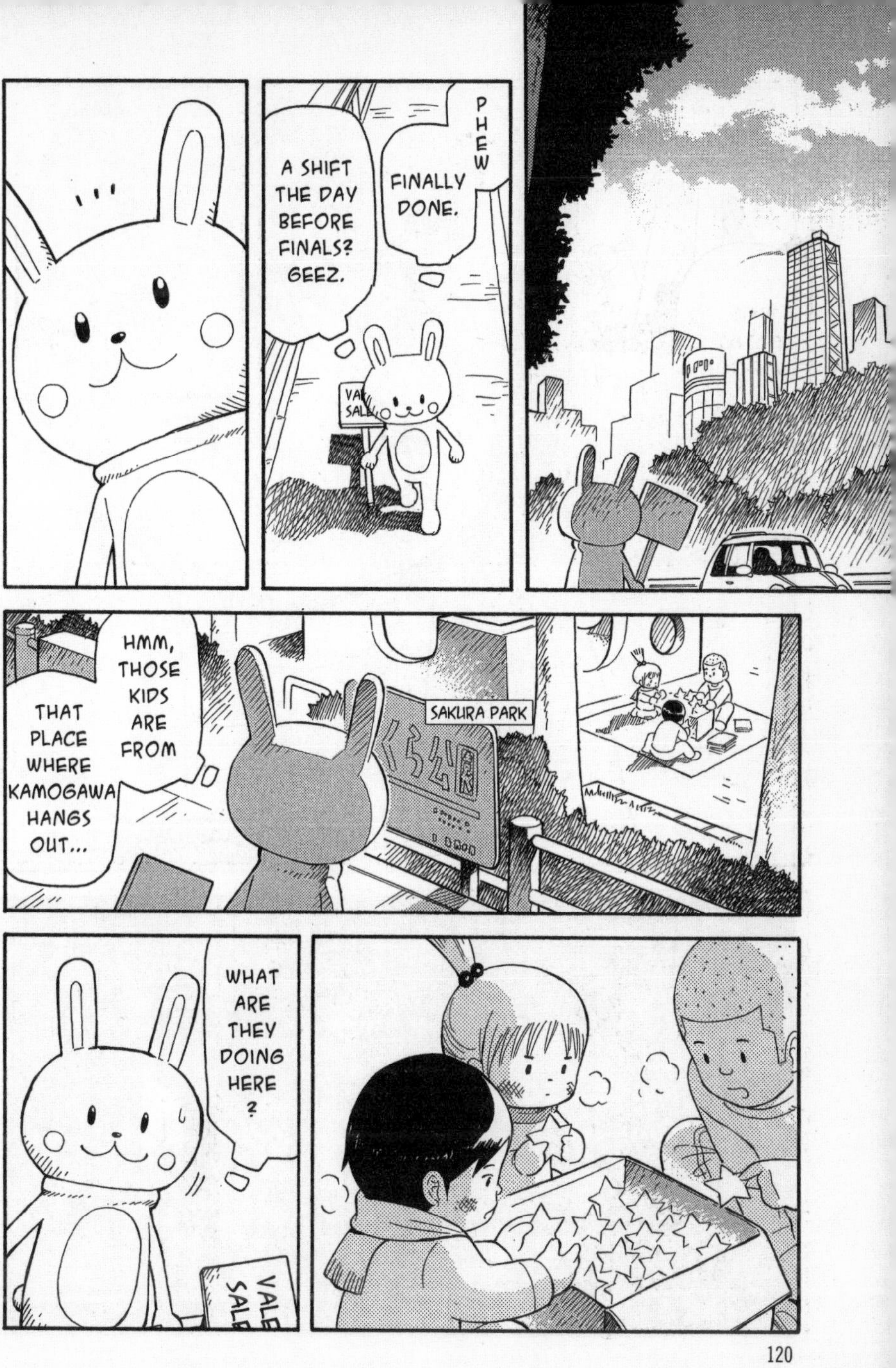
PHEW
FINALLY DONE.
A SHIFT THE DAY BEFORE FINALS? GEEZ.
SAKURA PARK
HMM, THOSE KIDS ARE FROM
THAT PLACE WHERE KAMOGAWA HANGS OUT...
WHAT ARE THEY DOING HERE?

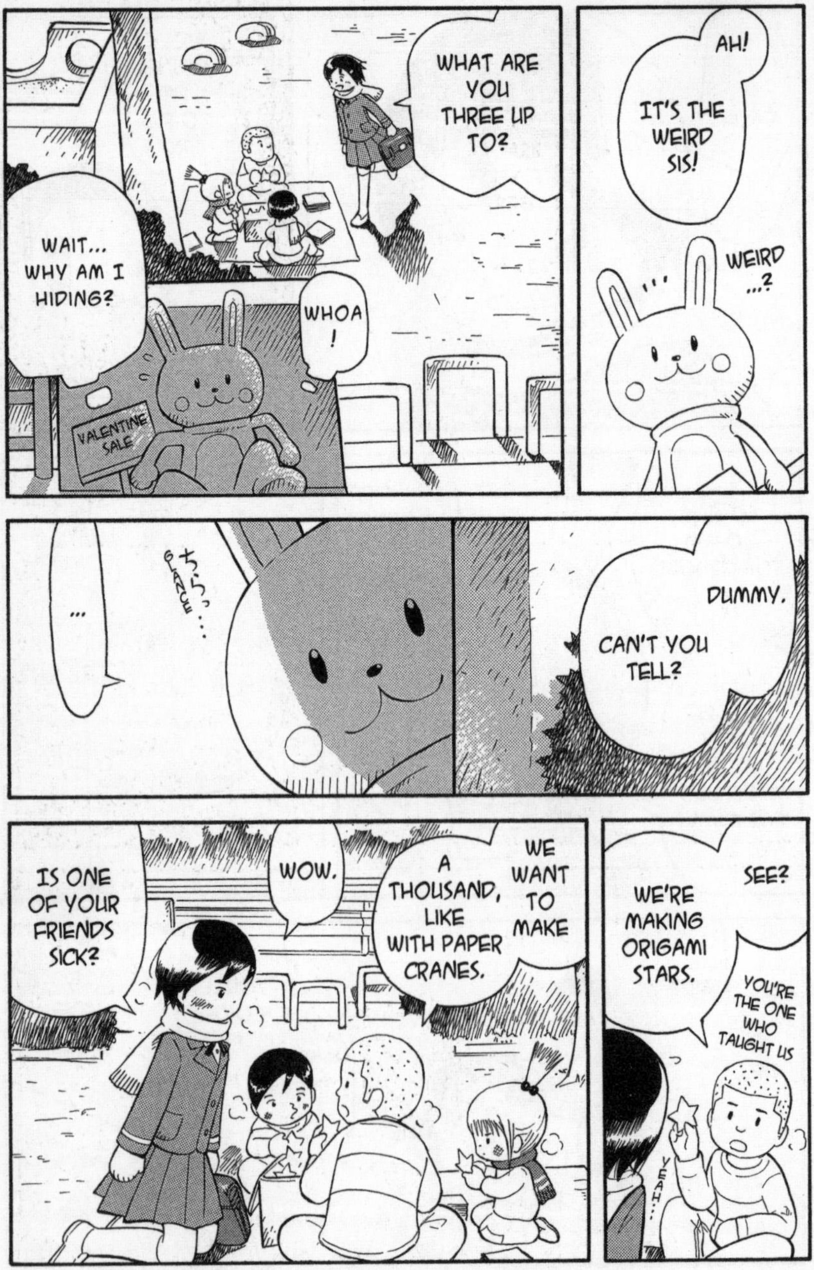
AH!
IT'S THE WEIRD SIS!
...
WEIRD ...?
WHAT ARE YOU THREE UP TO?
WHOA !
WAIT... WHY AM I HIDING?
VALENTINE SALE
DUMMY.
CAN'T YOU TELL?
ちらっ GLANCE...
...
SEE?
WE'RE MAKING ORIGAMI STARS.
YOU'RE THE ONE WHO TAUGHT US
YEAH...
WE WANT TO MAKE
A THOUSAND, LIKE WITH PAPER CRANES.
WOW.
IS ONE OF YOUR FRIENDS SICK?

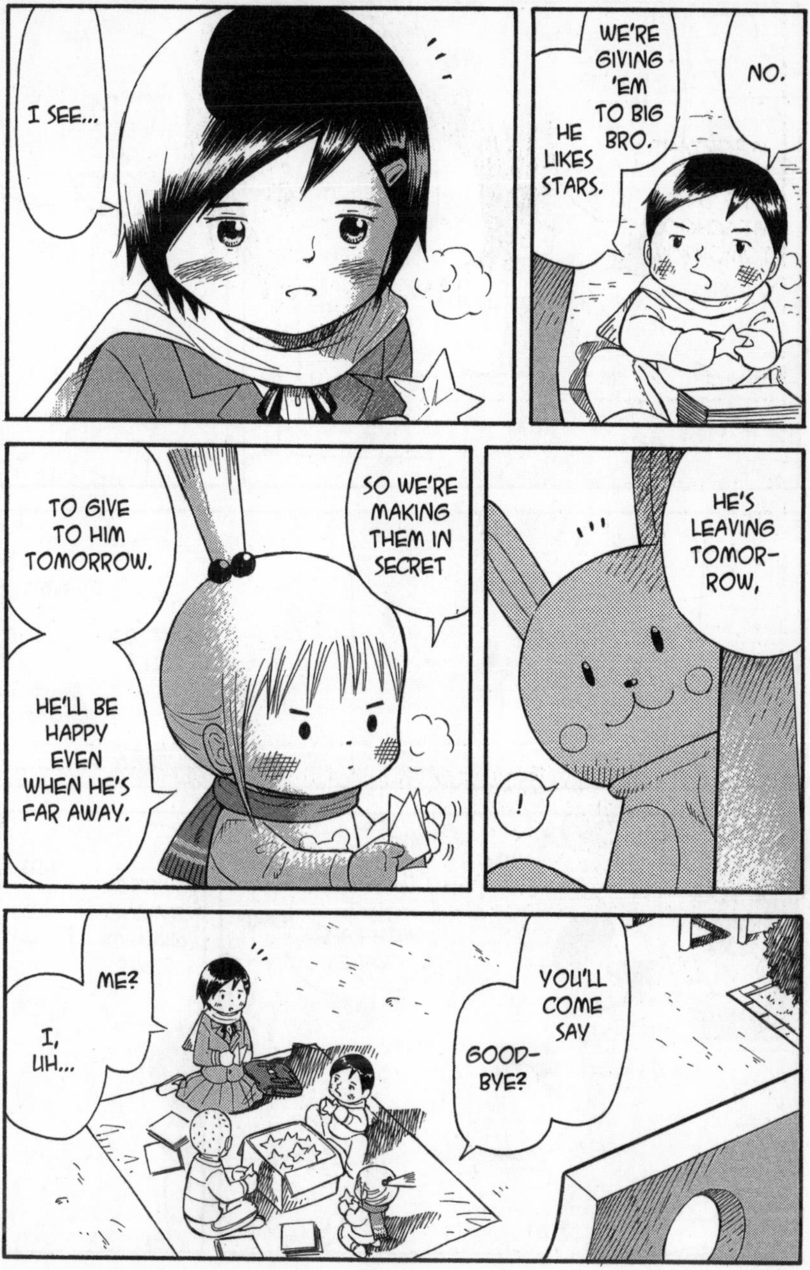
NO.
WE'RE GIVING 'EM TO BIG BRO.
HE LIKES STARS.
I SEE...
HE'S LEAVING TOMOR-ROW,
!
SO WE'RE MAKING THEM IN SECRET
TO GIVE TO HIM TOMORROW.
HE'LL BE HAPPY EVEN WHEN HE'S FAR AWAY.
YOU'LL COME SAY GOOD-BYE?
ME?
I, UH...

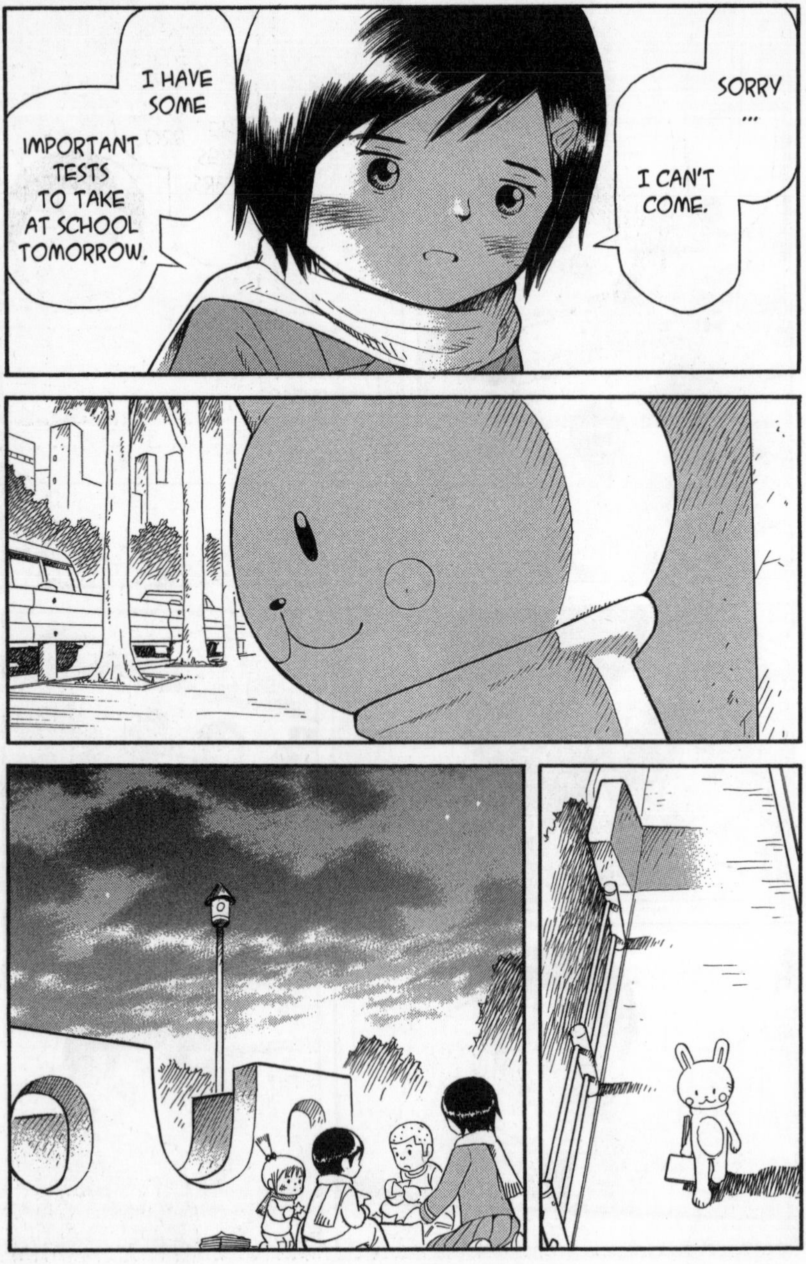
SORRY ... I CAN'T COME.
I HAVE SOME IMPORTANT TESTS TO TAKE AT SCHOOL TOMORROW.

10:00 ～ 11:00

PLEASE BEGIN.

キーンコーン
DING DONG
カーンコーン

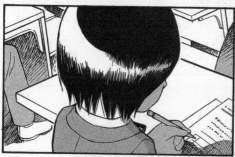

URR
...

TSK
!

...

STOP
ACTING
!

124

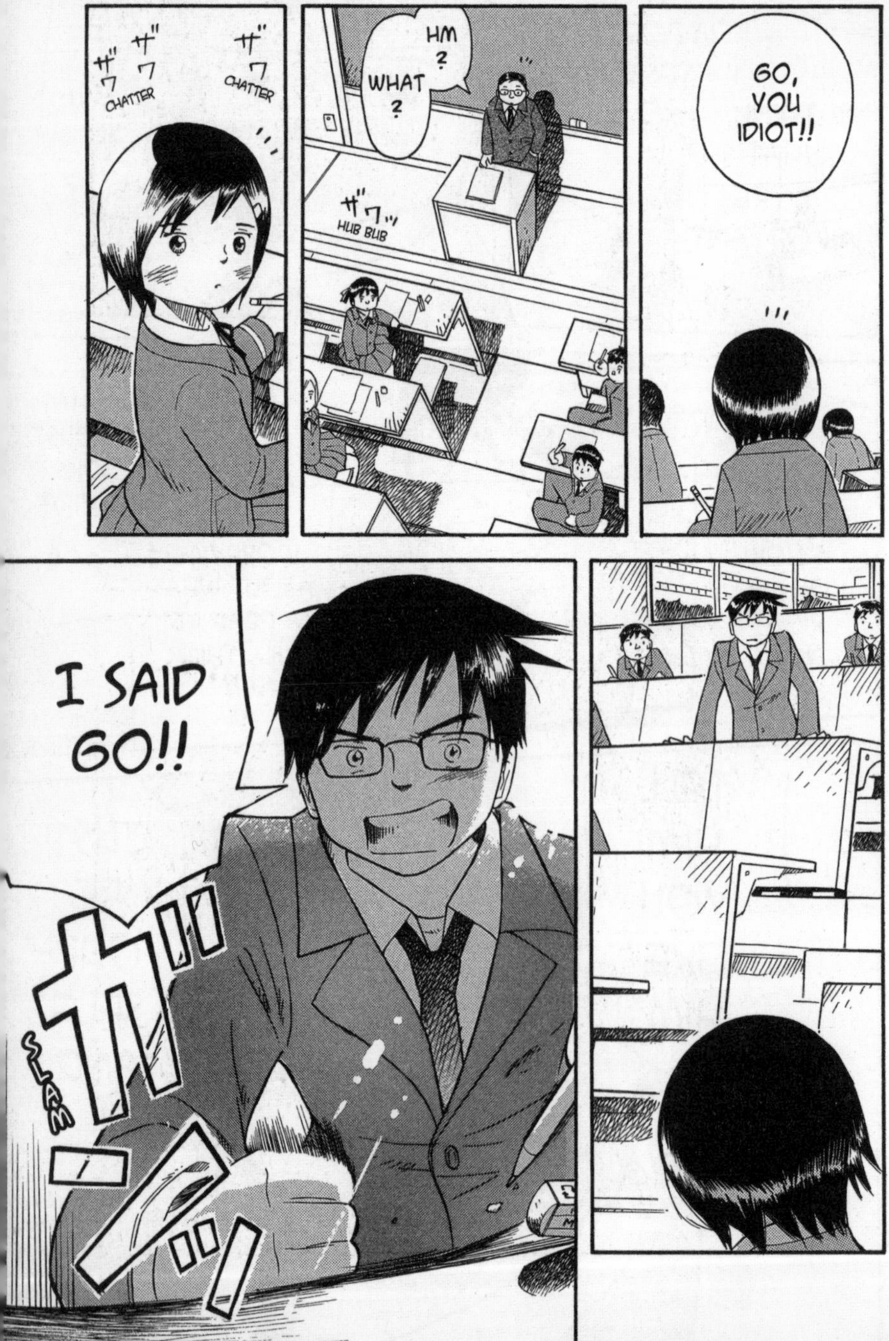

GO, YOU IDIOT!!
HM? WHAT?
ザワッ
HUB BUB
ザワ
CHATTER
ザワ
CHATTER
I SAID GO!!
ガッ
SLAM

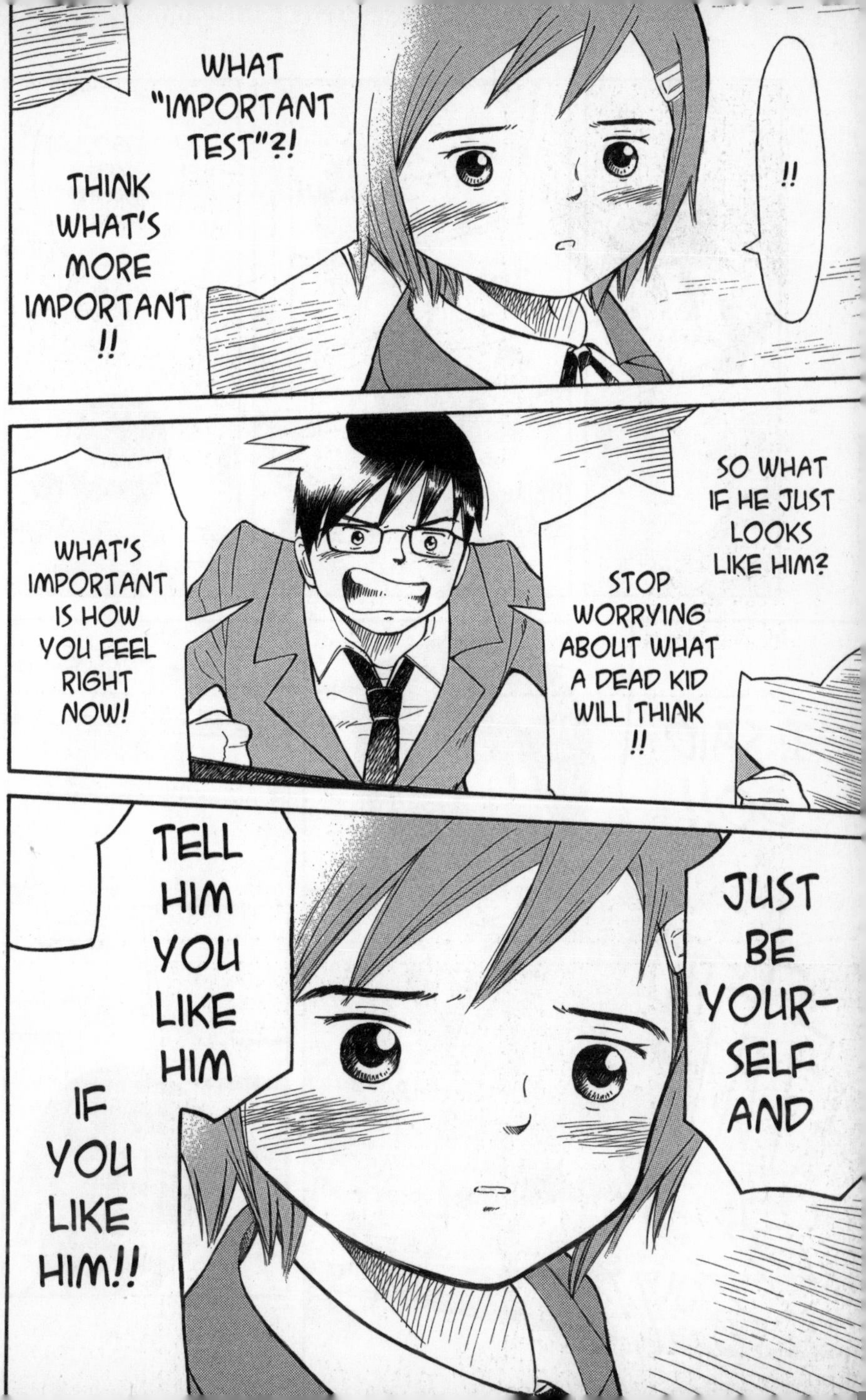
!!
WHAT "IMPORTANT TEST"?!
THINK WHAT'S MORE IMPORTANT!!
SO WHAT IF HE JUST LOOKS LIKE HIM?
STOP WORRYING ABOUT WHAT A DEAD KID WILL THINK!!
WHAT'S IMPORTANT IS HOW YOU FEEL RIGHT NOW!
JUST BE YOUR-SELF AND
TELL HIM YOU LIKE HIM
IF YOU LIKE HIM!!

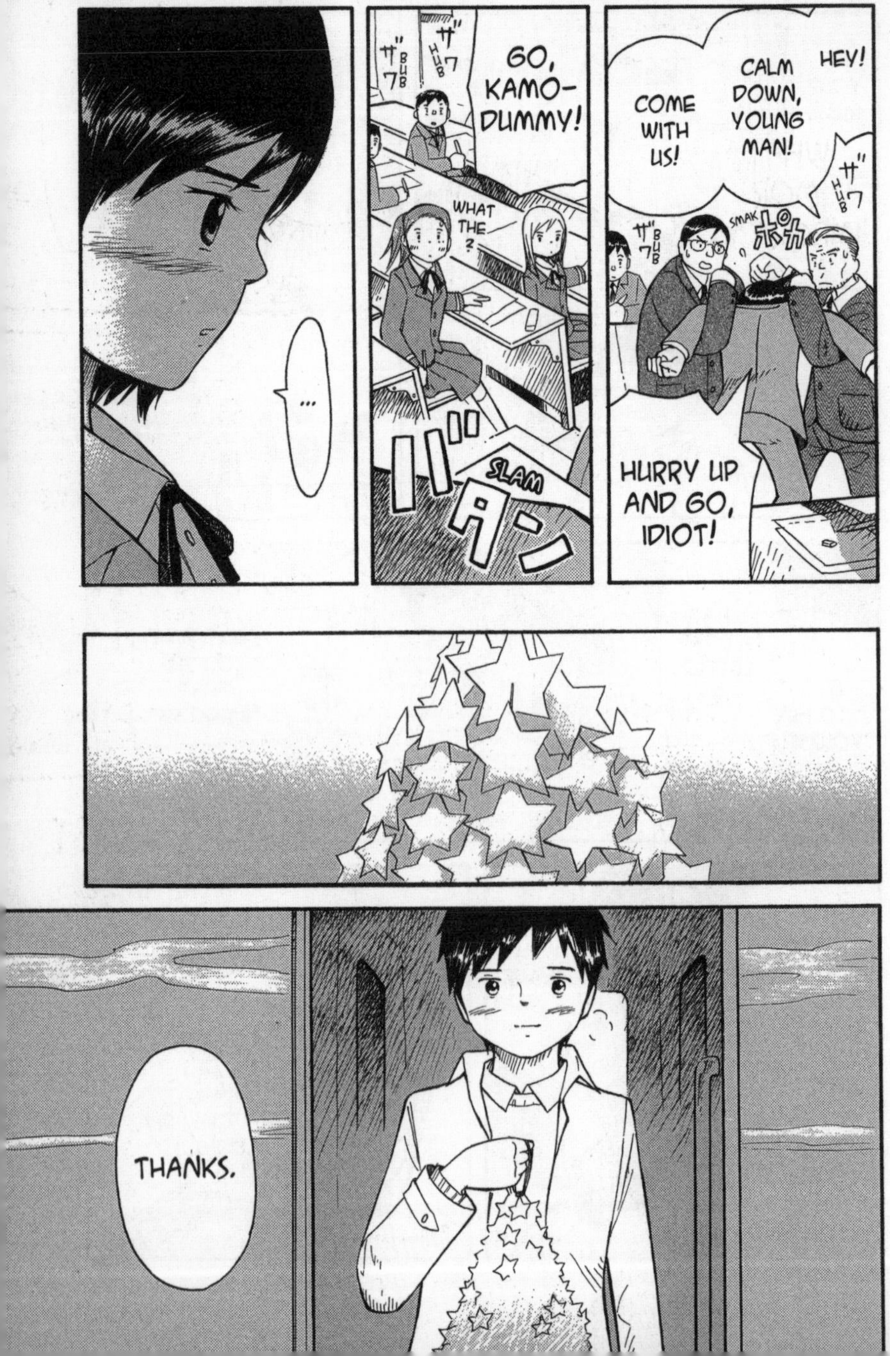
HEY!
CALM DOWN, YOUNG MAN!
COME WITH US!
ザワ HUB
ザワ BUB
ポカ SMAK
HURRY UP AND GO, IDIOT!
GO, KAMO-DUMMY!
ザワ HUB
ザワ BUB
WHAT THE ?
バタン SLAM
...
THANKS.

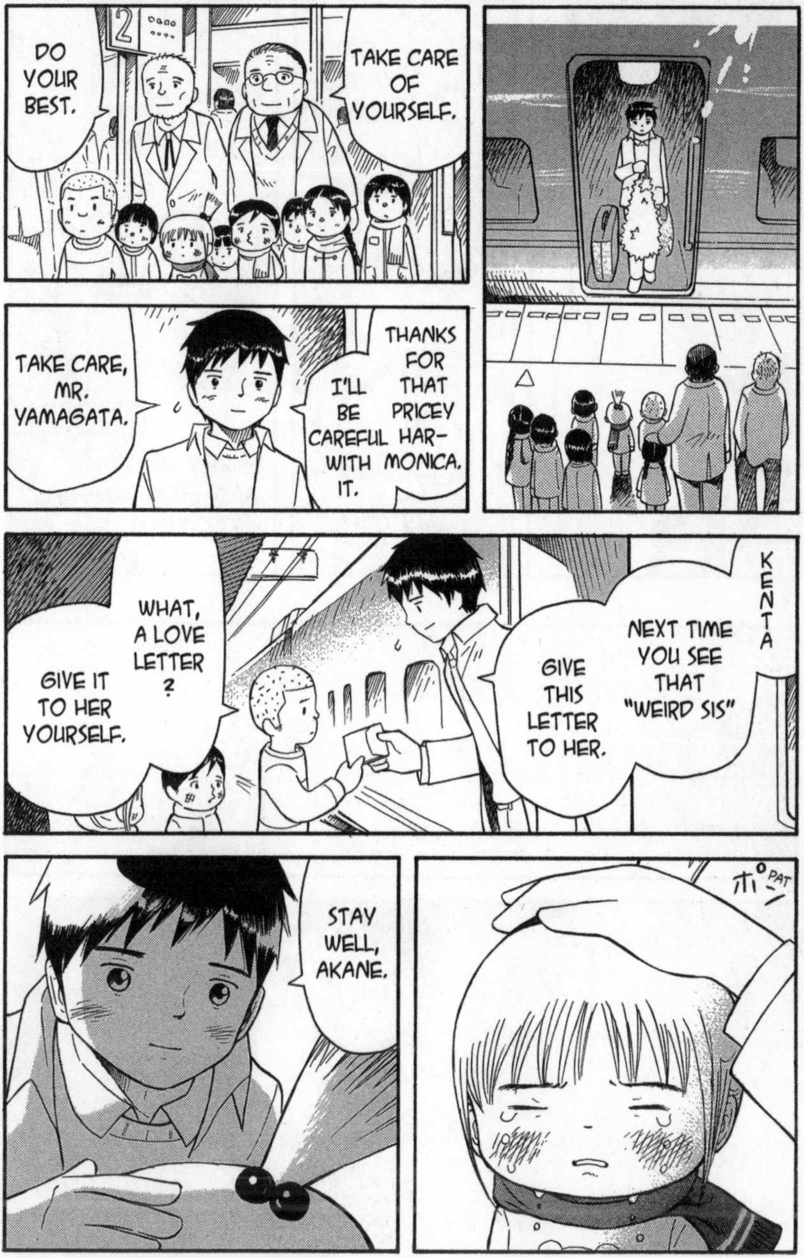
TAKE CARE OF YOURSELF.
DO YOUR BEST.
THANKS FOR THAT PRICEY HARMONICA.
I'LL BE CAREFUL WITH IT.
TAKE CARE, MR. YAMAGATA.
KENTA
NEXT TIME YOU SEE THAT "WEIRD SIS"
GIVE THIS LETTER TO HER.
WHAT, A LOVE LETTER?
GIVE IT TO HER YOURSELF.
PAT
STAY WELL, AKANE.

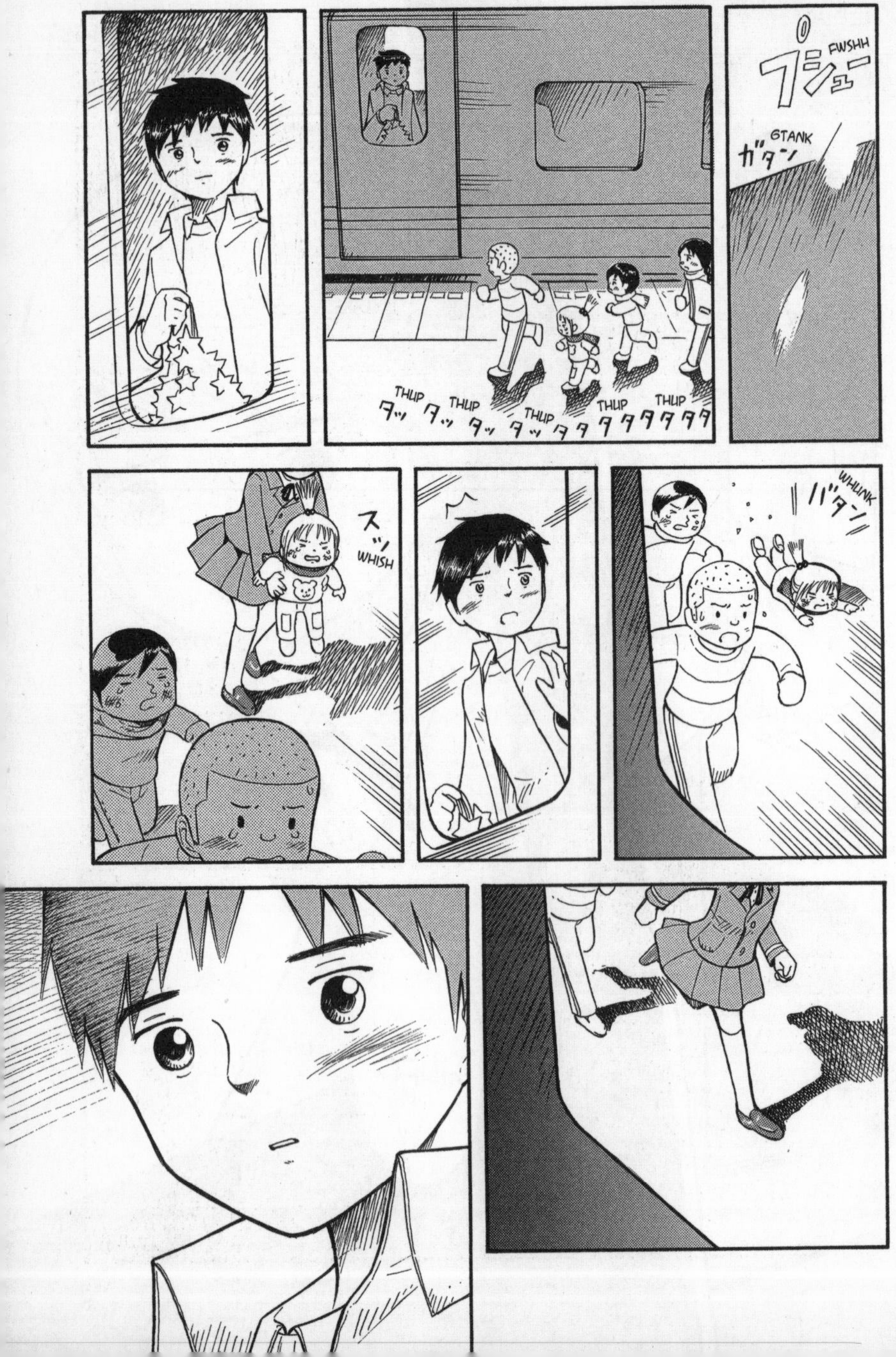

プシュー
FWSHH
ガタン
GTANK
タッ タッ タッ タッ タタタタタタ
THUP THUP THUP THUP THUP
バタン
WHUNK
スッ
WHISH

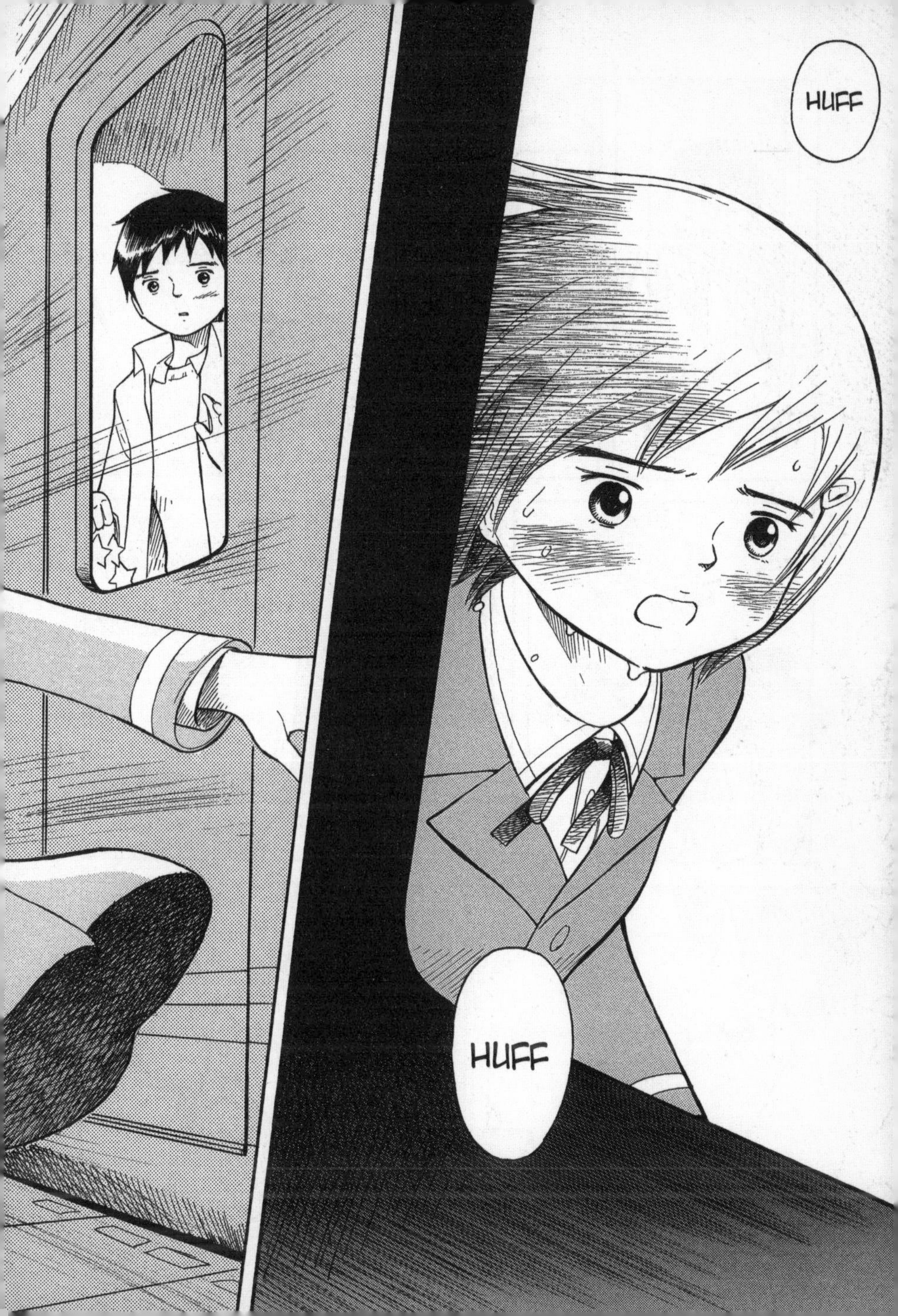
HUFF
HUFF

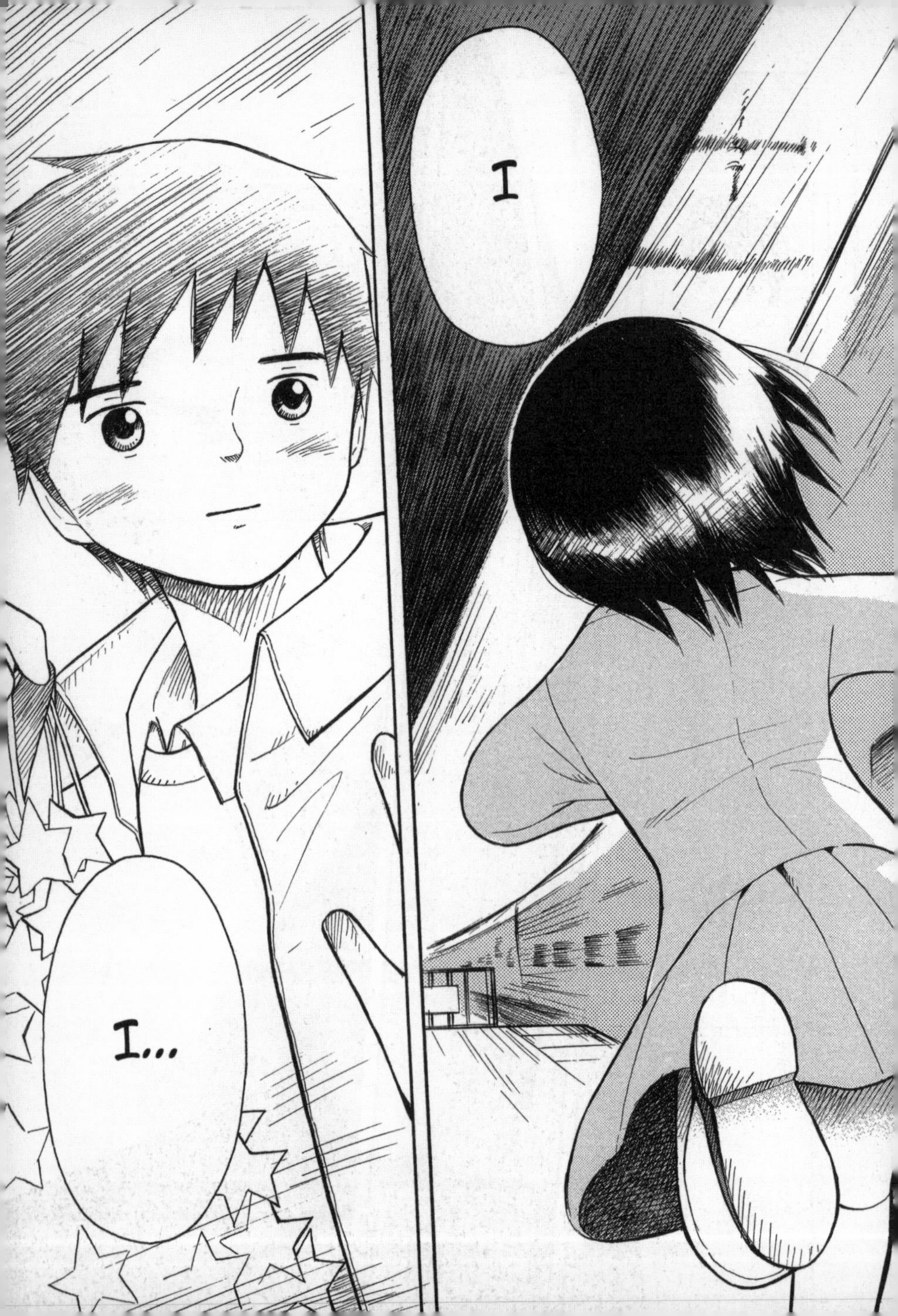
I
I...

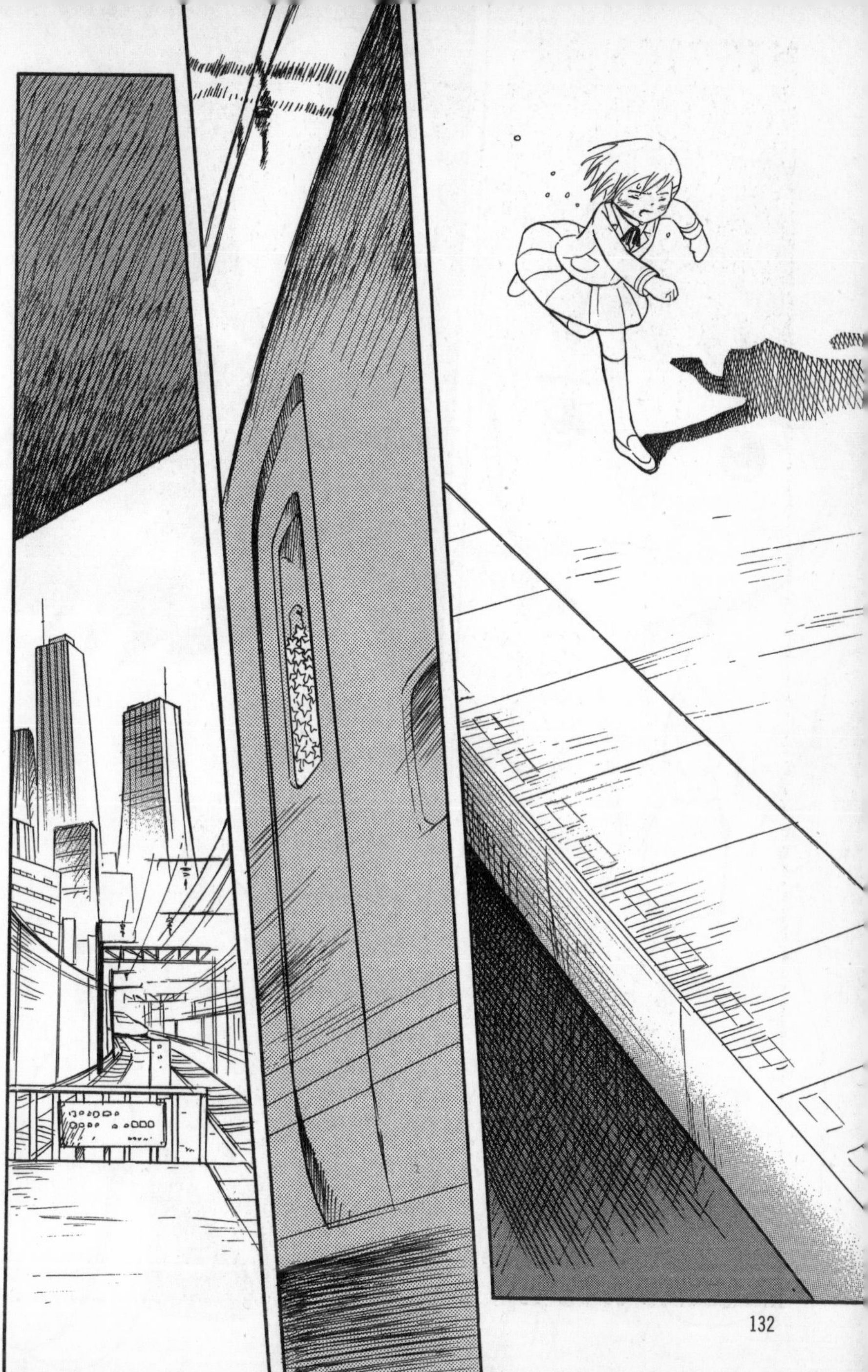

MISSION:43

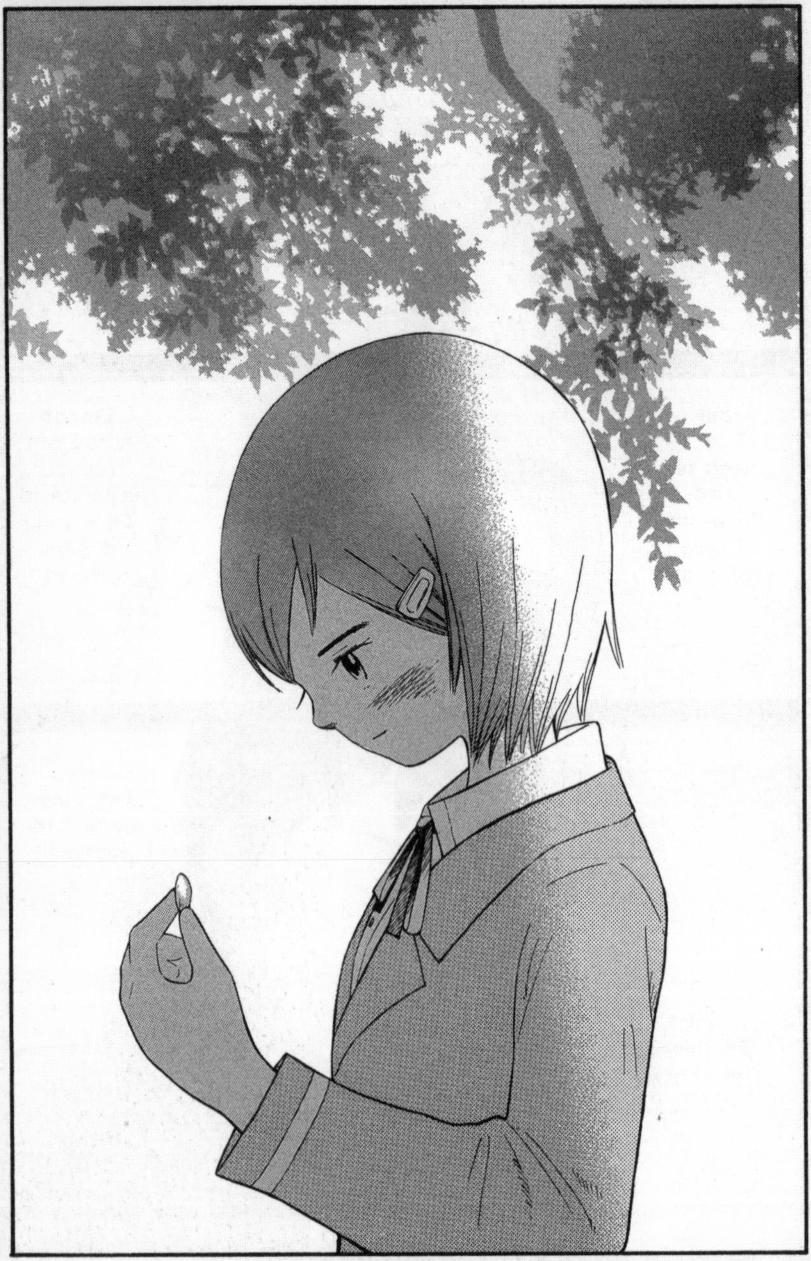

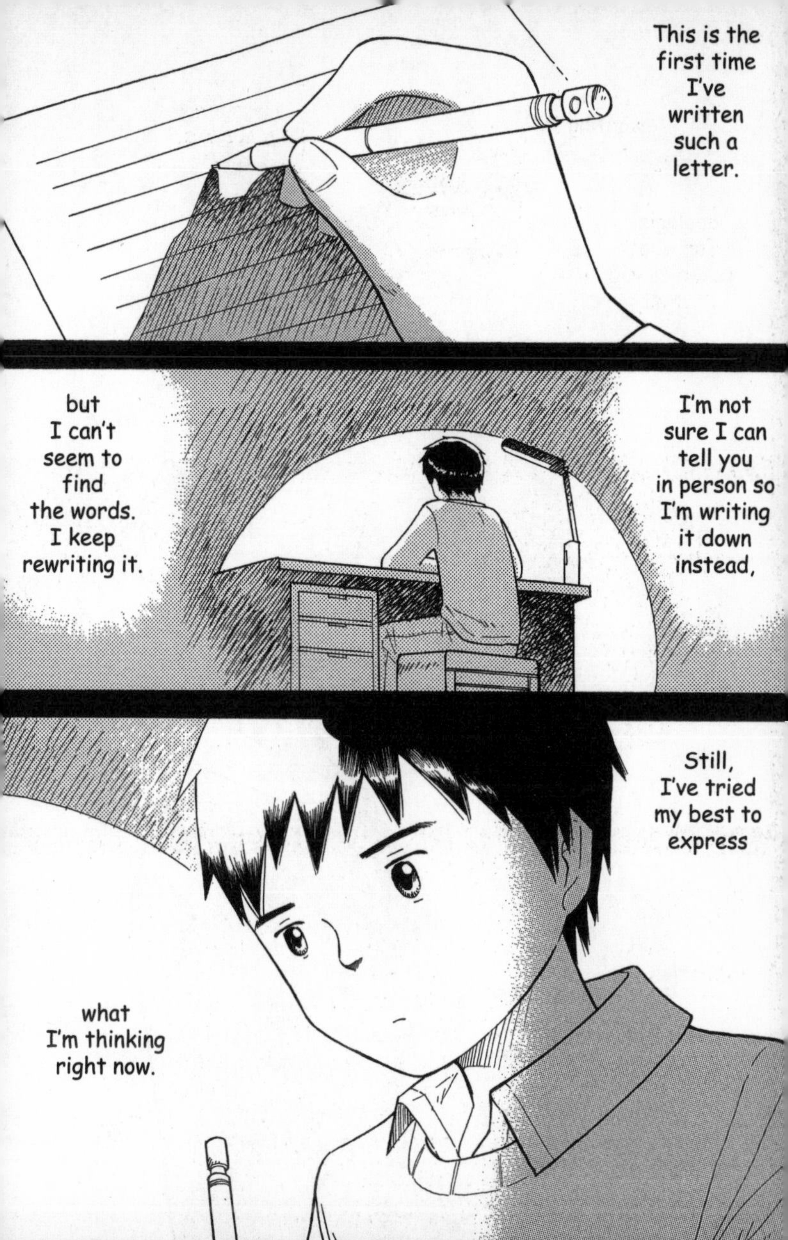
This is the first time I've written such a letter.
I'm not sure I can tell you in person so I'm writing it down instead,
but I can't seem to find the words. I keep rewriting it.
Still, I've tried my best to express
what I'm thinking right now.

THOSE UNIFORMS MAKE ME SICK.
I'd been wanting to
apologize for what I said to you that day.
Back then, I took part in anti-rocket demonstrations,
NO MORE ROCKET LAUNCHES!!
ANTI-ROCKET
making the time for marches and gatherings.

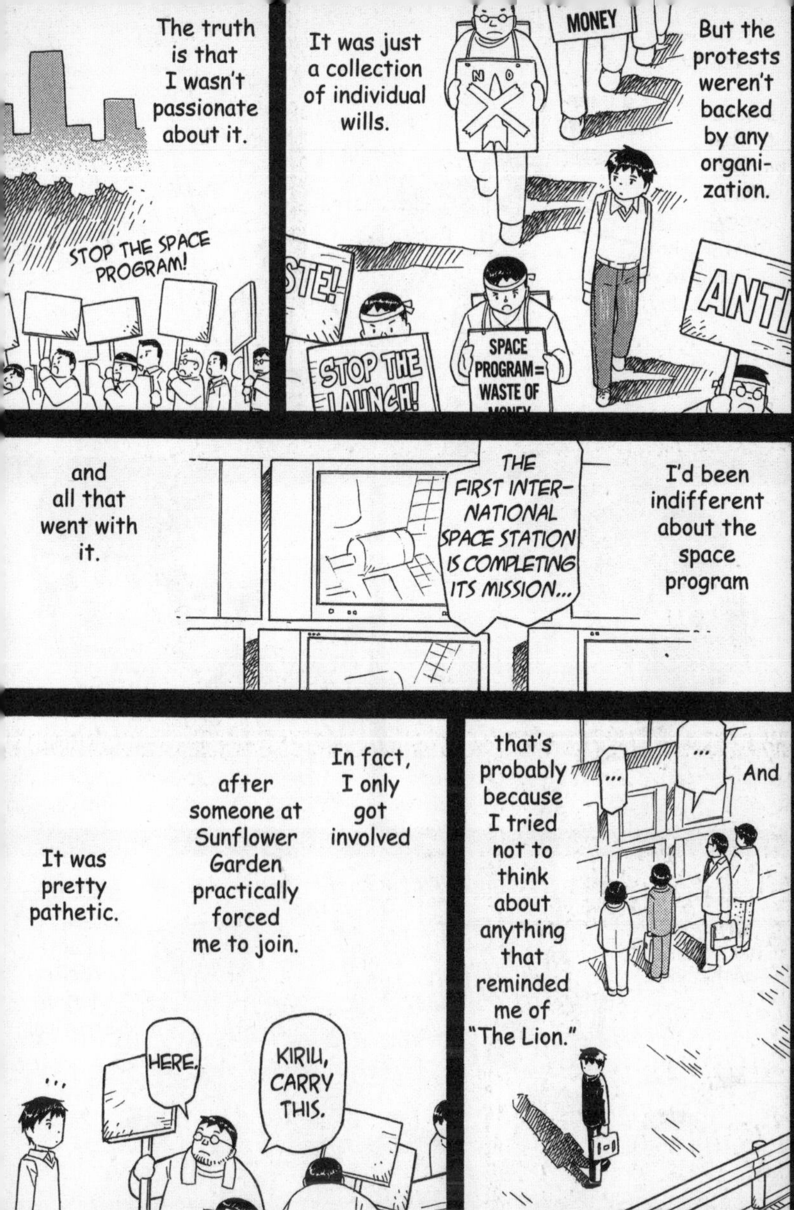

MONEY
But the protests weren't backed by any organization.
It was just a collection of individual wills.
NO
ANTI
SPACE PROGRAM= WASTE OF
STOP THE LAUNCH!
STE!
The truth is that I wasn't passionate about it.
STOP THE SPACE PROGRAM!
I'd been indifferent about the space program
THE FIRST INTERNATIONAL SPACE STATION IS COMPLETING ITS MISSION...
and all that went with it.
And
...
...
that's probably because I tried not to think about anything that reminded me of "The Lion."
In fact, I only got involved
after someone at Sunflower Garden practically forced me to join.
It was pretty pathetic.
KIRIU, CARRY THIS.
HERE.
...

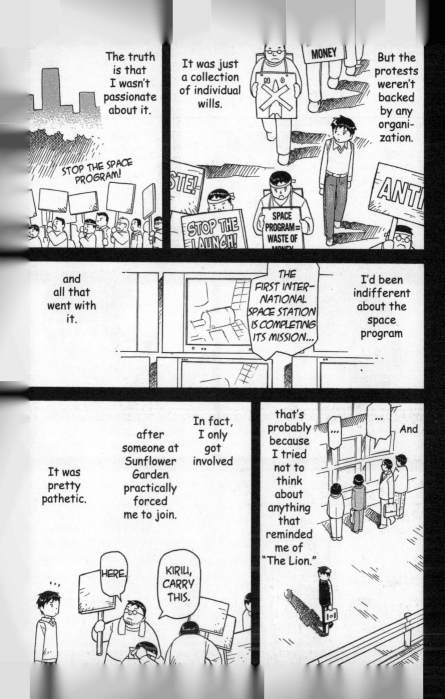

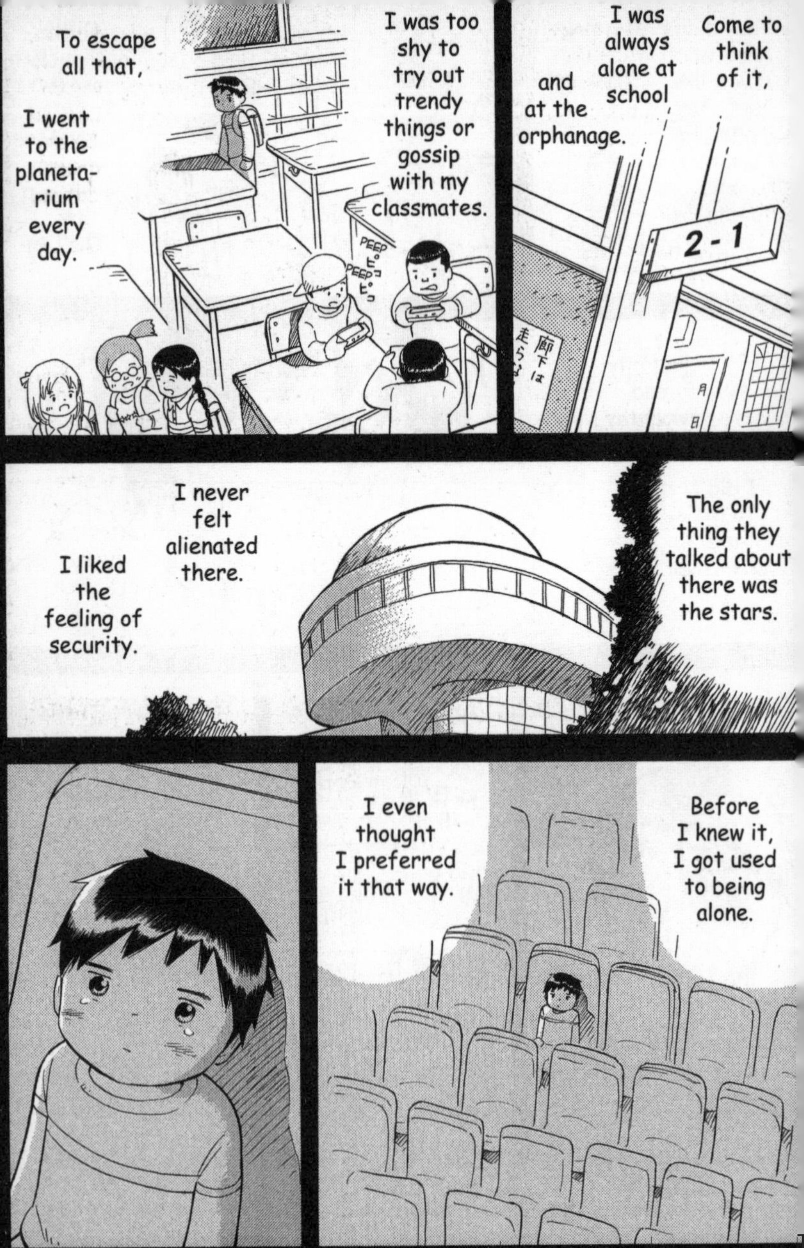
Come to think of it,
I was always alone at school
and at the orphanage.
2 - 1
I was too shy to try out trendy things or gossip with my classmates.
PEEP ピコ PEEP ピコ
To escape all that,
I went to the planetarium every day.
The only thing they talked about there was the stars.
I never felt alienated there.
I liked the feeling of security.
Before I knew it, I got used to being alone.
I even thought I preferred it that way.

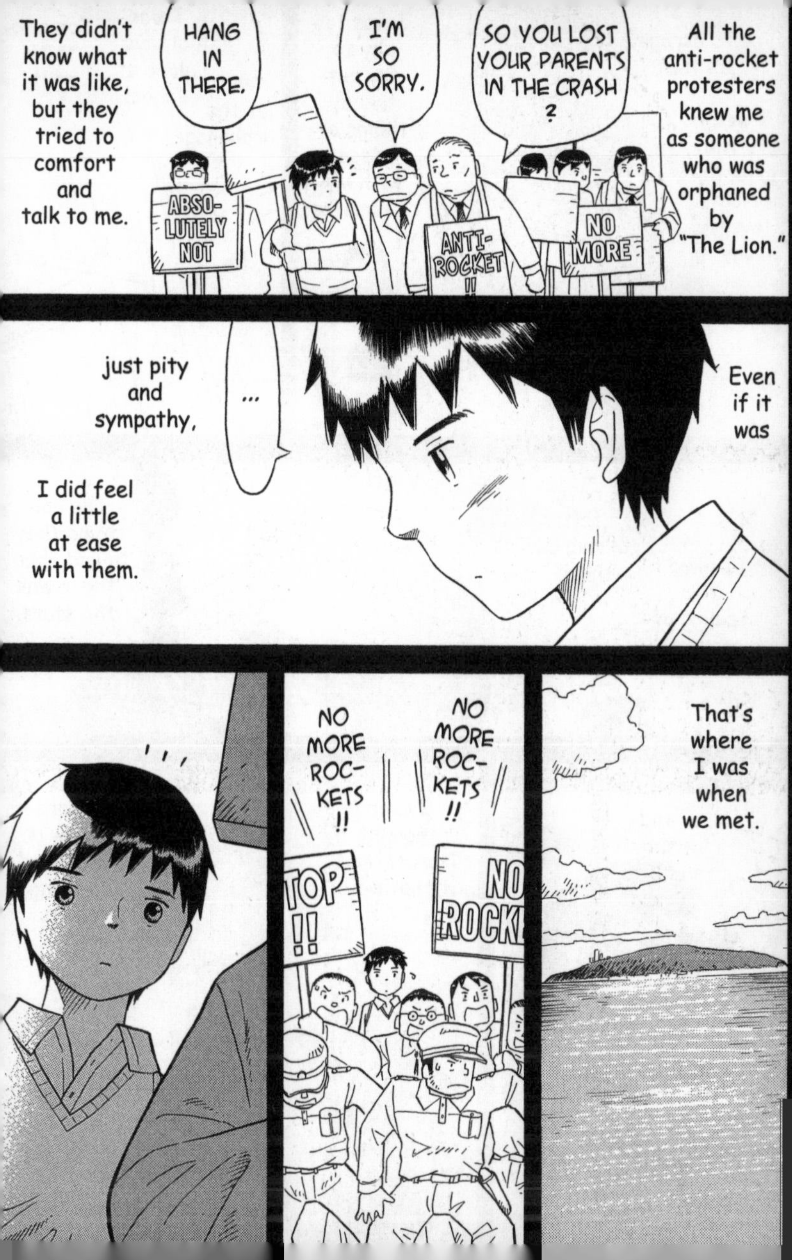
All the anti-rocket protesters knew me as someone who was orphaned by "The Lion."
SO YOU LOST YOUR PARENTS IN THE CRASH?
NO MORE
ANTI-ROCKET!!
I'M SO SORRY.
HANG IN THERE.
ABSO-LUTELY NOT
They didn't know what it was like, but they tried to comfort and talk to me.
Even if it was
...
just pity and sympathy,
I did feel a little at ease with them.
That's where I was when we met.
NO MORE ROC-KETS!!
NO MORE ROC-KETS!!
NO ROCK
TOP!!

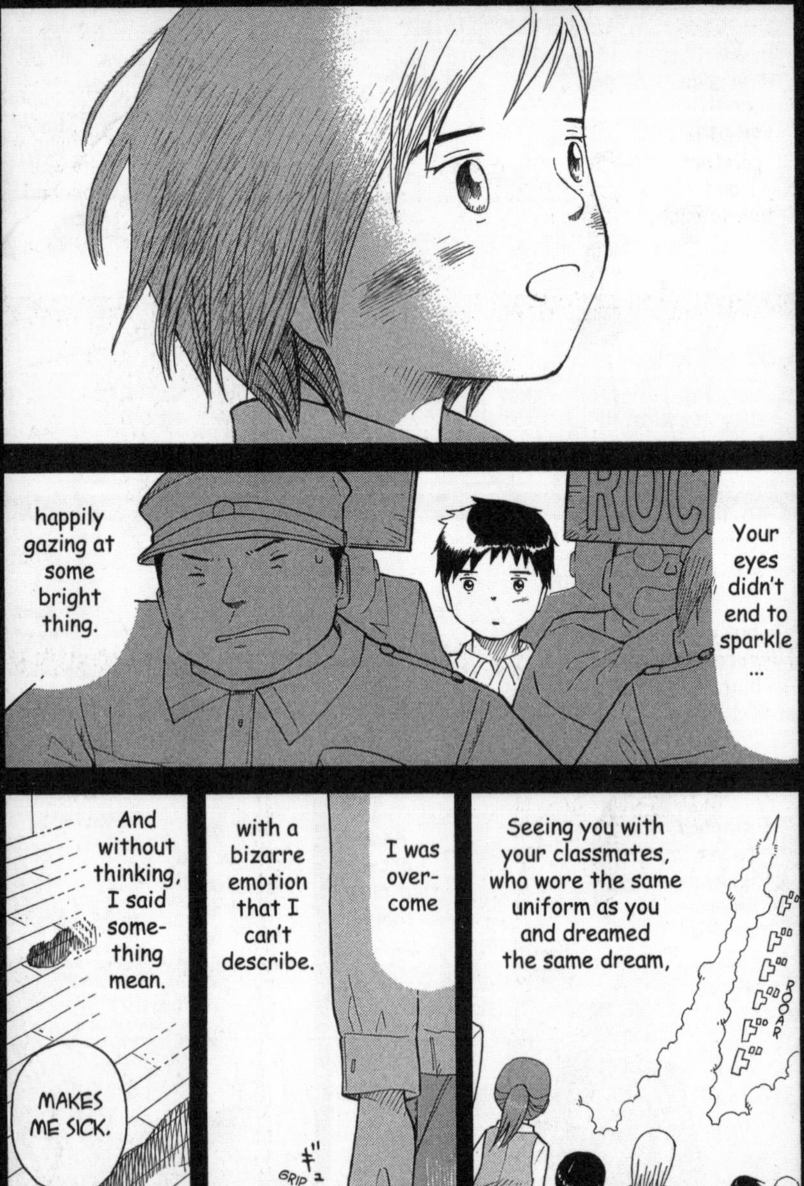
Your eyes didn't end to sparkle ...
happily gazing at some bright thing.
Seeing you with your classmates, who wore the same uniform as you and dreamed the same dream,
ROOAR
I was over-come
with a bizarre emotion that I can't describe.
GRIP
And without thinking, I said some-thing mean.
MAKES ME SICK.

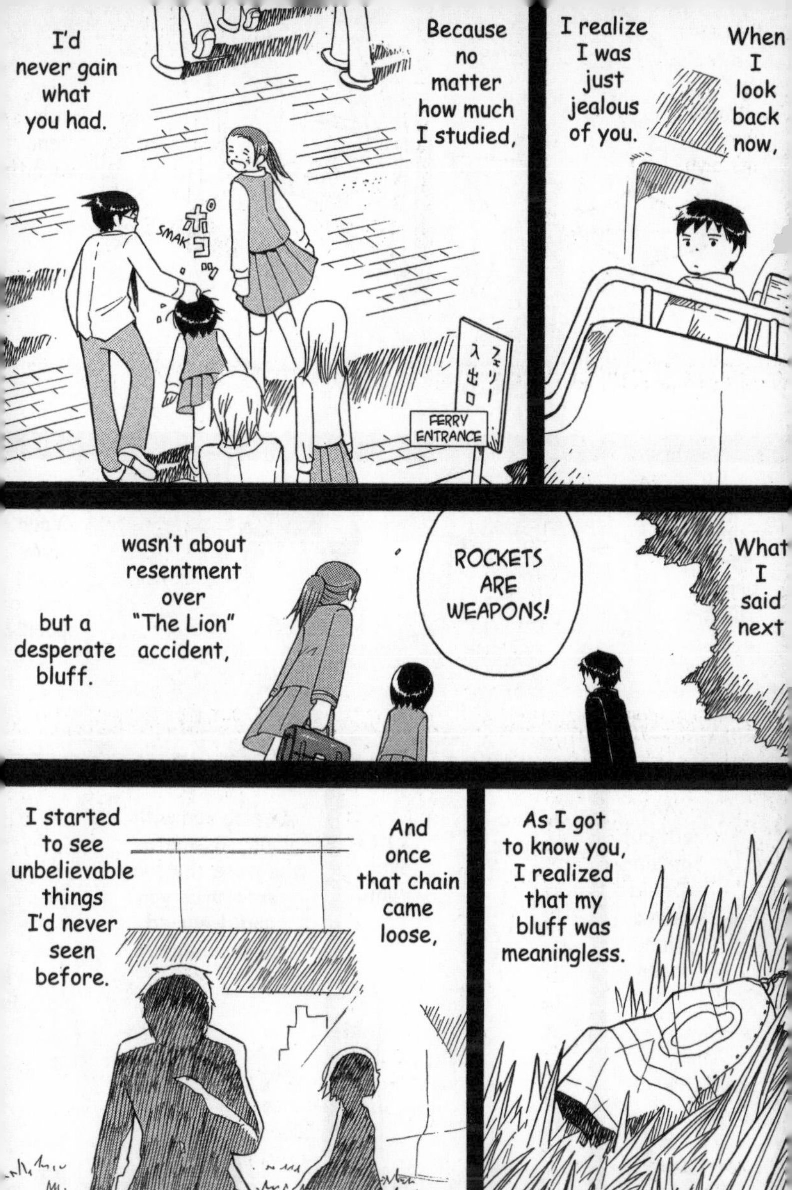
When I look back now,
I realize I was just jealous of you.
Because no matter how much I studied,
I'd never gain what you had.
ポコッ
SMAK
フェリー入出口
FERRY ENTRANCE
What I said next
ROCKETS ARE WEAPONS!
wasn't about resentment over "The Lion" accident,
but a desperate bluff.
As I got to know you, I realized that my bluff was meaningless.
And once that chain came loose,
I started to see unbelievable things I'd never seen before.

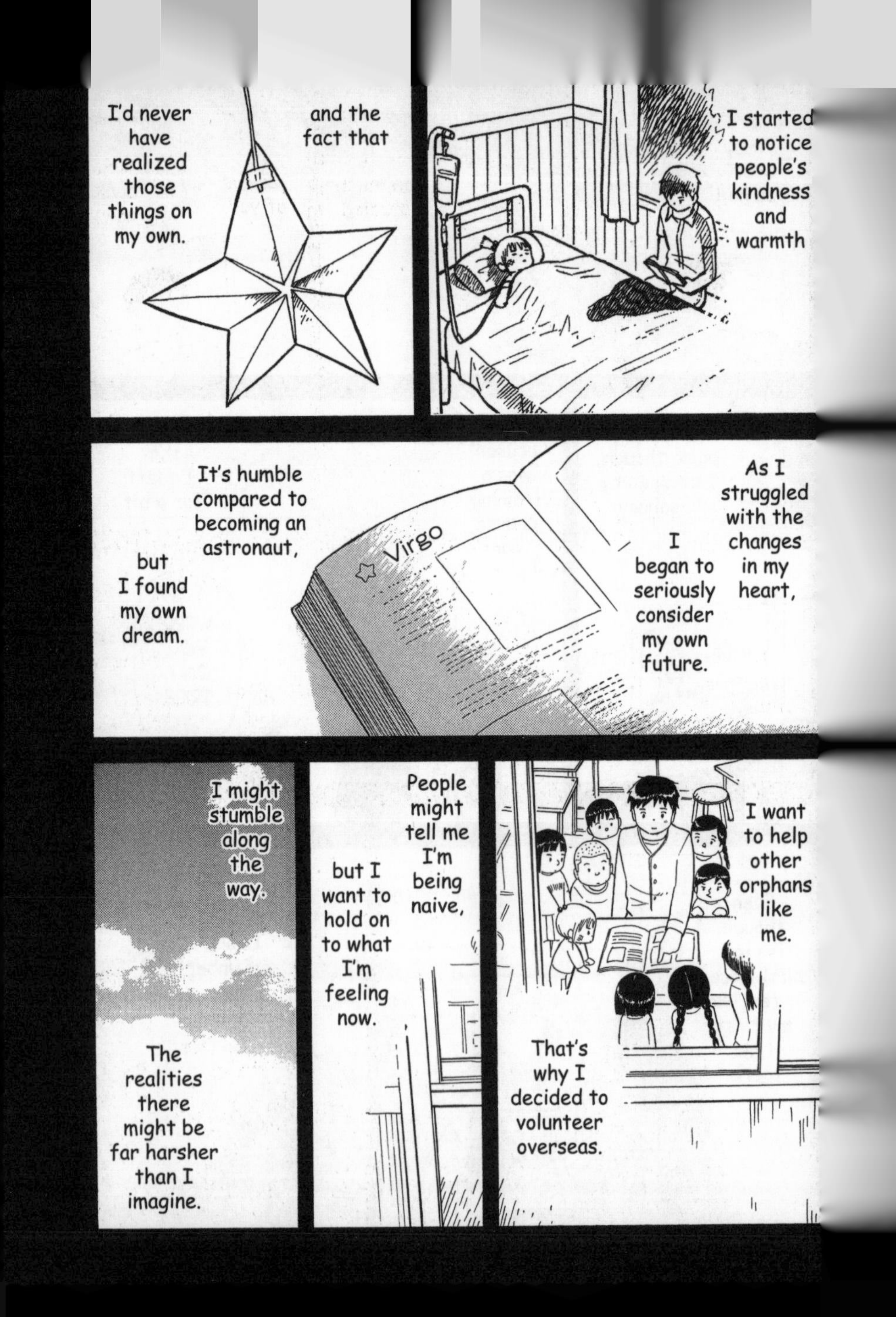
I started to notice people's kindness and warmth
and the fact that
I'd never have realized those things on my own.
As I struggled with the changes in my heart,
I began to seriously consider my own future.
Virgo
It's humble compared to becoming an astronaut,
but I found my own dream.
I want to help other orphans like me.
That's why I decided to volunteer overseas.
People might tell me I'm being naive,
but I want to hold on to what I'm feeling now.
I might stumble along the way.
The realities there might be far harsher than I imagine.

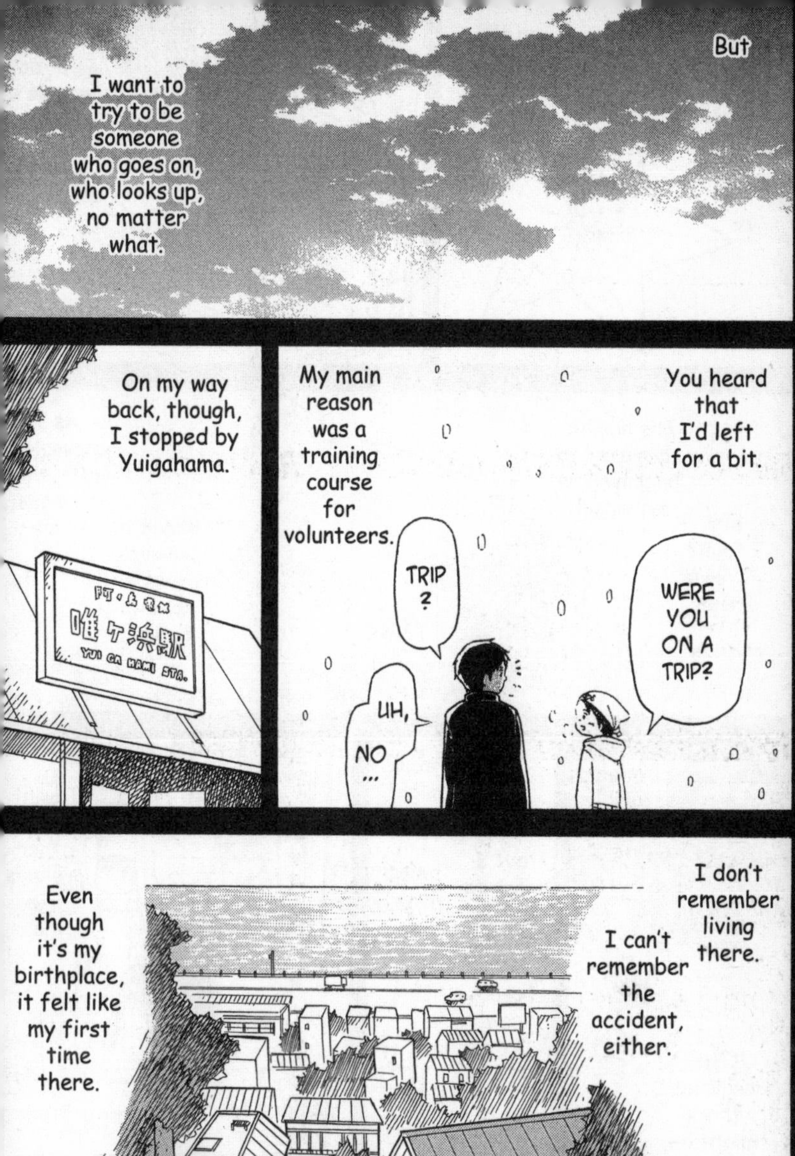
But
I want to try to be someone who goes on, who looks up, no matter what.
You heard that I'd left for a bit.
WERE YOU ON A TRIP?
My main reason was a training course for volunteers.
TRIP?
UH, NO ...
On my way back, though, I stopped by Yuigahama.
唯ヶ浜駅
YUI GA HAMA STA.
I don't remember living there.
I can't remember the accident, either.
Even though it's my birthplace, it felt like my first time there.

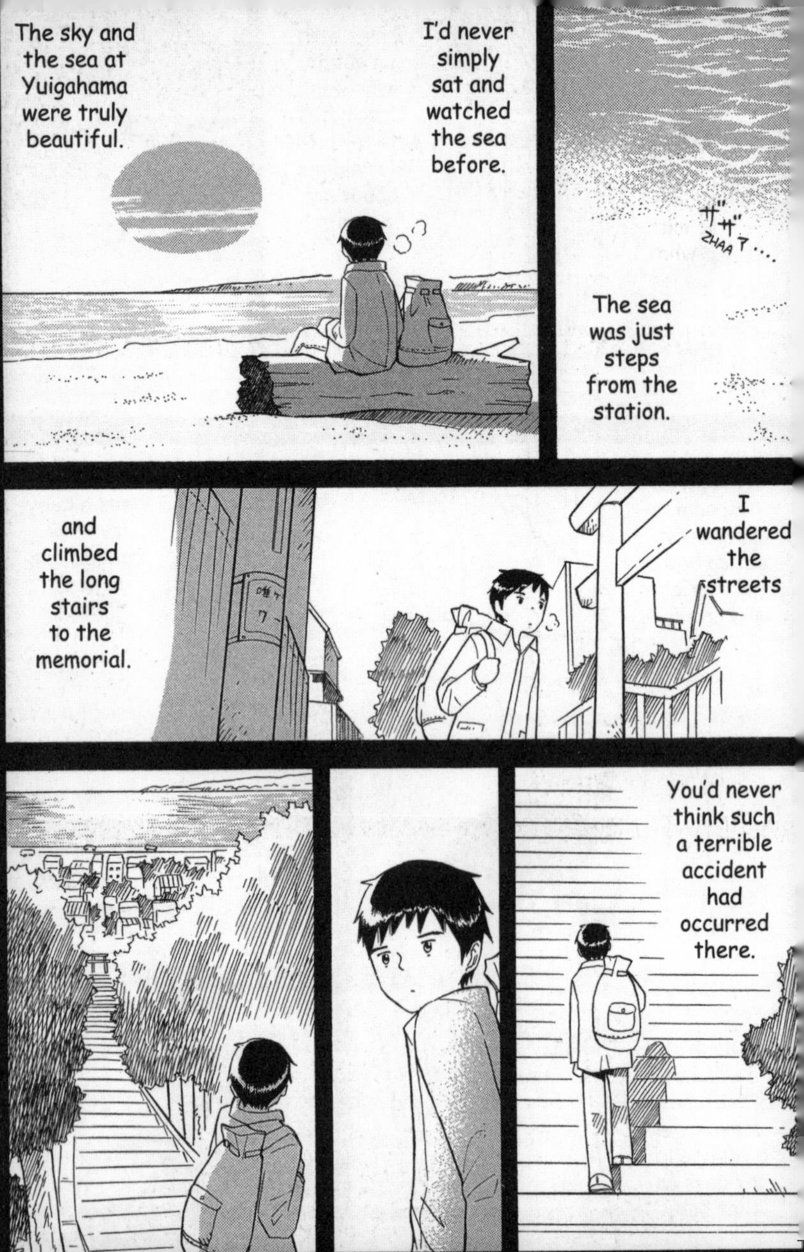

ZHAA...
The sea was just steps from the station.
I'd never simply sat and watched the sea before.
The sky and the sea at Yuigahama were truly beautiful.
I wandered the streets
and climbed the long stairs to the memorial.
You'd never think such a terrible accident had occurred there.

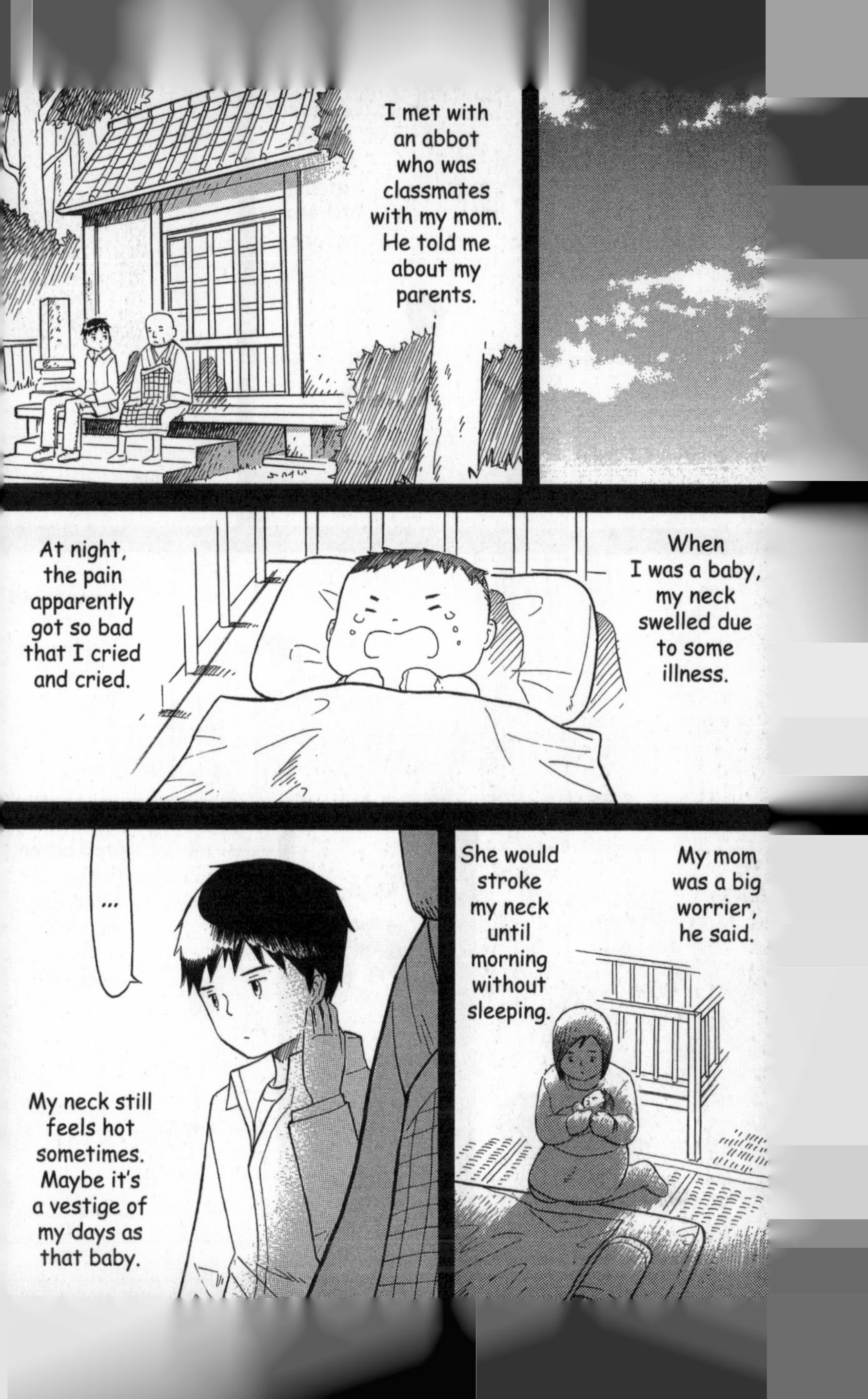
I met with an abbot who was classmates with my mom. He told me about my parents.
When I was a baby, my neck swelled due to some illness.
At night, the pain apparently got so bad that I cried and cried.
My mom was a big worrier, he said.
She would stroke my neck until morning without sleeping.
...
My neck still feels hot sometimes. Maybe it's a vestige of my days as that baby.

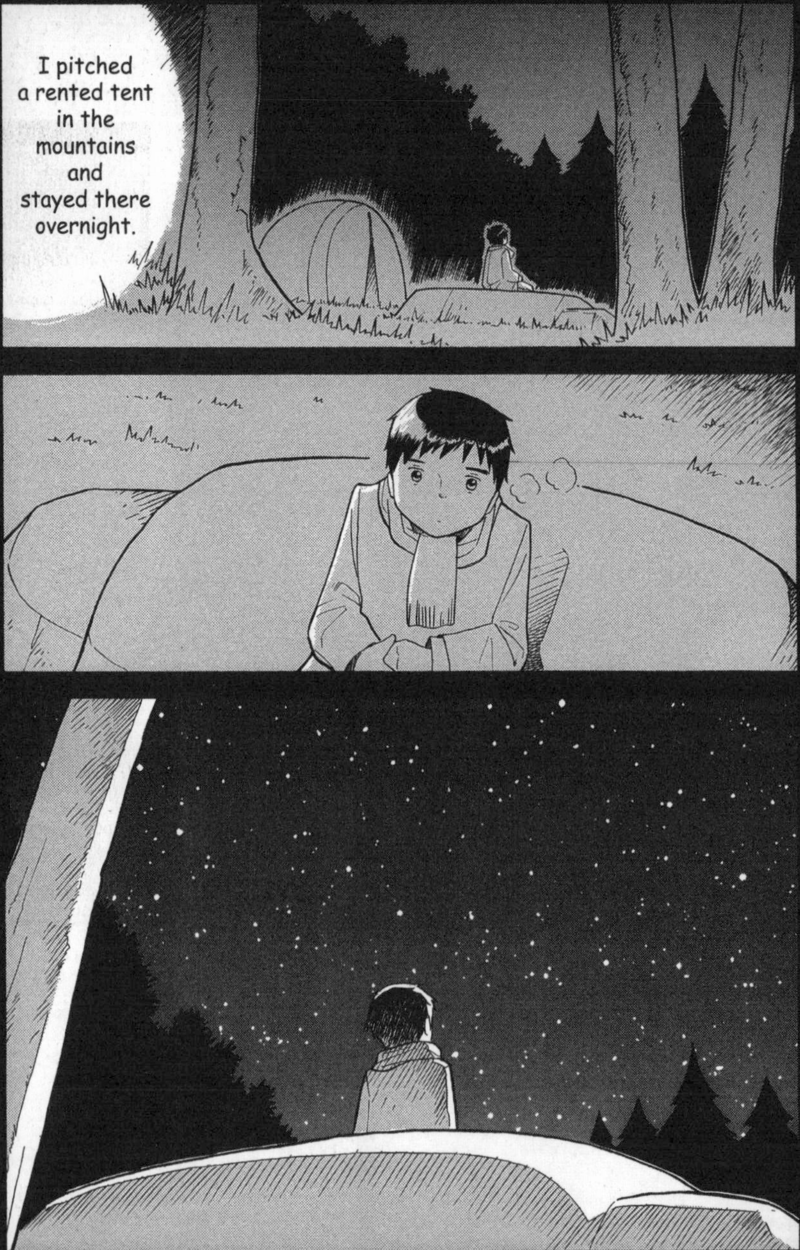
I pitched a rented tent in the mountains and stayed there overnight.

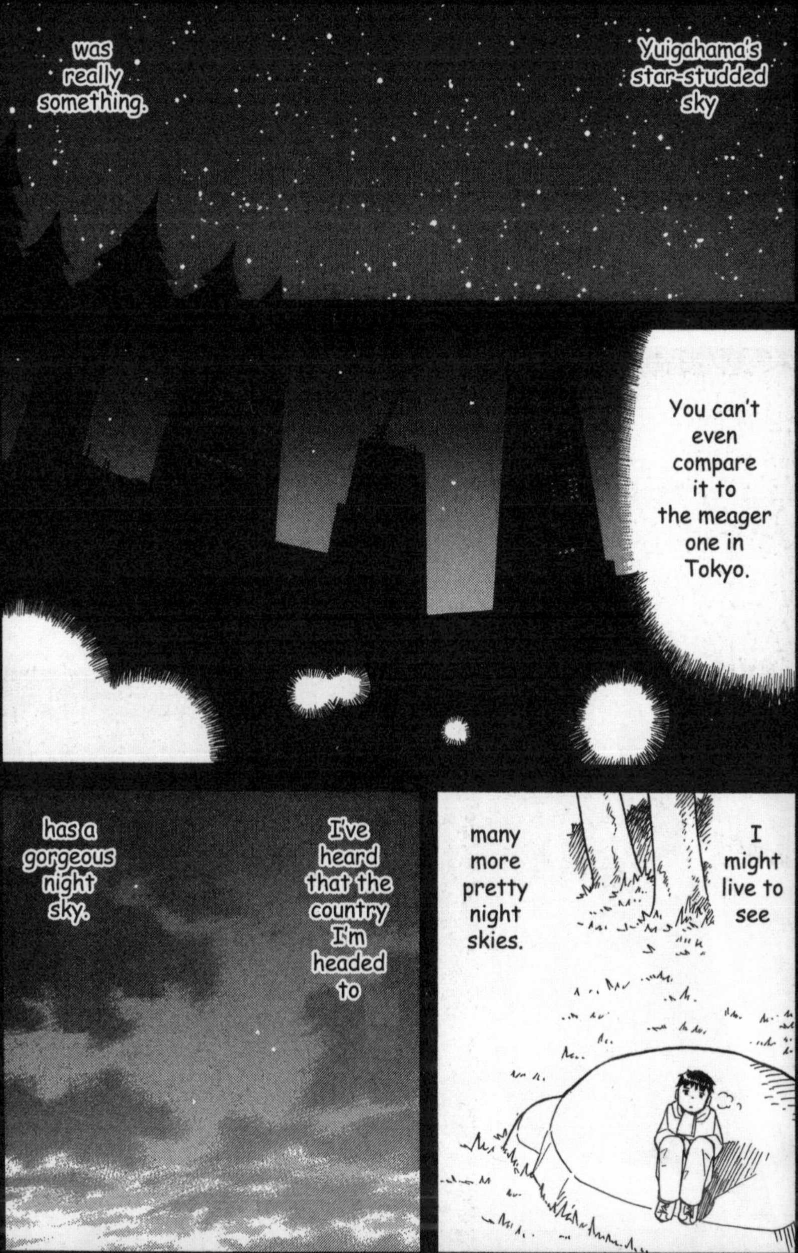
Yuigahama's star-studded sky
was really something.
You can't even compare it to the meager one in Tokyo.
I might live to see
many more pretty night skies.
I've heard that the country I'm headed to
has a gorgeous night sky.

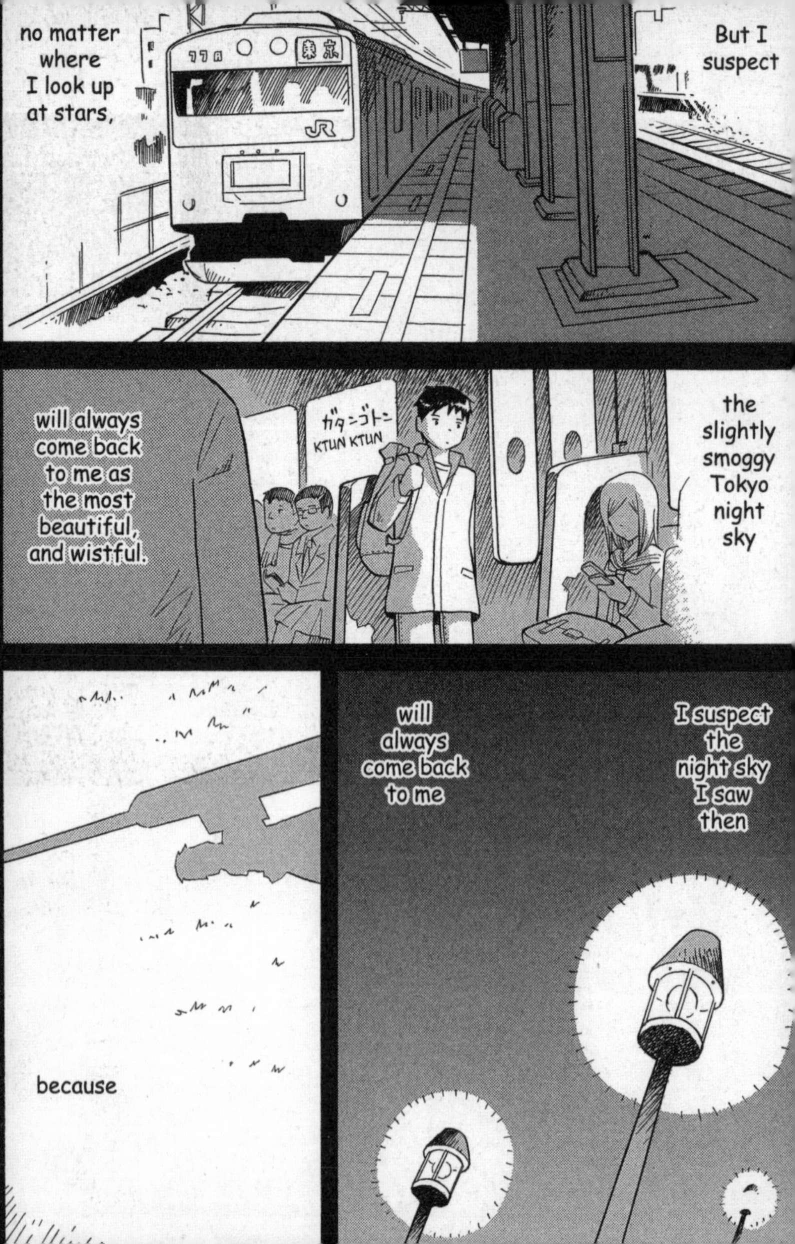
But I suspect
no matter where I look up at stars,
the slightly smoggy Tokyo night sky
ガタンゴトン
KTUN KTUN
will always come back to me as the most beautiful, and wistful.
I suspect the night sky I saw then
will always come back to me
because

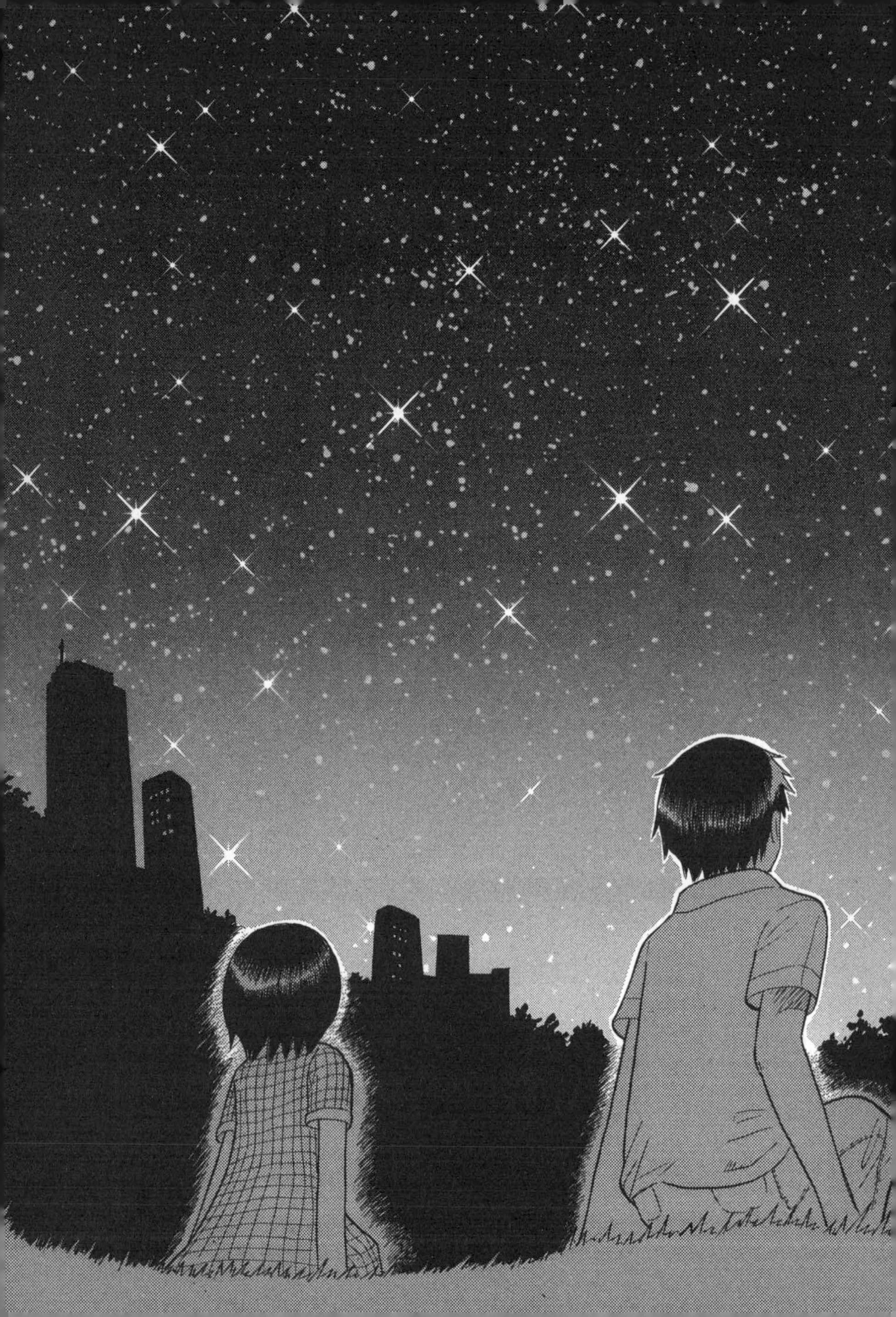

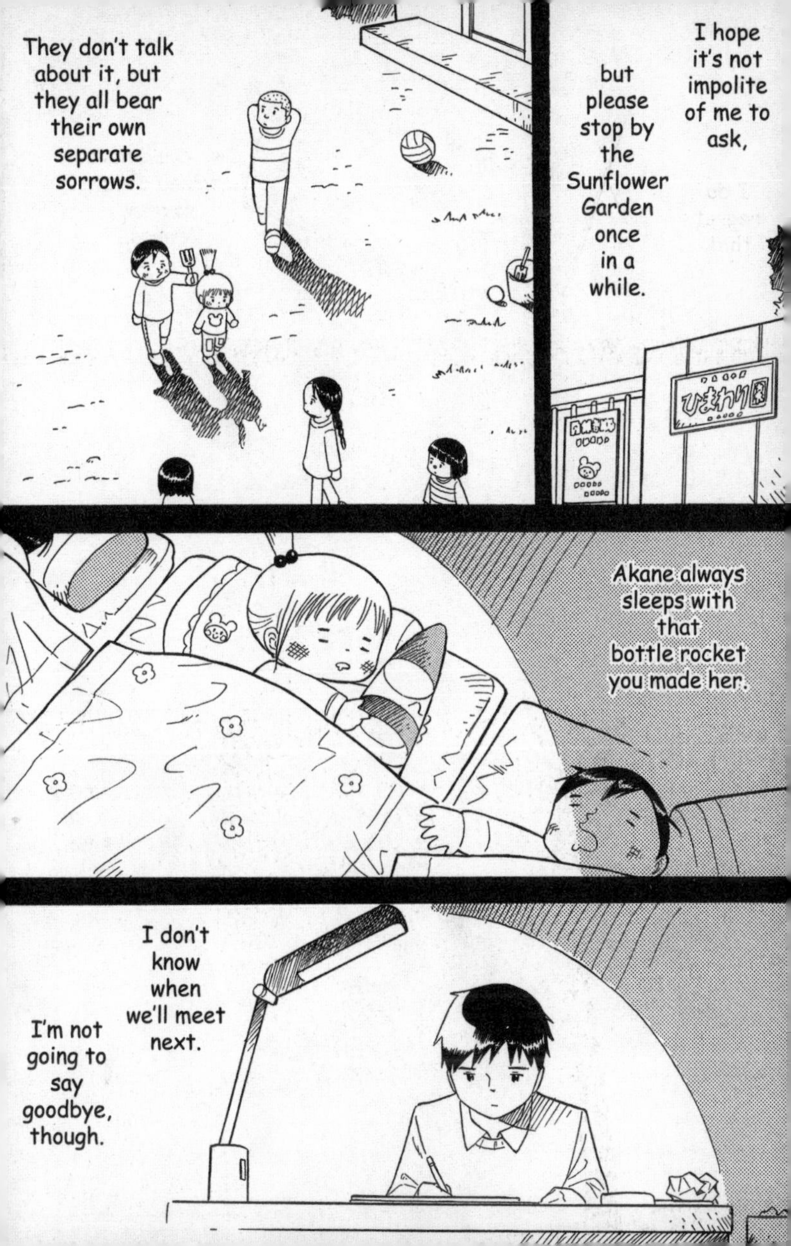
I hope it's not impolite of me to ask,
but please stop by the Sunflower Garden once in a while.
ひまわり園
They don't talk about it, but they all bear their own separate sorrows.
Akane always sleeps with that bottle rocket you made her.
I don't know when we'll meet next.
I'm not going to say goodbye, though.

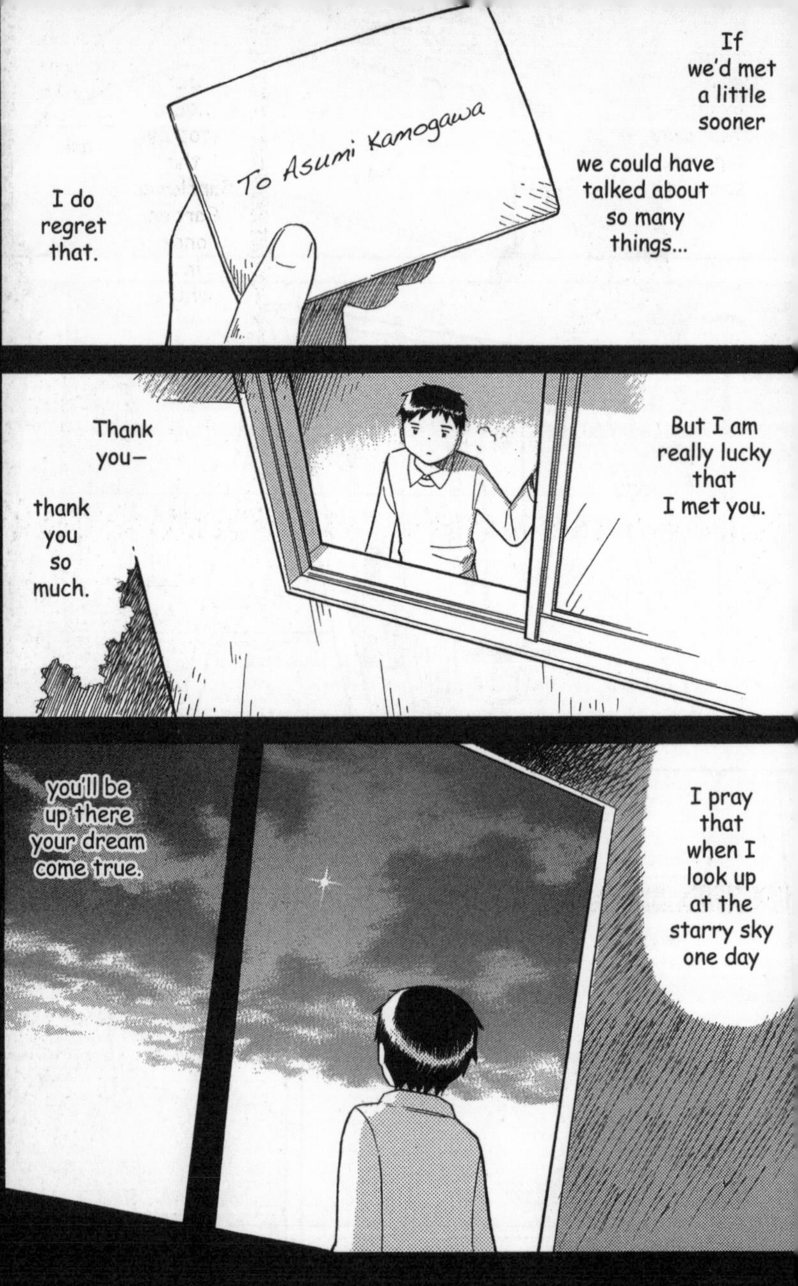
If we'd met a little sooner
we could have talked about so many things...
To Asumi Kamogawa
I do regret that.
But I am really lucky that I met you.
Thank you—
thank you so much.
I pray that when I look up at the starry sky one day
you'll be up there your dream come true.

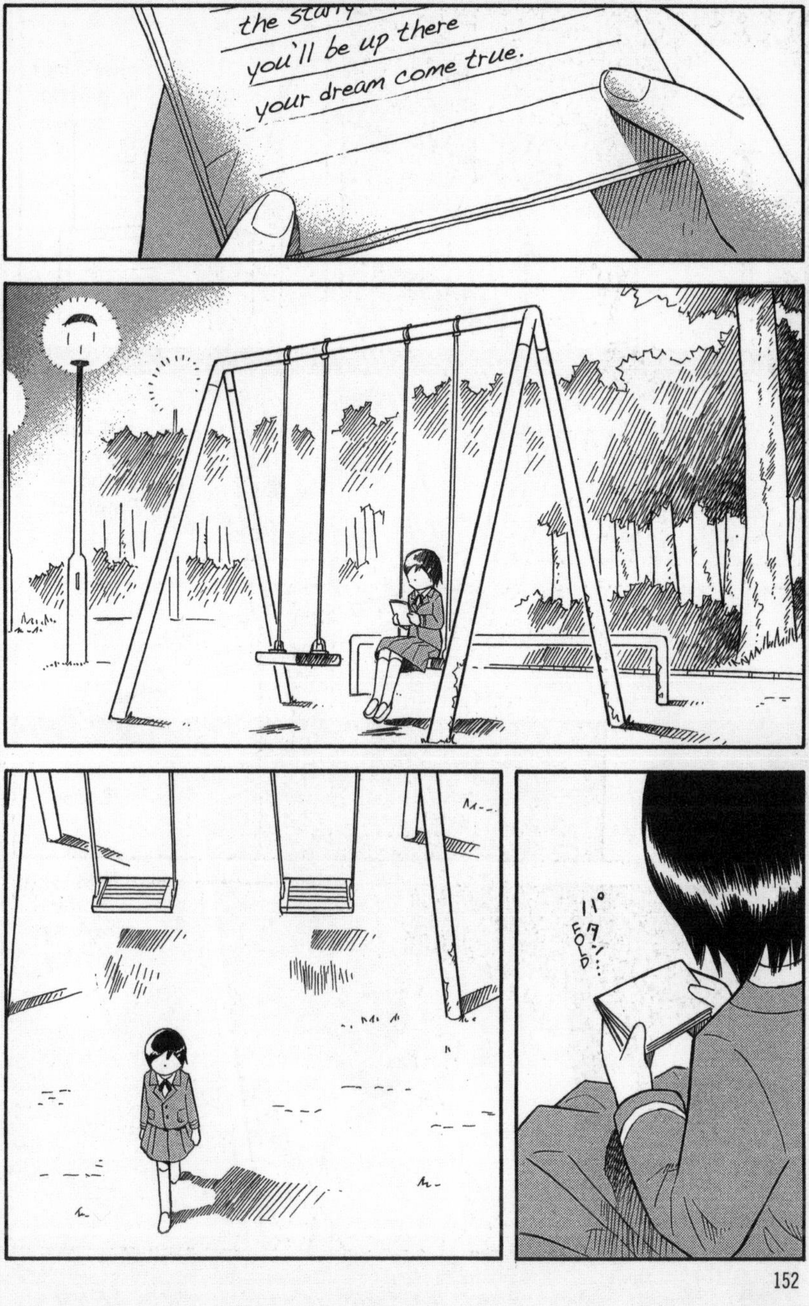
the
you'll be up there
your dream come true.
パタン…
FOLD

パカ…
KREAK
ギ…
KREE

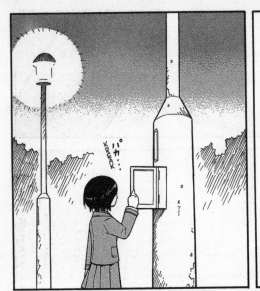

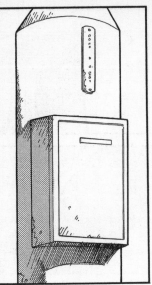

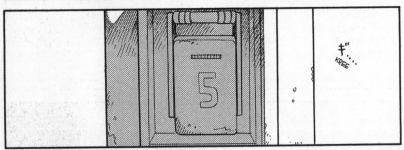

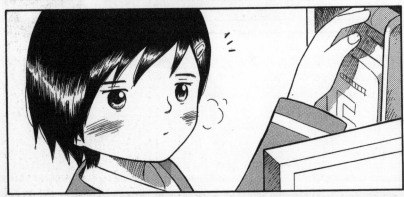

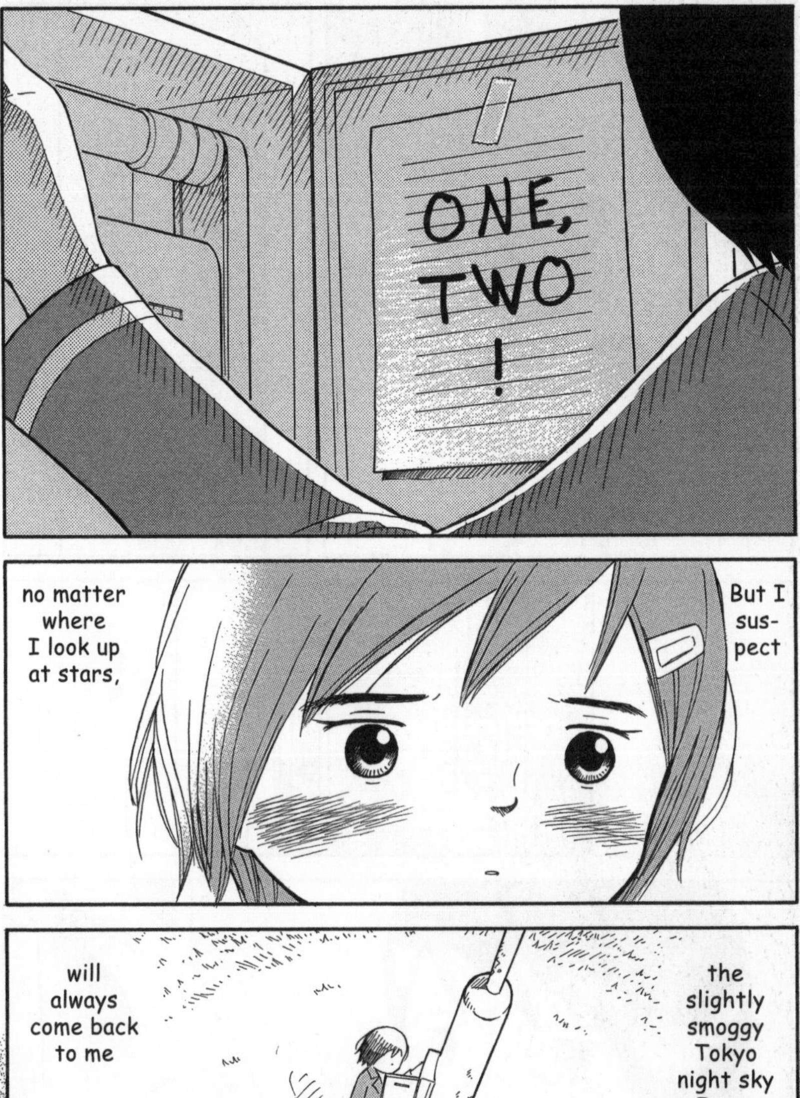
ONE, TWO !
But I suspect
no matter where I look up at stars,
the slightly smoggy Tokyo night sky I saw then
will always come back to me

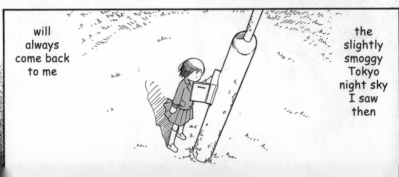

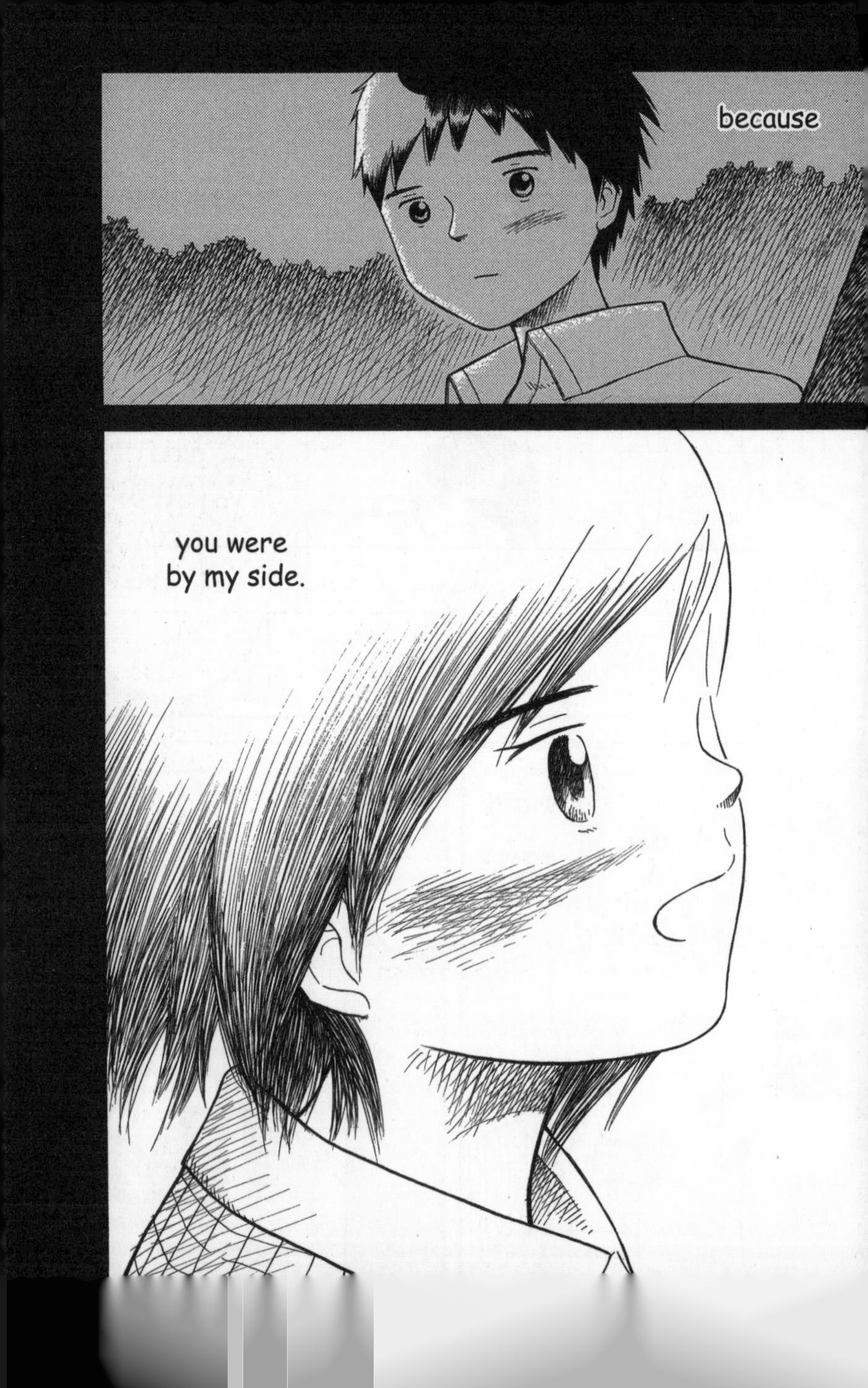
because
you were by my side.

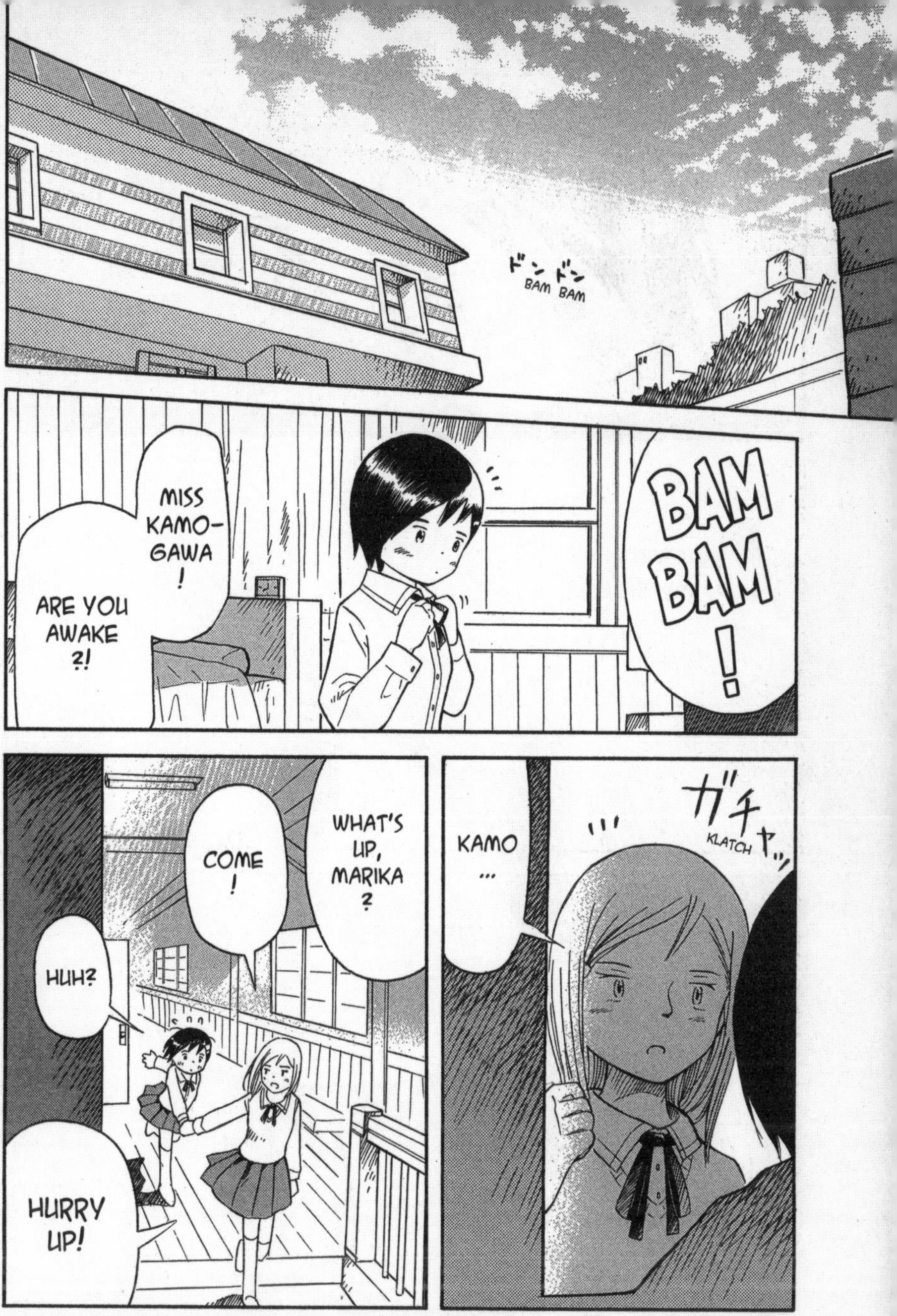
ドンドン
BAM BAM
BAM BAM!
MISS KAMO-GAWA!
ARE YOU AWAKE?!
ガチャッ
KLATCH
KAMO...
WHAT'S UP, MARIKA?
COME!
HUH?
HURRY UP!

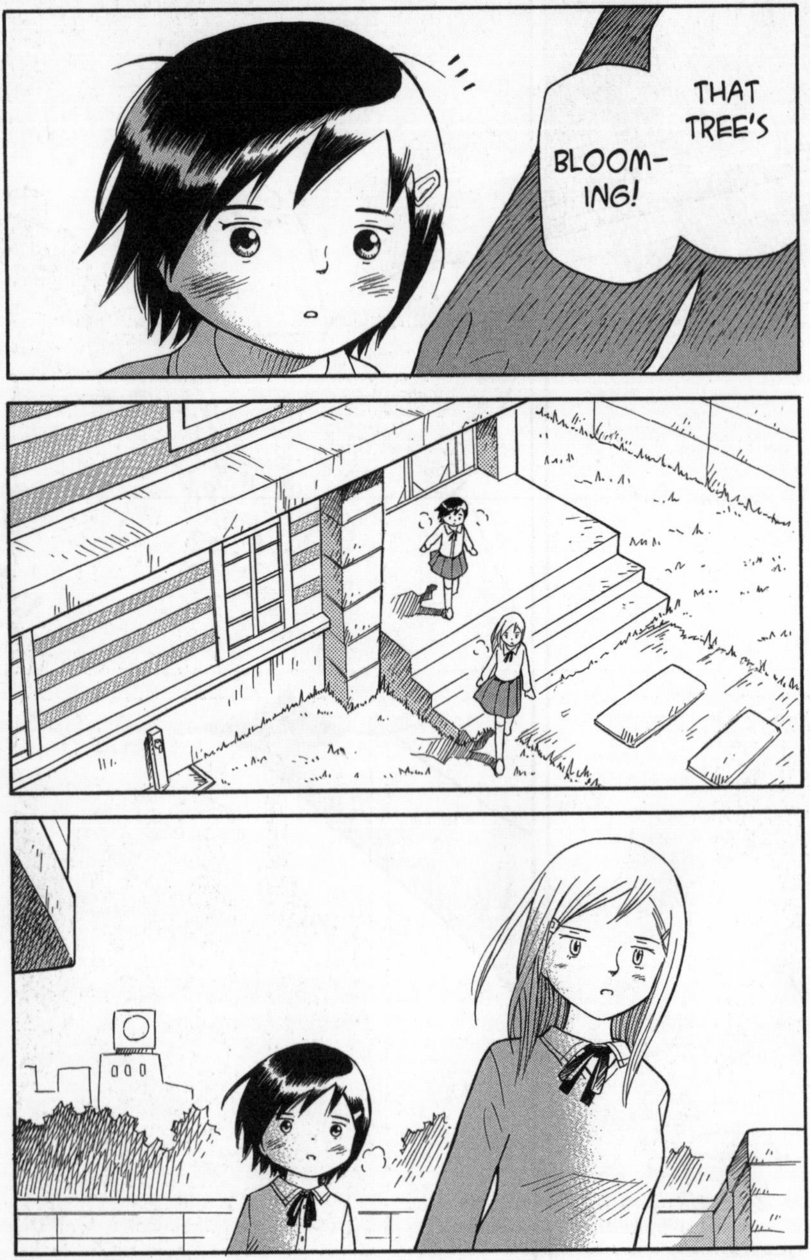
THAT TREE'S BLOOM-ING!

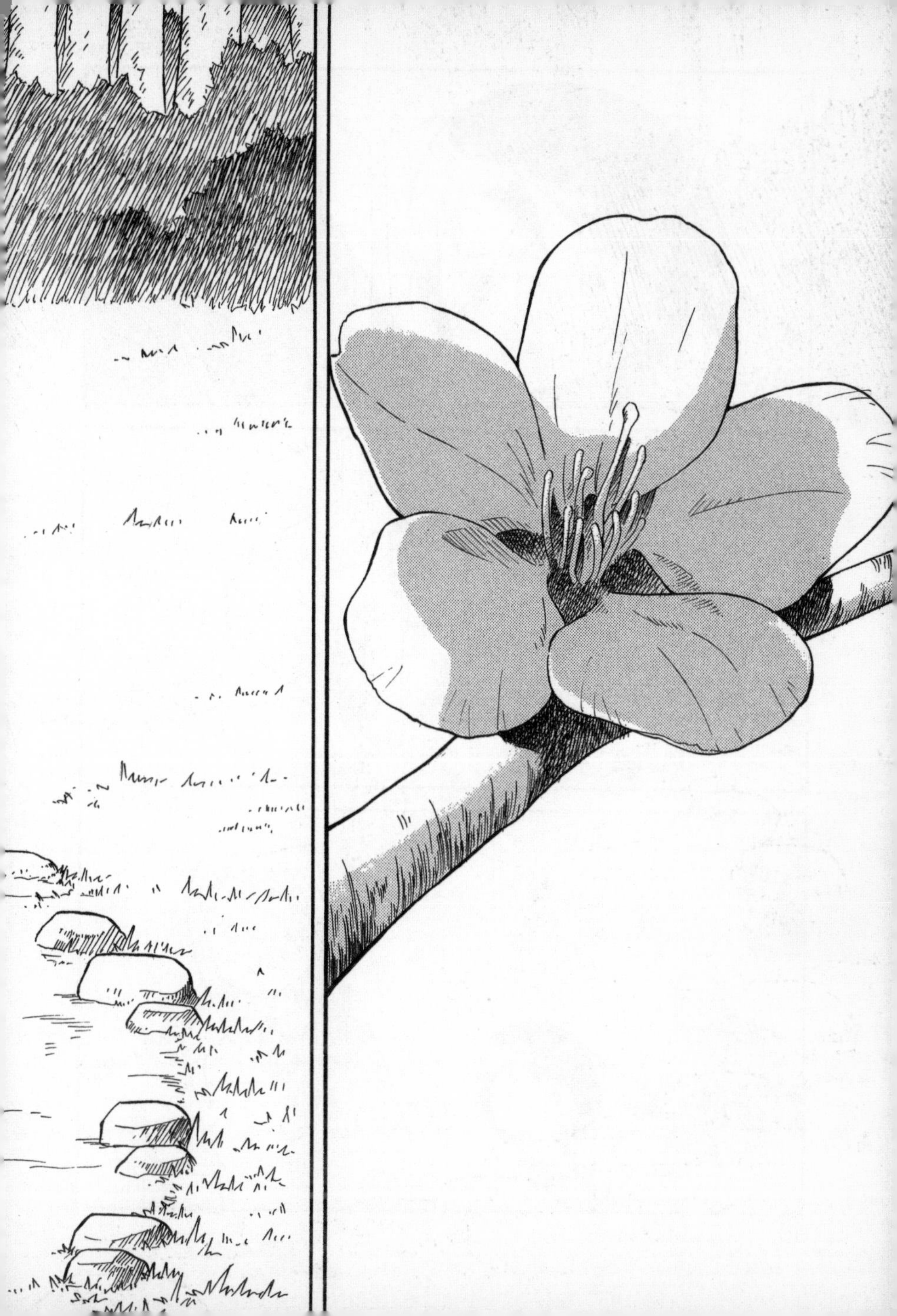

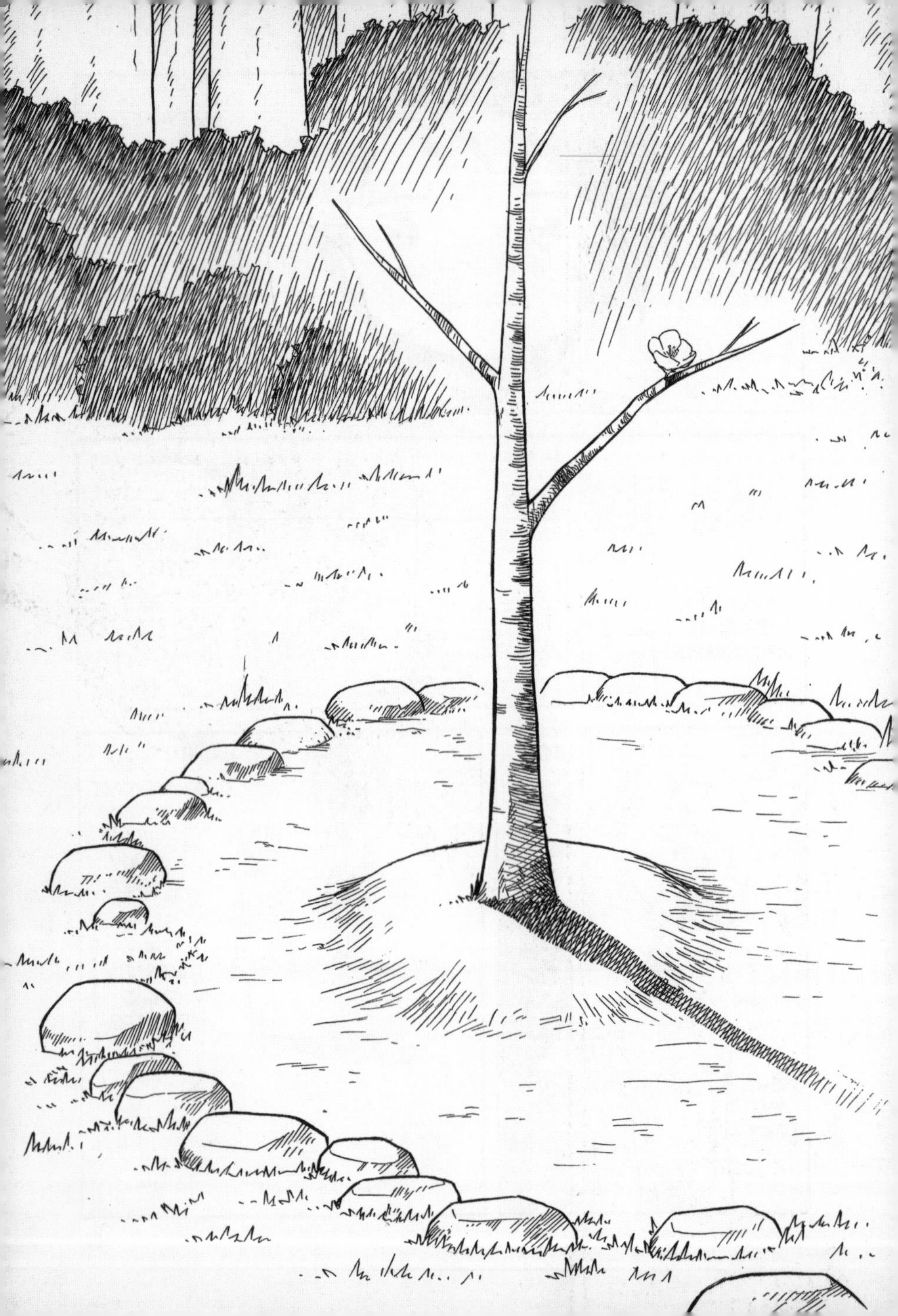

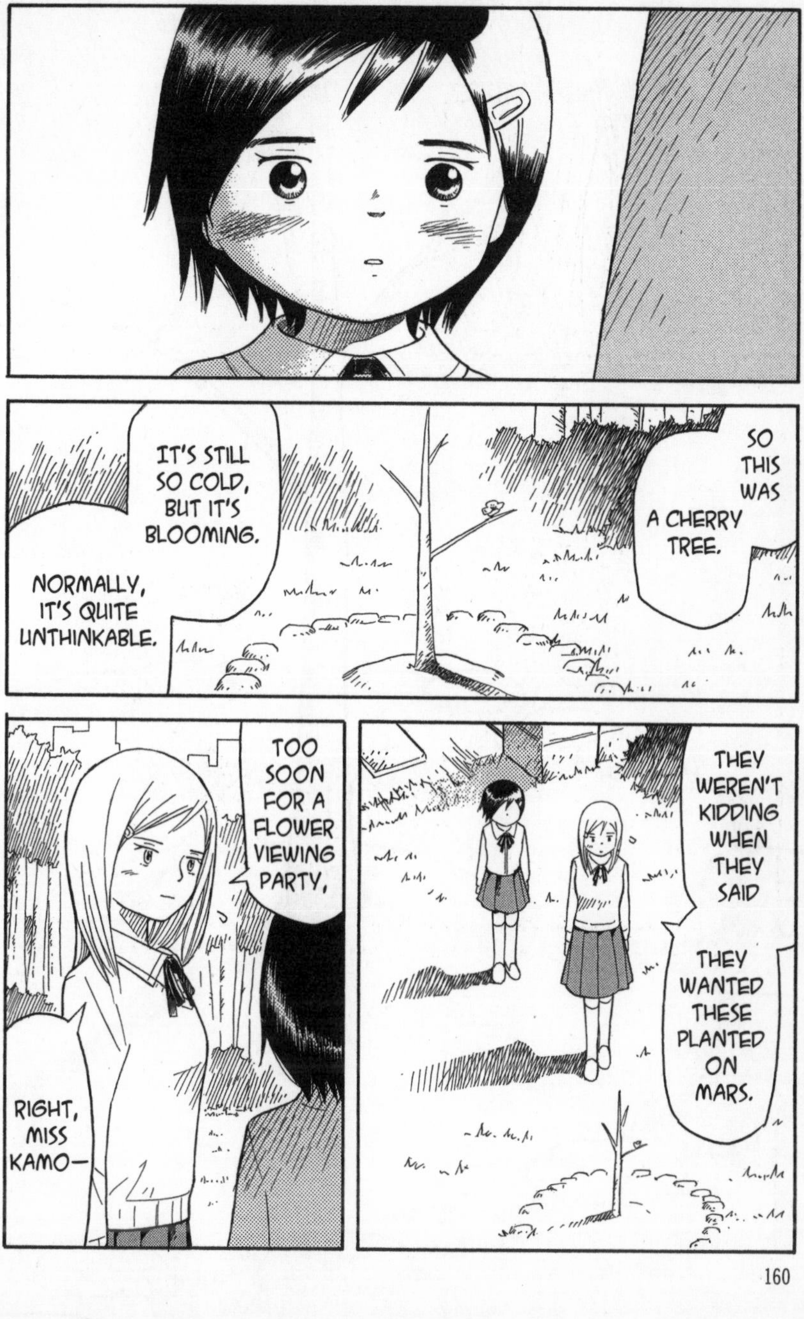
SO THIS WAS A CHERRY TREE.
IT'S STILL SO COLD, BUT IT'S BLOOMING.
NORMALLY, IT'S QUITE UNTHINKABLE.
THEY WEREN'T KIDDING WHEN THEY SAID
THEY WANTED THESE PLANTED ON MARS.
TOO SOON FOR A FLOWER VIEWING PARTY,
RIGHT, MISS KAMO—

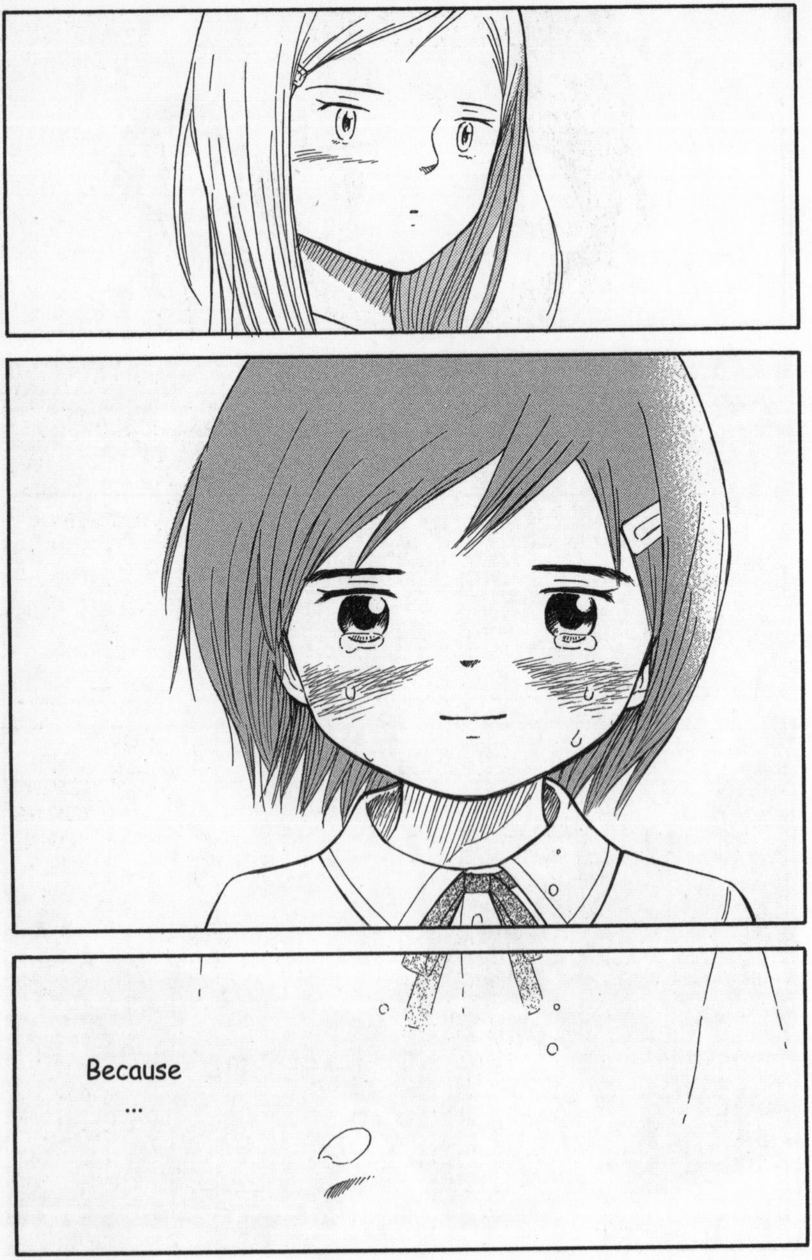
Because
...

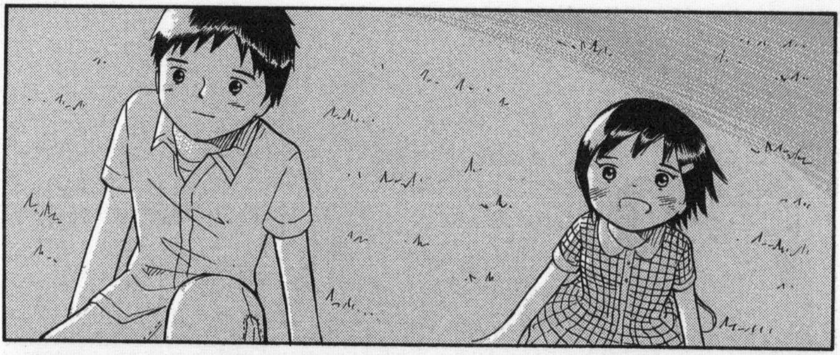

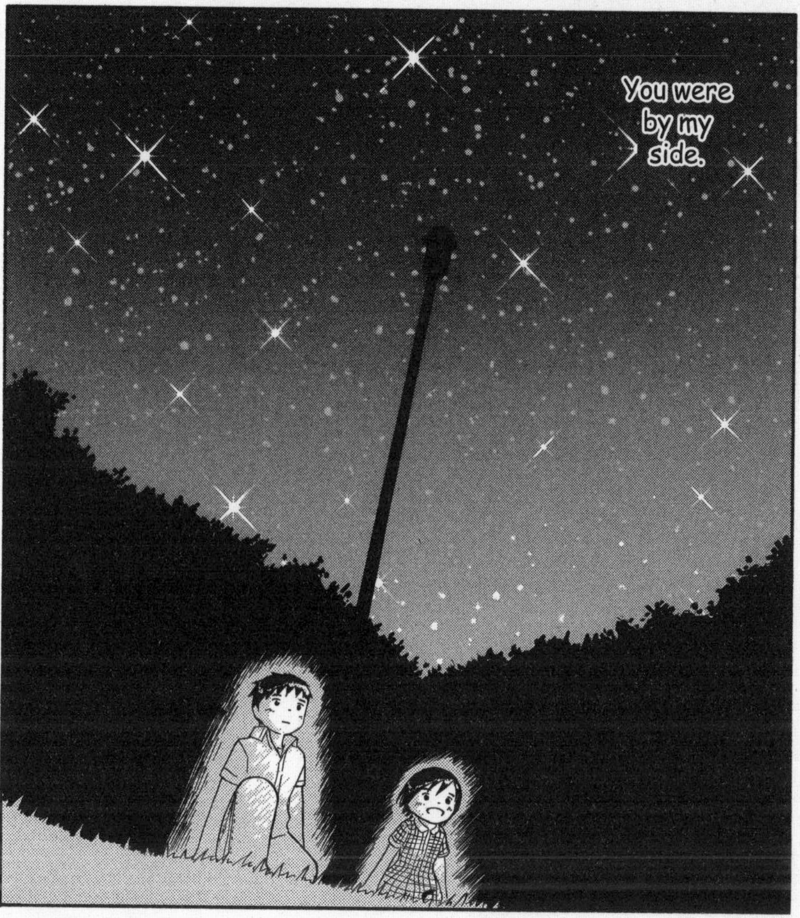
You were by my side.

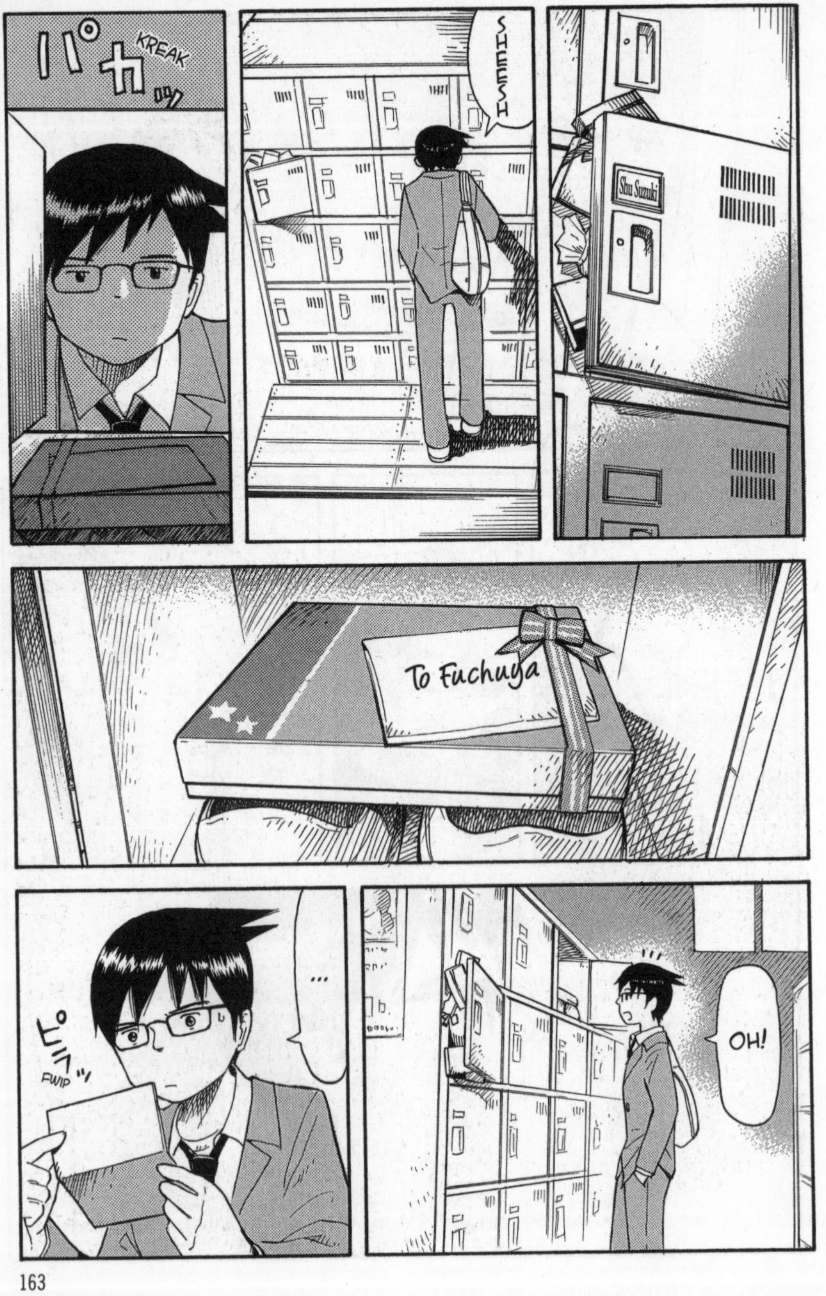
Shu Suzuki
SHEESH
パカッ
KREAK
To Fuchuya
OH!
...
ピラッ
FWIP

Fucchy
Happy Valentine's day♡
We made these ourselves!!
Kei & Asumi
IT'S JUST FRIEND CHOCOLATE!
DON'T GET MY HOPES UP!
パクッ
PLOMP
BITTER ...
ポリ…
CRUNCH

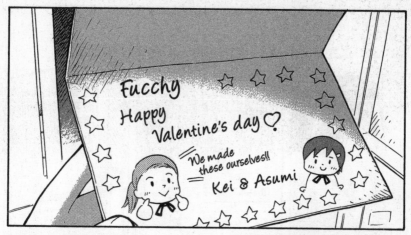

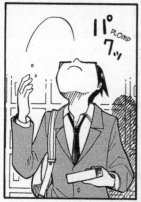

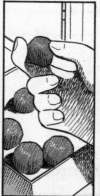

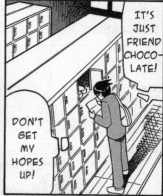

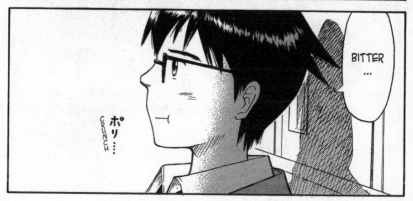

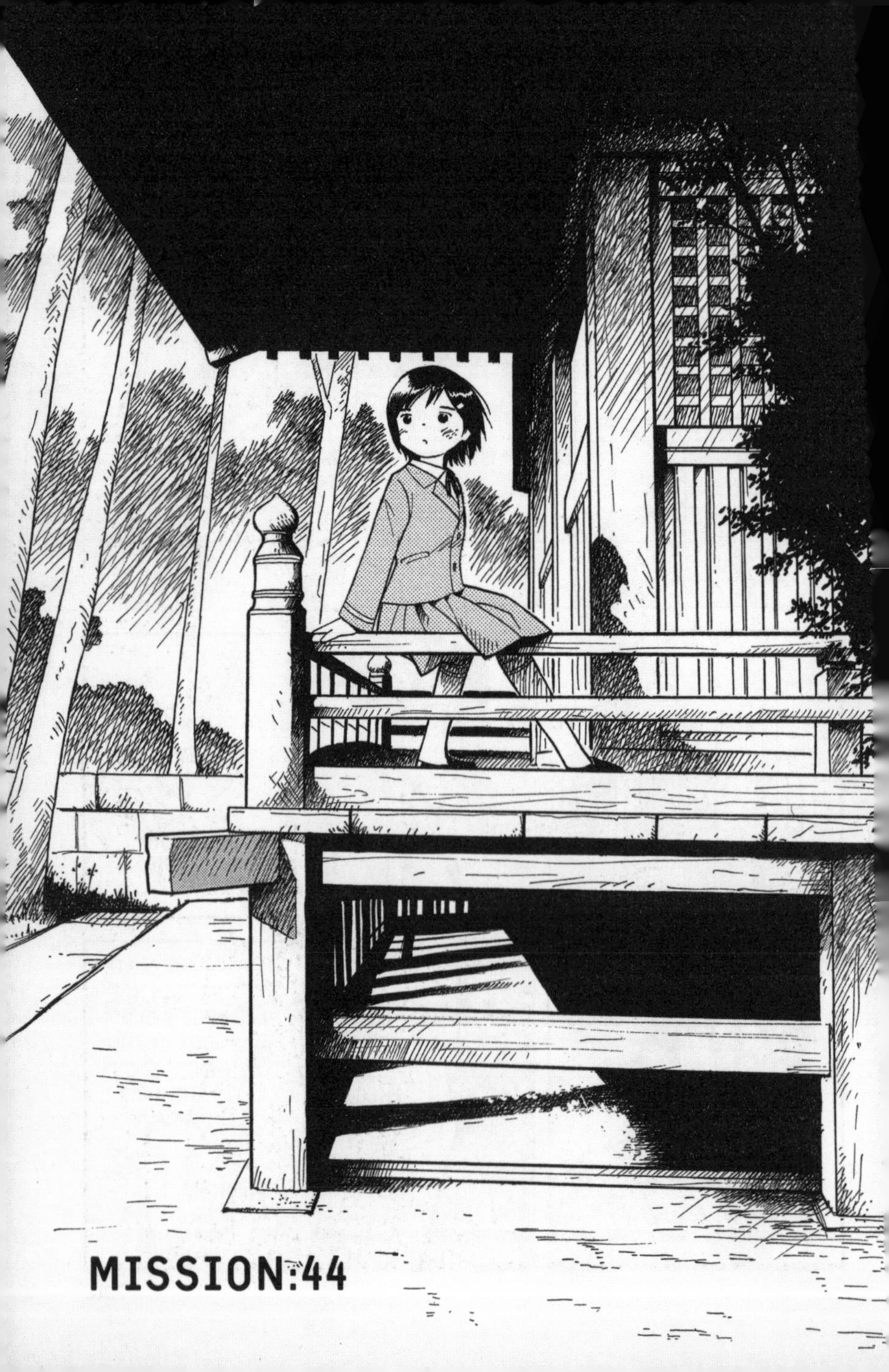

MISSION:44

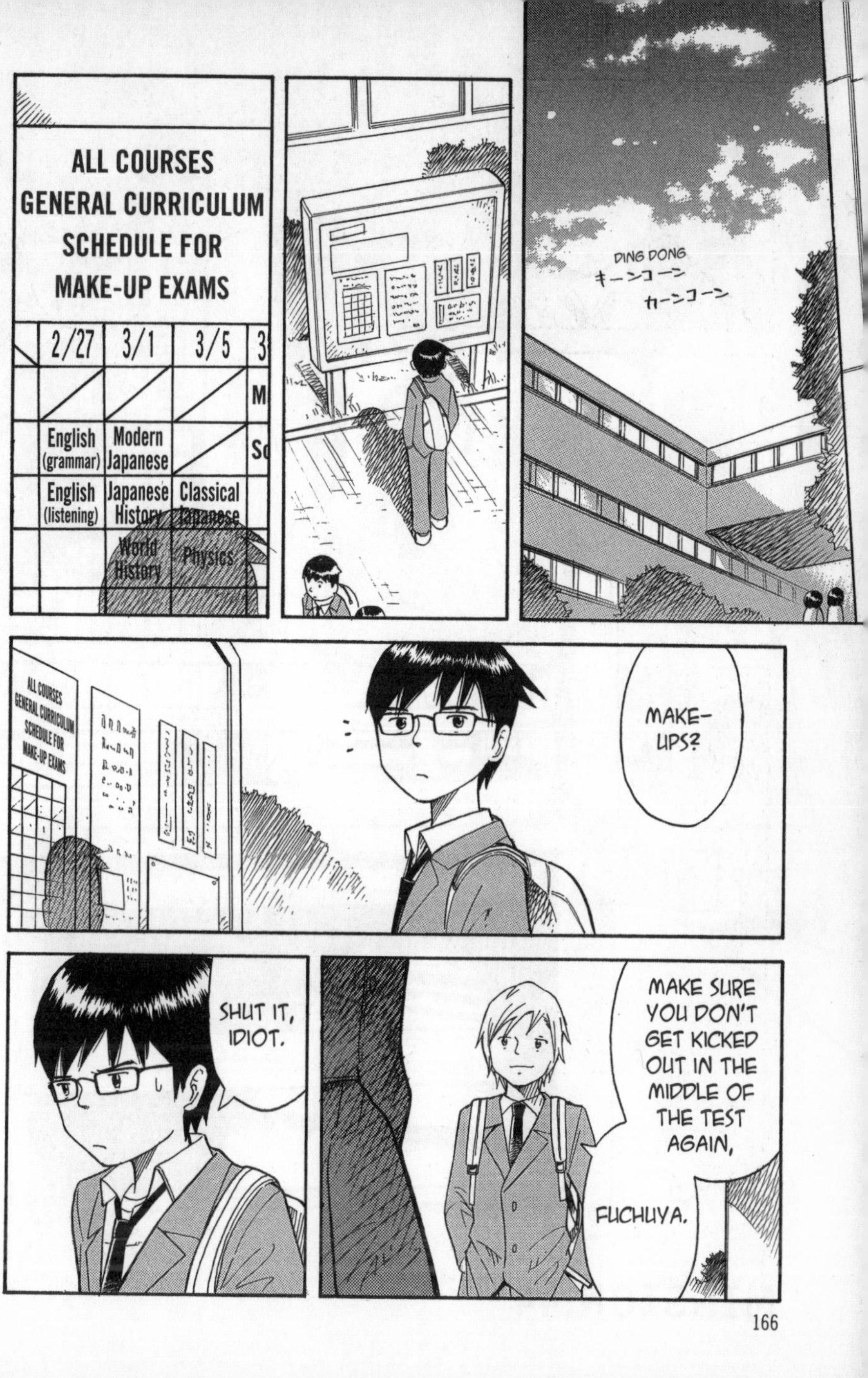
DING DONG
キーンコーン
カーンコーン
ALL COURSES
GENERAL CURRICULUM
SCHEDULE FOR
MAKE-UP EXAMS
2/27
3/1
3/5
English (grammar)
Modern Japanese
English (listening)
Japanese History
Classical Japanese
World History
Physics
ALL COURSES GENERAL CURRICULUM SCHEDULE FOR MAKE-UP EXAMS
MAKE-UPS?
MAKE SURE YOU DON'T GET KICKED OUT IN THE MIDDLE OF THE TEST AGAIN,
FUCHUYA.
SHUT IT, IDIOT.

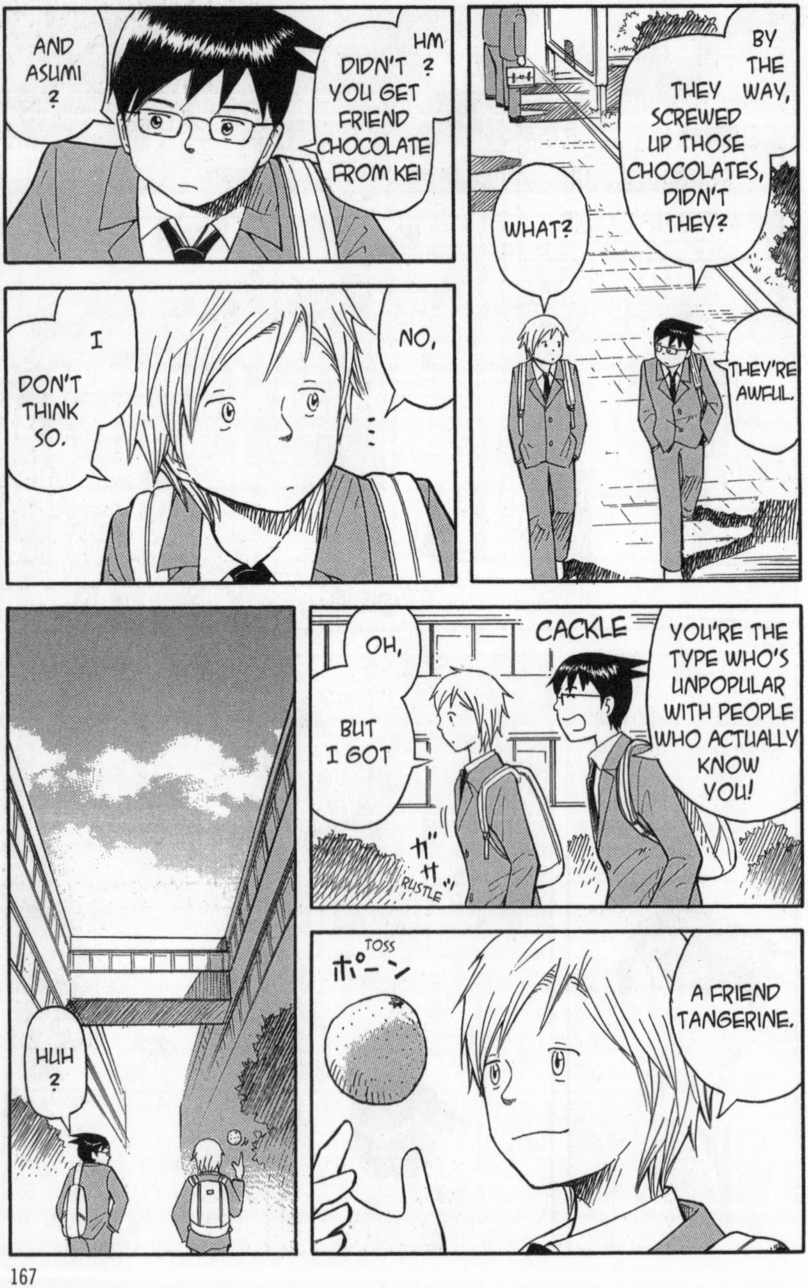
BY THE WAY, THEY SCREWED UP THOSE CHOCOLATES, DIDN'T THEY?
WHAT?
THEY'RE AWFUL.
HM? DIDN'T YOU GET FRIEND CHOCOLATE FROM KEI
AND ASUMI?
NO, ...
I DON'T THINK SO.
YOU'RE THE TYPE WHO'S UNPOPULAR WITH PEOPLE WHO ACTUALLY KNOW YOU!
CACKLE
OH,
BUT I GOT
ガサッ
RUSTLE
A FRIEND TANGERINE.
ポーン
TOSS
HUH?

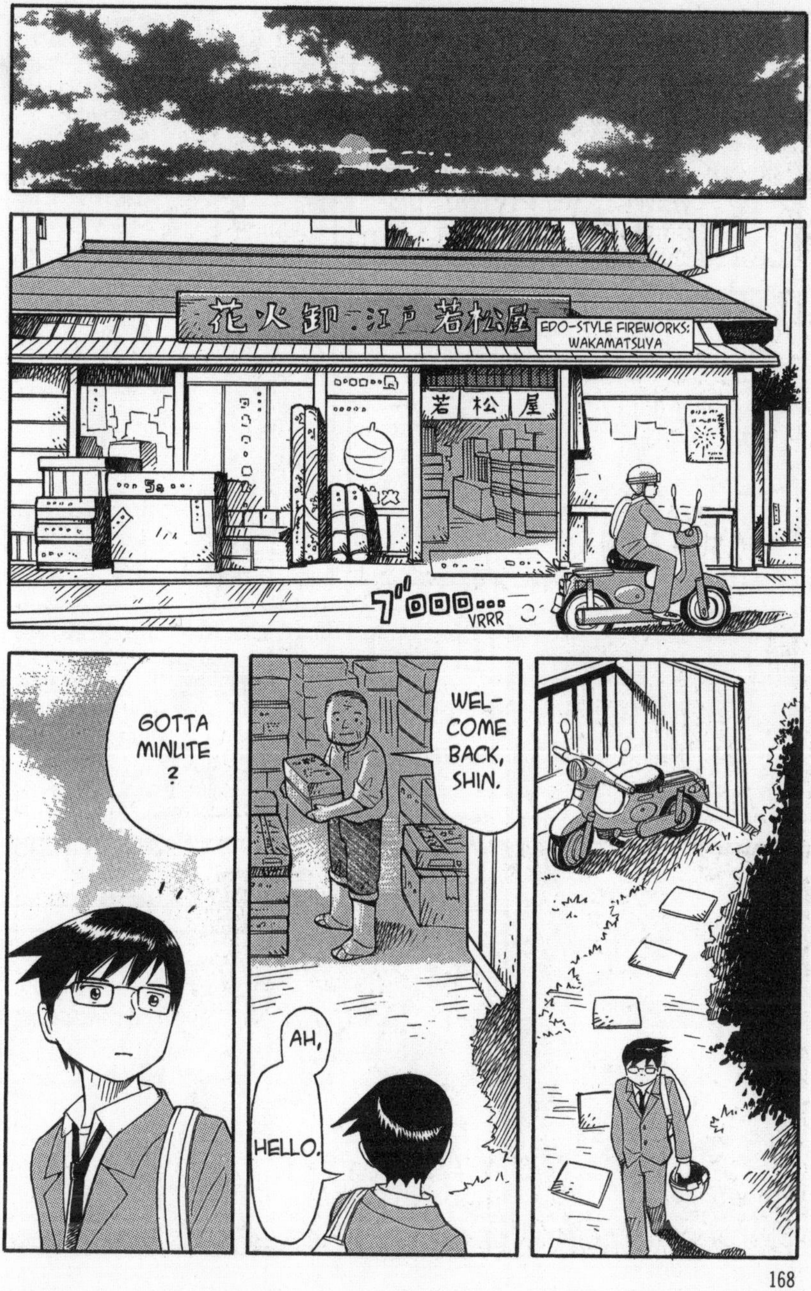
花火卸・江戸 若松屋
EDO-STYLE FIREWORKS: WAKAMATSUYA
若松屋
VRRR
WEL-COME BACK, SHIN.
AH,
HELLO.
GOTTA MINUTE?

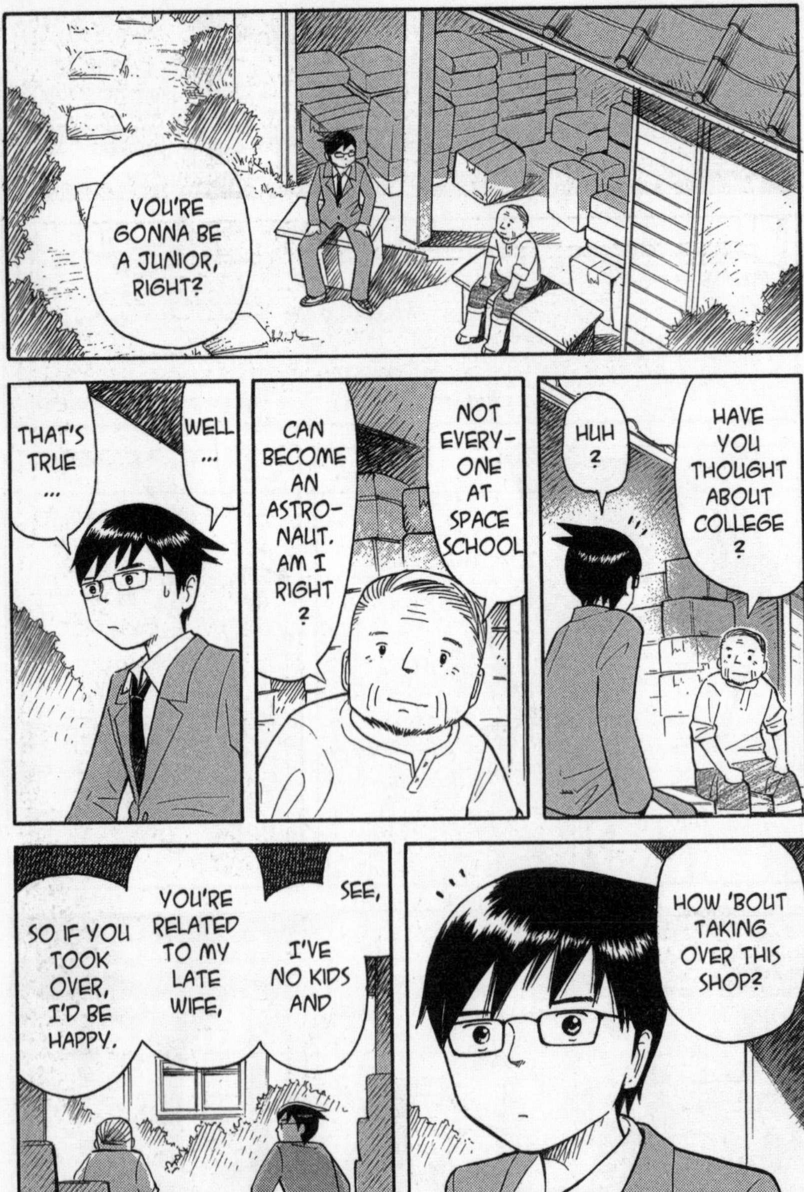
YOU'RE GONNA BE A JUNIOR, RIGHT?
HAVE YOU THOUGHT ABOUT COLLEGE?
HUH?
NOT EVERY-ONE AT SPACE SCHOOL
CAN BECOME AN ASTRO-NAUT. AM I RIGHT?
WELL ...
THAT'S TRUE ...
HOW 'BOUT TAKING OVER THIS SHOP?
SEE,
I'VE NO KIDS AND
YOU'RE RELATED TO MY LATE WIFE,
SO IF YOU TOOK OVER, I'D BE HAPPY.

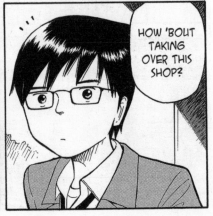

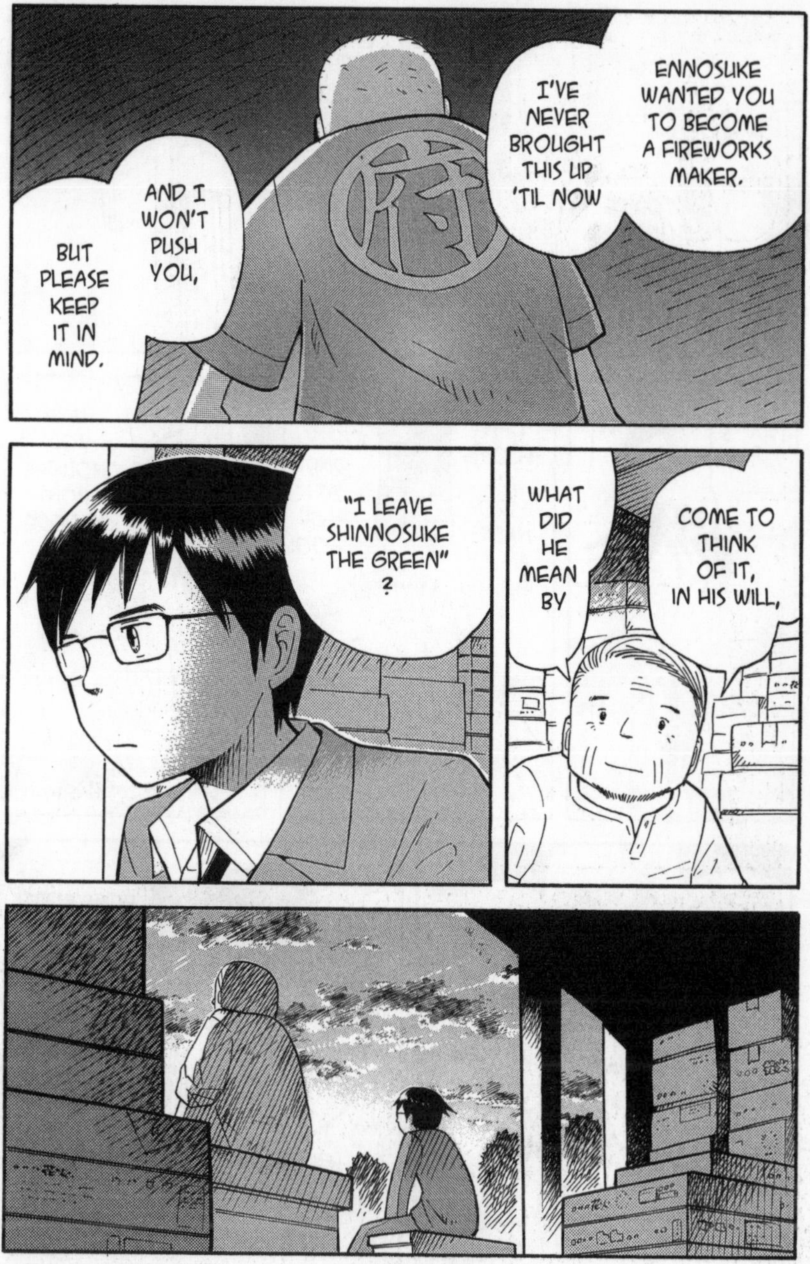
ENNOSUKE WANTED YOU TO BECOME A FIREWORKS MAKER.
I'VE NEVER BROUGHT THIS UP 'TIL NOW
AND I WON'T PUSH YOU,
BUT PLEASE KEEP IT IN MIND.
COME TO THINK OF IT, IN HIS WILL,
WHAT DID HE MEAN BY
"I LEAVE SHINNOSUKE THE GREEN" ?

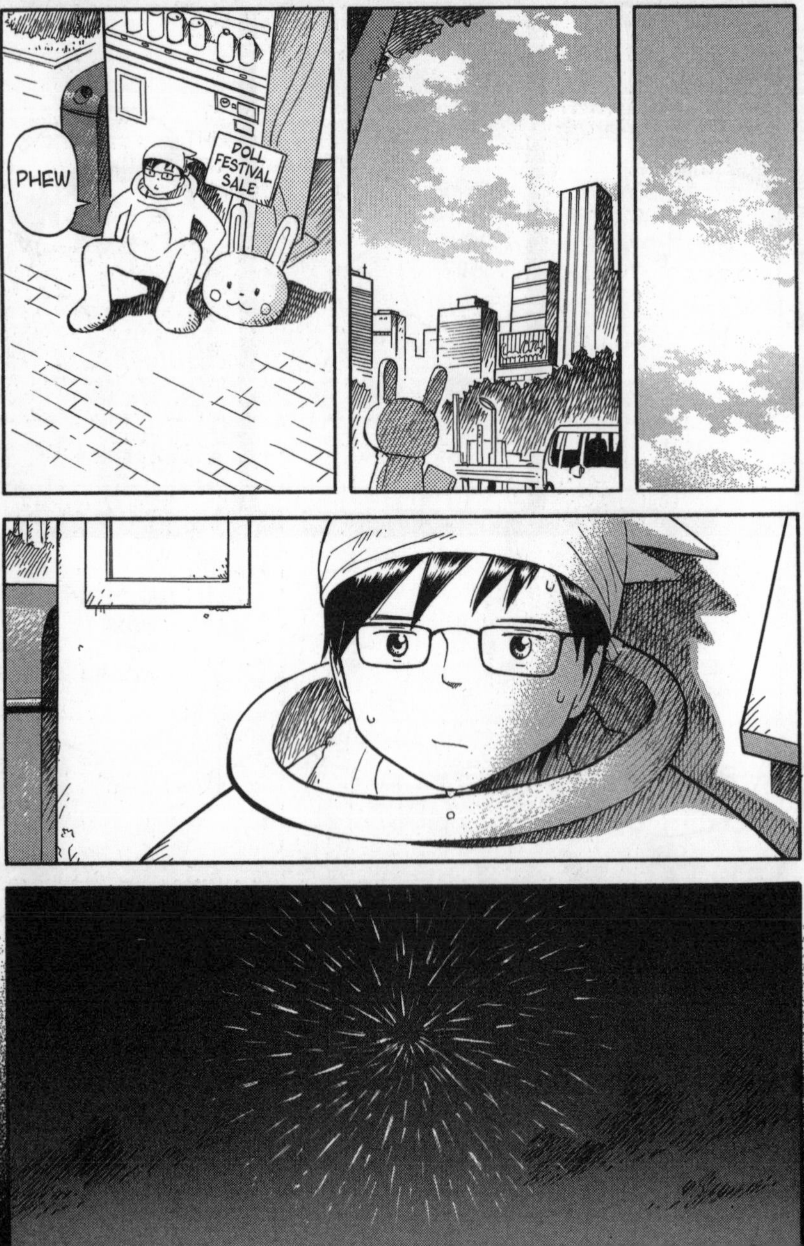
PHEW
DOLL FESTIVAL SALE

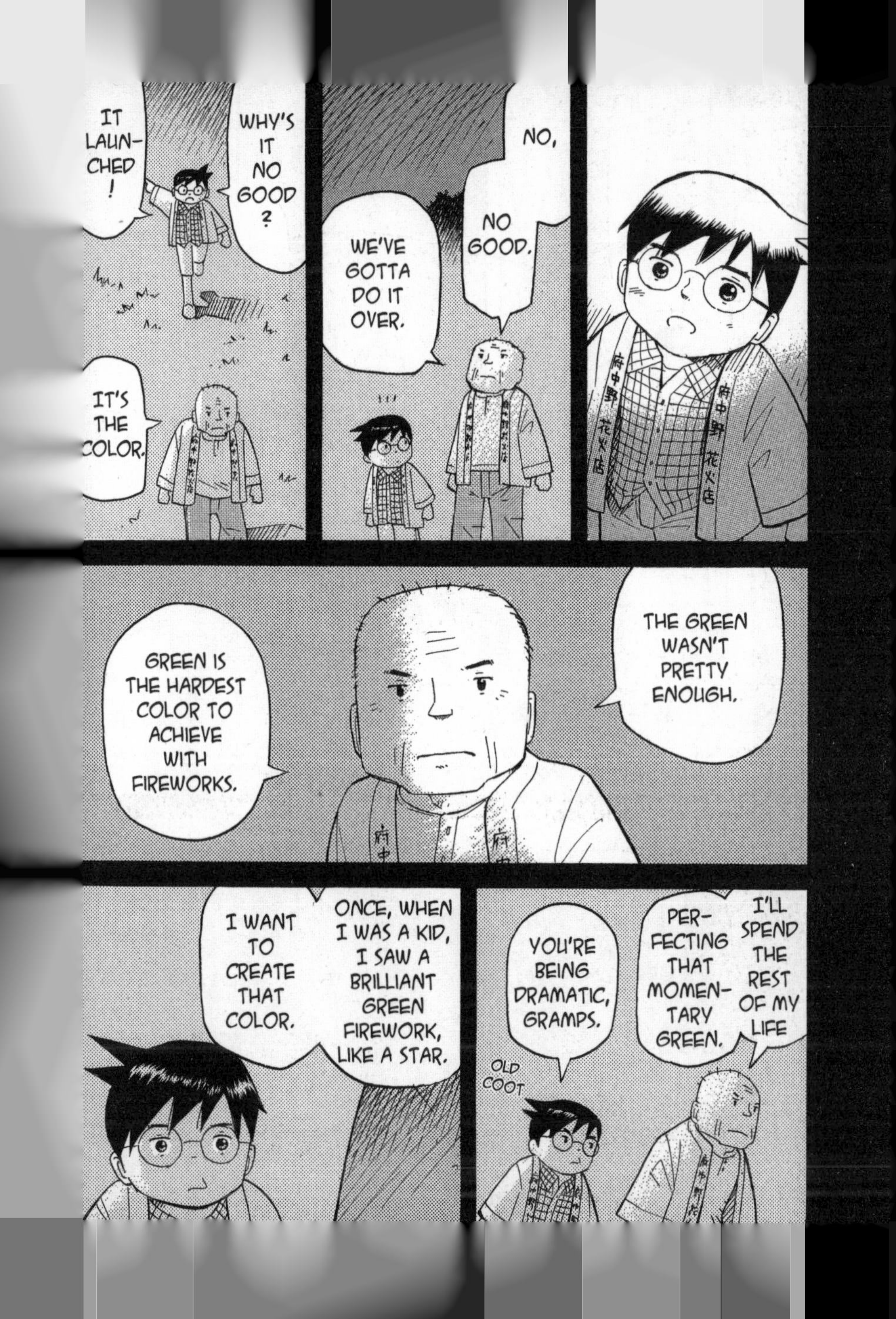
NO,
NO GOOD.
WE'VE GOTTA DO IT OVER.
WHY'S IT NO GOOD?
IT LAUN-CHED!
IT'S THE COLOR.
THE GREEN WASN'T PRETTY ENOUGH.
GREEN IS THE HARDEST COLOR TO ACHIEVE WITH FIREWORKS.
I'LL SPEND THE REST OF MY LIFE
PER-FECTING THAT MOMEN-TARY GREEN.
YOU'RE BEING DRAMATIC, GRAMPS.
OLD COOT
ONCE, WHEN I WAS A KID, I SAW A BRILLIANT GREEN FIREWORK, LIKE A STAR.
I WANT TO CREATE THAT COLOR.

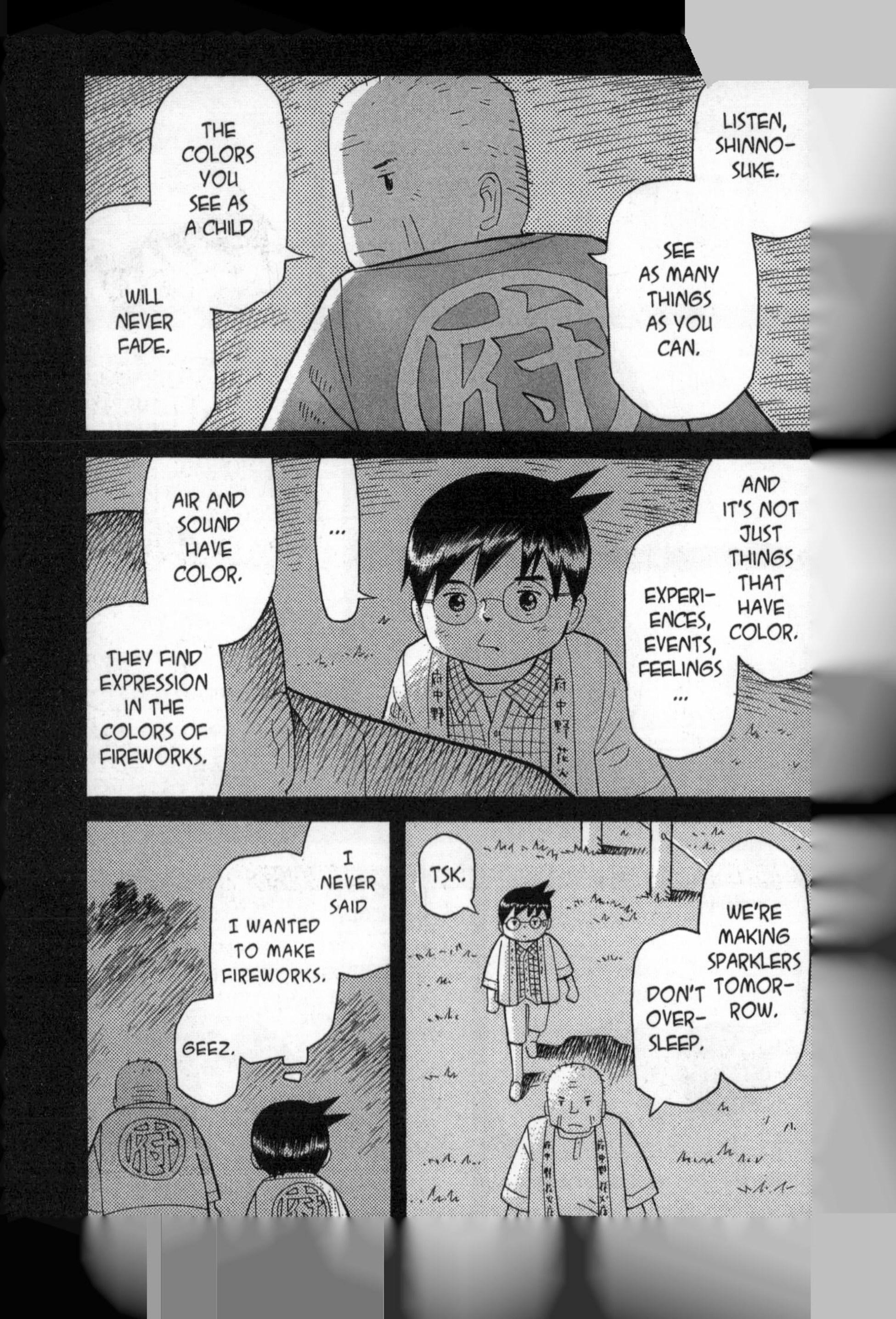
LISTEN, SHINNO-SUKE.
SEE AS MANY THINGS AS YOU CAN.
THE COLORS YOU SEE AS A CHILD
WILL NEVER FADE.
AND IT'S NOT JUST THINGS THAT HAVE COLOR.
EXPERI-ENCES, EVENTS, FEELINGS ...
...
AIR AND SOUND HAVE COLOR.
THEY FIND EXPRESSION IN THE COLORS OF FIREWORKS.
WE'RE MAKING SPARKLERS TOMOR-ROW.
DON'T OVER-SLEEP.
TSK.
I NEVER SAID
I WANTED TO MAKE FIREWORKS.
GEEZ.

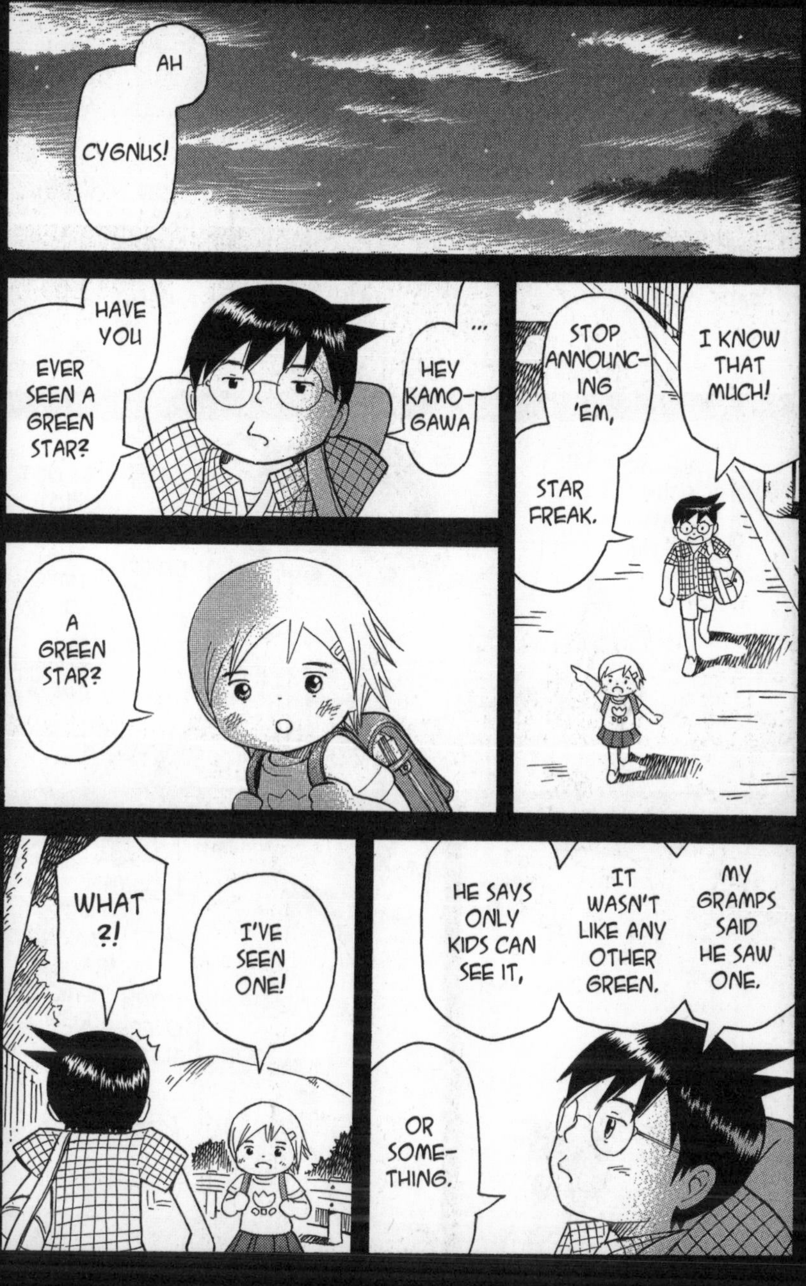
AH CYGNUS!
I KNOW THAT MUCH!
STOP ANNOUNCING-ING 'EM, STAR FREAK.
... HEY KAMO-GAWA
HAVE YOU EVER SEEN A GREEN STAR?
A GREEN STAR?
MY GRAMPS SAID HE SAW ONE.
IT WASN'T LIKE ANY OTHER GREEN.
HE SAYS ONLY KIDS CAN SEE IT,
OR SOME-THING.
I'VE SEEN ONE!
WHAT ?!

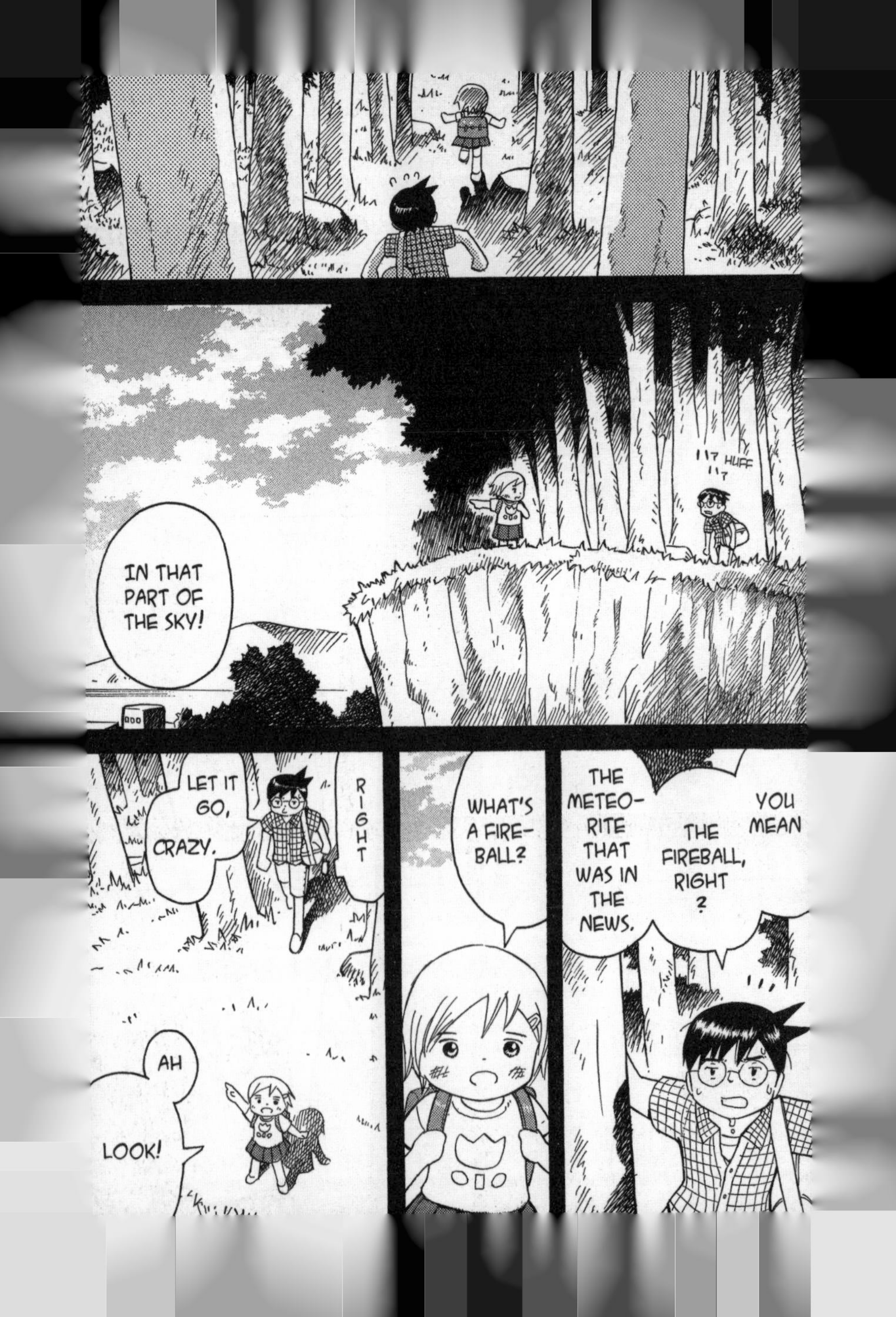
HUFF
IN THAT PART OF THE SKY!
YOU MEAN THE FIREBALL, RIGHT?
THE METEORITE THAT WAS IN THE NEWS.
WHAT'S A FIRE-BALL?
RIGHT
LET IT GO, CRAZY.
AH
LOOK!

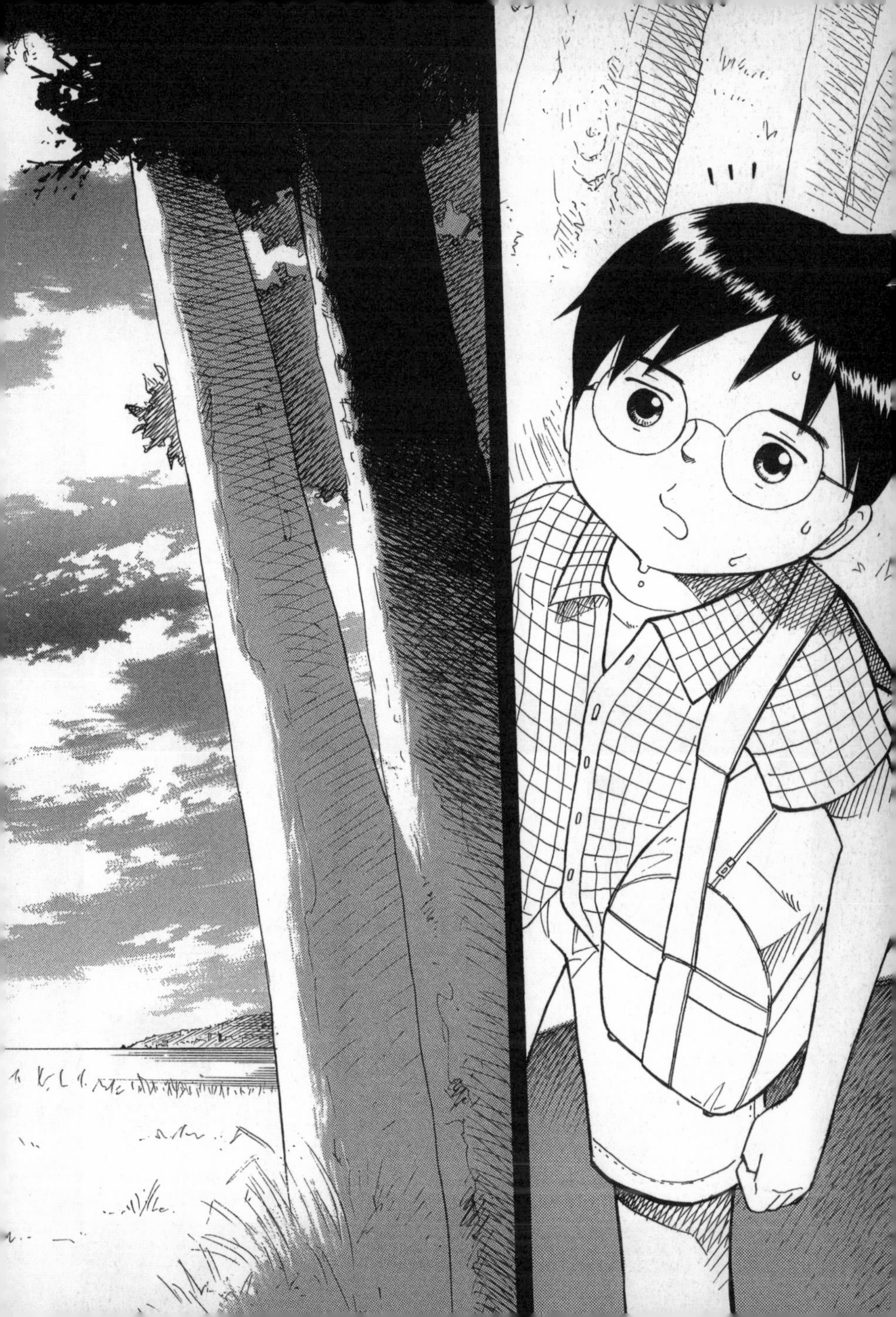

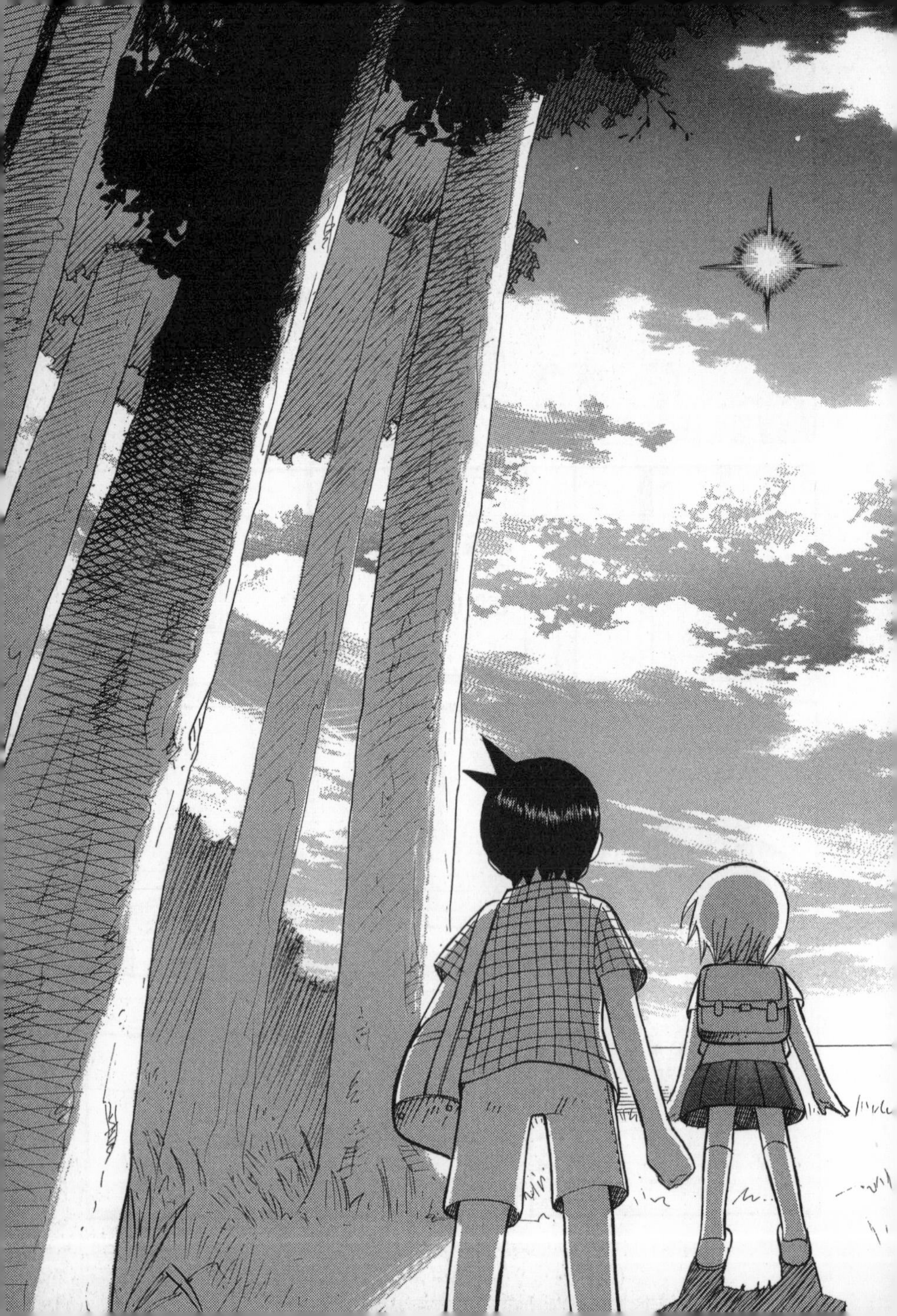

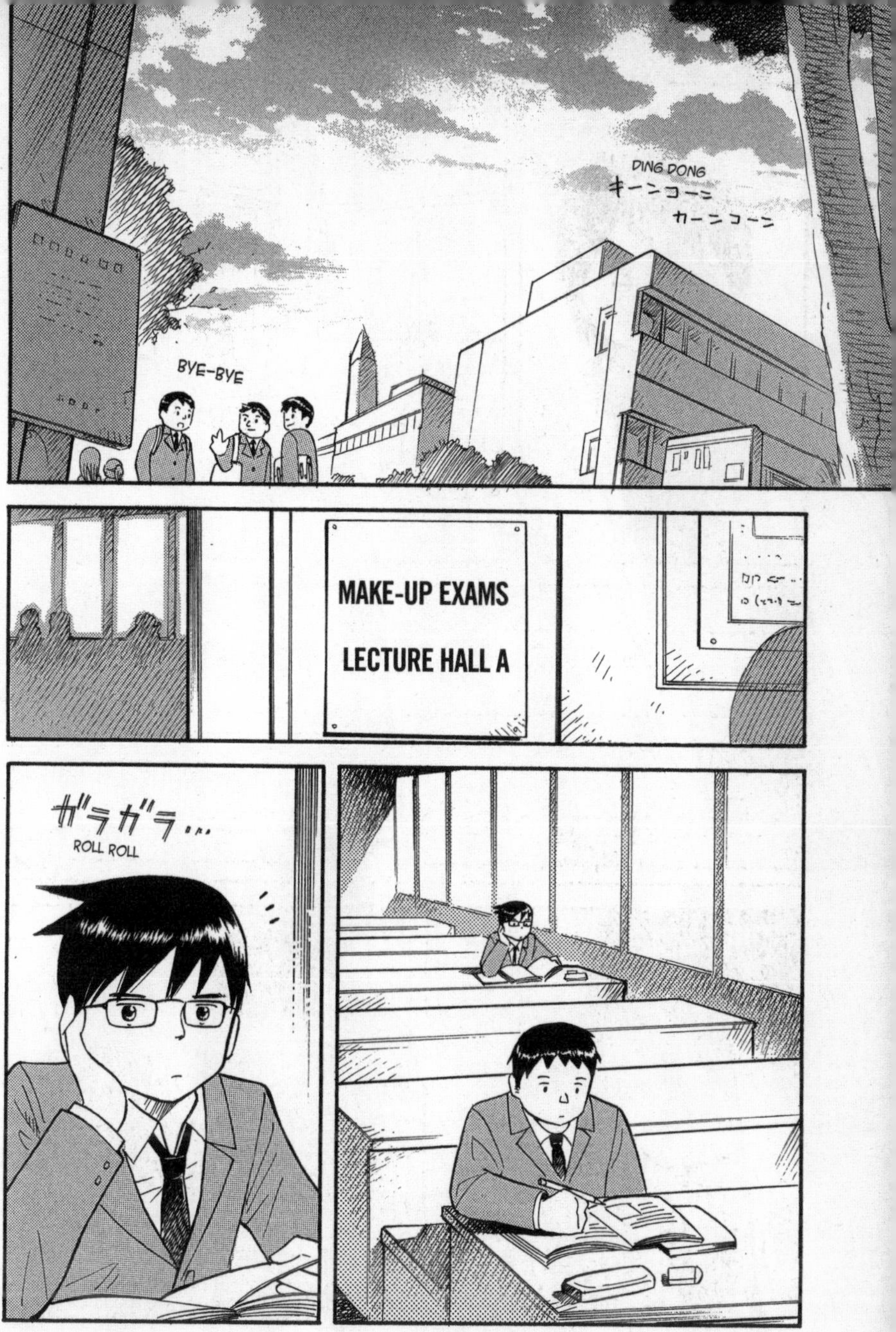
DING DONG
キーンコーン
カーンコーン
BYE-BYE
MAKE-UP EXAMS
LECTURE HALL A
ガラガラ…
ROLL ROLL

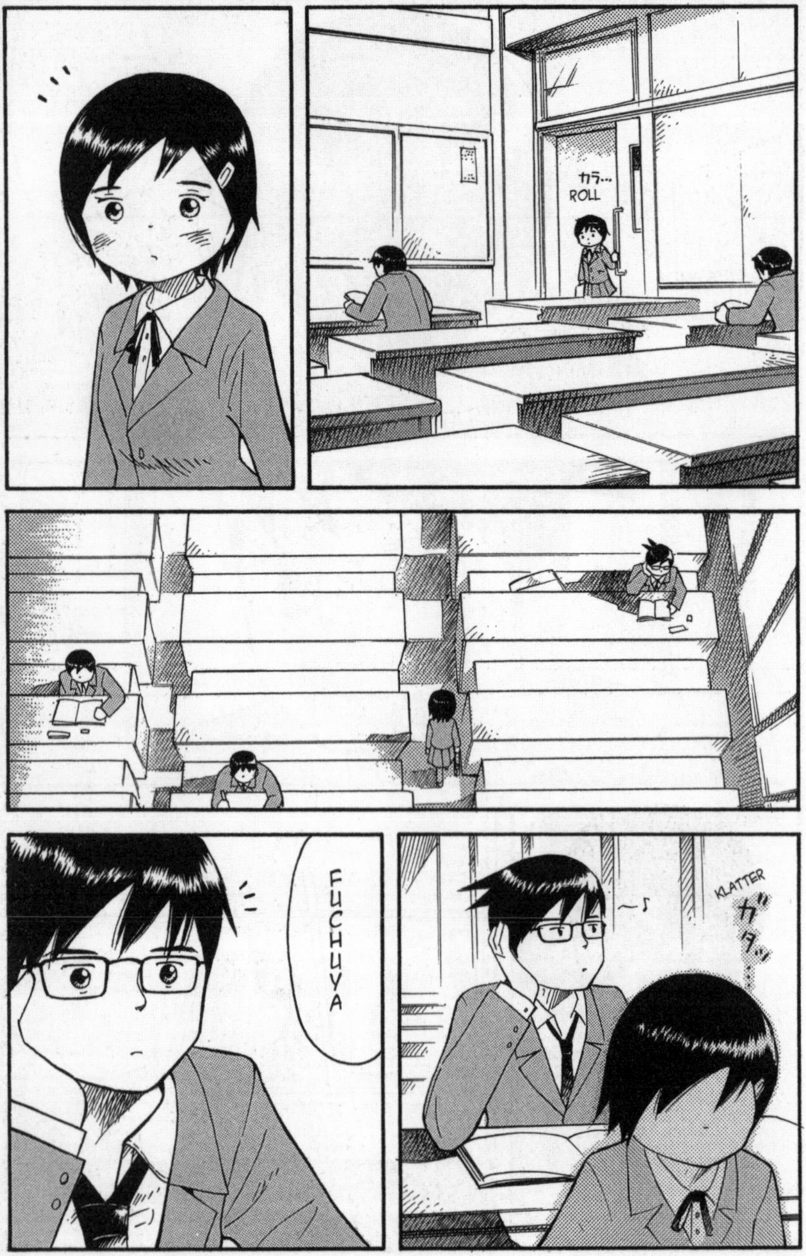
カラ…
ROLL
KLATTER
ガタッ
～♪
FUCHUYA

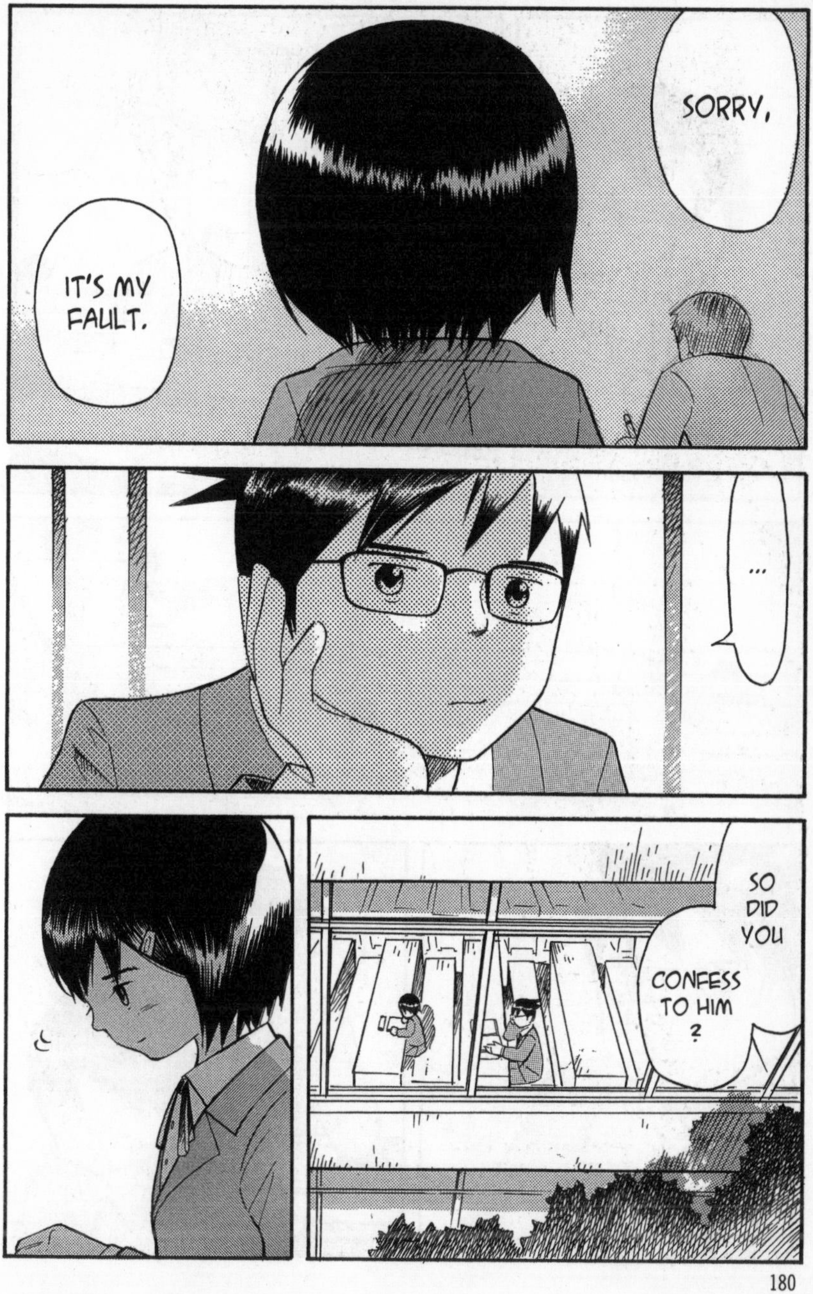
SORRY,
IT'S MY FAULT.
...
SO DID YOU CONFESS TO HIM ?

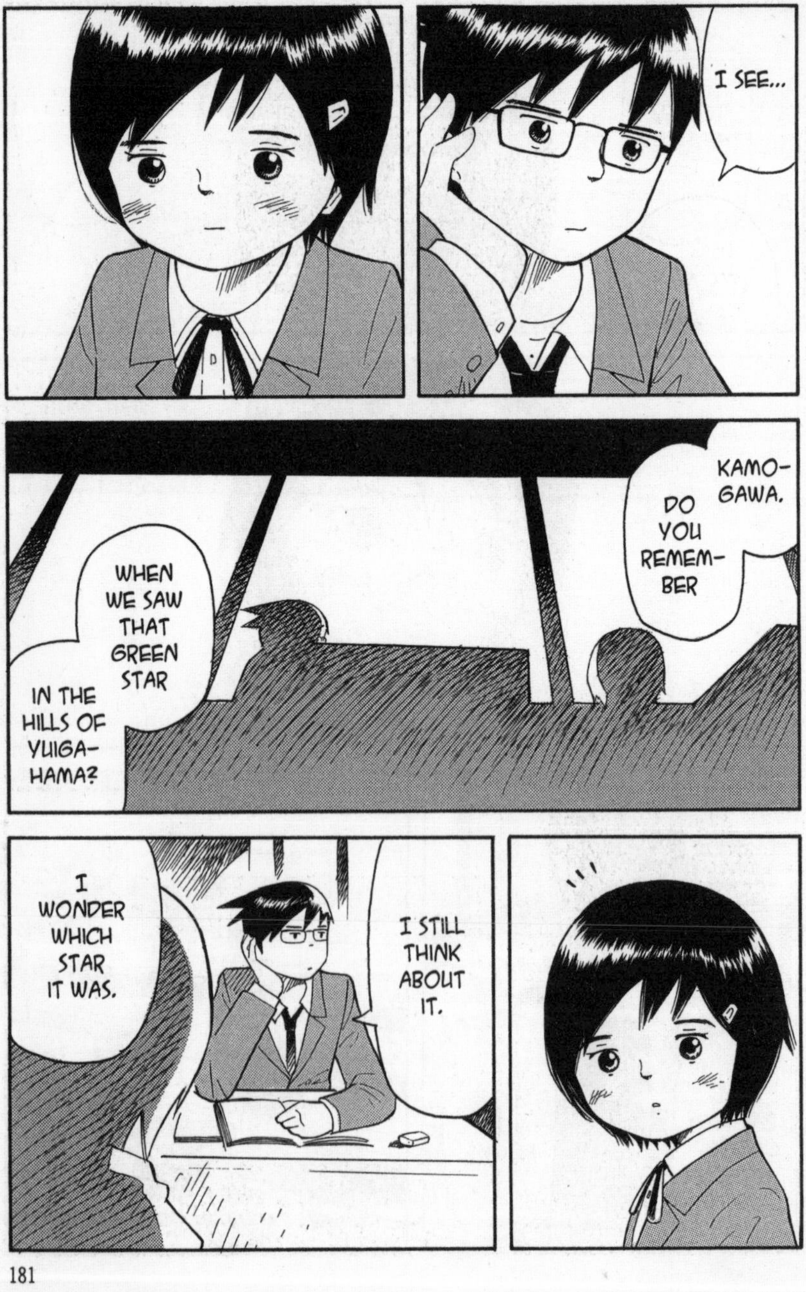
I SEE...
KAMO-GAWA. DO YOU REMEM-BER
WHEN WE SAW THAT GREEN STAR IN THE HILLS OF YUIGA-HAMA?
I STILL THINK ABOUT IT.
I WONDER WHICH STAR IT WAS.

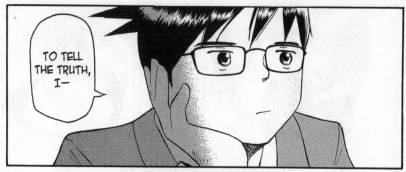

TO TELL THE TRUTH, I—
ガラッ
SLAM
OK, CLOSE YOUR BOOKS.
I'M PASSING OUT THE ANSWER FORMS.

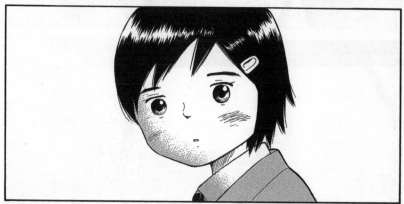

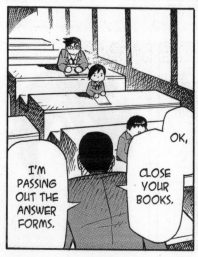

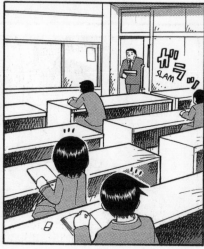

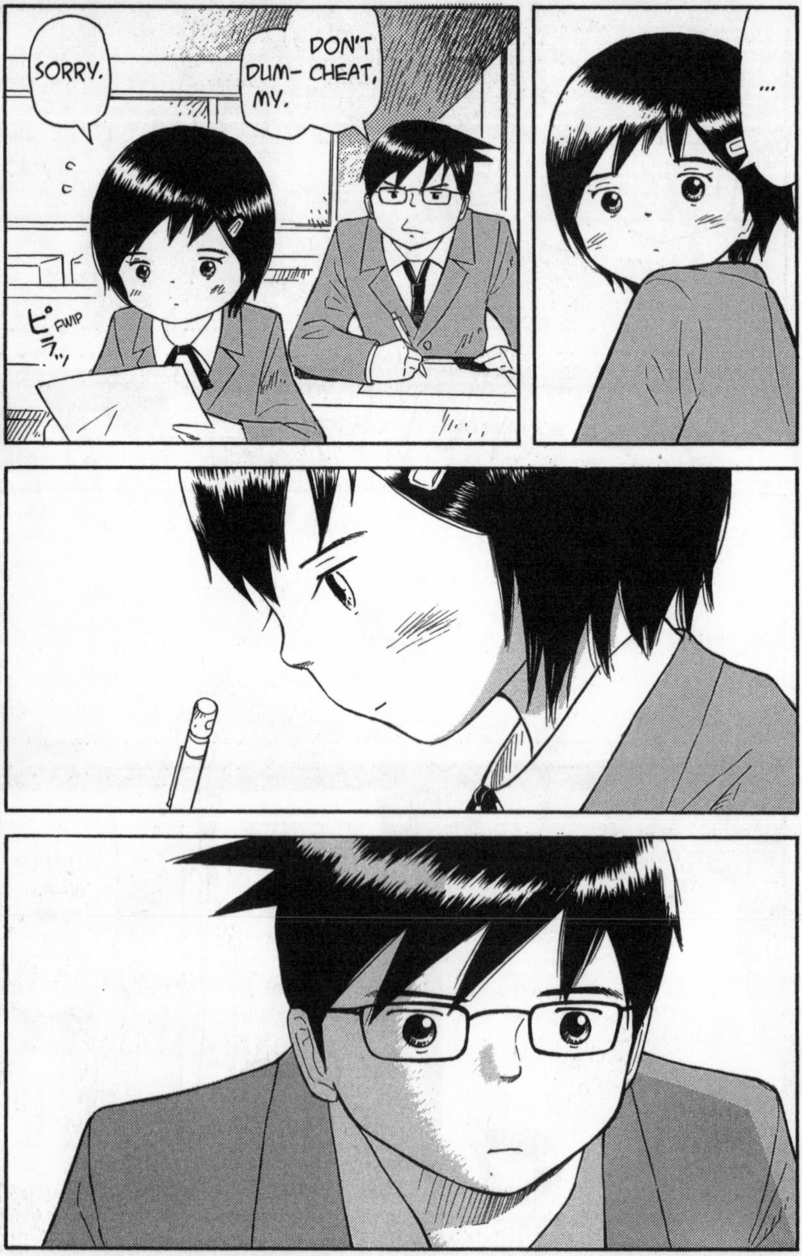
...
DON'T CHEAT, DUM-MY.
SORRY.
ピラッ FWIP

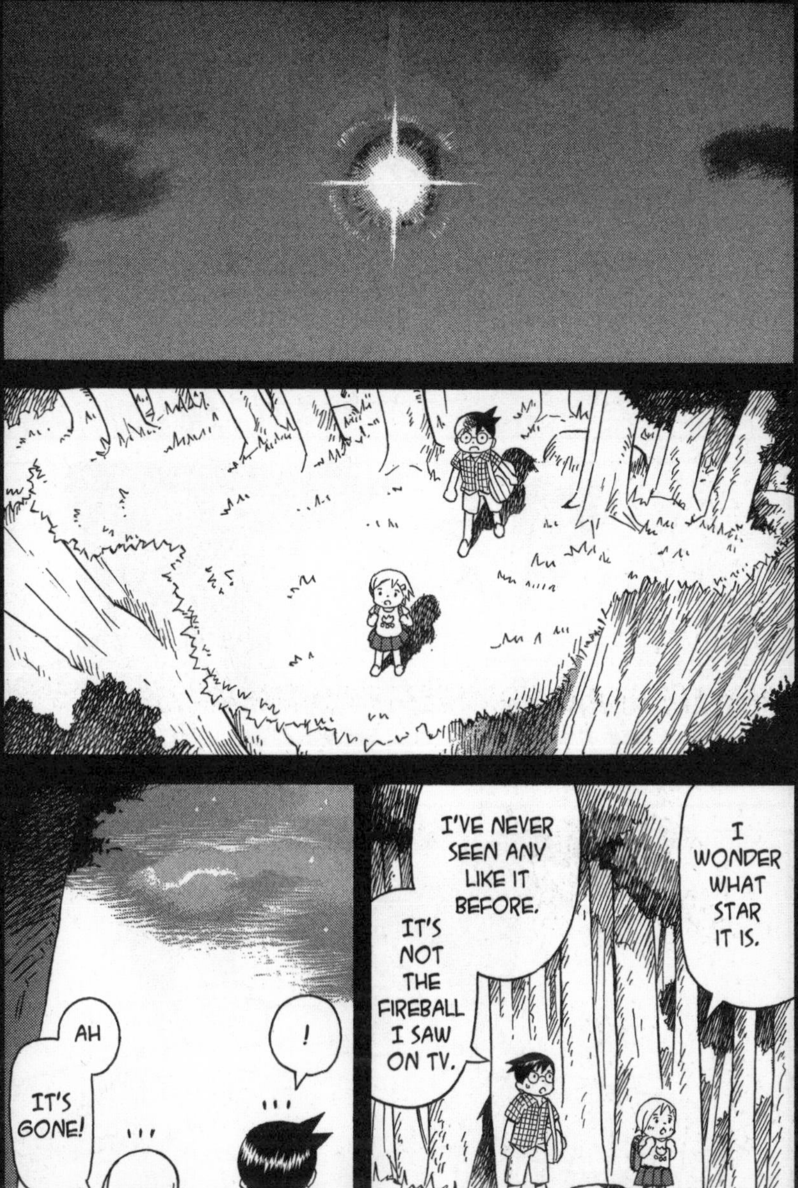
I WONDER WHAT STAR IT IS.
I'VE NEVER SEEN ANY LIKE IT BEFORE.
IT'S NOT THE FIREBALL I SAW ON TV.
!
AH
...
IT'S GONE!
...

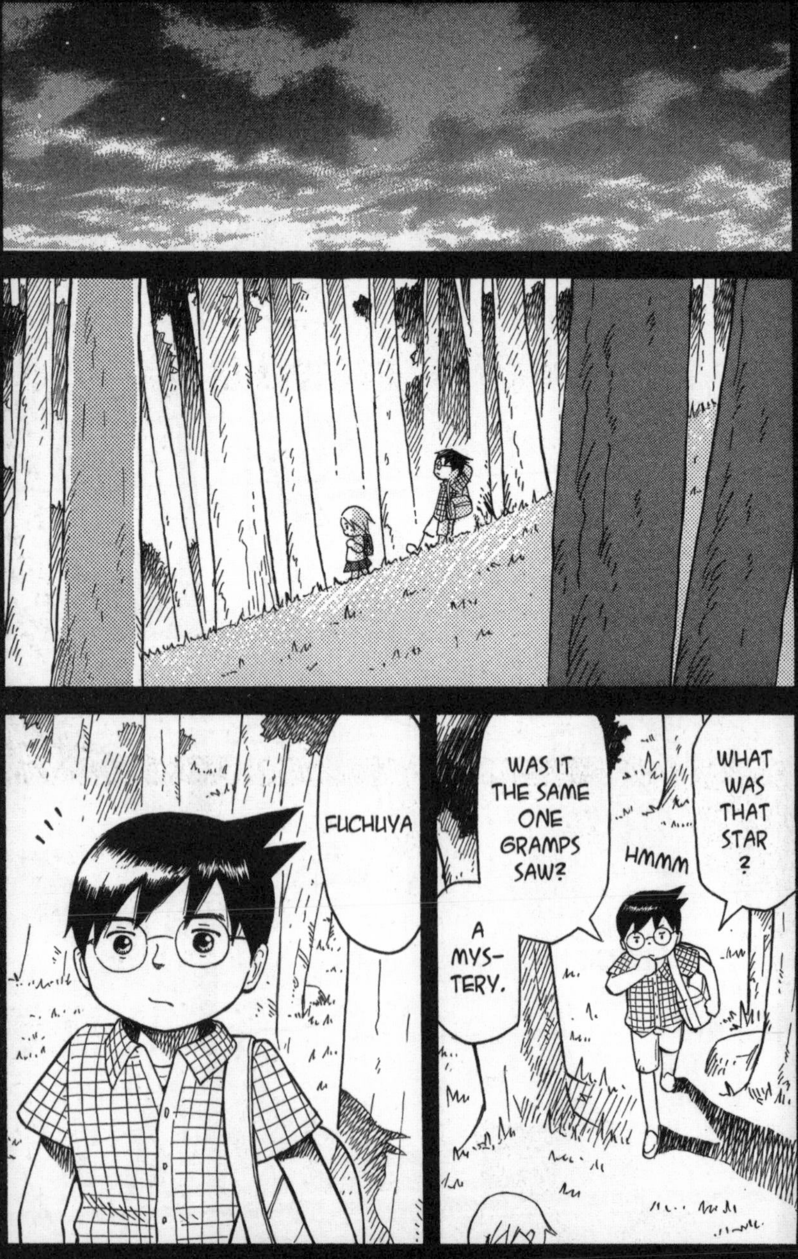
WHAT WAS THAT STAR?
WAS IT THE SAME ONE GRAMPS SAW?
HMMM
A MYS-TERY.
FUCHUYA

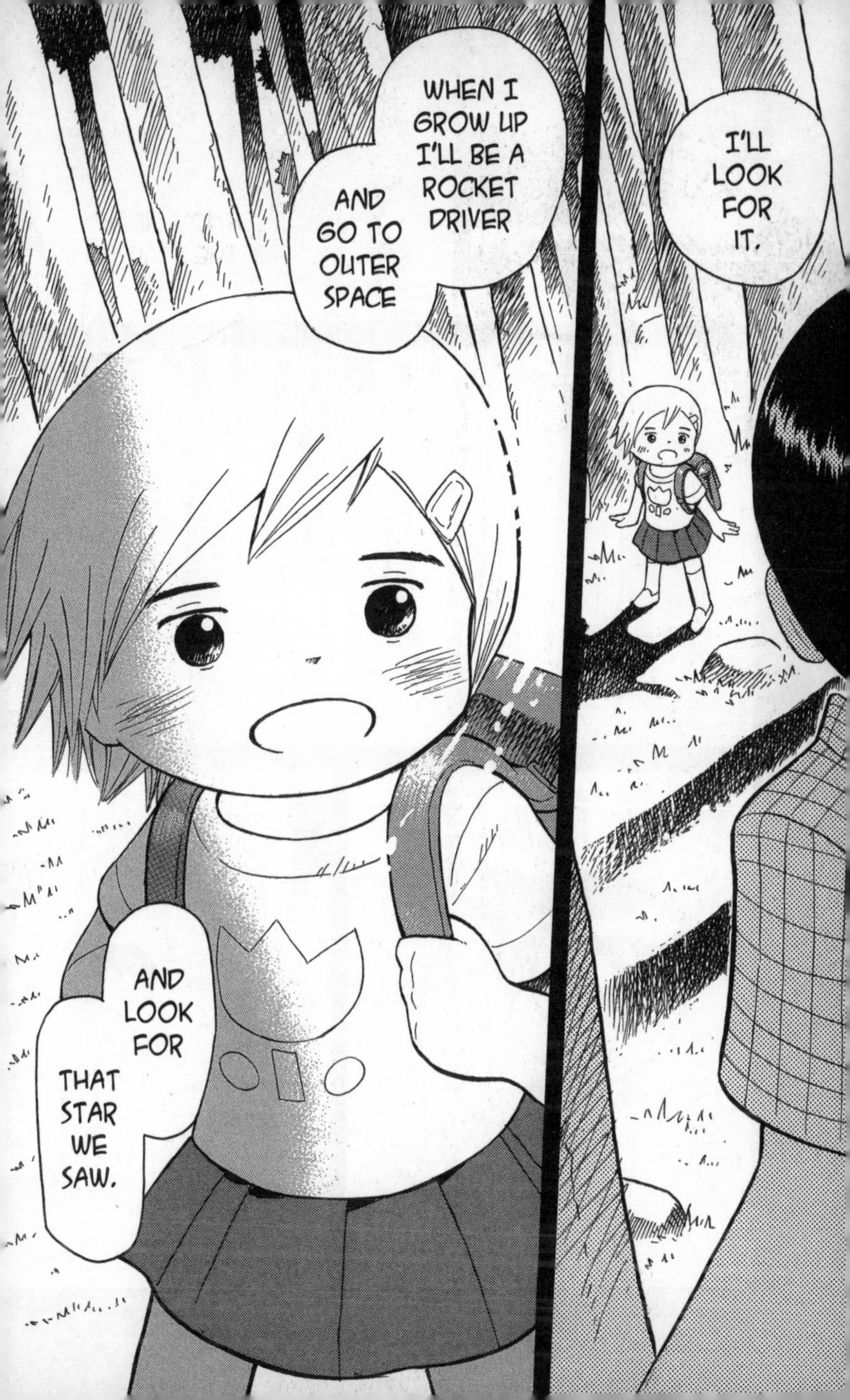
I'LL LOOK FOR IT.
WHEN I GROW UP I'LL BE A ROCKET DRIVER
AND GO TO OUTER SPACE
AND LOOK FOR THAT STAR WE SAW.

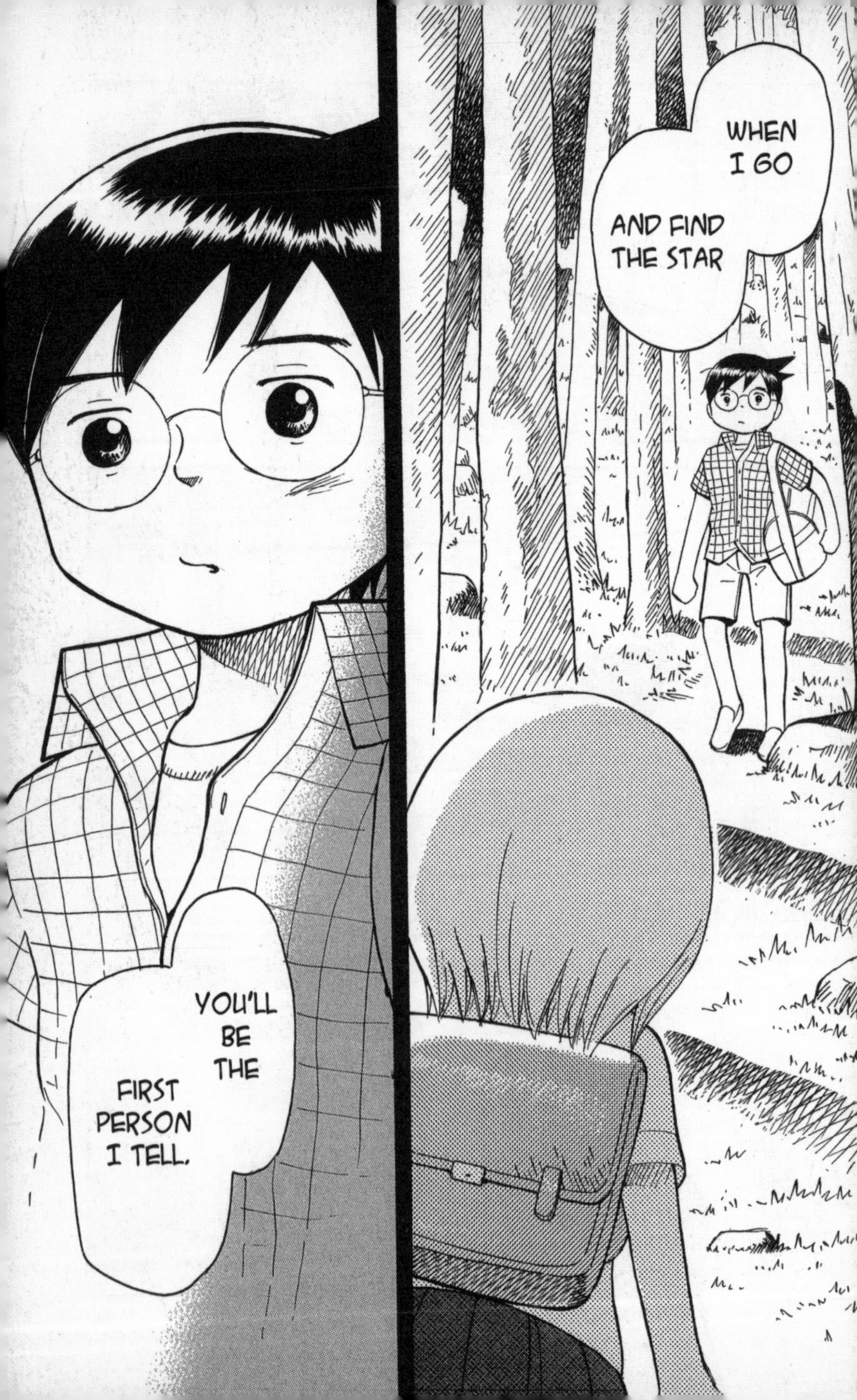
WHEN I GO
AND FIND THE STAR
YOU'LL BE THE FIRST PERSON I TELL.

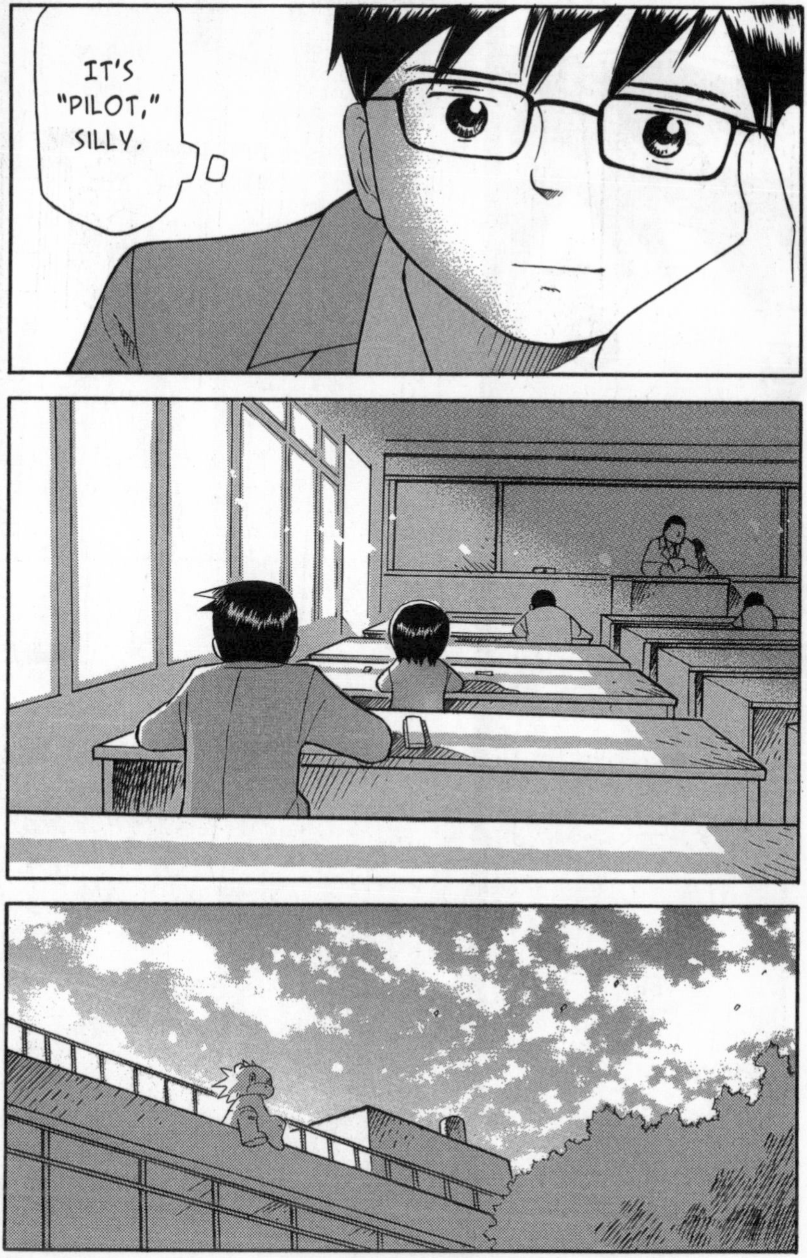
IT'S "PILOT," SILLY.

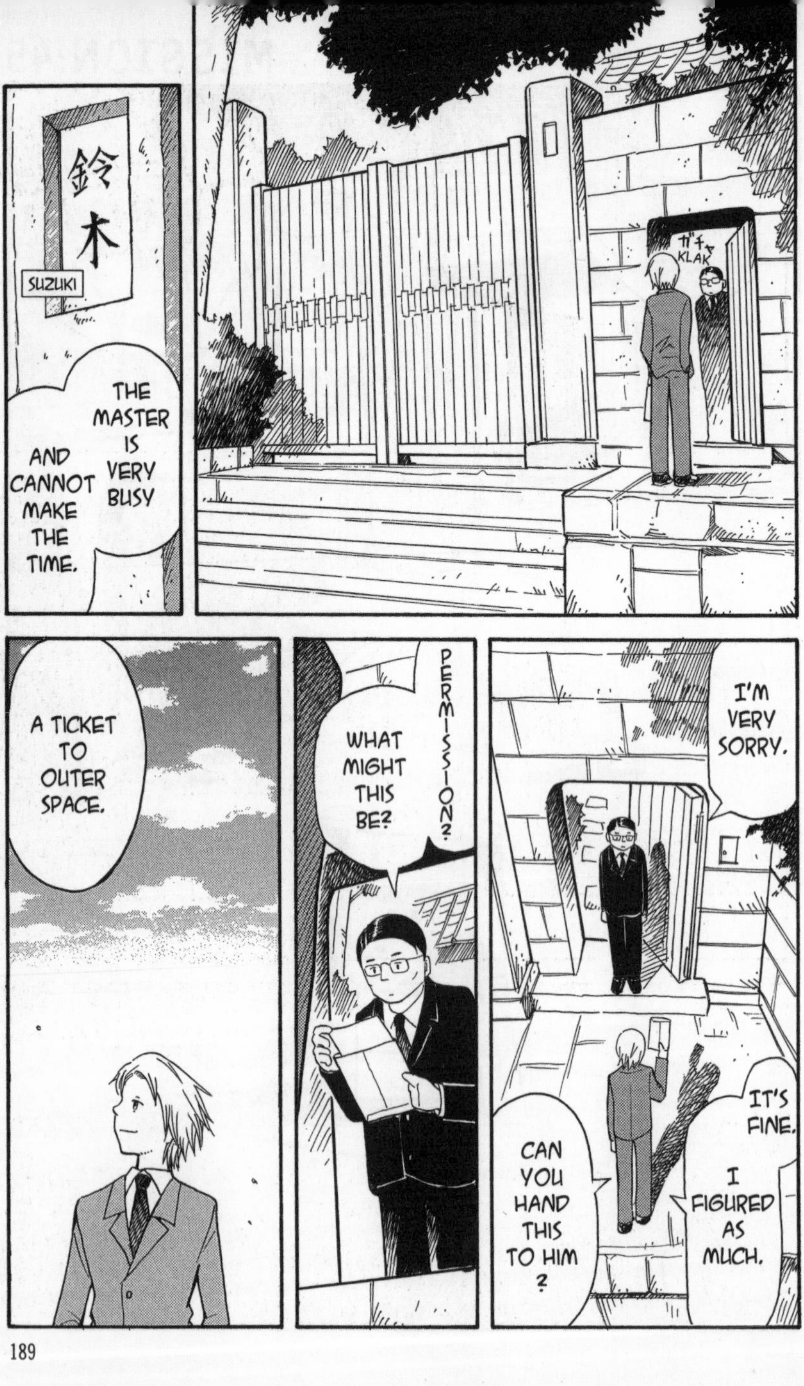
ガチャ
KLAK
鈴木
SUZUKI
THE MASTER IS VERY BUSY AND CANNOT MAKE THE TIME.
I'M VERY SORRY.
IT'S FINE. I FIGURED AS MUCH.
CAN YOU HAND THIS TO HIM?
PERMISSION?
WHAT MIGHT THIS BE?
A TICKET TO OUTER SPACE.

MISSION:45

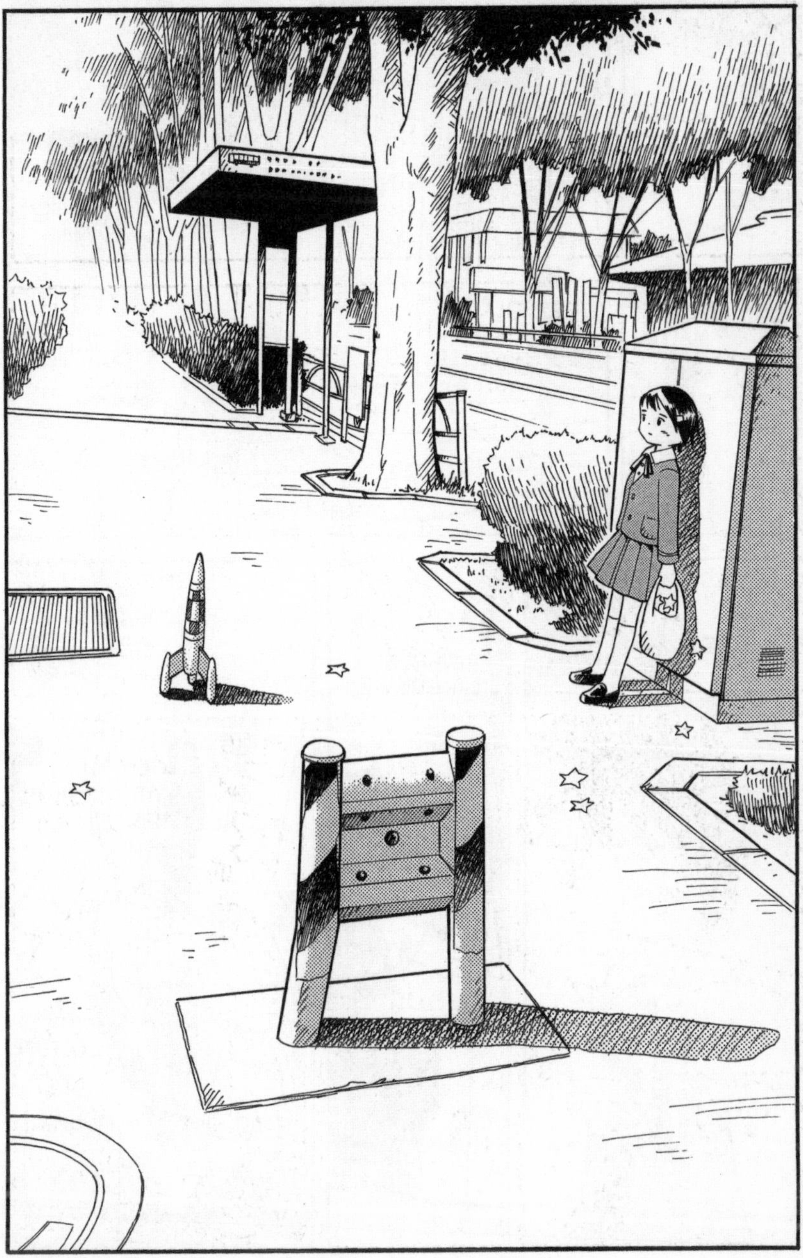

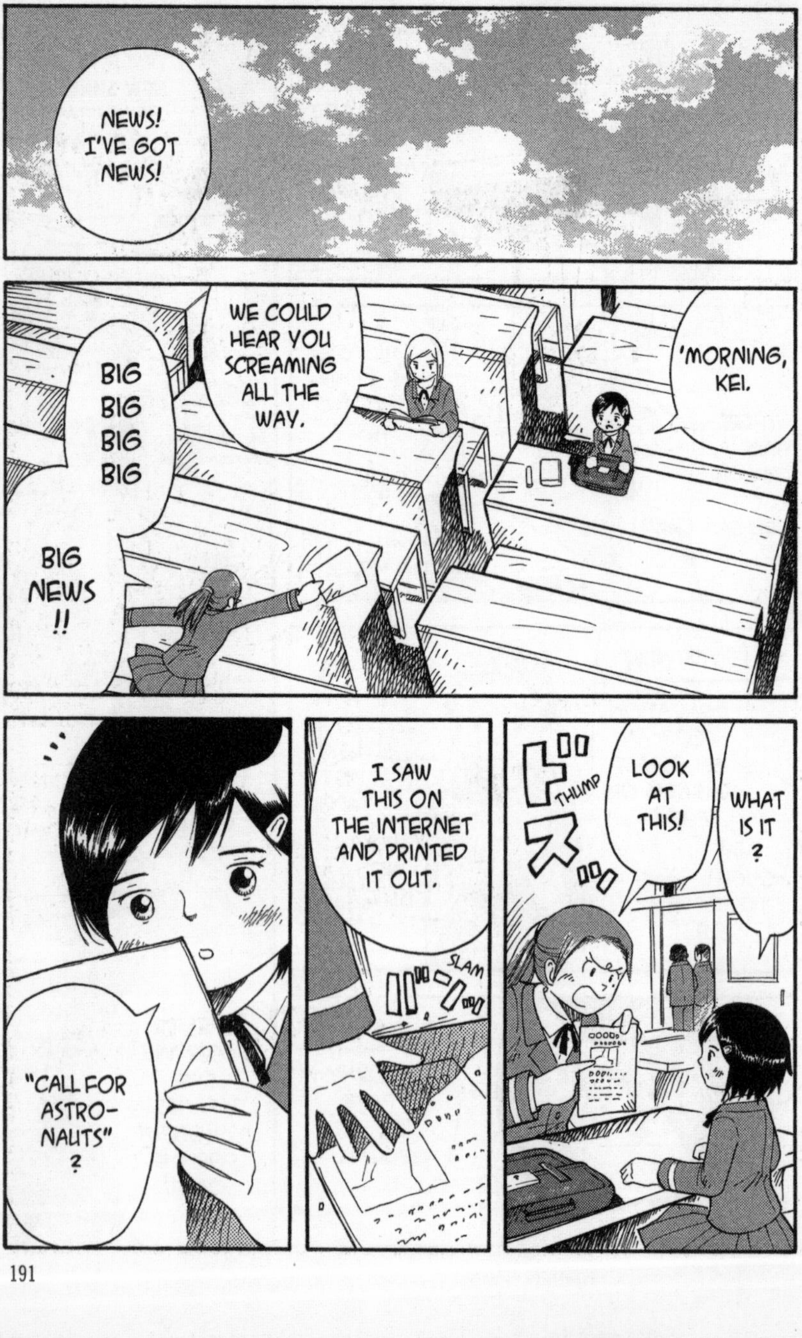
NEWS! I'VE GOT NEWS!
'MORNING, KEI.
WE COULD HEAR YOU SCREAMING ALL THE WAY.
BIG BIG BIG BIG
BIG NEWS !!
WHAT IS IT ?
LOOK AT THIS!
THUMP
I SAW THIS ON THE INTERNET AND PRINTED IT OUT.
SLAM
...
"CALL FOR ASTRO-NAUTS" ?

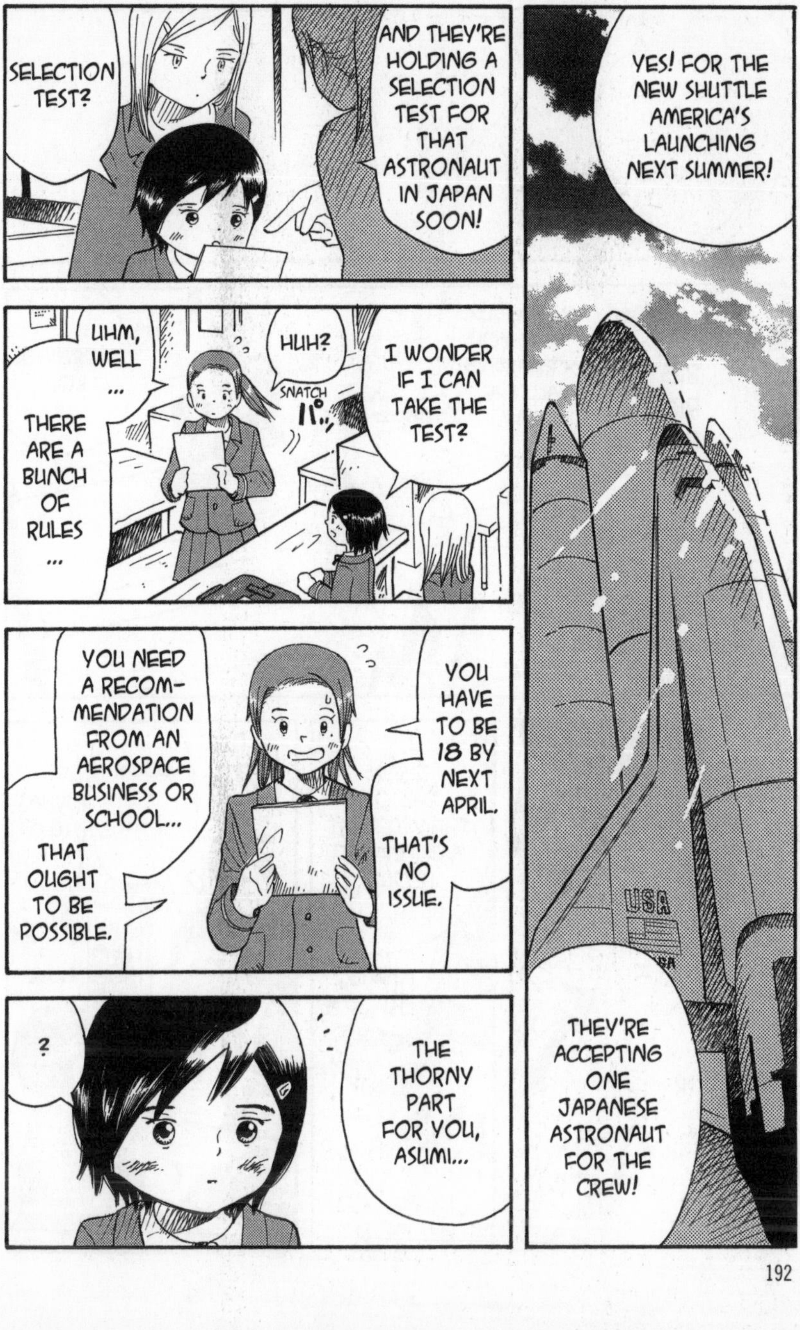
YES! FOR THE NEW SHUTTLE AMERICA'S LAUNCHING NEXT SUMMER!
USA
THEY'RE ACCEPTING ONE JAPANESE ASTRONAUT FOR THE CREW!
AND THEY'RE HOLDING A SELECTION TEST FOR THAT ASTRONAUT IN JAPAN SOON!
SELECTION TEST?
I WONDER IF I CAN TAKE THE TEST?
SNATCH
HUH?
UHM, WELL ...
THERE ARE A BUNCH OF RULES ...
YOU HAVE TO BE 18 BY NEXT APRIL.
THAT'S NO ISSUE.
YOU NEED A RECOMMENDATION FROM AN AEROSPACE BUSINESS OR SCHOOL...
THAT OUGHT TO BE POSSIBLE.
THE THORNY PART FOR YOU, ASUMI...
?

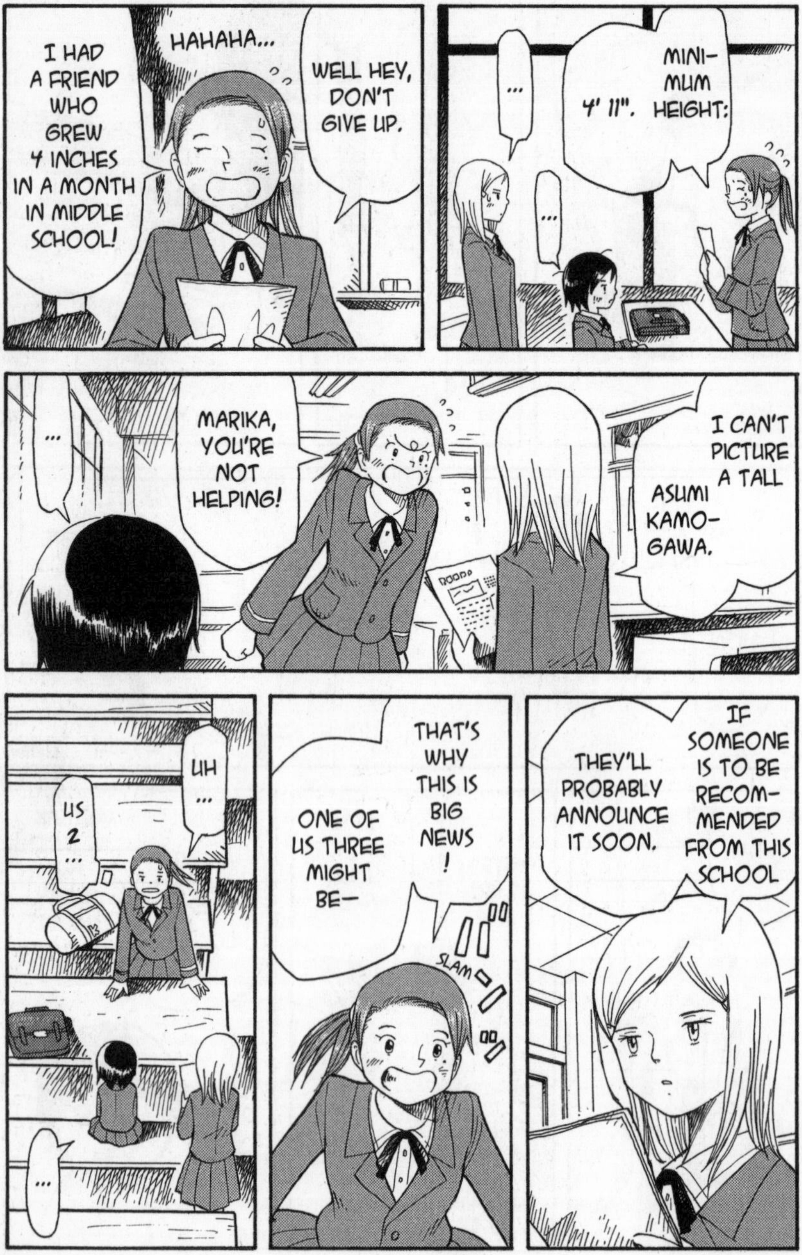

MINI-MUM HEIGHT:
4' 11".
...
...
WELL HEY, DON'T GIVE UP.
HAHAHA...
I HAD A FRIEND WHO GREW 4 INCHES IN A MONTH IN MIDDLE SCHOOL!
I CAN'T PICTURE A TALL
ASUMI KAMO-GAWA.
MARIKA, YOU'RE NOT HELPING!
...
IF SOMEONE IS TO BE RECOM-MENDED FROM THIS SCHOOL
THEY'LL PROBABLY ANNOUNCE IT SOON.
THAT'S WHY THIS IS BIG NEWS!
ONE OF US THREE MIGHT BE—
SLAM
UH...
US 2...
...

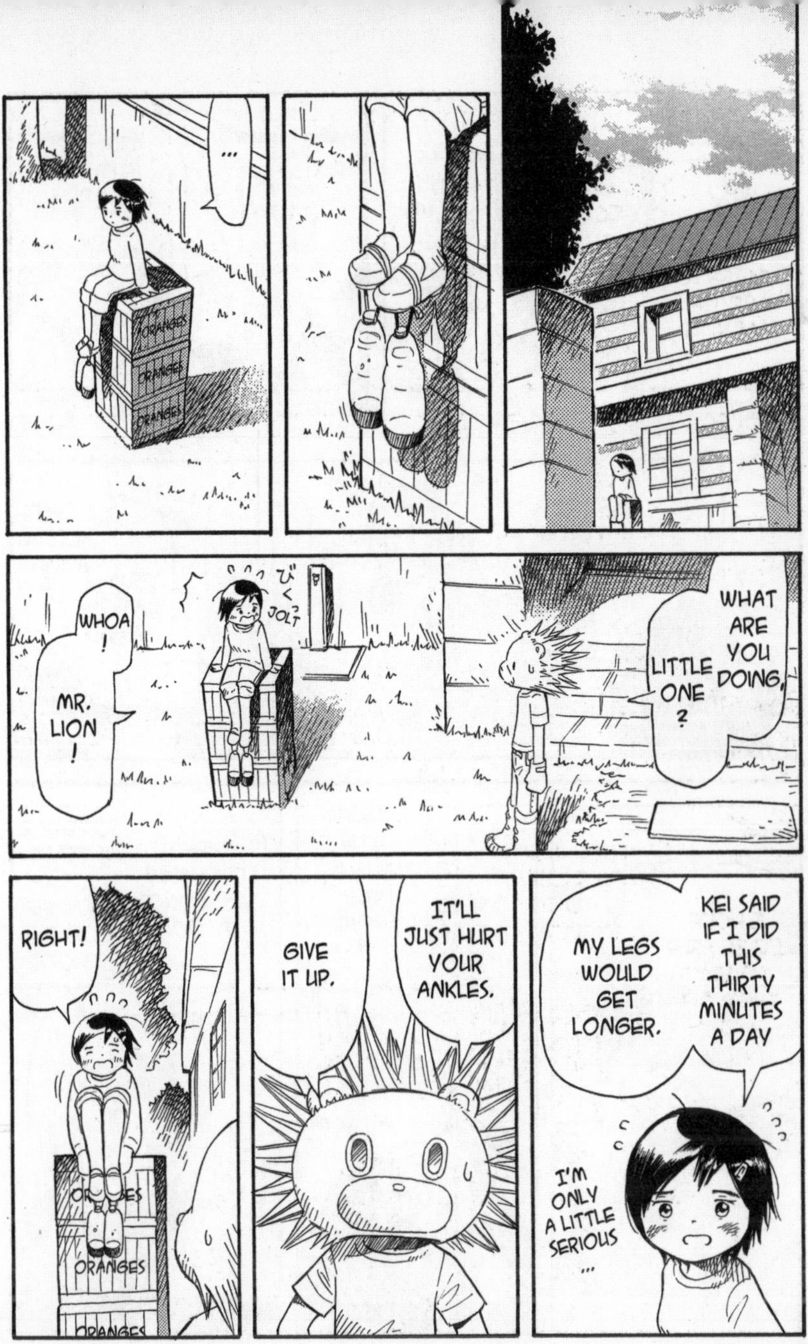

ORANGES
ORANGES
ORANGES
...
WHAT ARE YOU DOING, LITTLE ONE?
びく
JOLT
WHOA! MR. LION!
KEI SAID IF I DID THIS THIRTY MINUTES A DAY
MY LEGS WOULD GET LONGER.
I'M ONLY A LITTLE SERIOUS ...
IT'LL JUST HURT YOUR ANKLES.
GIVE IT UP.
RIGHT!
ORANGES
ORANGES

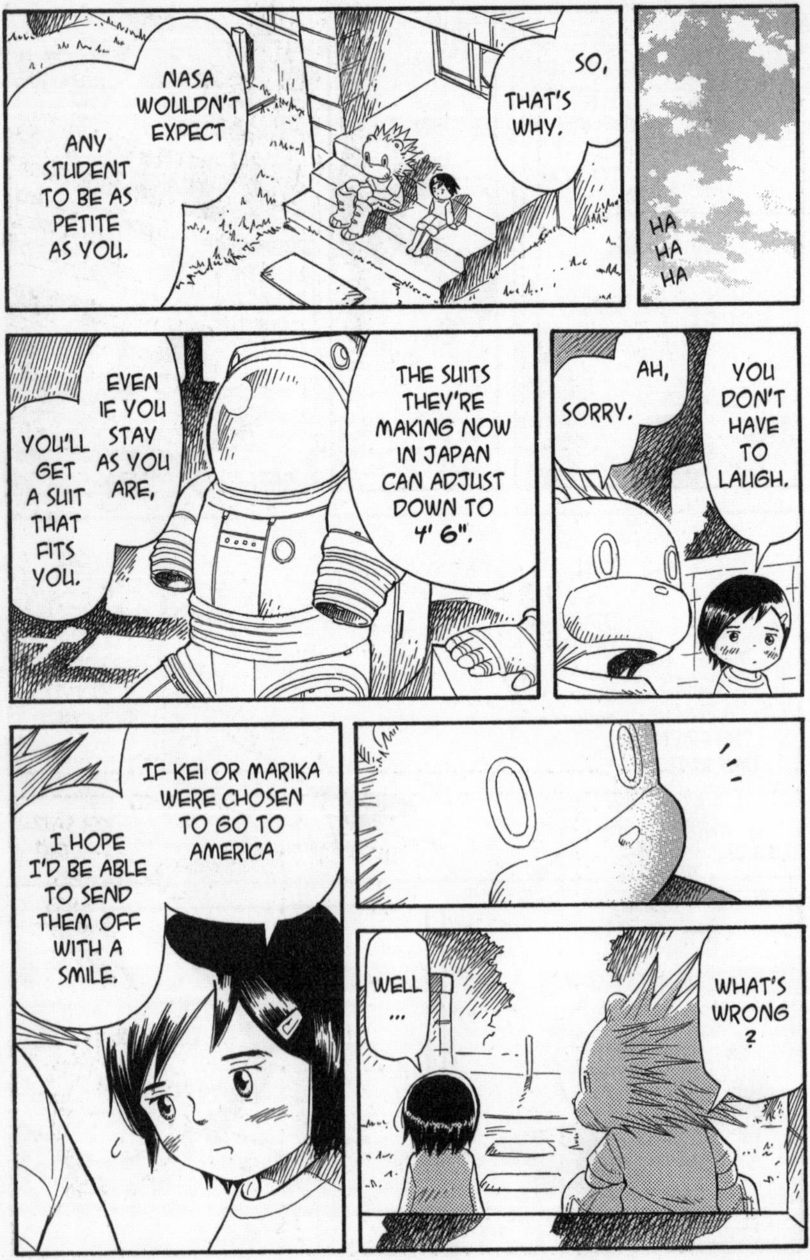
HA HA HA
SO, THAT'S WHY.
NASA WOULDN'T EXPECT
ANY STUDENT TO BE AS PETITE AS YOU.
YOU DON'T HAVE TO LAUGH.
AH, SORRY.
THE SUITS THEY'RE MAKING NOW IN JAPAN CAN ADJUST DOWN TO 4' 6".
EVEN IF YOU STAY AS YOU ARE,
YOU'LL GET A SUIT THAT FITS YOU.
WHAT'S WRONG?
WELL ...
IF KEI OR MARIKA WERE CHOSEN TO GO TO AMERICA
I HOPE I'D BE ABLE TO SEND THEM OFF WITH A SMILE.

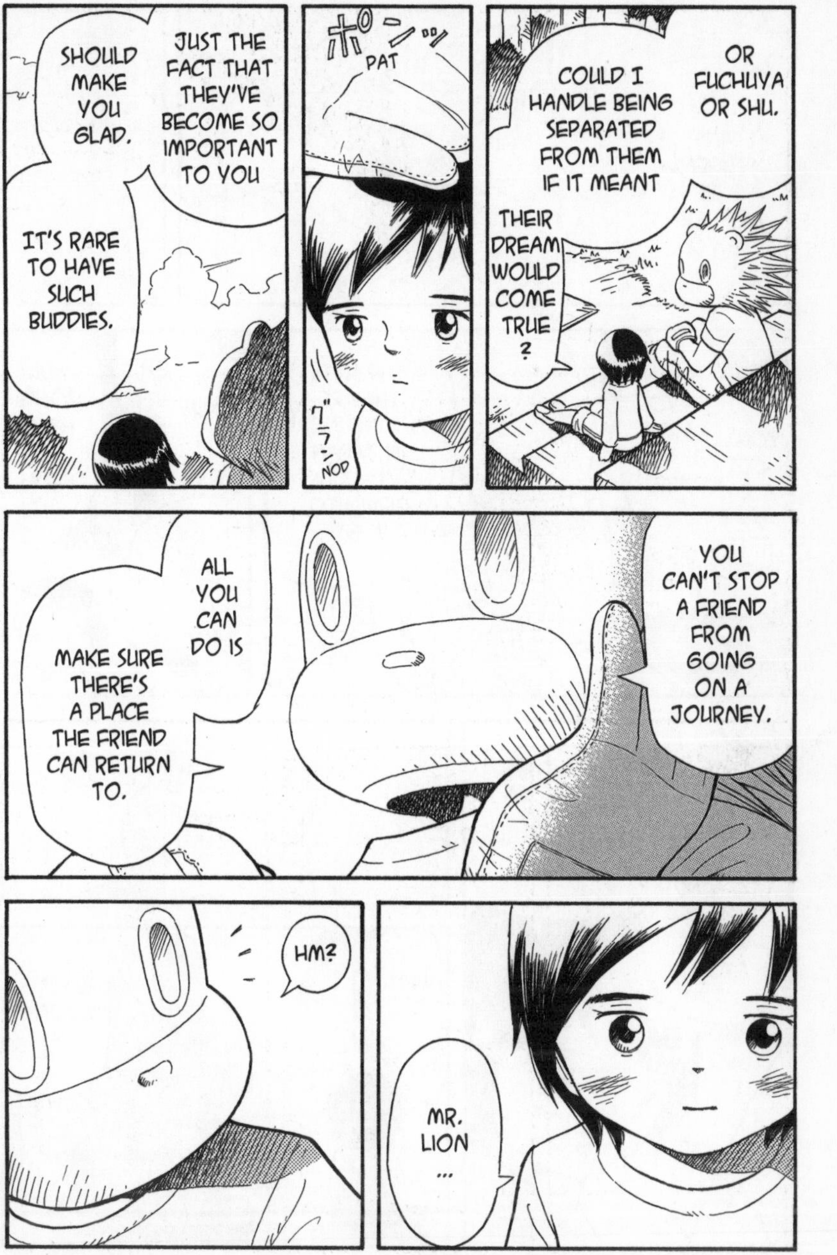
OR FUCHUYA OR SHU.
COULD I HANDLE BEING SEPARATED FROM THEM IF IT MEANT
THEIR DREAM WOULD COME TRUE?
PAT
NOD
JUST THE FACT THAT THEY'VE BECOME SO IMPORTANT TO YOU
SHOULD MAKE YOU GLAD.
IT'S RARE TO HAVE SUCH BUDDIES.
YOU CAN'T STOP A FRIEND FROM GOING ON A JOURNEY.
ALL YOU CAN DO IS
MAKE SURE THERE'S A PLACE THE FRIEND CAN RETURN TO.
MR. LION ...
HM?

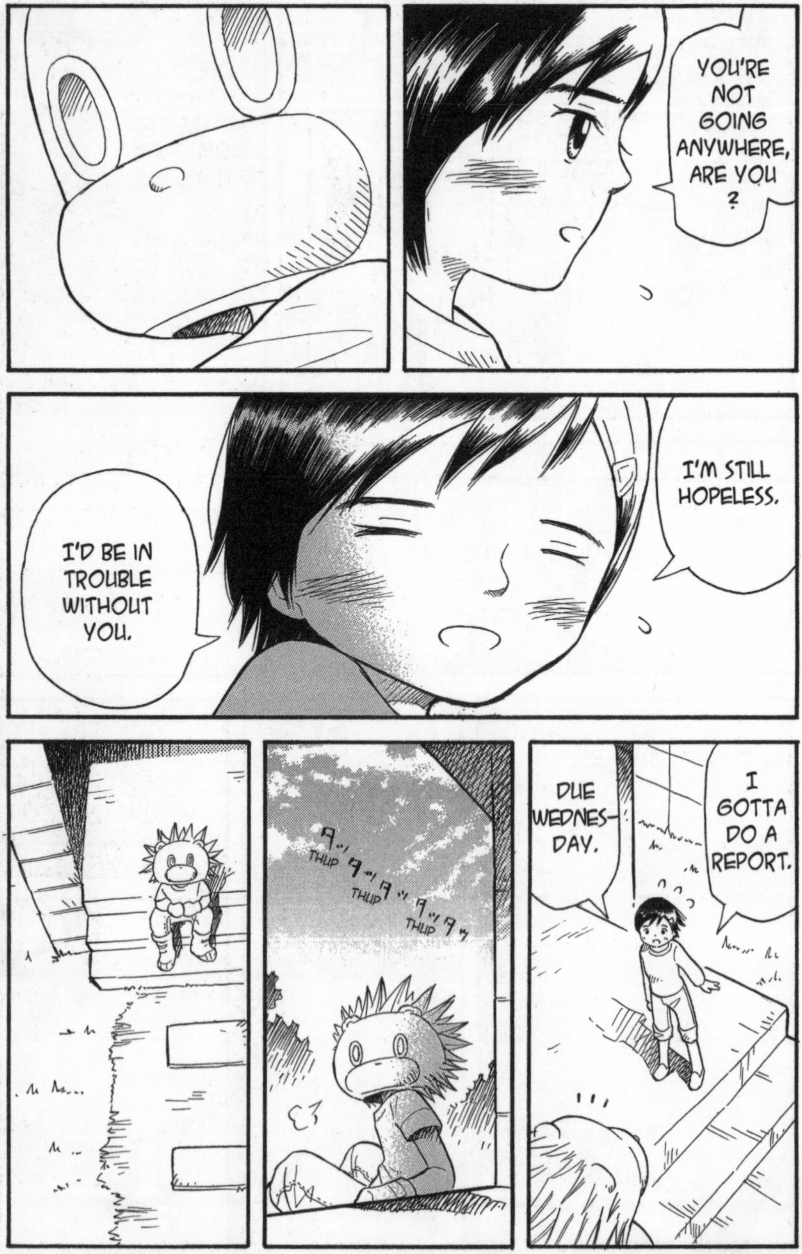
YOU'RE NOT GOING ANYWHERE, ARE YOU ?
I'M STILL HOPELESS.
I'D BE IN TROUBLE WITHOUT YOU.
I GOTTA DO A REPORT.
DUE WEDNES-DAY.
タッ THUP
タッ THUP
タッ THUP
タッ

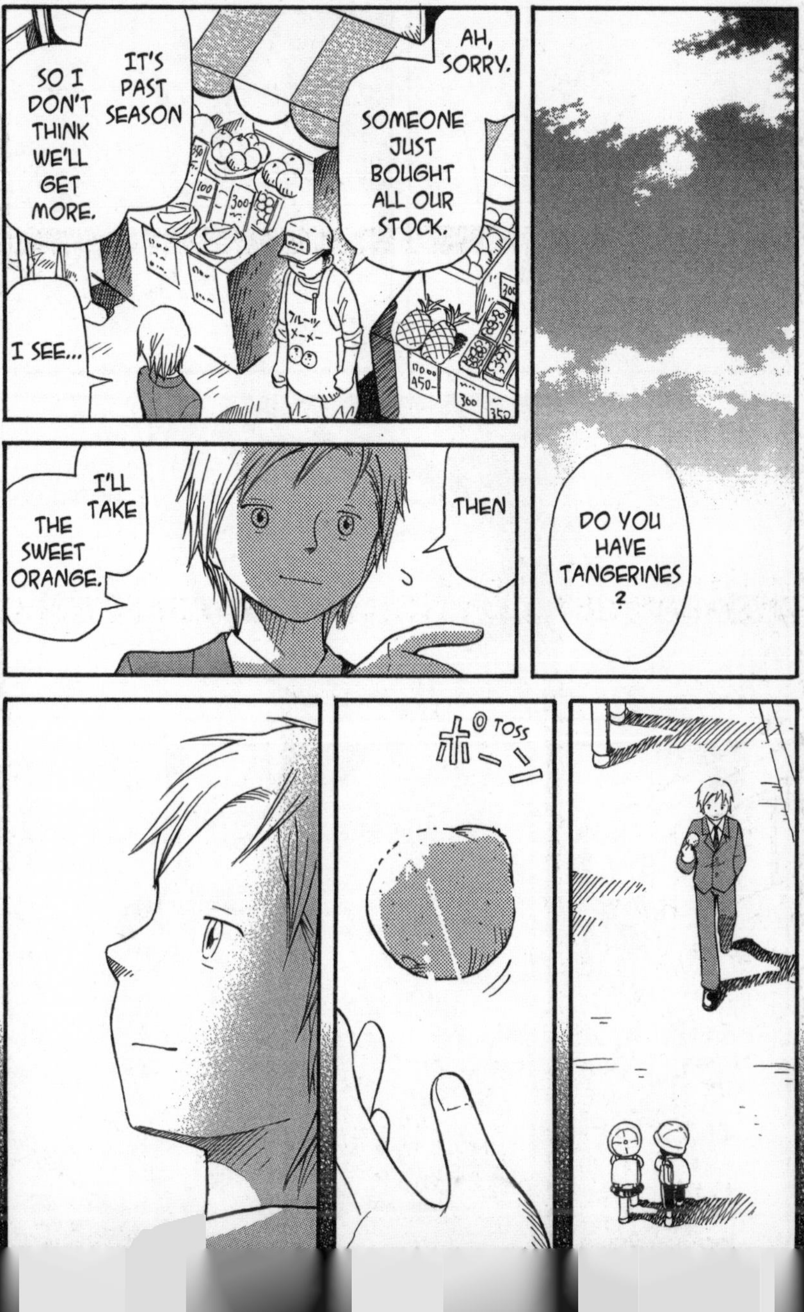
DO YOU HAVE TANGERINES?
AH, SORRY.
SOMEONE JUST BOUGHT ALL OUR STOCK.
IT'S PAST SEASON
SO I DON'T THINK WE'LL GET MORE.
I SEE...
THEN
I'LL TAKE THE SWEET ORANGE.
TOSS

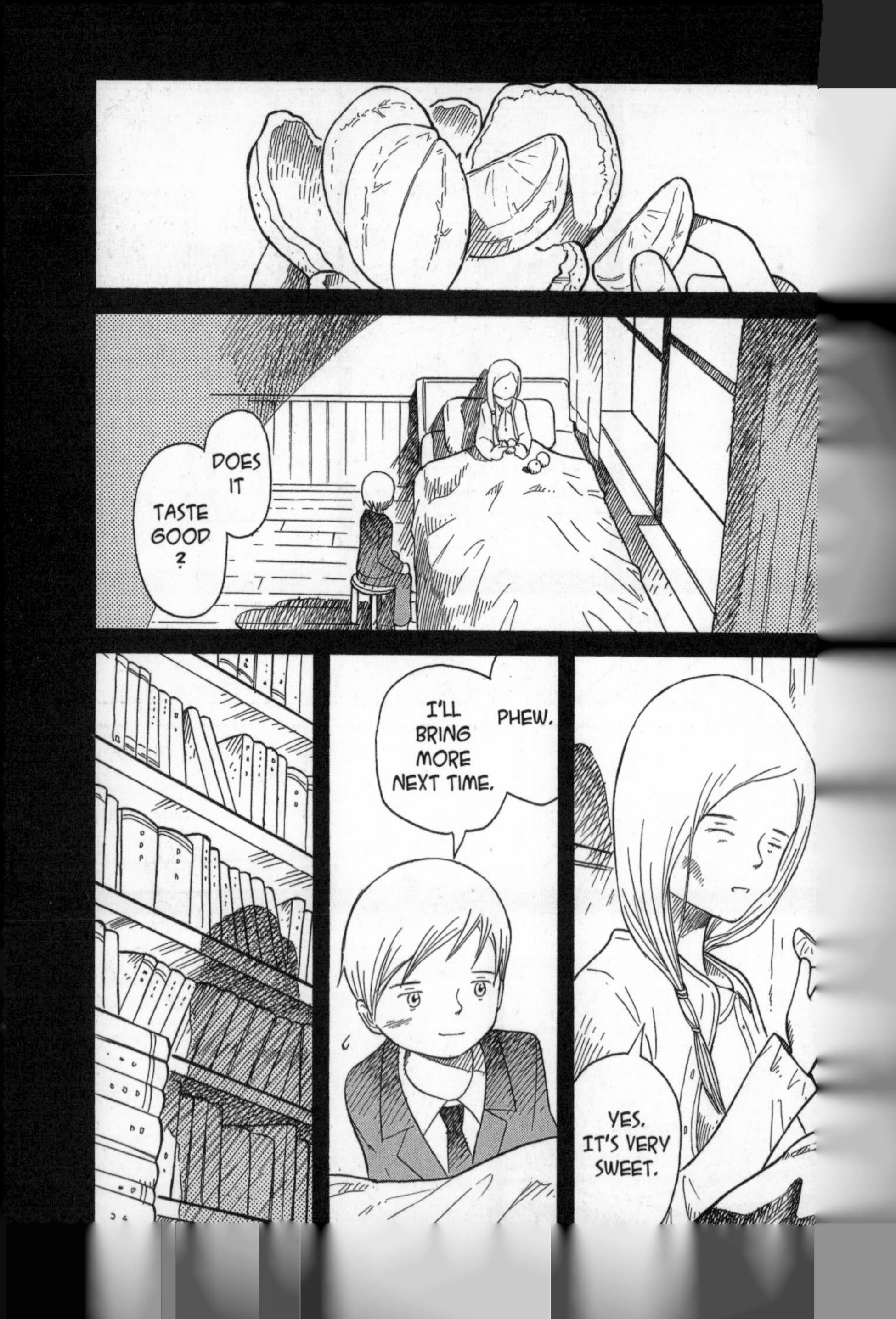
DOES IT TASTE GOOD?
YES. IT'S VERY SWEET.
PHEW.
I'LL BRING MORE NEXT TIME.

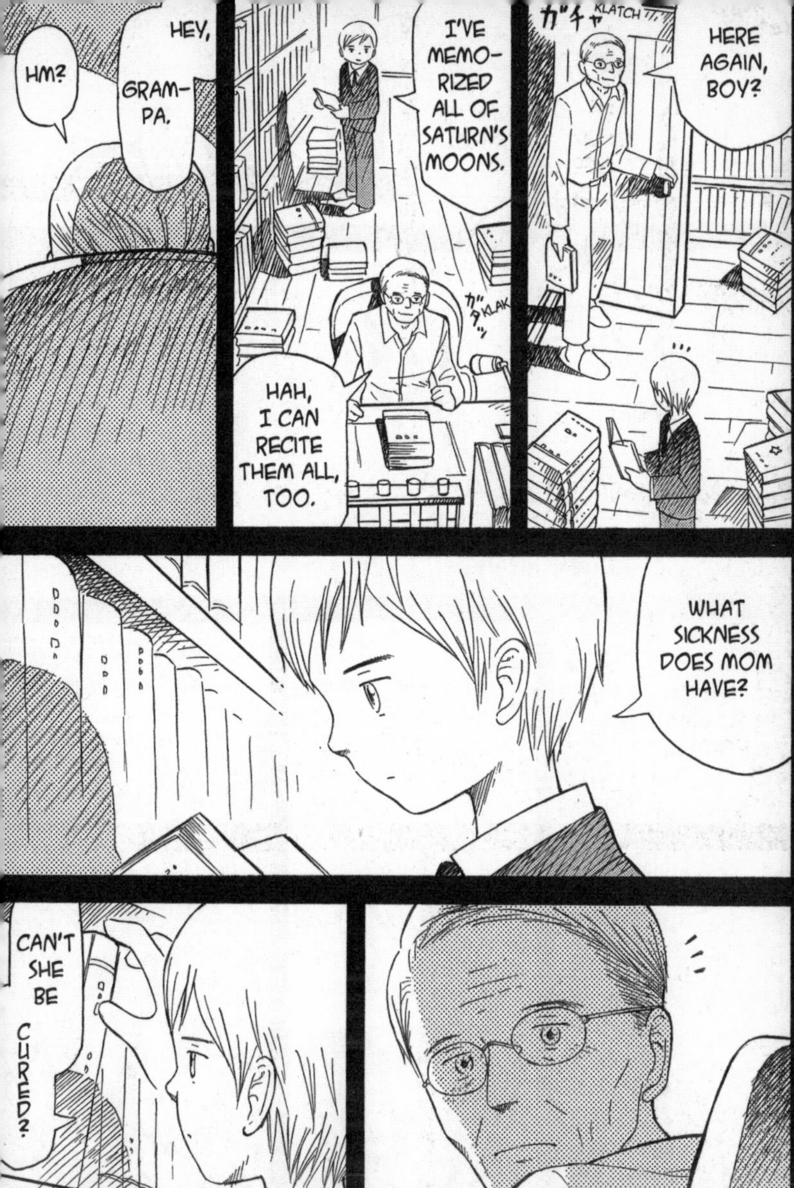
ガチャ KLATCH
HERE AGAIN, BOY?
...
I'VE MEMORIZED ALL OF SATURN'S MOONS.
ガタッ KLAK
HAH, I CAN RECITE THEM ALL, TOO.
HEY, GRAMPA.
HM?
WHAT SICKNESS DOES MOM HAVE?
CAN'T SHE BE CURED?

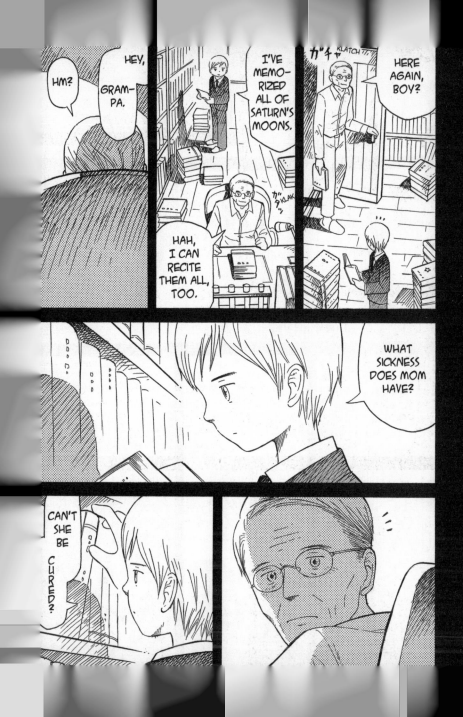

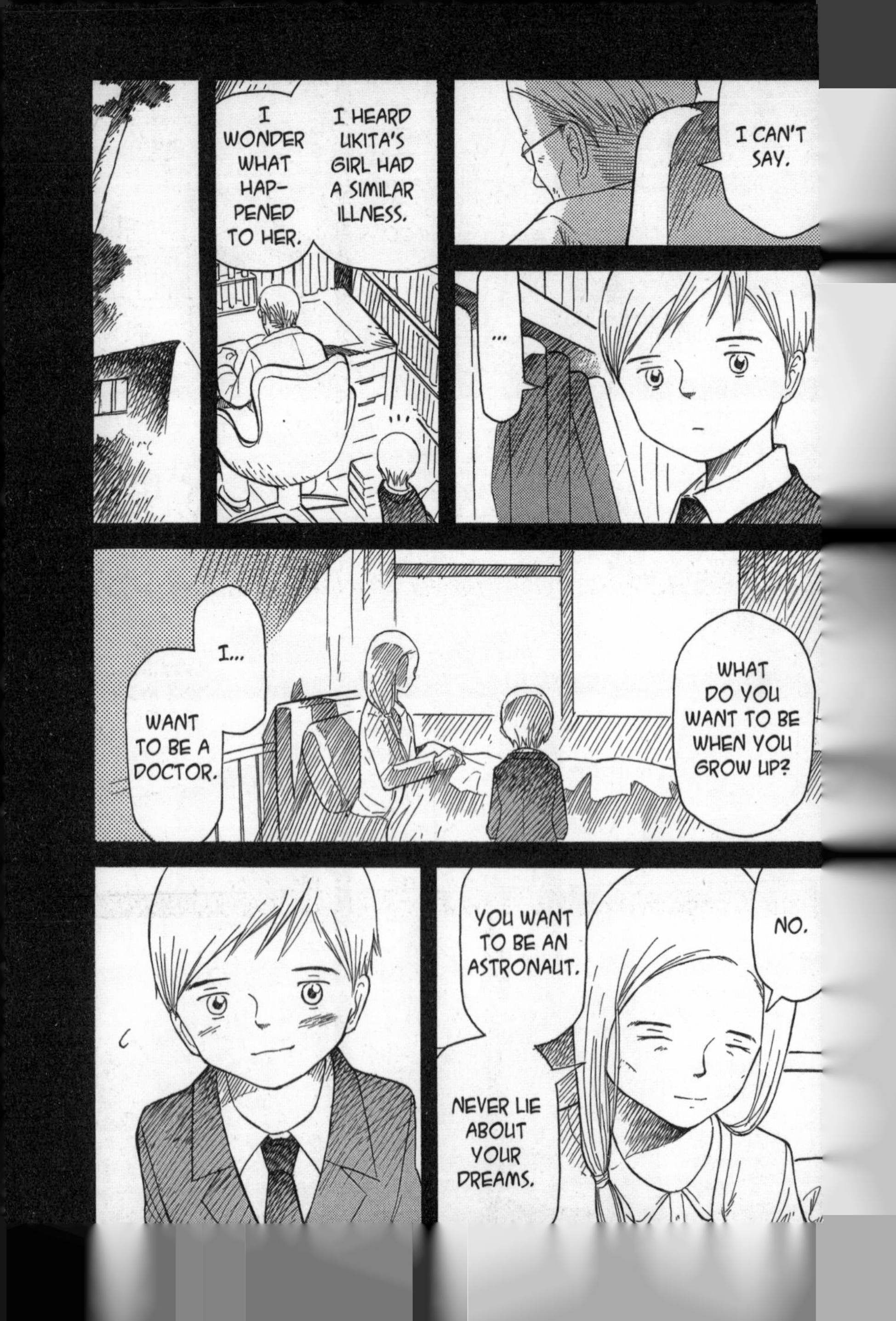
I CAN'T SAY.
...
I HEARD UKITA'S GIRL HAD A SIMILAR ILLNESS.
I WONDER WHAT HAP-PENED TO HER.
WHAT DO YOU WANT TO BE WHEN YOU GROW UP?
I...
WANT TO BE A DOCTOR.
NO.
YOU WANT TO BE AN ASTRONAUT.
NEVER LIE ABOUT YOUR DREAMS.

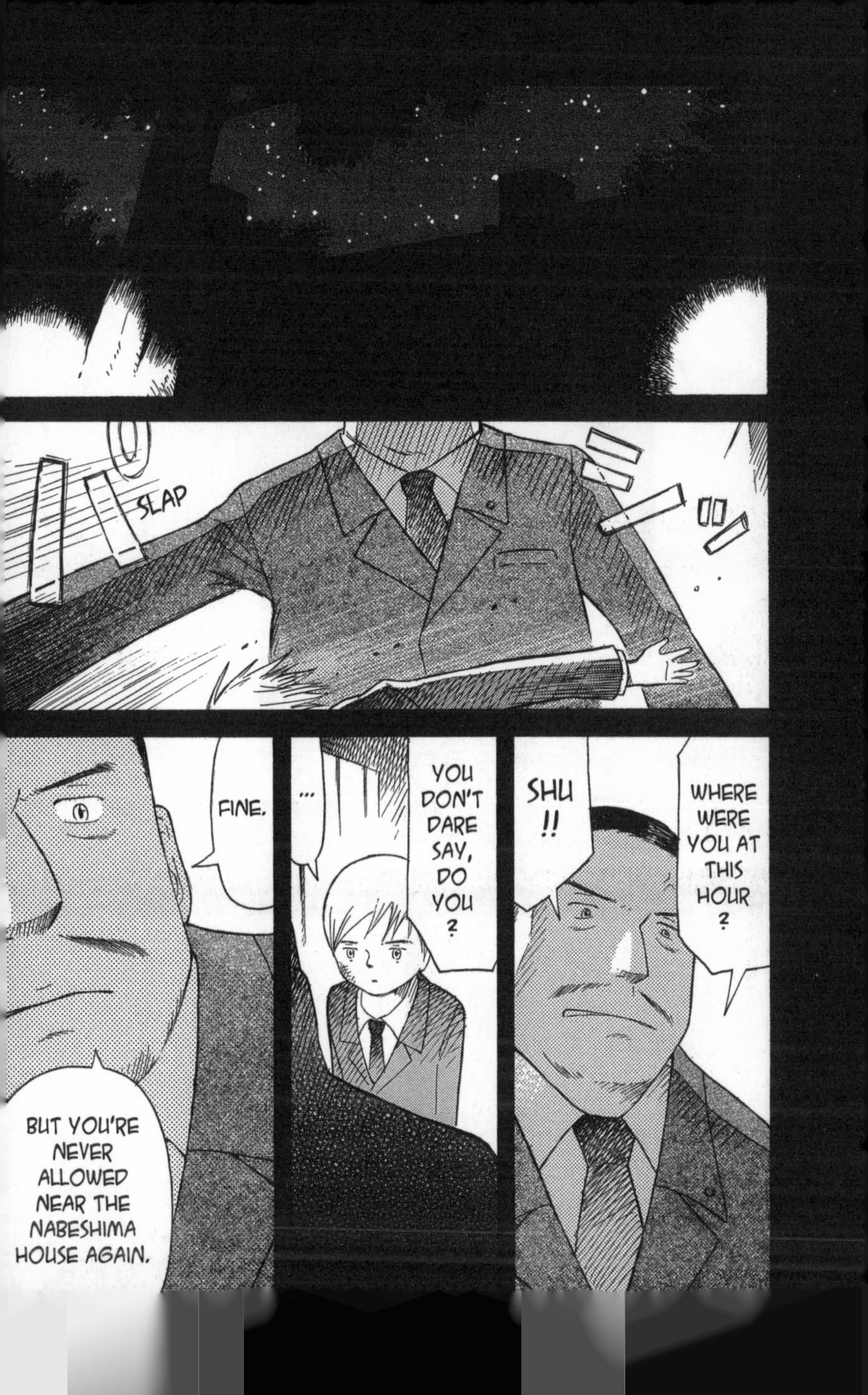
SLAP
WHERE WERE YOU AT THIS HOUR?
SHU!!
YOU DON'T DARE SAY, DO YOU?
...
FINE.
BUT YOU'RE NEVER ALLOWED NEAR THE NABESHIMA HOUSE AGAIN.

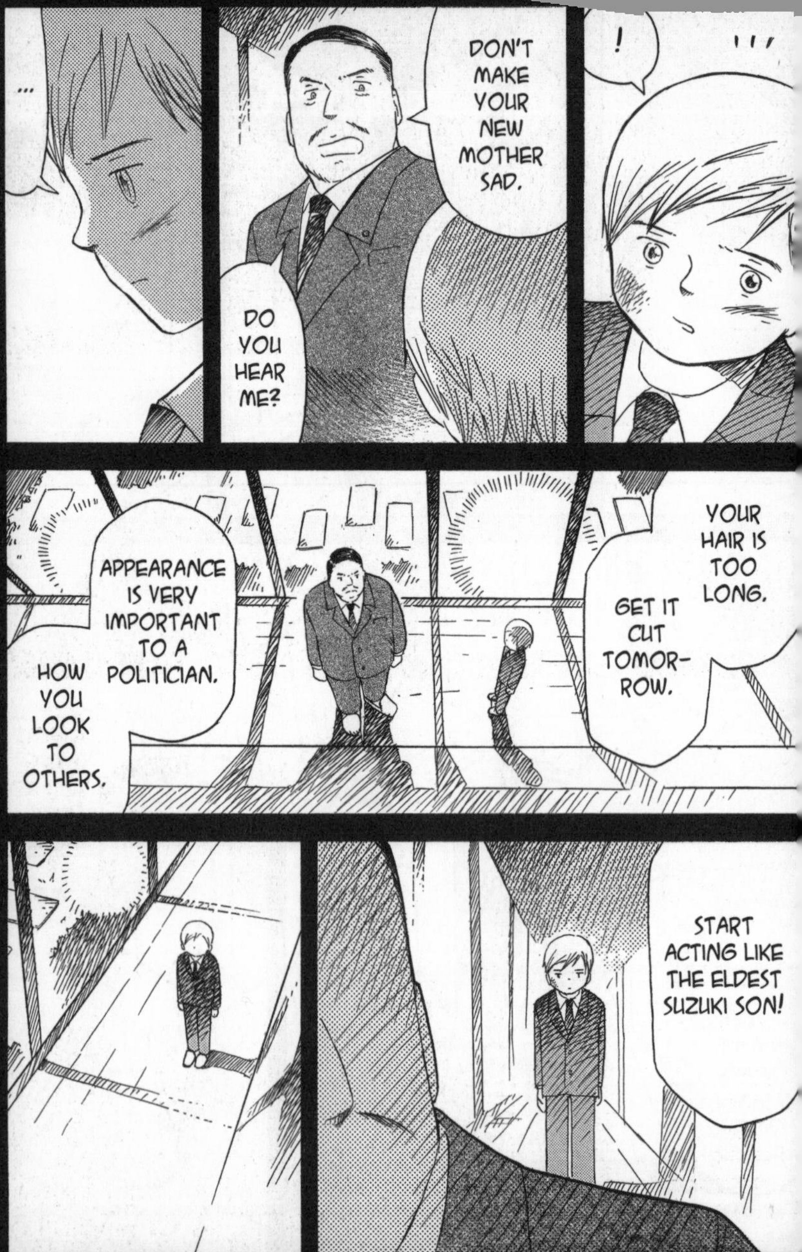
!
DON'T MAKE YOUR NEW MOTHER SAD.
DO YOU HEAR ME?
...
YOUR HAIR IS TOO LONG.
GET IT CUT TOMOR-ROW.
APPEARANCE IS VERY IMPORTANT TO A POLITICIAN.
HOW YOU LOOK TO OTHERS.
START ACTING LIKE THE ELDEST SUZUKI SON!

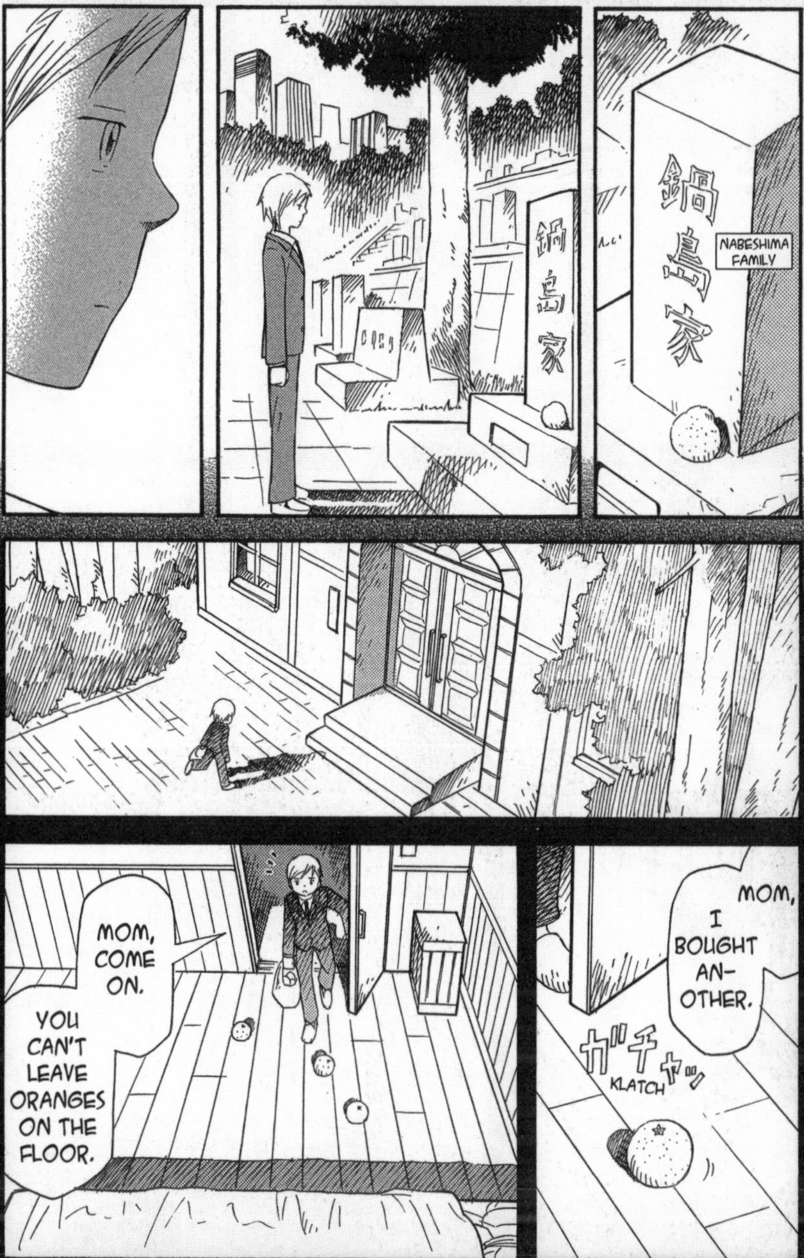
鍋島家
NABESHIMA FAMILY
鍋島家
MOM, I BOUGHT AN-OTHER.
ガチャッ
KLATCH
MOM, COME ON.
YOU CAN'T LEAVE ORANGES ON THE FLOOR.

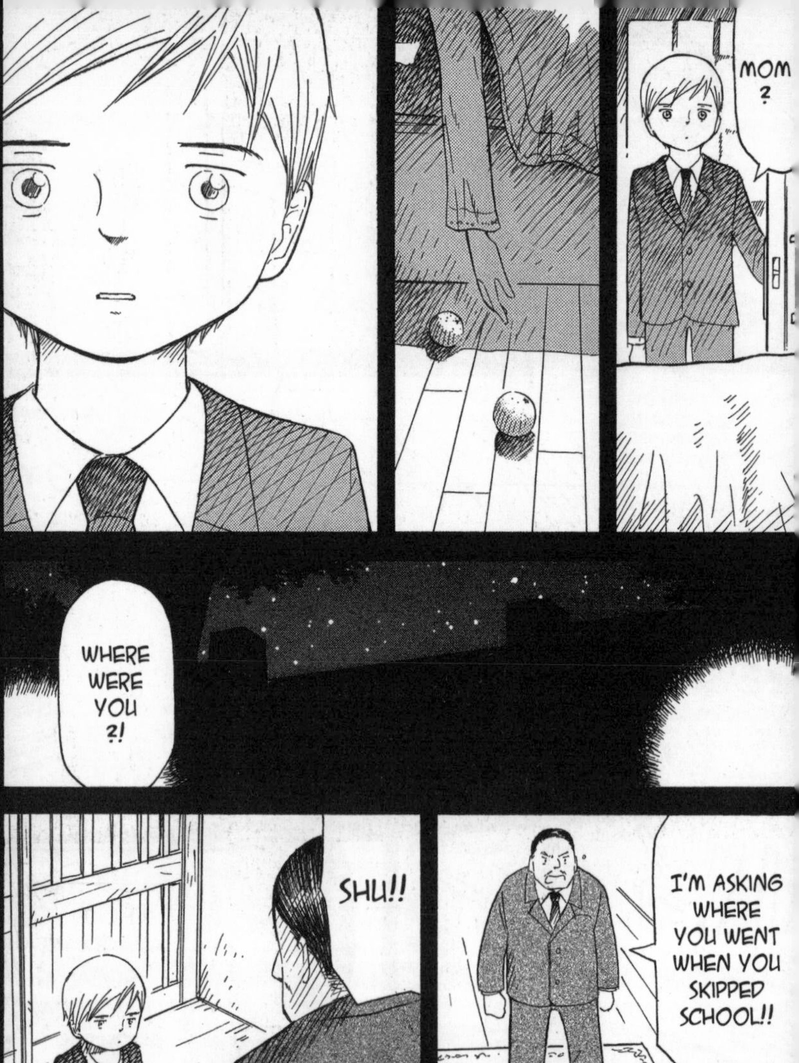
MOM ?
WHERE WERE YOU ?!
I'M ASKING WHERE YOU WENT WHEN YOU SKIPPED SCHOOL!!
SHU!!

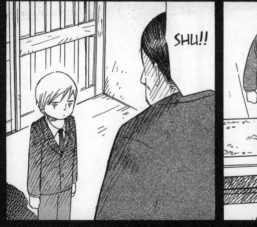

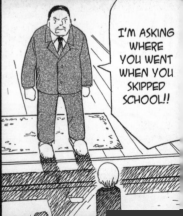

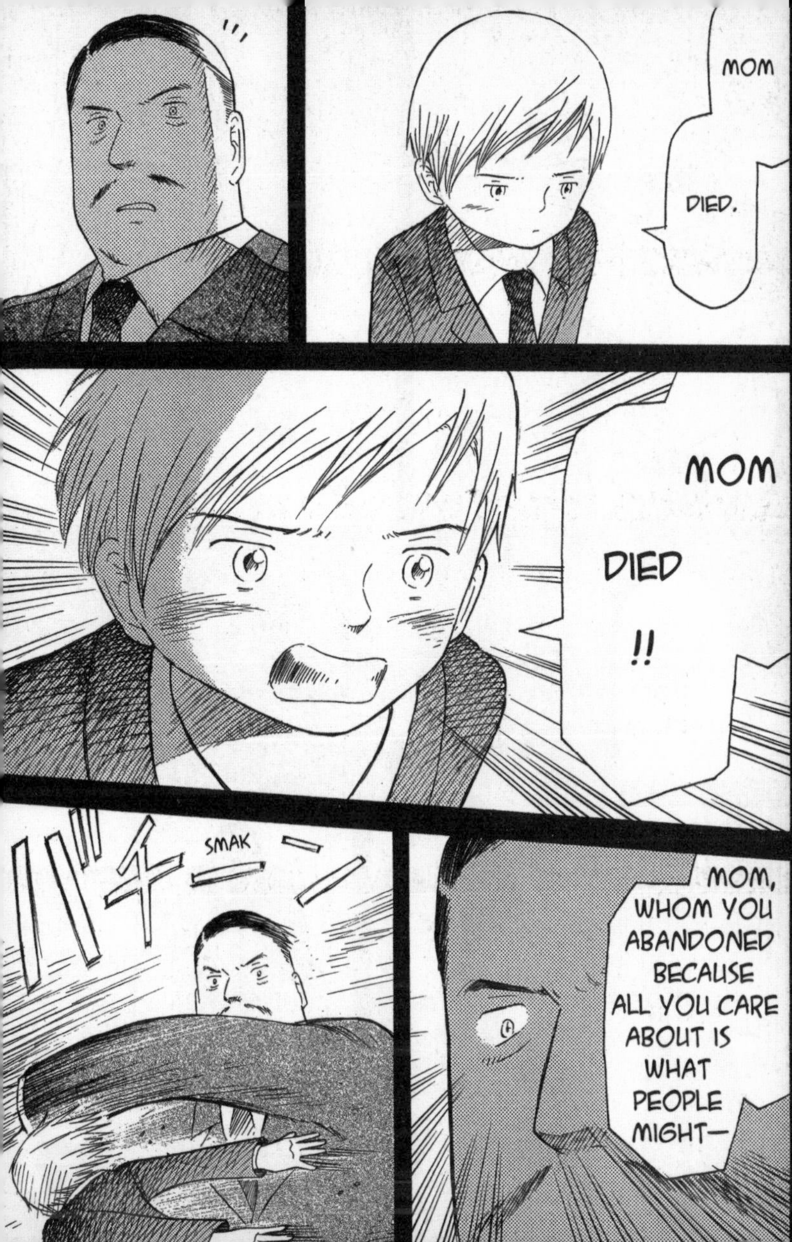
MOM
DIED.
MOM
DIED
!!
MOM, WHOM YOU ABANDONED BECAUSE ALL YOU CARE ABOUT IS WHAT PEOPLE MIGHT—
SMAK

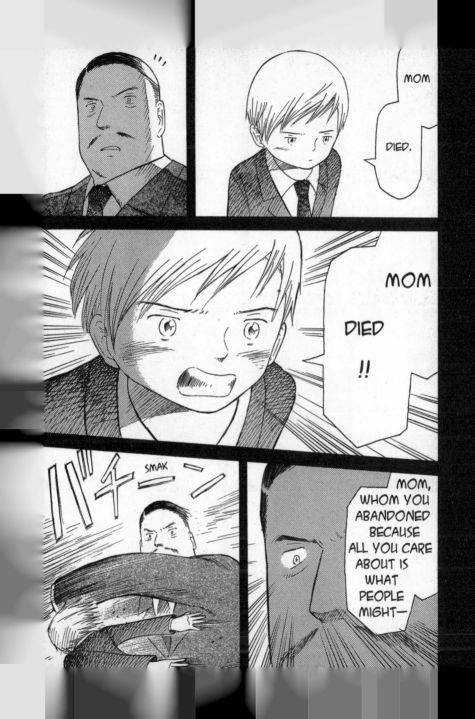

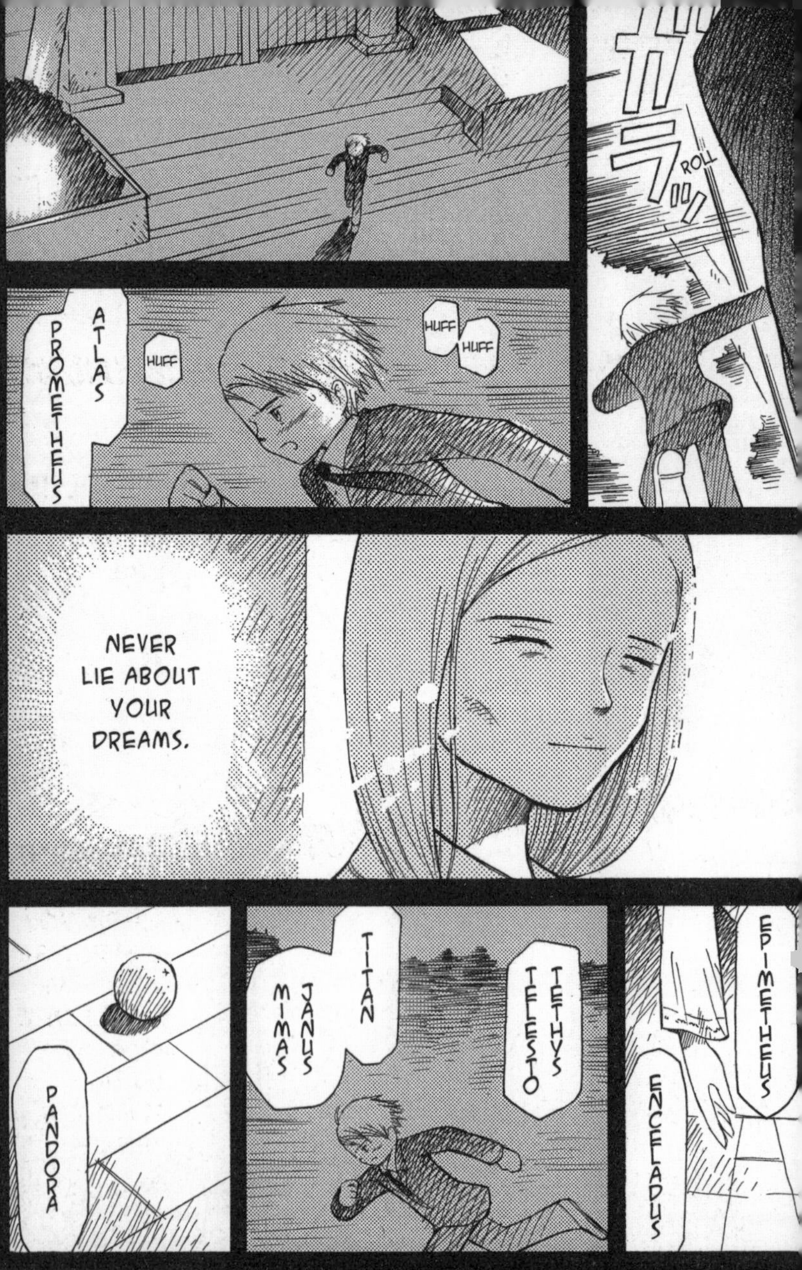
ガラ
ROLL
HUFF
HUFF
HUFF
ATLAS
PROMETHEUS
NEVER LIE ABOUT YOUR DREAMS.
EPIMETHEUS
ENCELADUS
TETHYS
TELESTO
TITAN
JANUS
MIMAS
PANDORA

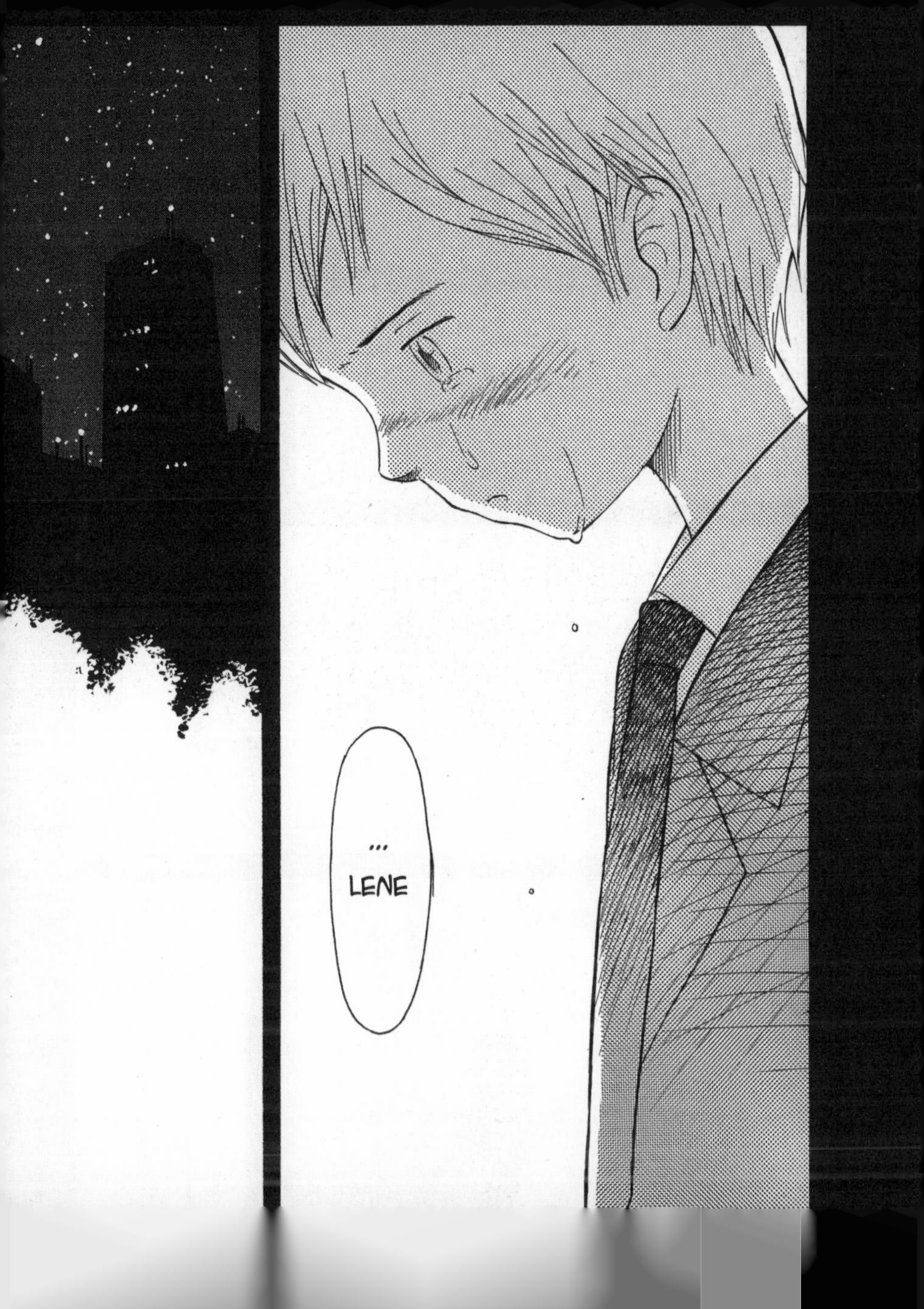
... LENE

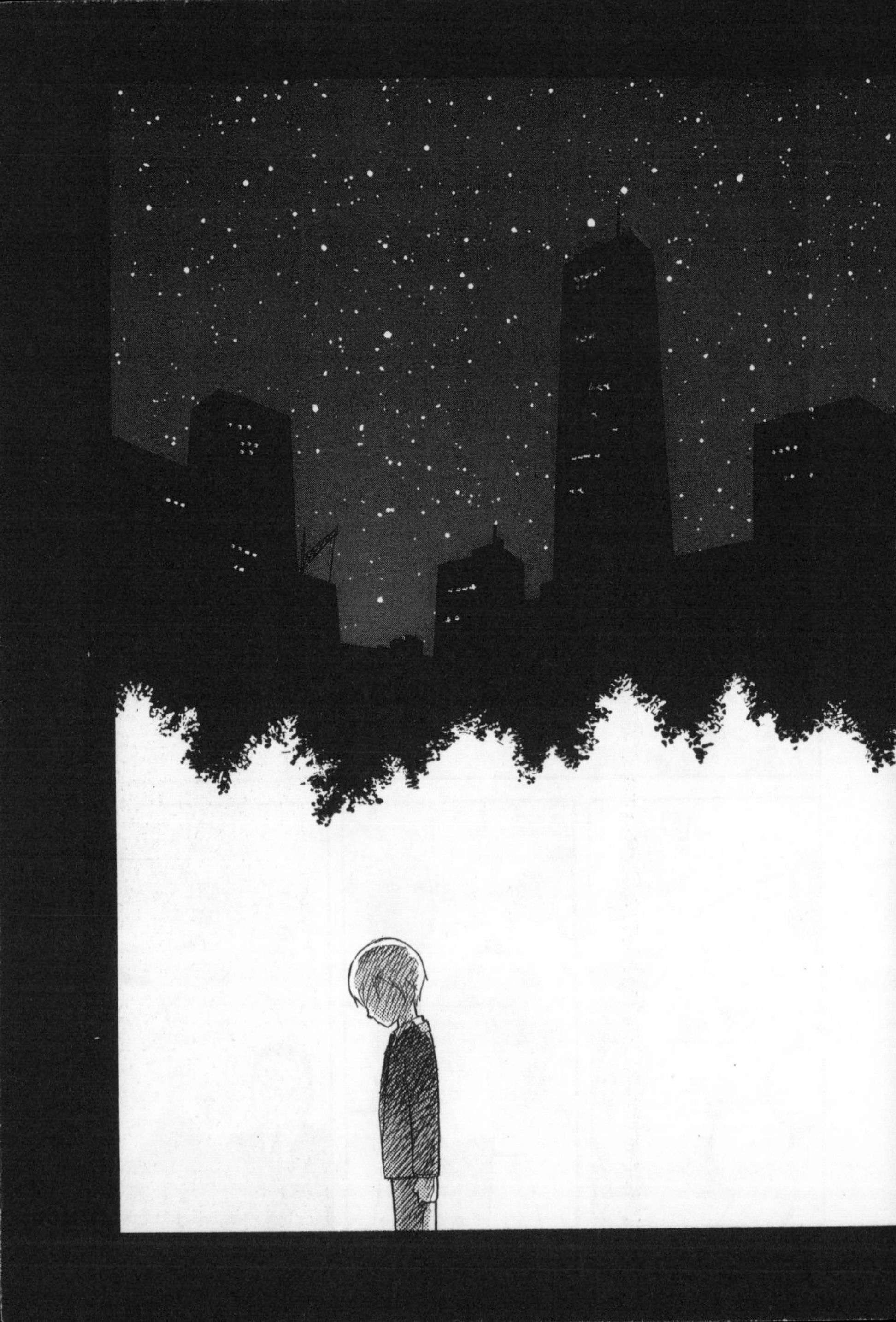

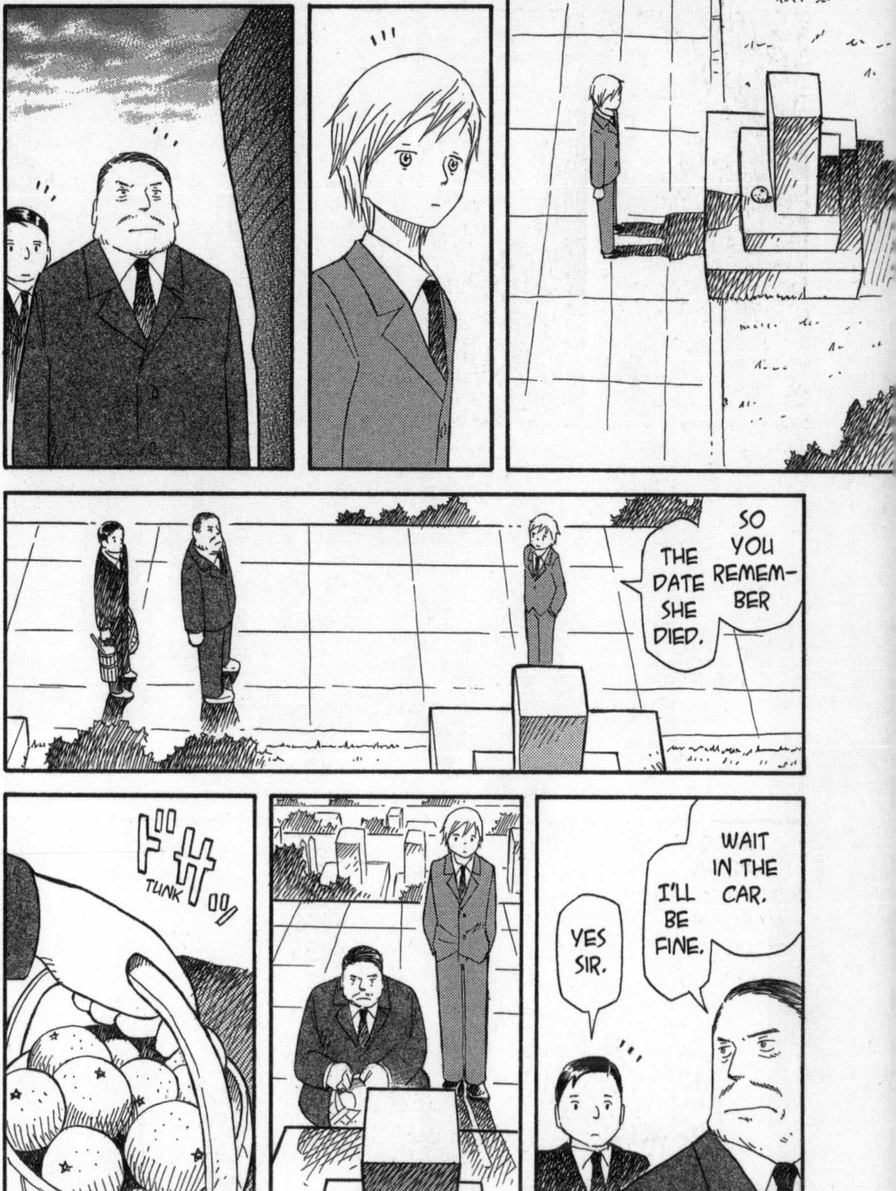
SO YOU REMEM-BER THE DATE SHE DIED.
WAIT IN THE CAR. I'LL BE FINE.
YES SIR.
ドサッ
TUNK

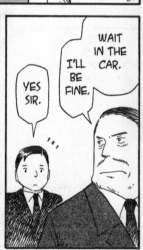

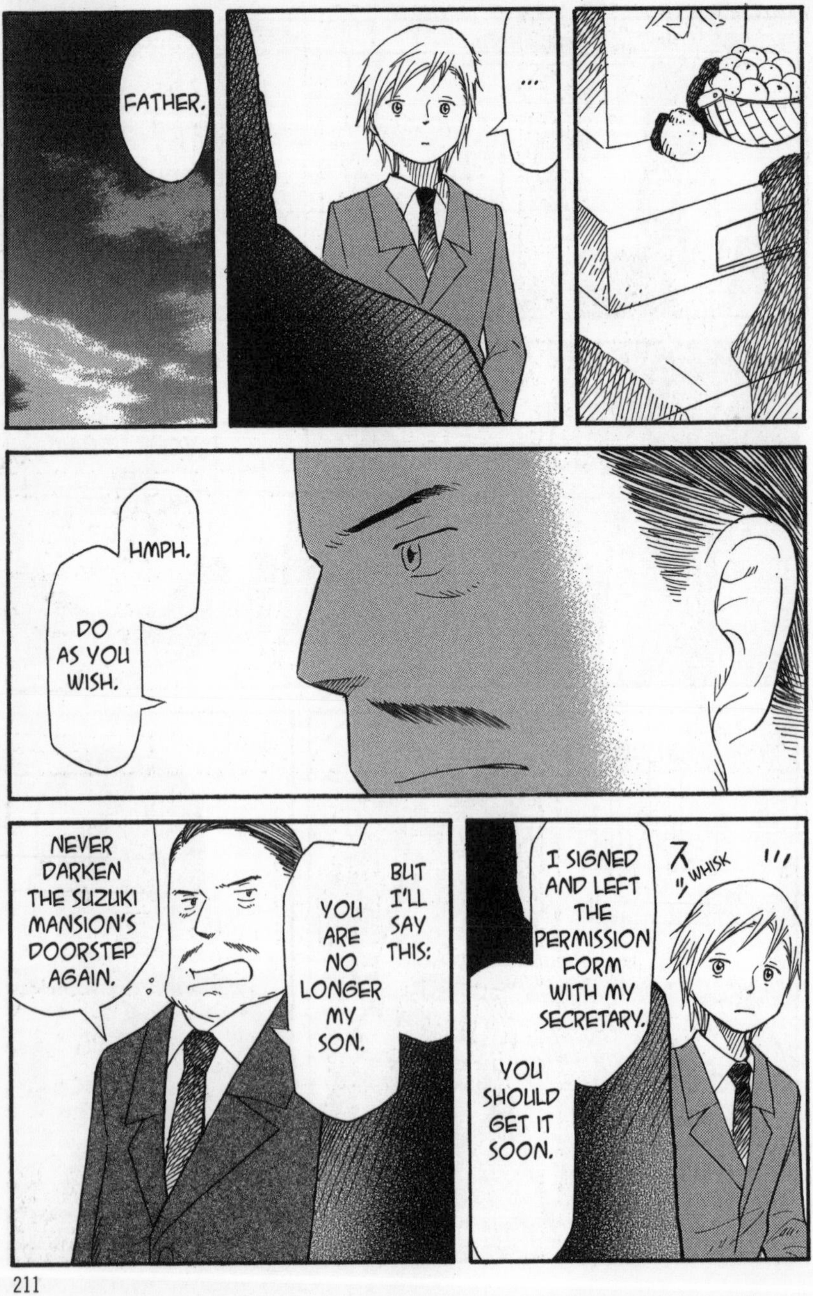
...
FATHER.
HMPH.
DO AS YOU WISH.
I SIGNED AND LEFT THE PERMISSION FORM WITH MY SECRETARY.
ス WHISK
YOU SHOULD GET IT SOON.
BUT I'LL SAY THIS:
YOU ARE NO LONGER MY SON.
NEVER DARKEN THE SUZUKI MANSION'S DOORSTEP AGAIN.

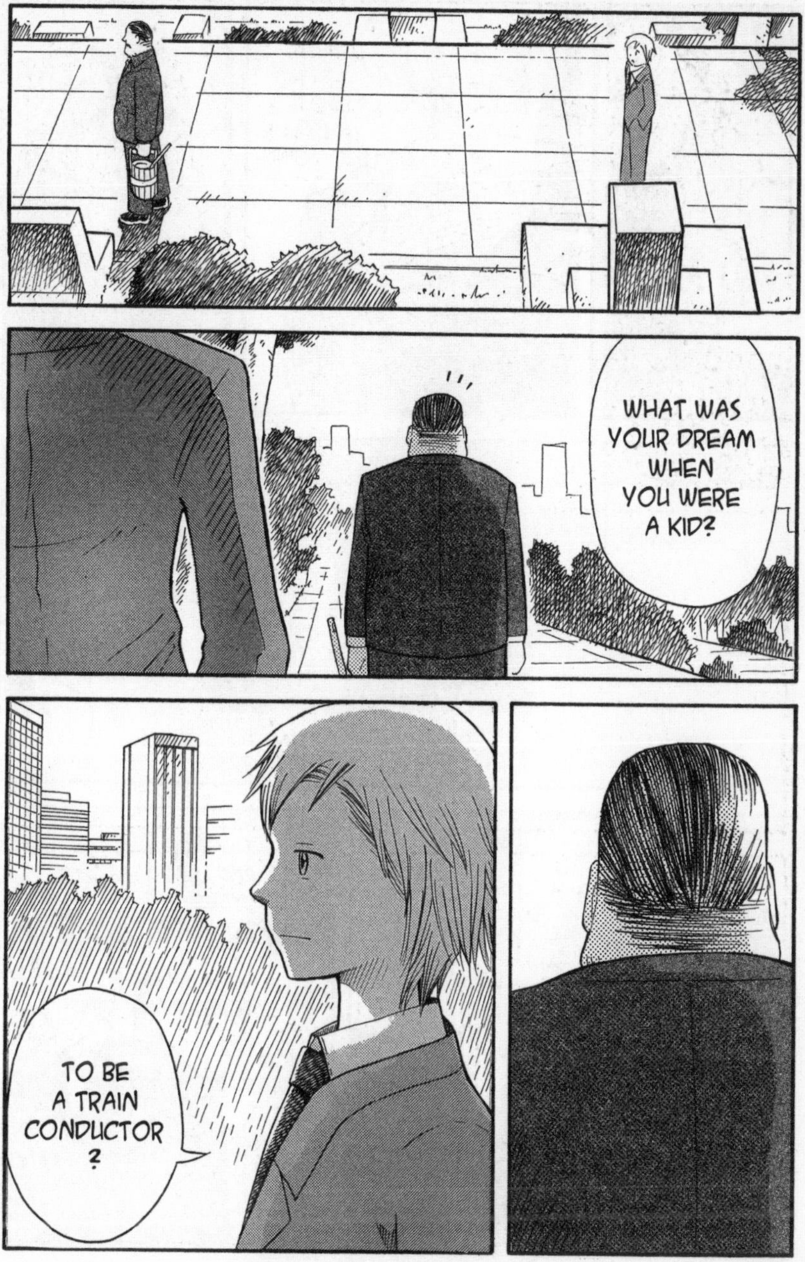
WHAT WAS YOUR DREAM WHEN YOU WERE A KID?
TO BE A TRAIN CONDUCTOR?

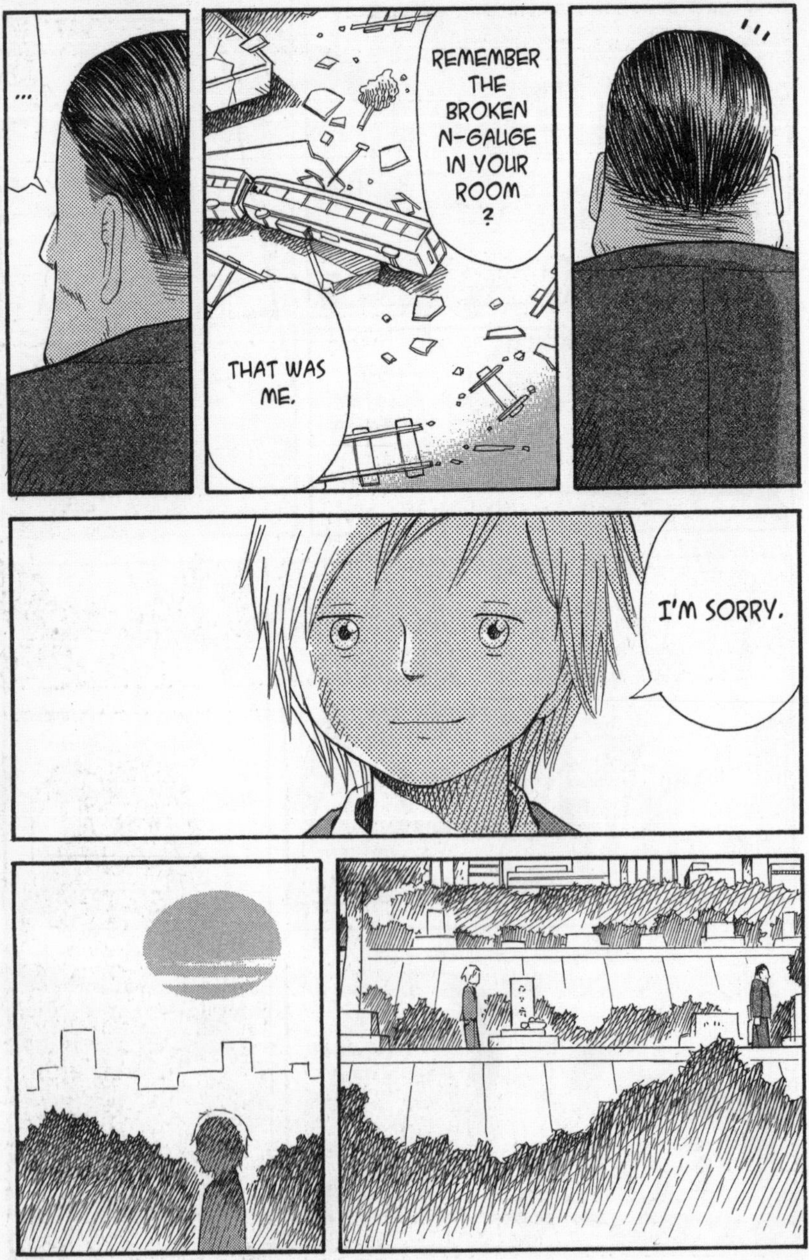
REMEMBER THE BROKEN N-GAUGE IN YOUR ROOM?
THAT WAS ME.
...
I'M SORRY.

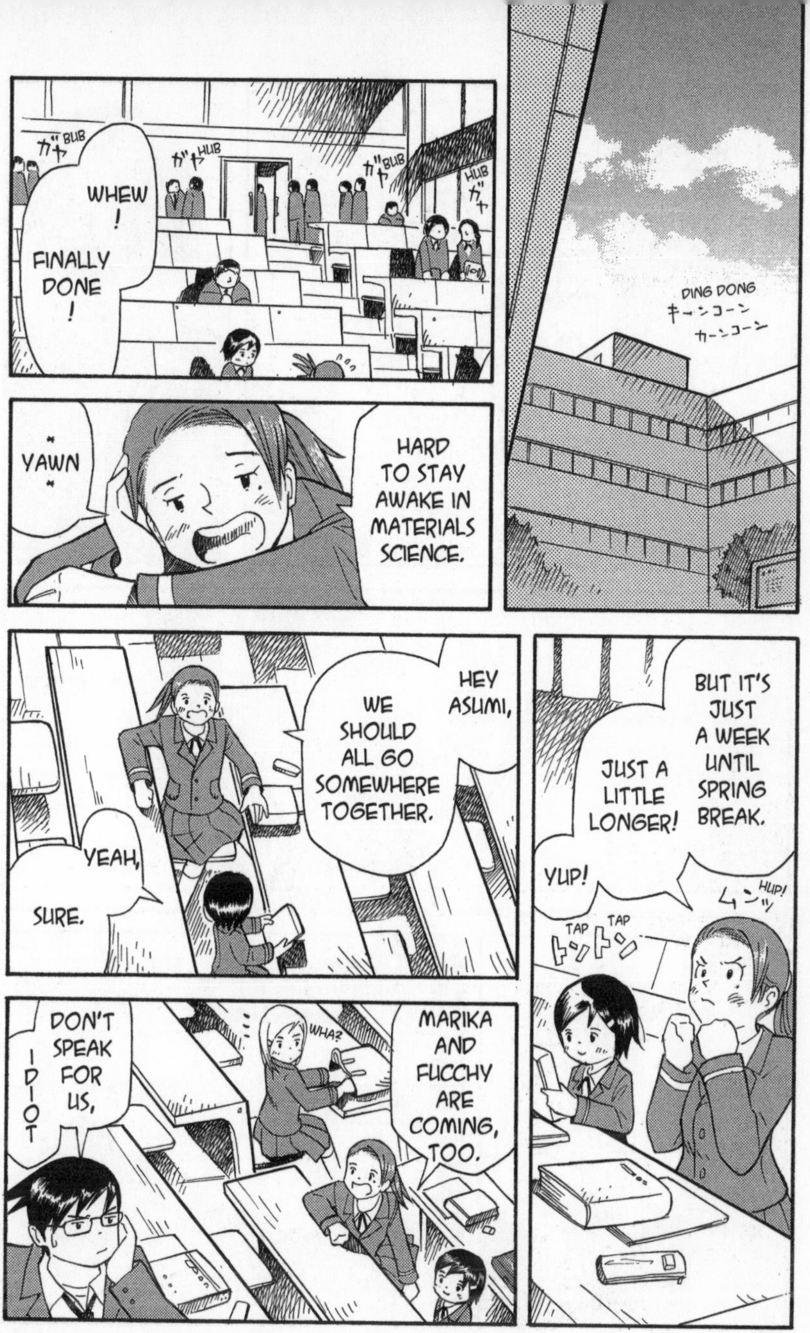
DING DONG
キーンコーン
カーンコーン
BUB
ガヤ
HUB
ガヤ
BUB
ガヤ
HUB
ガヤ
WHEW!
FINALLY DONE!
HARD TO STAY AWAKE IN MATERIALS SCIENCE.
YAWN
BUT IT'S JUST A WEEK UNTIL SPRING BREAK.
JUST A LITTLE LONGER!
HUP!
ムンッ
YUP!
TAP TAP
トントン
HEY ASUMI,
WE SHOULD ALL GO SOMEWHERE TOGETHER.
YEAH,
SURE.
MARIKA AND FUCCHY ARE COMING, TOO.
WHA?
DON'T SPEAK FOR US,
IDIOT

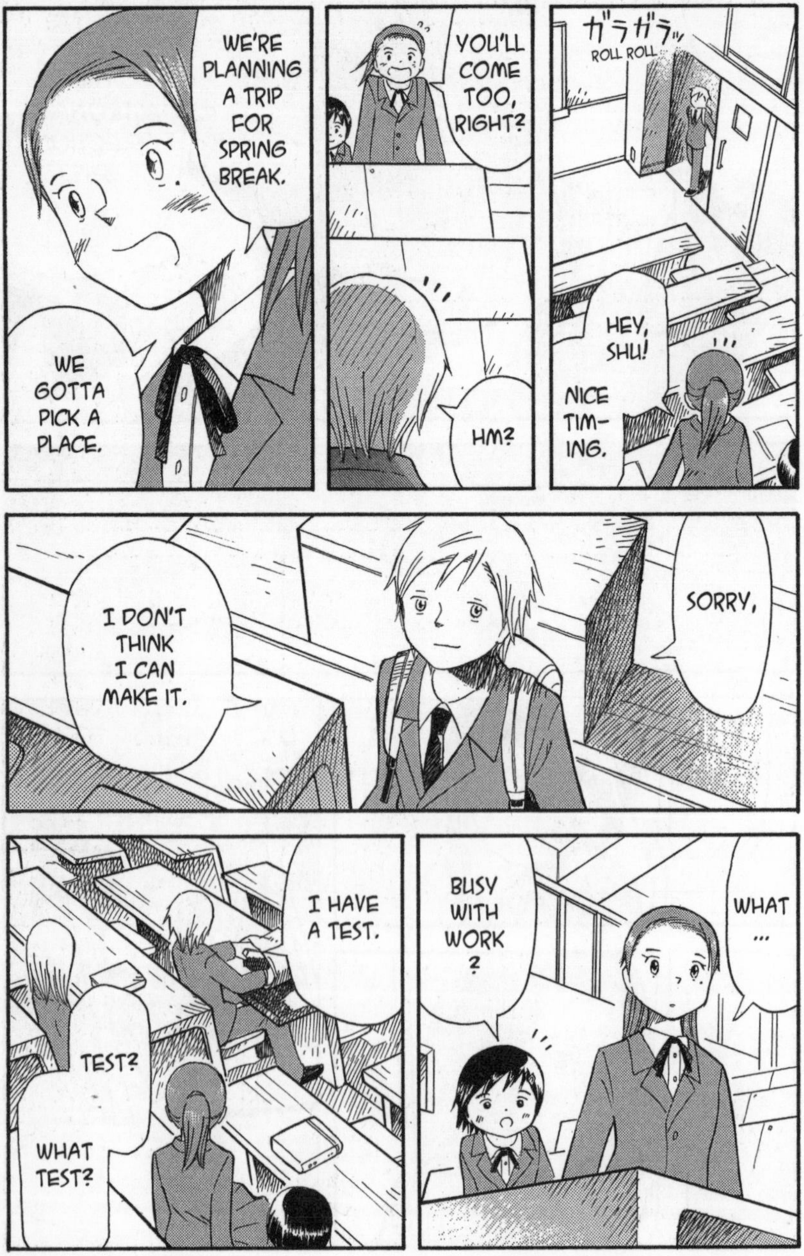
ガラガラッ
ROLL ROLL
HEY, SHU!
NICE TIM-ING.
YOU'LL COME TOO, RIGHT?
HM?
WE'RE PLANNING A TRIP FOR SPRING BREAK.
WE GOTTA PICK A PLACE.
SORRY,
I DON'T THINK I CAN MAKE IT.
WHAT ...
BUSY WITH WORK?
I HAVE A TEST.
TEST?
WHAT TEST?

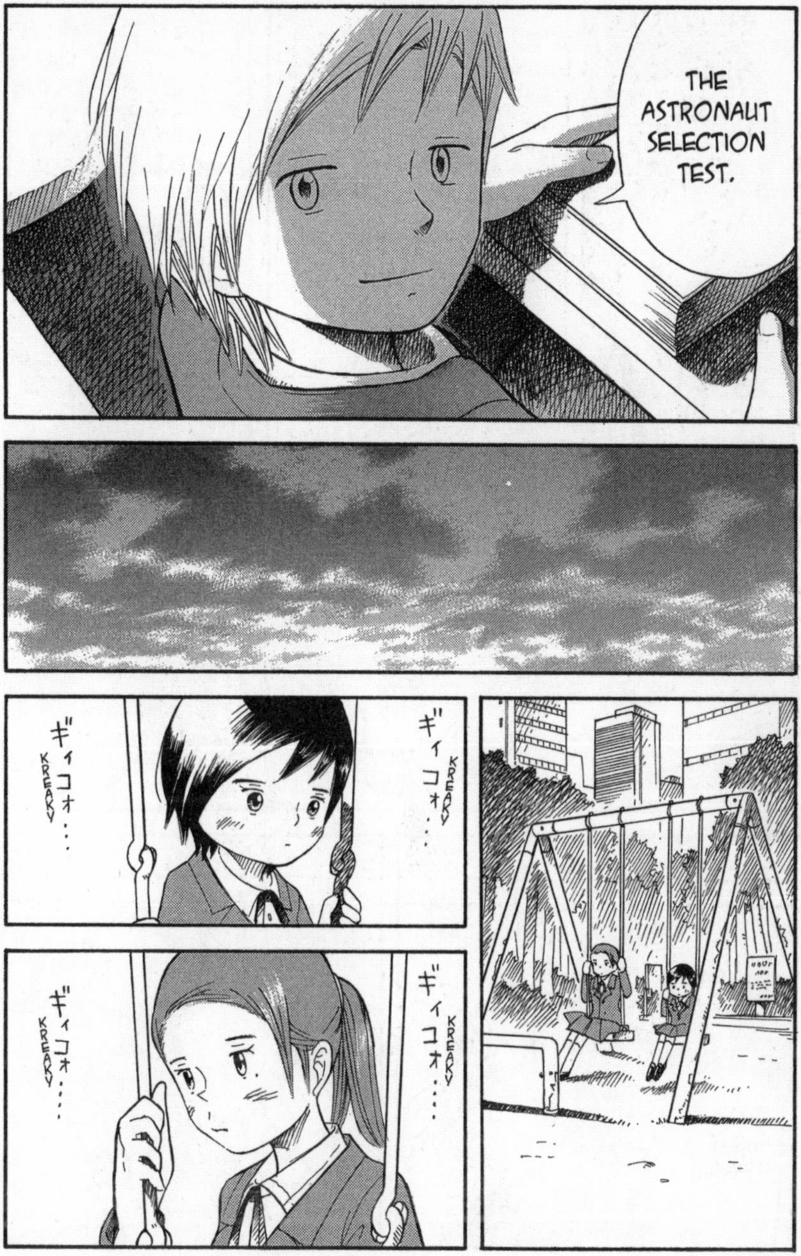
THE ASTRONAUT SELECTION TEST.
ギィコォ・・・
KREAKY
ギィコォ・・・
KREAKY
ギィコォ・・・
KREAKY
ギィコォ・・・
KREAKY

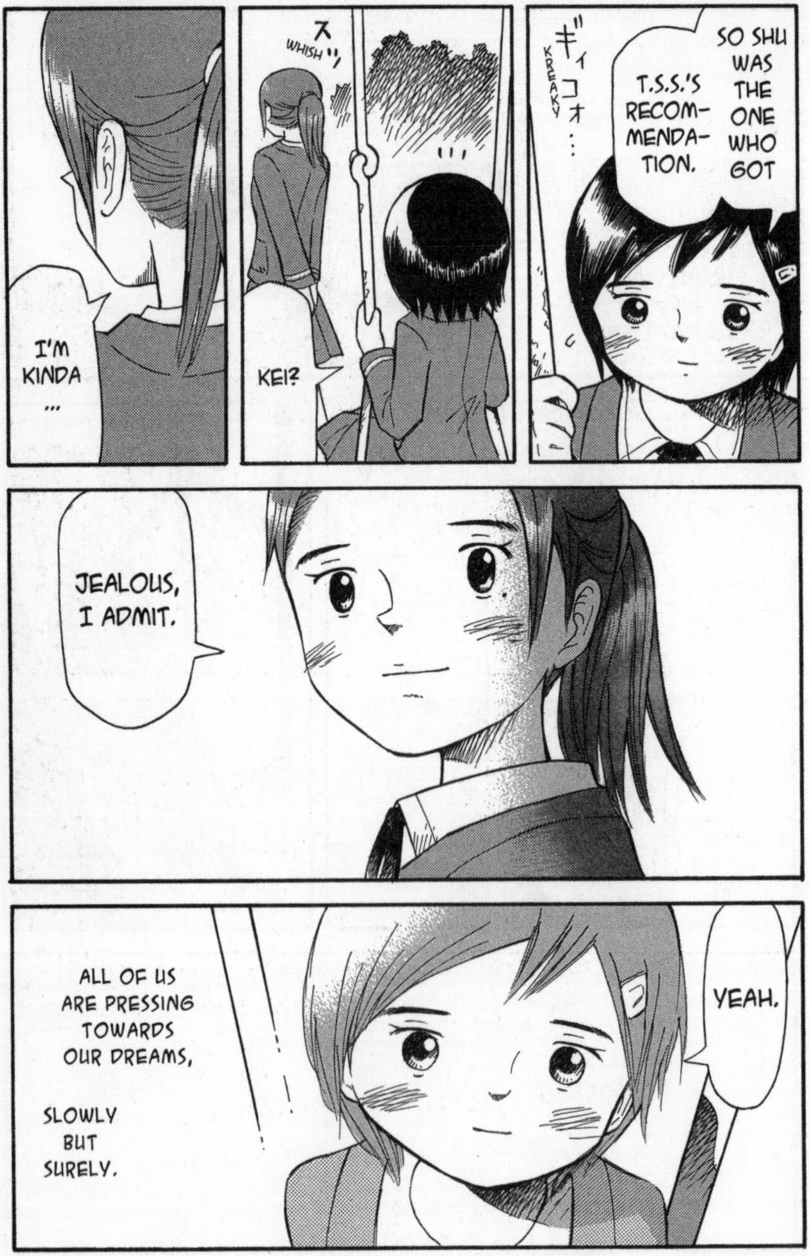
ギィコォ…
KREAKY
SO SHU WAS THE ONE WHO GOT T.S.S.'S RECOM-MENDA-TION.
ス
WHISH
ツ
KEI?
I'M KINDA ...
JEALOUS, I ADMIT.
YEAH.
ALL OF US ARE PRESSING TOWARDS OUR DREAMS,
SLOWLY BUT SURELY.

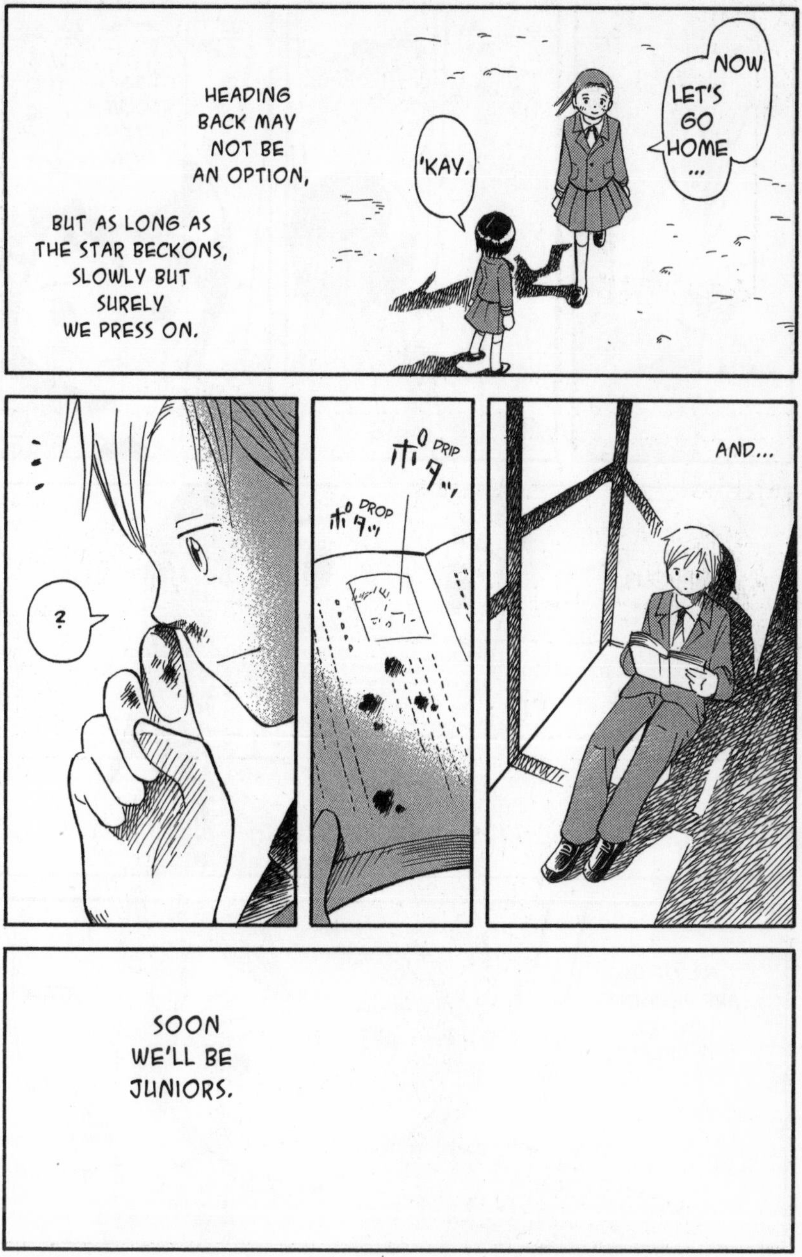
NOW LET'S GO HOME...
'KAY.
HEADING BACK MAY NOT BE AN OPTION,
BUT AS LONG AS THE STAR BECKONS, SLOWLY BUT SURELY WE PRESS ON.
AND...
ポタッ DRIP
ポタッ DROP
?
SOON WE'LL BE JUNIORS.

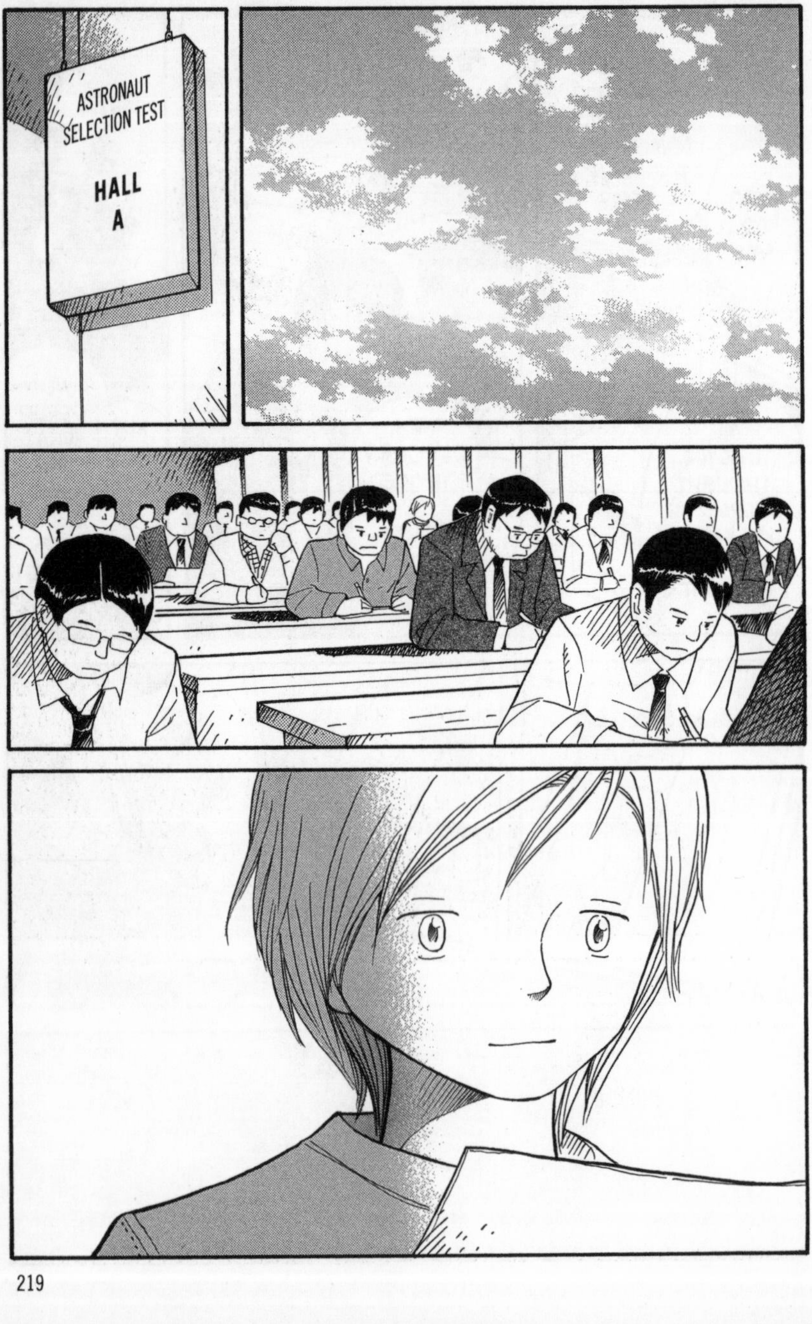
ASTRONAUT
SELECTION TEST
HALL
A

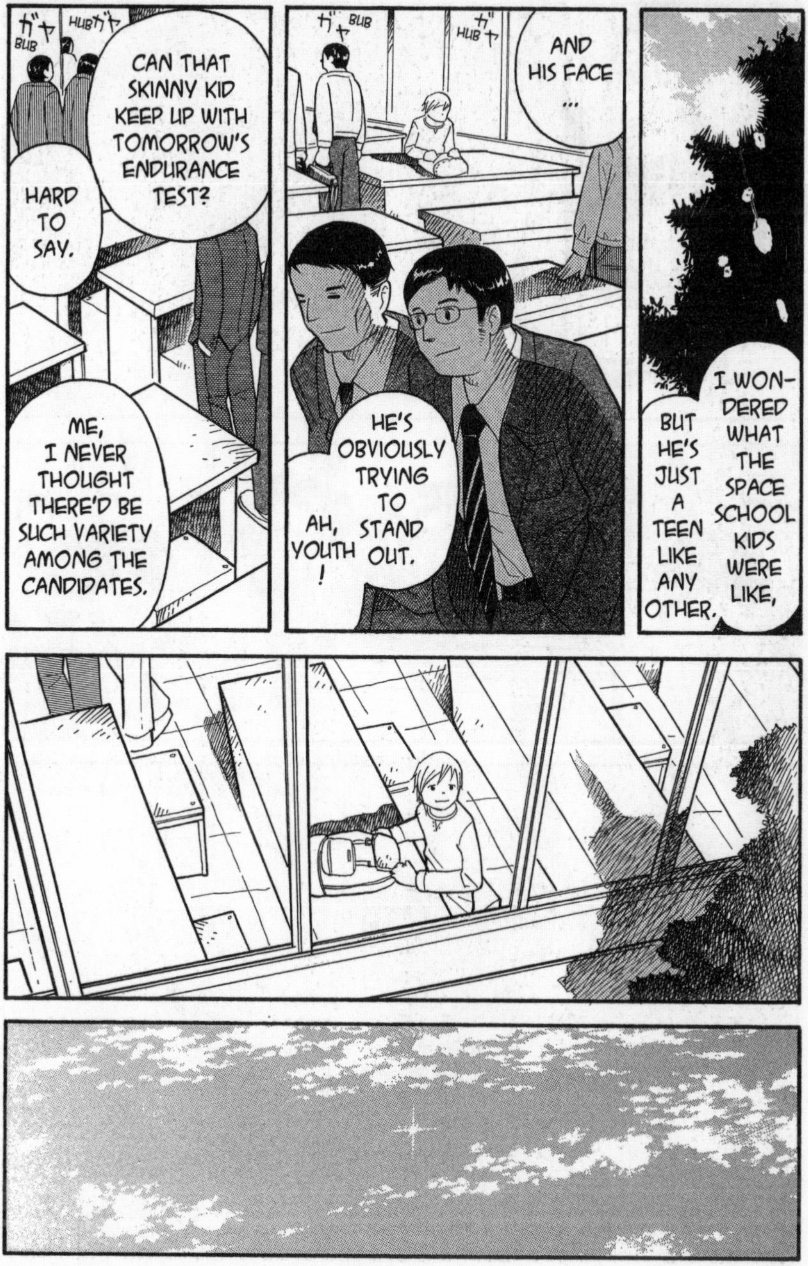
I WONDERED WHAT THE SPACE SCHOOL KIDS WERE LIKE,
BUT HE'S JUST A TEEN LIKE ANY OTHER.
ガヤ HUB
ガヤ BUB
AND HIS FACE ...
HE'S OBVIOUSLY TRYING TO STAND OUT.
AH, YOUTH!
ガヤ HUB
ガヤ BUB
CAN THAT SKINNY KID KEEP UP WITH TOMORROW'S ENDURANCE TEST?
HARD TO SAY.
ME, I NEVER THOUGHT THERE'D BE SUCH VARIETY AMONG THE CANDIDATES.

MISSION:46

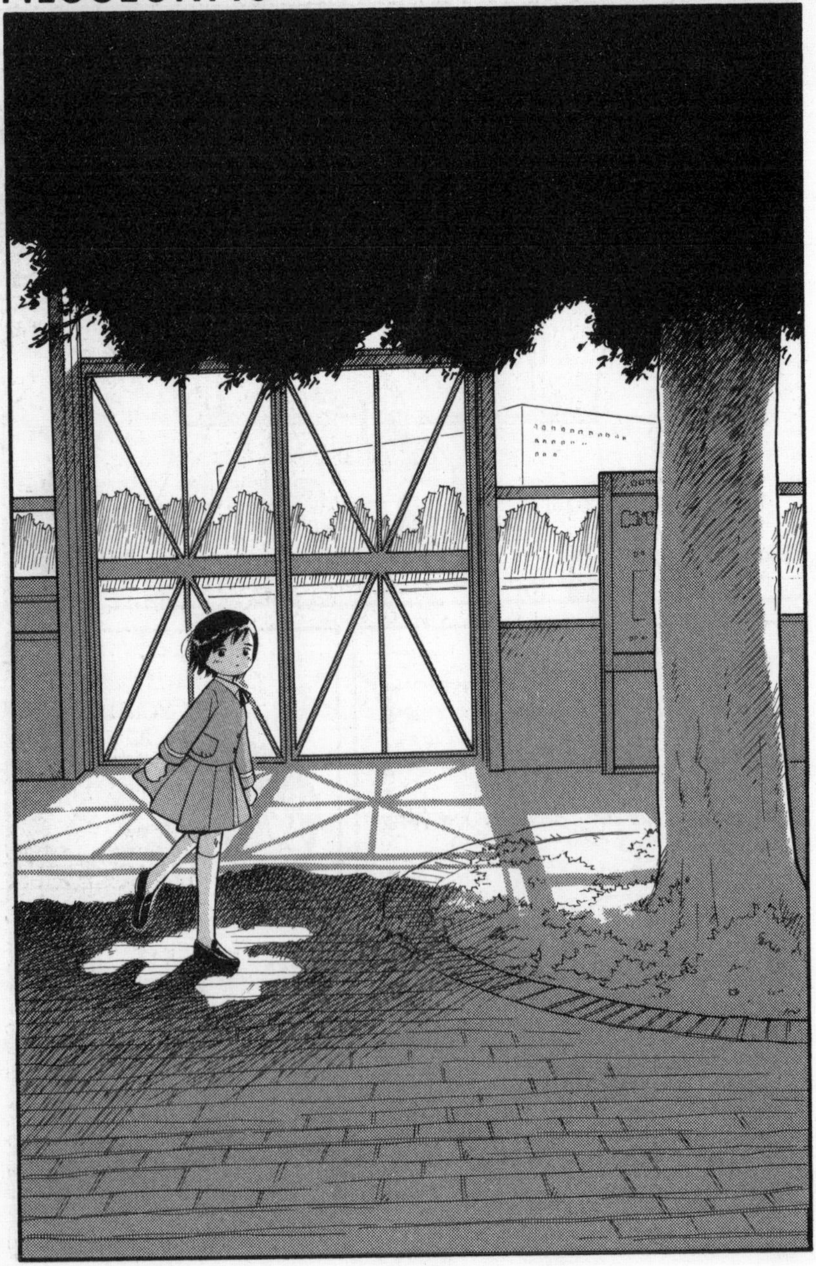

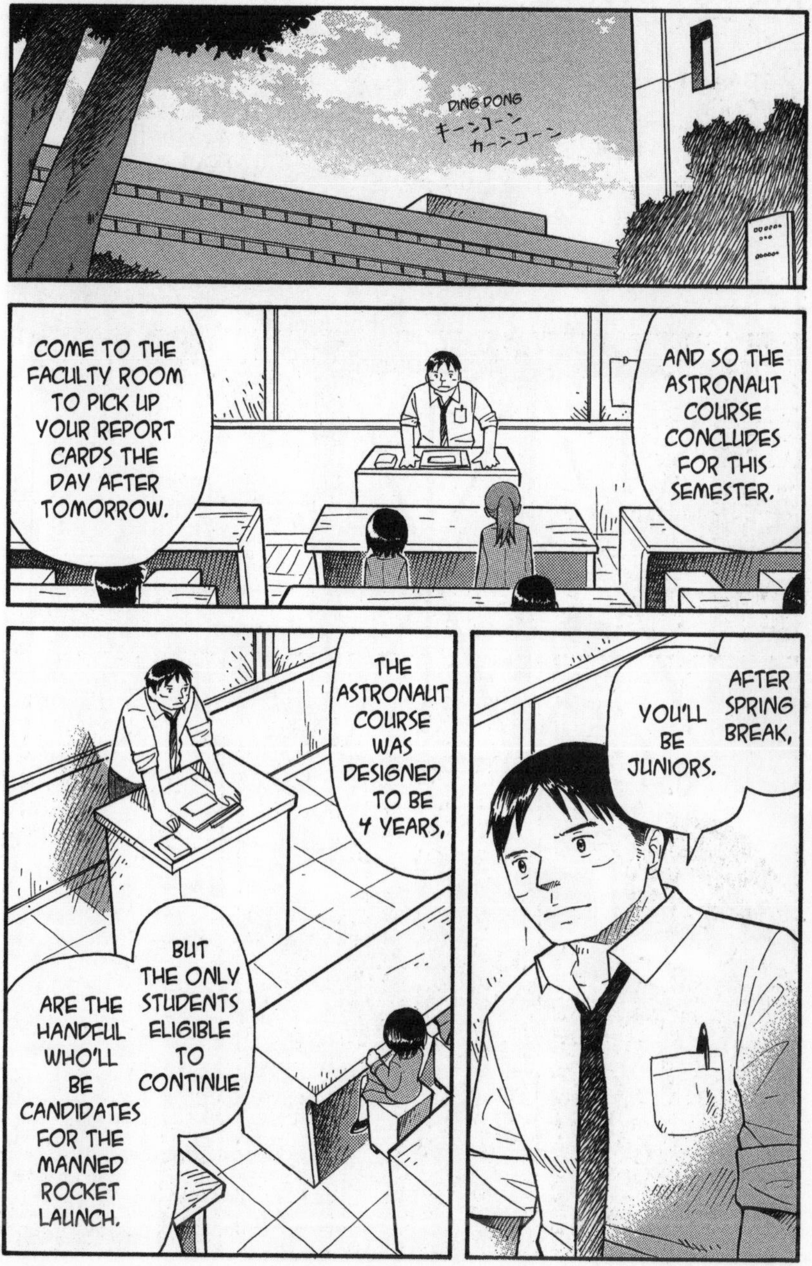
DING DONG
キーンコーン カーンコーン
AND SO THE ASTRONAUT COURSE CONCLUDES FOR THIS SEMESTER.
COME TO THE FACULTY ROOM TO PICK UP YOUR REPORT CARDS THE DAY AFTER TOMORROW.
AFTER SPRING BREAK,
YOU'LL BE JUNIORS.
THE ASTRONAUT COURSE WAS DESIGNED TO BE 4 YEARS,
BUT THE ONLY STUDENTS ELIGIBLE TO CONTINUE
ARE THE HANDFUL WHO'LL BE CANDIDATES FOR THE MANNED ROCKET LAUNCH.

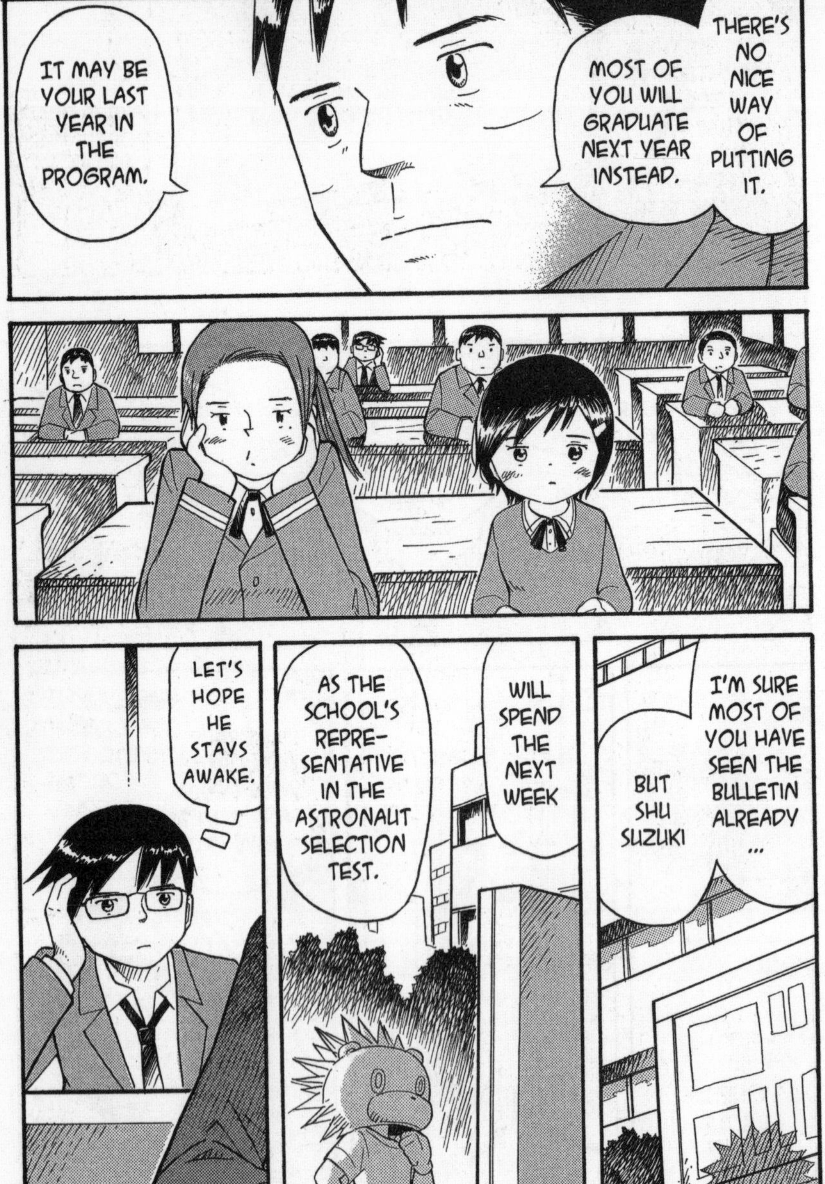
THERE'S NO NICE WAY OF PUTTING IT.
MOST OF YOU WILL GRADUATE NEXT YEAR INSTEAD.
IT MAY BE YOUR LAST YEAR IN THE PROGRAM.
I'M SURE MOST OF YOU HAVE SEEN THE BULLETIN ALREADY ...
BUT SHU SUZUKI
WILL SPEND THE NEXT WEEK
AS THE SCHOOL'S REPRESENTATIVE IN THE ASTRONAUT SELECTION TEST.
LET'S HOPE HE STAYS AWAKE.

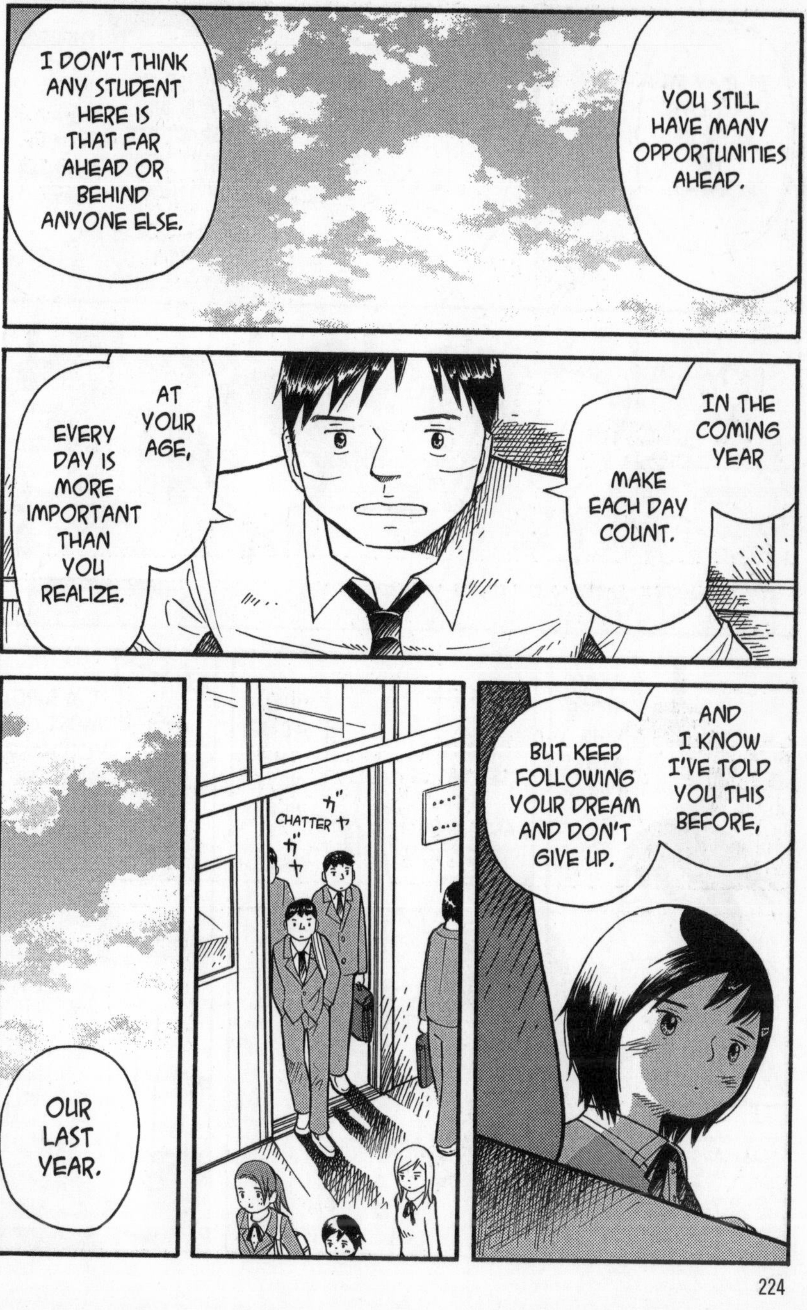
YOU STILL HAVE MANY OPPORTUNITIES AHEAD.
I DON'T THINK ANY STUDENT HERE IS THAT FAR AHEAD OR BEHIND ANYONE ELSE.
IN THE COMING YEAR
MAKE EACH DAY COUNT.
AT YOUR AGE,
EVERY DAY IS MORE IMPORTANT THAN YOU REALIZE.
AND I KNOW I'VE TOLD YOU THIS BEFORE,
BUT KEEP FOLLOWING YOUR DREAM AND DON'T GIVE UP.
ガヤ
CHATTER
ガヤ
OUR LAST YEAR.

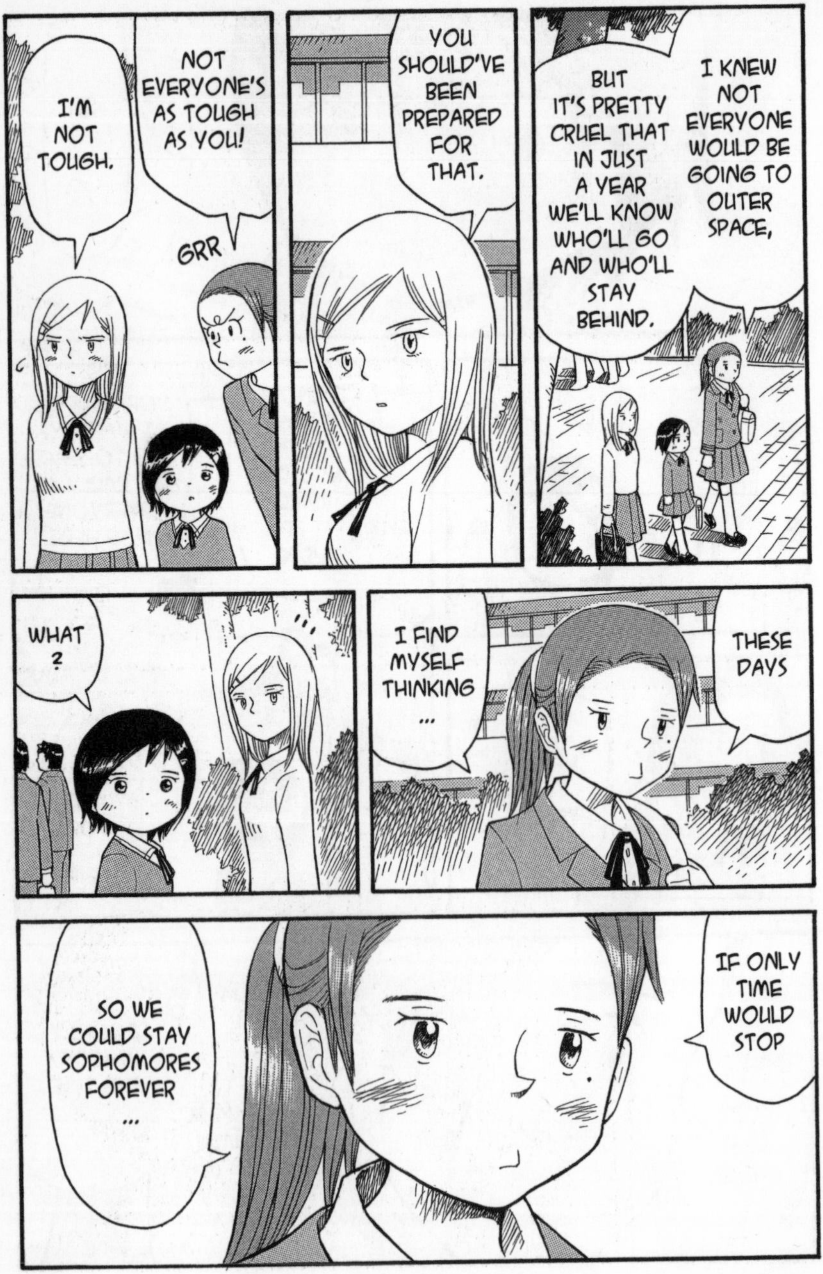
I KNEW NOT EVERYONE WOULD BE GOING TO OUTER SPACE,
BUT IT'S PRETTY CRUEL THAT IN JUST A YEAR WE'LL KNOW WHO'LL GO AND WHO'LL STAY BEHIND.
YOU SHOULD'VE BEEN PREPARED FOR THAT.
NOT EVERYONE'S AS TOUGH AS YOU!
GRR
I'M NOT TOUGH.
THESE DAYS
I FIND MYSELF THINKING ...
WHAT ?
IF ONLY TIME WOULD STOP
SO WE COULD STAY SOPHOMORES FOREVER ...

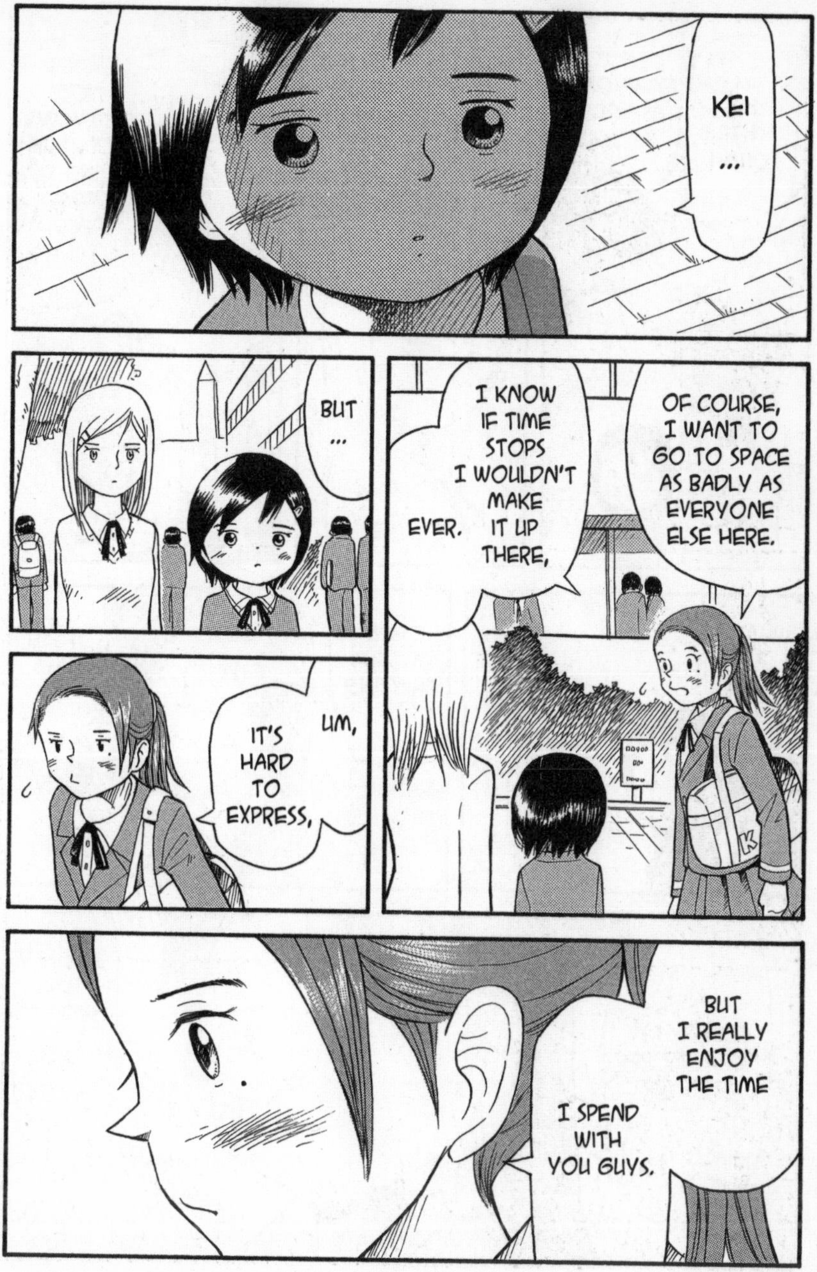
KEI ...
OF COURSE, I WANT TO GO TO SPACE AS BADLY AS EVERYONE ELSE HERE.
I KNOW IF TIME STOPS I WOULDN'T MAKE IT UP THERE,
EVER.
BUT ...
UM, IT'S HARD TO EXPRESS,
BUT I REALLY ENJOY THE TIME
I SPEND WITH YOU GUYS.

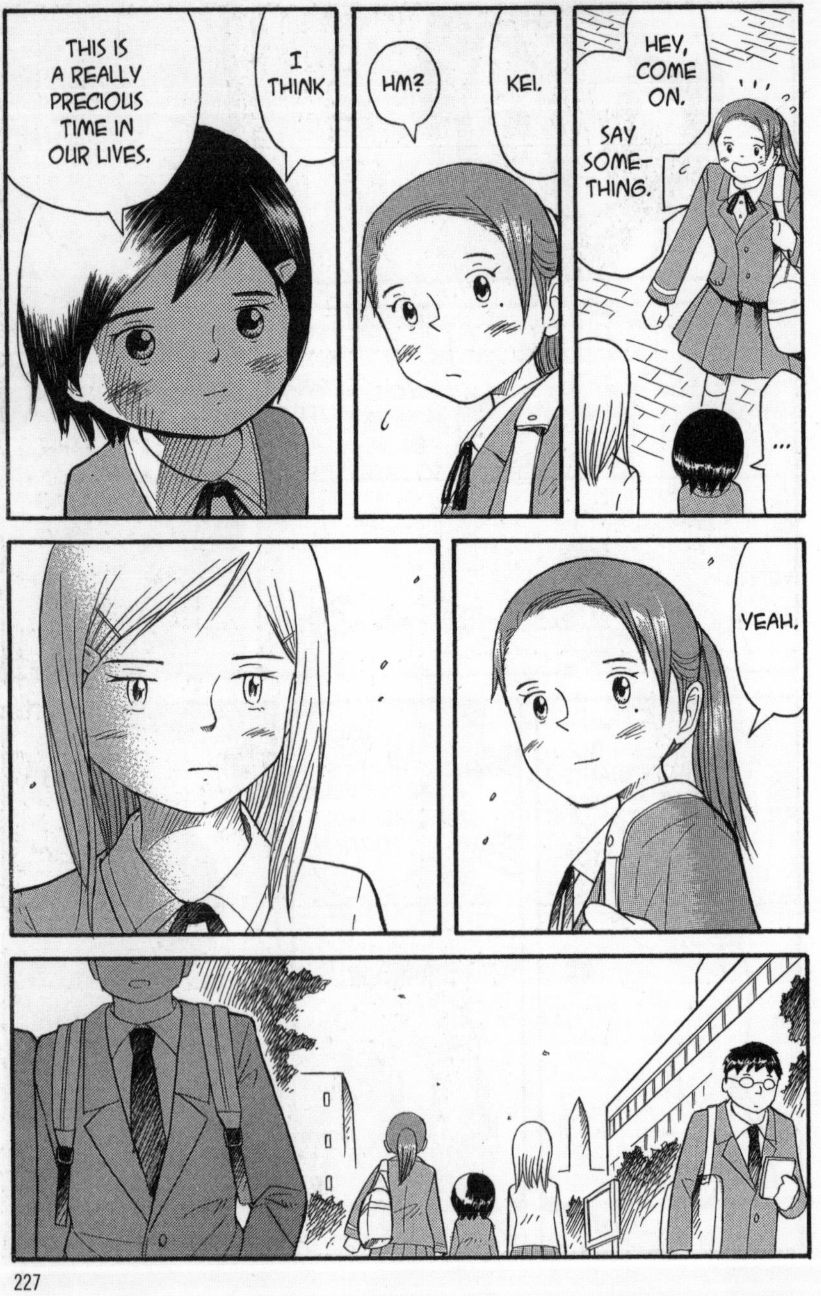
HEY, COME ON.
SAY SOME-THING.
...
KEI.
HM?
I THINK
THIS IS A REALLY PRECIOUS TIME IN OUR LIVES.
YEAH.

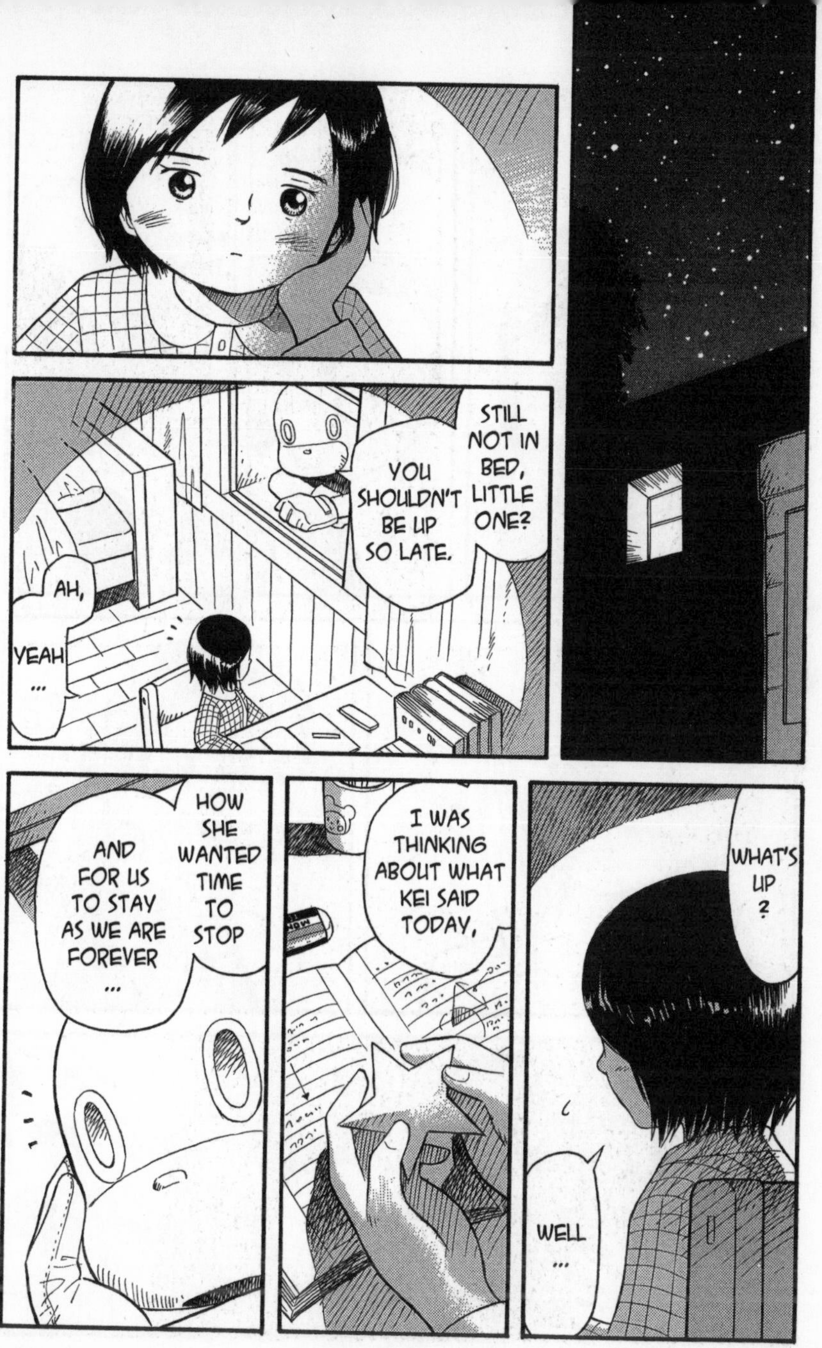
STILL NOT IN BED, LITTLE ONE?
YOU SHOULDN'T BE UP SO LATE.
AH, YEAH ...
WHAT'S UP ?
WELL ...
I WAS THINKING ABOUT WHAT KEI SAID TODAY,
HOW SHE WANTED TIME TO STOP
AND FOR US TO STAY AS WE ARE FOREVER ...

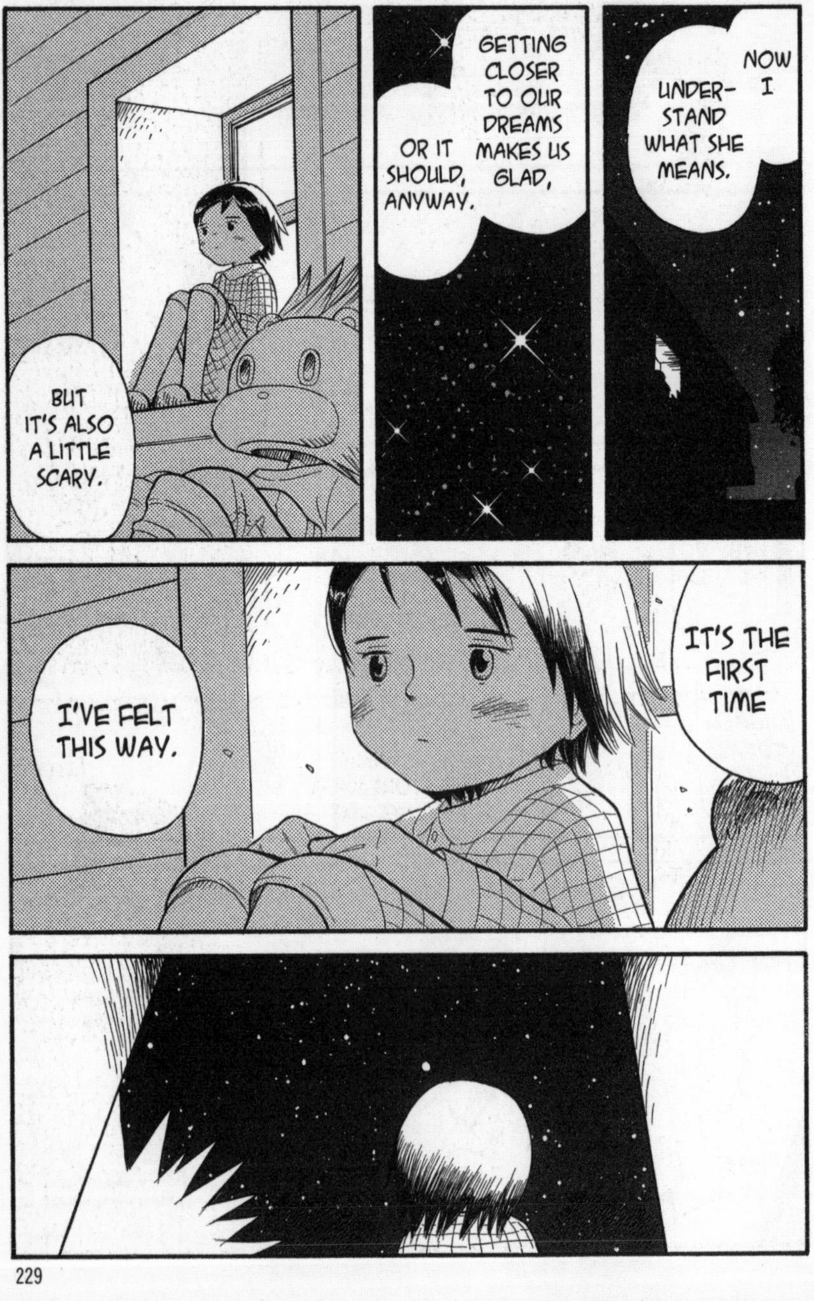
NOW I UNDER-STAND WHAT SHE MEANS.
GETTING CLOSER TO OUR DREAMS MAKES US GLAD,
OR IT SHOULD, ANYWAY.
BUT IT'S ALSO A LITTLE SCARY.
IT'S THE FIRST TIME
I'VE FELT THIS WAY.

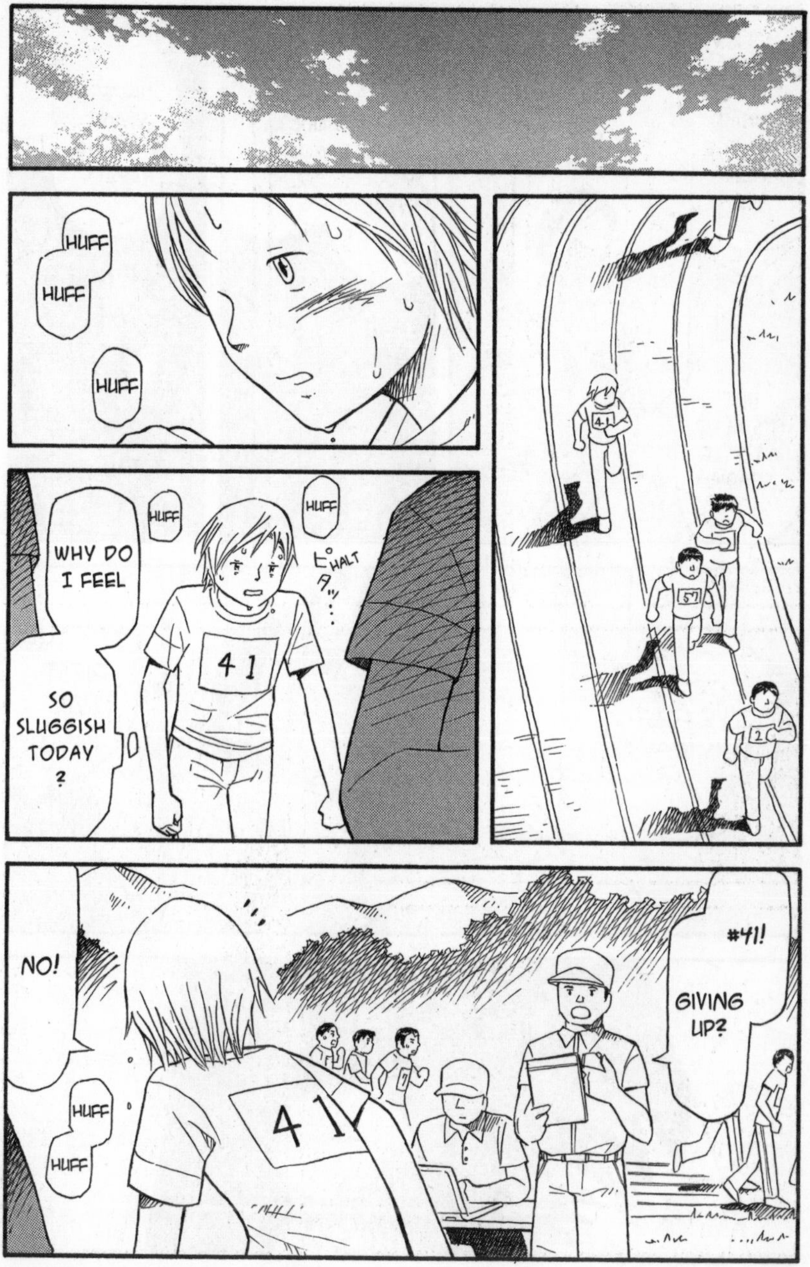
HUFF
HUFF
HUFF
HUFF
HUFF
HALT
WHY DO I FEEL SO SLUGGISH TODAY?
#41! GIVING UP?
NO!
HUFF
HUFF

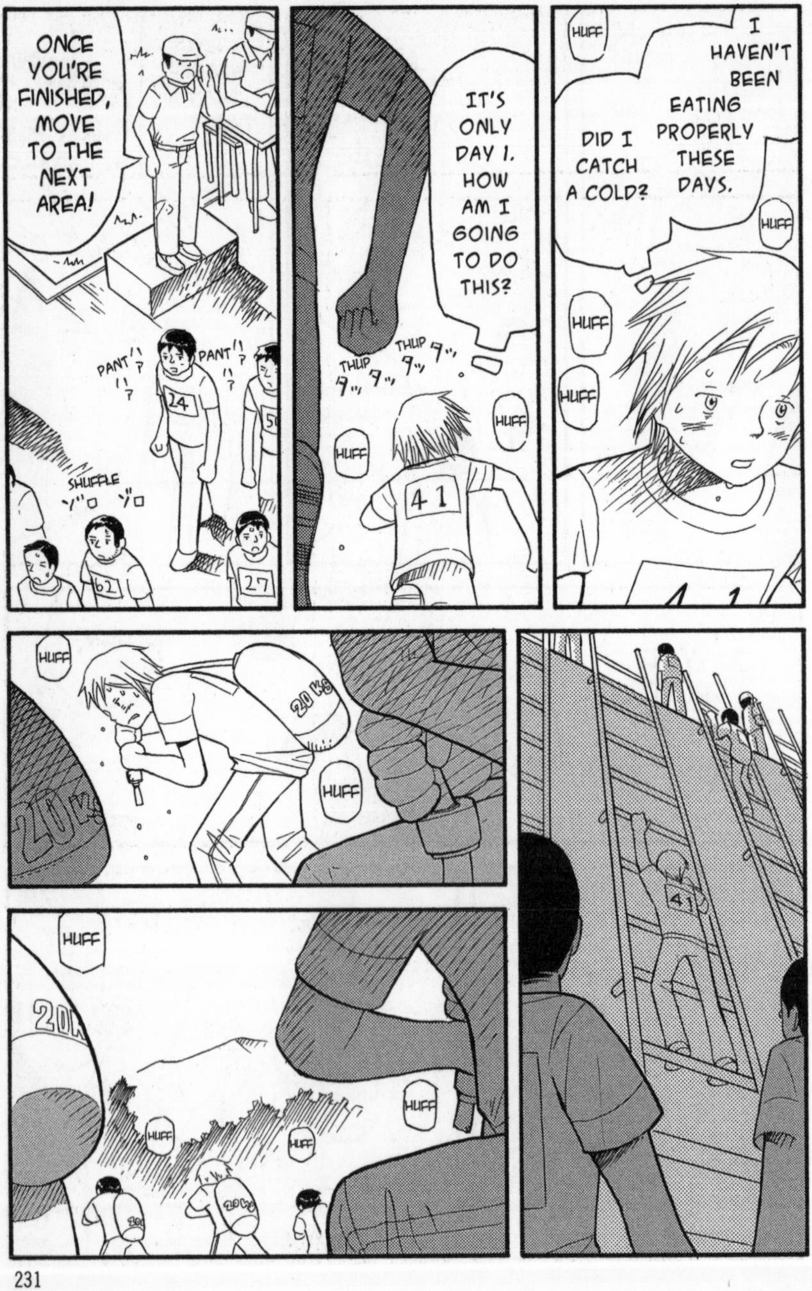
HUFF
I HAVEN'T BEEN EATING PROPERLY THESE DAYS.
DID I CATCH A COLD?
HUFF
HUFF
HUFF
IT'S ONLY DAY 1. HOW AM I GOING TO DO THIS?
THUP タッ タッ
THUP タッ タッ
HUFF
HUFF
ONCE YOU'RE FINISHED, MOVE TO THE NEXT AREA!
PANT ハァ ハァ
PANT ハァ ハァ
SHUFFLE ゾロ ゾロ
HUFF
HUFF
HUFF
HUFF
HUFF
HUFF

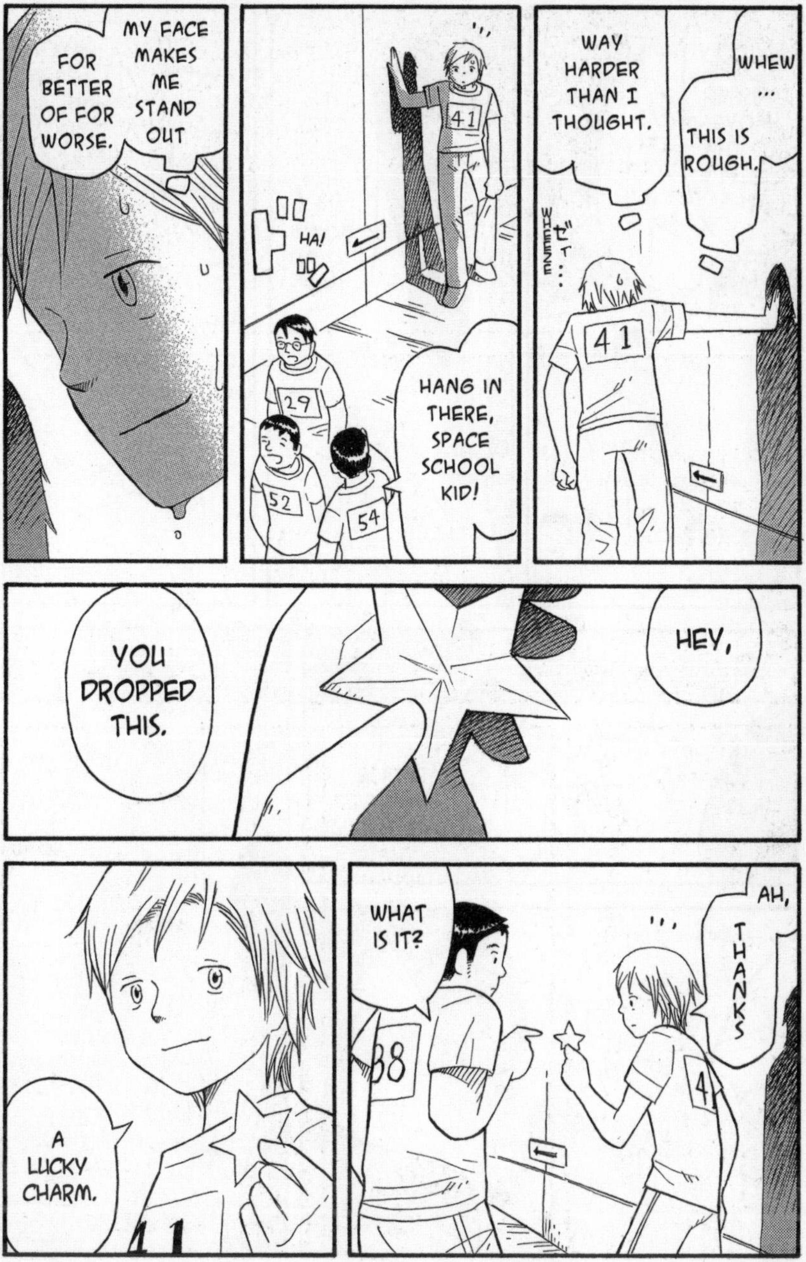
WHEW ... THIS IS ROUGH.
WAY HARDER THAN I THOUGHT.
WHEEZE
HA!
HANG IN THERE, SPACE SCHOOL KID!
MY FACE MAKES ME STAND OUT
FOR BETTER OF FOR WORSE.
HEY,
YOU DROPPED THIS.
AH, THANKS
WHAT IS IT?
A LUCKY CHARM.

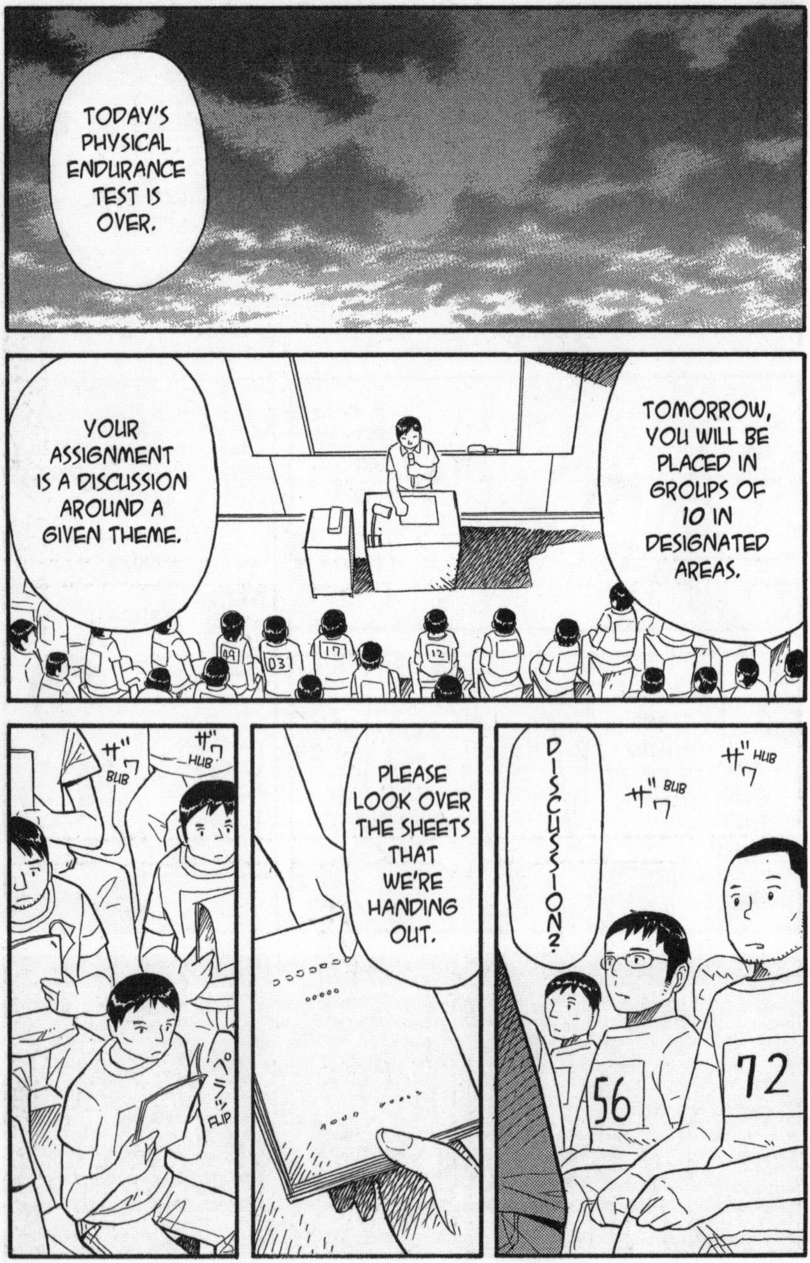
TODAY'S PHYSICAL ENDURANCE TEST IS OVER.
TOMORROW, YOU WILL BE PLACED IN GROUPS OF 10 IN DESIGNATED AREAS.
YOUR ASSIGNMENT IS A DISCUSSION AROUND A GIVEN THEME.
ザワ HUB
ザワ BUB
DISCUSSION?
PLEASE LOOK OVER THE SHEETS THAT WE'RE HANDING OUT.
ザワ BUB
ザワ HUB
ペラッ FLIP

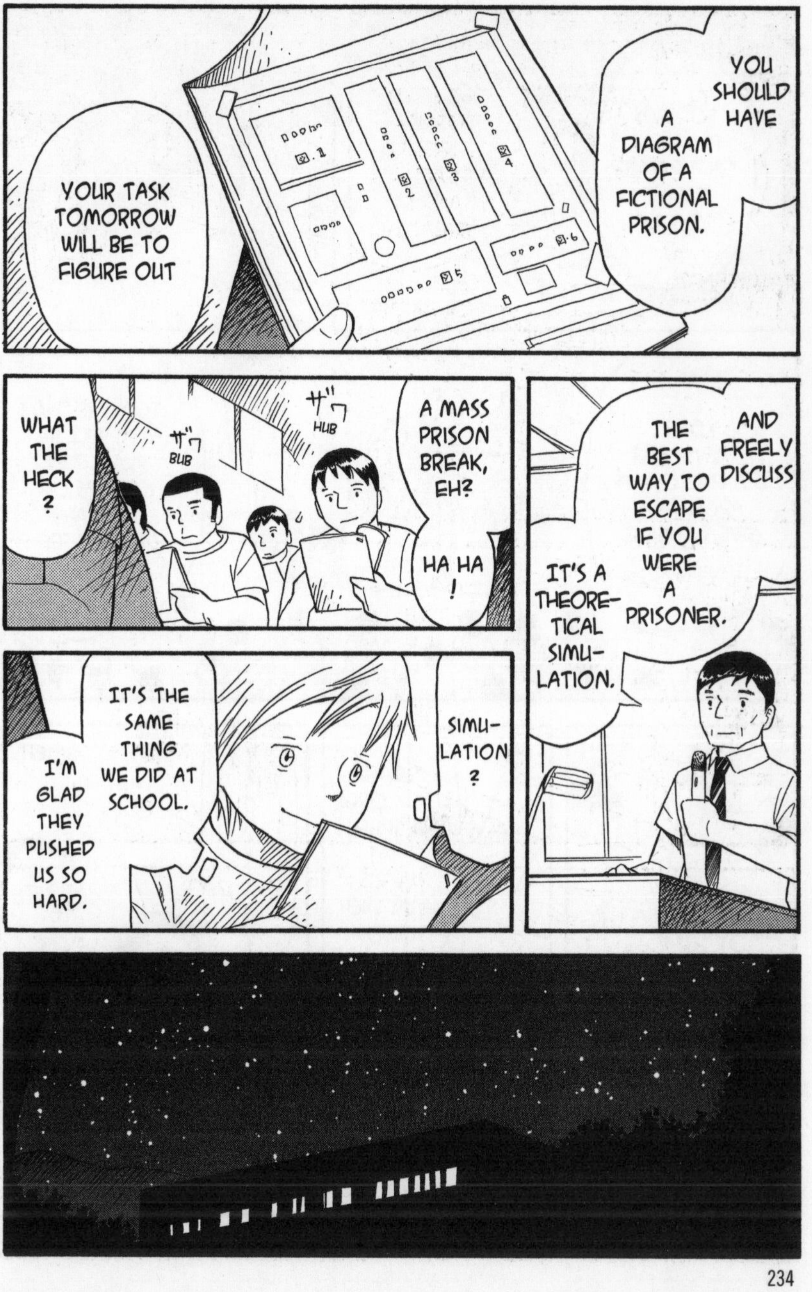
YOU SHOULD HAVE A DIAGRAM OF A FICTIONAL PRISON.
YOUR TASK TOMORROW WILL BE TO FIGURE OUT
AND FREELY DISCUSS
THE BEST WAY TO ESCAPE IF YOU WERE A PRISONER.
IT'S A THEORE-TICAL SIMU-LATION.
A MASS PRISON BREAK, EH?
HA HA!
ザワ HUB
ザワ BUB
WHAT THE HECK?
SIMU-LATION?
IT'S THE SAME THING WE DID AT SCHOOL.
I'M GLAD THEY PUSHED US SO HARD.

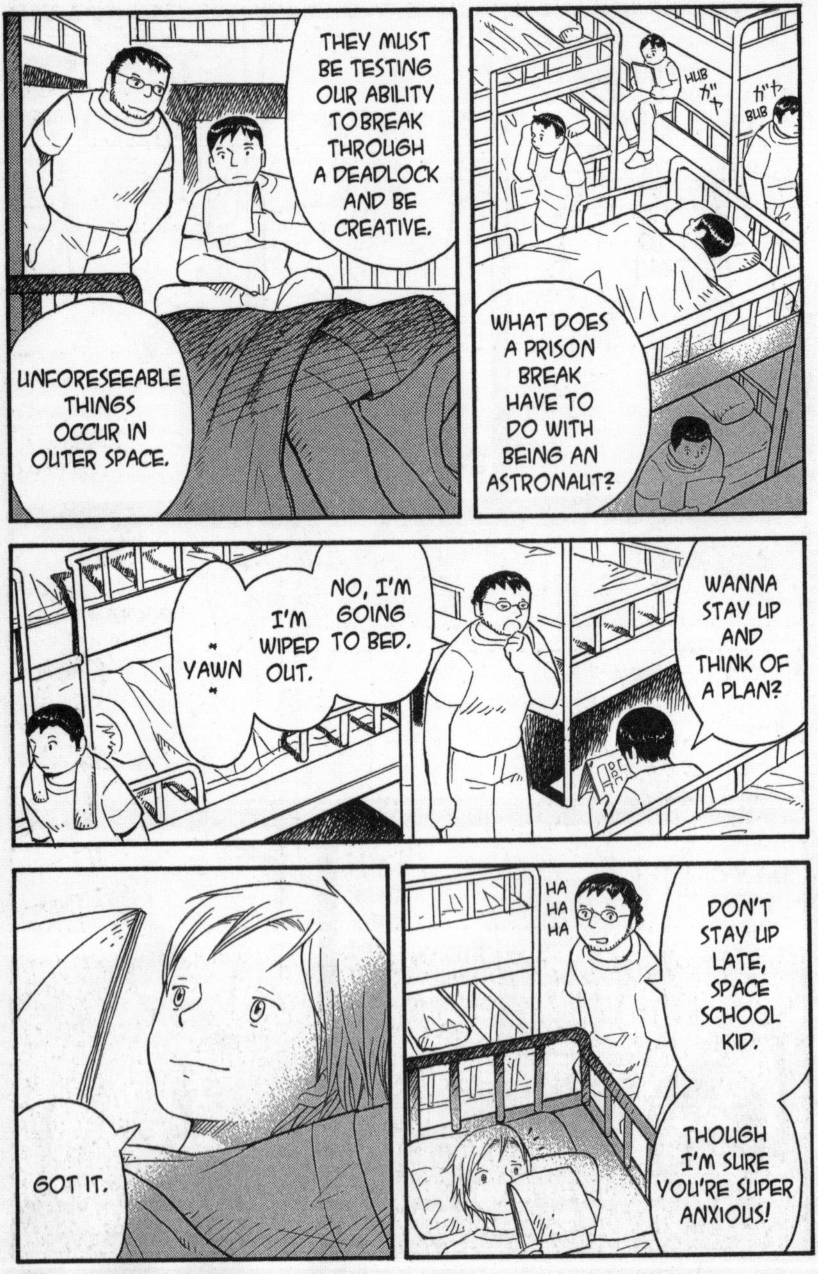
HUB ガヤ
ガヤ BUB
WHAT DOES A PRISON BREAK HAVE TO DO WITH BEING AN ASTRONAUT?
THEY MUST BE TESTING OUR ABILITY TO BREAK THROUGH A DEADLOCK AND BE CREATIVE.
UNFORESEEABLE THINGS OCCUR IN OUTER SPACE.
WANNA STAY UP AND THINK OF A PLAN?
NO, I'M GOING TO BED.
I'M WIPED OUT.
* YAWN *
DON'T STAY UP LATE, SPACE SCHOOL KID.
THOUGH I'M SURE YOU'RE SUPER ANXIOUS!
HA HA HA
GOT IT.

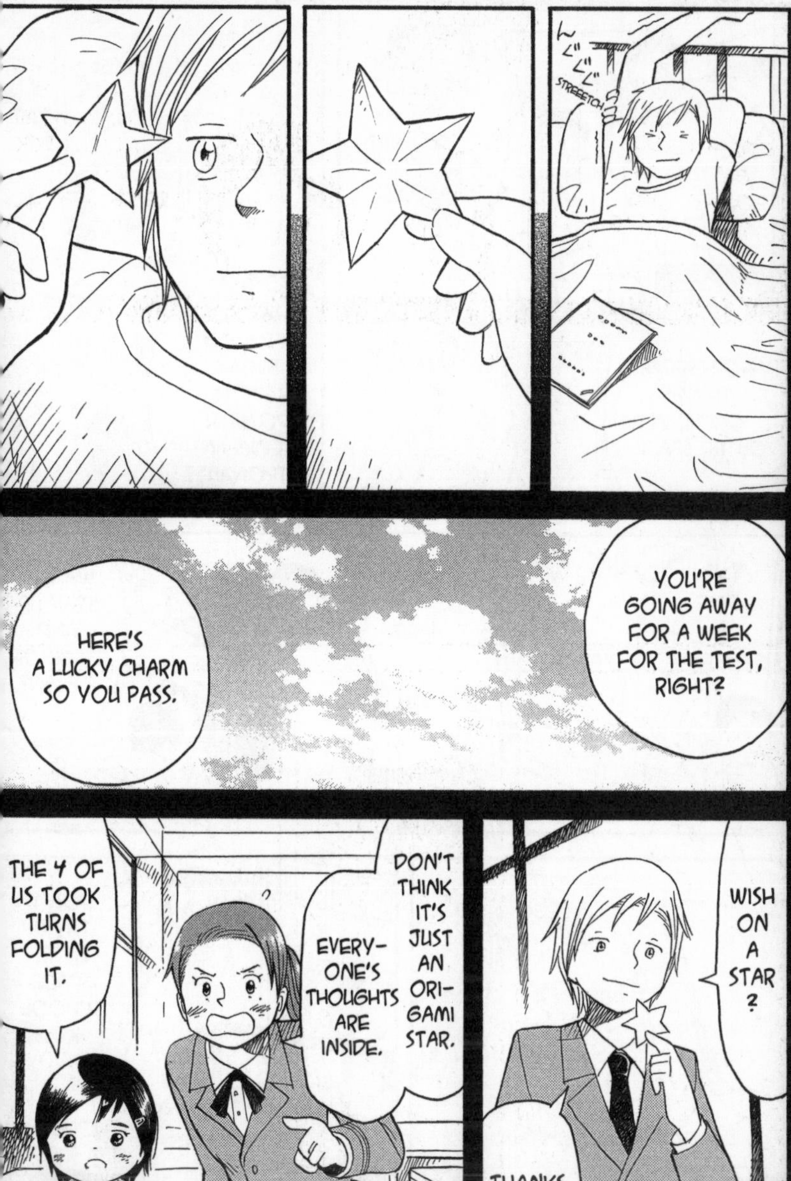
んーぐぐぐ
STREEETCH
YOU'RE GOING AWAY FOR A WEEK FOR THE TEST, RIGHT?
HERE'S A LUCKY CHARM SO YOU PASS.
WISH ON A STAR?
THANKS.
DON'T THINK IT'S JUST AN ORIGAMI STAR.
EVERYONE'S THOUGHTS ARE INSIDE.
THE 4 OF US TOOK TURNS FOLDING IT.

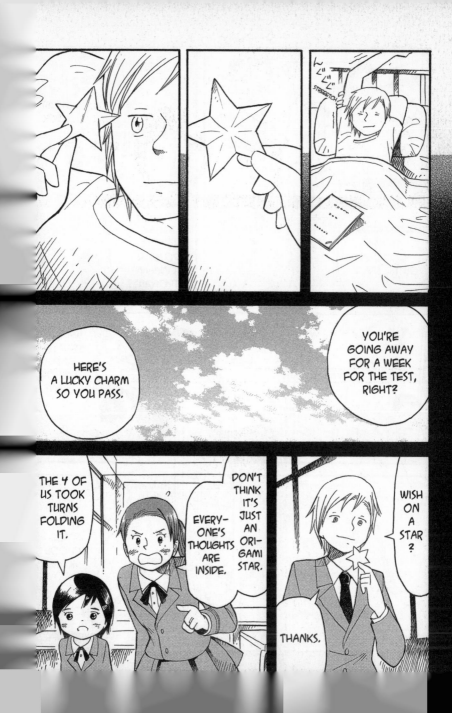

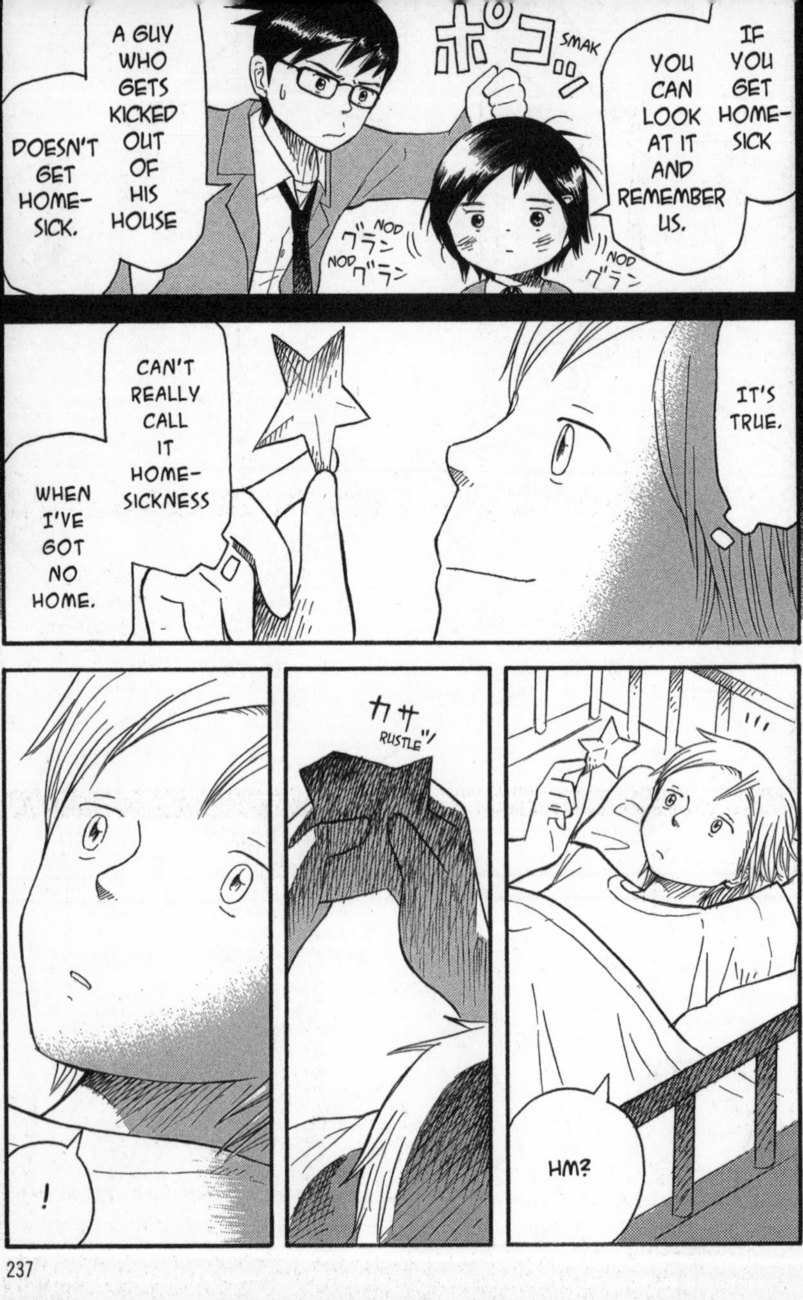
IF YOU GET HOME-SICK YOU CAN LOOK AT IT AND REMEMBER US.
ポコッ SMAK
A GUY WHO GETS KICKED OUT OF HIS HOUSE DOESN'T GET HOME-SICK.
グラン NOD
グラン NOD
グラン NOD
IT'S TRUE.
CAN'T REALLY CALL IT HOME-SICKNESS WHEN I'VE GOT NO HOME.
HM?
カサ RUSTLE
!

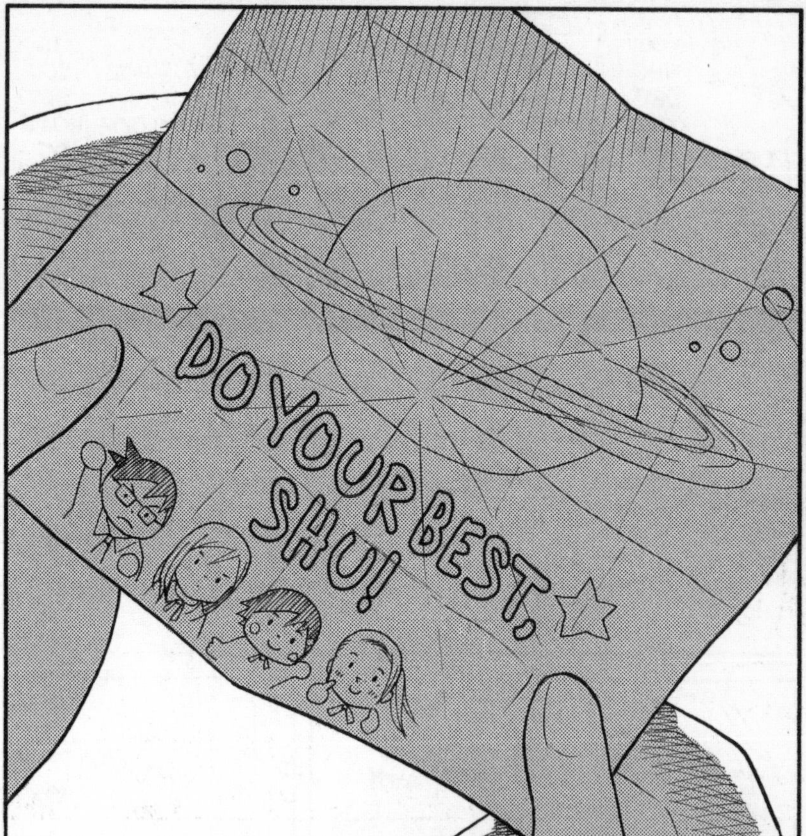
DO YOUR BEST, SHU!
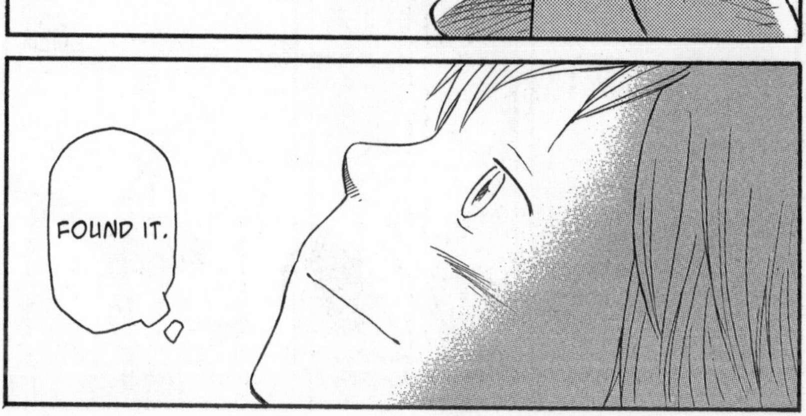
FOUND IT.

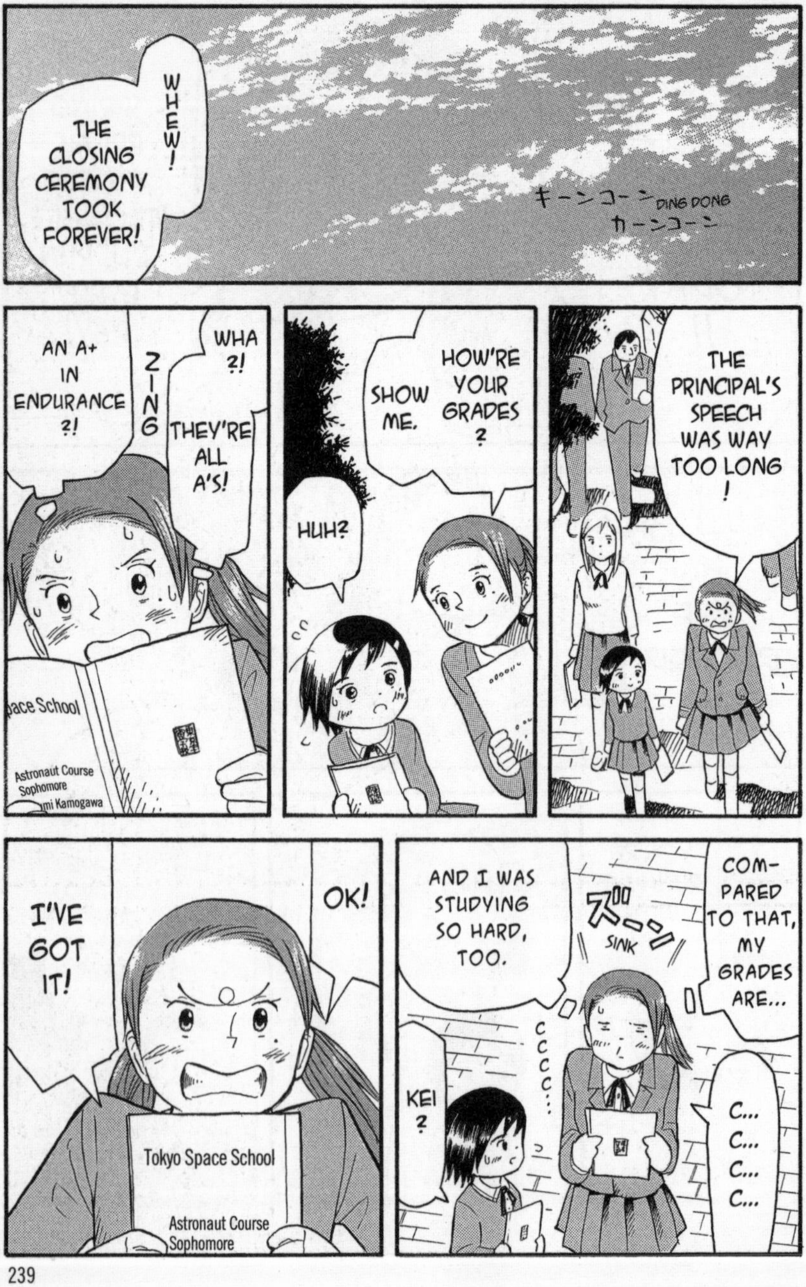
キーンコーン DING DONG カーンコーン
WHEW!
THE CLOSING CEREMONY TOOK FOREVER!
THE PRINCIPAL'S SPEECH WAS WAY TOO LONG!
HOW'RE YOUR GRADES?
SHOW ME.
HUH?
WHA?!
THEY'RE ALL A'S!
ZING
AN A+ IN ENDURANCE?!
Astronaut Course
Sophomore
COM-PARED TO THAT, MY GRADES ARE...
AND I WAS STUDYING SO HARD, TOO.
SINK
C... C... C... C...
CCCC...
KEI?
OK!
I'VE GOT IT!
Tokyo Space School
Astronaut Course
Sophomore

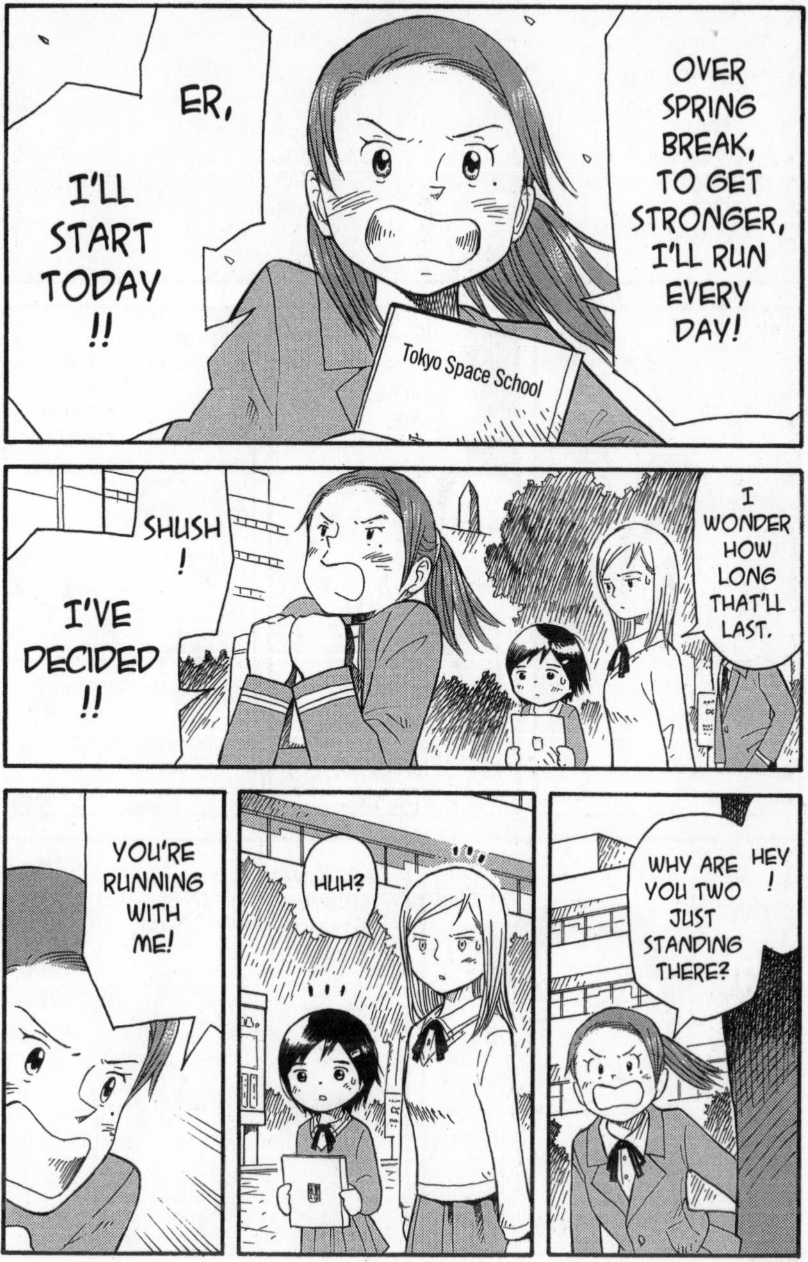
OVER SPRING BREAK, TO GET STRONGER, I'LL RUN EVERY DAY!
ER,
I'LL START TODAY !!
Tokyo Space School
I WONDER HOW LONG THAT'LL LAST.
SHUSH !
I'VE DECIDED !!
HEY !
WHY ARE YOU TWO JUST STANDING THERE?
HUH?
YOU'RE RUNNING WITH ME!

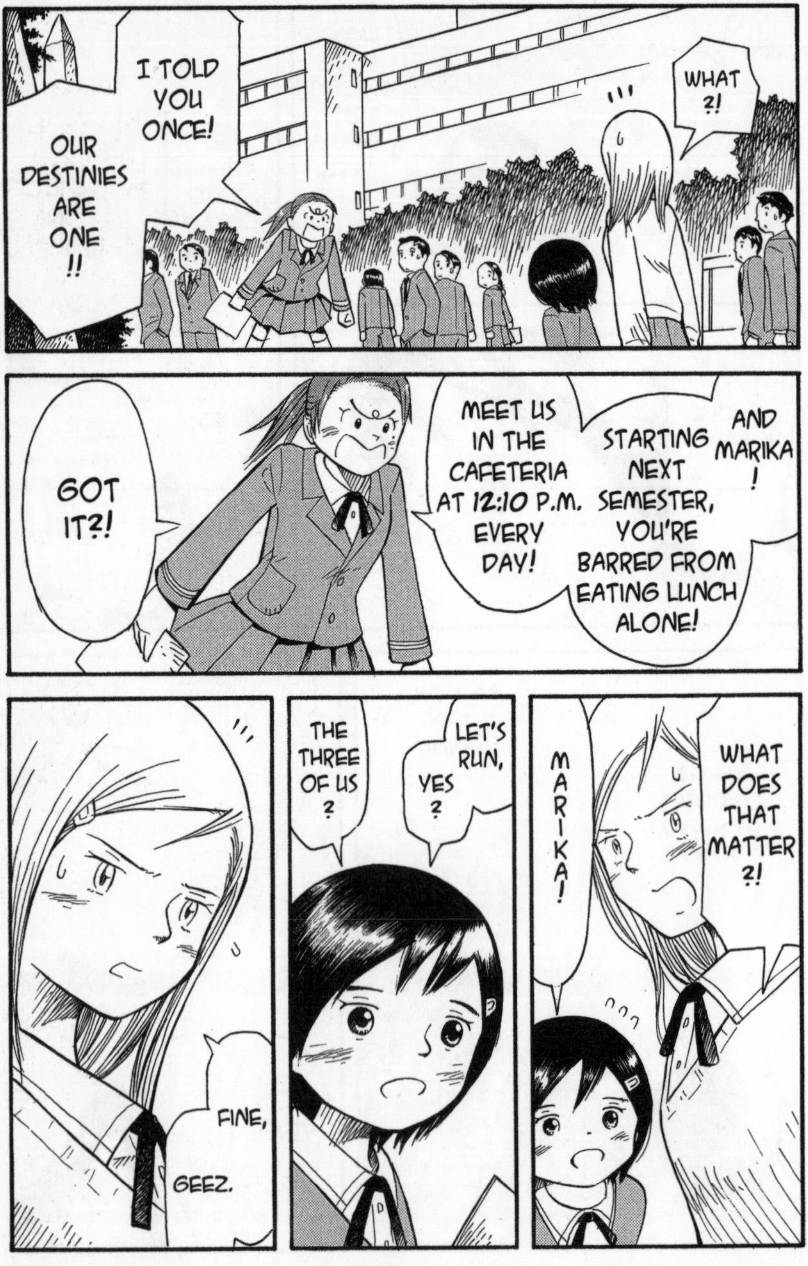
WHAT ?!
I TOLD YOU ONCE!
OUR DESTINIES ARE ONE !!
AND MARIKA !
STARTING NEXT SEMESTER, YOU'RE BARRED FROM EATING LUNCH ALONE!
MEET US IN THE CAFETERIA AT 12:10 P.M. EVERY DAY!
GOT IT?!
WHAT DOES THAT MATTER ?!
MARIKA!
LET'S RUN, YES ?
THE THREE OF US ?
FINE,
GEEZ.

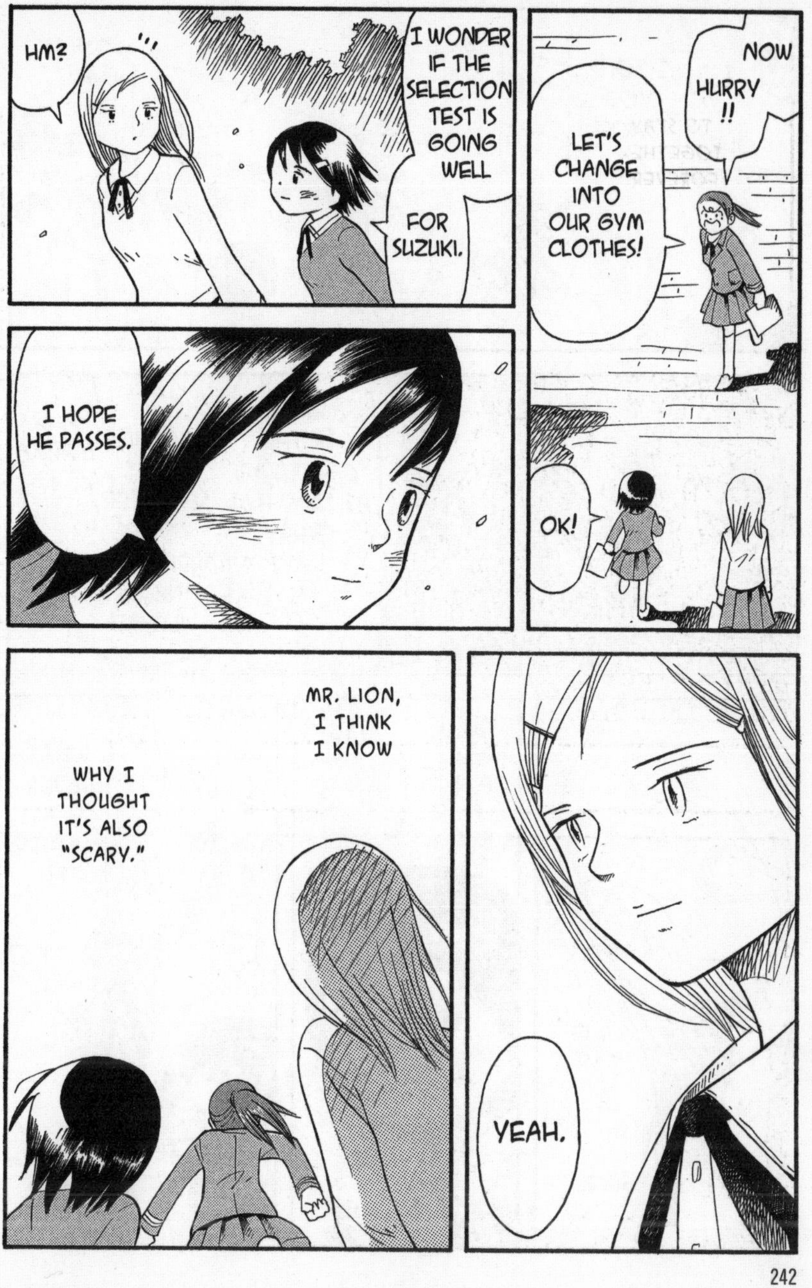
NOW HURRY!!
LET'S CHANGE INTO OUR GYM CLOTHES!
OK!
I WONDER IF THE SELECTION TEST IS GOING WELL
FOR SUZUKI.
HM?
I HOPE HE PASSES.
YEAH.
MR. LION, I THINK I KNOW
WHY I THOUGHT IT'S ALSO "SCARY."

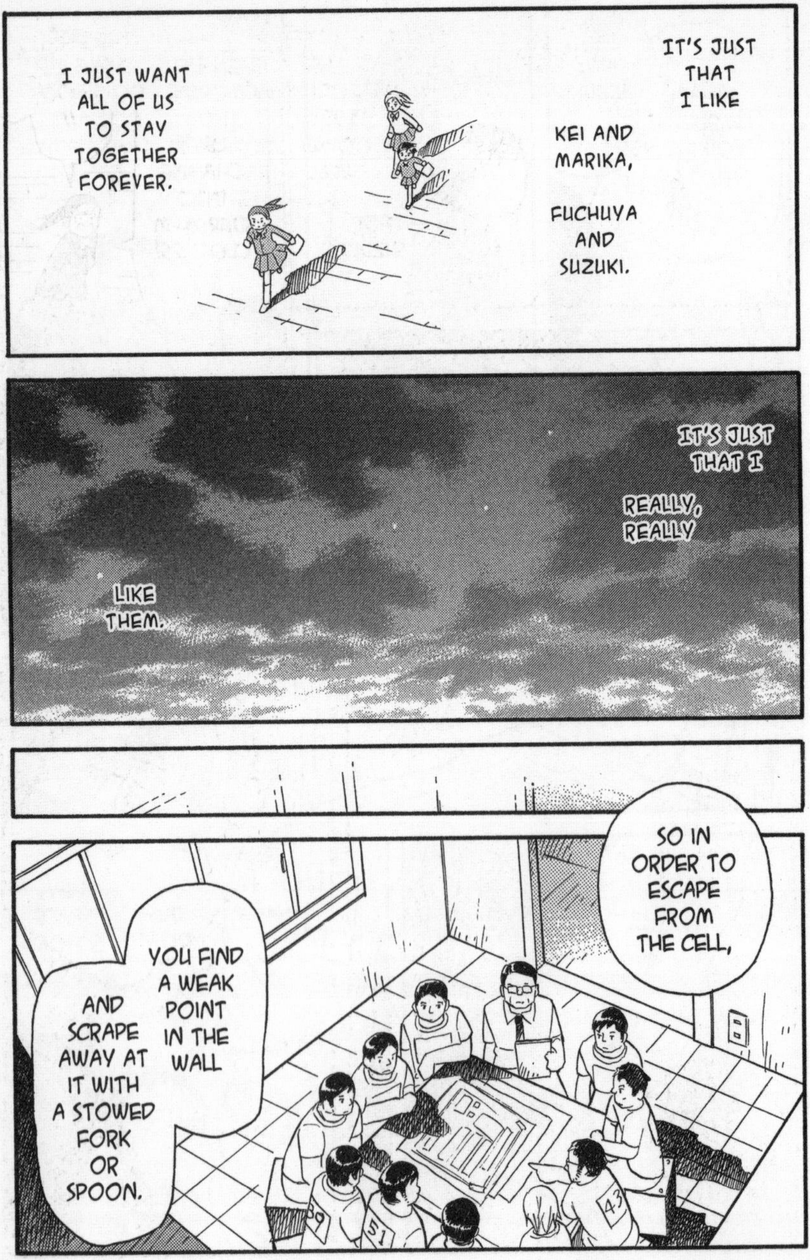
IT'S JUST THAT I LIKE
KEI AND MARIKA,
FUCHUYA AND SUZUKI.
I JUST WANT ALL OF US TO STAY TOGETHER FOREVER.
IT'S JUST THAT I
REALLY, REALLY
LIKE THEM.
SO IN ORDER TO ESCAPE FROM THE CELL,
YOU FIND A WEAK POINT IN THE WALL
AND SCRAPE AWAY AT IT WITH A STOWED FORK OR SPOON.

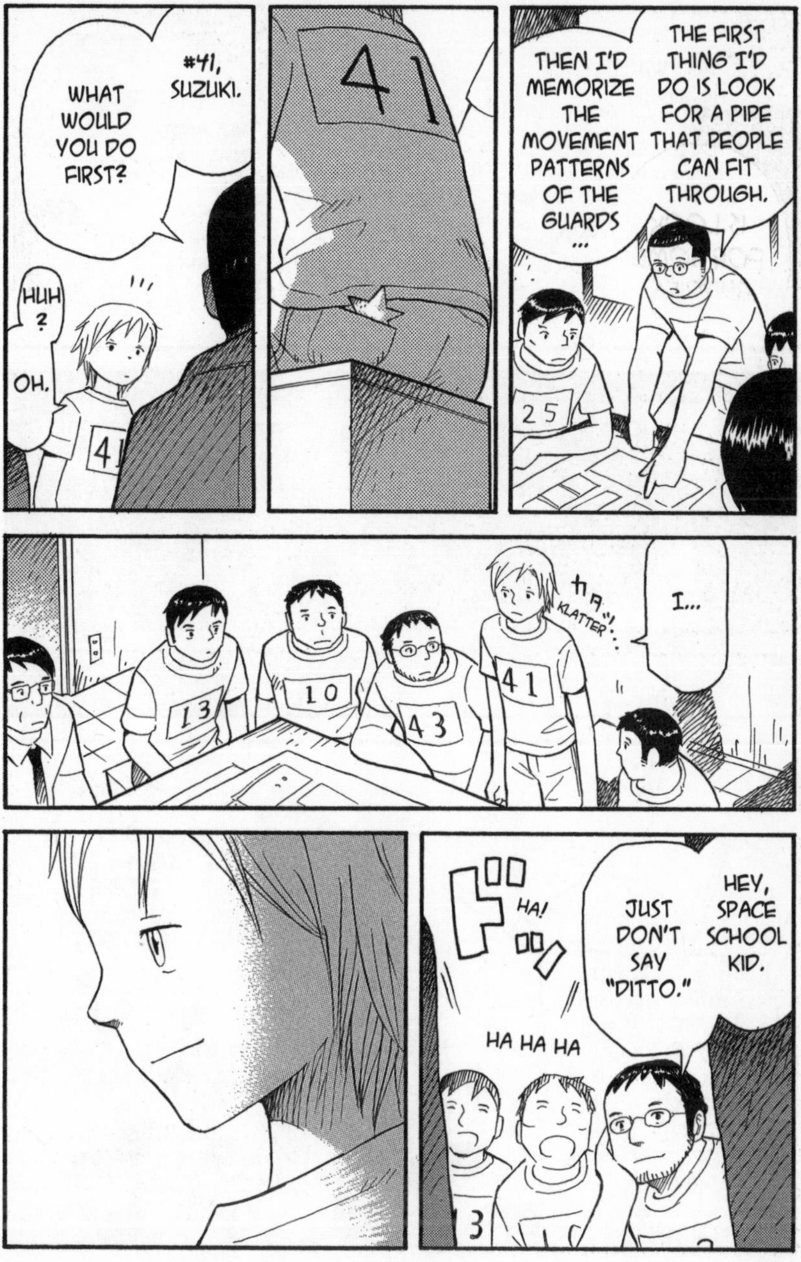
THE FIRST THING I'D DO IS LOOK FOR A PIPE THAT PEOPLE CAN FIT THROUGH.
THEN I'D MEMORIZE THE MOVEMENT PATTERNS OF THE GUARDS ...
#41, SUZUKI.
WHAT WOULD YOU DO FIRST?
HUH ?
OH.
I...
KLATTER
HEY, SPACE SCHOOL KID.
JUST DON'T SAY "DITTO."
HA!
HA HA HA

THE FIRST THING I'D DO
IS LOOK FOR SOME BUDDIES.
BEST, SHU!
YOU CAN'T
GO TO SPACE ALONE.

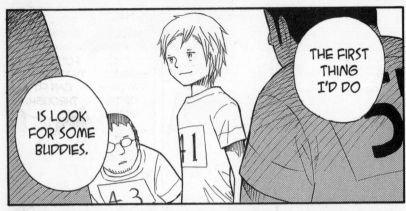

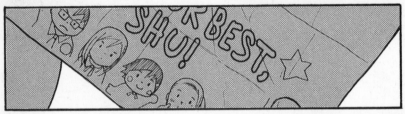

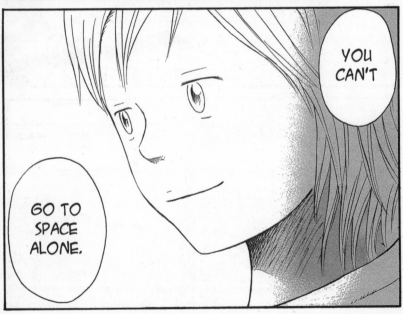

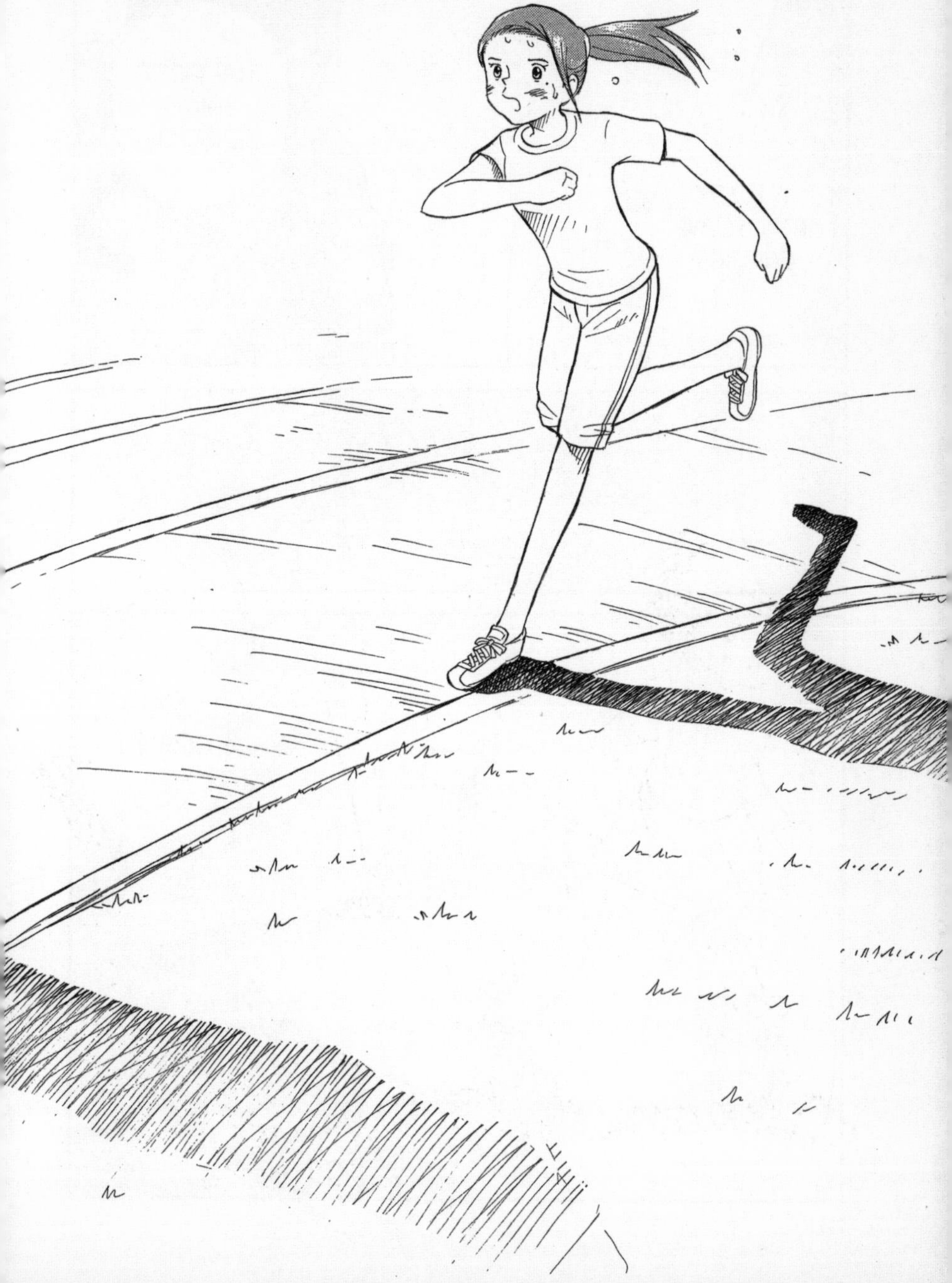

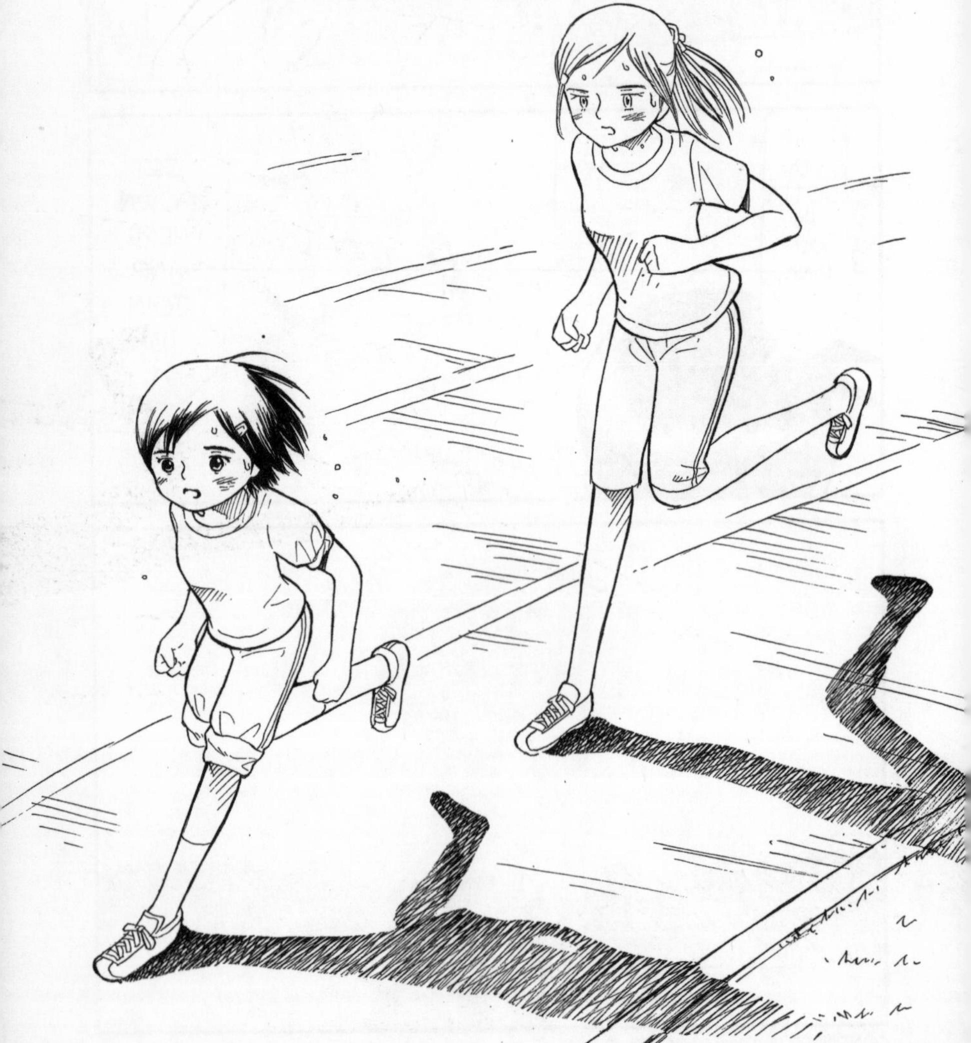

HEY!! FUCCHY!
HM?
GET DOWN HERE AND JOIN US!
ULP!
YOU GOTTA BE KID-DING, IDIOT!

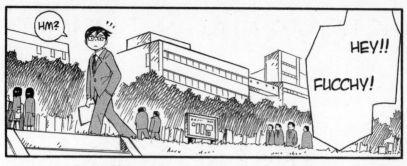

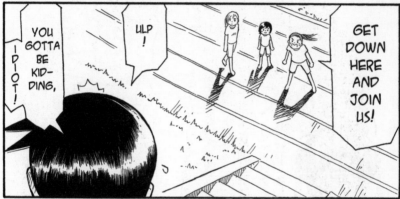

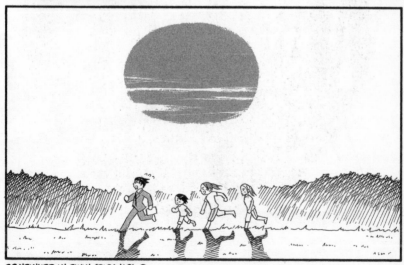

CONTINUED IN TWIN SPICA VOL.9

GIOVANNI'S TICKET

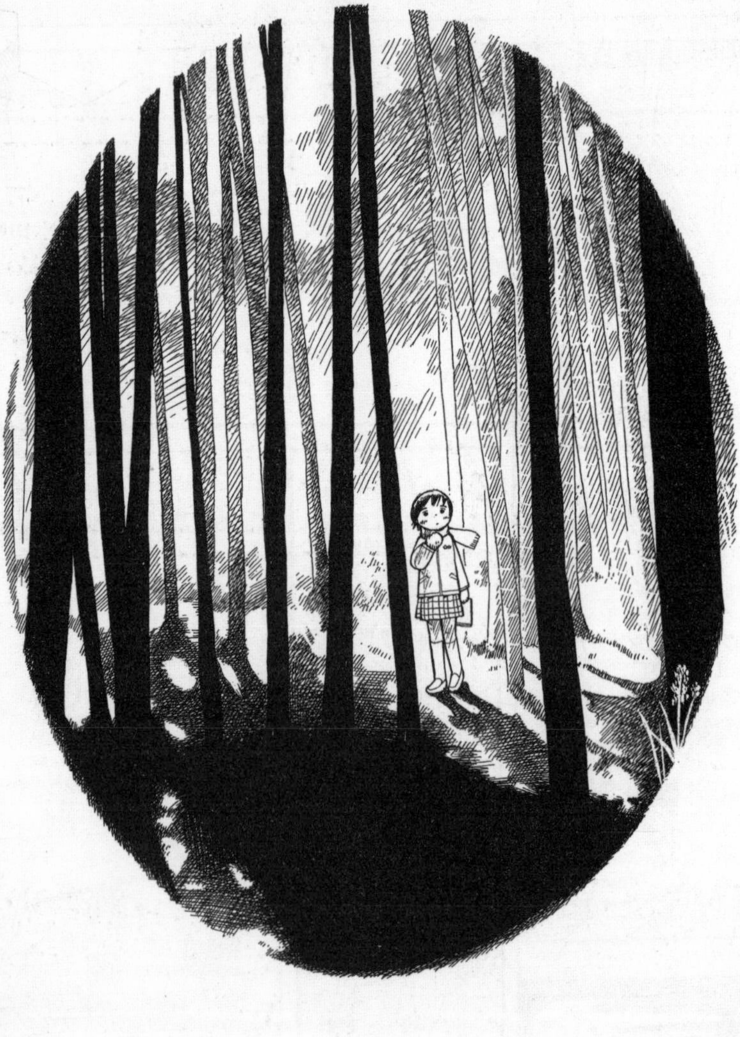

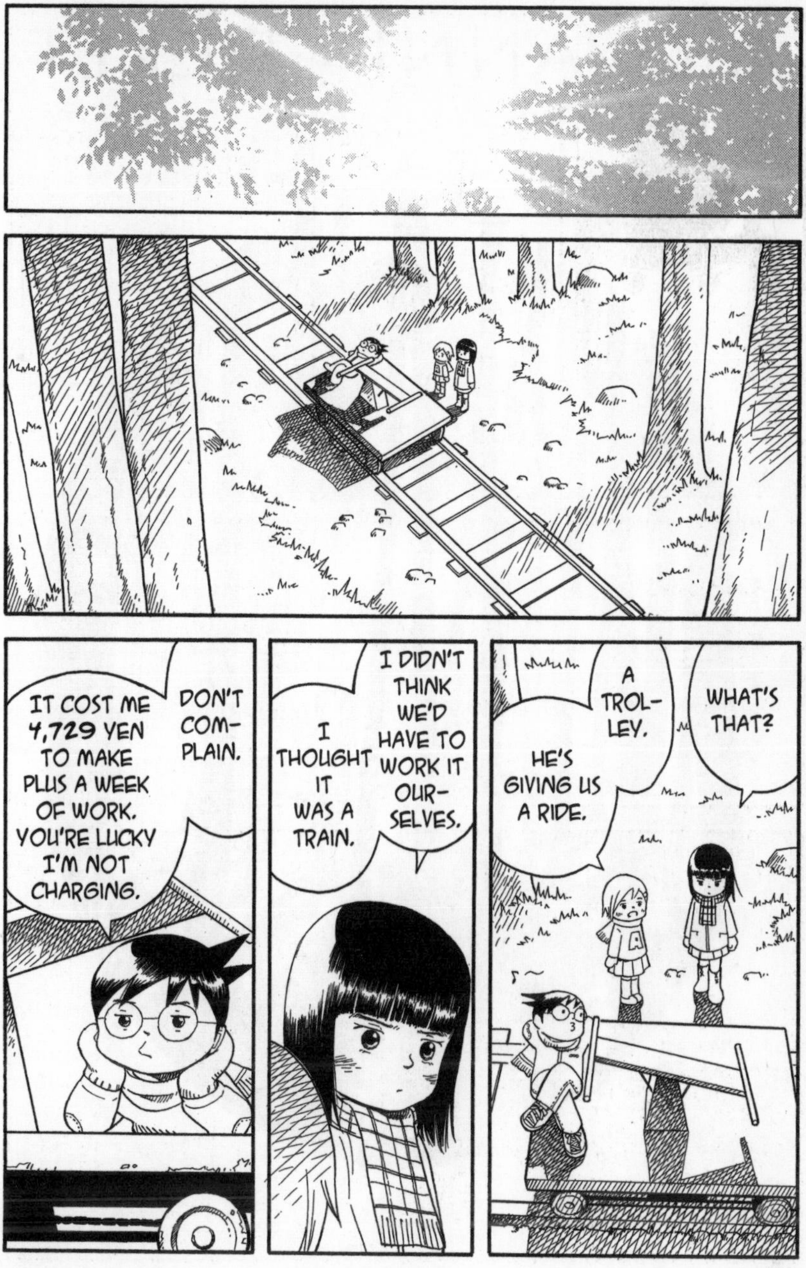
WHAT'S THAT?
A TROL-LEY.
HE'S GIVING US A RIDE.
I DIDN'T THINK WE'D HAVE TO WORK IT OUR-SELVES.
I THOUGHT IT WAS A TRAIN.
DON'T COM-PLAIN.
IT COST ME 4,729 YEN TO MAKE PLUS A WEEK OF WORK. YOU'RE LUCKY I'M NOT CHARGING.

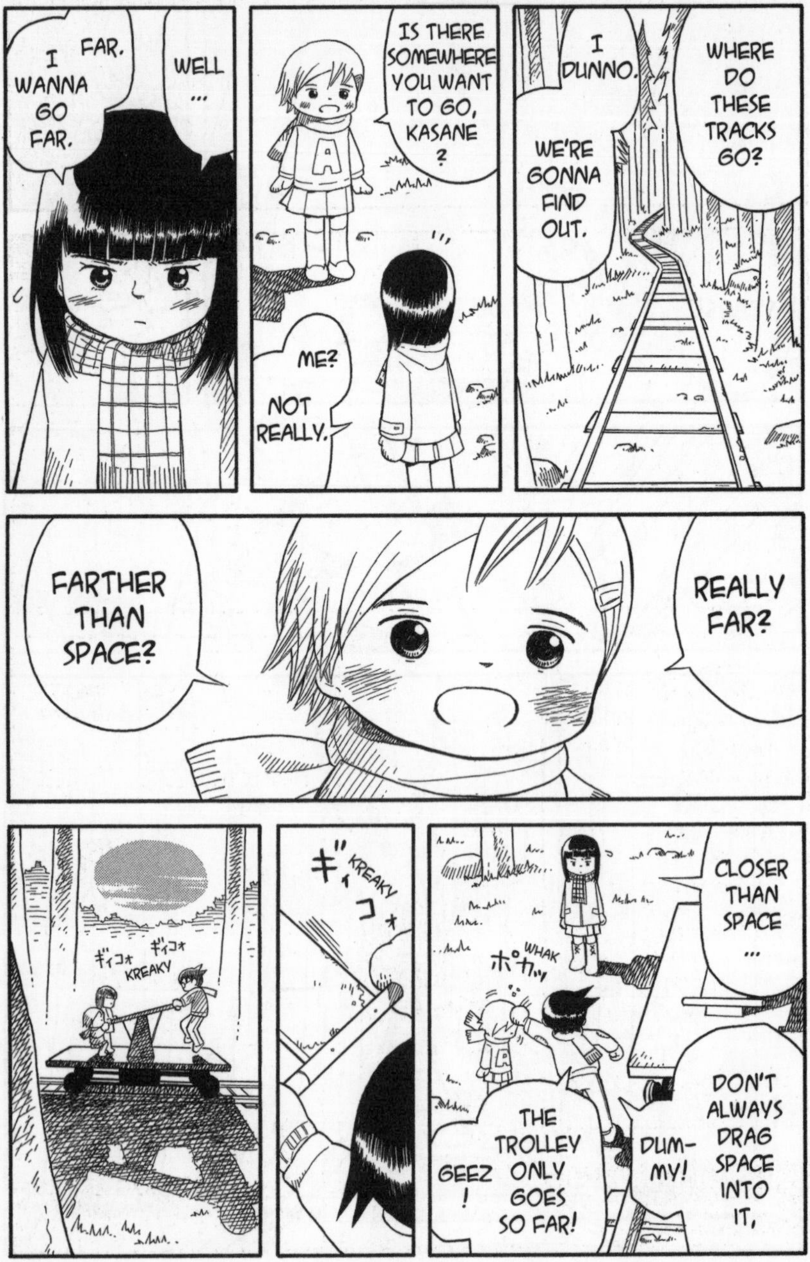

WHERE DO THESE TRACKS GO?
I DUNNO.
WE'RE GONNA FIND OUT.
IS THERE SOMEWHERE YOU WANT TO GO, KASANE?
ME?
NOT REALLY.
WELL ...
FAR.
I WANNA GO FAR.
REALLY FAR?
FARTHER THAN SPACE?
CLOSER THAN SPACE ...
ポカッ WHAK
DON'T ALWAYS DRAG SPACE INTO IT,
DUM-MY!
THE TROLLEY ONLY GOES SO FAR!
GEEZ!
ギィコォ KREAKY
ギィコォ ギィコォ KREAKY

STARS!

AH!

"GIOVANNI'S TICKET" —END

Guide to Cherry Blossoms

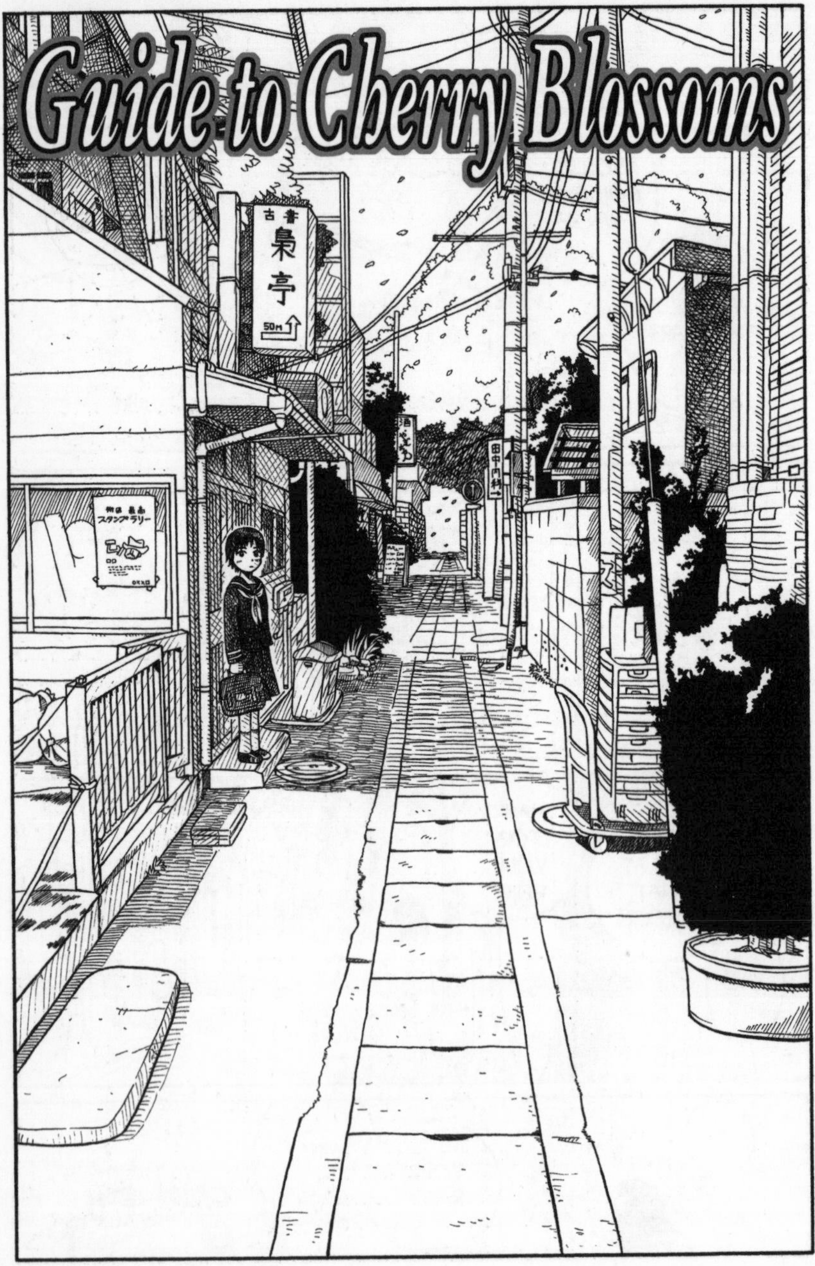
古書
梟亭
50M
スタンプラリー

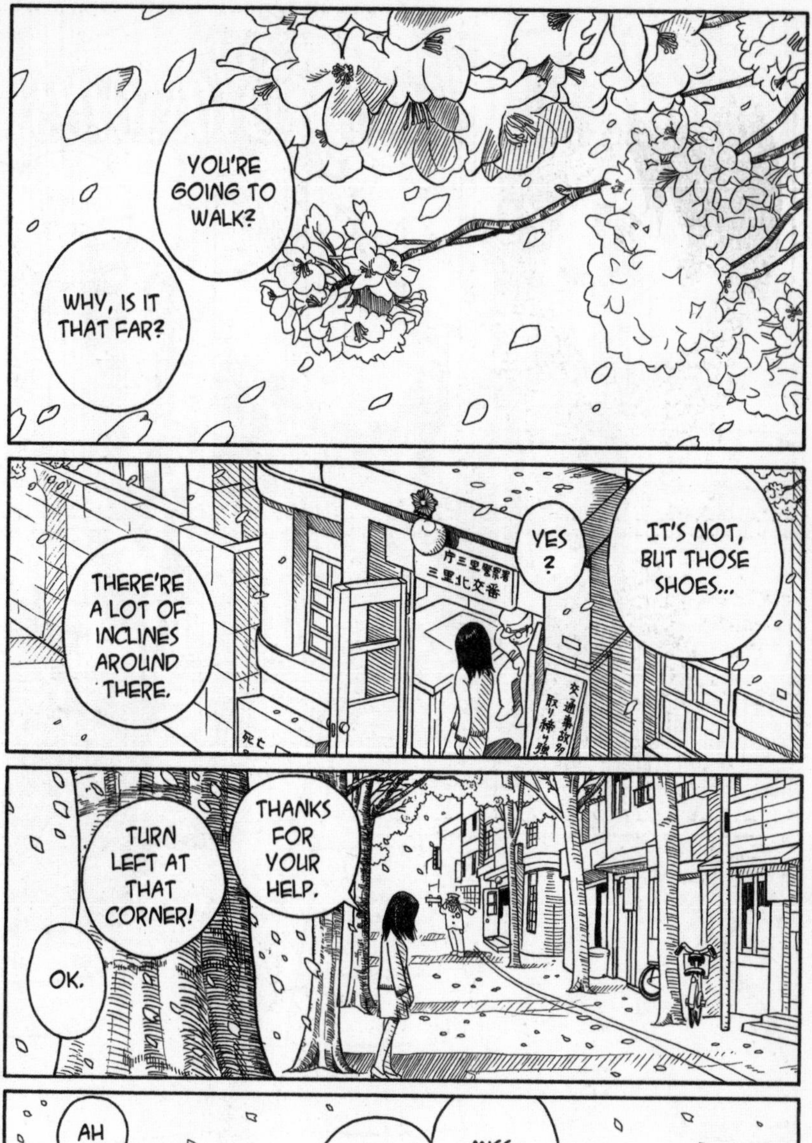
YOU'RE GOING TO WALK?
WHY, IS IT THAT FAR?
IT'S NOT, BUT THOSE SHOES...
YES?
三里北交番
THERE'RE A LOT OF INCLINES AROUND THERE.
THANKS FOR YOUR HELP.
TURN LEFT AT THAT CORNER!
OK.
MISS,
YOUR BAG!!
AH
...

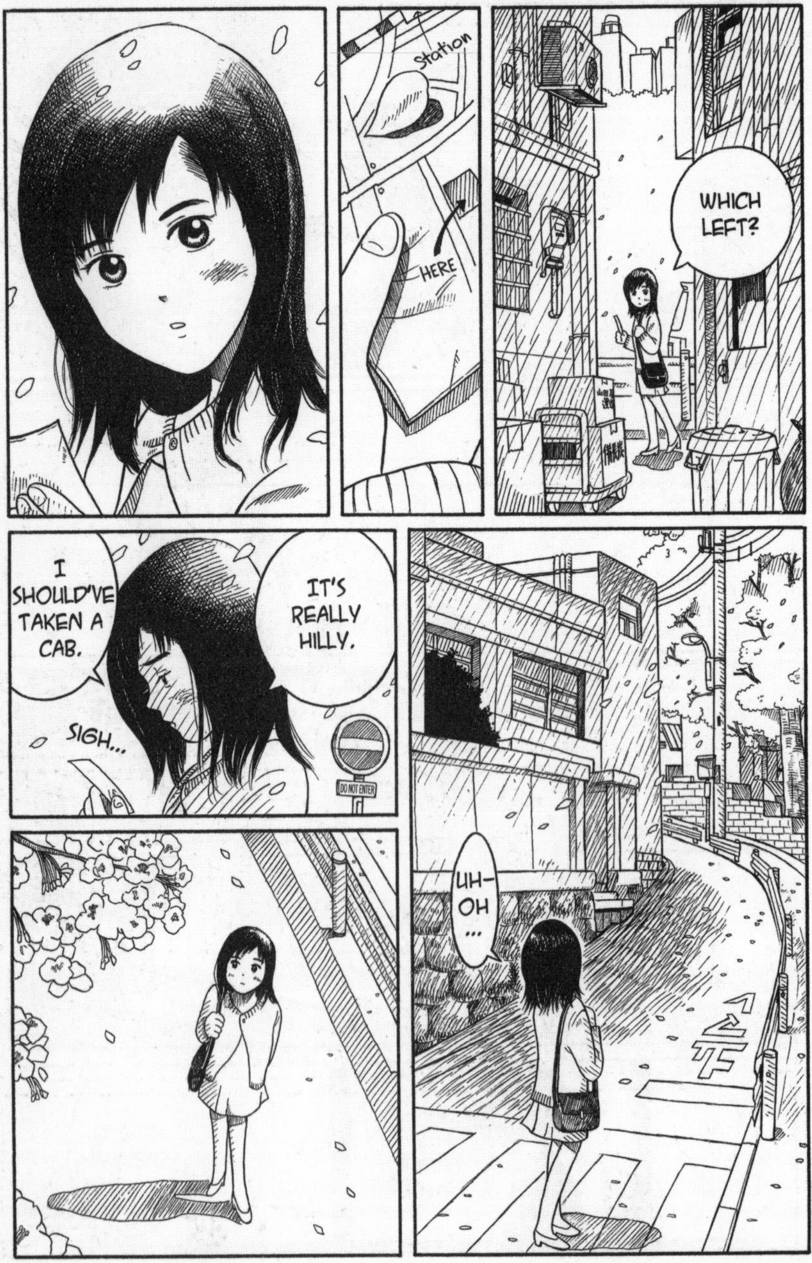
WHICH LEFT?
Station
HERE
UH-OH ...
IT'S REALLY HILLY.
I SHOULD'VE TAKEN A CAB.
SIGH...
DO NOT ENTER

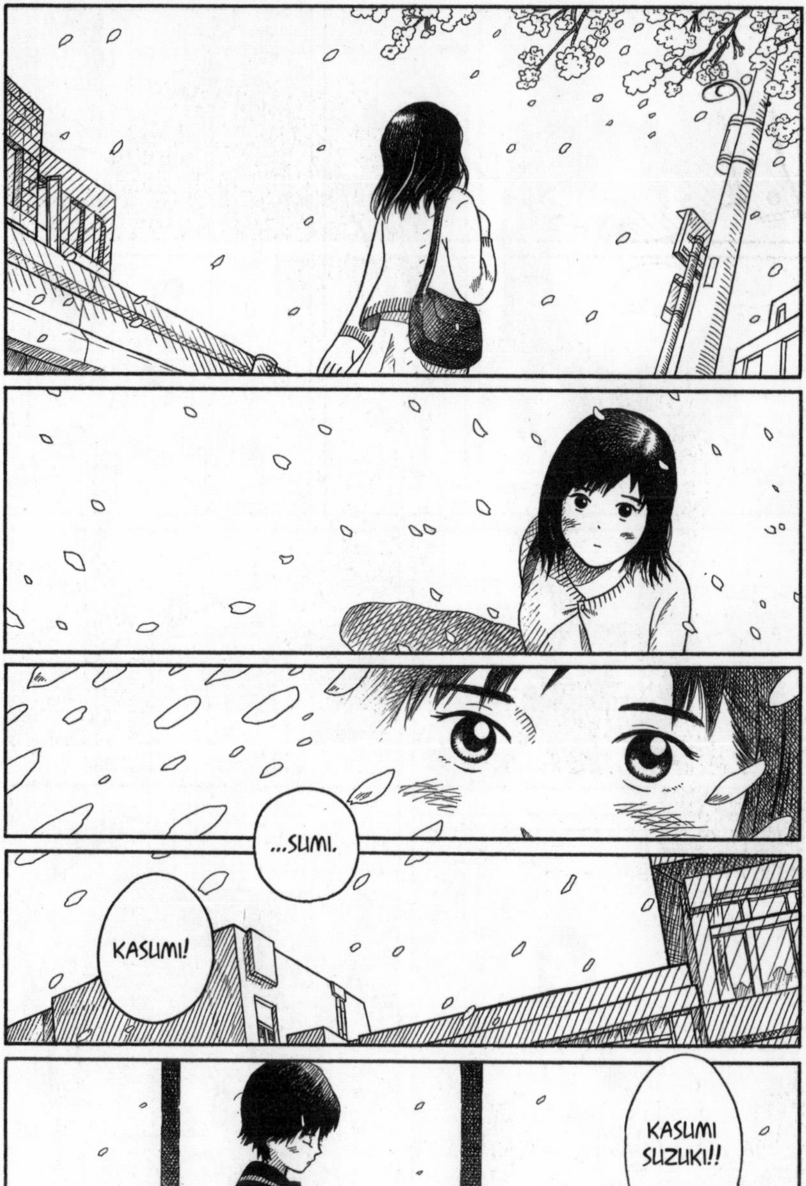
...SUMI.
KASUMI!
KASUMI SUZUKI!!

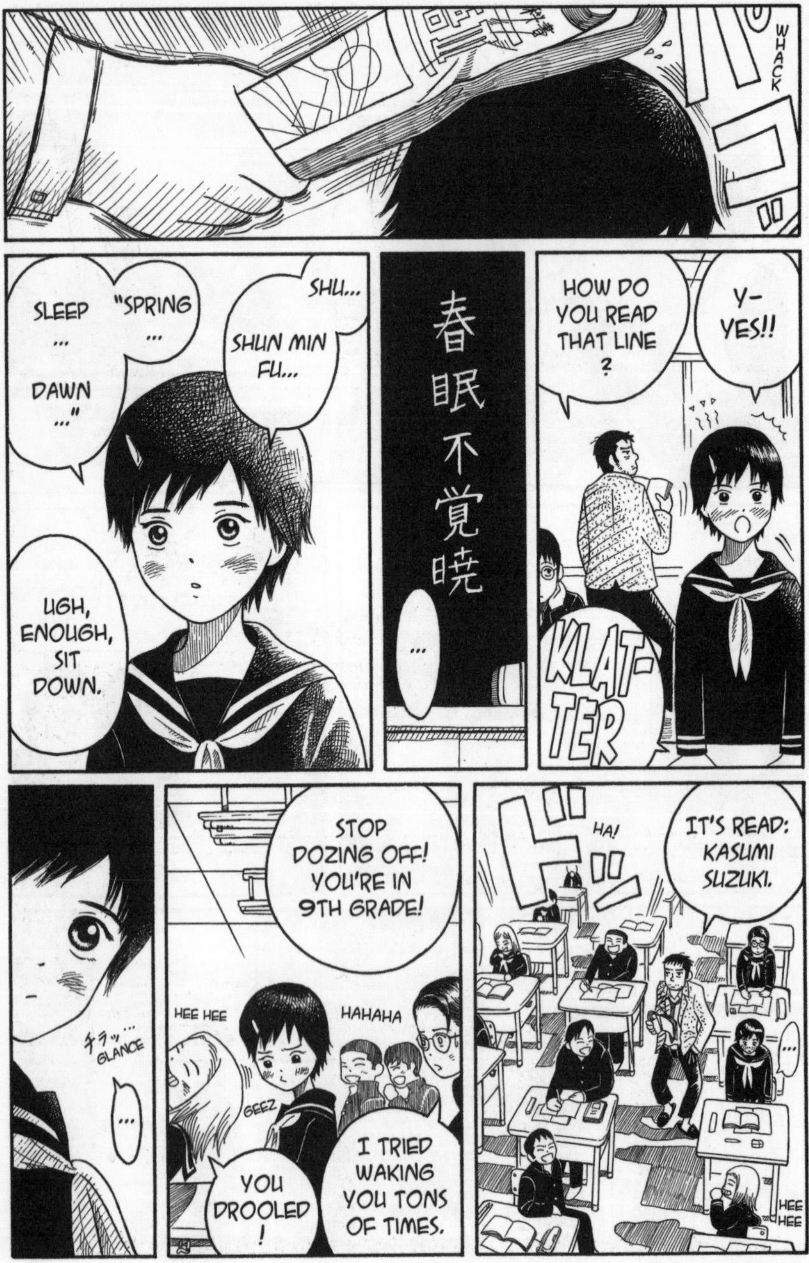

WHACK
Y- YES!!
HOW DO YOU READ THAT LINE?
KLAT-TER
春眠不覚暁
...
SHU...
SHUN MIN FU...
"SPRING ...
SLEEP ... DAWN ..."
UGH, ENOUGH, SIT DOWN.
IT'S READ: KASUMI SUZUKI.
HA!
...
HEE HEE
STOP DOZING OFF! YOU'RE IN 9TH GRADE!
HAHAHA
HEE HEE
GEEZ
I TRIED WAKING YOU TONS OF TIMES.
YOU DROOLED!
チラッ… GLANCE
...

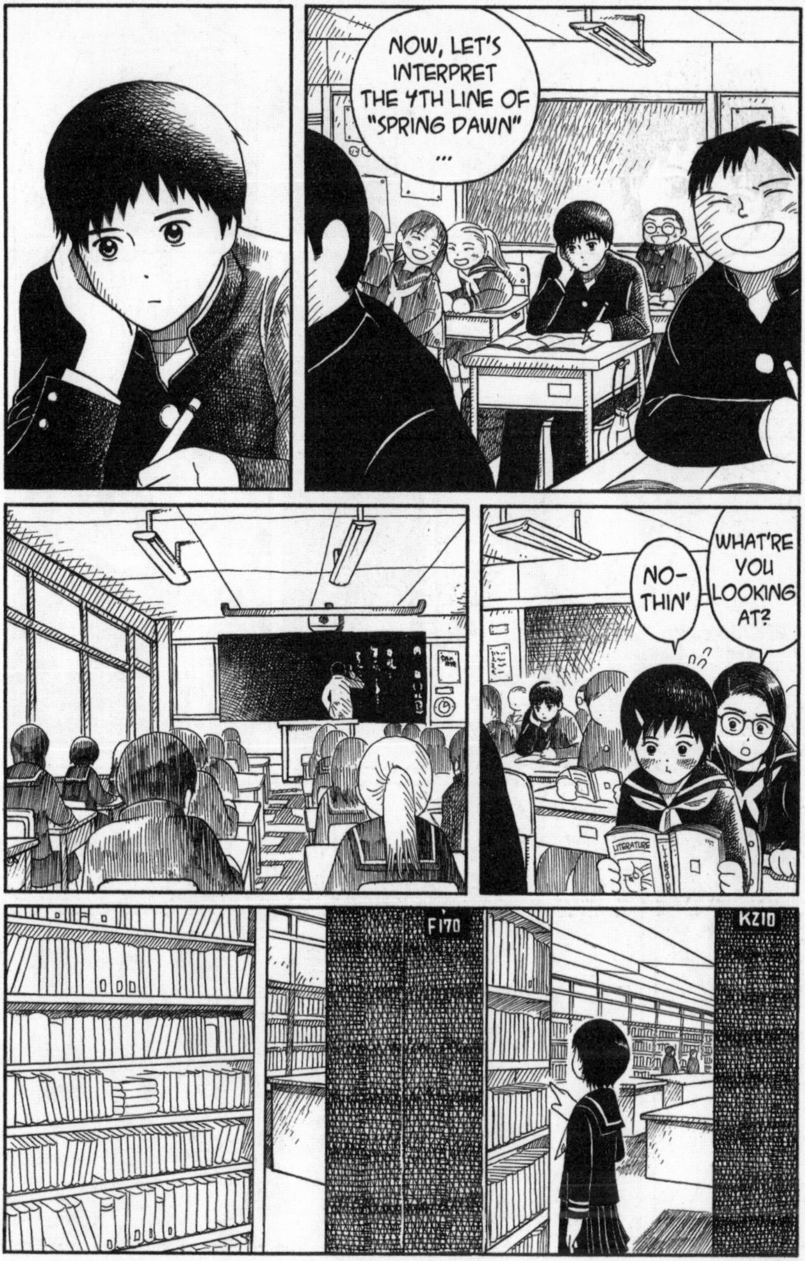
NOW, LET'S INTERPRET THE 4TH LINE OF "SPRING DAWN" ...
WHAT'RE YOU LOOKING AT?
NO-THIN'
LITERATURE
KZ10
F170

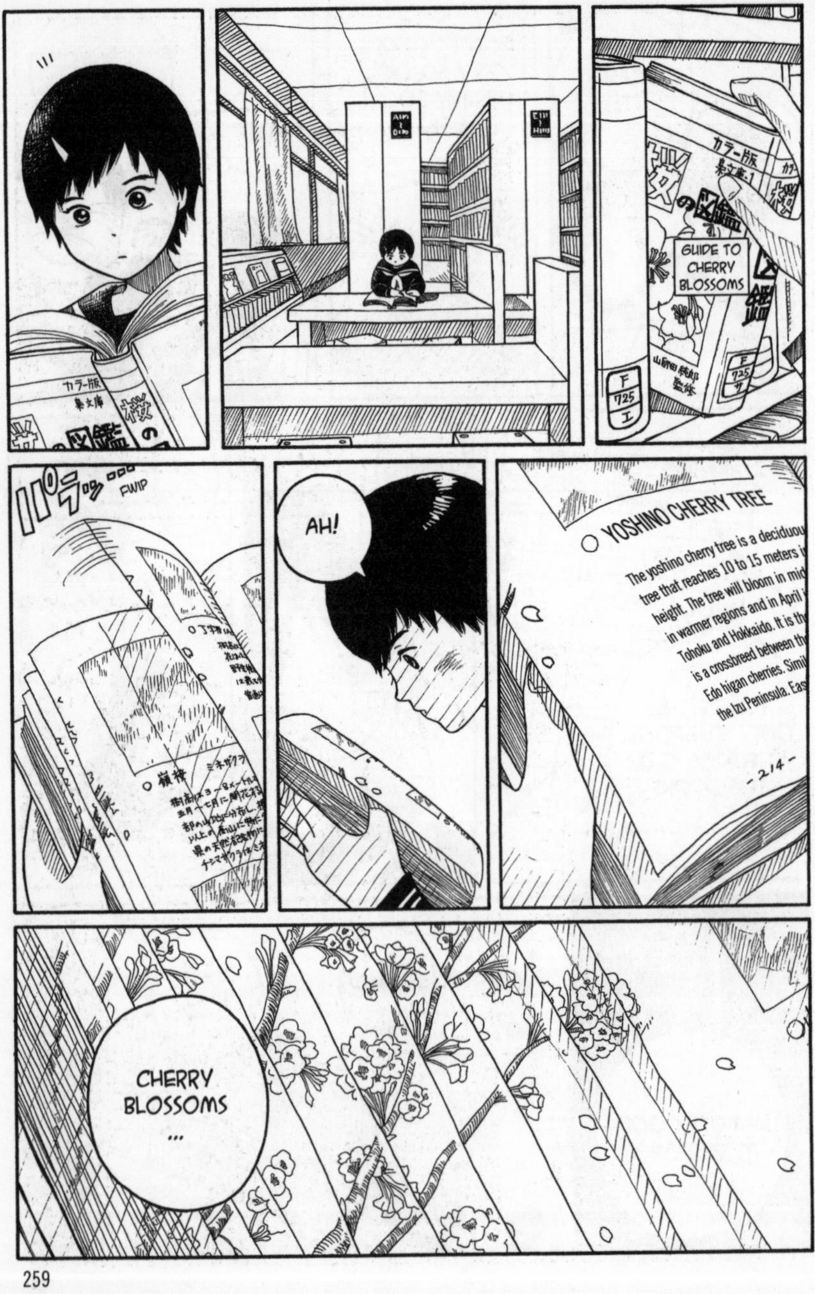
GUIDE TO CHERRY BLOSSOMS
YOSHINO CHERRY TREE
The yoshino cherry tree is a deciduou
tree that reaches 10 to 15 meters i
height. The tree will bloom in mid
in warmer regions and in April i
Tohoku and Hokkaido. It is the
is a crossbreed between th
Edo higan cherries. Simil
the Izu Peninsula. Eas
-214-
AH!
FWIP
CHERRY BLOSSOMS ...

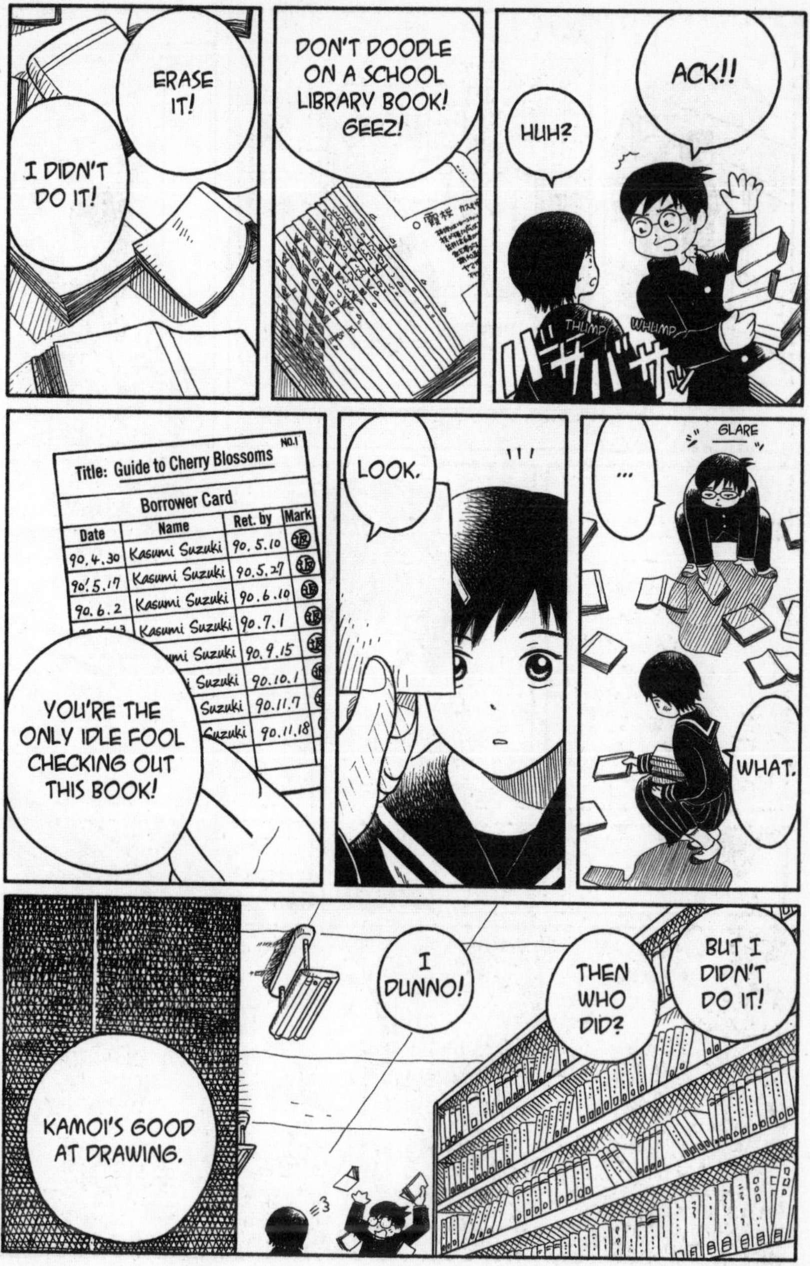
ACK!!
HUH?
THUMP
WHUMP
DON'T DOODLE ON A SCHOOL LIBRARY BOOK! GEEZ!
ERASE IT!
I DIDN'T DO IT!
GLARE
...
WHAT.
LOOK.
NO.1
Title: Guide to Cherry Blossoms
Borrower Card
Date Name Ret. by Mark
90.4.30 Kasumi Suzuki 90.5.10
90.5.17 Kasumi Suzuki 90.5.27
90.6.2 Kasumi Suzuki 90.6.10
Kasumi Suzuki 90.7.1
90.9.15
90.10.1
90.11.7
90.11.18
YOU'RE THE ONLY IDLE FOOL CHECKING OUT THIS BOOK!
BUT I DIDN'T DO IT!
THEN WHO DID?
I DUNNO!
KAMOI'S GOOD AT DRAWING.

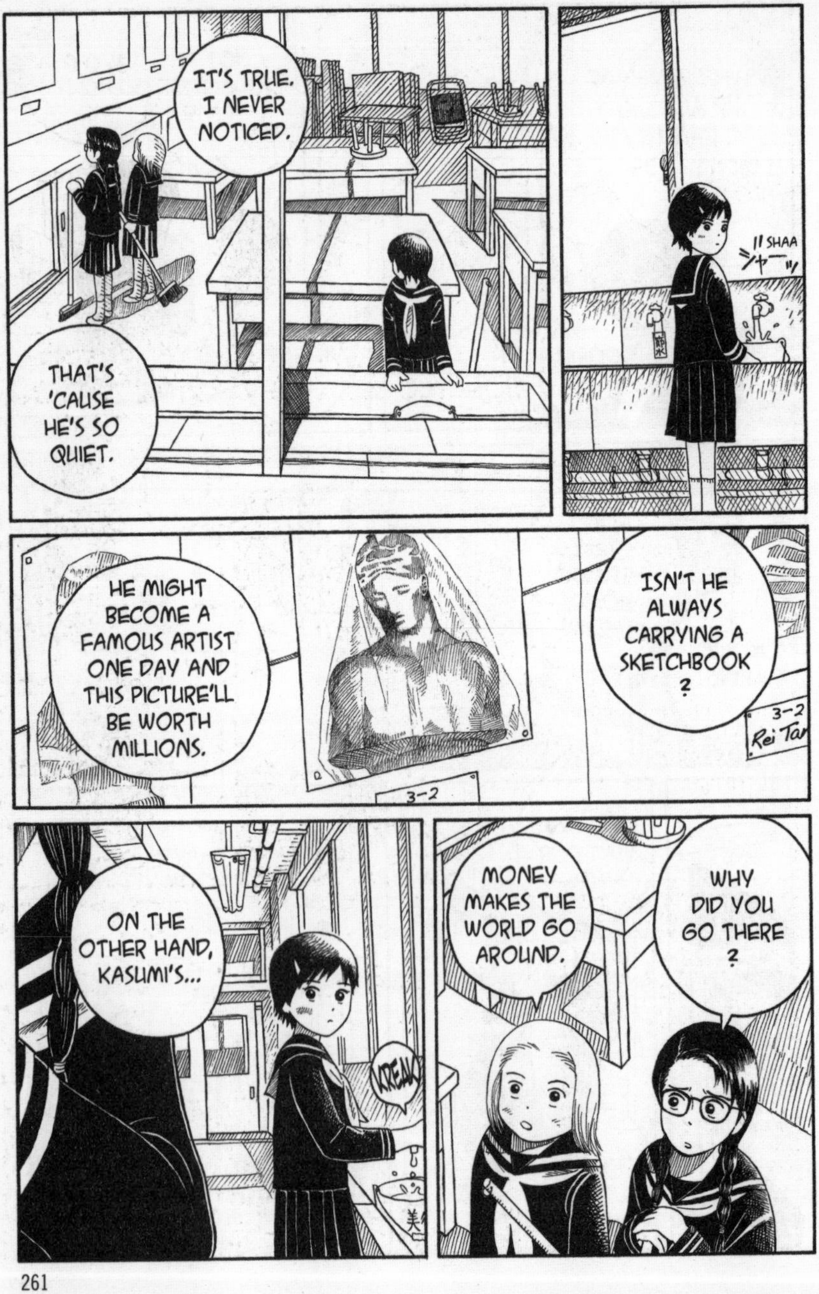
SHAA
シャー
IT'S TRUE. I NEVER NOTICED.
THAT'S 'CAUSE HE'S SO QUIET.
ISN'T HE ALWAYS CARRYING A SKETCHBOOK?
HE MIGHT BECOME A FAMOUS ARTIST ONE DAY AND THIS PICTURE'LL BE WORTH MILLIONS.
3-2
WHY DID YOU GO THERE?
MONEY MAKES THE WORLD GO AROUND.
ON THE OTHER HAND, KASUMI'S...
KREAK

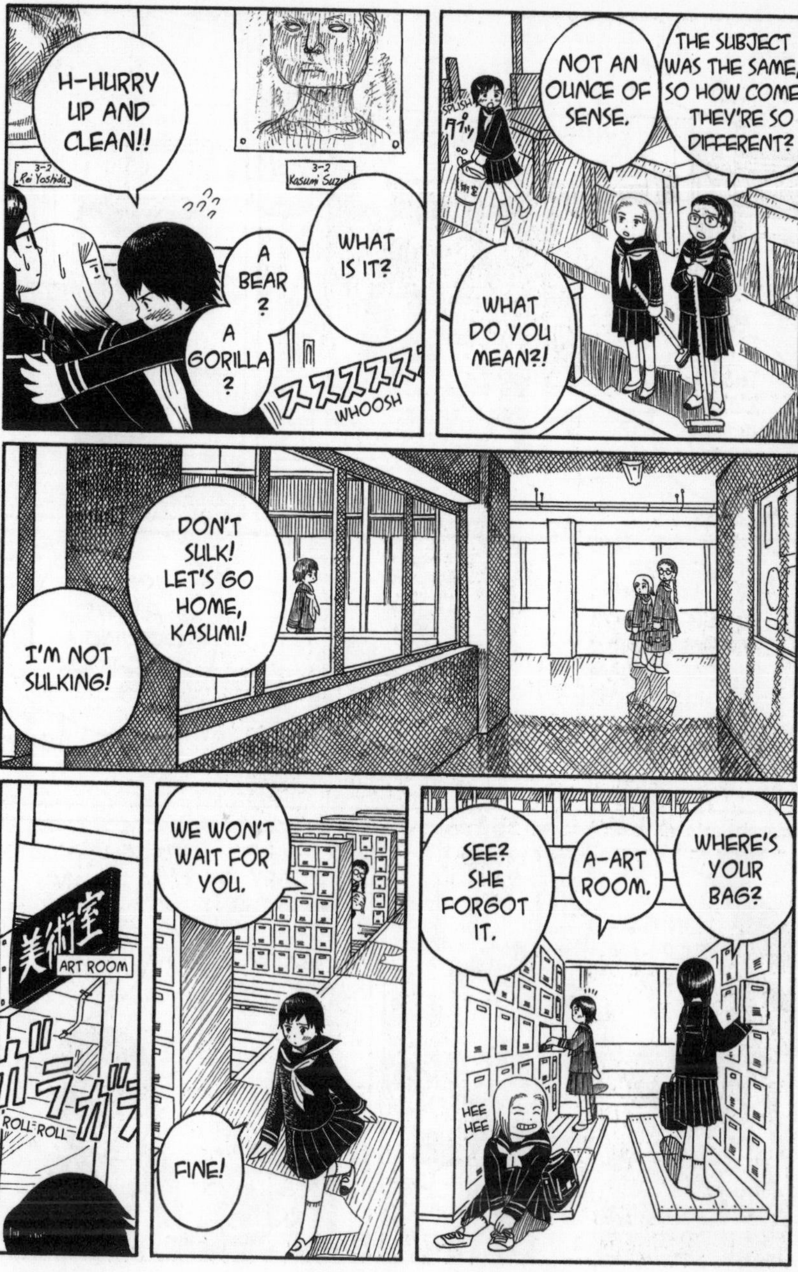
THE SUBJECT WAS THE SAME, SO HOW COME THEY'RE SO DIFFERENT?
NOT AN OUNCE OF SENSE.
SPLISH
WHAT DO YOU MEAN?!
3-2 Kasumi Suzu
3-2 Rei Yoshida
WHAT IS IT?
A BEAR?
A GORILLA?
H-HURRY UP AND CLEAN!!
WHOOSH
DON'T SULK! LET'S GO HOME, KASUMI!
I'M NOT SULKING!
WHERE'S YOUR BAG?
A-ART ROOM.
SEE? SHE FORGOT IT.
HEE HEE
WE WON'T WAIT FOR YOU.
FINE!
美術室
ART ROOM
ROLL ROLL

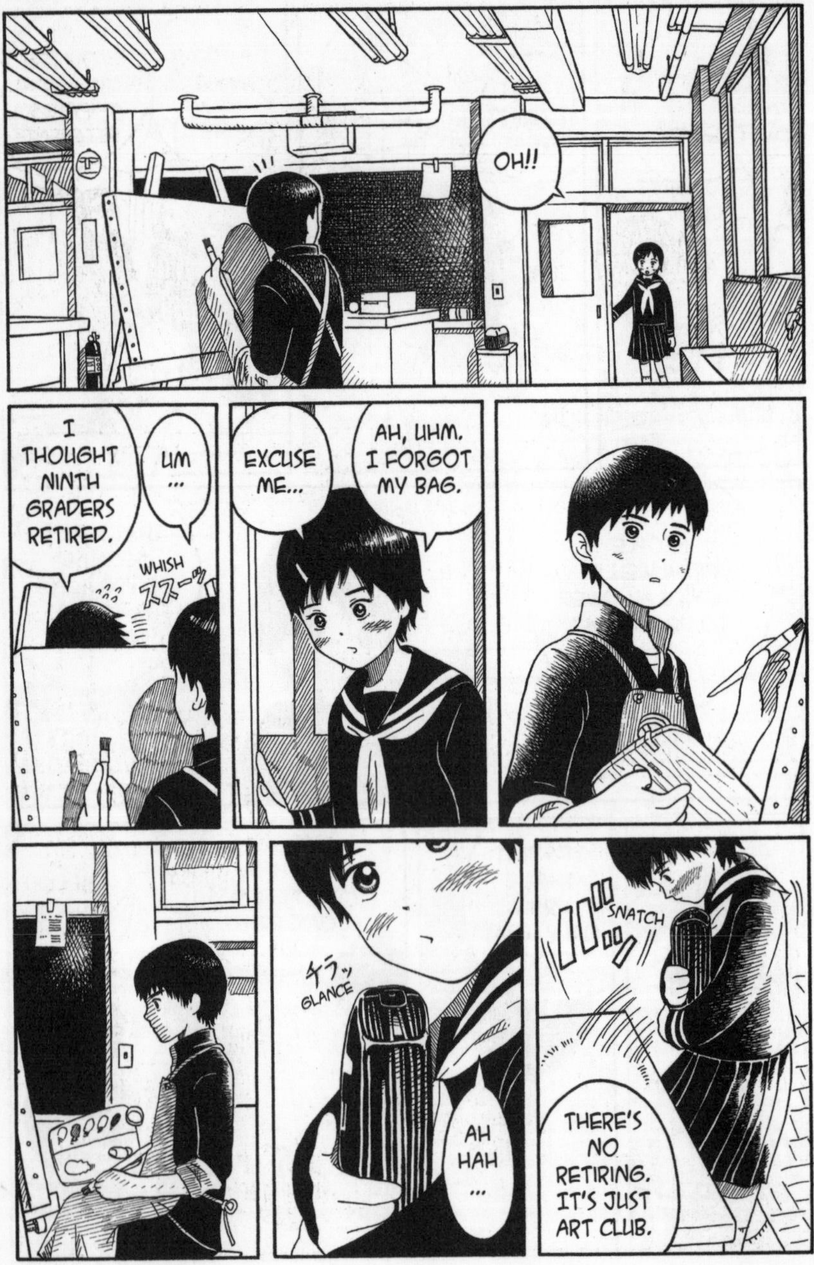
OH!!
AH, UHM. I FORGOT MY BAG.
EXCUSE ME...
UM ...
I THOUGHT NINTH GRADERS RETIRED.
WHISH
スス－ッ
SNATCH
THERE'S NO RETIRING. IT'S JUST ART CLUB.
チラッ
GLANCE
AH HAH ...

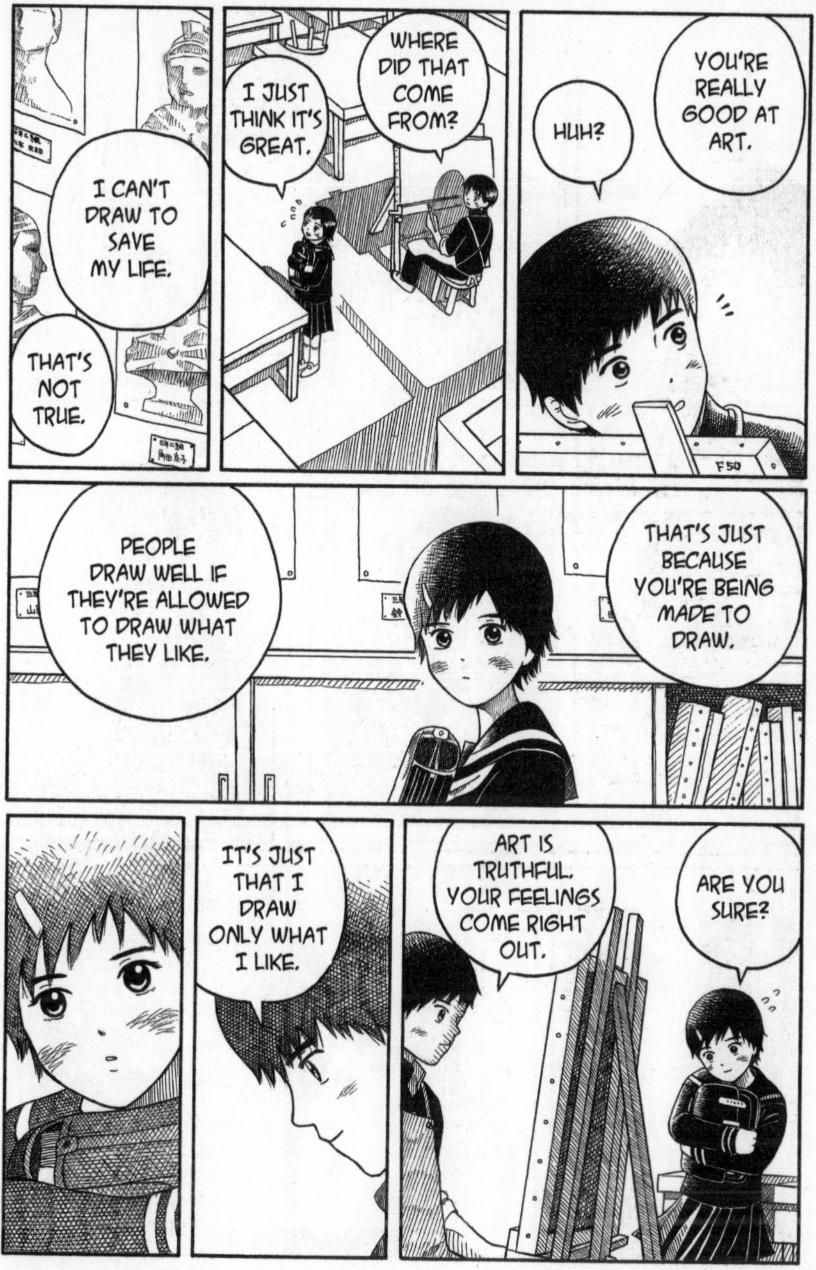
YOU'RE REALLY GOOD AT ART.
HUH?
F50
WHERE DID THAT COME FROM?
I JUST THINK IT'S GREAT.
I CAN'T DRAW TO SAVE MY LIFE.
THAT'S NOT TRUE.
THAT'S JUST BECAUSE YOU'RE BEING MADE TO DRAW.
PEOPLE DRAW WELL IF THEY'RE ALLOWED TO DRAW WHAT THEY LIKE.
ARE YOU SURE?
ART IS TRUTHFUL. YOUR FEELINGS COME RIGHT OUT.
IT'S JUST THAT I DRAW ONLY WHAT I LIKE.

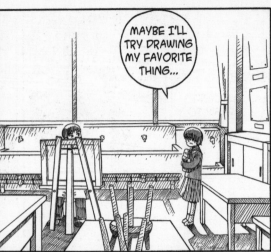

MAYBE I'LL TRY DRAWING MY FAVORITE THING...

RUSTLE

HEH, IT STILL WON'T BE MUCH.

UH, THANKS

USE THIS.

Sketc

265

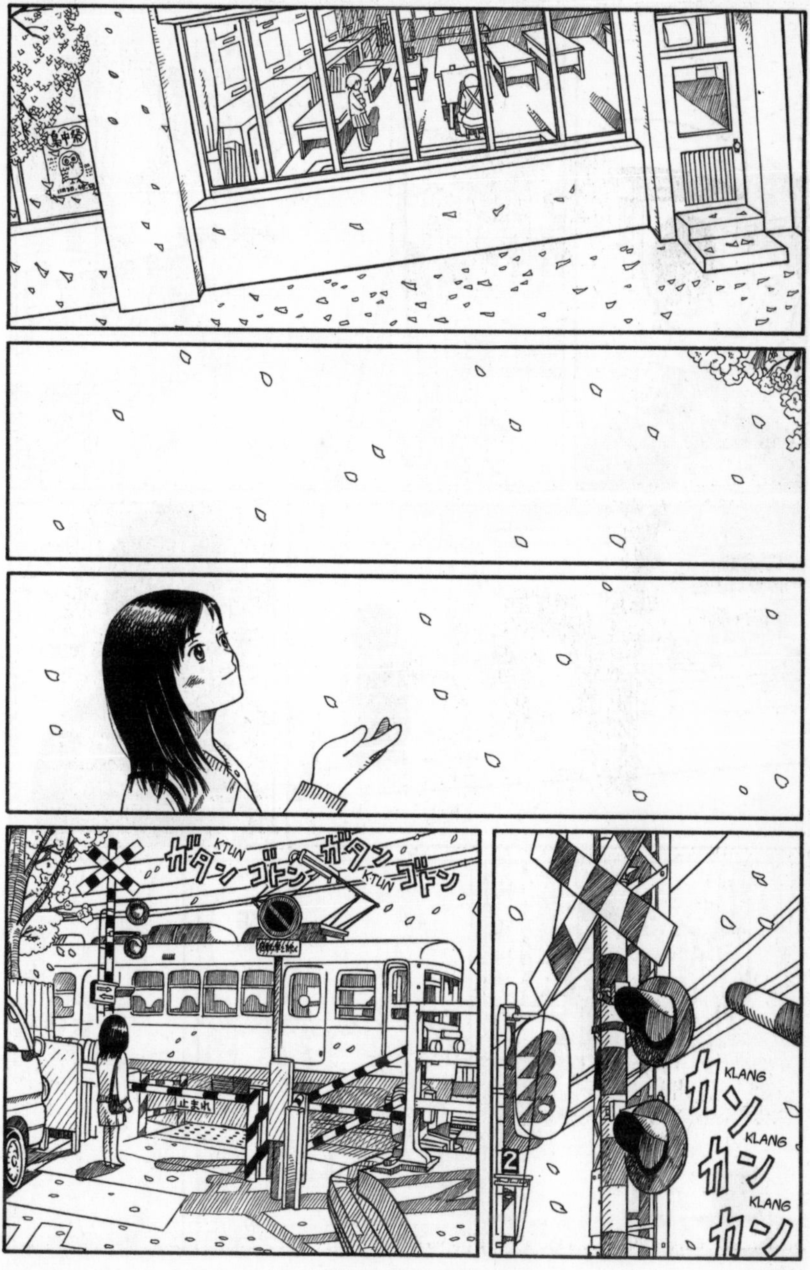
KLANG
カーン
KLANG
カーン
KLANG
カーン
ガタン
ゴトン
KTUN
ガタン
ゴトン
KTUN
止まれ

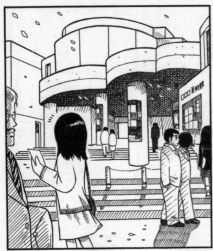

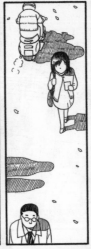

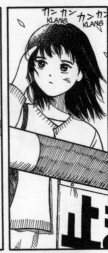

カンカン
KLANG
カンカン
KLANG
第十二回
新人作家芸術展
12TH ANNUAL NEW ARTIST EXHIBIT
デゾン美術館
FINALLY FOUND IT...
WHEW...
MY SENSE OF DIRECTION IS TERRIBLE.
...
I DON'T GET IT.

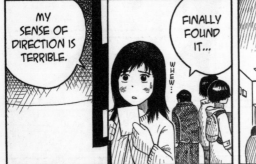

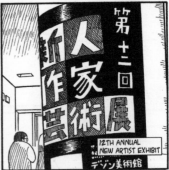

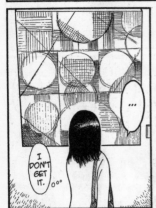

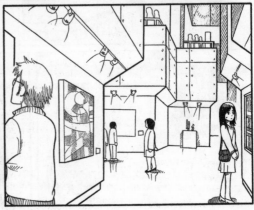

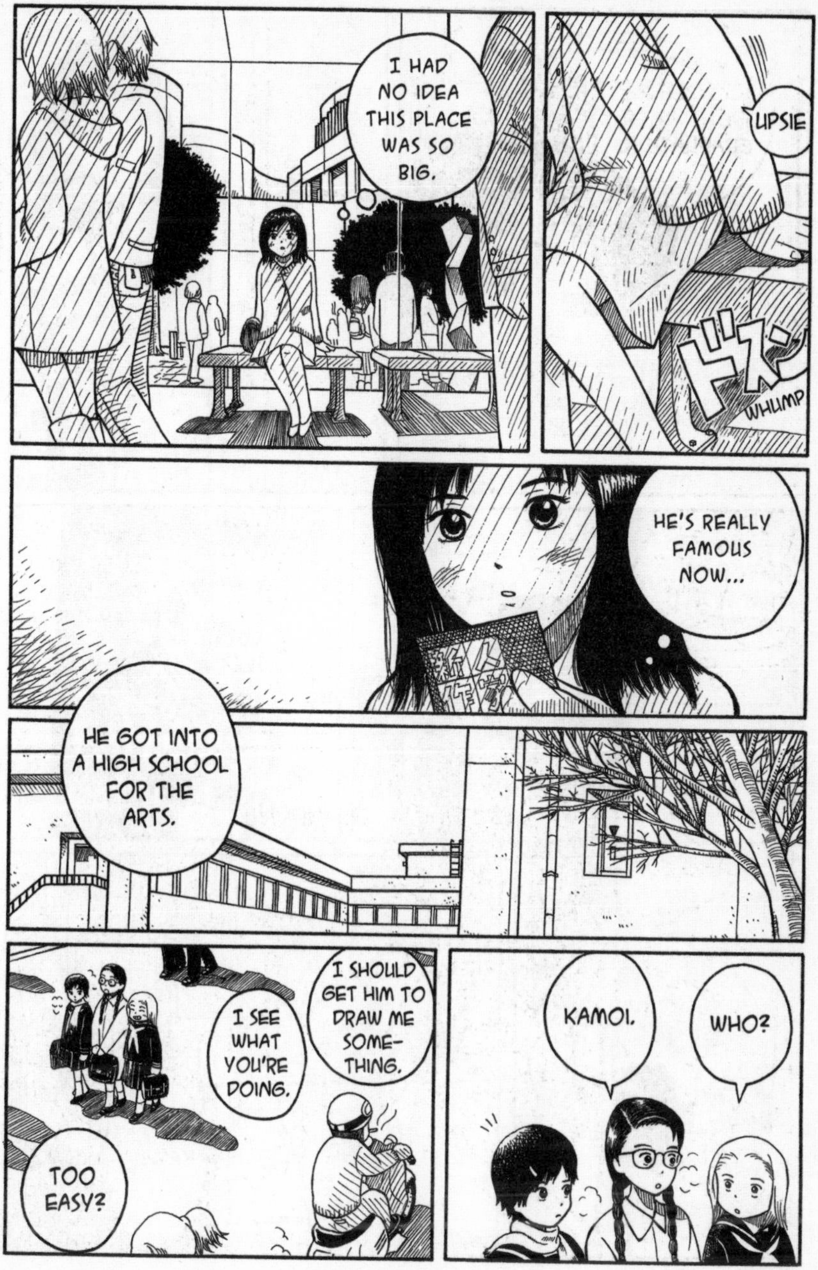
UPSIE
ドスン
WHUMP
I HAD NO IDEA THIS PLACE WAS SO BIG.
HE'S REALLY FAMOUS NOW...
HE GOT INTO A HIGH SCHOOL FOR THE ARTS.
WHO?
KAMOI.
I SHOULD GET HIM TO DRAW ME SOME-THING.
I SEE WHAT YOU'RE DOING.
TOO EASY?

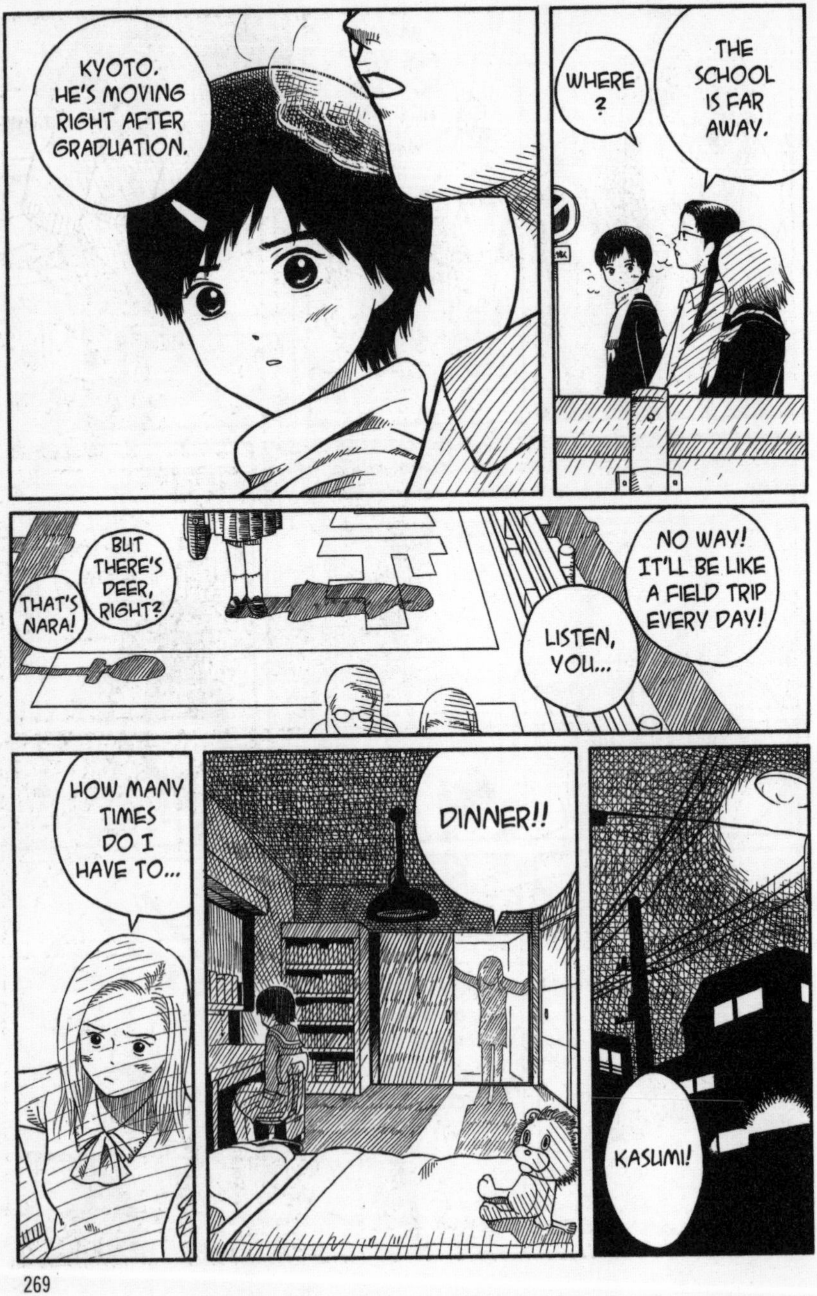
THE SCHOOL IS FAR AWAY.
WHERE?
KYOTO. HE'S MOVING RIGHT AFTER GRADUATION.
NO WAY! IT'LL BE LIKE A FIELD TRIP EVERY DAY!
LISTEN, YOU...
BUT THERE'S DEER, RIGHT?
THAT'S NARA!
KASUMI!
DINNER!!
HOW MANY TIMES DO I HAVE TO...

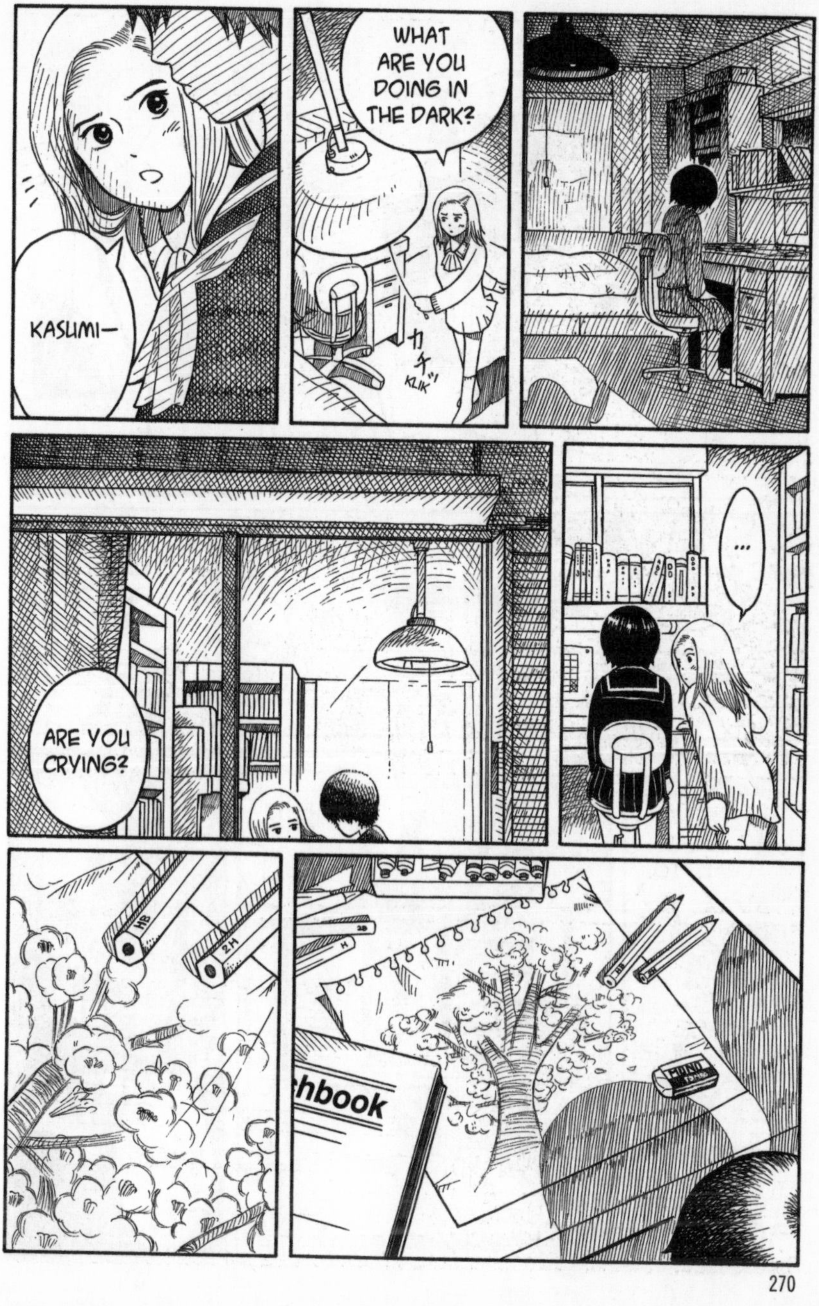
WHAT ARE YOU DOING IN THE DARK?
カチッ
KLIK
KASUMI—
...
ARE YOU CRYING?

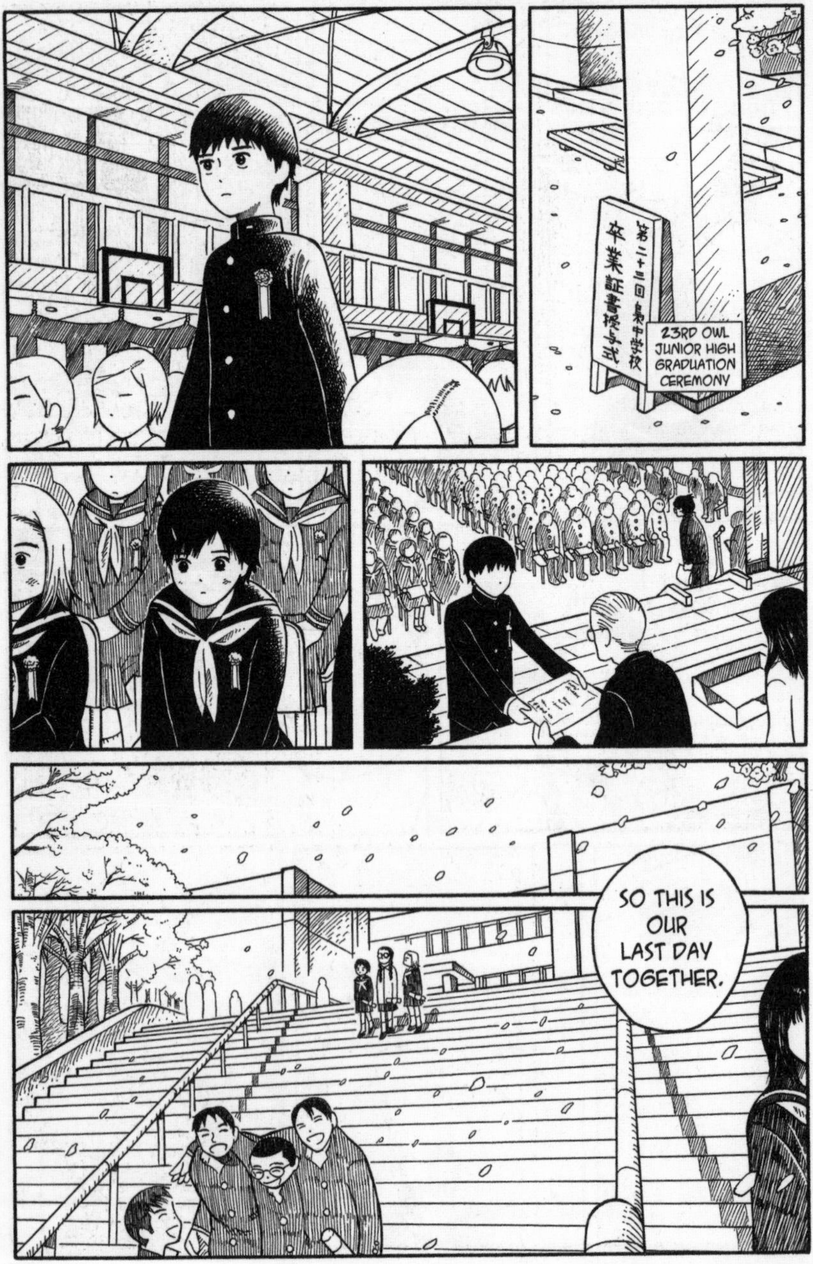
第二十三回梟中学校
卒業証書授与式
23RD OWL JUNIOR HIGH GRADUATION CEREMONY
SO THIS IS OUR LAST DAY TOGETHER.

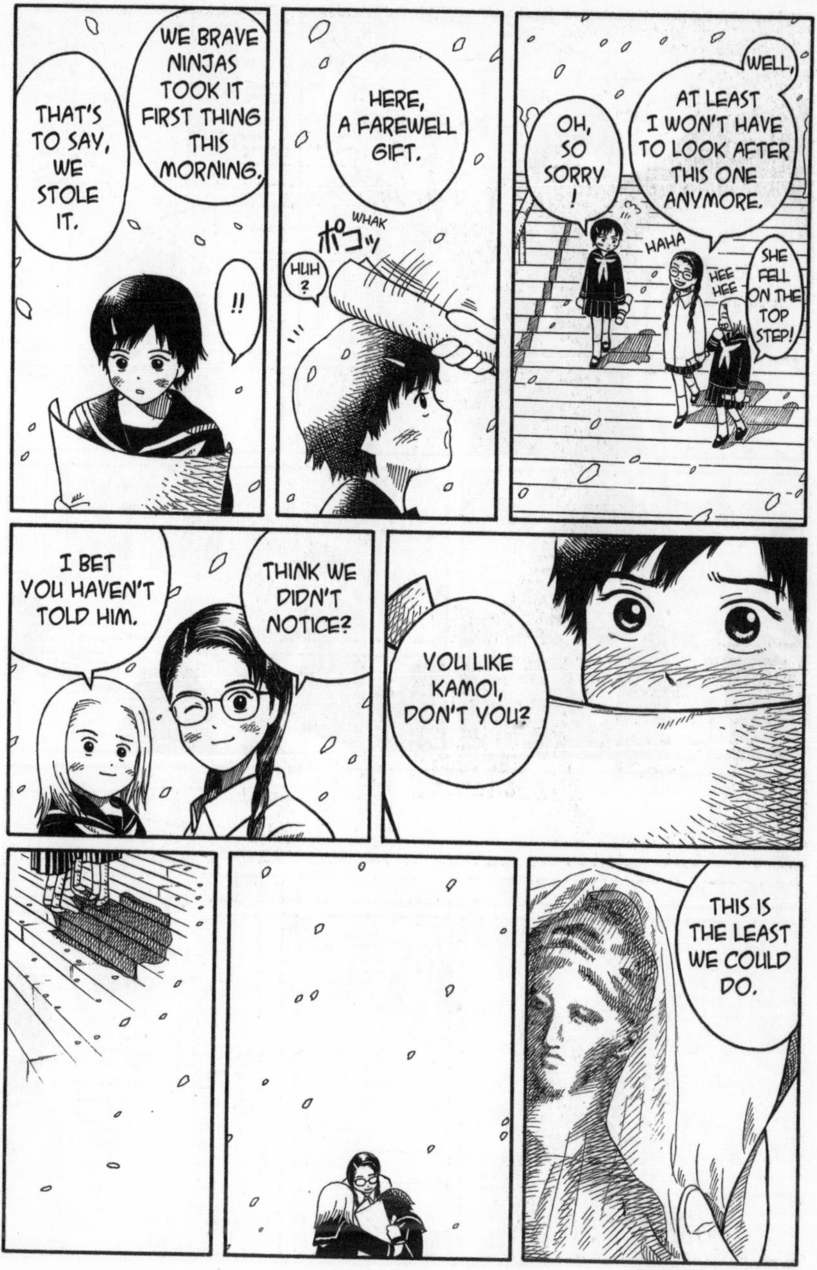
WELL, AT LEAST I WON'T HAVE TO LOOK AFTER THIS ONE ANYMORE.
OH, SO SORRY!
SHE FELL ON THE TOP STEP!
HEE HEE
HAHA
HERE, A FAREWELL GIFT.
ポコッ WHAK
HUH?
WE BRAVE NINJAS TOOK IT FIRST THING THIS MORNING.
THAT'S TO SAY, WE STOLE IT.
!!
YOU LIKE KAMOI, DON'T YOU?
THINK WE DIDN'T NOTICE?
I BET YOU HAVEN'T TOLD HIM.
THIS IS THE LEAST WE COULD DO.

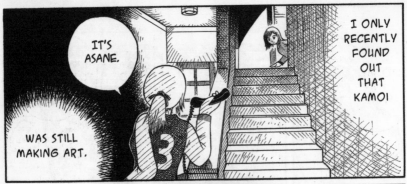

I ONLY RECENTLY FOUND OUT THAT KAMOI
IT'S ASANE.
WAS STILL MAKING ART.
DAISON MUSEUM
デゾン美術館
新人作家
WHERE'S THE WORK BY YUSUKE KAMOI?
AH YES, BACK THERE.

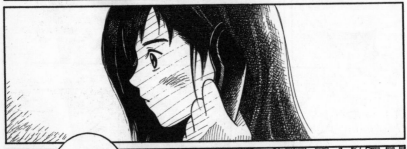

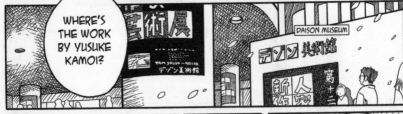

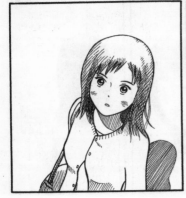

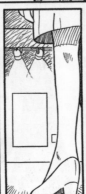

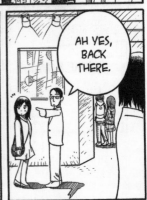

CHERRY BLOS-SOMS?
YUSUKE KAMOI
"Guide to Cherry Blossoms"
YUSUKE KAMOI
"Guide to Cherry Blossoms"
油彩 170×250

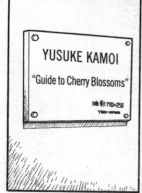

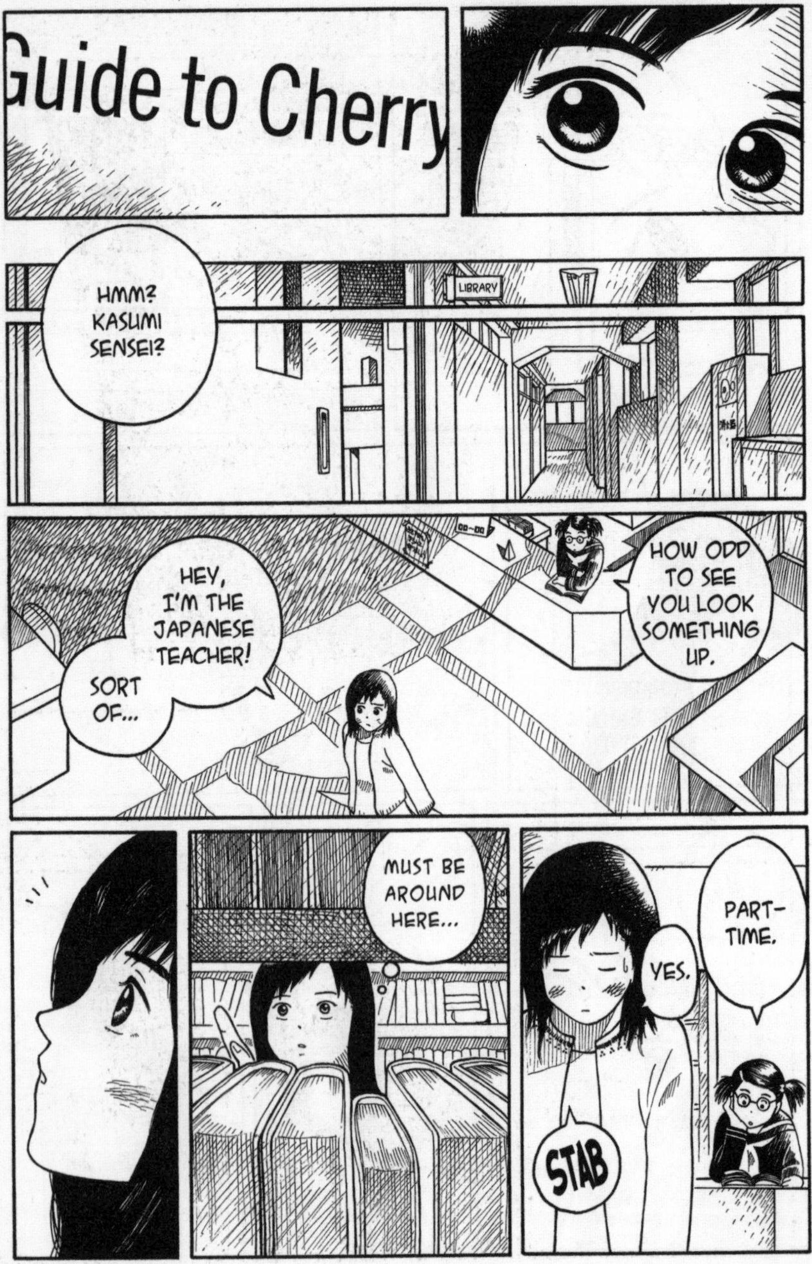
Guide to Cherry
LIBRARY
HMM? KASUMI SENSEI?
HOW ODD TO SEE YOU LOOK SOMETHING UP.
HEY, I'M THE JAPANESE TEACHER!
SORT OF...
PART-TIME.
YES.
STAB
MUST BE AROUND HERE...

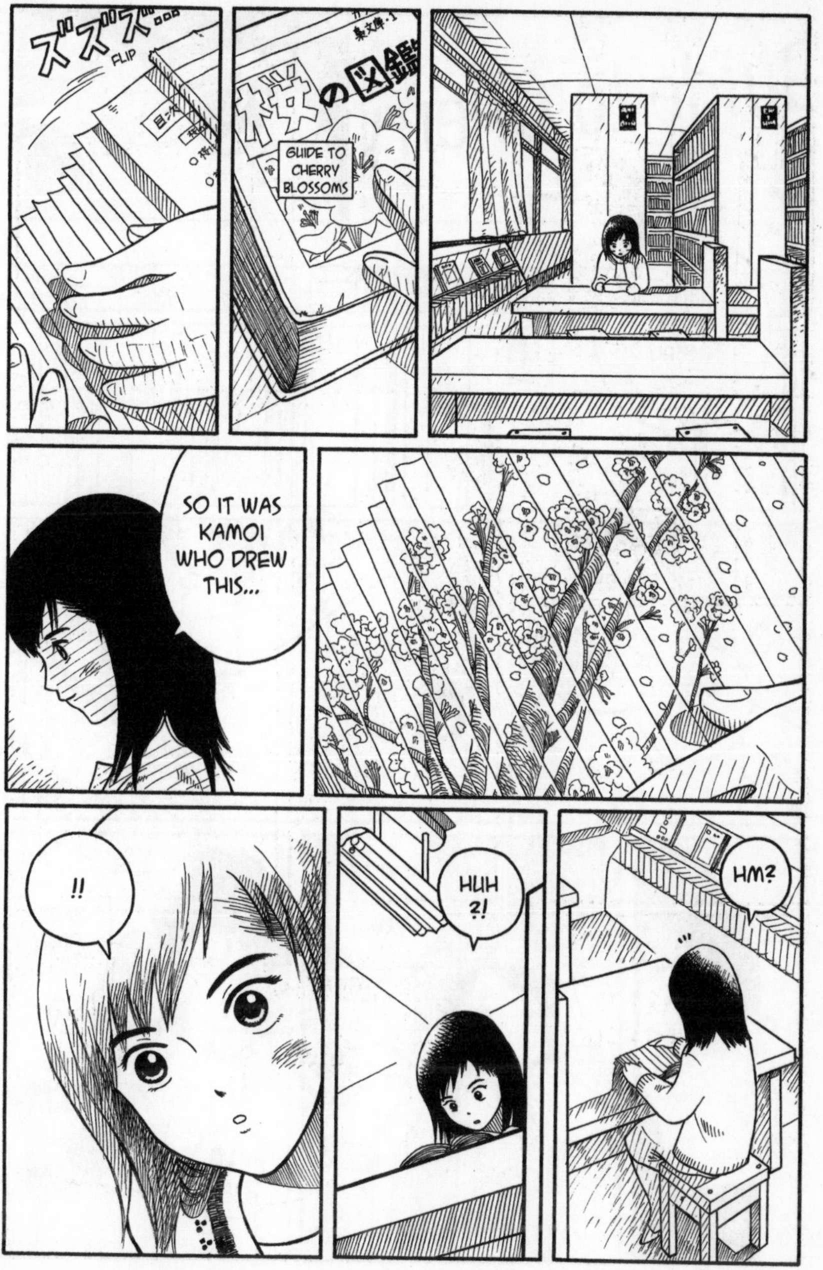
桜の図鑑
GUIDE TO CHERRY BLOSSOMS
ズズズ...
FLIP
目次
SO IT WAS KAMOI WHO DREW THIS...
HM?
HUH ?!
!!

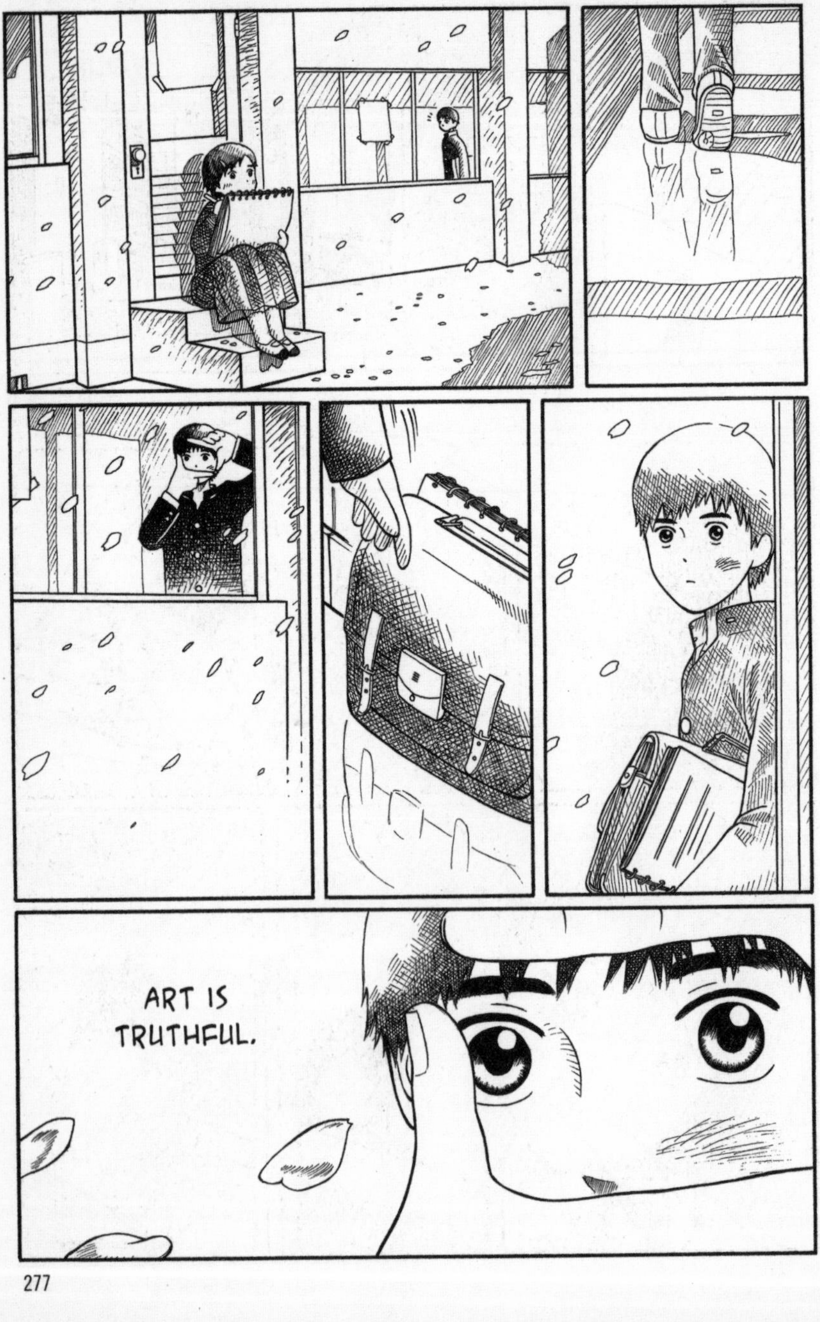
ART IS
TRUTHFUL.

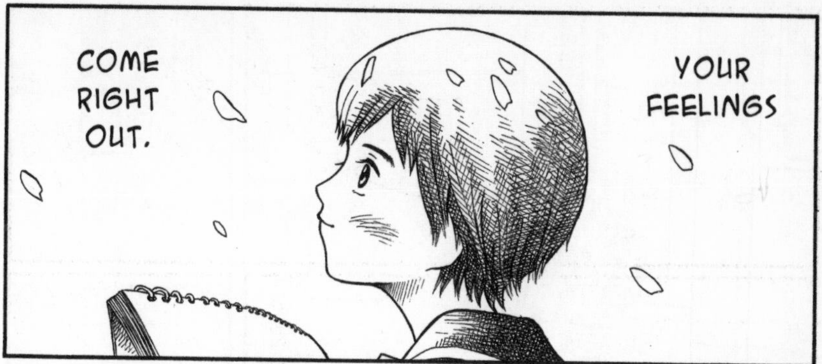
YOUR FEELINGS
COME RIGHT OUT.

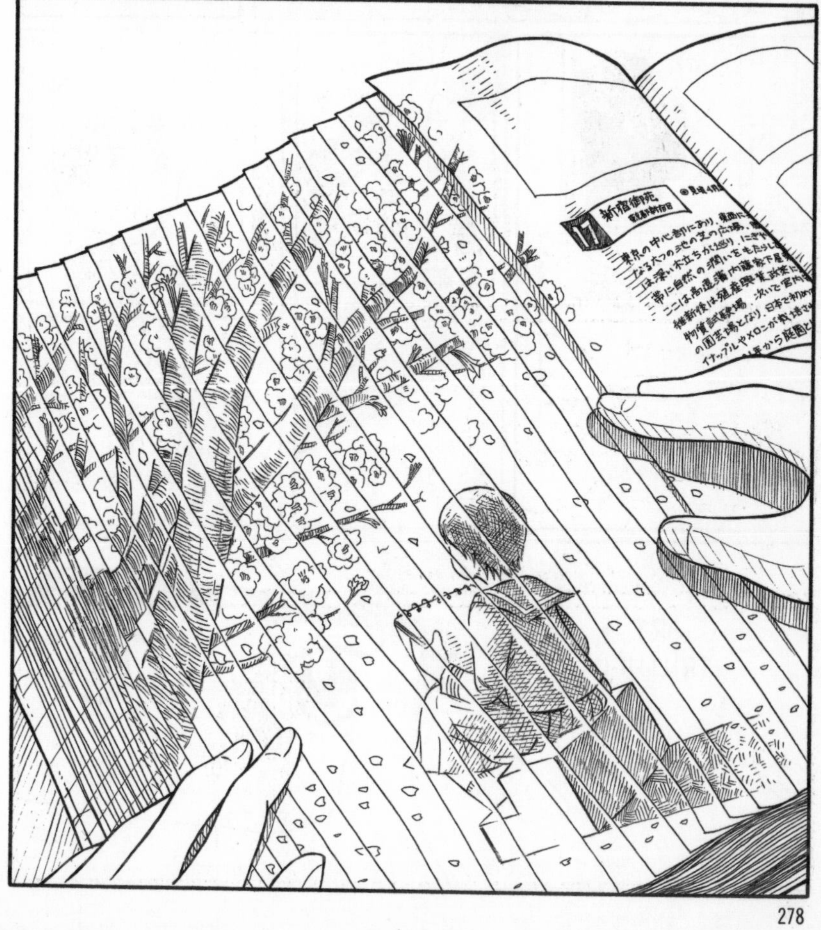
17
新宿御苑

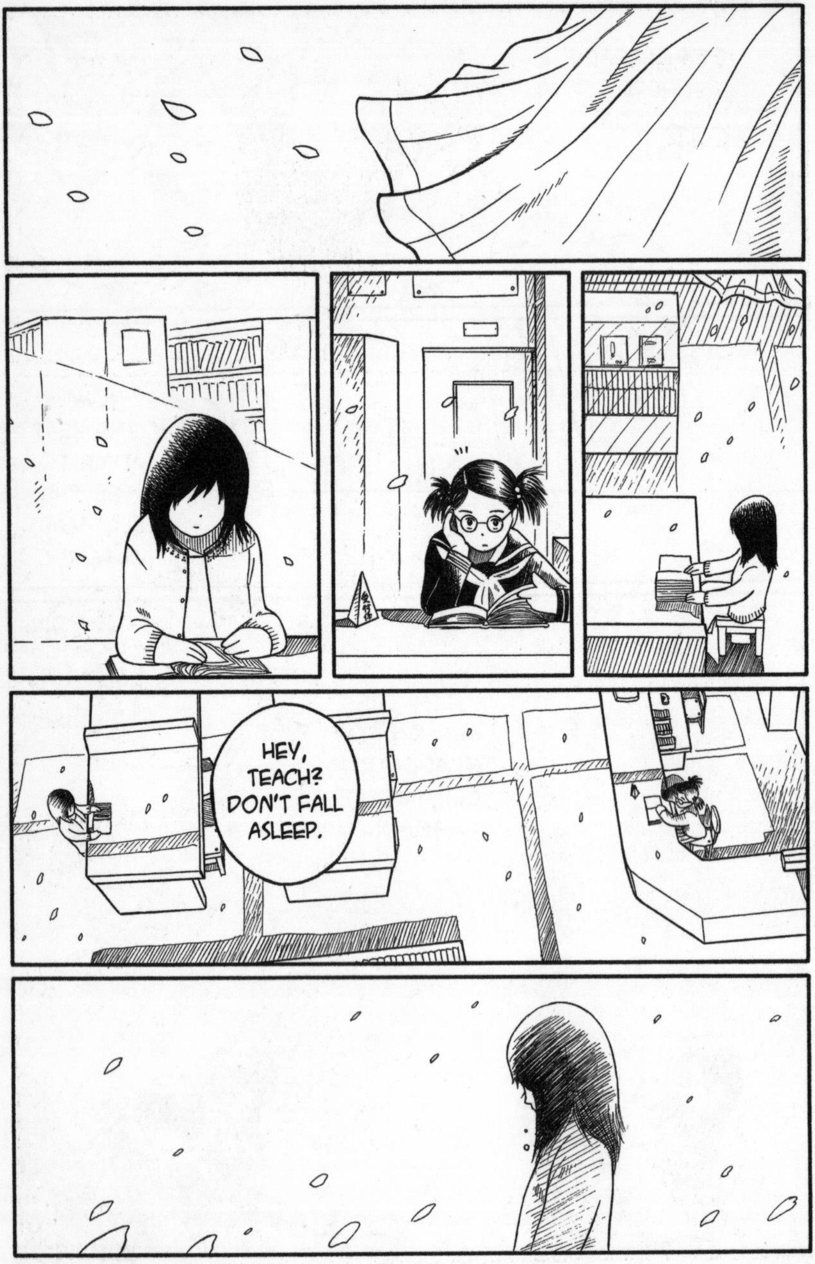
HEY, TEACH? DON'T FALL ASLEEP.

IT'S ALREADY CHERRY BLOSSOM SEASON.

NOW IS THE BEST TIME TO SEE THE BLOSSOMS IN TOKYO.

IT'S THE SEASON FOR GRADUATION CEREMONIES AGAIN.

"GUIDE TO CHERRY BLOSSOMS" —END

ANOTHER SPICA

KOU YAGINUMA

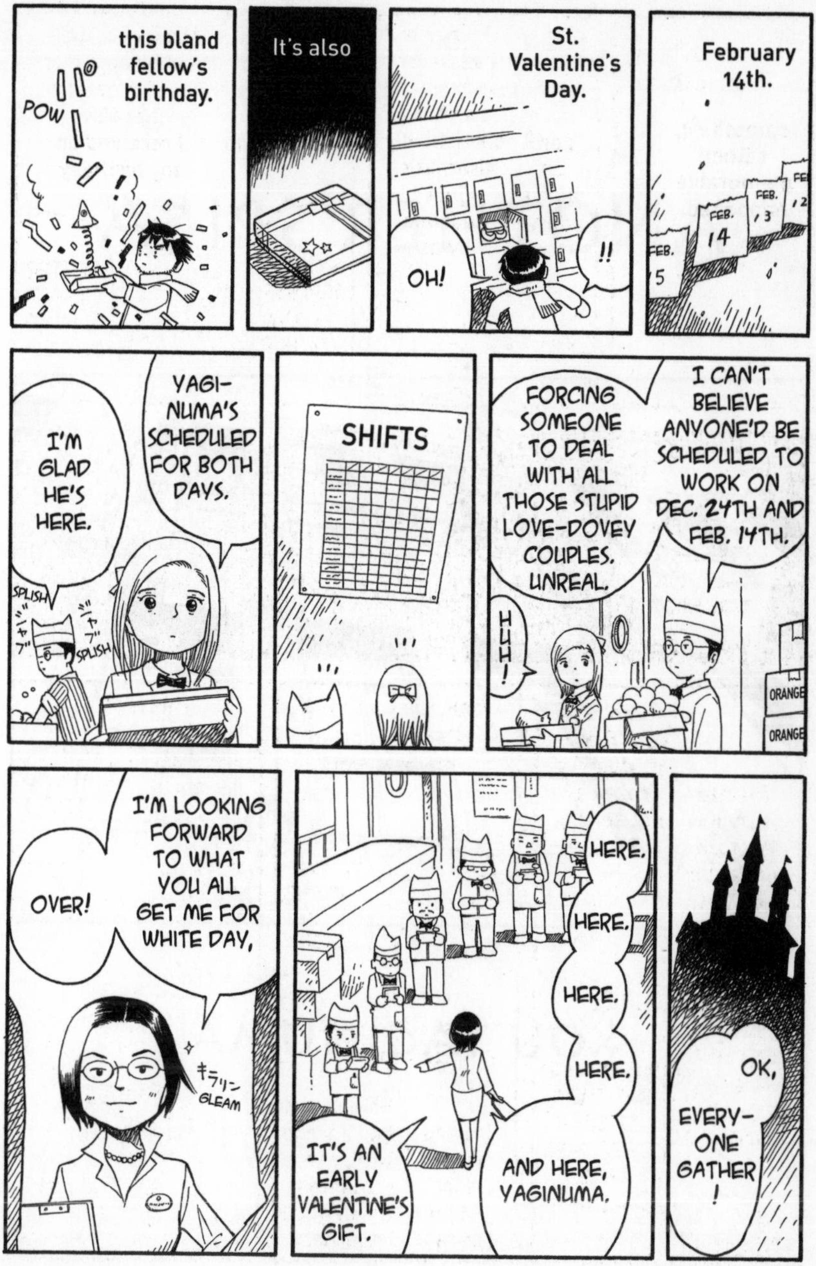
February 14th.
St. Valentine's Day.
!!
OH!
It's also
this bland fellow's birthday.
POW
I CAN'T BELIEVE ANYONE'D BE SCHEDULED TO WORK ON DEC. 24TH AND FEB. 14TH.
FORCING SOMEONE TO DEAL WITH ALL THOSE STUPID LOVE-DOVEY COUPLES. UNREAL.
HUH!
ORANGE
ORANGE
SHIFTS
YAGI-NUMA'S SCHEDULED FOR BOTH DAYS.
I'M GLAD HE'S HERE.
SPLISH
SPLISH
OK, EVERY-ONE GATHER!
HERE.
HERE.
HERE.
HERE.
AND HERE, YAGINUMA.
IT'S AN EARLY VALENTINE'S GIFT.
I'M LOOKING FORWARD TO WHAT YOU ALL GET ME FOR WHITE DAY,
OVER!
キラリン
GLEAM

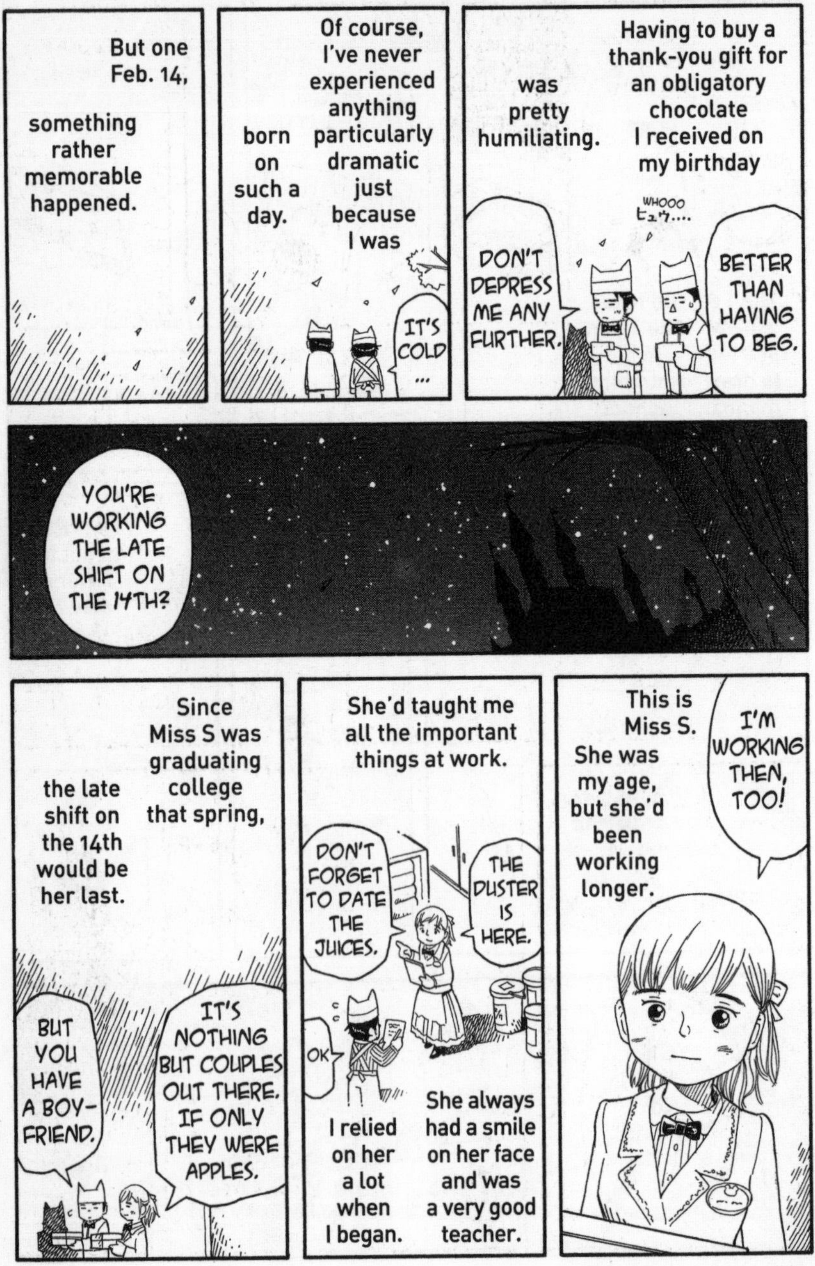
Having to buy a thank-you gift for an obligatory chocolate I received on my birthday
was pretty humiliating.
WHOOO ヒュゥ....
BETTER THAN HAVING TO BEG.
DON'T DEPRESS ME ANY FURTHER.
Of course, I've never experienced anything particularly dramatic just because I was
born on such a day.
IT'S COLD ...
But one Feb. 14,
something rather memorable happened.
YOU'RE WORKING THE LATE SHIFT ON THE 14TH?
I'M WORKING THEN, TOO!
This is Miss S.
She was my age, but she'd been working longer.
She'd taught me all the important things at work.
THE DUSTER IS HERE.
DON'T FORGET TO DATE THE JUICES.
OK
She always had a smile on her face and was a very good teacher.
I relied on her a lot when I began.
Since Miss S was graduating college that spring,
the late shift on the 14th would be her last.
IT'S NOTHING BUT COUPLES OUT THERE. IF ONLY THEY WERE APPLES.
BUT YOU HAVE A BOY-FRIEND.

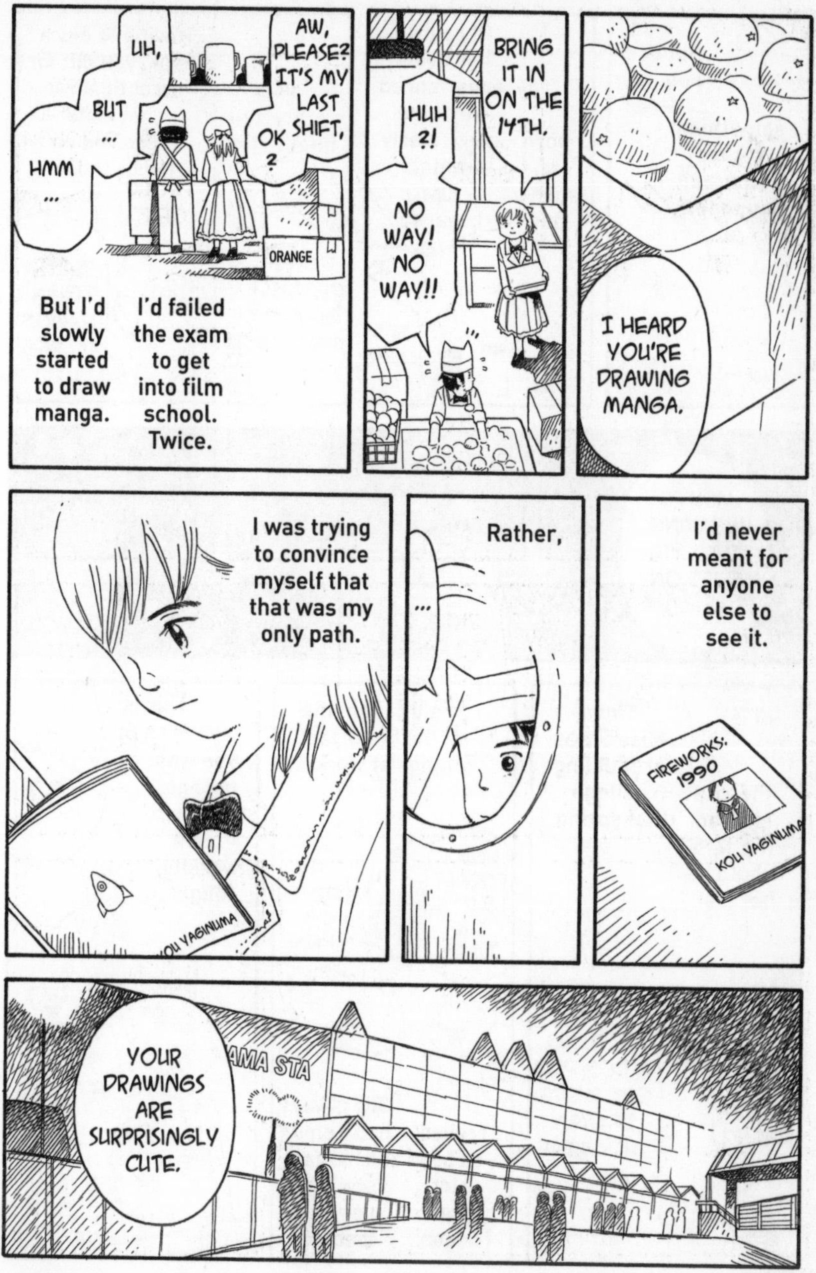
I HEARD YOU'RE DRAWING MANGA.
BRING IT IN ON THE 14TH.
HUH ?!
NO WAY! NO WAY!!
AW, PLEASE? IT'S MY LAST SHIFT, OK ?
UH, BUT ...
HMM ...
ORANGE
I'd failed the exam to get into film school. Twice.
But I'd slowly started to draw manga.
I'd never meant for anyone else to see it.
FIREWORKS: 1990
KOU YAGINUMA
Rather,
...
I was trying to convince myself that that was my only path.
KOU YAGINUMA
YOUR DRAWINGS ARE SURPRISINGLY CUTE.
AMA STA

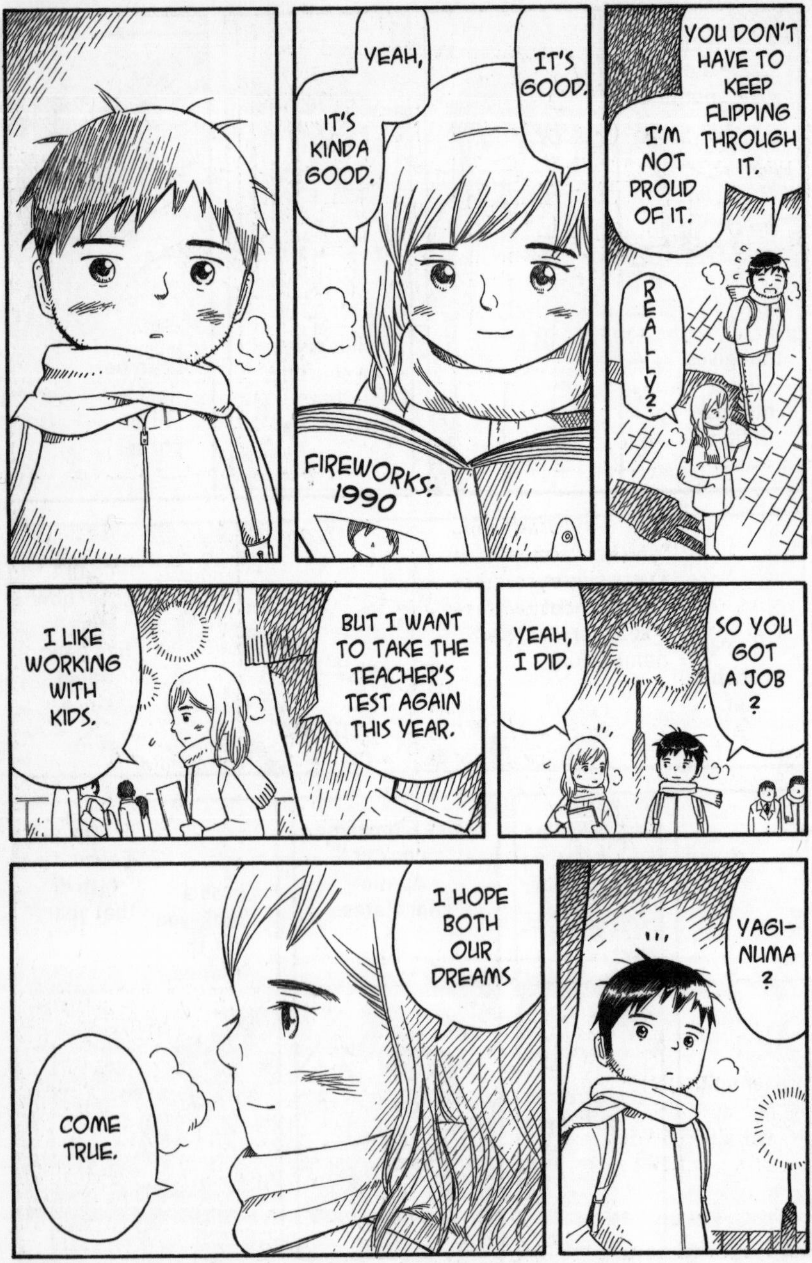
YOU DON'T HAVE TO KEEP FLIPPING THROUGH IT.
I'M NOT PROUD OF IT.
REALLY?
IT'S GOOD.
YEAH, IT'S KINDA GOOD.
FIREWORKS: 1990
SO YOU GOT A JOB?
YEAH, I DID.
BUT I WANT TO TAKE THE TEACHER'S TEST AGAIN THIS YEAR.
I LIKE WORKING WITH KIDS.
YAGI-NUMA?
I HOPE BOTH OUR DREAMS
COME TRUE.

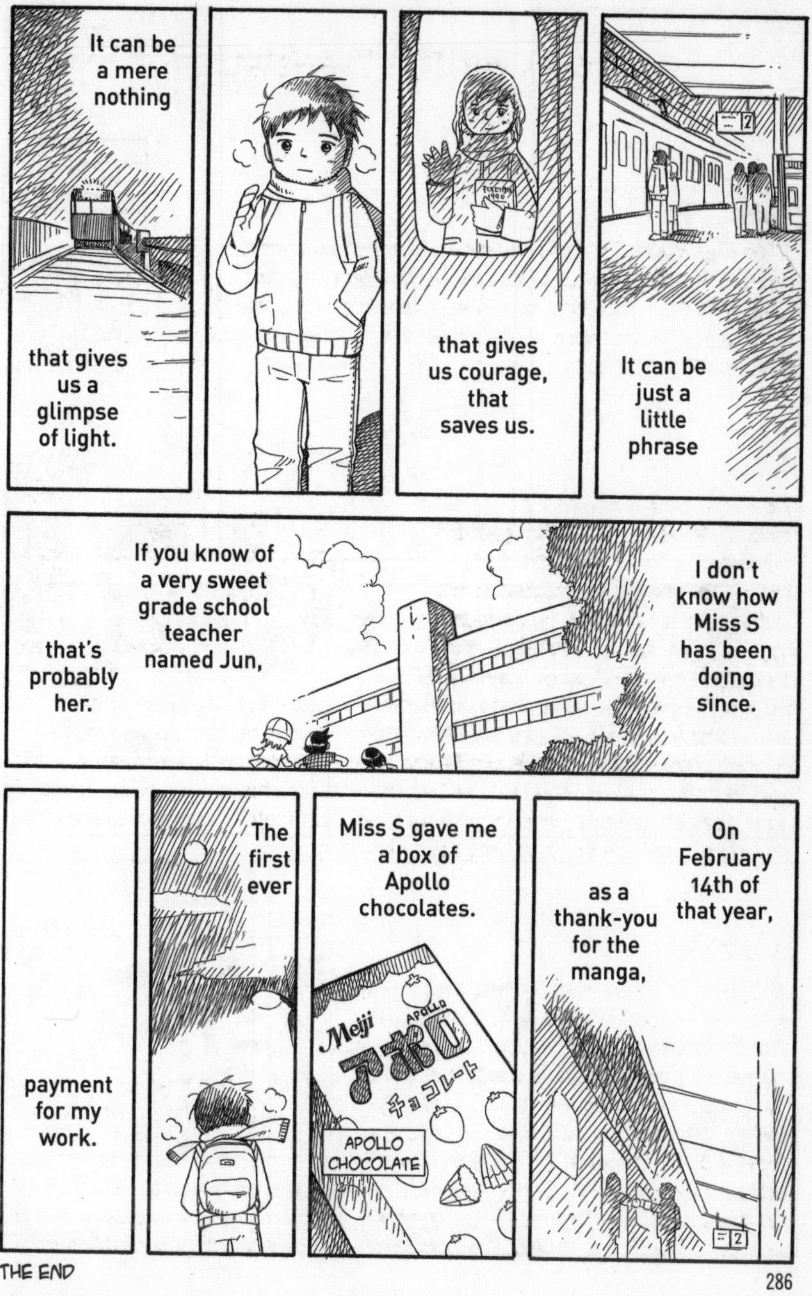
It can be just a little phrase
that gives us courage, that saves us.
It can be a mere nothing
that gives us a glimpse of light.
I don't know how Miss S has been doing since.
If you know of a very sweet grade school teacher named Jun,
that's probably her.
On February 14th of that year,
as a thank-you for the manga,
Miss S gave me a box of Apollo chocolates.
Meiji
APOLLO
アポロ
チョコレート
APOLLO CHOCOLATE
The first ever
payment for my work.

THE END